New Perspectives on

Microsoft® Office 2003

Second Edition

Brief

Ann Shaffer
Patrick Carey
June Jamrich Parsons
Dan Oja

Kathleen T. Finnegan
Lisa Ruffolo
Robin M. Romer

Roy Ageloff
University of Rhode Island

S. Scott Zimmerman
Brigham Young University

Joseph J. Adamski
Grand Valley State University

Beverly B. Zimmerman
Brigham Young University

THOMSON
COURSE TECHNOLOGY ™

Australia • Canada • Mexico • Singapore • Spain • United Kingdom • United States

THOMSON
COURSE TECHNOLOGY

New Perspectives on Microsoft® Office 2003—Brief, Second Edition
is published by Thomson Course Technology.

Executive Editor:
Rachel Goldberg

Senior Product Manager:
Kathy Finnegan

Product Manager:
Brianna Hawes

Associate Product Manager:
Shana Rosenthal

Editorial Assistant:
Janine Tangney

Marketing Manager:
Joy Stark

Marketing Coordinator:
Melissa Marcoux

Developmental Editors:
Pam Conrad, Kim Crowley, Jane Pedicini, Katherine T. Pinard, Robin Romer, Lisa Ruffolo

Production Editors:
Jennifer Goguen McGrail, Summer Hughes, Philippa Lehar, Elena Montillo, Kelly Robinson

Composition:
GEX Publishing Services

Text Designer:
Steve Deschene

Cover Designer:
Nancy Goulet

Cover Artist:
Ed Carpenter
www.edcarpenter.net

COPYRIGHT © 2007 Thomson Course Technology, a division of Thomson Learning, Inc. Thomson Learning™ is a trademark used herein under license.

Printed in China

3 4 5 6 7 8 9 C&C 10 09 08 07

For more information, contact Thomson Course Technology, 25 Thomson Place, Boston, Massachusetts, 02210.

Or find us on the World Wide Web at: www.course.com

ALL RIGHTS RESERVED. No part of this work covered by the copyright hereon may be reproduced or used in any form or by any means—graphic, electronic, or mechanical, including photocopying, recording, taping, Web distribution, or information storage and retrieval systems—without the written permission of the publisher.

For permission to use material from this text or product, submit a request online at www.thomsonrights.com

Any additional questions about permissions can be submitted by e-mail to thomsonrights@thomson.com

Disclaimer
Thomson Course Technology reserves the right to revise this publication and make changes from time to time in its content without notice.

Some of the product names and company names used in this book have been used for identification purposes only and may be trademarks or registered trademarks of their respective manufacturers and sellers.

Disclaimer: Any fictional URLs used throughout this book are intended for instructional purposes only. At the time this book was printed, any such URLs were fictional and not belonging to any real persons or companies.

Microsoft and the Office logo are either registered trademarks or trademarks of Microsoft Corporation in the United States and/or other countries. Course Technology is an independent entity from the Microsoft Corporation, and not affiliated with Microsoft in any manner.

ISBN-13: 978-1-4188-6092-9
ISBN-10: 1-4188-6092-1

Preface

Real, Thought-Provoking, Engaging, Dynamic, Interactive—these are just a few of the words that are used to describe the New Perspectives Series' approach to learning and building computer skills.

Without our critical-thinking and problem-solving methodology, computer skills could be learned but not retained. By teaching with a case-based approach, the New Perspectives Series challenges students to apply what they've learned to real-life situations.

Our ever-growing community of users understands why they're learning what they're learning. Now you can too!

See what instructors and students are saying about the best-selling New Perspectives Series:

"The New Perspectives format is a pleasure to use. The Quick Checks and the tutorial Review Assignments help students view topics from a real world perspective."
— Craig Shaw, Central Community College – Hastings

...and about New Perspectives on Microsoft Office 2003:

"Our school has used the New Perspectives on Microsoft Office book for several years, and we have found no reason to consider changing to another textbook, despite considerable efforts from other publishers. We recently completed another textbook evaluation project, and we determined there simply is not a better solution for our student population. The book is extremely student friendly, the screen shots are very meaningful and visually appealing, and the actual student instructions are easily identifiable, easy to follow and accurate."
— Glen Johansson, Spokane Community College

"The layout in this textbook is thoughtfully designed and organized. It is very easy to locate concepts and step-by-step instructions. The Case Problems provide different scenarios that cover material in the tutorial with plenty of exercises."
— Shui-lien Huang, Mt. San Antonio College

"The 'Managing Your Files' tutorial covers all the basic skills students need to have a good working knowledge of files and file management. It is clear, concise, and easy to understand."
— Mary Logan, Delgado Community College

www.course.com/NewPerspectives

Why *New Perspectives* will work for you

Context

Each tutorial begins with a problem presented in a "real-world" case that is meaningful to students. The case sets the scene to help students understand what they will do in the tutorial.

Hands-on Approach

Each tutorial is divided into manageable sessions that combine reading and hands-on, step-by-step work. Colorful screenshots help guide students through the steps. **Trouble?** tips anticipate common mistakes or problems to help students stay on track and continue with the tutorial.

Review

In New Perspectives, retention is a key component to learning. At the end of each session, a series of Quick Check questions helps students test their understanding of the concepts before moving on. Each tutorial also contains an end-of-tutorial summary and a list of key terms for further reinforcement.

Assessment

Engaging and challenging Review Assignments and Case Problems have always been a hallmark feature of the New Perspectives Series. Colorful icons and brief descriptions accompany the exercises, making it easy to understand, at a glance, both the goal and level of challenge a particular exercise holds.

Reference

While contextual learning is excellent for retention, there are times when students will want a high-level understanding of how to accomplish a task. Within each tutorial, Reference Windows appear before a set of steps to provide a succinct summary and preview of how to perform a task. In addition, a complete Task Reference at the back of the book provides quick access to information on how to carry out common tasks. Finally, each book includes a combination Glossary/Index to promote easy reference of material.

Lab Assignments

Certain tutorials in this book contain Lab Assignments, which provide additional reinforcement of important skills in a simulated environment. These labs have been hailed by students and teachers alike for years as the most comprehensive and accurate on the market. Great for pre-work or remediation, the labs help students learn concepts and skills in a structured environment.

Student Online Companion

This book has an accompanying online companion Web site designed to enhance learning. This Web site includes:

- Internet Assignments and Lab Assignments for selected tutorials
- Student Data Files
- PowerPoint presentations

Review

Apply

Reference Window

Task Reference

Reinforce

www.course.com/NewPerspectives

New Perspectives offers an entire system of instruction

The New Perspectives Series is more than just a handful of books. It's a complete system of offerings:

New Perspectives catalog

Our online catalog is never out of date! Go to the catalog link on our Web site to check out our available titles, request a desk copy, download a book preview, or locate online files.

Coverage to meet your needs!

Whether you're looking for just a small amount of coverage or enough to fill a semester-long class, we can provide you with a textbook that meets your needs.

- Brief books typically cover the essential skills in just 2 to 4 tutorials.
- Introductory books build and expand on those skills and contain an average of 5 to 8 tutorials.
- Comprehensive books are great for a full-semester class, and contain 9 to 12+ tutorials.
- Power Users or Advanced books are perfect for a highly accelerated introductory class or a second course in a given topic.

So if the book you're holding does not provide the right amount of coverage for you, there's probably another offering available. Go to our Web site or contact your Course Technology sales representative to find out what else we offer.

Instructor Resources

We offer more than just a book. We have all the tools you need to enhance your lectures, check students' work, and generate exams in a new, easier-to-use and completely revised package. This book's Instructor's Manual, ExamView testbank, PowerPoint presentations, data files, solution files, figure files, and a sample syllabus are all available on a single CD-ROM or for downloading at www.course.com.

How will your students master Microsoft Office?

SAM (Skills Assessment Manager) 2003 helps you energize your class exams and training assignments by allowing students to learn and test important computer skills in an active, hands-on environment. With SAM 2003, you create powerful interactive exams on critical Microsoft Office 2003 applications, including Word, Excel, Access, and PowerPoint. The exams simulate the application environment, allowing your students to demonstrate their knowledge and to think through the skills by performing real-world tasks. Designed to be used with the New Perspectives Series, SAM 2003 includes built-in page references so students can create study guides that match the New Perspectives textbooks you use in class. Powerful administrative options allow you to schedule exams and assignments, secure your tests, and run reports with almost limitless flexibility. Find out more about SAM 2003 by going to www.course.com or speaking with your Course Technology sales representative.

Distance Learning

Enhance your course with any of our online learning platforms. Go to www.course.com or speak with your Course Technology sales representative to find the platform or the content that's right for you.

www.course.com/NewPerspectives

About This Book

This book offers a case-based, problem-solving approach to learning the fundamentals of both Microsoft Office 2003 and Windows XP. In this book, students learn key skills and tasks working with all four applications—Word, Excel, Access, and PowerPoint—as well as Outlook and Windows. This Second Edition also includes the following features, **new to this edition**:

- Updated coverage of USB drives and how students can use these popular storage devices is presented in the "Managing Your Files" tutorial.
- Two new Case Problems in each Word, Excel, Access, and PowerPoint tutorial allow you to keep your assignments fresh and encourage students to think critically.
- Increased emphasis on file management is provided with the new tear-off File Management FastCARD on the back of the book, giving students a handy way to have file management tips and techniques at their fingertips.

Brief Contents

Table of Contents

Office   OFF 1

Using Common Features of Microsoft Office 2003   OFF 3

Word

Tutorial 1   WD 3

Excel

Access

Tutorial 1   AC 3

Tutorial 2   AC 35

PowerPoint

Tutorial 1   PPT 3

Outlook

Tutorial 1   OUT 3

New Perspectives on

Exploring the Basics of Microsoft® Windows XP

Investigating the Windows XP Operating System   **WIN 3**

New Perspectives Series

Read This Before You Begin

To the Student

Data Files

The Exploring the Basics of Microsoft Windows XP tutorial does not require any starting student Data Files. Also, you do not have to save any files for the tutorial or any end-of-tutorial exercises, so you will not need a floppy disk or other storage medium in order to complete this tutorial.

Course Labs

The Exploring the Basics of Microsoft Windows XP tutorial features two interactive Course Labs to help you understand mouse and keyboard concepts. There are Lab Assignments at the end of the tutorial that relate to these labs. Contact your instructor or technical support person for assistance in accessing the labs.

To the Instructor

The Course Labs are available on the Instructor Resources CD for this title. Follow the instructions in the Help file on the CD to install the programs to your network or standalone computer.

You are granted a license to copy the Course Labs to any computer or computer network used by students who have purchased this book.

System Requirements

If you are going to work through this book using your own computer, you need:

- **Computer System** This tutorial assumes a typical installation of Microsoft Windows XP Professional (although the Microsoft Windows XP Home version is acceptable as well).

- **Course Labs** See your instructor or technical support person to obtain the Course Lab software for use on your own computer.

www.course.com/NewPerspectives

Objectives

Session 1
- Start Windows XP and tour the desktop
- Explore the Start menu
- Run software programs, switch between them, and close them
- Manipulate windows
- Identify and use the controls in menus, toolbars, and dialog boxes

Session 2
- Navigate your computer with Windows Explorer and My Computer
- Change the view of the items in your computer
- Get help when you need it
- Shut down Windows

Exploring the Basics of Microsoft Windows XP

Investigating the Windows XP Operating System

Case

Your Computer Training

Your Computer Training is a small business in Tampa, Florida, that provides lessons and instruction on how to use a computer, offering courses for beginning, intermediate, and advanced computer users. The instruction includes detailed explanations, definitions, and descriptions as well as hands-on practice of computer skills. First-time and novice users learn a full range of basic tasks—from starting the computer and opening and closing programs to shutting down the computer. Steve Laslow teaches an introductory course on the fundamentals of using the Microsoft Windows XP operating system.

In this tutorial you will start Windows XP and practice some basic computer skills. Then you'll learn how to navigate with My Computer and Windows Explorer. Finally, you'll use the Windows XP Help system.

Labs

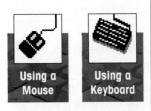

Student Data Files

There are no student Data Files needed for this tutorial.

Starting Windows XP

Steve Laslow begins the course by discussing the operating system. The **operating system** is software that helps the computer perform essential tasks such as displaying information on the computer screen and saving data on disks. (Software refers to the **programs**, or **applications**, that a computer uses to complete tasks.) Your computer uses the **Microsoft Windows XP** operating system—**Windows XP** for short. Windows is the name of the operating system, and XP indicates the version you are using. Microsoft has released many versions of Windows since 1985, and is currently developing new versions.

Much of the software created for Windows XP shares the same look and works the same way. This similarity in design means that once you learn how to use one Windows XP program, such as Microsoft Word (a word-processing program), you are well on your way to understanding how to use other Windows XP programs. Windows XP allows you to use more than one program at a time, so you can easily switch between your word-processing program and your appointment book program, for example. Windows XP also makes it easy to access the **Internet**, a worldwide collection of computers connected to one another to enable communication. All in all, Windows XP makes your computer an effective and easy-to-use productivity tool.

Windows XP starts automatically when you turn on your computer. After completing some necessary startup tasks, Windows XP displays a Welcome screen. Depending on the way your computer is set up, the Welcome screen might simply welcome you to Windows XP or it might list all the users for the computer. If a list of users appears, you must click your user name and perhaps type a password to start using Windows XP. A **user name** is a unique name that identifies you to Windows XP, and a **password** is text—often a confidential combination of letters and numbers—that you must enter before you can work with Windows XP. The Welcome screen might reappear if there's been no activity on the computer for a while.

To start Windows XP:

▶ **1.** Turn on your computer. After a moment, Windows XP starts and the Welcome screen appears.

Trouble? If you are asked to select an operating system, do not take action. Windows XP should start automatically after a designated number of seconds. If it does not, ask your instructor or technical support person for help.

Trouble? If this is the first time you have started your computer with Windows XP, messages might appear on your screen informing you that Windows is setting up components of your computer.

▶ **2.** On the Welcome screen, click your user name, if necessary. The Windows XP screen appears, as shown in Figure 1.

Trouble? If your user name does not appear in the list of users on the Welcome screen, ask your instructor or technical support person which name you should click.

Trouble? If you need to enter a user name and a password, type your assigned user name, press the Tab key, type your password, and then click the Continue button or press the Enter key to continue.

Windows XP desktop ◀ **Figure 1**

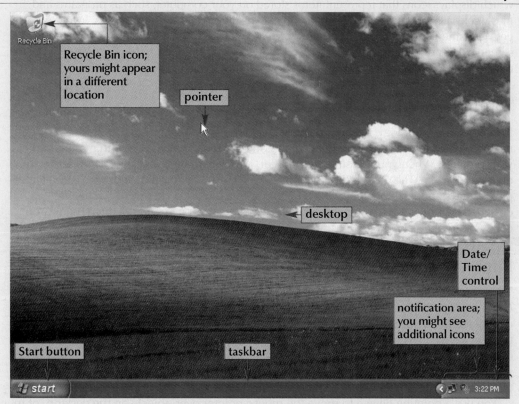

Recycle Bin icon; yours might appear in a different location

pointer

desktop

Date/ Time control

notification area; you might see additional icons

Start button

taskbar

3. Look at your screen and locate the objects labeled in Figure 1. The objects on your screen might appear larger or smaller than those in Figure 1, depending on your monitor's settings. Figure 2 describes the function of each of these objects.

Elements of the Windows XP desktop ◀ **Figure 2**

Element	Description
Icon	A small picture that represents an object available to your computer
Pointer	A small object, such as an arrow, that moves on the screen when you move the mouse
Desktop	Your workplace on the screen
Date/Time control	Shows the current date and time and lets you set the clock
Taskbar	Contains buttons that give you quick access to common tools and the programs currently running
Start button	Provides access to Windows XP programs, documents, and information on the Internet
Notification area	Displays icons corresponding to services running in the background, such as an Internet connection

Trouble? If a blank screen or animated design replaces the Windows XP desktop, your computer might be set to use a screen saver, a program that causes a monitor to go blank or to display an animated design after a specified amount of idle time. Press any key to restore the Windows XP desktop.

The Windows XP screen uses a **graphical user interface** (**GUI**, pronounced "gooey"), which displays icons that represent items stored on your computer, such as programs and files. **Icons** are pictures of familiar objects, such as file folders and documents. Windows XP gets its name from the rectangular work areas, called "windows," that appear on your screen as you work (although no other windows should be open right now). You will learn more about windows later in this tutorial.

Touring the Windows XP Desktop

In Windows terminology, the area displayed on your screen when Windows XP starts represents a **desktop**—a workspace for projects and the tools that you need to manipulate your projects. When you first start a computer, it uses **default** settings, those preset by the operating system. The default desktop you see after you first install Windows XP, for example, displays an image of green hills and clouds in a blue sky. However, Microsoft designed Windows XP so that you can easily change the appearance of the desktop. You can, for example, change images or add patterns and text to the desktop background.

Using a Mouse

Interacting with the Desktop

To interact with the objects on your desktop, you use a **pointing device**. Pointing devices come in many shapes and sizes. The most common one is called a **mouse**, so this book uses that term. If you are using a different pointing device, such as a trackball, substitute that device whenever you see the term "mouse." Some pointing devices are designed to ensure that your hand won't suffer fatigue while using them. Some are attached directly to your computer via a cable, whereas others work like a TV remote control and allow you to access your computer without being right next to it.

You use a pointing device to move the mouse pointer over objects on the desktop, or to **point** to them. The pointer is usually shaped like an arrow ⊾, although it changes shape depending on the pointer's location on the screen and what tasks you are performing. As you move the mouse on a surface, such as a mouse pad, the pointer on the screen moves in a corresponding direction.

When you point to certain objects, such as the objects on the taskbar, a "tip" appears in a yellow box. These tips are called **ScreenTips**, and they tell you the purpose or function of the object to which you are pointing.

To view ScreenTips:

▶ **1.** Use the mouse to point to the **Start** button on the taskbar. After a few seconds, you see the ScreenTip "Click here to begin," as shown in Figure 3.

| Figure 3 | **Viewing ScreenTips** |

▶ **2.** Point to the time displayed at the right end of the taskbar. A ScreenTip for today's date (or the date to which your computer's time clock is set) appears.

Clicking refers to pressing a mouse button and immediately releasing it. Clicking sends a signal to your computer that you want to perform an action on the object you click. In Windows XP you perform most actions with the left mouse button. If you are told to click an object, position the mouse pointer on that object and click the left mouse button, unless instructed otherwise.

When you click the Start button, the Start menu opens. A **menu** is a group or list of commands, and a **menu command** is a word that you can click to complete tasks. If a right-pointing arrow follows a menu command, then you can point to the command to open a **submenu**, which is a list of additional choices related to the command. The **Start menu** provides you with access to programs, documents, and much more. You can click the Start button to open the Start menu.

To open the Start menu:

1. Point to the **Start** button on the taskbar.
2. Click the left mouse button. The Start menu opens. An arrow ▷ follows the All Programs command on the Start menu, indicating that you can view additional choices by navigating to a submenu. See Figure 4; your Start menu might show different commands.

Start menu ◁ Figure 4

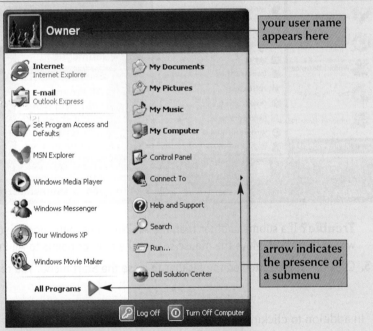

3. Click the **Start** button on the taskbar to close the Start menu.

You need to select an object to work with it. To **select** an object in Windows XP, you point to and then click that object. Windows XP shows you which object is selected by highlighting it, usually by changing the object's color, putting a box around it, or making the object appear to be pushed in.

In Windows XP, depending on your computer's settings, you can select certain objects by pointing to them and others by clicking them. You'll point to the All Programs command on the Start menu to open the All Programs submenu.

To select a menu command:

1. Click the **Start** button on the taskbar. The button appears to be pushed in, indicating that it is selected.
2. Point to (but don't click) **All Programs** on the Start menu. When you first point to the All Programs command, it is highlighted to indicate it is selected. After a short pause, the All Programs submenu opens. See Figure 5.

Figure 5   All Programs submenu

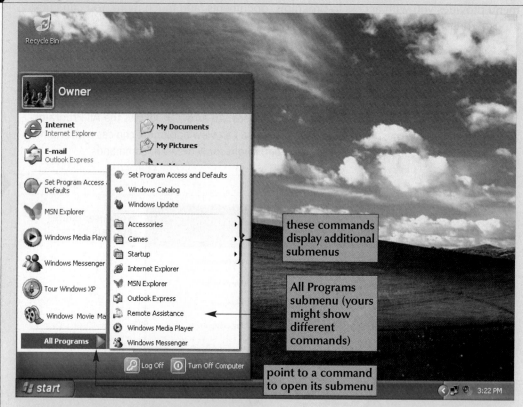

Trouble? If a submenu other than the All Programs menu opens, you pointed to the wrong command. Move the mouse so that the pointer points to All Programs.

3. Click the **Start** button on the taskbar to close the Start menu. You return to the desktop.

In addition to clicking an object to select it, you can double-click an object to open or start the item associated with it. For example, you can double-click a folder icon to open the folder and see its contents. Or you can double-click a program icon to start the program. **Double-clicking** means to click the left mouse button twice in quick succession.

You can practice double-clicking now by opening the Recycle Bin. The Recycle Bin holds deleted items such as folders until you remove them permanently.

To view the contents of the Recycle Bin:

1. Click the desktop, and then point to the **Recycle Bin** icon on the desktop. After a few moments, a ScreenTip appears that describes the Recycle Bin.
2. Click the left mouse button twice quickly to double-click the **Recycle Bin** icon. The Recycle Bin window opens, as shown in Figure 6.

Contents of the Recycle Bin ◢ Figure 6

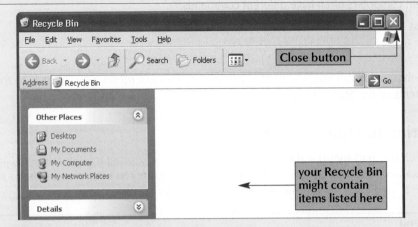

Trouble? If the Recycle Bin window does not open, and you see only the Recycle Bin name highlighted below the icon, you double-clicked too slowly. Double-click the icon again more quickly.

Now you can close the Recycle Bin window.

3. Click the **Close** button ☒ in the upper-right corner of the Recycle Bin window.

You'll learn more about opening and closing windows later in this session.

Your mouse has more than one button—in addition to the left button, the mouse has a right button that you can use for performing certain actions in Windows XP. However, the term "clicking" continues to refer to the left button; clicking an object with the *right* button is called **right-clicking**.

In Windows XP, right-clicking selects an object and opens its **shortcut menu**, which is a list of commands directly related to the object that you right-clicked. You can right-click practically any object—the Start button, a desktop icon, the taskbar, and even the desktop itself—to view commands associated with that object. Recall that you clicked the Start button with the left mouse button to open the Start menu. Now you can right-click the Start button to open the shortcut menu for the Start button.

To right-click an object:

1. Position the pointer over the **Start** button on the taskbar.

2. Right-click the **Start** button on the taskbar to open its shortcut menu. This menu offers a list of commands related to the Start button. See Figure 7.

Start button shortcut menu ◢ Figure 7

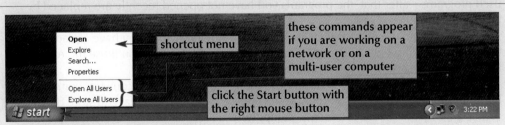

Trouble? If the shortcut menu does not open and you are using a trackball or a mouse with three buttons or a wheel, make sure you click the button on the far right, not the one in the middle.

> **Trouble?** If your menu looks slightly different from the one in Figure 7, don't worry; different computers often have different commands.
>
> ▶ **3.** Press the **Esc** key to close the shortcut menu. You return to the desktop.

Now that you've opened the Start menu and its shortcut menu, you're ready to explore the contents of the Start menu.

Exploring the Start Menu

Recall that the Start menu is the central point for accessing programs, documents, and other resources on your computer. The Start menu is organized into two panels, as shown in Figure 8, and each panel lists items you can point to or click.

Figure 8 ▶ **Start menu**

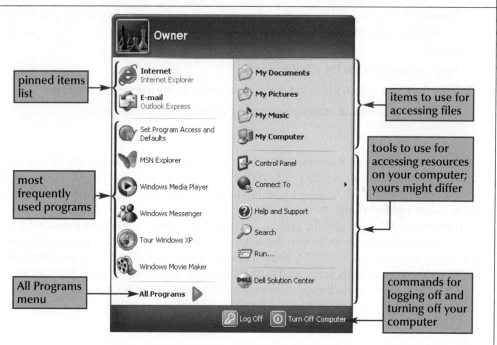

The left panel organizes programs for easy access. The area at the top of the left panel is called the **pinned items list**. Pinned items stay on the Start menu unless you remove them. By default, Windows XP lists the Web browser and e-mail program on your computer in the pinned items list. You can pin other items to this list if you like. When you use a program, Windows XP adds it to the **most frequently used programs list**, which appears below the pinned items list. Windows XP can list only a certain number of frequently used programs—after that, the programs you have not opened recently are replaced by the programs you used last.

The last item in the left panel is the All Programs menu, which you have already used to display a list of programs currently installed on your computer. You'll use the All Programs menu shortly to start a program.

From the right panel, you can access common locations and tools on your computer. For example, **My Documents** is your personal folder, a convenient place to store documents, graphics, and other work. **My Computer** is a tool that you use to view, organize, and access the programs, files, and drives on your computer.

From the lower section of the right panel, you can open windows that help you work effectively with Windows XP, including the **Control Panel**, which contains specialized tools that you can use to change the way Windows XP looks and behaves, and the **Help and Support Center**, which provides tutorials, demonstrations, and steps for performing tasks in Windows XP. (You'll explore the Help and Support Center later in this tutorial.) Finally, you also log off and turn off your computer from the Start menu. When you **log off**, you end your session with Windows XP but leave the computer turned on.

Now that you've explored the Start menu, you're ready to use it to start a program.

Reference Window

Starting a Program

- Click the Start button on the taskbar, and then point to All Programs.
- If necessary, point to the submenu that contains the program you want to start.
- Click the name of the program you want to start.

or

- Click the name or icon of the program you want to start in the pinned items list or the most frequently used programs list on the Start menu.

Windows XP includes an easy-to-use word-processing program called WordPad. Suppose you want to start the WordPad program and use it to write a letter or report. You open Windows XP programs from the Start menu. Programs are usually located on the All Programs submenu or on one of its submenus. To start WordPad, for example, you navigate to the All Programs and Accessories submenus.

To start the WordPad program from the Start menu:

▶ **1.** Click the **Start** button on the taskbar to open the Start menu.

▶ **2.** Point to **All Programs** to open the All Programs submenu.

▶ **3.** Point to **Accessories**. The Accessories submenu opens. Figure 9 shows the open menus.

Start menu and related submenus   ◀ **Figure 9**

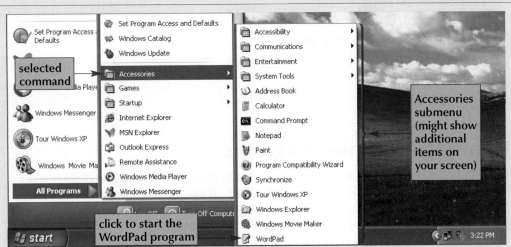

Trouble? If a different menu opens, you might have paused the pointer over a different menu command, which opened its submenu. Move the pointer back to All Programs, and then move the pointer up or down to point to Accessories.

> **4.** Click **WordPad** on the Accessories submenu. The WordPad program window opens, as shown in Figure 10.

Figure 10 ▶ **WordPad program window**

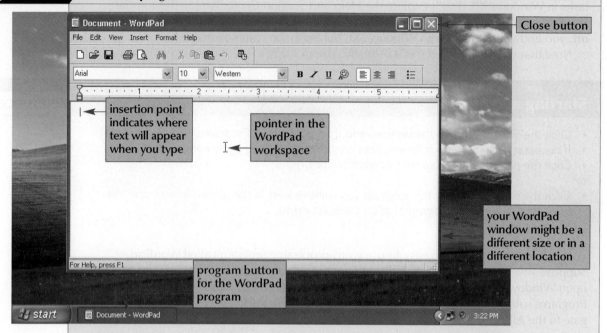

Trouble? If the WordPad program window fills the entire screen, don't worry. You will learn how to manipulate windows shortly.

When a program is started, it is said to be open or running. A **program button** appears on the taskbar for each open program. You click a program button to switch between open programs. When you are finished using a program, you can click the Close button located in the upper-right corner of the program window to **exit**, or close, that program.

To exit the WordPad program:

> **1.** Click the **Close** button ⊠ on the WordPad title bar. The WordPad program closes and you return to the Windows XP desktop.

Running Multiple Programs

One of the most useful features of Windows XP is its ability to run multiple programs at the same time. This feature, known as **multitasking**, allows you to work on more than one task at a time and to switch quickly between projects. For example, you can start WordPad and leave it running while you start the Paint program.

To run WordPad and Paint at the same time:

▶ 1. Start WordPad again.

▶ 2. Click the **Start** button on the taskbar.

▶ 3. Point to **All Programs**, and then point to **Accessories**.

▶ 4. Click **Paint**. The Paint program window opens, as shown in Figure 11. Now two programs are running at the same time.

Two programs open ◀ **Figure 11**

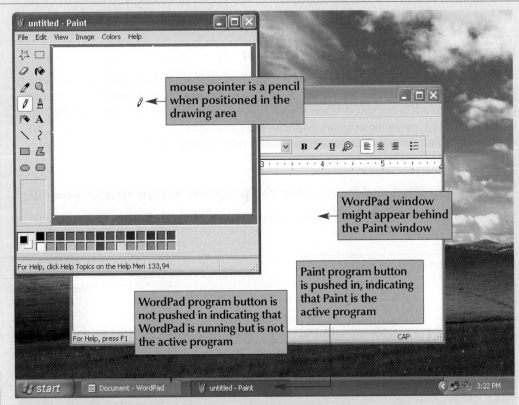

mouse pointer is a pencil when positioned in the drawing area

WordPad window might appear behind the Paint window

Paint program button is pushed in, indicating that Paint is the active program

WordPad program button is not pushed in indicating that WordPad is running but is not the active program

Trouble? If the Paint program fills the entire screen, continue with the next set of steps. You will learn how to manipulate windows shortly.

The **active program** is the one you are currently using—Windows XP applies your next keystroke or command to the active program. Paint is the active program because it is the one in which you are currently working. The WordPad program button is still on the taskbar, indicating that WordPad is still running even if you can't see its program window. Imagine that the WordPad program window is stacked behind the Paint program window.

Switching Between Programs

Because only one program is active at a time, you'll need to switch between programs if you want to work in one or the other. The easiest way to switch between programs is to use the program buttons on the taskbar.

To switch between WordPad and Paint:

▶ 1. Click the program button labeled **Document - WordPad** on the taskbar. The WordPad program window moves to the front, and now the Document - WordPad button looks pushed in, indicating that WordPad is the active program.

▶ 2. Click the program button labeled **untitled - Paint** on the taskbar to switch to the Paint program. The Paint program is again the active program.

In addition to using the taskbar to switch between open programs, you can also close programs from the taskbar.

Closing Programs from the Taskbar

You should always close a program when you are finished using it. Each program uses computer resources, such as memory, so Windows XP works more efficiently when only the programs you need are open. You've already seen how to close an open program using the Close button on the title bar of the program window. You can also close a program, whether active or inactive, by using the shortcut menu associated with the program button on the taskbar.

To close WordPad and Paint using the program button shortcut menus:

▶ 1. Right-click the **untitled - Paint** button on the taskbar. The shortcut menu for the Paint program button opens. See Figure 12.

Figure 12 ▶ **Program button shortcut menu**

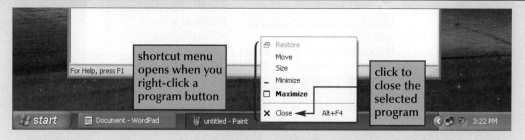

For Help, press F1

shortcut menu opens when you right-click a program button

	Restore
-	Move
	Size
-	Minimize
☐	**Maximize**
✕	Close ◀— Alt+F4

click to close the selected program

⊞ start | 📄 Document - WordPad | ✍ untitled - Paint | 3:22 PM

▶ 2. Click **Close** on the shortcut menu. The Paint program closes and the program button labeled "untitled - Paint" disappears from the taskbar.

▶ 3. Right-click the **Document - WordPad** button on the taskbar, and then click **Close** on the shortcut menu. The WordPad program closes and its program button no longer appears on the taskbar.

Now that you've learned the basics of using the Windows XP desktop, you're ready to explore other Windows XP features, including windows and dialog boxes.

Using Windows and Dialog Boxes

Recall that when you run a program in Windows XP, the program appears in a window. A **window** is a rectangular area of the screen that contains a program, text, graphics, or data. Windows, spelled with an uppercase "W," is the name of the Microsoft operating system. The word "window" with a lowercase "w" refers to one of the rectangular areas on the screen. A window also contains **controls**, which are graphical or textual objects used for manipulating the window and for using the program. Figure 13 describes the controls you are likely to see in most windows.

Window controls ◀ Figure 13

Control	Description
Menu bar	Contains the titles of menus, such as File, Edit, and Help
Sizing buttons	Let you enlarge, shrink, or close a window
Status bar	Provides you with messages relevant to the task you are performing
Title bar	Contains the window title and basic window control buttons
Toolbar	Contains buttons that provide you with shortcuts to common menu commands
Window title	Identifies the program and document contained in the window
Workspace	Part of the window you use to enter your work—to enter text, draw pictures, set up calculations, and so on

The WordPad program is a good example of a typical window. You'll start WordPad and identify its window controls.

To look at the window controls in WordPad:

▶ **1.** Make sure that Windows XP is running and the Windows XP desktop is displayed.

▶ **2.** Start WordPad.

▶ **3.** On your screen, identify the controls that are labeled in Figure 14.

WordPad window controls ◀ Figure 14

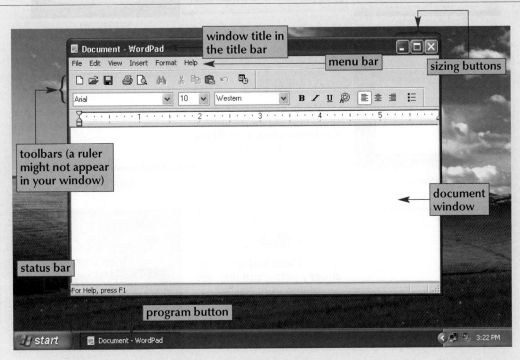

Trouble? If your WordPad program window fills the entire screen or differs in size, you can still identify all the controls.

After you open a window, you can manipulate it by changing its size and position.

Manipulating Windows

On the right side of the title bar are three buttons. The Minimize button, which is the first of the three buttons, hides a window so that only its program button is visible on the taskbar. The other button changes name and function depending on the status of the window (it either maximizes the window or restores it to a predefined size). You are already familiar with the last button—the Close button. Figure 15 shows how these buttons work.

Figure 15 ▶ **Window buttons**

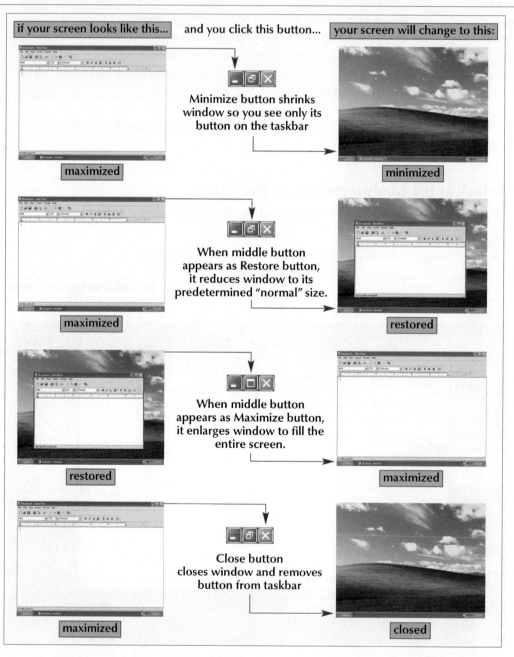

You can use the Minimize button when you want to temporarily hide a window but keep the program running.

To minimize the WordPad window:

▶ **1.** Click the **Minimize** button 🔲 on the WordPad title bar. The WordPad window shrinks so that only the Document - WordPad button on the taskbar is visible.

Trouble? If the WordPad program window closed, you accidentally clicked the Close button. Use the Start button to start WordPad again, and then repeat Step 1. If you accidentally clicked the Maximize or Restore button, repeat Step 1.

You can redisplay a minimized window by clicking the program's button on the taskbar. When you redisplay a window, it becomes the active window.

To redisplay the WordPad window:

▶ **1.** Click the **Document - WordPad** button on the taskbar. The WordPad window is restored to its previous size.

The taskbar button provides another way to switch a window between its minimized and active states.

▶ **2.** Click the **Document - WordPad** button on the taskbar again to minimize the window.

▶ **3.** Click the **Document - WordPad** button once more to redisplay the window.

The Maximize button enlarges a window so that it fills the entire screen. You will probably do most of your work using maximized windows because they allow you to see more of the program and your data.

To maximize the WordPad window:

▶ **1.** Click the **Maximize** button 🔲 on the WordPad title bar.

Trouble? If the window is already maximized, it will fill the entire screen, and the Maximize button won't appear. Instead, you'll see the Restore button. Skip Step 1.

The Restore button reduces the window so that it is smaller than the entire screen. This feature is useful if you want to see more than one window at a time. Also, because the window is smaller, you can move the window to another location on the screen or change the dimensions of the window.

To restore a window:

▶ **1.** Click the **Restore** button 🔲 on the WordPad title bar. Once a window is restored, the Restore button 🔲 changes to the Maximize button 🔲.

You can use the mouse to move a window to a new position on the screen. When you click an object and then press and hold down the mouse button while moving the mouse, you are said to be **dragging** the object. You can move objects on the screen by dragging them to a new location. If you want to move a window, you drag the window by its title bar. You cannot move a maximized window.

To drag the restored WordPad window to a new location:

▶ **1.** Position the mouse pointer on the WordPad title bar.

▶ **2.** Press and hold down the left mouse button, and then move the mouse up or down a little to drag the window. The window moves as you move the mouse.

▶ **3.** Position the window anywhere on the desktop, and then release the left mouse button. The WordPad window appears in the new location.

▶ **4.** Drag the WordPad window to the upper-left corner of the desktop.

You can also use the mouse to change the size of a window. Notice the sizing handle ⊞ at the lower-right corner of the window. The **sizing handle** provides a visible control for changing the size of a window.

To change the size of the WordPad window:

▶ **1.** Position the pointer over the sizing handle ⊞ in the lower-right corner of the WordPad window. The pointer changes to ⬦. See Figure 16.

| **Figure 16** ▶ | **Preparing to resize a window** |

▶ **2.** Press and hold down the mouse button, and then drag the sizing handle down and to the right.

▶ **3.** Release the mouse button. Now the window is larger.

▶ **4.** Practice using the sizing handle to make the WordPad window larger or smaller, and then maximize the WordPad window.

You can also use the resize pointer to drag the left, right, top, or bottom window borders left, right, up, or down to change a window's size in any one direction.

Selecting Options from a Menu

Most Windows XP programs use menus to organize the program's features and available functions. The menu bar is typically located at the top of the program window and shows the names of the menus, such as File, Edit, and Help. Windows XP menus are relatively standardized—most programs designed for Windows XP include similar menus. This makes it easier to learn new programs because you can make a pretty good guess about which menu contains the task you want to perform.

When you click any menu name, the choices for that menu appear below the menu bar. Like choices on the Start menu, these choices are referred to as menu commands. To select a menu command, you click it. For example, the File menu is a standard feature in most Windows XP programs and contains the commands typically related to working with a file: creating, opening, saving, and printing. Menu commands that are followed by an ellipsis open a dialog box. A **dialog box** is a special kind of window where you enter or choose settings for how you want to perform a task. For example, you use the Page Setup dialog box to set margins and some printing options. If you open a menu, and then decide not to select a command, you can close the menu by clicking its name again or pressing the Esc key.

To select the Page Setup menu command from the File menu:

▶ **1.** Click **File** on the WordPad menu bar to open the File menu. See Figure 17.

File menu ◀ **Figure 17**

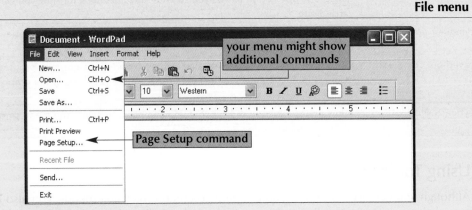

▶ **2.** Click **Page Setup** to open the Page Setup dialog box.

▶ **3.** After examining the dialog box, click the **Cancel** button to close the Page Setup dialog box.

If you had selected options in the Page Setup dialog box that you wanted to retain, you would click the OK button instead of the Cancel button.

Not all menu items and commands immediately carry out an action—some show submenus or ask you for more information about what you want to do. The menu gives you visual hints about what to expect when you select an item. These hints are sometimes referred to as **menu conventions**. Figure 18 shows examples of these menu conventions.

Examples of menu conventions ◀ **Figure 18**

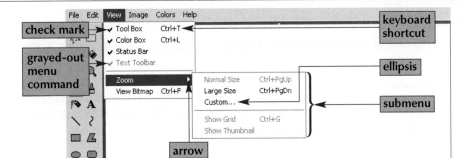

Figure 19 describes the Windows XP menu conventions.

Figure 19 Menu conventions

Convention	Description
Check mark	Indicates a toggle, or "on-off" switch (like a light switch) that is either checked (turned on) or not checked (turned off).
Ellipsis	Three dots that indicate you must make additional selections after you select that command. Commands without dots do not require additional choices—they take effect as soon as you click them. If a command is followed by an ellipsis, a dialog box opens that allows you to enter specifications for how you want a task carried out.
Triangular arrow	Indicates the presence of a submenu. When you point to a menu option that has a triangular arrow, a submenu automatically appears.
Grayed-out command	Command that is not currently available. For example, a graphics program might display the Text Toolbar command in gray if there is no text in the graphic to work with.
Keyboard shortcut	A key or combination of keys that you can press to select the menu command without actually opening the menu.

Using Toolbars

Although you can usually perform all program commands by using menus, you also have one-click access to frequently used commands on the toolbars in the program window. Using the buttons on the toolbars, you can quickly access common commands. Just as menu commands are grouped on menus according to task, the buttons on a toolbar are also grouped and organized by task.

Recall that Windows XP programs often display ScreenTips, which indicate the purpose and function of a window component such as a button. You'll explore the WordPad toolbar buttons by looking at their ScreenTips.

To determine the names and descriptions of the buttons on the WordPad toolbar:

1. Position the pointer over the **Print Preview** button 🔍 on the WordPad toolbar. After a short pause, the ScreenTip for the button appears below the button, and a description of the button appears in the status bar just above the Start button.

   Trouble? If you closed WordPad after the previous set of steps, restart the program.

2. Move the pointer to each button on the toolbar to display its name and purpose.

You select a toolbar button by clicking it, which performs the button's command. One of the buttons you pointed to on the WordPad toolbar is called the Undo button. Clicking the Undo button reverses the effects of your last action.

To use the Undo button on the WordPad toolbar:

1. Type your name in the WordPad window.
2. Click the **Undo** button 🔄 on the WordPad toolbar. WordPad reverses your last action by removing your name from the WordPad window.

Besides menus and toolbars, windows can contain list boxes and scroll bars, which you'll learn about next.

Using List Boxes and Scroll Bars

As you might guess from the name, a **list box** displays a list of available choices from which you can select one item. In WordPad, you can choose a date and time format from the Available formats list box in the Date/Time dialog box. List box controls usually include arrow buttons, a scroll bar, and a scroll box. A scroll bar appears when the list of available options is too long or wide to fit in the list box. The arrows and scroll box enable you to move through the complete list.

To use the Date/Time list box:

1. Click the **Date/Time** button 🖳 on the WordPad toolbar to open the Date and Time dialog box, which lists the current date in many formats. See Figure 20.

List box ◀ **Figure 20**

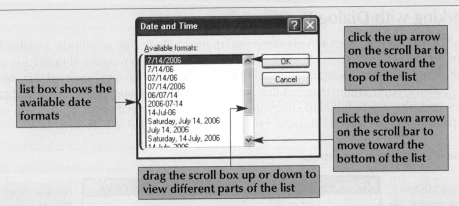

list box shows the available date formats

click the up arrow on the scroll bar to move toward the top of the list

click the down arrow on the scroll bar to move toward the bottom of the list

drag the scroll box up or down to view different parts of the list

2. To scroll down the list, click the **down arrow** button on the scroll bar three times.

3. Drag the **scroll box** to the top of the scroll bar by pointing to the scroll box, pressing and holding down the left mouse button, dragging the scroll box up, and then releasing the left mouse button. The list scrolls back to the beginning.

4. Find a date format similar to "July 14, 2006" in the Available formats list box, and then click that date format to select it.

5. Click the **OK** button to close the Date and Time dialog box. The current date is inserted into your document.

A list box is helpful because it only includes options that are appropriate for your current task. For example, you can select only dates and times in the available formats from the list box in the Date and Time dialog box—no matter which format you choose, WordPad will recognize it. Sometimes a list might not include every possible option, so you can type the option you want to select. In this case, the list box includes a **list arrow** on its right side. You can click the list arrow to view options and then select one, or you can type appropriate text.

Buttons can also have list arrows. The list arrow indicates that there is more than one option for that button. Rather than crowding the window with a lot of buttons, one for each possible option, including a list arrow on a button organizes its options logically and compactly into a list. Toolbars often include list boxes and buttons with list arrows. For example, the Font Size button list box on the WordPad toolbar includes a list arrow. To select an option other than the one shown in the list box or on the button, you click the list arrow, and then click the option that you want to use.

To select a new font size from the Font Size button list box:

▶ **1.** Click the **Font Size** button list arrow 10 ▾ on the WordPad toolbar.

▶ **2.** Click **18**. The Font Size list closes, and the font size you selected appears in the list box.

▶ **3.** Type a few characters to test the new font size.

▶ **4.** Click the **Font Size** button list arrow 10 ▾ on the WordPad toolbar again.

▶ **5.** Click **12**.

▶ **6.** Type a few characters to test this type size. The text appears in the smaller font size.

Dialog boxes also contain scroll bars and list boxes. You'll examine a typical dialog box next.

Working with Dialog Boxes

Recall that when you select a menu command or item followed by an ellipsis, a dialog box opens that allows you to provide more information about how a program should carry out a task. Some dialog boxes organize different kinds of information into bordered rectangular areas called groups. Within these groups, you will usually find tabs, option buttons, check boxes, and other controls that the program uses to collect information about how you want it to perform a task. Figure 21 displays examples of common dialog box controls.

Figure 21 ▶ **Examples of dialog box controls**

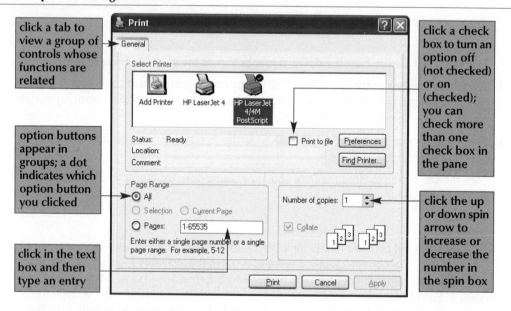

Now you can open a typical Windows XP dialog box in WordPad. To learn how dialog box controls work, you'll open the Options dialog box, which you use to determine how text fits in the WordPad window and which toolbars appear. You'll remove the check mark from a check box and select an option button, and then see how these settings affect the WordPad window. Note that by default the status bar appears at the bottom of the WordPad window and that the ruler uses inches.

To work with a typical Windows XP dialog box:

▶ **1.** Click **View** on the WordPad menu bar, and then click **Options**. The Options dialog box opens, by default, to the Rich Text tab.

Trouble? If the Options dialog box does not display the Rich Text options, click the Rich Text tab.

▶ **2.** Click the **Status bar** check box to remove the check mark.

▶ **3.** Click the **Options** tab to select the measurement units that the WordPad ruler uses.

▶ **4.** Click the **Centimeters** option button.

▶ **5.** Click the **OK** button. WordPad accepts your changes and closes the Options dialog box.

Examine the WordPad window and note that the ruler now uses centimeters instead of inches and the status bar no longer appears at the bottom of the window. You can use the Options dialog box again to restore the WordPad window to its original condition.

To restore the WordPad window:

▶ **1.** Click **View** on the WordPad menu bar, and then click **Options**. The Options dialog box opens.

▶ **2.** On the Rich Text tab, click the **Status bar** check box to insert a check mark.

▶ **3.** Click the **Options** tab, and then click the **Inches** option button.

▶ **4.** Click the **OK** button. The WordPad window now includes a status bar and a ruler that uses inches as its measurement unit.

▶ **5.** Click the **Close** button ⊠ on the WordPad title bar to close WordPad.

▶ **6.** When you see the message "Save changes to Document?" click the **No** button.

In this session, you started Windows XP and toured the desktop, learning how to interact with the items on the desktop and on the Start menu. You also started two Windows programs, manipulated windows, and learned how to select options from a menu, toolbar, and dialog box.

Session 1 Quick Check

Review

1. What is the purpose of the taskbar?
2. What is a ScreenTip?
3. The _____ is a list of options that provides you with access to programs, documents, submenus, and more.
4. Which feature of Windows XP allows you to run more than one program at a time?
5. Even if you can't see an open program on your desktop, the program might be running. How can you tell if a program is running?
6. Why should you close each program when you are finished using it?
7. A(n) _____ consists of a group of buttons, each of which provides one-click access to important program functions.
8. A(n) _____ is helpful because it only includes options that are appropriate for your current task.

Session 2

Exploring Your Computer

To discover the contents and resources on your computer, you explore, or navigate, it. **Navigating**, in this context, means to move from one location to another on your computer, such as from one window to another. Windows XP provides two different ways to navigate, view, and work with the contents and resources on your computer—My Computer and Windows Explorer.

Navigating with My Computer

The My Computer icon on the Start menu represents your computer, its storage devices, printers, and other objects. The My Computer icon opens the My Computer window, which contains an icon for each of the storage devices on your computer, as shown in Figure 22. These icons appear in the right pane of the My Computer window. By default, the My Computer window also has a left pane, which shows icons and links to other resources. You'll learn more about the left pane shortly.

| Figure 22 | Relationship between computer and My Computer window |

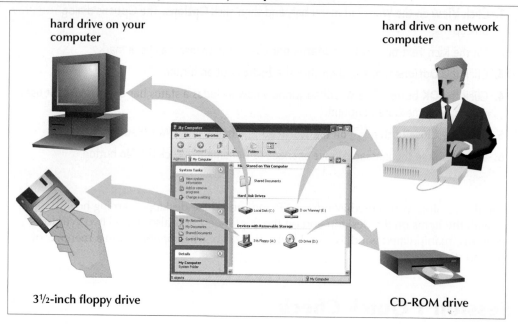

Each storage device you have access to on your computer has a letter associated with it. The first floppy drive on a computer is usually designated as drive A (if you add a second drive, it is usually designated as drive B), and the first hard drive is usually designated as drive C (if you add additional hard drives, they are usually designated D, E, and so on). If you have a CD or DVD drive, it usually has the next letter in the alphabetic sequence. If you have access to hard drives located on other computers in a network, those drives will sometimes (although not always) have letters associated with them as well. Naming conventions for network drives vary. In the example shown in Figure 22, the network drive has the drive letter E.

You can use the My Computer window to keep track of where your files are stored and to organize your files. In this session, you will explore the contents of your hard disk, which is assumed to be located in drive C. If you use a different drive on your computer, such as drive E, substitute its letter for "C" throughout this session.

Now you'll open the My Computer window and explore the contents of your computer.

To explore the contents of your computer using the My Computer window:

1. If you took a break after the previous session, make sure that your computer is on and Windows XP is running.

2. Click the **Start** button on the taskbar, and then click **My Computer**. The My Computer window opens. See Figure 23. Your window might look different. For example, in addition to the Shared Documents folder, your window probably lists folders with names for each user on your computer, such as "Andrea's Documents."

My Computer window | Figure 23

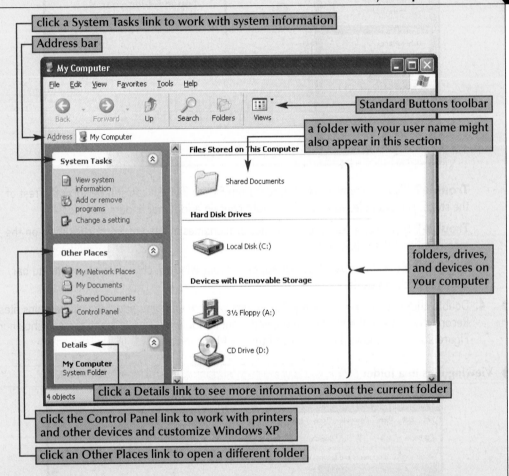

click a System Tasks link to work with system information

Address bar

Standard Buttons toolbar

a folder with your user name might also appear in this section

folders, drives, and devices on your computer

click a Details link to see more information about the current folder

click the Control Panel link to work with printers and other devices and customize Windows XP

click an Other Places link to open a different folder

3. In the Files Stored on This Computer section, double-click the folder with your user name. A window opens showing the contents of that folder. See Figure 24.

Figure 24 ▶ **Contents of the folder with your user name**

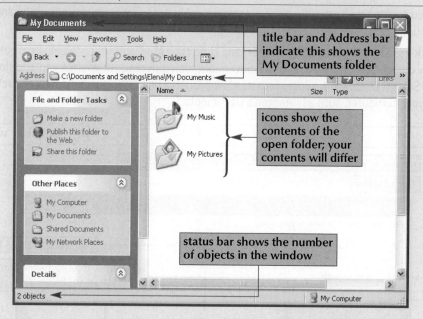

Trouble? If your window looks different from Figure 24, you can still perform the rest of the steps. For example, your window might contain additional folders and files.

Trouble? If you see a list of folder names or filenames instead of icons, click View on the menu bar, and then click Tiles.

Trouble? If the status bar does not appear in your window, click View on the menu bar, and then click Status Bar.

▶ **4.** Double-click each folder in the My Documents window until you find one that contains files. Record the name of the folder you opened. Your window will be similar to the one shown in Figure 25, which shows the contents of the My Music folder.

Figure 25 ▶ **Viewing files in a folder**

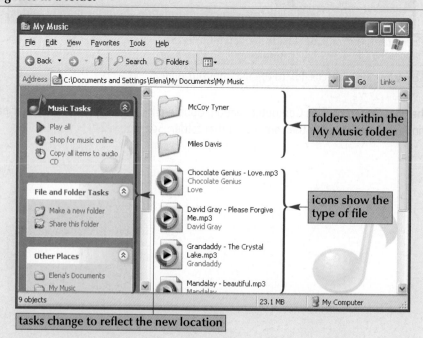

The tasks in the left pane change so that they are appropriate for the new location—in Figure 25, the left pane lists music tasks and other folders you might want to open. The right pane shows the contents of the folder you double-clicked. The file icon indicates its type. In Figure 25, the icon indicates that these are music files.

You can change the appearance of most windows to suit your preferences. You'll change the view of the My Computer window next.

Changing the View

Windows XP offers several options that control how toolbars, icons, and buttons appear in the My Computer window. The My Computer window, in addition to featuring a Standard Buttons toolbar, allows you to display the same toolbars that can appear on the Windows XP taskbar, such as the Address bar or the Links toolbar. You can use these toolbars to access the Web from the My Computer window. In this tutorial, however, you need to see only the Address bar and Standard Buttons toolbar.

To display only the Address bar and Standard Buttons toolbar:

1. Click **View** on the menu bar, and then point to **Toolbars**. The Standard Buttons and Address Bar commands on the Toolbars submenu should be checked, indicating that they are displayed in the My Computer window. The Links option should not be checked.

2. If the Standard Buttons or Address Bar commands *are not checked*, click the command to select it. Or if the Links command *is checked*, click it to deselect it. You must display the Toolbars submenu to select or deselect each command.

3. If necessary, click **View** on the menu bar, and then point to **Toolbars**. Make sure that only Standard Buttons, Address Bar, and Lock the Toolbars are checked.

4. Press the **Esc** key twice to close the menus.

Windows XP also provides five ways to view the contents of a disk—Thumbnails, Tiles, Icons, List, and Details. The default view, Tiles view, displays a large icon, title, file type, and file size for each file. The icon provides a visual cue to the type of file. You can also find this same information with the smaller icons displayed in the Icons and List views, but in less screen space. In Icons and List views, you can see more files and folders at one time, which is helpful when you have many files in one location.

All of the three icon views (Tiles, Icons, and List) help you quickly identify a file and its type, but what if you want more information about a set of files? Details view shows more information than the other three views. Details view shows the file icon, filename, file size, program used to create the file, and the date and time the file was created or last modified.

If you have graphic files, you can use Thumbnails view, which displays a small preview image of the graphic. In Thumbnails view, you can quickly see not only the filename, but also which picture or drawing the file contains. Thumbnails view is great for browsing a large collection of graphic files, but switching to this view can be time-consuming because Windows XP must first create all the preview images.

To practice switching from one view to another, you'll start by displaying the contents of the folder you opened earlier in Details view. So far, you've used the View menu to change the window view. Now you can use the Views button, which displays the same commands for changing views as the View menu.

To view a detailed list of files:

1. Click the **Views** button ▦ on the Standard Buttons toolbar, and then click **Details** to display details for the files on your disk. See Figure 26. Your files might differ or be listed in a different order.

Figure 26	Details view

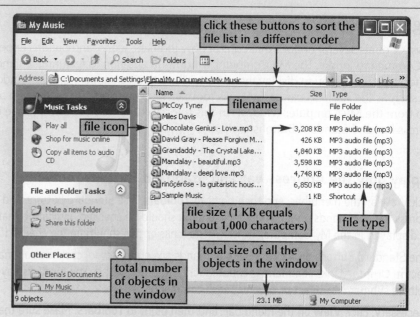

2. Look at the file sizes. Which files are the largest?
3. Look at the Type column. Which file is a shortcut?

Note that in Figure 26, the Sample Music item is a **shortcut**, a special type of file that serves as a direct link to another location that your computer can access, such as a folder, a document in a file, a program, a Windows tool, or a Web site.

One of the advantages of Details view is that you can sort the file list by filename, size, type, or date. This helps if you're looking for a particular file in a long file listing. For example, suppose you know that you created a file recently, but can't remember its name. You could sort the file list by date so that the most recent files appear at the top of the list.

To sort the file list by date:

1. Click **View** on the menu bar, click **Choose Details**, click the **Date Modified** check box if it is not checked, and then click the **OK** button.

2. Click the **Date Modified** button at the top of the list of files. The files are now sorted in descending order by date, starting with the most recent files.

3. Click the **Date Modified** button again. The sort order is reversed, with the oldest files now at the top of the list.

4. Click the **Name** button at the top of the file list. The files are now sorted in alphabetical order by filename.

Now that you have looked at the file details, you can switch back to Tiles view.

To switch to Tiles view:

▶ **1.** Click the **Views** button ⊞ on the Standard Buttons toolbar, and then click **Tiles** to return to Tiles view.

▶ **2.** Click the **Close** button ⊠ to close the window.

Now you can compare My Computer to Windows Explorer, another navigation tool.

Navigating with Windows Explorer

Like My Computer, Windows Explorer also lets you easily navigate the resources on your computer. Many of the techniques you use with the My Computer window apply to Windows Explorer—and vice versa. Both let you display and work with files and folders. By default, however, Windows Explorer also lets you see the hierarchy of all the folders on your computer. Viewing this hierarchy makes it easier to navigate your computer, especially if it contains many files and folders.

You will use Windows Explorer to open the same folders you opened in My Computer. As with other Windows XP programs, you start Windows Explorer using the Start menu.

To start Windows Explorer:

▶ **1.** Click the **Start** button on the taskbar, point to **All Programs**, point to **Accessories**, and then click **Windows Explorer**. The Windows Explorer window opens, as shown in Figure 27. By default, this window shows the contents of your My Documents folder when you first open it.

Windows Explorer window ◀ **Figure 27**

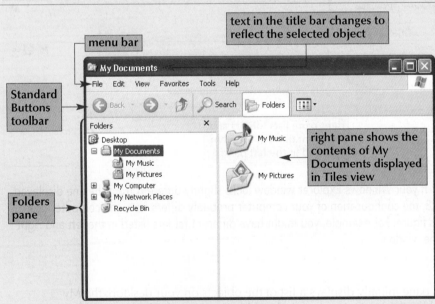

Trouble? If your Windows Explorer window looks slightly different from the one displayed in Figure 27, the configuration of your computer probably differs from the computer used to take this figure. Continue with Step 2.

▶ **2.** If the Windows Explorer window is not maximized, click the **Maximize** button ▢ on the Windows Explorer title bar.

Windows Explorer is divided into two sections called **panes**. The left pane, also called the **Explorer bar**, shows different ways of locating specific files or folders on your computer. The right pane lists the contents of these files and folders, similar to the view of files and folders in My Computer.

The Explorer bar can be displayed in one of five ways: as a Search, Favorites, Media, History, or Folders pane. The Search pane includes tools to help you search for a particular file or folder on your computer. The Favorites pane lists your favorite files and folders on your computer and sites on the World Wide Web. The Media pane lists multimedia files, such as videos and music. The History pane organizes the files and folders on your computer by the date you last worked with them. The Folders pane organizes your files and folders based on their location in the hierarchy of objects on your computer. To move between these different panes, you click the appropriate command on the View menu. You can also quickly open the Search and Folders panes by clicking either the Search button ⌕ or the Folders button 📁 on the Standard Buttons toolbar. Note that the Explorer bar is available in any Windows XP window that displays files and folders. You can, for example, use the Explorer bar in the My Computer window.

You'll start working with Windows Explorer using the Folders pane.

To view the Folders pane:

▶ 1. Click **View** on the menu bar, and then point to **Explorer Bar**.

▶ 2. If necessary, click **Folders** to check that option; otherwise, click a blank area of the screen to close the View menu. Your Windows Explorer window should now resemble Figure 28.

| Figure 28 | Folders pane in the Windows Explorer window |

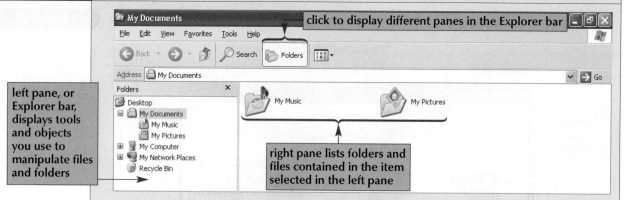

Trouble? If your Windows Explorer window looks slightly different from the one displayed in Figure 28, the configuration of your computer probably differs from the computer used to take this figure. For example, you might have different folders listed in the left and right panes of the window.

The Folders pane initially displays a list of the objects on your desktop: the My Documents folder, the My Computer window, the My Network Places window, and the Recycle Bin. If your desktop contains other folders or objects, those are displayed as well. The right pane of the Windows Explorer window displays the contents of the object selected in the Folders pane. In this case, the My Documents folder is the selected object, and it contains two items—the My Music and My Pictures folders. Icons for these objects are therefore displayed in the right pane.

Now you can open the same folder you opened before in the My Computer window.

To open a folder:

▶ **1.** Double-click the folder you double-clicked earlier in the My Computer window, such as the My Music folder. The contents of that folder appear in the right pane of the Windows Explorer window, and the folder you opened is selected in the left pane.

▶ **2.** Click the **Close** button ☒ on the title bar to close the window.

Getting Help

Windows XP **Help** provides on-screen information about the program you are using. Help for the Windows XP operating system is available by clicking the Start button on the taskbar and then clicking Help and Support on the Start menu. If you want Help for a particular program, such as WordPad, you must first start the program, and then click Help on the program's menu bar.

When you start Help for Windows XP, a Windows Help and Support Center window opens, which gives you access to Help files stored on your computer as well as Help information stored on Microsoft's Web site. If you are not connected to the Web, you only have access to the Help files stored on your computer.

To start Windows XP Help:

▶ **1.** Click the **Start** button on the taskbar.

▶ **2.** Click **Help and Support**. The Help and Support Center window opens. See Figure 29.

Windows XP Help and Support Center window ◀ **Figure 29**

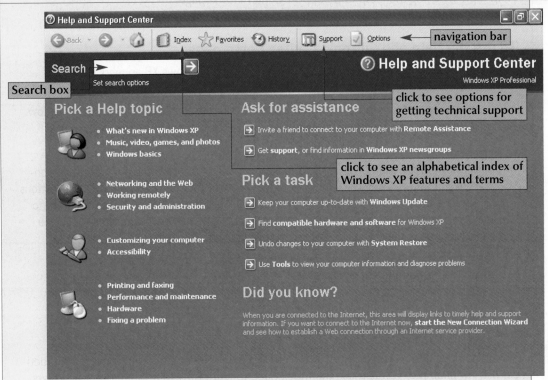

Trouble? If the Help and Support window does not display the information you see in Figure 29, click the Home icon on the navigation bar at the top of the window to view Help contents.

The Windows XP Help and Support Center window organizes the vast amount of help and support information into pages. These six pages—the Home, Index, Favorites, History, Support, and Options page—are designed to aid users in locating information on a particular topic quickly. To open one of these pages, click its button on the navigation bar. The Home page lists common tasks under the heading "Pick a Help topic" in the left pane on the page. Click a task to see detailed information or instructions about that task in the right pane of the page. The right pane of the Home page lists common tasks, tips, and ways you can ask for assistance. For example, you can contact a support professional or download the latest version of Windows XP.

The Index page displays an alphabetical list of all the Help topics from which you can choose. The Favorites page shows Help topics you've added to your Favorites list. To add a topic to the Favorites list, open the topic, and then click the Favorites button on the Help window. The History page lists links you've recently selected in Help. The Support page includes links that you can click to connect to the Microsoft Web site, if possible, for additional assistance. The Options page provides ways you can customize Help. For example, you can change the appearance of the navigation bar.

If you can't find the topic you want listed on any of the six Help and Support Center pages, the word that you are using for a feature or topic might be different from the word that Windows XP uses. You can use the Search box to search for all keywords contained in the Help pages, not just the topic titles. In the Search box, you can type any word or phrase, click the Search button, and Windows XP lists all the Help topics that contain that word or phrase.

Viewing Topics on the Windows XP Help and Support Center Home Page

Windows XP Help includes instructions on using Help itself. You can learn how to find a Help topic by using the Help and Support Center Home page.

To use the Help and Support Center Home page:

▶ 1. Click **Windows basics**. A list of topics related to using Windows XP appears in the left pane of the Help and Support Center window.

▶ 2. Click **Tips for using Help**. A list of Help topics appears in the right pane of the Help window.

▶ 3. Click **Change fonts in Help and Support Center**. The instructions appear in the right pane of the Help and Support Center window.

Besides listing the pages in the Help and Support Center window, the navigation bar contains two buttons—the Back button 🔙 and the Forward button 🔜 . You use these buttons to navigate the pages you've already opened. You'll use the Back button next to return to the previous page you viewed. Once you do, you activate the Forward button, which you can click to go to the next page of those you've opened.

▶ 4. Click the **Back** button 🔙 on the navigation bar. You return to the Tips for using Help page. The Forward button is now active.

Using a Keyboard

Selecting a Topic from the Index

The Index page allows you to jump to a Help topic by selecting a topic from an alphabetical list. For example, you can use the Index page to learn how to arrange open windows on your desktop.

To find a Help topic using the Index page:

1. Click **Index** 📖 on the navigation bar. A long list of indexed Help topics appears in the left pane.

2. Drag the **scroll box** down to view additional topics in the list box.

   You can quickly jump to any part of the list by typing the first few characters of a word or phrase in the box that appears above the Index list.

3. If necessary, click in the Type in the keyword to find text box above the Index list, and then type **windows**. As you type each character in the word, the list of Index topics scrolls and eventually displays topics that relate to windows.

4. Under the "windows and panes on your computer screen" topic, click the topic **reducing windows to taskbar buttons**, and then click the **Display** button. When there is just one topic, it appears immediately in the right pane; otherwise, the Topics Found window opens, listing all topics indexed under the selected entry.

   The information you requested appears in the right pane. This topic has two underlined phrases, "taskbar" and "Related Topics," which you can click to view definitions or additional information.

5. Click the underlined phrase **taskbar**. A ScreenTip shows the definition of "taskbar."

6. Click a blank area of the Help and Support Center window to close the ScreenTip.

If you have an Internet connection, you can use another Help page, Support, to contact Microsoft support or get in touch with other users of Windows XP. The Support page works like the Home page. To get support on a particular feature, you click a support option and then click the topic for which you need help. Continue clicking topics, if necessary, until you get help from a Microsoft support person or an experienced Windows XP user.

Searching the Help Pages

If you can't find the topic you need by using the Home or Index pages, or if you want to quickly find Help pages related to a particular topic, you can use the Search box. Suppose you want to know how to exit Windows XP, but you don't know if Windows refers to this as exiting, quitting, closing, or shutting down. You can search the Help pages to find just the right topic.

To search the Help pages for information on exiting Windows XP:

1. Click in the Search box. A blinking insertion point appears.

2. Type **shutdown** and then click the **Start Searching** button ➡. A list of Help pages containing the word "shutdown" appears in the left pane of the Help and Support Center window. The ones listed under Suggested Topics are topics where "shutdown" has been assigned as a keyword—meaning the topics have to do with shutting something down.

3. Click the **Full-text Search Matches** button. In these topics, "shutdown" is included in the text of the Help topic.

4. Click the **Suggested Topics** button, and then click **Turn off the computer**. A Help topic appears in the right pane of the Help and Support Center window, as shown in Figure 30.

Figure 30 | **Using search to find a Help page**

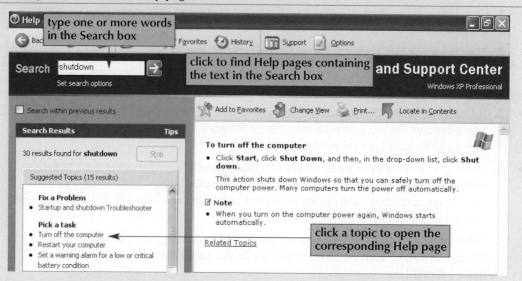

If this topic were longer than the Help and Support Center window, you could use the scroll bar to read the entire topic.

5. Click the **Close** button ⊠ on the title bar to close the Help and Support Center window.

Now that you know how Windows XP Help works, don't forget to use it. Use Help when you need to perform a new task or when you forget how to complete a procedure.

Shutting Down Windows XP

You should always shut down Windows XP before you turn off your computer. If you turn off your computer without shutting it down correctly, you might lose data and damage your files.

Typically you will use the Turn Off Computer command on the Start menu when you want to turn off your computer. However, your school might prefer that you select the Log Off command on the Start menu. This command logs you out of Windows XP but leaves the computer turned on, allowing another user to log on without restarting the computer. Check with your instructor or technical support person for the preferred method at your lab.

When you select the Turn Off Computer command on the Start menu, the Turn Off Computer dialog box opens with four buttons: Standby, Turn Off, Restart, and Cancel. You choose Standby when you want to put your computer into an idle state in which it consumes less power, but is still available for immediate use. Choose Turn Off to shut down Windows and turn off the power, and choose Restart to shut down Windows and then immediately start it again. Choose Cancel if you do not want to end your Windows session, but want to return to your previous task.

To shut down Windows XP:

1. Click the **Start** button on the taskbar.

2. Click the **Turn Off Computer** command at the bottom of the Start menu. The Turn Off Computer dialog box opens. See Figure 31.

Shutting down the computer ◀ Figure 31

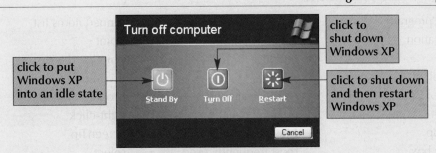

Trouble? If you are supposed to log off rather than shut down, click Log Off instead and follow your school's logoff procedure.

▶ 3. Click the **Turn Off** button.

▶ 4. Wait until you see a message indicating that it is safe to turn off your computer. If your lab procedure includes switching off your computer after shutting it down, do so now; otherwise, leave the computer running. Some computers turn themselves off automatically.

In this session you learned how to start and close programs and how to use multiple programs at the same time. You learned how to work with windows and the controls they employ. Finally, you learned how to get help when you need it and shut down Windows XP. After completing Steve's introductory course, you are well on your way to mastering the fundamentals of using the Windows XP operating system.

Session 2 Quick Check

1. The _____ icon on the Start menu represents your computer, its storage devices, printers, and other objects.
2. Explain the difference between the left pane in My Computer (the Tasks pane) and the Folders pane in Windows Explorer.
3. What information does Details view supply about a list of folders and files?
4. True or false: A shortcut is a special type of file that serves as a direct link to another location that your computer can access, such as a folder or a document in a file.
5. Name the five ways that you can display the Explorer bar in Windows Explorer.
6. In the Help and Support Center window, the _____ page displays an alphabetical list of all the Help topics from which you can choose.
7. To learn how to perform new tasks, you can use _____.
8. You should always _____ Windows XP before you turn off your computer.

Tutorial Summary

In this tutorial, you learned the basics of Windows XP. You toured the desktop and learned how to open objects on the desktop. You explored the Start menu and opened its submenus. You started programs from the Start menu, and then switched between multiple programs. You worked with windows by manipulating them. You selected options from a menu and buttons on a toolbar. You also examined typical dialog boxes and their controls. Then you explored your computer with My Computer and Windows Explorer, learned how to get help when you need it, and finally shut down Windows XP.

Key Terms

active program	list arrow	pinned items list
application	list box	point
click	log off	pointing device
control	menu	program
Control Panel	menu command	program button
default	menu convention	right-click
desktop	Microsoft Windows XP	ScreenTip
dialog box	most frequently used	select
double-click	programs list	shortcut
drag	mouse	shortcut menu
exit	multitask	sizing handle
Explorer bar	My Computer	Start menu
graphical user interface (GUI)	My Documents	submenu
Help	navigate	user name
Help and Support Center	operating system	window
icon	pane	Windows XP
Internet	password	

Practice

Practice the skills you learned in the tutorial.

Review Assignments

There are no Data Files needed for the Review Assignments.

Steve Laslow offers a practice session as a follow-up to his basic Windows XP course. You'll start working on the Windows XP desktop, with no windows opened or minimized. Complete the following steps, recording your answers to any questions according to your instructor's preferences:

1. Start Windows XP and log on, if necessary.
2. Use the mouse to point to each object on your desktop. Record the names of each object as they appear in the ScreenTips.
3. Click the Start button. How many menu items or commands are on the Start menu?
4. Run the WordPad program located on the Accessories menu. How many program buttons are now on the taskbar (don't count toolbar buttons or items in the notification area)?
5. Run the Paint program and maximize the Paint window. How many programs are running now?
6. Switch to WordPad. What are two visual clues that tell you that WordPad is the active program?
7. Close WordPad, and then restore the Paint window.
8. Open the Recycle Bin window. Record the number of items it contains.
9. Drag the Recycle Bin window so that you can see it and the Paint window.
10. Close the Paint window from the taskbar.
11. Open the File menu in the Recycle Bin window. Write down the commands on the menu. Press the Esc key to close the menu.
12. Use any menu in the Recycle Bin window to open a dialog box. What steps did you perform? What dialog box did you open? For what do you think you use this dialog box? Click Cancel to close the dialog box.
13. Close the Recycle Bin window.

14. Open the My Computer window, and then open the My Documents folder that is designed to contain your documents.
15. Open a folder in the My Documents window that you did not open in the tutorial. List the name and contents of that folder.
16. Close the My Documents window.
17. Start Windows Explorer. Use the Folders pane to navigate to the same folder you opened in Step 14. What steps did you perform?
18. Change the view of the icons in the right pane of the Windows Explorer window. What view did you select? Describe the icons in the Windows Explorer window.
19. Close the Windows Explorer window.
20. Open the Help and Support Center window.
21. Use the Help and Support Center window to learn something new about Windows Explorer. What did you learn? How did you find this topic?
22. Use the Index page to find information about the topic of speech recognition, a feature new to Windows XP. How many topics are listed? What is their primary subject matter?
23. Use the Search box to find information about the topic of speech recognition. How many topics are listed?
24. Open the Home page in the Help and Support Center window, click What's new in Windows XP, and then click Windows XP Articles: Walkthrough ways to use your PC.
25. Click Walkthrough: Making Music.
26. Read the Get Started page. (*Hint:* The contents of the article are listed in a box in the upper-left corner of the window. Each topic is a link you can click to go to another page in the article.)
27. Click the links in the contents box, and then answer the following questions using the information you find:
    a. How can you listen to music using Windows XP?
    b. What is a playlist? What is the first step you take to create one?
    c. What is the advantage of listening to Internet radio?
28. Close Help, and then close WordPad.
29. Shut down or log off Windows.

Case Problem 1

Apply

Use the skills you learned in the tutorial to explore the contents of other folders on your computer for JL Productions.

There are no Data Files needed for this Case Problem.

JL Productions JL Productions is a company in Fort Wayne, Indiana, that produces videos and hosts advertising events for businesses in the Midwest. You have recently been hired by Julian Letice, the owner of JL Productions, to help him with office management. Your first task is to explore Julian's new Windows XP computer. Because he is visually oriented, he is particularly interested in features that improve the appearance of his desktop or that would enhance the materials he sends to his clients. Complete the following steps:

1. Start Windows XP and log on, if necessary.
2. From the desktop or the Start menu, open My Computer, and then maximize the window.

Explore

3. If necessary, change the My Computer window to Tiles view, arrange icons by type, and organize icons by group. (*Hint:* Click View on the menu bar, point to Arrange Icons by, and then click Show in Groups.) List the names of the drives on your computer.
4. Click the Shared Documents link in the Other Places area of the Tasks pane. What are the names of the Shared folders within this folder?
5. Display the Folders pane in the My Computer window. (*Hint:* Click the Folders button on the Standard Buttons toolbar.) Where is the Shared Documents folder located in the folder structure of your computer? Describe its relation to the My Documents folder.

6. Close the Folders pane, open the My Pictures folder, click the View as a slide show link in the Picture Tasks dynamic menu, and enjoy the slide show. When you are ready to exit the slide show, press the Esc key.

7. Navigate to a folder that contains graphics, music, or other media files, such as My Pictures or My Music. Switch to Details view. What types of files are contained in this folder?

8. Double-click the icon for one of the files in this folder. What happens? Close any windows that open.

9. Close the My Computer window, if necessary, and then start Windows Explorer. Open the Search pane in the Windows Explorer window. (*Hint:* Click the Search button on the Standard Buttons toolbar.)

10. Open the Help and Support Center window and then find and read topics that explain how to use the Search pane to find types of files.

Explore

11. Use the Search pane to find .bmp files, a common type of graphics file, on your computer. (*Hint:* Use *.bmp as the search text.) Name at least two locations where your computer stores .bmp files.

12. Close all open windows.

Apply

Apply what you learned in the tutorial to work with Windows XP installed on a computer for a landscaping business.

Case Problem 2

There are no Data Files needed for this Case Problem.

Rolling Hills Landscaping After working for a number of gardening and landscaping firms in Towson, Maryland, Elaine Rodriguez founded her own company, named Rolling Hills Landscaping. She works with property owners and businesses to create garden and landscaping designs, and contracts with local professional gardeners to plant and maintain the landscapes. She hired you to help her perform office tasks, and asks you to start by teaching her the basics of using her computer, which runs Windows XP. She especially wants to know which programs are installed on her computer and what they do. Complete the following:

1. Open the Start menu and write down the programs on the pinned items list.

2. Start one of the programs on the pinned items list and then describe what it does. Close the program.

3. Open the Start menu and write down the programs on the most frequently used programs list.

4. Start one of the programs on the most frequently used programs list and then describe what it does. Close the program.

5. Open the All Programs menu, point to the Accessories folder, and then open a program in the Accessories folder. What program did you start?

6. Use the Help and Support Center to research the program you started in Step 5. Find out how to perform a task using that program.

7. Perform the steps you researched in Step 6. What task did you complete? Write down the steps you performed and the results.

8. Close all open windows.

9. Start another program using the Start menu. Make sure the program includes a Help menu on its menu bar. Describe the steps you performed.

10. Click Help on the menu bar and then click each command on the menu until you open a window listing Help topics for this program. Describe the typical tasks users perform when they use this program.

Explore

11. If possible, perform one set of steps you researched in Step 10. Describe the task you performed and the results. Then close the program.

Challenge

Extend what you've learned to customize the My Computer window for a consumer research organization.

Explore

Explore

Explore

Explore

Case Problem 3

There are no Data Files needed for this Case Problem.

Yamamoto Research   Ken Yamamoto runs a small business called Yamamoto Research, which researches and tests consumer products, focusing on those used in the home health care industry. Ken has created many files and folders on his new Windows XP computer, and asks you to catalog his options for working in the My Computer window. Complete the following steps:

1. Open the My Computer window. Open each menu in the My Computer window, and write down any items that seem related to changing the appearance of the window.
2. Display the My Computer window so that no toolbars appear. Then restore the window to its original condition.
3. Navigate to a folder containing graphic files. Display the icons using Thumbnail view.
4. Change the view to Icons view. Describe the differences among Icons, Thumbnail, and Tiles view.
5. In Icons view, arrange the icons by type. Then arrange them by name.
6. Switch to Details view. On the View menu, open a dialog box that lets you choose the details displayed in Details view. Note which items are currently checked.
7. Use the Choose Details dialog box to show only the name, type, and size of the items in Details view. Close the Choose Details dialog box and then sort the contents of the My Computer window by size.
8. Use the Choose Details dialog box to restore your original settings. Then sort the contents of the My Computer window by name.
9. On the Tools menu, click Folder Options to open the Folder Options dialog box. Select the option that uses Windows Classic folders, and then click the OK button. Describe the changes in the My Computer window.
10. Open the Folder Options dialog box again and click the Restore Defaults button.
11. Open the Help and Support Center window from the My Computer window and search for information about folder options. Find a definition of hidden files, and how to hide and show hidden files in the My Computer window. Record your findings.
12. Close all open windows.

Research

Work with the skills you've learned, and use the Internet, to provide information to a translation company.

Explore

Case Problem 4

There are no Data Files needed for this Case Problem.

Janus Translation   Several years ago, Doug Janus and Mohammed Amos started a company that translates software programs so that they can be used in Europe, Asia, and South America. Doug often works from home, and recently set up a computer running Windows XP. He asks you to help him get connected to the Internet. You suggest using the Help and Support Center to find information. Doug also needs to know more about the Help and Support Center itself. Complete the following steps:

1. In the Help and Support Center, find information about the hardware and software Doug needs to connect to the Internet.
2. Use the Help and Support Center to find two ways that Doug can connect to the Internet. Describe these two methods.
3. Choose a topic you'd like to research using the Windows XP online Help system. Look for information on your topic using the Help and Support Center Home page, Index page, Search box, and Support page. (*Hint*: Click the Support button on the navigation bar to open the Support page.) From the Support page, go to a Windows Web site forum to research your topic. (You must be connected to the Internet to complete this step.)

4. Once you've found all the information you can, compare the four methods (Home page, Index page, Search box, and Support page) of looking for information. Write a paragraph that discusses which method proved the most useful. Did you reach the same information topics using all four methods? In a second paragraph, summarize what you learned about your topic. Finally, in a third paragraph, indicate under what circumstances you'd use which method.

Assess

SAM Assessment and Training

If you have a SAM user profile, you may have access to hands-on instruction, practice, and assessment of the skills covered in this tutorial. Log in to your SAM account and go to your assignments page to see what your instructor has assigned.

Reinforce

Lab Assignments

Using a Mouse   Using a Keyboard

The New Perspectives Labs are designed to help you master some of the key concepts and skills presented in this text. The steps for completing this Lab are located on the Course Technology Web site. Log on to the Internet and use your Web browser to go to the Student Online Companion for New Perspectives Office 2003 at **www.course.com/np/office2003**. Click the Lab Assignments link, and then navigate to the assignments for this tutorial.

Review

Quick Check Answers

Session 1

1. to provide access to common tools and programs currently running
2. text that displays the purpose and function of a window component, such as a button
3. Start menu
4. multitasking
5. its button appears on the taskbar
6. to conserve computer resources such as memory
7. toolbar
8. list box

Session 2

1. My Computer
2. The Tasks pane (the left pane) of My Computer lists tasks that change so that they are appropriate for the new location. When the left pane in Windows Explorer shows the Folders pane, it shows different ways of locating specific files or folders on your computer.
3. filename, file size, file type, and date modified
4. true
5. Search, Favorites, Media, History, and Folders panes
6. Index
7. online Help or Help and Support Center
8. shut down

New Perspectives on
Managing Your Files

Creating and Working with Files   FM 3
and Folders in Windows XP

Read This Before You Begin

To the Student

Data Files

To complete the Managing Your Files (FM) tutorial, you need the starting student Data Files. Your instructor will either provide you with these Data Files or ask you to obtain them yourself.

The Managing Your Files tutorial requires the folder named "FM" to complete the Tutorial, Review Assignments, and Case Problems. You will need to copy this folder from a file server, a standalone computer, or the Web to the drive and folder where you will be storing your Data Files. Your instructor will tell you which computer, drive letter, and folder(s) contain the files you need. You can also download the files by going to www.course.com; see the inside back or front cover for more information on downloading the files, or ask your instructor or technical support person for assistance.

If you are storing your Data Files on floppy disks, you will need **two** blank, formatted, high-density disks for this tutorial. Label your disks as shown, and place on them the folders indicated.

▼ **FM Data Disk 1: Tutorial**
  FM\Tutorial folder
▼ **FM Data Disk 2: Exercises**
  FM\Review folder
  FM\Cases folder

When you begin this tutorial, refer to the Student Data Files section at the bottom of the tutorial opener page, which indicates which folders and files you need for the tutorial. Each end-of-tutorial exercise also indicates the files you need to complete that exercise

Course Labs

The Managing Your Files tutorial features an interactive Course Lab to help you understand file management concepts. There are Lab Assignments at the end of the tutorial that relate to this lab. Contact your instructor or technical support person for assistance in accessing the labs.

To the Instructor

The Data Files and Course Labs are available on the Instructor Resources CD for this title. Follow the instructions in the Help file on the CD to install the programs to your network or standalone computer. See the "To the Student" section above for information on how to set up the Data Files that accompany this text.

You are granted a license to copy the Data Files and Course Labs to any computer or computer network used by students who have purchased this book.

System Requirements

If you are going to work through this book using your own computer, you need:

• **Computer System** This tutorial assumes a typical installation of Microsoft Windows XP Professional (although the Microsoft Windows XP Home version is acceptable as well).

• **Data Files** You will not be able to complete the tutorials or exercises in this book using your own computer until you have the necessary starting Data Files.

• **Course Labs** See your instructor or technical support person to obtain the Course Lab software for use on your own computer.

www.course.com/NewPerspectives

Objectives

- Develop file management strategies
- Explore files and folders
- Create, name, copy, move, and delete folders
- Name, copy, move, and delete files
- Work with compressed files

Managing Your Files

Creating and Working with Files and Folders in Windows XP

Case

Distance Learning Company

The Distance Learning Company specializes in distance learning courses for individuals who want to participate in college-level classes to work toward a degree or for personal enrichment. Distance learning is formalized education that typically takes place using a computer and the Internet, replacing normal classroom interaction with modern communications technology. The company's goal is to help students gain new skills and stay competitive in the job market. The head of the Customer Service Department, Shannon Connell, interacts with the Distance Learning Company's clients on the phone and from her computer. Shannon, like all other employees, is required to learn the basics of managing files on her computer.

In this tutorial, you'll help Shannon devise a strategy for managing files. You'll learn how Windows XP organizes files and folders, and you'll examine Windows XP file management tools. You'll create folders and organize files within them. You'll also explore options for working with compressed files.

Lab

Using Files

Student Data Files

▼**FM folder**

▽ **Tutorial folder**

    Agenda.doc
    Holiday.bmp
    New Logo.bmp
    Proposal.doc
    Resume.doc
    Salinas members.eml
    Stationery.bmp
    Vinca.jpg

▽ **Review folder**

    Billing Worksheet.wk4
    Car Savings Plan.xls
    Commissions.xls
    Contracts.xls
    Customer Accounts.xls
    Filenames.pps
    Personal Loan.doc
    Speech.wav
    Water lilies.jpg

▽ **Cases folder**

    Invoice Feb.xls
    Invoice Jan.xls
    Invoice March.xls
    Painting Class - Agenda.doc
    Painting Class - Questionnaire.doc
    Painting Class - Teaching Manual.doc
    Paris.jpg
    Vegetables.jpg

Using Files

Organizing Files and Folders

Knowing how to save, locate, and organize computer files makes you more productive when you are working with a computer. A **file**, often referred to as a **document**, is a collection of data that has a name and is stored in a computer. Once you create a file, you can open it, edit its contents, print it, and save it again—usually using the same program you used to create it. You organize files by storing them in **folders**, which are containers for your files. You need to organize files so you can find them easily and work efficiently.

A file cabinet is a common metaphor for computer file organization. A computer is like a file cabinet that has two or more drawers—each drawer is a storage device, or **disk**. Each disk contains folders that hold documents, or files. To make it easy to retrieve files, you arrange them logically into folders. For example, one folder might contain financial data, another might contain your creative work, and another could contain information you're collecting for an upcoming vacation.

A computer can store folders and files on different types of disks, ranging from removable media—such as **USB drives** (also called USB flash drives), **compact discs (CDs)**, and **floppy disks**—to **hard disks**, or fixed disks, which are permanently stored in a computer. Hard disks are the most popular type of computer storage because they can contain many gigabytes of data, millions of times more data than a floppy disk, and are economical.

To have your computer access a removable disk, you must insert the disk into a **drive**, which is a computer device that can retrieve and sometimes record data on a disk. See Figure 1. A hard disk is already contained in a drive, so you don't need to insert it each time you use the computer.

Figure 1 ▶ **Computer drives and disks**

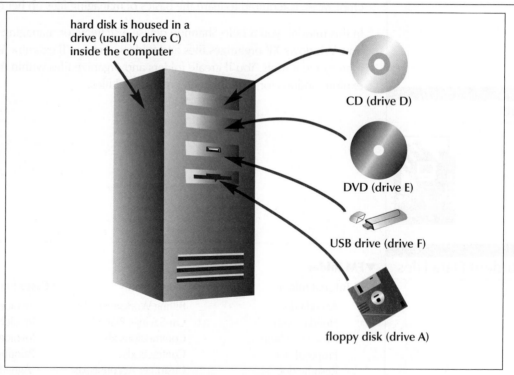

hard disk is housed in a
drive (usually drive C)
inside the computer

CD (drive D)

DVD (drive E)

USB drive (drive F)

floppy disk (drive A)

A computer distinguishes one drive from another by assigning each a drive letter. The floppy disk drive is drive A. (Most computers have only one floppy disk drive—if your computer has two, the second one is called drive B.) The hard disk is usually assigned to drive C. The remaining drives can have any other letters, but are usually assigned in the order that the drives were installed on the computer—so your USB drive might be drive D or drive F.

Understanding the Need for Organizing Files and Folders

Windows XP stores thousands of files in many folders on the hard disk of your computer. These are system files that Windows XP needs to display the desktop, use drives, and perform other operating system tasks. To ensure system stability and find files quickly, Windows organizes the folders and files in a hierarchy, or **file system**. At the top of the hierarchy, Windows stores folders and important files that it needs when you turn on the computer. This location is called the **root directory**, and is usually drive C (the hard disk). The term "root" refers to another popular metaphor for visualizing a file system—an upside-down tree, which reflects the file hierarchy that Windows uses. In Figure 2, the tree trunk corresponds to the root directory, the branches to the folders, and the leaves to files.

Windows file hierarchy | **Figure 2**

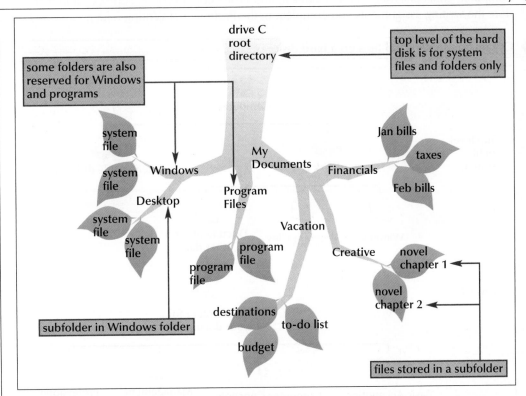

Note that some folders contain other folders. An effectively organized computer contains a few folders in the root directory, and those folders contain other folders, also called **subfolders**.

The root directory, or top level, of the hard disk is for system files and folders only—you should not store your own work here because it could interfere with Windows or a program. (If you are working in a computer lab, you might not be allowed to access the root directory.)

Do not delete or move any files or folders from the root directory of the hard disk—doing so could mean that you cannot run or start the computer. In fact, you should not reorganize or change any folder that contains installed software, because Windows XP expects to find the files for specific programs within certain folders. If you reorganize or change these folders, Windows XP cannot locate and start the programs stored in that folder. Likewise, you should not make changes to the folder that contains the Windows XP operating system (usually named Windows or Winnt).

Because the top level of the hard disk is off limits for your files—the ones that you create, open, and save on the hard disk—you must store your files in subfolders. If you are working on your own computer, you should store your files within the My Documents folder. If you are working in a computer lab, you will probably use a different location that your instructor specifies. If you simply store all your files in one folder, however, you will soon have trouble finding the ones you want. Instead, you should create folders within a main folder to separate files in a way that makes sense for you.

Likewise, if you store most of your files on removable media, such as USB drives, you need to organize those files into folders and subfolders. Before you start creating folders, whether on a hard disk or removable disk, you should plan the organization you will use.

Developing Strategies for Organizing Files and Folders

The type of disk you use to store files determines how you organize those files. Figure 3 shows how you could organize your files on a hard disk if you were taking a full semester of distance learning classes. To duplicate this organization, you would open the main folder for your documents, create four folders—one each for the Basic Accounting, Computer Concepts, Management Skills II, and Professional Writing courses—and then store the writing assignments you complete in the Professional Writing folder.

Figure 3 ▶ **Organizing folders and files on a hard disk**

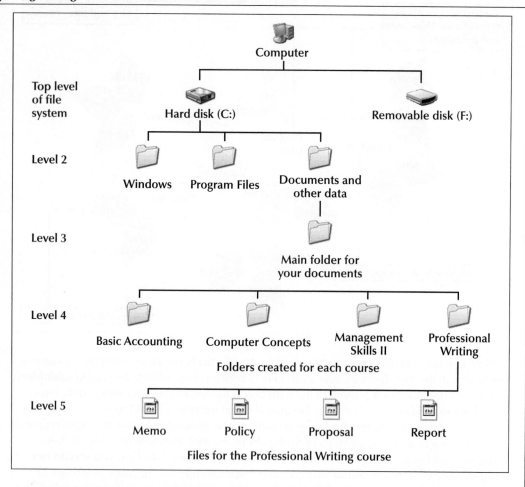

If you store your files on removable media, such as a USB drive or rewritable CD, you can use a simpler organization because you do not have to account for system files. In general, the larger the medium, the more levels of folders you should use because large media can store more files, and therefore need better organization. For example, you could organize your files on a 128 MB USB drive. In the top level of the USB drive, you could create folders for each general category of documents you store—one each for Courses, Creative, Financials, and Vacation. The Courses folder could then include one folder for each course, and each of those folders could contain the appropriate files.

You could organize these files on 1.44 MB floppy disks. Because the storage capacity of a floppy disk is much less than that of a USB drive, you would probably use one floppy disk for your courses, another for creative work, and so on. If you had to create large documents for your courses, you could use one floppy disk for each course.

If you work on two computers, such as one computer at an office or school and another computer at home, you can duplicate the folders you use on both computers to simplify transferring files from one computer to another. For example, if you have four folders in your My Documents folder on your work computer, you would create these same four folders on your removable media as well as in the My Documents folder of your home computer. If you change a file on the hard disk of your home computer, you can copy the most recent version of the file to the corresponding folder on your removable media so that it is available when you are at work. You also then have a **backup**, or duplicate copy, of important files that you need.

Planning Your Organization

Now that you've explored the basics of organizing files on a computer, you can plan the organization of your files for this book by writing in your answers to the following questions:

1. How do you obtain the files for this book (on a USB drive from your instructor, for example)? _____
   _____

2. On what drive do you store your files for this book (drive A, C, D, for example)? _____
   _____

3. Do you use a particular folder on this drive? If so, which folder do you use? _____
   _____

4. Is this folder contained within another folder? If so, what is the name of that main folder?
   _____

5. On what type of disk do you save your files for this book (hard disk, USB drive, CD, or network drive, for example)? _____

   If you cannot answer any of these questions, ask your instructor for help.

Exploring Files and Folders

Windows XP provides two tools for exploring the files and folders on your computer—Windows Explorer and My Computer. Both display the contents of your computer, using icons to represent drives, folders, and files. However, by default, each presents a different view of your computer. **Windows Explorer** shows the files, folders, and drives on your computer, making it easy to navigate, or move from one location to another within the file hierarchy. **My Computer** shows the drives on your computer and makes it easy to perform system tasks, such as viewing system information.

The Windows Explorer window is divided into two sections, called **panes**. The left pane, also called the **Explorer bar** or **Folders pane**, shows the hierarchy of the folders and other locations on your computer. The right pane lists the contents of these folders and other locations. If you select a folder in the left pane, for example, the files stored in that folder appear in the right pane. The My Computer window is also divided into panes—the left pane, called the task pane, lists tasks related to the items displayed in the right pane.

If the Folders pane in Windows Explorer showed all the folders on your computer at once, it could be a very long list. Instead, Windows Explorer allows you to open drives and folders only when you want to see what they contain. If a folder contains subfolders, an expand icon ✛ appears to the left of the folder icon. (The same is true for drives.) To view the folders contained in an object, you click the expand icon. A collapse icon ⊟ then appears next to the folder icon; click the collapse icon to close the folder. To view the files contained in a folder, you click the folder icon, and the files appear in the right pane. See Figure 4.

Figure 4	Viewing folder contents in Windows Explorer

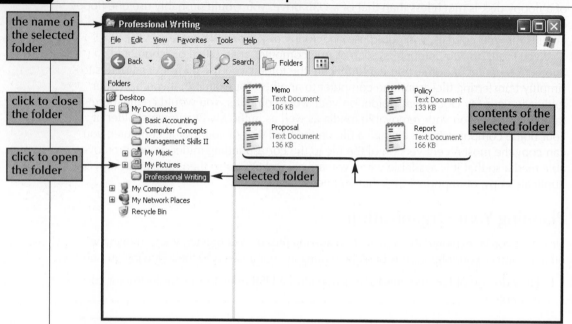

Using the Folders pane helps you navigate your computer and orients you to your current location. As you move, copy, delete, and perform other tasks with the files in the right pane of Windows Explorer, you can refer to the Folders pane to see how your changes affect the overall organization.

Like Windows Explorer, My Computer also lets you view, organize, and access the drives, folders, and files on your computer. Instead of using the Folders pane, however, you can navigate your computer in four other ways:

- **Opening drives and folders in the right pane:** To view the contents of a drive or folder, double-click the drive or folder icon in the right pane of the My Computer window. For example, to view the contents of the Professional Writing folder shown in Figure 5, you open the My Documents folder and then the Professional Writing folder.
- **Using the Standard Buttons toolbar:** Click the buttons on the Standard Buttons toolbar to navigate the hierarchy of drives, folders, subfolders, and other objects in your computer.
- **Using the Address bar:** By clicking the Address bar list arrow, you can view a list of drives, folders, and other locations on your computer. This gives you a quick way of moving to an upper level of the Windows XP file system without navigating the intermediate levels.
- **Using the task pane:** The Other Places area of the My Computer task pane lists links you can click to quickly open folders or navigate to other useful places.

By default, when you first open My Computer, it shows all the drives available on your computer, whereas Windows Explorer shows the files, folders, and drives on your computer. However, by changing window settings, you can make the two tools interchangeable. You can change settings in the My Computer window to show the Folders pane instead of the task pane. If you do, you have the same setup as Windows Explorer. Likewise, if you close the Folders pane in the Windows Explorer window, the task pane opens, giving you the same setup as in the My Computer window.

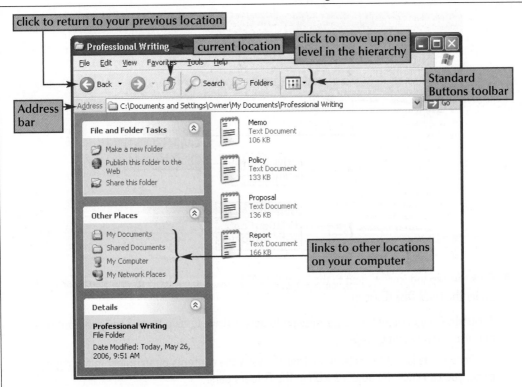

Viewing folder contents in My Computer — Figure 5

Shannon prefers to use Windows Explorer to manage her files. You'll use Windows Explorer to manage files in the rest of this tutorial.

Using Windows Explorer

Windows XP also provides a folder for your documents—the **My Documents folder**, which is designed to store the files and folders you work with regularly. On your own computer, this is where you can keep your data files—the memos, videos, graphics, music, and other files that you create, edit, and manipulate in a program. If you are working in a computer lab, you might not be able to access the My Documents folder, or you might be able to store files there only temporarily because that folder is emptied every night. Instead, you might permanently store your Data Files on removable media or in a different folder on your computer or network.

When you start Windows Explorer, it opens to the My Documents folder by default. If you cannot access the My Documents folder, the screens you see as you perform the following steps will differ. However, you can still perform the steps accurately.

To examine the organization of your computer using Windows Explorer:

1. Click the **Start** button on the taskbar, point to **All Programs**, point to **Accessories**, and then click **Windows Explorer**. The Windows Explorer window opens.

2. Click the **expand** icon ➕ next to the My Computer icon. The drives and other useful locations on your computer appear under the My Computer icon, as shown in Figure 6. The contents of your computer will differ.

Figure 6 ▶ **Viewing the contents of your computer**

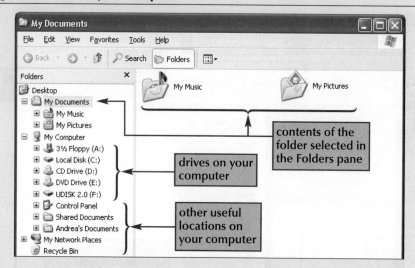

3. Click the **expand** icon ➕ next to the Local Disk (C:) icon. The contents of your hard disk appear under the Local Disk (C:) icon.

   Trouble? If you do not have permission to access drive C, skip Step 3 and read but do not perform the remaining steps.

   My Documents is still the selected folder. To view the contents of an object in the right pane, you can click the object's icon in the Folders pane.

4. Click **Documents and Settings** in the Folders pane. Its contents appear in the right pane. Documents and Settings is a built-in Windows XP folder that contains a folder for each user installed on the system.

You've already mastered the basics of navigating your computer with Windows Explorer. You click expand icons in the left pane until you find the folder that you want. Then you click the folder icon in the left pane to view the files it contains in the right pane.

Navigating to Your Data Files

The **file path** is a notation that indicates a file's location on your computer. The file path leads you through the Windows file system to your file. For example, the Holiday file is stored in the Tutorial subfolder of the FM folder. If you are working on a USB drive, for example, the path to this file might be as follows:

F:\FM\Tutorial\Holiday.bmp

This path has four parts, and each part is separated by a backslash (\ ):

- **F**: The drive name; for example, drive F might be the name for the USB drive. If this file were stored on the hard disk, the drive name would be C.
- **FM**: The top-level folder on drive F.
- **Tutorial**: A subfolder in the FM folder.
- **Holiday.bmp**: The full filename with the file extension.

If someone tells you to find the file F:\FM\Tutorial\Holiday.bmp, you know you must navigate to your USB drive, open the FM folder, and then open the Tutorial folder to find the Holiday file. My Computer and Windows Explorer can display the full file path in their Address bars so you can keep track of your current location as you navigate.

You can use Windows Explorer to navigate to the Data Files you need for the rest of this tutorial. Refer back to the information you provided in the "Planning Your Organization" section and note the drive on your system that contains your Data Files. In the following steps, this is drive F, a USB drive. If necessary, substitute the appropriate drive on your system when you perform the steps.

To navigate to your Data Files:

▶ 1. Make sure your computer can access your Data Files for this tutorial. For example, if you are using a USB drive, insert the drive into the USB port.

   Trouble? If you don't have the Data Files, you need to get them before you can proceed. Your instructor will either give you the Data Files or ask you to obtain them from a specified location (such as a network drive). In either case, be sure that you make a backup copy of your Data Files before you start using them, so that the original files will be available on your copied disk in case you need to start over because of an error or problem. If you have any questions about the Data Files, see your instructor or technical support person for assistance.

▶ 2. In the Windows Explorer window, click the **expand** icon ＋ next to the drive containing your Data Files, such as UDISK 2.0 (F:). A list of the folders on that drive appears.

▶ 3. If the list of folders does not include the FM folder, continue clicking the **expand** icon ＋ to navigate to the folder that contains the FM folder.

▶ 4. Click the **FM** folder. Its contents appear in the Folders pane and in the right pane of the Windows Explorer window. The FM folder contains the Cases, Review, and Tutorial folders, as shown in Figure 7. The other folders on your system might vary.

Navigating to the FM folder ◀ **Figure 7**

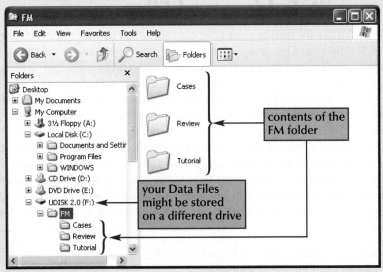

▶ 5. In the left pane, click the **Tutorial** folder. The files it contains appear in the right pane. You want to view them as a list.

▶ 6. Click the **Views** button on the Standard Buttons toolbar, and then click **List**. The files appear in List view in the Windows Explorer window. See Figure 8.

Figure 8 ▸ Files in the Tutorial folder in List view

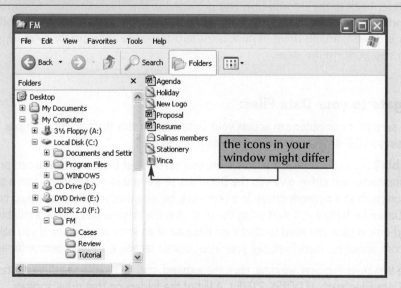

The file icons in your window depend on the programs installed on your computer, so they might be different from the ones shown in Figure 8.

Leave the Windows Explorer window open so you can work with the files in the Tutorial folder.

Working with Folders and Files

After you devise a plan for storing your files, you are ready to get organized by creating folders that will hold your files. You can do so using My Computer or Windows Explorer. For this tutorial, you'll create folders in the Tutorial folder. When you are working on your own computer, you will usually create folders within the My Documents folder.

Examine the files shown in Figure 8 again and determine which files seem to belong together. Holiday, New Logo, and Vinca are all graphics files containing pictures or photographs. The Resume and Stationery files were created for a summer job hunt. The other files were created for the Salinas neighborhood association project to update a playground.

One way to organize these files is to create three folders—one for graphics, one for the job hunt files, and another for the Salinas files. When you create a folder, you give it a name, preferably one that describes its contents. A folder name can have up to 255 characters, except / \ : * ? " < > or |. With these guidelines in mind, you could create three folders as follows:

- **Graphics folder**: Holiday, New Logo, and Vinca files
- **Job Hunt folder**: Resume and Stationery files
- **Playground folder**: Agenda, Proposal, and Salinas members files

Shannon asks you to create three new folders. Then you'll move the files to the appropriate subfolder.

Creating Folders

You've already seen folder icons in the windows you've examined. Now, you'll create folders in the Tutorial folder using the Windows Explorer menu bar.

Creating a Folder Using Windows Explorer

- In the left pane, click the drive or folder where you want to create a folder.
- Click File on the menu bar, point to New, and then click Folder (*or* right-click a blank area in the folder window, point to New, and then click Folder).
- Type a name for the folder, and then press the Enter key.

Now you can create three folders in your Tutorial folder as you planned—the Graphics, Job Hunt, and Playground folders. The Windows Explorer window should show the contents of the Tutorial folder in List view.

To create folders using Windows Explorer:

1. Click **File** on the menu bar, point to **New** to display the submenu, and then click **Folder**. A folder icon with the label "New Folder" appears in the right pane, and the expand icon appears next to the Tutorial folder because it now contains a subfolder. See Figure 9.

Creating a folder in the Tutorial folder | Figure 9

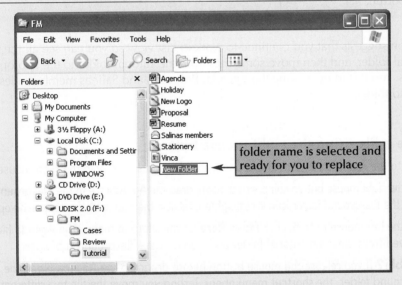

> folder name is selected and ready for you to replace

Trouble? If the "New Folder" name is not selected, right-click the new folder, click Rename, and then continue with Step 2.

Windows uses "New Folder" as a placeholder, and selects the text so that you can replace it with the name you want.

2. Type **Graphics** as the folder name, and then press the **Enter** key. The new folder is named "Graphics" and is the selected item in the right pane.

You are ready to create a second folder. This time you'll use a shortcut menu to create a folder.

3. Right-click a blank area next to the Graphics folder, point to **New** on the shortcut menu, and then click **Folder**. A folder icon with the label "New Folder" appears in the right pane with the "New Folder" text selected.

4. Type **Job Hunt** as the name of the new folder, and then press the **Enter** key.

5. Using the menu bar or the shortcut menu, create a folder named **Playground**. The Tutorial folder contains three new subfolders.

Now that you've created three folders, you're ready to organize your files by moving them into the appropriate folders.

Moving and Copying Files and Folders

If you want to place a file into a folder from another location, you can either move the file or copy it. **Moving** a file removes it from its current location and places it in a new location you specify. **Copying** places the file in both locations. Windows XP provides several techniques for moving and copying files. The same principles apply to folders—you can move and copy folders using a variety of methods.

Reference Window | **Moving a File or Folder in Windows Explorer or My Computer**

- Right-click and drag the file you want to move to the destination folder.
- Click Move Here on the shortcut menu.

or

- Click the file you want to move, and then click Move this file in the File and Folder Tasks area.
- In the Move Items dialog box, navigate to the destination folder, and then click the Move button.

Shannon suggests that you continue to work in List view so you can see all the files in the Tutorial folder, and then move some files from the Tutorial folder to the appropriate subfolders. You'll start by moving the Agenda, Proposal, and Salinas members files to the Playground folder.

To move a file using the right mouse button:

1. Point to the **Agenda** file in the right pane, and then press and hold the *right* mouse button.

2. With the right mouse button still pressed down, drag the **Agenda** file to the **Playground** folder. When the Playground folder icon is highlighted, release the button. A shortcut menu opens.

3. With the left mouse button, click **Move Here** on the shortcut menu. The Agenda file is removed from the main Tutorial folder and stored in the Playground subfolder.

   Trouble? If you release the mouse button before dragging the Agenda file to the Playground folder, the shortcut menu opens, letting you move the file to a different folder. Press the Esc key to close the shortcut menu without moving the file, and then repeat Steps 1 through 3.

4. In the right pane, double-click the **Playground** folder. The Agenda file is in the Playground folder.

5. In the left pane, click the **Tutorial** folder to see its contents. The Tutorial folder no longer contains the Agenda file.

The advantage of moving a file or folder by dragging with the right mouse button is that you can efficiently complete your work with one action. However, this technique requires polished mouse skills so that you can drag the file comfortably. Another way to move files and folders is to use the File and Folder Tasks links in the task pane of the Windows Explorer or My Computer window. Although using the File and Folder Tasks links takes more steps, some users find it easier than dragging with the right mouse button.

You'll move the Resume file to the Job Hunt folder next. First, you'll close the Folders pane so that the task pane replaces it.

To move files using the File and Folder Tasks area:

1. Click the **Folders** button on the Standard Buttons toolbar. The task pane replaces the Folders pane, so that this window now resembles the My Computer window. Switch to List view, if necessary.

2. Click the **Resume** file to select it. The task pane links change so that they are appropriate for working with files.

3. In the File and Folder Tasks area, click **Move this file**. The Move Items dialog box opens. See Figure 10.

Move Items dialog box ◀ **Figure 10**

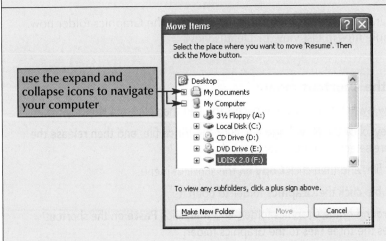

use the expand and collapse icons to navigate your computer

4. Click the **expand** icon + next to the drive containing your Data Files. Continue clicking **expand** icons + to navigate to the Tutorial folder provided with your Data Files.

5. Click the **Job Hunt** folder.

6. Click the **Move** button. The Move Items dialog box closes; Windows moves the Resume file to the Job Hunt folder, and then displays the contents of the Tutorial folder, which no longer contains the Resume file.

   You'll move the Stationery file from the Tutorial folder to the Job Hunt folder.

7. Click the **Stationery** file in the Tutorial window, and then click **Move this file** in the File and Folder Tasks area. The Move Items dialog box opens again, with the Job Hunt folder already selected for you.

8. Click the **Move** button.

You can also copy a file using the same techniques as when you move a file—by dragging with the right mouse button or by using the File and Folder Tasks links. Another easy way to copy a file is to use the file's shortcut menu. You can copy more than one file at the same time by selecting all the files you want to copy, and then clicking them as a group. To select files that are listed together in a window, click the first file in the list, hold down the Shift key, click the last file in the list, and then release the Shift key. To select files that are not listed together, click one file, hold down the Ctrl key, click the other files, and then release the Ctrl key.

Copying a File or Folder in Windows Explorer or My Computer

- Click the file or folder you want to copy, and then click Copy this file or Copy this folder in the File and Folder Tasks area.
- In the Copy Items dialog box, navigate to the destination folder, and then click the Copy button.

or

- Right-click the file or folder you want to copy, and then click Copy on the shortcut menu.
- Navigate to the destination folder.
- Right-click a blank area of the destination folder window, and then click Paste on the shortcut menu.

You'll copy the three graphics files from the Tutorial folder to the Graphics folder now. It's easiest to select multiple files in List view or Details view.

To copy files using the shortcut menu:

1. In the Tutorial window, switch to List view, if necessary, and then click the **Holiday** file.

2. Hold down the **Ctrl** key, click the **New Logo** file, click the **Vinca** file, and then release the **Ctrl** key. Three files are selected in the Tutorial window.

3. Right-click a selected file, and then click **Copy** on the shortcut menu.

4. In the right pane, double-click the **Graphics** folder to open it.

5. Right-click the background of the Graphics folder, and then click **Paste** on the shortcut menu. Windows copies the three files to the Graphics folder.

6. Switch to List view, if necessary.

Now that you are familiar with two ways to copy files, you can use the technique you prefer to copy the Proposal and Salinas members files to the Playground folder.

To copy the two files:

1. In the Graphics folder window, click the **Back** button on the Standard Buttons toolbar to return to the Tutorial folder.

2. Use any technique you've learned to copy the **Proposal** and **Salinas members** files from the Tutorial folder to the Playground folder.

You can move and copy folders in the same way that you move and copy files. When you do, you move or copy all the files contained in the folder. You'll practice moving and copying folders in the Case Problems at the end of this tutorial.

Naming and Renaming Files

As you work with files, pay attention to **filenames**—they provide important information about the file, including its contents and purpose. A filename such as Car Sales.doc has three parts:

- **Main part of the filename:** The name you provide when you create a file, and the name you associate with a file
- **Dot:** The period (.) that separates the main part of the filename from the file extension
- **File extension:** Usually three characters that follow the dot in the filename

The main part of a filename can have up to 255 characters—this gives you plenty of room to name your file accurately enough so that you'll know the contents of the file just by looking at the filename. You can use spaces and certain punctuation symbols in your filenames. Like folder names, however, filenames cannot contain the symbols \ / ? : * " < > | because these characters have special meaning in Windows XP.

A filename might display an **extension**—three or more characters following a dot—that identifies the file's type and indicates the program in which the file was created. For example, in the filename Car Sales.doc, the extension "doc" identifies the file as one created by Microsoft Word, a word-processing program. You might also have a file called Car Sales.xls—the "xls" extension identifies the file as one created in Microsoft Excel, a spreadsheet program. Though the main parts of these filenames are identical, their extensions distinguish them as different files. You usually do not need to add extensions to your filenames because the program that you use to create the file adds the file extension automatically. Also, although Windows XP keeps track of extensions, not all computers are set to display them.

Be sure to give your files and folders meaningful names that will help you remember their purpose and contents. You can easily rename a file or folder by using the Rename command on the file's shortcut menu.

Shannon recommends that you rename the Agenda file in the Playground folder to give it a more descriptive filename—that file could contain the agenda for any meeting. The Agenda file was originally created to store a list of topics to discuss at a meeting of the Salinas neighborhood association. You'll rename the file "Salinas Meeting Agenda."

To rename the Agenda file:

1. Click **Tutorial** in the Other Places menu, and then double-click the **Playground** folder.

2. In the Playground window, right-click the **Agenda** file, and then click **Rename** on the shortcut menu. The filename is highlighted and a box appears around it.

3. Type **Salinas Meeting Agenda**, and then press the **Enter** key. The file now appears with the new name.

   Trouble? If you make a mistake while typing and you haven't pressed the Enter key yet, press the Backspace key until you delete the mistake, and then complete Step 3. If you've already pressed the Enter key, repeat Steps 1 through 3 to rename the file again.

   Trouble? If your computer is set to display file extensions, a message might appear asking if you are sure you want to change the file extension. Click the No button, right-click the Agenda file, click Rename on the shortcut menu, type "Salinas Meeting Agenda.doc", and then press the Enter key.

All the files that originally appeared in the Tutorial folder are now stored in appropriate subfolders. Shannon mentions that you can streamline the organization of the Tutorial folder by deleting the files you no longer need.

Deleting Files and Folders

You should periodically delete files and folders you no longer need so that your main folders and disks don't get cluttered. In My Computer or Windows Explorer, you delete a file or folder by deleting its icon. Be careful when you delete a folder, because you also delete all the files it contains. When you delete a file from a hard disk, Windows XP removes the filename from the folder, but stores the file contents in the Recycle Bin. The **Recycle Bin** is an area on your hard disk that holds deleted files until you remove them permanently; an icon on the desktop allows you easy access to the Recycle Bin. If you change your mind and want to retrieve a file deleted from your hard disk, you can use the Recycle Bin to recover it or return it to its original location. However, after you empty the Recycle Bin, you can no longer recover the files that were in it.

When you delete a file from removable media, it does not go into the Recycle Bin. Instead, it is deleted as soon as its icon disappears—and you cannot recover it.

Shannon reminds you that because you copied the Holiday, New Logo, Proposal, Salinas members, and Vinca files to the Graphics and Playground folders, you can safely delete the original files in the Tutorial folder. As with moving, copying, and renaming files and folders, you can delete a file or folder in many ways, including using a shortcut menu or the File and Folder Tasks menu.

To delete files in the Tutorial folder:

▶ **1.** Use any technique you've learned to navigate to and open the **Tutorial** folder.

▶ **2.** Switch to List view (if necessary), click **Holiday** (the first file in the file list), hold down the **Shift** key, click **Vinca** (the last file in the file list), and then release the **Shift** key. All the files in the Tutorial folder are now selected. None of the subfolders should be selected.

▶ **3.** Right-click the selected files, and then click **Delete** on the shortcut menu. Windows XP asks if you're sure you want to delete these files.

▶ **4.** Click the **Yes** button.

So far, you've worked with files using Windows Explorer and My Computer, but you haven't viewed any of their contents. To view file contents, you open the file. When you double-click a file in Windows Explorer or My Computer, Windows XP starts the appropriate program and opens the file.

Working with Compressed Files

If you transfer files from one location to another, such as from your hard disk to a removable disk or vice versa, or from one computer to another via e-mail, you can store the files in a **compressed (zipped) folder** so that they take up less disk space. You can then transfer the files more quickly. When you create a compressed folder, Windows XP displays a zipper on the folder icon.

You compress a folder so that the files it contains use less space on the disk. Compare two folders—a folder named My Pictures that contains about 8.6 MB of files and a compressed folder containing the same files, but requiring only 6.5 MB of disk space. In this case, the compressed files use about 25 percent less disk space than the uncompressed files.

You can create a compressed folder using the Compressed (zipped) Folder command on the New submenu of the File menu or shortcut menu in Windows Explorer or My Computer. Then you can compress files or other folders by dragging them into the compressed folder. You can open files directly from a compressed folder, or you can extract the files first. When you **extract** a file, you create an uncompressed copy of the file and folder in a folder you specify. The original file remains in the compressed folder.

If a different compression program has been installed on your computer, such as WinZip or PKZip, the Compressed (zipped) Folder command does not appear on the New submenu. Instead, it is replaced by the name of your compression program. In this case, refer to your compression program's Help system for instructions on working with compressed files.

Shannon suggests you compress the files and folders in the Tutorial folder so you can more quickly transfer them to another location.

To compress the folders and files in the Tutorial folder:

1. In Windows Explorer, navigate to the Tutorial folder.

2. Right-click a blank area of the right pane, point to **New** on the shortcut menu, and then click **Compressed (zipped) Folder**. A new compressed folder with a zipper icon appears in the Tutorial window. See Figure 11. Your window might appear in a different view.

Creating a compressed folder ◀ **Figure 11**

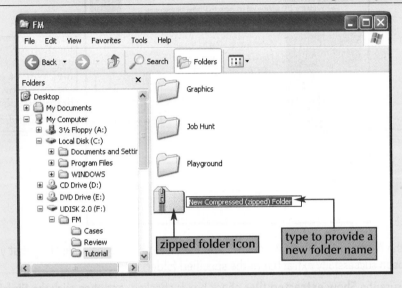

Trouble? If the Compressed (zipped) Folder command does not appear on the New sub-menu, a different compression program is probably installed on your computer. Click a blank area of the Tutorial window to close the shortcut menu, and then read but do not perform the remaining steps.

3. Type **Final Tutorial files**, and then press the **Enter** key. Windows XP creates the com-pressed folder in the Tutorial folder.

4. Click the **Graphics** folder in the right pane, hold down the **Shift** key, click the **Playground** folder in the right pane, and then release the **Shift** key. Three folders are selected in the Tutorial window.

5. Drag the three folders to the **Final Tutorial files** compressed folder. Windows XP copies the files to the folder, compressing them to save space.

You open a compressed folder by double-clicking it. You can then move and copy files and folders in a compressed folder, though you cannot rename them. If you want to open, edit, and save files in a compressed folder, you should first extract them. When you do, Windows XP uncompresses the files and copies them to a location that you specify, pre-serving them in their folders as appropriate.

To extract the compressed files:

1. Right-click the **Final Tutorial files** compressed folder, and then click **Extract All** on the shortcut menu. The Extraction Wizard starts and opens the Welcome to the Compressed (zipped) Folders Extraction Wizard dialog box.

2. Click the **Next** button. The Select a Destination dialog box opens.

3. Press the **End** key to deselect the path in the text box, press the **Backspace** key as many times as necessary to delete "Final Tutorial files," and then type **Extracted**. The last three parts of the path in the text box should be "\FM\Tutorial\Extracted." See Figure 12.

| Figure 12 | Select a Destination dialog box |

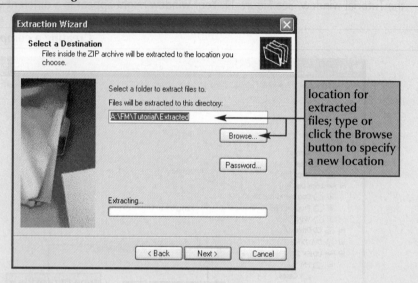

location for extracted files; type or click the Browse button to specify a new location

4. Click the **Next** button. The Extraction Complete dialog box opens, indicating that your files have been successfully extracted to the specified folder.

5. Make sure the **Show extracted files** check box is checked, and then click the **Finish** button. The Extracted folder opens, showing the Graphics, Job Hunt, and Playground folders.

6. Open each folder to make sure it contains the files you worked with in this tutorial.

7. Close all open windows.

Shannon says you have successfully completed basic Windows XP file management tasks, and are ready to use Windows XP to organize your files.

| Review |

Quick Check

1. What is the term for a collection of data that has a name and is stored on a disk or other storage medium?
2. Name two types of removable media for storing files.
3. The letter C is typically used for the _____ drive of a computer.
4. What are the two tools that Windows XP provides for exploring the files and folders on your computer?
5. What is the notation you can use to indicate a file's location on your computer?
6. True or False: The advantage of moving a file or folder by dragging with the right mouse button is that you can efficiently complete your work with one action.
7. In a filename, the _____ identifies the file's type and indicates the program in which the file was created.
8. True or False: When you extract a file, the original file is deleted from the compressed folder.

Review

Tutorial Summary

In this tutorial, you examined Windows XP file organization, noting that you need to organize files and folders to work efficiently. You learned about typical file management strategies, whether you are working on a hard disk or a removable disk. Then you applied these strategies to organizing files and folders by creating folders, moving and copying files, and renaming and deleting files. You also learned how to copy files to a compressed (zipped) folder, and then extract files from a compressed folder.

Key Terms

backup	extract	move
compact disc (CD)	file	My Computer
compressed (zipped) folder	file path	My Documents folder
copy	file system	pane
disk	filename	Recycle Bin
document	floppy disk	root directory
drive	folder	subfolder
Explorer bar	Folders pane	USB drive
extension	hard disk	Windows Explorer

Practice

Practice the skills you learned in the tutorial.

Review Assignments

Data Files needed for the Review Assignments: Commissions.xls, Contracts.xls, Customer Accounts.xls, Billing Worksheet.wk4, Car Savings Plan.xls, Personal Loan.doc, Speech.wav, Filenames.pps, Water lilies.jpg

Complete the following steps, recording your answers to any questions in the spaces provided:

1. Use My Computer or Windows Explorer as necessary to record the following information:
   - Where are you supposed to store the files you use in the Review Assignments for this tutorial? _____
   - Describe the method you will use to navigate to the location where you save your files for this book. _____
   _____
   - Do you need to follow any special guidelines or conventions when naming the files your save for this book? For example, should all the filenames start with your course number or tutorial number? If so, describe the conventions. _____
   _____
   - When you are instructed to open a file for this book, what location are you supposed to use? _____
   - Describe the method you will use to navigate to this location. _____
   _____

2. Use My Computer or Windows Explorer to navigate to and open the FM\Review folder provided with your Data Files.

3. Examine the nine files in the Review folder included with your Data Files, and then answer the following questions:
   - How will you organize these files? _____
   _____
   - What folders will you create? _____
   _____

- Which files will you store in these folders? _____
  _____

- Will you use any built-in Windows folders? If so, which ones? For which files?
  _____

4. In the Review folder, create three folders: Business, Personal Finances, and Project Media.
5. Move the **Commissions**, **Contracts**, **Customer Accounts**, and **Billing Worksheet** files from the Review folder to the Business folder.
6. Move the **Car Savings Plan** and **Personal Loan** files to the Personal Finances folder.
7. Copy the remaining files to the Project Media folder.
8. Delete the files in the Review folder (do *not* delete any folders).
9. Rename the **Speech** file in the Project Media folder to **Ask Not**.
10. Create a compressed (zipped) folder in the Review folder named **Final Review files** that contains all the files and folders in the Review folder.
11. Extract the contents of the Final Review files folder to a new folder named **Extracted**. (*Hint:* The file path will end with "\FM\Review\Extracted.")
12. Use Windows Explorer or My Computer to locate all copies of the **Personal Loan** file in the subfolders of the Review folder. In which locations did you find this file?
    _____

13. Close all open windows.

Apply

Use the skills you learned in the tutorial to manage files and folders for an arts organization.

Case Problem 1

Data Files needed for this Case Problem: Invoice Jan.xls, Invoice Feb.xls, Invoice March.xls, Painting Class – Agenda.doc, Painting Class – Questionnaire.doc, Painting Class – Teaching Manual.doc, Paris.jpg, Vegetables.jpg

Jefferson Street Fine Arts Center Rae Wysnewski owns the Jefferson Street Fine Arts Center (JSFAC) in Pittsburgh, and offers classes and gallery, studio, and practice space for aspiring and fledgling artists, musicians, and dancers. Rae opened JSFAC two years ago, and this year the center has a record enrollment in its classes. Knowing you are multitalented, she hires you to teach a painting class for three months and to show her how to manage her files on her new Windows XP computer. Complete the following steps:

1. In the FM\Cases folder provided with your Data Files, create two folders: Invoices and Painting Class.
2. Move the **Invoice Jan**, **Invoice Feb**, and **Invoice March** files from the Cases folder to the Invoices folder.
3. Rename the three files in the Invoices folder to remove "Invoice" from each name.
4. Move the three text documents from the Cases folder to the Painting Class folder. Rename the three documents, using shorter but still descriptive names.
5. Copy the remaining files to the Painting Class folder.

Explore

6. Using My Computer or Windows Explorer, switch to Details view and then answer the following questions:
    a. What is the largest file in the Painting Class folder? _____
    b. How many files (don't include folders) are in the Cases folder? _____
    c. How many word-processed documents are in the Cases folder and its subfolders? ____
    d. How many files in the Painting Class folder are JPEG images? (*Hint:* Look in the Type column to identify JPEG images.) _____
7. Delete the **Paris** and **Vegetables** files from the Painting Class folder.

8. Open the Recycle Bin folder by double-clicking the Recycle Bin icon on the desktop. Do the Paris and Vegetables files appear in the Recycle Bin folder? Explain why or why not. _____

9. Copy the Painting Class folder to the Cases folder. The name of the duplicate folder appears as "Copy of Painting Class." Rename the "Copy of Painting Class" folder as "Graphics."

10. Create a new folder in the Cases folder named "JSFAC." Move the Invoices, Painting Class, and Graphics folders to the JSFAC folder.

Challenge

Extend what you've learned to discover other methods of managing files for a social service organization.

Case Problem 2

There are no Data Files needed for this Case Problem.

First Call Outreach   Victor Crillo is the director of a social service organization named First Call Outreach in Toledo, Ohio. Its mission is to connect people who need help from local and state agencies to the appropriate service. Victor has a dedicated staff, but they are all relatively new to Windows XP. In particular, they have trouble finding files that they have saved on their hard disks. He asks you to demonstrate how to find files in Windows XP. Complete the following:

Explore

1. Windows XP Help and Support includes topics that explain how to search for files on a disk without looking through all the folders. Click the Start button and then click Help and Support to start Windows Help and Support. Use one of the following methods to locate topics on searching for files.
   - On the Home page, click the Windows Basics link. On the Windows Basics page, click the Finding and organizing files link, and then click the Searching for files or folders topic. In the article, click the Related Topics link, and then click Search for a file or folder.
   - On the Index page, type "files" (no quotation marks) in the Type in the keyword to find text box. In the list of entries for "files," double-click "searching for." In the Topics found dialog box, double-click "Searching for files or folders."
   - In the Search box, type "searching for files," and then click Search. Click the Searching for files or folders link.

Explore

2. Read the topic and click the Related Topics link at the end of the topic, if necessary, to provide the following information:
   a. To display the Search dialog box, you must click the _____ button, point to _____ from the menu, and finally click _____ from the submenu.
   b. Do you need to type in the entire filename to find the file? _____
   c. Name three file characteristics you can use as search options. _____
   _____
   _____

Explore

3. Use the Index page in Windows XP Help and Support to locate topics related to managing files and folders. Write out two procedures for managing files and folders that were not covered in the tutorial. _____
   _____
   _____
   _____
   _____

SAM Assessment and Training

If you have a SAM user profile, you may have access to hands-on instruction, practice, and assessment of the skills covered in this tutorial. Log in to your SAM account and go to your assignments page to see what your instructor has assigned.

Reinforce

Lab Assignments

The New Perspectives Labs are designed to help you master some of the key concepts and skills presented in this text. The steps for completing this Lab are located on the Course Technology Web site. Log on to the Internet and use your Web browser to go to the Student Online Companion for New Perspectives Office 2003 site at **www.course.com/np/office2003**. Click the Lab Assignments link, and then navigate to the assignments for this tutorial.

Review

Quick Check Answers

1. file
2. USB drives, CDs, DVDs, and floppy disks
3. hard disk
4. Windows Explorer and My Computer
5. file path
6. true
7. extension
8. false

New Perspectives on

Using Common Features of Microsoft® Office 2003

Preparing Promotional Materials   OFF 3

Read This Before You Begin

To the Student

Data Files

To complete the Using Common Features of Microsoft Office 2003 tutorial, you need the starting student Data Files. Your instructor will either provide you with these Data Files or ask you to obtain them yourself.

The Using Common Features of Microsoft Office 2003 tutorial requires the folder named "OFF" to complete the Tutorial, Review Assignments, and Case Problems. You will need to copy this folder from a file server, a stand-alone computer, or the Web to the drive and folder where you will be storing your Data Files. Your instructor will tell you which computer, drive letter, and folder(s) contain the files you need. You can also download the files by going to www.course.com; see the inside back or front cover for more information on downloading the files, or ask your instructor or technical support person for assistance.

If you are storing your Data Files on floppy disks, you will need one blank, formatted, high-density disk for this tutorial. Label your disk as shown, and place on it the folder indicated.

▼ **Common Features of Office: Data Disk**
   OFF folder

When you begin this tutorial, refer to the Student Data Files section at the bottom of the tutorial opener page, which indicates which folders and files you need for the tutorial. Each end-of-tutorial exercise also indicates the files you need to complete that exercise.

To the Instructor

The Data Files are available on the Instructor Resources CD for this title. Follow the instructions in the Help file on the CD to install the programs to your network or standalone computer. See the "To the Student" section above for information on how to set up the Data Files that accompany this text.

You are granted a license to copy the Data Files to any computer or computer network used by students who have purchased this book.

System Requirements

If you are going to work through this book using your own computer, you need:

• **Computer System** Microsoft Windows 2000 or Windows XP Professional or higher must be installed on your computer. This tutorial assumes a typical installation of Microsoft Office 2003. Additionally, to complete the steps for accessing Microsoft's Online Help for Office, an Internet connection and a Web browser are required.

• **Data Files** You will not be able to complete the tutorals or exercises in this book using your own computer until you have the necessary starting Data Files.

www.course.com/NewPerspectives

Objectives

- Explore the programs that comprise Microsoft Office
- Start programs and switch between them
- Explore common window elements
- Minimize, maximize, and restore windows
- Use personalized menus and toolbars
- Work with task panes
- Create, save, close, and open a file
- Use the Help system
- Print a file
- Exit programs

Using Common Features of Microsoft Office 2003

Preparing Promotional Materials

Case

Delmar Office Supplies

Delmar Office Supplies, a company in Wisconsin founded by Jake Alexander in 1996, sells recycled office supplies to businesses and home-based offices around the world. The demand for quality recycled papers, reconditioned toner cartridges, and renovated office furniture has been growing each year. Jake and all his employees use Microsoft Office 2003, which provides everyone in the company the power and flexibility to store a variety of information, create consistent files, and share data. In this tutorial, you'll review how the company's employees use Microsoft Office 2003.

Student Data Files

▼OFF folder

▽ Tutorial folder

    (no starting Data Files)

▽ Review folder

    Finances.xls

    Letter.doc

Exploring Microsoft Office 2003

Microsoft Office 2003, or simply **Office**, is a collection of the most popular Microsoft programs: Word, Excel, PowerPoint, Access, and Outlook. Each Office program contains valuable tools to help you accomplish many tasks, such as composing reports, analyzing data, preparing presentations, compiling information, sending e-mail, and planning schedules.

Microsoft Word 2003, or simply **Word**, is a word-processing program you use to create text documents. The files you create in Word are called **documents**. Word offers many special features that help you compose and update all types of documents, ranging from letters and newsletters to reports, brochures, faxes, and even books—all in attractive and readable formats. You can also use Word to create, insert, and position figures, tables, and other graphics to enhance the look of your documents. The Delmar Office Supplies sales representatives create their business letters using Word.

Microsoft Excel 2003, or simply **Excel**, is a spreadsheet program you use to display, organize, and analyze numerical data. You can do some of this in Word with tables, but Excel provides many more tools for recording and formatting numbers as well as performing calculations. The graphics capabilities in Excel also enable you to display data visually. You might, for example, generate a pie chart or a bar chart to help readers quickly see the significance of and the connections between information. The files you create in Excel are called **workbooks**. The Delmar Office Supplies operations department uses a line chart in an Excel workbook to visually track the company's financial performance.

Microsoft Access 2003, or simply **Access**, is a database program you use to enter, organize, display, and retrieve related information. The files you create in Access are called **databases**. With Access you can create data entry forms to make data entry easier, and you can create professional reports to improve the readability of your data. The Delmar Office Supplies operations department tracks the company's inventory in a table in an Access database.

Microsoft PowerPoint 2003, or simply **PowerPoint**, is a presentation graphics program you use to create a collection of slides that can contain text, charts, pictures, and so on. The files you create in PowerPoint are called **presentations**. You can show these presentations on your computer monitor, project them onto a screen as a slide show, print them, share them over the Internet, or display them on the World Wide Web. You can also use PowerPoint to generate presentation-related documents such as audience handouts, outlines, and speakers' notes. The Delmar Office Supplies sales department has created an effective slide presentation with PowerPoint to promote the company's latest product line.

Microsoft Outlook 2003, or simply **Outlook**, is an information management program you use to send, receive, and organize e-mail; plan your schedule; arrange meetings; organize contacts; create a to-do list; and jot down notes. You can also use Outlook to print schedules, task lists, phone directories, and other documents. Jake Alexander uses Outlook to send and receive e-mail, plan his schedule, and create a to-do list.

Although each Office program individually is a strong tool, their potential is even greater when used together.

Integrating Office Programs

One of the main advantages of Office is **integration**, the ability to share information between programs. Integration ensures consistency and accuracy, and it saves time because you don't have to re-enter the same information in several Office programs. The staff at Delmar Office Supplies uses the integration features of Office daily, including the following examples:

- The accounting department created an Excel bar chart on the previous two years' fourth-quarter results, which they inserted into the quarterly financial report created in Word. They included a hyperlink in the Word report that employees can click to open the Excel workbook and view the original data.
- The operations department included an Excel pie chart of sales percentages by divisions of Delmar Office Supplies on a PowerPoint slide, which is part of a presentation to stockholders.
- The marketing department produced a mailing to promote the company's newest products by combining a form letter created in Word with an Access database that stores the names and addresses of customers.
- A sales representative wrote a letter in Word about a sales incentive program and merged the letter with an Outlook contact list containing the names and addresses of his customers.

These are just a few examples of how you can take information from one Office program and integrate it into another.

Starting Office Programs

You can start any Office program by clicking the Start button on the Windows taskbar, and then selecting the program you want from the All Programs menu. Once the program starts, you can immediately begin to create new files or work with existing ones. If you or another user has recently used one of the Office programs, then that program might appear on the most frequently used programs list on the left side of the Start menu. You can click the program name to start the program.

Reference Window

Starting Office Programs

- Click the Start button on the taskbar.
- Point to All Programs.
- Point to Microsoft Office.
- Click the name of the program you want to start.

or

- Click the name of the program you want to start on the most frequently used programs list on the left side of the Start menu.

You'll start Excel using the Start button.

To start Excel and open a new, blank workbook:

▶ **1.** Make sure your computer is on and the Windows desktop appears on your screen.

Trouble? If your screen varies slightly from those shown in the figures, then your computer might be set up differently. The figures in this book were created while running Windows XP in its default settings, but how your screen looks depends on a variety of things, including the version of Windows, background settings, and so forth.

▶ **2.** Click the **Start** button on the taskbar, and then point to **All Programs** to display the All Programs menu.

▶ **3.** Point to **Microsoft Office** on the All Programs menu, and then point to **Microsoft Office Excel 2003**. See Figure 1. Depending on how your computer is set up, your desktop and menu might contain different icons and commands.

Figure 1	Start menu with All Programs submenu displayed

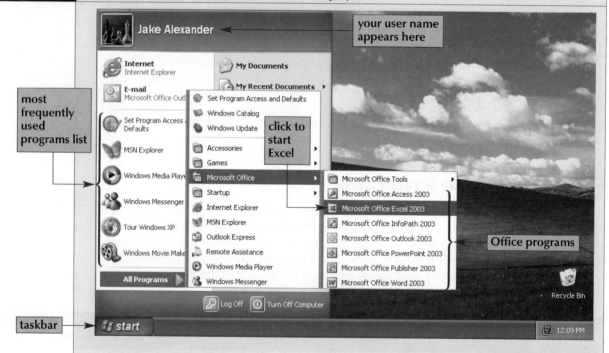

Trouble? If you don't see Microsoft Office on the All Programs menu, point to Microsoft Office Excel 2003. If you still don't see Microsoft Office Excel 2003, ask your instructor or technical support person for help.

▶ **4.** Click **Microsoft Office Excel 2003** to start Excel and open a new, blank workbook. See Figure 2.

New, blank Excel workbook   **Figure 2**

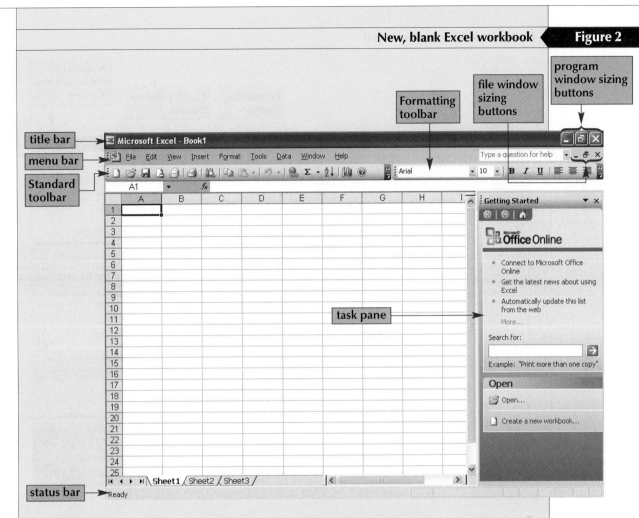

Trouble? If the Excel window doesn't fill your entire screen, the window is not maximized, or expanded to its full size. You'll maximize the window shortly.

You can have more than one Office program open at once. You'll use this same method to start Word and open a new, blank document.

To start Word and open a new, blank document:

1. Click the **Start** button on the taskbar.

2. Point to **All Programs** to display the All Programs menu.

3. Point to **Microsoft Office** on the All Programs menu.

   Trouble? If you don't see Microsoft Office on the All Programs menu, point to Microsoft Office Word 2003. If you still don't see Microsoft Office Word 2003, ask your instructor or technical support person for help.

4. Click **Microsoft Office Word 2003**. Word opens with a new, blank document. See Figure 3.

| Figure 3 | New, blank document in Word |

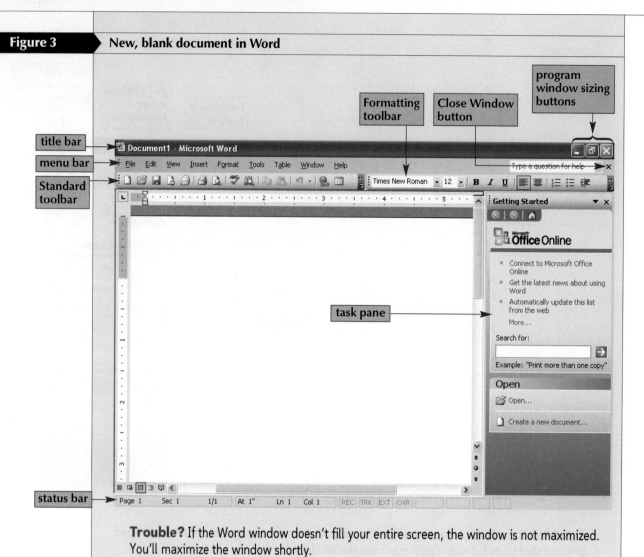

Trouble? If the Word window doesn't fill your entire screen, the window is not maximized. You'll maximize the window shortly.

When you have more than one program or file open at a time, you can switch between them.

Switching Between Open Programs and Files

Two programs are running at the same time—Excel and Word. The taskbar contains buttons for both programs. When you have two or more programs running, or two files within the same program open, you can use the taskbar buttons to switch from one program or file to another. The employees at Delmar Office Supplies often work in several programs at once.

To switch between Word and Excel:

▶ 1. Click the **Microsoft Excel – Book1** button on the taskbar to switch from Word to Excel. See Figure 4.

Excel and Word programs opened simultaneously ◀ **Figure 4**

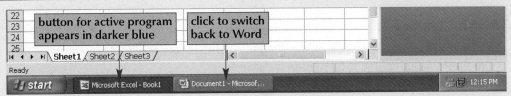

▶ 2. Click the **Document1 – Microsoft Word** button on the taskbar to return to Word.

As you can see, you can start multiple programs and switch between them in seconds.

Exploring Common Window Elements

The Office programs consist of windows that have many similar features. As you can see in Figures 2 and 3, many of the elements you see in both the Excel program window and the Word program window are the same. In fact, all the Office programs have these same elements. Figure 5 describes some of the most common window elements.

Common window elements ◀ **Figure 5**

Element	Description
Title bar	A bar at the top of the window that contains the filename of the open file, the program name, and the program window sizing buttons
Menu bar	A collection of menus for commonly used commands
Toolbars	Collections of buttons that are shortcuts to commonly used menu commands
Sizing buttons	Buttons that resize and close the program window or the file window
Task pane	A window that provides access to commands for common tasks you'll perform in Office programs
Status bar	An area at the bottom of the program window that contains information about the open file or the current task on which you are working

Because these elements are the same in each program, once you've learned one program, it's easy to learn the others. The next sections explore the primary common features—the window sizing buttons, the menus and toolbars, and the task panes.

Using the Window Sizing Buttons

There are two sets of sizing buttons. The top set controls the program window and the bottom set controls the file window. There are three different sizing buttons. The Minimize button ⬜, which is the left button, hides a window so that only its program button is visible on the taskbar. The middle button changes name and function depending on the status of the window—the Maximize button ⬜ expands the window to the full screen size or to the program window size, and the Restore button ⬜ returns the window to a predefined size. The right button, the Close button ⬜, exits the program or closes the file.

Most often you'll want to maximize the program and file windows as you work to take advantage of the full screen size you have available. If you have several files open, you might want to restore the files so that you can see more than one window at a time or you might want to minimize the programs with which you are not working at the moment. You'll try minimizing, maximizing, and restoring windows now.

To resize windows:

▶ 1. Click the **Minimize** button ▬ on the Word title bar to reduce the Word program window to a taskbar button. The Excel window is visible again.

▶ 2. If necessary, click the **Maximize** button ☐ on the Excel title bar. The Excel program window expands to fill the screen.

▶ 3. Click the **Restore Window** button ⧉ on the Excel menu bar. The file window, referred to as the workbook window in Excel, resizes smaller than the full program window. See Figure 6.

Figure 6	Resized Excel windows

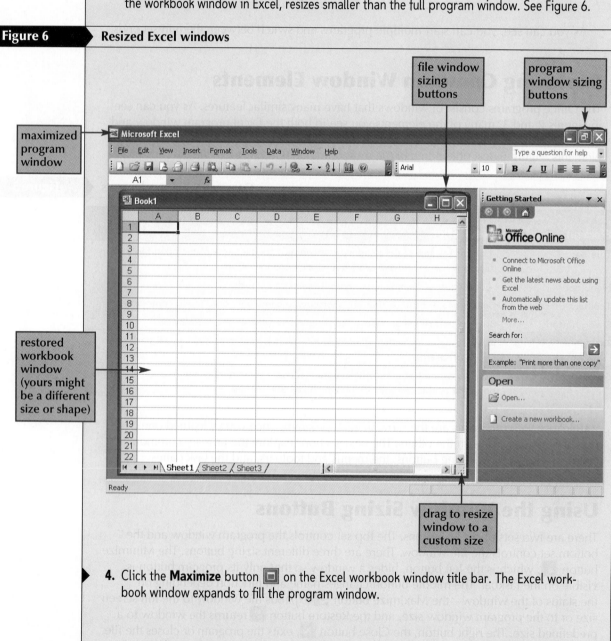

file window sizing buttons

program window sizing buttons

maximized program window

restored workbook window (yours might be a different size or shape)

drag to resize window to a custom size

▶ 4. Click the **Maximize** button ☐ on the Excel workbook window title bar. The Excel workbook window expands to fill the program window.

5. Click the **Document1 - Microsoft Word** button on the taskbar. The Word program window returns to its previous size.

6. If necessary, click the **Maximize** button ▣ on the Word title bar. The Word program window expands to fill the screen.

The sizing buttons give you the flexibility to arrange the program and file windows on your screen to best fit your needs.

Using Menus and Toolbars

In each Office program, you can perform tasks using a menu command, a toolbar button, or a keyboard shortcut. A **menu command** is a word on a menu that you click to execute a task; a **menu** is a group of related commands. For example, the File menu contains commands for managing files, such as the Open command and the Save command. The File, Edit, View, Insert, Format, Tools, Window, and Help menus appear on the menu bar in all the Office programs, although some of the commands they include differ from program to program. Other menus are program specific, such as the Table menu in Word and the Data menu in Excel.

A **toolbar** is a collection of buttons that correspond to commonly used menu commands. For example, the Standard toolbar contains an Open button and a Save button. The Standard and Formatting toolbars (as well as other toolbars) appear in all the Office programs, although some of the buttons they include differ from program to program. The Standard toolbar has buttons related to working with files. The Formatting toolbar has buttons related to changing the appearance of content. Each program also has program-specific toolbars, such as the Tables and Borders toolbar in Word for working with tables and the Chart toolbar in Excel for working with graphs and charts.

A **keyboard shortcut** is a combination of keys you press to perform a command. For example, Ctrl+S is the keyboard shortcut for the Save command (you hold down the Ctrl key while you press the S key). Keyboard shortcuts appear to the right of many menu commands.

Viewing Personalized Menus and Toolbars

When you first use a newly installed Office program, the menus and toolbars display only the basic and most commonly used commands and buttons, streamlining the program window. The other commands and buttons are available, but you have to click an extra button to see them (the Expand button on a menu and the Toolbar Options button on a toolbar). As you select commands and click buttons, the ones you use often are put on the short, personalized menu and on the visible part of the toolbars. The ones you don't use remain available on the full menus and toolbars. This means that the Office menus and toolbars might display different commands and buttons on each person's computer.

To view a personalized and full menu:

1. Click **Insert** on the Word menu bar to display the short, personalized menu. See Figure 7. The Bookmark command, for example, does not appear on the short menu.

Figure 7 | Short, personalized menu

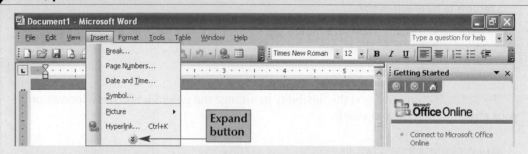

Trouble? If the Insert menu displays different commands than those shown in Figure 7, you need to reset the menus. Click Tools on the menu bar, click Customize (you might need to pause until the full menu appears to see the command), and then click the Options tab in the Customize dialog box. Click the Always show full menus check box to remove the check mark, if necessary, and then click the Show full menus after a short delay check box to insert a check mark, if necessary. Click the Reset menu and toolbar usage data button, and then click the Yes button to confirm that you want to reset the commands. Click the Close button. Repeat Step 1.

You can display the full menu in one of three ways: (1) pause until the full menu appears, which might happen as you read this; (2) click the Expand button at the bottom of the menu; or (3) double-click the menu name on the menu bar.

▸ **2.** Pause until the full Insert menu appears, as shown in Figure 8. The Bookmark command and other commands are now visible.

Figure 8 | Full, expanded menu

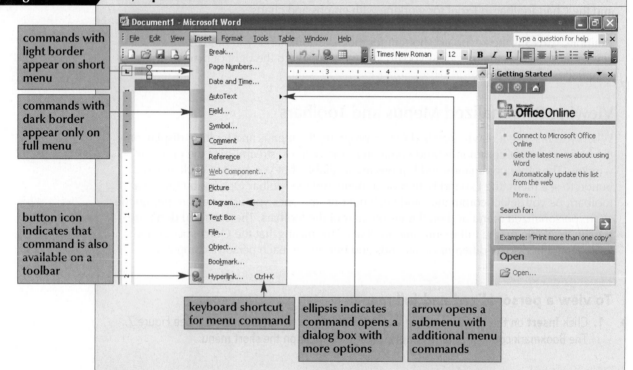

▸ **3.** Click the **Bookmark** command. A dialog box opens when you click a command whose name is followed by an ellipsis (...). In this case, the Bookmark dialog box opens.

4. Click the **Cancel** button to close the Bookmark dialog box.

5. Click **Insert** on the menu bar again to display the short, personalized menu. The Bookmark command appears on the short, personalized menu because you have recently used it.

6. Press the **Esc** key on the keyboard twice to close the menu.

As you can see, the menu changed based on your actions. Over time, only the commands you use frequently will appear on the personalized menu. The toolbars work similarly.

To use the personalized toolbars:

1. Observe that the Standard and Formatting toolbars appear side by side below the menu bar.

Trouble? If the toolbars appear on two rows, you need to reset them to their default state. Click Tools on the menu bar, click Customize, and then click the Options tab in the Customize dialog box. Click the Show Standard and Formatting toolbars on two rows check box to remove the check mark. Click the Reset menu and toolbar usage data button, and then click the Yes button to confirm you want to reset the commands. Click the Close button. Repeat Step 1.

2. Click the **Toolbar Options** button on the Standard toolbar. See Figure 9.

Toolbar Options palette ◄ **Figure 9**

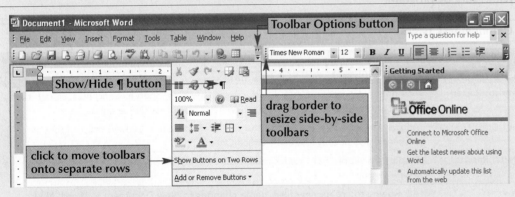

Trouble? If you see different buttons on the Toolbar Options palette, your side-by-side toolbars might be sized differently than the ones shown in Figure 9. Continue with Step 3.

3. Click the **Show/Hide ¶** button ¶ on the Toolbar Options palette to display the nonprinting screen characters. The Show/Hide ¶ button moves to the visible part of the Standard toolbar, and another button may be moved onto the Toolbar Options palette to make room for the new button.

Trouble? If the Show/Hide ¶ button already appears on the Standard toolbar, click another button on the Toolbar Options palette. Then click that same button again in Step 4 to turn off that formatting, if necessary.

Some buttons, like the Show/Hide ¶ button, act as a toggle switch—one click turns on the feature and a second click turns it off.

4. Click the **Show/Hide ¶** button ¶ on the Standard toolbar again to hide the nonprinting screen characters.

Some people like that the menus and toolbars change to meet their work habits. Others prefer to see all the menu commands or to display the default toolbars on two rows so that all the buttons are always visible. You'll change the toolbar setting now.

To turn off the personalized toolbars:

▶ 1. Click the **Toolbar Options** button ▮ on the right side of the Standard toolbar.

▶ 2. Click the **Show Buttons on Two Rows** command. The toolbars move to separate rows (the Standard toolbar on top) and you can see all the buttons on each toolbar.

You can easily access any button on the Standard and Formatting toolbars with one mouse click. The drawback is that when the toolbars are displayed on two rows, they take up more space in the program window, limiting the space you have to work.

Using Task Panes

A **task pane** is a window that provides access to commands for common tasks you'll perform in Office programs. For example, the Getting Started task pane, which opens when you first start any Office program, enables you to create new files and open existing ones. Task panes also help you navigate through more complex, multi-step procedures. All the Office programs include the task panes described in Figure 10. The other available task panes vary by program.

Figure 10 ▶ **Common task panes**

Task pane	Description
Getting Started	The home task pane; allows you to create new files, open existing files, search the online and offline Help system by keyword, and access Office online
Help	Allows you to search the online and offline Help system by keyword or table of contents, and access Microsoft Office Online
Search Results	Displays available Help topics related to entered keyword and enables you to initiate a new search
New	Allows you to create new files; name changes to New Document in Word, New Workbook in Excel, New File in Access, and New Presentation in PowerPoint
Clip Art	Allows you to search for all types of media clips (pictures, sound, video) and insert clips from the results
Clipboard	Allows you to paste some or all of the items that have been cut or copied from any Office program during the current work session
Research	Allows you to search a variety of reference material and other resources from within a file

No matter what their purpose, you use the same processes to open, close, and navigate between the task panes.

Opening and Closing Task Panes

When you first start any Office program, the Getting Started task pane opens by default along the right edge of the program window. You can resize or move the task pane to suit your work habits. You can also close the task pane to display the open file in the full available program window. For example, you might want to close the task pane when you are typing the body of a letter in Word or entering a lot of data in Excel.

You will open and close the task pane.

To open and close the task pane:

▶ 1. If necessary, click **View** on the menu bar, and then click **Task Pane**. The most recently viewed task pane opens on the right side of the screen. See Figure 11.

Getting Started task pane ◀ **Figure 11**

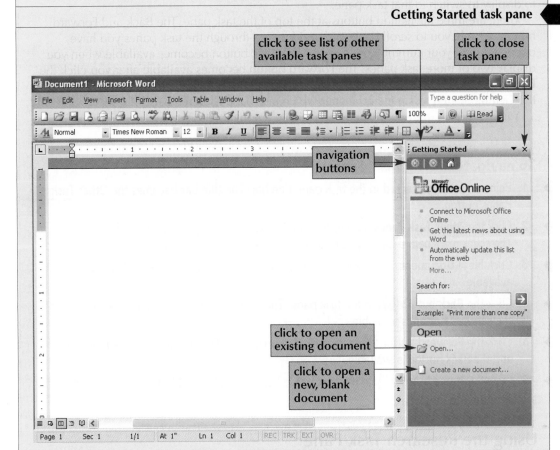

click to see list of other available task panes

click to close task pane

navigation buttons

click to open an existing document

click to open a new, blank document

Trouble? If you do not see the task pane, you probably closed the open task pane in Step 1. Repeat Step 1 to reopen the task pane.

Trouble? If a different task pane than the Getting Started task pane opens, then another task pane was the most recently viewed task pane. You'll learn how to open different task panes in the next section; continue with Step 2.

▶ 2. Click the **Close** button ✕ on the task pane title bar. The task pane closes, leaving more room on the screen for the open file.

▶ 3. Click **View** on the menu bar, and then click **Task Pane**. The task pane reopens.

There are several ways to display different task panes.

Navigating Among Task Panes

Once the task pane is open, you can display different task panes to suit the task you are trying to complete. For example, you can display the New task pane when you want to create a new file from a template. The name of the New task pane varies, depending on the program you are using: Word has the New Document task pane, Excel has the New Workbook task pane, PowerPoint has the New Presentation task pane, and Access has the New File task pane.

One of the quickest ways to display a task pane is to use the Other Task Panes button. When you point to the name of the open task pane in the task pane title bar, it becomes the Other Task Panes button. When you click the Other Task Panes button, all the available task panes for that Office program are listed. Just click the name of the task pane you want to display to switch to that task pane.

There are three navigation buttons at the top of the task pane. The Back and Forward buttons enable you to scroll backward and forward through the task panes you have opened during your current work session. The Back button becomes available when you display two or more task panes. The Forward button becomes available after you click the Back button to return to a previously viewed task pane. The Home button returns you to the Getting Started task pane no matter which task pane is currently displayed.

You'll use each of these methods to navigate among the task panes.

To navigate among task panes:

1. Point to **Getting Started** in the task pane title bar. The title bar becomes the Other Task Panes button.

2. Click the **Other Task Panes** button. A list of the available task panes for Word is displayed. The check mark before Getting Started indicates that this is the currently displayed task pane.

3. Click **New Document**. The New Document task pane appears and the Back button is available.

4. Click the **Back** button ⊕ in the task pane. The Getting Started task pane reappears and the Forward button is available.

5. Click the **Forward** button ⊕ in the task pane. The New Document task pane reappears and the Back button is available.

6. Click the **Home** button ⌂ in the task pane. The Getting Started task pane reappears.

Using the Research Task Pane

The Research task pane allows you to search a variety of reference materials and other resources to find specific information while you are working on a file. You can insert the information you find directly into your open file. The thesaurus and language translation tools are installed with Office and therefore are stored locally on your computer. If you are connected to the Internet, you can also use the Research task pane to access a dictionary, an encyclopedia, research sites, as well as business and financial sources. Some of the sites that appear in the search results are fee-based, meaning that you'll need to pay to access information on that site.

To use the Research task pane, you type a keyword or phrase into the Search for text box and then select whether you want to search all the books, sites, and sources; one category; or a specific source. The search results appear in the Research task pane. Some of the results appear as links, which you can click to open your browser window and display that information. If you are using Internet Explorer 5.01 or later as your Web browser, the Research task pane is tiled (appears side by side) with your document. If you are using another Web browser, you'll need to return to the task pane in your open file to click another link.

The Research task pane functions independently in each file. So you can open multiple files and perform a different search in each. In addition, each Research task pane stores the results of up to 10 searches, so you can quickly return to the results from any of your most recent searches. To move among the saved searches, click the Back and Forward buttons in the task pane.

Using the Research Task Pane

- Type a keyword or phrase into the Search for text box.
- Select a search category, individual source, or all references.
- If necessary, click a link in the search results to display more information.
- Copy and paste selected content from the task pane into your file.

Jake plans to send a copy of the next quarter's sales report to the office in France. You'll use the bilingual dictionaries in the Research task pane to begin entering labels in French into an Excel workbook for the sales report.

To use the bilingual dictionaries in the Research task pane:

1. Click the **Microsoft Excel – Book1** button on the taskbar to switch to the Excel window.

2. Click the **Other Task Panes** button on the Getting Started task pane, and then click **Research**. The Research task pane opens.

3. Click in the **Search for** text box, and then type **paper**.

4. Click the **Search for** list arrow and then click **Translation**. The bilingual dictionary opens in the Research task pane. You can choose from among 12 languages to translate to and from, including Japanese, Russian, Spanish, Dutch, German, and French.

   Trouble? If a dialog box opens stating the translation feature is not installed, click the Yes button to install it.

5. If necessary, click the **To** list arrow, and then click **French (France)**. See Figure 12.

Research task pane | **Figure 12**

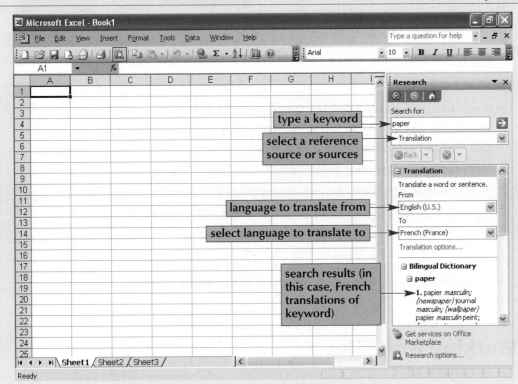

6. Scroll to read the different translations of "paper" in French.

After you locate specific information, you can quickly insert it into your open file. The information can be inserted by copying the selected content you want to insert, and then pasting it in the appropriate location in your file. In some instances, such as MSN Money Stock Quotes, a button appears enabling you to quickly insert the indicated information in your file at the location of the insertion point. Otherwise, you can use the standard Copy and Paste commands.

You'll copy the translation for "paper" into the Excel workbook.

To copy information from the Research task pane into a file:

▶ 1. Select **papier** in the Research task pane. This is the word you want to copy to the workbook.

▶ 2. Right-click the selected text, and then click **Copy** on the shortcut menu. The text is duplicated on the Office Clipboard.

▶ 3. Right-click cell **A1**, and then click **Paste**. The word "papier" is entered into the cell. See Figure 13.

Figure 13 ▶ **Translation copied into Excel**

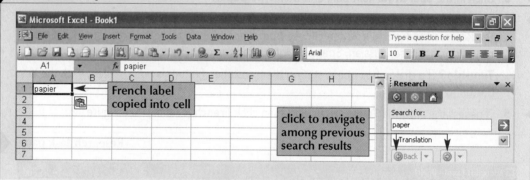

You'll repeat this process to look up the translation for "furniture" and copy it into cell A2.

To translate and copy another word into Excel:

▶ 1. Double-click **paper** in the Search for text box to select the text, type **furniture**, and then click the **Start searching** button ➡ in the Research task pane.

▶ 2. Verify that you're translating from English (U.S) to French (France).

▶ 3. Select **meubles** in the translation results, right-click the selected text, and then click **Copy**.

▶ 4. Right-click cell **A2**, and then click **Paste**. The second label appears in the cell.

The Research task pane works similarly in all the Office programs. You'll use other task panes later in this tutorial to perform specific tasks, including opening a file and getting assistance.

Working with Files

The most common tasks you'll perform in any Office program are to create, open, save, and close files. The processes for each of these tasks are the same in all the Office programs. In addition, there are several methods for performing most tasks in Office. This flexibility enables you to use Office in a way that fits how you like to work.

Creating a File

To begin working in a program, you need to create a new file or open an existing file. When you start Word, Excel, or PowerPoint, the program opens along with a blank file—ready for you to begin working on a new document, workbook, or presentation. When you start Access, the Getting Started task pane opens, displaying options for opening a new database or an existing one.

Jake has asked you to start working on the agenda for the stockholder meeting, which he suggests you create using Word. You enter text in a Word document by typing.

To enter text in a document:

▶ 1. Click the **Document1 – Microsoft Word** button on the taskbar to activate the Word program window.

▶ 2. Type **Delmar Office Supplies**, and then press the **Enter** key. The text you typed appears on one line in the Word document.

   Trouble? If you make a typing error, press the Backspace key to delete the incorrect letters, and then retype the text.

▶ 3. Type **Stockholder Meeting Agenda**, and then press the **Enter** key. The text you typed appears on the second line.

Next, you'll save the file.

Saving a File

As you create and modify Office files, your work is stored only in the computer's temporary memory, not on a hard disk. If you were to exit the programs, turn off your computer, or experience a power failure, your work would be lost. To prevent losing work, save your file to a disk frequently—at least every 10 minutes. You can save files to the hard disk located inside your computer or to portable storage disks, such as floppy disks, Zip disks, or read-write CD-ROMs.

The first time you save a file, you need to name it. This name is called a **filename**. When you choose a filename, select a descriptive one that accurately reflects the content of the document, workbook, presentation, or database, such as "Shipping Options Letter" or "Fourth Quarter Financial Analysis." Filenames can include a maximum of 255 letters, numbers, hyphens, and spaces in any combination. Office appends a **file extension** to the filename, which identifies the program in which that file was created. The file extensions are .doc for Word, .xls for Excel, .ppt for PowerPoint, and .mdb for Access. Whether you see file extensions depends on how Windows is set up on your computer.

You also need to decide where to save the file—on which disk and in what folder. A **folder** is a container for your files. Just as you organize paper documents within folders stored in a filing cabinet, you can organize your files within folders stored on your computer's hard disk or a removable disk. Store each file in a logical location that you will remember whenever you want to use the file again.

Saving a File

- Click the Save button on the Standard toolbar (*or* click File on the menu bar, and then click Save or Save As).
- In the Save As dialog box, click the Save in list arrow, and then navigate to the location where you want to save the file.
- Type a filename in the File name text box.
- Click the Save button.
- To resave the named file to the same location, click the Save button on the Standard toolbar (*or* click File on the menu bar, and then click Save).

The two lines of text you typed are not yet saved on disk. You'll do that now.

To save a file for the first time:

▶ 1. Click the **Save** button 🔲 on the Standard toolbar. The Save As dialog box opens. The first few words of the first line appear in the File name text box, as a suggested filename. You'll replace this with a more descriptive filename.

▶ 2. Click the **Save in** list arrow, and then click the location that contains your Data Files.

Trouble? If you don't have the Common Office Features Data Files, you need to get them before you can proceed. Your instructor will either give you the Data Files or ask you to obtain them from a specified location (such as a network drive). In either case, be sure that you make a backup copy of your Data Files before you start using them, so that the original files will be available on your copied disk in case you need to start over because of an error or problem. If you have any questions about the Data Files, see your instructor or technical support person for assistance.

▶ 3. Double-click the **OFF** folder in the list box, and then double-click the **Tutorial** folder. This is the location where you want to save the document. See Figure 14.

▶ 4. Type **Stockholder Meeting Agenda** in the File name text box.

Figure 14

Completed Save As dialog box

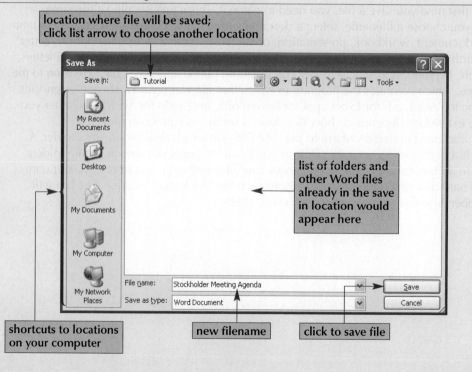

location where file will be saved;
click list arrow to choose another location

list of folders and other Word files already in the save in location would appear here

shortcuts to locations on your computer

new filename

click to save file

Trouble? If the .doc file extension appears after the filename, then your computer is configured to show file extensions. Continue with Step 5.

▶ **5.** Click the **Save** button. The Save As dialog box closes, and the name of your file appears in the program window title bar.

The saved file includes everything in the document at the time you last saved it. Any edits or additions you then make to the document exist only in the computer's memory and are not saved in the file on the disk. As you work, remember to save frequently so that the file is updated to reflect the latest content of the document.

Because you already named the document and selected a storage location, the second and subsequent times you save, the Save As dialog box doesn't open. If you wanted to save a copy of the file with a different filename or to a different location, you would reopen the Save As dialog box by clicking File on the menu bar, and then clicking Save As. The previous version of the file remains on your disk as well.

You need to add your name to the agenda. Then you'll save your changes.

To modify and save a file:

▶ **1.** Type your name, and then press the **Enter** key. The text you typed appears on the next line.

▶ **2.** Click the **Save** button 🖫 on the Standard toolbar to save your changes.

When you're done with a file, you can close it.

Closing a File

Although you can keep multiple files open at one time, you should close any file you are no longer working on to conserve system resources as well as to ensure that you don't inadvertently make changes to the file. You can close a file by clicking the Close command on the File menu or by clicking the Close Window button in the upper-right corner of the menu bar.

As a standard practice, you should save your file before closing it. If you're unsure whether the file is saved, it cannot hurt to save it again. However, Office has an added safeguard: If you attempt to close a file or exit a program without saving your changes, a dialog box opens asking whether you want to save the file. Click the Yes button to save the changes to the file before closing the file and program. Click the No button to close the file and program without saving changes. Click the Cancel button to return to the program window without saving changes or closing the file and program. This feature helps to ensure that you always save the most current version of any file.

You'll add the date to the agenda. Then, you'll attempt to close the document without saving.

To modify and close a file:

▶ **1.** Type the date, and then press the **Enter** key. The text you typed appears under your name in the document.

▶ **2.** Click the **Close Window** button ⊠ on the Word menu bar to close the document. A dialog box opens, asking whether you want to save the changes you made to the document.

3. Click the **Yes** button. The current version of the document is saved to the file, and then the document closes, and Word is still running.

   Trouble? If Word is not running, then you closed the program in Step 2. Start Word, click the Close Window button on the menu bar to close the blank document.

Once you have a program open, you can create additional new files for the open program or you can open previously created and saved files.

Opening a File

When you want to open a blank document, workbook, presentation, or database, you create a new file. When you want to work on a previously created file, you must first open it. Opening a file transfers a copy of the file from the storage disk (either a hard disk or a portable disk) to the computer's memory and displays it on your screen. The file is then in your computer's memory and on the disk.

Reference Window | **Opening an Existing or a New File**

- Click the Open button on the Standard toolbar (*or* click File on the menu bar, and then click Open *or* click the More link in the Open section of the Getting Started task pane).
- In the Open dialog box, click the Look in list arrow, and then navigate to the storage location of the file you want to open.
- Click the filename of the file you want to open.
- Click the Open button.

or

- Click the New button on the Standard toolbar (*or* click File on the menu bar, click New, and then (depending on the program) click the Blank document, Blank workbook, Blank presentation, or Blank database link in the New task pane).

Jake asks you to print the agenda. To do that, you'll reopen the file. You'll use the Open button on the Standard toolbar.

To open an existing file:

1. Click the **Open** button 📂 on the Standard toolbar. The Open dialog box, which works similarly to the Save As dialog box, opens.

2. Click the **Look in** list arrow, and then navigate to the **OFF\Tutorial** folder included with your Data Files. This is the location where you saved the agenda document.

3. Click **Stockholder Meeting Agenda** in the file list. See Figure 15.

Open dialog box | **Figure 15**

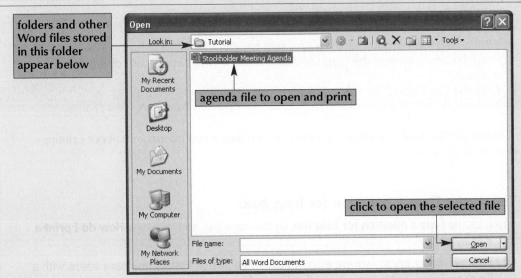

folders and other Word files stored in this folder appear below

agenda file to open and print

click to open the selected file

4. Click the **Open** button. The file containing the agenda opens in the Word program window.

Next, you'll get information about printing files in Word.

Getting Help

If you don't know how to perform a task or want more information about a feature, you can turn to Office itself for information on how to use it. This information, referred to simply as **Help**, is like a huge encyclopedia available from your desktop. You can access Help in a variety of ways, including ScreenTips, the Type a question for help box, the Help task pane, and Microsoft Office Online.

Using ScreenTips

ScreenTips are a fast and simple method you can use to get help about objects you see on the screen. A **ScreenTip** is a yellow box with the button's name. Just position the mouse pointer over a toolbar button to view its ScreenTip.

Using the Type a Question for Help Box

For answers to specific questions, you can use the **Type a question for help box**, located on the menu bar of every Office program, to find information in the Help system. You simply type a question using everyday language about a task you want to perform or a topic you need help with, and then press the Enter key to search the Help system. The Search Results task pane opens with a list of Help topics related to your query. You click a topic to open a Help window with step-by-step instructions that guide you through a specific procedure and explanations of difficult concepts in clear, easy-to-understand language. For example, you might ask how to format a cell in an Excel worksheet; a list of Help topics related to the words you typed will appear.

Getting Help from the Type a Question for Help Box

- Click the Type a question for help box on the menu bar.
- Type your question, and then press the Enter key.
- Click a Help topic in the Search Results task pane.
- Read the information in the Help window. For more information, click other topics or links.
- Click the Close button on the Help window title bar.

You'll use the Type a question for help box to obtain more information about printing a document in Word.

To use the Type a question for help box:

1. Click the **Type a question for help box** on the menu bar, and then type **How do I print a document?**

2. Press the **Enter** key to retrieve a list of topics. The Search Results task pane opens with a list of topics related to your query. See Figure 16.

Figure 16 | **Search Results task pane displaying Help topics**

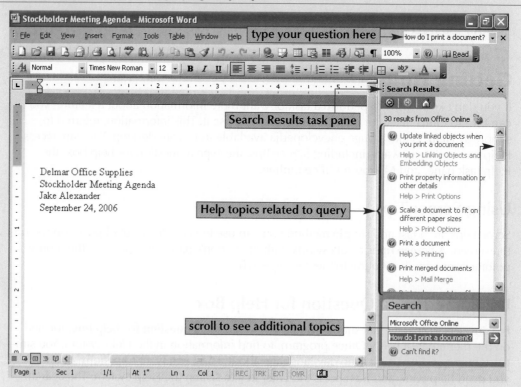

Trouble? If your search results list differs from the one shown in Figure 16, your computer is not connected to the Internet or Microsoft has updated the list of available Help topics since this book was published. Continue with Step 3.

3. Scroll through the list to review the Help topics.

4. Click **Print a document** to open the Help window and learn more about the various ways to print a document. See Figure 17.

Print a document Help window ◀ Figure 17

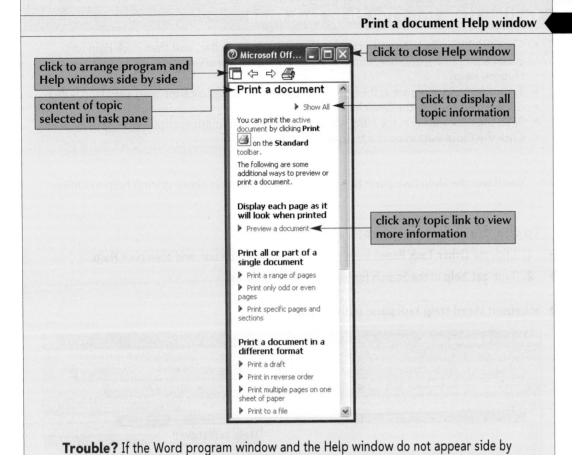

click to arrange program and Help windows side by side

content of topic selected in task pane

click to close Help window

click to display all topic information

click any topic link to view more information

Trouble? If the Word program window and the Help window do not appear side by side, then you need to tile the windows. Click the Auto Tile button on the toolbar in the Help window.

5. Read the information, and then when you're done, click the **Close** button ☒ on the Help window title bar to close the Help window.

The Help task pane works similarly.

Using the Help Task Pane

For more in-depth help, you can use the **Help task pane**, a task pane that enables you to search the Help system using keywords or phrases. You type a specific word or phrase in the Search for text box, and then click the Start searching button. The Search Results task pane opens with a list of topics related to the keyword or phrase you entered. If your computer is connected to the Internet, you might see more search results because some Help topics are stored only online and not locally on your computer. The task pane also has a Table of Contents link that organizes the Help system by subjects and topics, like in a book. You click main subject links to display related topic links.

Reference Window

Getting Help from the Help Task Pane

- Click the Other Task Panes button on the task pane title bar, and then click Help (*or* click Help on the menu bar, and then click Microsoft Word/Excel/PowerPoint/Access/Outlook Help).
- Type a keyword or phrase in the Search for text box, and then click the Start searching button.
- Click a Help topic in the Search Results task pane.
- Read the information in the Help window. For more information, click other topics or links.
- Click the Close button on the Help window title bar.

You'll use the Help task pane to obtain more information about getting help in Office.

To use the Help task pane:

▶ **1.** Click the **Other Task Panes** button on the task pane title bar, and then click **Help**.

▶ **2.** Type **get help** in the Search for text box. See Figure 18.

Figure 18 ▶ **Microsoft Word Help task pane with keyword**

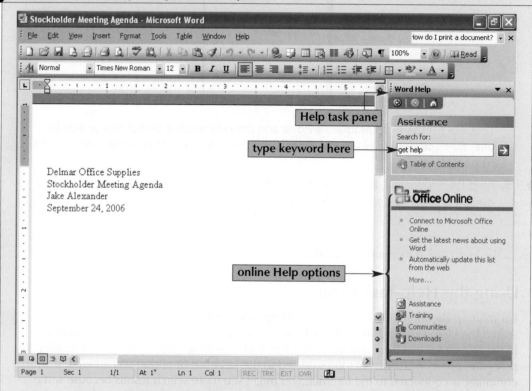

▶ **3.** Click the **Start searching** button ➡. The Search Results task pane opens with a list of topics related to your keywords.

▶ **4.** Scroll through the list to review the Help topics.

▶ **5.** Click **About getting help while you work** to open the Microsoft Word Help window and learn more about the various ways to obtain help in Word. See Figure 19.

About getting help while you work Help window ◀ **Figure 19**

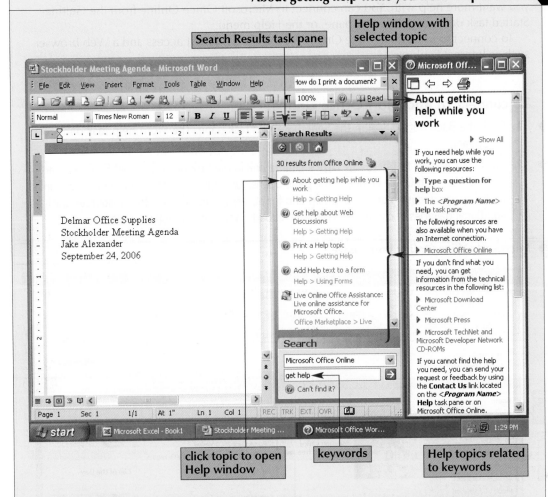

Search Results task pane

Help window with selected topic

click topic to open Help window

keywords

Help topics related to keywords

Trouble? If your search results list differs from the one shown in Figure 19, your computer is not connected to the Internet or Microsoft has updated the list of available Help topics since this book was published. Continue with Step 6.

Trouble? If the Word program window and the Help window do not appear side by side, then you need to tile the windows. Click the Auto Tile button on the toolbar in the Help window.

6. Click **Microsoft Office Online** in the right pane to display information about that topic. Read the information.

7. Click the other links about this feature and read the information.

8. When you're done, click the **Close** button ☒ on the Help window title bar to close the Help window. The task pane remains open.

If your computer has a connection to the Internet, you can get more help information from Microsoft Office Online.

Using Microsoft Office Online

Microsoft Office Online is a Web site maintained by Microsoft that provides access to additional Help resources. For example, you can access current Help topics, read how-to articles, and find tips for using Office. You can search all or part of a site to find information about tasks you want to perform, features you want to use, or anything else you want more help with. You can connect to Microsoft Office Online from the Getting Started task pane, the Help task pane, or the Help menu.

To connect to Microsoft Office Online, you'll need Internet access and a Web browser such as Internet Explorer.

To connect to Microsoft Office Online:

▶ 1. Click the **Back** button ⊕ in the Search Results task pane. The Word Help task pane reappears.

▶ 2. Click the **Connect to Microsoft Office Online** link in the task pane. Internet Explorer starts and the Microsoft Office Online home page opens. See Figure 20. This Web page offers links to Web pages focusing on getting help and for accessing additional Office resources, such as additional galleries of clip art, software downloads, and training opportunities.

Figure 20	Microsoft Office Online home page

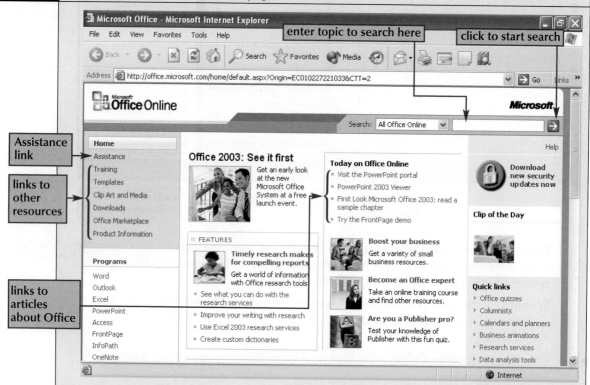

Trouble? If the content you see on the Microsoft Office Online home page differs from the figure, the site has been updated since this book was published. Continue with Step 3.

▶ 3. Click the **Assistance** link. The Assistance page opens. From this page, you browse for help in each of the different Office programs. You can also enter a keyword or phrase pertaining to a particular topic you wish to search for information on using the Search box in the upper-right corner of the window.

▶ 4. Click the **Close** button ☒ on the Internet Explorer title bar to close the browser.

The Help features enable the staff at Delmar Office Supplies to get answers to questions they have about any task or procedure when they need it. The more you practice getting information from the Help system, the more effective you will be at using Office to its full potential.

Printing a File

At times, you'll want a paper copy of your Office file. The first time you print during each session at the computer, you should use the Print menu command to open the Print dialog box so you can verify or adjust the printing settings. You can select a printer, the number of copies to print, the portion of the file to print, and so forth; the printing settings vary slightly from program to program. For subsequent print jobs, you can use the Print button to print without opening the dialog box, if you want to use the same default settings.

Reference Window

Printing a File

- Click File on the menu bar, and then click Print.
- Verify the print settings in the Print dialog box.
- Click the OK button.

or

- Click the Print button on the Standard toolbar.

Now that you know how to print, you'll print the agenda for Jake.

To print a file:

1. Make sure your printer is turned on and contains paper.

2. Click **File** on the menu bar, and then click **Print**. The Print dialog box opens. See Figure 21.

Print dialog box | **Figure 21**

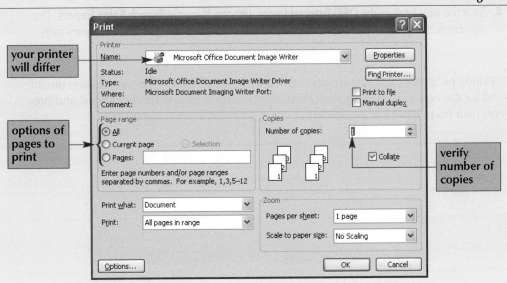

3. Verify that the correct printer appears in the Name list box in the Printer area. If the wrong printer appears, click the **Name** list arrow, and then click the correct printer from the list of available printers.

4. Verify that **1** appears in the Number of copies text box.

5. Click the **OK** button to print the document.

Trouble? If the document does not print, see your instructor or technical support person for help.

Now that you have printed the agenda, you can close Word and Excel.

Exiting Programs

Whenever you finish working with a program, you should exit it. As with many other aspects of Office, you can exit programs with a button or from a menu. You'll use both methods to close Word and Excel. You can use the Exit command to exit a program and close an open file in one step. If you haven't saved the final version of the open file, a dialog box opens, asking whether you want to save your changes. Clicking the Yes button saves the open file, closes the file, and then exits the program.

To exit a program:

1. Click the **Close** button ⊠ on the Word title bar to exit Word. The Word document closes and the Word program exits. The Excel window is visible again on your screen.

Trouble? If a dialog box opens, asking whether you want to save the document, you may have inadvertently made a change to the document. Click the No button.

2. Click **File** on the Excel menu bar, and then click **Exit**. A dialog box opens asking whether you want to save the changes you made to the workbook.

3. Click the **Yes** button. The Save As dialog box opens.

4. Save the workbook in the **OFF\Tutorial** folder with the filename **French Sales Report**. The workbook closes, saving a copy to the location you specified, and the Excel program exits.

Exiting programs after you are done using them keeps your Windows desktop uncluttered for the next person using the computer, frees up your system's resources, and prevents data from being lost accidentally.

Review

Quick Check

1. List the five programs included in Office.
2. How do you start an Office program?
3. Explain the difference between Save As and Save.
4. What is one method for opening an existing Office file?
5. What happens if you attempt to close a file or exit a program without saving the current version of the open file?
6. What are four ways to get help?

Review

Tutorial Summary

You have learned how to use features common to all the programs included in Microsoft Office 2003, including starting and exiting programs; resizing windows; using menus and toolbars; working with task panes; saving, opening, closing, and printing files; and getting help.

Key Terms

Access	menu	Outlook
database	menu bar	PowerPoint
document	menu command	presentation
Excel	Microsoft Access 2003	ScreenTip
file extension	Microsoft Excel 2003	task pane
filename	Microsoft Office 2003	toolbar
folder	Microsoft Office Online	Type a question for help box
Help	Microsoft Outlook 2003	Word
Help task pane	Microsoft PowerPoint 2003	workbook
integration	Microsoft Word 2003	
keyboard shortcut	Office	

Practice

Practice the skills you learned in the tutorial using the same case scenario.

Review Assignments

Data Files needed for the Review Assignments: Finances.xls, Letter.doc

Before the stockholders meeting at Delmar Office Supplies, you'll open and print documents for the upcoming presentation. Complete the following steps:

1. Start PowerPoint.
2. Use the Help task pane to learn how to change the toolbar buttons from small to large, and then do it. Use the same procedure to change the buttons back to regular size. Close the Help window when you're done.
3. Start Excel.
4. Switch to the PowerPoint window using the taskbar, and then close the presentation but leave open the PowerPoint program. (*Hint:* Click the Close Window button on the menu bar.)
5. Open a new, blank PowerPoint presentation from the Getting Started task pane. (*Hint:* Click Create a new presentation in the Open section of the Getting Started task pane.)
6. Close the PowerPoint presentation and program using the Close button on the PowerPoint title bar; do not save changes if asked.

7. Open the **Finances** workbook located in the **OFF\Review** folder included with your Data Files using the Open button on the Standard toolbar in Excel.
8. Use the Save As command to save the workbook as **Delmar Finances** in the **OFF\Review** folder.
9. Type your name, press the Enter key to insert your name at the top of the worksheet, and then save the workbook.
10. Print one copy of the worksheet using the Print command on the File menu.
11. Exit Excel using the File menu.
12. Start Word, and then use the Getting Started task pane to open the **Letter** document located in the **OFF\Review** folder included with your Data Files. (*Hint:* Click the More link in the Getting Started task pane to open the Open dialog box.)
13. Use the Save As command to save the document with the filename **Delmar Letter** in the **OFF\Review** folder.
14. Press and hold the Ctrl key, press the End key, and then release both keys to move the insertion point to the end of the letter, and then type your name.
15. Use the Save button on the Standard toolbar to save the change to the Delmar Letter document.
16. Print one copy of the document, and then close the document.
17. Exit the Word program using the Close button on the title bar.

Assess

SAM Assessment and Training

If you have a SAM user profile, you may have access to hands-on instruction, practice, and assessment of the skills covered in this tutorial. Log in to your SAM account and go to your assignments page to see what your instructor has assigned.

Review

Quick Check Answers

1. Word, Excel, PowerPoint, Access, Outlook
2. Click the Start button on the taskbar, point to All Programs, point to Microsoft Office, and then click the name of the program you want to open.
3. Save As enables you to change the filename and storage location of a file. Save updates a file to reflect its latest contents using its current filename and location.
4. Either click the Open button on the Standard toolbar or click the More link in the Getting Started task pane to open the Open dialog box.
5. A dialog box opens asking whether you want to save the changes to the file.
6. ScreenTips, Type a question for help box, Help task pane, Microsoft Office Online

New Perspectives on

Microsoft® Office Word 2003

Read This Before You Begin: Tutorials 1-2

To the Student

Data Files

To complete Word Tutorials 1 and 2, you need the starting student Data Files. Your instructor will either provide you with these Data Files or ask you to obtain them yourself.

Word Tutorials 1 and 2 require the folders shown in the next column to complete the Tutorials, Review Assignments, and Case Problems. You will need to copy these folders from a file server, a standalone computer, or the Web to the drive and folder where you will be storing your Data Files. Your instructor will tell you which computer, drive letter, and folder(s) contain the files you need. You can also download the files by going to www.course.com; see the inside back or front cover for more information on downloading the files, or ask your instructor or technical support person for assistance.

If you are storing your Data Files on floppy disks, you will need **one** blank, formatted, high-density disk for these tutorials. Label your disk as shown, and place on it the folders indicated.

▼ **Word 2003 Tutorials 1-2: Data Disk**

 Tutorial.01 folder

 Tutorial.02 folder

When you begin a tutorial, refer to the Student Data Files section at the bottom of the tutorial opener page, which indicates which folders and files you need for the tutorial. Each end-of-tutorial exercise also indicates the files you need to complete that exercise.

Course Labs

The Word tutorials feature an interactive Course Lab to help you understand word processing concepts. There are Lab Assignments at the end of Tutorial 1 that relate to this lab. Contact your instructor or technical support person for assistance in accessing the lab.

To the Instructor

The Data Files and Course Labs are available on the Instructor Resources CD for this title. Follow the instructions in the Help file on the CD to install the programs to your network or standalone computer. See the "To the Student" section above for information on how to set up the Data Files that accompany this text.

You are granted a license to copy the Data Files and Course Labs to any computer or computer network used by students who have purchased this book.

System Requirements

If you are going to work through this book using your own computer, you need:

- **Computer System** Microsoft Windows 2000, Windows XP or higher must be installed on your computer. These tutorials assume a typical installation of Microsoft Word 2003.

- **Data Files** You will not be able to complete the tutorials or exercises in this book using your own computer until you have the necessary starting Data Files.

- **Course Labs** See your instructor or technical support person to obtain the Course Lab software for use on your own computer.

www.course.com/NewPerspectives

Objectives

Lab

Student Data Files

There are no student Data Files needed for this tutorial.

Creating a Document

Writing a Business Letter

Case

Art4U, Inc.

Megan Grahs is the owner and manager of Art4U, Inc., a graphics design firm in Tucson, Arizona. When Megan founded Art4U in the early 1980s, the company drew most of its revenue from design projects for local magazines, newspapers, advertising circulars, and other print publications. The artists at Art4U laboriously created logos, diagrams, and other illustrations by hand, using watercolors, ink, pastels, and a variety of other media. Since the advent of the Internet, however, Art4U has become one of the Southwest's leading creators of electronic artwork. The firm's artists now work exclusively on computers, saving each piece of art as an electronic file that they can e-mail to a client in a matter of minutes.

Thanks to e-mail, Art4U is no longer limited to the local Tucson market. As a result, Art4U has nearly doubled in size over the past ten years. Most of the increase in business has come from Web page designers, who continually need fresh and innovative graphics to use in their Web pages. In fact, Megan has just signed a contract with Web Time Productions agreeing to create a series of logos for a high-profile Web site. She needs to return the signed contract to Web Time Productions' office in Chicago.

In this tutorial, you will create the cover letter that will accompany the contract. You will create the letter using **Microsoft Office Word 2003** (or simply **Word**), a popular word-processing program. Before you begin typing the letter, you will learn how to start the Word program, identify and use the elements of the Word screen, and adjust some Word settings. Next, you will create a new Word document, type the text of the cover letter, save the letter, and then print the letter for Megan. In the process of entering the text, you'll learn several ways to correct typing errors.

Four Steps to a Professional Document

Word helps you produce quality work in minimal time. Not only can you type a document in Word, but you can also quickly make revisions and corrections, adjust margins and spacing, create columns and tables, and add graphics to your documents. The most efficient way to produce a document is to follow these four steps: (1) planning, (2) creating and editing, (3) formatting, and (4) printing.

In the long run, planning saves time and effort. First, you should determine what you want to say. State your purpose clearly and include enough information to achieve that purpose without overwhelming or boring your reader. Be sure to organize your ideas logically. Decide how you want your document to look as well. In this case, your letter to Web Time Productions will take the form of a standard business letter. It should be addressed to Web Time's president, Nicholas Brower. Megan has given you a handwritten note indicating what she would like you to say in the letter. This note is shown in Figure 1-1.

| Figure 1-1 | Megan's notes for the contract letter |

Notes for Contract Letter

Please include the following questions in the Web Time Productions cover letter:

• When will we receive a complete schedule for the project?

• How many preliminary designs do you require?

• Will you be available to discuss the project with our artists via a conference call next week?

Send the letter to Web Time Productions' president, Nicholas Brower. The address is: 2015 Dubuque Avenue, Chicago, IL 60025.

After you plan your document, you can go ahead and create and edit it using Word. Creating the document generally means typing the text of your document. Editing consists of reading the document you've created, correcting your errors, and, finally, adding or deleting text to make the document easy to read.

Once your document is error-free, you can format it to make it visually appealing. Formatting features, such as adjusting margins to create white space (blank areas of a page), setting line spacing, and using bold and italic, can help make your document easier to read.

Printing is the final phase in creating an effective document. In this tutorial, you will preview your document before you spend time and resources to print it.

Exploring the Word Window

Before you can apply these four steps to produce a letter in Word, you need to start Word and learn about the general organization of the Word window. You'll do that now.

To start Microsoft Word:

1. Click the **Start** button on the taskbar, point to **All Programs**, point to **Microsoft Office**, and then click **Microsoft Office Word 2003**. The Word window opens. See Figure 1-2.

   Trouble? If you don't see the Microsoft Office Word 2003 option on the Microsoft Office submenu, look for it in a different submenu or as an option on the All Programs menu. If you still can't find the Microsoft Office Word 2003 option, ask your instructor or technical support person for help.

Maximized Word window ◀ **Figure 1-2**

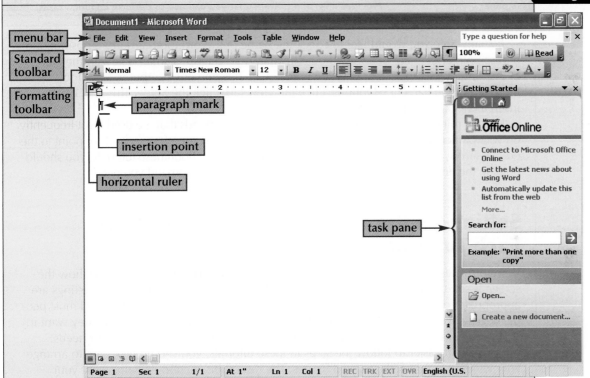

2. If the Word window does not fill the entire screen, click the **Maximize** button 🔲 in the upper-right corner of the Word window. Your screen should now resemble Figure 1-2.

   Trouble? If your screen looks slightly different from Figure 1-2, just continue with the steps. You will learn how to change the appearance of the Word window shortly.

   Word is now running and ready to use. Don't be concerned if you don't see everything shown in Figure 1-2. You'll learn how to adjust the appearance of the Word window soon.

The Word window is made up of a number of elements, which are described in Figure 1-3. You are already familiar with some of these elements, such as the menu bar and toolbars, because they are common to all Windows programs.

Figure 1-3 ▶ **Parts of the Word window**

Screen Element	Description
Formatting toolbar	Contains buttons that affect how the document looks.
horizontal ruler	Shows page margins, tabs, and column widths.
insertion point	Shows where characters will appear when you start typing.
menu bar	Contains lists, or menus, of all the Word commands. When you first display a menu, you see a short list of the most frequently used commands. To see the full list of commands in the menu, you can click the menu and then wait a few seconds for the remaining commands to appear, double-click the menu, or click the menu and then click or point to the downward-facing double-arrow at the bottom of the menu.
paragraph mark	Marks the end of a paragraph.
Standard toolbar	Contains buttons for activating frequently used commands.
task pane	Provides links and buttons that you can use to perform common tasks.

If at any time you would like to check the name of a Word toolbar button, position the mouse pointer over the button without clicking. A ScreenTip, a small box with the name of the button, will appear. (If you don't see ScreenTips on your computer, click Tools on the Word menu bar, click Options, click the View tab, click the ScreenTips check box to insert a check, and then click OK.)

Keep in mind that the menus initially display the commands that are used most frequently on your particular computer. When you leave a menu open for a few seconds or point to the double-arrow, a complete list of commands appears. Throughout these tutorials, you should point to the double-arrow on a menu if you do not see the command you need.

Setting Up the Window Before You Begin Each Tutorial

Word provides a set of standard settings, called **default settings**, which control how the screen is set up and how a document looks when you first start typing. These settings are appropriate for most situations. However, these settings are easily changed, and most people begin a work session by adjusting Word to make sure it is set up the way they want it.

As you gain experience, you will learn how to customize Word to suit your needs. But to make it easier to follow the steps in these tutorials, you should take care to arrange your window to match the tutorial figures. The rest of this section explains what your window should look like and how to make it match those in the tutorials. Depending on how many people use your computer (and how much they adjust Word's appearance), you might have to set up the window to match the figures each time you start Word.

Setting the Document View to Normal

The View buttons in the lower-left corner of the Word window change the way your document is displayed. You will learn how to select the appropriate view for a document in a later tutorial. For now, you want the document displayed in Normal view.

To make sure the document is displayed in Normal view:

1. Click the **Normal View** button ☰ to the left of the horizontal scroll bar. See Figure 1-4. If your Document window was not in Normal view, it changes to Normal view now. The Normal View button is now highlighted, indicating that it is selected.

Changing to Normal view ◀ **Figure 1-4**

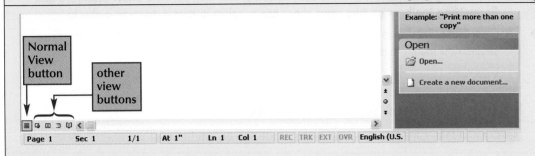

Displaying the Toolbars, Task Pane, and Ruler

The Word toolbars allow you to perform common tasks quickly by clicking a button. To eliminate on-screen clutter while you work through these tutorials, you should check to make sure that only the Formatting and Standard toolbars appear on your screen. The Standard toolbar should be positioned on top of the Formatting toolbar, as shown previously in Figure 1-2.

Depending on the choices made by the last person to use your computer, you may not see both toolbars or you may see both toolbars on one row. You also may see additional toolbars. In the following steps, you will make sure that your Word window shows only the Standard and Formatting toolbars. At the same time, you will verify that the task pane is displayed as it is in Figure 1-2.

To verify that your Word window shows the correct toolbars and the task pane:

1. Position the pointer over any toolbar and click the right mouse button. A shortcut menu appears. The menu lists all available toolbars with a check mark next to those currently displayed. If the Standard and Formatting toolbars are currently displayed on your computer, you should see check marks next to their names. You should also see a check mark next to "Task Pane," indicating that the task pane is displayed on the right side of the screen. (You saw the task pane earlier in Figure 1-2.)

2. Verify that you see a check mark next to the word "Standard" in the shortcut menu. If you do not see a check mark, click **Standard** now. (Clicking any item on the shortcut menu closes the menu, so you will need to re-open it in the next step.)

3. Redisplay the shortcut menu, and click **Formatting** if you don't see a check mark next to it.

4. If you don't see the task pane, click View on the menu bar and then click **Task Pane**.

5. Redisplay the shortcut menu. If any toolbar besides the Formatting and Standard toolbars is open, click the toolbar name to remove the check mark and hide the toolbar.

   Trouble? If you see a task pane other than the Getting Started task pane, click the down pointing arrow at the top of the task pane, and then click Getting Started.

If the toolbars appear on one row, perform the next steps to arrange them in two rows.

To arrange the Standard and Formatting toolbars on two rows:

1. Click **Tools** on the menu bar, and then click **Customize**. The Customize dialog box opens.
2. Click the **Options** tab if it is not already selected, and then click the **Show Standard and Formatting toolbars on two rows** check box to select it (that is, to insert a check).
3. Click **Close**. The Customize dialog box closes. The toolbars and task pane on your screen should now match those shown earlier in Figure 1-2.

Setting Up Other Screen Elements

Next, you'll take care of a few other parts of the screen, including:

- The horizontal ruler, which appears below the Formatting toolbar and is used to adjust margins and align parts of a document
- The Zoom setting, which controls the document's on-screen magnification; a setting of 100% displays the text in the same size as it will appear when printed
- The default font setting, which controls the size and shape of the characters that appear when you start typing

You'll learn more about these topics later. For now, you simply need to make your screen match the figures in this book by displaying the horizontal ruler, setting the Zoom setting to 100%, and verifying that 12-point Times New Roman is the default font.

To display the ruler, check your Zoom setting, and select the correct default font:

1. Click **View** on the menu bar, and then point to the double-arrow at the bottom of the menu to display the hidden menu commands.
2. If "Ruler" does not have a check mark next to it, click **Ruler**. The horizontal ruler should now be displayed, as shown earlier in Figure 1-2.
3. Click the **Zoom** list arrow $\boxed{100\% \ \blacktriangledown}$ on the Standard toolbar. A list of screen magnification settings appears. In Figure 1-5, the currently selected setting is 100%.

Figure 1-5 | **Zoom settings**

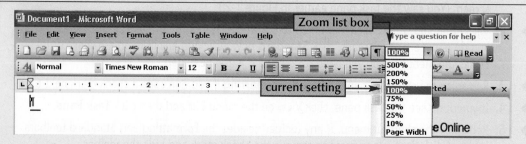

4. If 100% is not selected on your computer, click **100%** to select it. If you don't need to change your Zoom setting, press the **Esc** key to close the Zoom list. Next, you will check the default font setting.
5. Click **Format** on the menu bar, and then click **Font**. The Font dialog box opens. Click the **Font** tab if it is not already selected. See Figure 1-6.

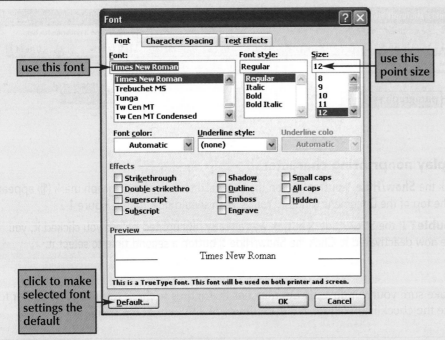

use this font

use this point size

click to make selected font settings the default

6. In the Font list box, click **Times New Roman**.

7. In the Size list box, click **12** if it is not already selected.

8. Click the **Default** button to make Times New Roman and 12 point the default settings. Word displays a message asking you to verify that you want to make 12-point Times New Roman the default font.

9. Click the **Yes** button.

Displaying Nonprinting Characters

Nonprinting characters are symbols that can appear on the screen but are not visible on the printed page. For example, one nonprinting character marks the end of a paragraph (¶) and another marks the space between words (•). It's helpful to display nonprinting characters so you can see whether you've typed an extra space, ended a paragraph, and so on.

Depending on how your computer is set up, nonprinting characters might have appeared automatically when you started Word. In Figure 1-7, you can see the paragraph symbol (¶) in the blank Document window. Also, the Show/Hide ¶ button is highlighted in the Standard toolbar. Both of these indicate that nonprinting characters are displayed. If they are not displayed on your screen, you need to perform the following step.

Figure 1-7   Nonprinting characters displayed

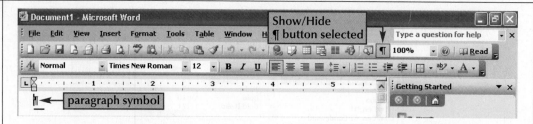

To display nonprinting characters:

1. Click the **Show/Hide ¶** button ¶ on the Standard toolbar. A paragraph mark (¶) appears at the top of the Document window. Your screen should now match Figure 1-7.

   Trouble? If the Show/Hide ¶ button was already highlighted before you clicked it, you have now deactivated it. Click the Show/Hide ¶ button a second time to select it.

To make sure your window always matches the figures in these tutorials, remember to complete the checklist in Figure 1-8 each time you sit down at the computer.

Figure 1-8   Word window checklist

Screen Element	Setting
Default font	Times New Roman
Default font size	12 point
Document view	Normal view
Formatting toolbar	Displayed below Standard toolbar
Horizontal ruler	Displayed
Nonprinting characters	Displayed
Other toolbars	Hidden
Standard toolbar	Displayed below menu bar
Task pane	Displayed
Word window	Maximized
Zoom box	Setting identical to setting shown in figures

Now that you have planned your letter, opened Word, identified screen elements, and adjusted settings, you are ready to begin typing a letter.

Beginning a Letter

You're ready to begin typing Megan's letter to Nicholas Brower at Web Time Productions. Figure 1-9 shows the completed letter printed on company letterhead. You will create this letter by completing the steps in this tutorial.

Art4U, Inc.
5725 Mesa Avenue
Tucson, AZ 85703
Art4U@Earth-World-Art.com

February 15, 2006

Nicholas Brower
Web Time Productions
2015 Dubuque Avenue
Chicago, IL 60025

Dear Nicholas:

Enclosed you will find the signed contract. As you can see, I am returning all three pages, with my signature on each.

Now that we have finalized the contract, I have a few questions: When will we receive a complete schedule for the project? Also, how many preliminary designs do you require? Finally, will you be available to discuss the project with our artists via a conference call some afternoon next week? Thursday or Friday afternoon would be ideal, if either of those options work for you.

Thanks again for choosing Art4U. We look forward to working with you.

Sincerely yours,

Megan L. Grahs

You'll begin by opening a new blank document (in case you accidentally typed something in the current page). Whenever you need to perform a common task such as opening a document, you can usually start with the task pane. In this case, you can use a special task pane that is devoted to creating new documents.

To open a new document:

▶ **1.** Click the **Create a new document** button 🗋 in the Open section at the bottom of the Getting Started task pane. Instead of the Getting Started task pane, you now see the New Document task pane. See Figure 1-10.

| Figure 1-10 | New Document task pane |

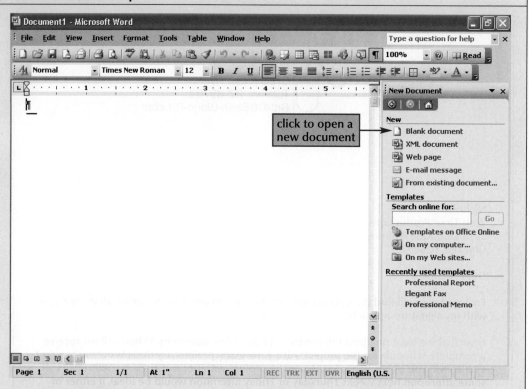

2. Click the **Blank document** button ☐ in the New Document task pane. A new document named Document2 opens and the task pane closes.

Now that you have opened a new document, you need to insert some blank lines in the document to ensure that you leave enough room for the company letterhead.

To insert blank lines in the document:

1. Press the **Enter** key eight times. Each time you press the Enter key, a nonprinting paragraph mark appears. In the status bar (at the bottom of the Document window), you should see the setting "At 2.5"," indicating that the insertion point is approximately 2.5 inches from the top of the page. Another setting in the status bar should read "Ln 9," indicating that the insertion point is in line 9 of the document. See Figure 1-11. (Your settings may be slightly different.)

Document window after inserting blank lines | **Figure 1-11**

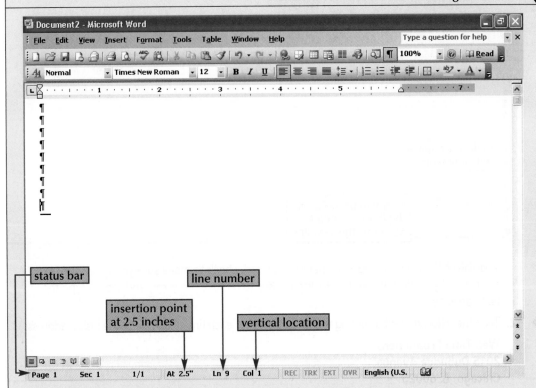

Trouble? If the paragraph mark doesn't appear each time you press the Enter key, the non-printing characters might be hidden. Click the Show/Hide ¶ button on the Standard toolbar.

Trouble? If you pressed the Enter key too many times, press the Backspace key to delete each extra line and paragraph mark. If you're on line 9 but the "At" number is not 2.5", don't worry. Different monitors produce slightly different measurements when you press the Enter key.

Pressing Enter is a simple, fast way to insert space in a document. When you are a more experienced Word user, you'll learn how to insert space without using the Enter key.

Entering Text

Normally, you begin typing a letter by entering the date. However, Megan tells you that she's not sure whether the contract will be ready to send today or tomorrow. So she asks you to skip the date for now and begin with the inside address. Making changes to documents is easy in Word, so you can easily add the date later.

In the following steps, you'll type the inside address (shown on Megan's note, in Figure 1-1). If you type a wrong character, press the Backspace key to delete the mistake and then retype the correct character.

To type the inside address:

1. Type **Nicholas Brower**, and then press the **Enter** key. As you type, a nonprinting character (•) appears between words to indicate a space. See Figure 1-12.

Figure 1-12 First line of inside address

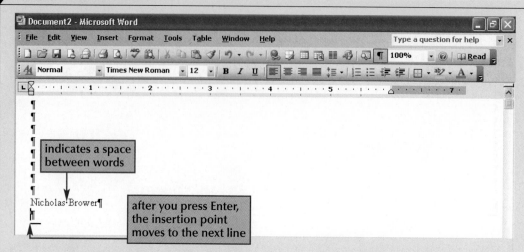

Trouble? If a wavy line appears beneath a word, check to make sure you typed the text correctly. If you did not, use the Backspace key to remove the error, and then retype the text correctly.

2. Type the following text, pressing the **Enter** key after each line to complete the inside address:

   Web Time Productions
   2015 Dubuque Avenue
   Chicago, IL 60025

   Be sure to press the Enter key after you type the ZIP code. Ignore the dotted underline below the street address. You'll learn the meaning of this underline later in this tutorial.

3. Press the **Enter** key again to add a blank line after the inside address. (You should see a total of two paragraph marks below the inside address.) Now you can type the salutation.

4. Type **Dear Nicholas:** and then press the **Enter** key twice to double space between the salutation and the body of the letter. See Figure 1-13.

Figure 1-13 Letter with inside address and salutation

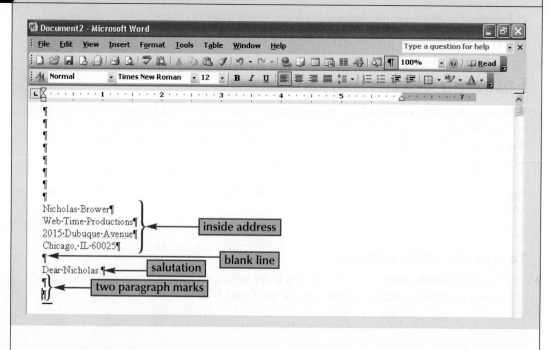

Before you continue with the rest of the letter, you should save what you have typed so far.

To save the document:

1. Click the **Save** button 🔲 on the Standard toolbar. The Save As dialog box opens. Note that Word suggests using the first few words of the letter ("Nicholas Brower") as the filename. You will replace the suggested filename with something more descriptive.

2. Type **Web Time Contract Letter** in the File name text box. Next, you need to tell Word where you want to save the document. In this case, you want to use the Tutorial subfolder in the Tutorial.01 folder.

3. Click the **Save in** list arrow, click the drive containing your Data Files, double-click the **Tutorial.01** folder, and then double-click the **Tutorial** folder. The word "Tutorial" is now displayed in the Save in box, indicating that the Tutorial folder is open and ready for you to save the document. See Figure 1-14.

   Trouble? The Tutorial.01 folder is included with the Data Files for this text. If you don't have the Word Data Files, you need to get them before you can proceed. Your instructor will either give you the Data Files or ask you to obtain them from a specified location (such as a network drive). In either case, be sure that you make a backup copy of your Data Files before you start using them, so that the original files will be available on your copied disk in case you need to start over because of an error or problem. If you have any questions about the Data Files, see your instructor or technical support person for assistance.

Save As dialog box | **Figure 1-14**

Tutorial subfolder in the Tutorial.01 folder of your Data Files

new filename

you might see the .doc file extension here

   Trouble? If Windows XP is configured for Web style, you can single-click, rather than double-click, folders to open them in the Save As dialog box.

   Trouble? If Word automatically adds the .doc extension to your filename, your computer is configured to show file extensions. Just continue with the tutorial.

4. Click the **Save** button in the Save As dialog box. The dialog box closes, and you return to the Document window. The new document name (Web Time Contract Letter) appears in the title bar.

Note that Word automatically appends the .doc extension to document filenames to identify them as Microsoft Word documents. However, unless your computer is set up to display file extensions, you won't see the .doc extension in any of the Word dialog boxes or in the title bar. These tutorials assume that file extensions are hidden.

You've made a good start on the letter, and you've saved your work so far. In the next session, you'll finish typing the letter and then you'll print it.

Review

Session 1.1 Quick Check

1. In your own words, list the steps in creating a document.
2. Define each of the following in your own words:
   a. nonprinting characters
   b. Zoom setting
   c. font settings
   d. default settings
3. Explain how to change the document view to Normal view.
4. Explain how to display or hide the Standard toolbar.
5. True or False: To display the Formatting toolbar, you need to use a button on the Standard toolbar.
6. True or False: Each time you press the Enter key, a nonprinting paragraph character (¶) appears in the status bar.
7. Word automatically appends the _____ extension to all document file names, even if you can't see the file extensions on the screen.

Session 1.2

Continuing Work on the Letter

Now that you have saved your document, you're ready to continue working on Megan's letter. As you type the body of the letter, you do not have to press the Enter key at the end of each line. Instead, when you type a word that extends into the right margin, both the insertion point and the word move automatically to the next line. This automatic line breaking is called **word wrap**. You'll see how word wrap works as you type the body of the letter.

To continue typing the letter:

1. If you took a break after the previous session, make sure that Word is running. Also, review the check list in Figure 1-8 and verify that your screen is set up to match the figures in this tutorial.

2. Make sure the insertion point is at Ln 16 (according to the setting in the status bar). If it's not, move it to line 16 by pressing the arrow keys.

3. Type the following sentence: **Enclosed you will find the signed contract.**

4. Press the **spacebar**.

5. Type the following sentence: **As you can see, I am returning all three pages, with my signature on each.** Notice how Word moves the last few words to a new line when the preceding line is full.

6. Press the **Enter** key to end the first paragraph, and then press the **Enter** key again to create a double space between the two paragraphs.

7. Type the following text:

Now that we have finalized the contract, I have a few questions: When will we receive a complete schedule for the project? Also, how many preliminary designs do you require?

When you are finished, your screen should look similar to Figure 1-15, although the line breaks on your screen might be slightly different.

Beginning of second main paragraph ◀ | **Figure 1-15**

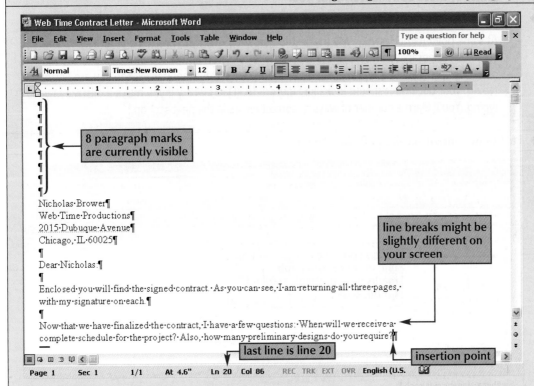

Trouble? If your screen does not match Figure 1-15 exactly, don't be concerned. The letter widths of the Times New Roman font can vary, which produces slightly different measurements on different monitors. As a result, the word or letter where the line wraps in your document might be different from the one shown in Figure 1-15.

Scrolling a Document

After you finish the last set of steps, the insertion point should be near the bottom of the Document window. Unless you are working on a large monitor, your screen probably looks like there's not enough room to type the rest of Megan's letter. However, as you continue to add text at the end of your document, the text that you typed earlier will **scroll** (or shift up) and disappear from the top of the Document window. You'll see how scrolling works as you enter the rest of the second paragraph.

To observe scrolling while you're entering text:

1. Make sure the insertion point is positioned to the right of the question mark after the word "require." The insertion point should be positioned at the end of line 20. See Figure 1-15.

2. Press the **spacebar**, and then type the following text:

   Finally, will you be available to discuss the project with our artists via a conference call some afternoon next week? Thursday or Friday afternoon would be ideal, if either of those options works for you.

3. Press the **Enter** key twice. The document scrolls up.

   At some point (either as you type the text in Step 2 or when you press the Enter key in Step 3), one or more paragraph marks at the top of the letter scroll off the top of the Document window. (Exactly when this happens depends on the size of your monitor.) When you are finished typing, your document should look like Figure 1-16. (Don't worry if you make a mistake in your typing. You'll learn a number of ways to correct errors in the next section.)

Figure 1-16	Part of document scrolled off the screen

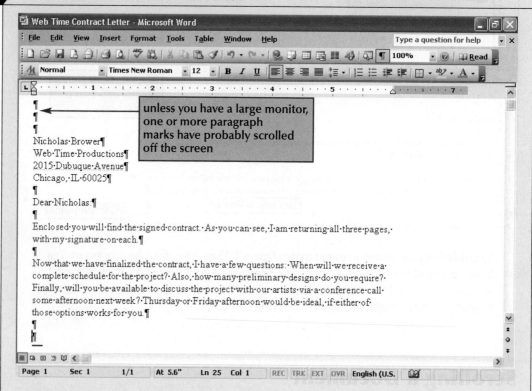

4. Type the following text:

   Thanks again for choosing Art4U. We look forward to working with you.

5. Press the **Enter** key twice.

6. Type **Sincerely yours,** (including the comma) to enter the complimentary closing.

7. Press the **Enter** key five times to allow space for a signature. Unless you have a very large monitor, part or even all of the inside address scrolls off the top of the Document window.

8. Type **Megan Grahs**, and then press the **Enter** key. A wavy red line appears below "Grahs." In Word, such lines indicate possible spelling errors. Because Megan's last name is not in the Word dictionary, Word suggests that it might be spelled incorrectly. You'll learn more about Word's error checking features in the next section. For now, you can ignore the wavy red line.

   You've completed the letter, so you should save your work.

9. Click the **Save** button 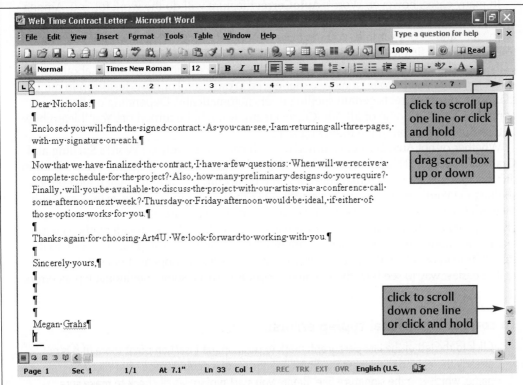 on the Standard toolbar. Word saves your letter with the same name and in the same location you specified earlier. Don't be concerned about any typing errors. You'll learn how to correct them in the next section.

In the last set of steps, you watched the text at the top of your document move off your screen. You can scroll this hidden text back into view so you can read the beginning of the letter. When you do, the text at the bottom of the screen will scroll out of view. To scroll the Document window, you can click the up or down arrows in the vertical scroll bar, click anywhere in the vertical scroll bar, or drag the scroll box. See Figure 1-17.

Note: If you are using a very large monitor, your insertion point may still be some distance from the bottom of the screen. In that case, you may not be able to perform the scrolling steps that follow. Read the steps to familiarize yourself with the process of scrolling. You'll have a chance to scroll longer documents later.

Parts of the scroll bar ◄ | **Figure 1-17**

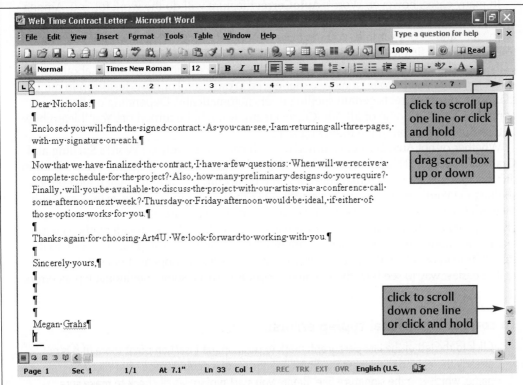

Web Time Contract Letter - Microsoft Word

File   Edit   View   Insert   Format   Tools   Table   Window   Help

Type a question for help

Normal   Times New Roman   12   B I U

Dear·Nicholas:¶
¶
Enclosed·you·will·find·the·signed·contract.··As·you·can·see,·I·am·returning·all·three·pages,·with·my·signature·on·each.¶
¶
Now·that·we·have·finalized·the·contract,·I·have·a·few·questions:··When·will·we·receive·a·complete·schedule·for·the·project?··Also,··how·many·preliminary·designs·do·you·require?··Finally,·will·you·be·available·to·discuss·the·project·with·our·artists·via·a·conference·call·some·afternoon·next·week?··Thursday·or·Friday·afternoon·would·be·ideal,··if·either·of·those·options·works·for·you.¶
¶
Thanks·again·for·choosing·Art4U.··We·look·forward·to·working·with·you.¶
¶
Sincerely·yours,¶
¶
¶
¶
Megan·Grahs¶

click to scroll up one line or click and hold

drag scroll box up or down

click to scroll down one line or click and hold

Page 1   Sec 1   1/1   At 7.1"   Ln 33   Col 1   REC   TRK   EXT   OVR   English (U.S.)

In the next set of steps, you will practice using the vertical scroll bar.

To scroll the document using the vertical scroll bar:

1. Position the mouse pointer on the up arrow at the top of the vertical scroll bar. Press and hold the mouse button to scroll the text. When the text stops scrolling, you have reached the top of the document and can see the beginning of the letter. Note that scrolling does not change the location of the insertion point in the document.

2. Click the down arrow on the vertical scroll bar several times. The document scrolls down one line at a time.

3. Click anywhere in the vertical scroll bar, below the scroll box. The document scrolls down one full screen.

4. Drag the scroll box up until the first line of the inside address ("Nicholas Brower") is positioned at the top of the Document window.

5. Scroll down to show the last line of the letter.

Correcting Errors

If you notice a typing error as soon as you make it, you can press the Backspace key, which deletes the characters and spaces to the left of the insertion point one at a time. Backspacing erases both printing and nonprinting characters. After you erase the error, you can type the correct character(s). You can also press the Delete key, which deletes characters to the right of the insertion point one at a time.

In many cases, however, Word's **AutoCorrect** feature will do the work for you. Among other things, AutoCorrect automatically corrects common typing errors, such as typing "adn" for "and." For example, you might have noticed AutoCorrect at work if you forgot to capitalize the first letter in a sentence as you typed the letter. AutoCorrect can automatically correct this error as you type the rest of the sentence. You'll learn more about using AutoCorrect as you become a more experienced Word user. For now, just keep in mind that AutoCorrect corrects certain spelling errors automatically. Depending on how your computer is set up, some or all AutoCorrect features might be turned off. You'll learn how to turn AutoCorrect on in the following steps.

Whether or not AutoCorrect is turned on, you can always rely on Word's **Spelling and Grammar checker**. This feature continually checks your document against Word's built-in dictionary and a set of grammar rules. If you type a word that doesn't match the correct spelling in Word's dictionary or if a word isn't in the dictionary at all (as is the case with Megan's last name, Grahs), a wavy red line appears beneath the word. A wavy red line also appears if you type duplicate words (such as "the the"). If you accidentally type an extra space between words or make a grammatical error (such as typing "He walk to the store." instead of "He walks to the store."), a wavy green line appears beneath the error.

The easiest way to see how these features work is to make some intentional typing errors.

To correct intentional typing errors:

1. Click to the left of the last paragraph mark to position the insertion point there (if it is not already there), and then press the **Enter** key to create a double space after Megan's last name, which is in the signature line. Before you start typing, you'll check to make sure AutoCorrect is turned on.

2. Click **Tools** on the menu bar, and then click **AutoCorrect Options**. The AutoCorrect: English (U.S.) dialog box opens.

3. Click the **Capitalize first letter of sentences** check box and the **Replace text as you type** check box to insert checks if these options are not already checked, and then click **OK**. (It is okay if other check boxes have checks.)

4. Carefully and slowly type the following sentence exactly as it is shown, including the spelling errors and the extra space between the last two words: **microsoft Word corects teh commen typing misTakes you make**. Press the **Enter** key when you are finished typing.

Notice that as you press the spacebar after the word "commen," a wavy red line appears beneath it, indicating that the word might be misspelled. Notice also that Word automatically capitalized the word "Microsoft" because it's the first word in the sentence. And, when you pressed the spacebar after the words "corects," "teh," and "misTakes," Word automatically corrected the spelling. After you pressed the Enter key, a wavy green line appeared under the last two words, alerting you to the extra space. See Figure 1-18.

Document with intentional typing errors ◄ **Figure 1-18**

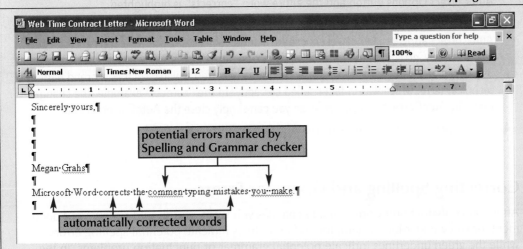

Trouble? If red and green wavy lines do not appear beneath mistakes, Word is probably not set to check spelling and grammar automatically as you type. Click Tools on the menu bar, and then click Options to open the Options dialog box. Click the Spelling & Grammar tab. If necessary, insert check marks in the "Check spelling as you type" and the "Check grammar as you type" check boxes, and then click OK.

Working with AutoCorrect

Whenever AutoCorrect makes a change, Word inserts an **AutoCorrect Options button** in the document. You can use this button to undo a change, or to prevent AutoCorrect from making the same change in the future. To see an AutoCorrect Options button, you position the mouse pointer over a word that has been changed by AutoCorrect.

To display an AutoCorrect Options button:

▶ **1.** Position the mouse pointer over the word "corrects." A small blue rectangle appears below the first few letters of the word, as shown in Figure 1-19.

Word changed by AutoCorrect ◄ **Figure 1-19**

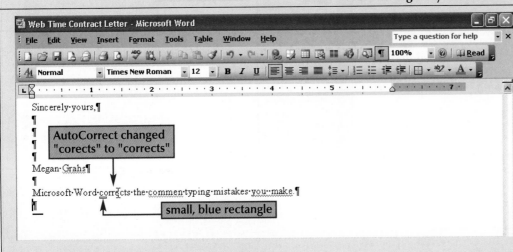

Trouble? If you see a blue button with a lightning bolt, move the pointer slightly to the right so that only the rectangle is visible, and then continue with the next step.

2. Point to the blue rectangle below "corrects." The blue rectangle is replaced by the AutoCorrect Options button and the entire word "corrects" is highlighted.

3. Click the **AutoCorrect Options** button [icon]. A menu with commands related to AutoCorrect appears. You could choose to change "corrects" back to "corects." You could also tell AutoCorrect to stop automatically correcting "corects." This second option might be useful if you found that AutoCorrect continually edited a word, such as a brand name or technical term, which was in fact spelled correctly. In the "corects" example, the change made by AutoCorrect is acceptable, so you can simply close the AutoCorrect menu.

4. Click anywhere in the document. The AutoCorrect menu closes.

Correcting Spelling and Grammar Errors

After you verify that AutoCorrect made changes you want, you should review your document for wavy underlines. Again, the red underlines indicate potential spelling errors, while the green underlines indicate potential grammar or punctuation problems. In the following steps, you will learn a quick way to correct such errors.

To correct spelling and grammar errors:

1. Position the I-Beam pointer over the word "commen," and then click the right mouse button. A shortcut menu appears with suggested spellings. See Figure 1-20.

| Figure 1-20 | Shortcut menu with suggested spellings |

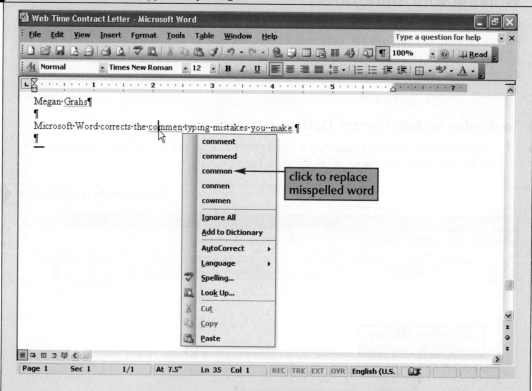

Trouble? If the shortcut menu doesn't appear, repeat Step 1, making sure you click the right mouse button, not the left one. If you see a different menu from the one shown in Figure 1-20, you didn't right-click exactly on the word "commen." Press the Esc key to close the menu, and then repeat Step 1.

2. Click **common** in the shortcut menu. The menu disappears, and the correct spelling appears in your document. Notice that the wavy red line disappears after you correct the error.

3. Click to the right of the letter "u" in the word "you." Press the **Delete** key to delete the extra space.

You can see how quick and easy it is to correct common typing errors with AutoCorrect and the Spelling and Grammar checker. Remember, however, to proofread each document you create thoroughly. AutoCorrect will not catch words that are spelled correctly, but used improperly (such as "your" for "you're").

Proofreading the Letter

Before you can proofread your letter, you need to delete the practice sentence.

To delete the practice sentence:

1. Confirm that the insertion point is to the right of "you" in the sentence you just typed, and then press the **Delete** key repeatedly to delete any spaces and characters to the right of the insertion point, including one paragraph mark.

2. Press the **Backspace** key repeatedly until the insertion point is to the left of the paragraph mark below Megan's name. There should only be one paragraph mark below her name. If you accidentally delete part of the letter, retype it, using Figure 1-17 as a guide.

Now you can proofread the letter for any typos. You can also get rid of the wavy red underline below Megan's last name.

To respond to possible spelling errors:

1. Be sure the signature line is visible. Because Word doesn't recognize "Grahs" as a word, it is marked as a potential error. You need to tell Word to ignore this name wherever it occurs in the letter.

2. Right-click **Grahs**. A shortcut menu opens.

3. Click **Ignore All**. The wavy red underline disappears from below "Grahs."

4. Scroll up to the beginning of the letter, and proofread it for typos. If a word has a wavy red or green underline, right-click it and choose an option in the shortcut menu. To correct other errors, click to the right or left of the error, use the Backspace or Delete key to remove it, and then type a correction.

5. Click the **Save** button on the Standard toolbar. Word saves your letter with the same name and to the same location you specified earlier.

Inserting a Date with AutoComplete

The beauty of using a word-processing program such as Microsoft Word is that you can easily make changes to text you have already typed. In this case, you need to insert the current date at the beginning of the letter. Megan tells you that she wants to send the contract to Web Time Productions on February 15, so you need to insert that date into the letter now.

Before you can enter the date, you need to move the insertion point to the right location. In a standard business letter, the date belongs approximately 2.5 inches from the top. (As you recall, this is where you started the inside address earlier.) You also need to insert some blank lines to allow enough space between the date and the inside address.

To move the insertion point and add some blank lines:

1. Scroll up to display the top of the document.

2. Click to the left of the "N" in "Nicholas Brower" in the inside address. The status bar indicates that the insertion point is on line 9, 2.5 inches from the top. (Your status bar might show slightly different measurements.)

3. Press the **Enter** key four times, and then press the ↑ key four times. Now the insertion point is positioned at line 9, with three blank lines between the inside address and the line where you will insert the date. See Figure 1-21.

Figure 1-21	Position of insertion point

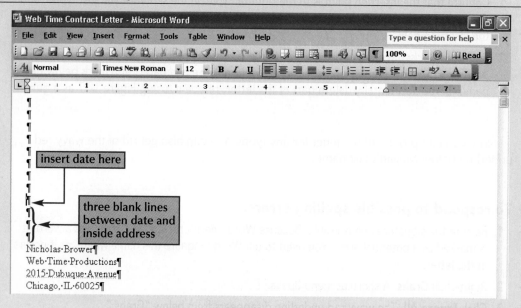

You're ready to insert the date. To do this you can take advantage of Word's **AutoComplete** feature, which automatically inserts dates and other regularly used items for you. In this case, you can type the first few characters of the month, and let Word insert the rest. (This only works for long month names like February.)

To insert the date:

▶ **1.** Type **Febr** (the first four letters of February). A rectangular box appears above the line, as shown in Figure 1-22. If you wanted to type something other than February, you could continue typing to complete the word. In this case, though, you want to accept the AutoComplete suggestion, which you will do in the next step.

AutoComplete suggestion ◀ | **Figure 1-22**

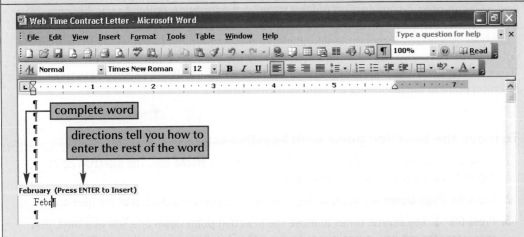

Trouble? If the AutoComplete suggestion doesn't appear, this feature may not be active. Click Tools on the menu bar, click AutoCorrect Options, click the AutoText tab, click the Show AutoComplete suggestions check box to insert a check, and then click OK. Delete the characters "Febr" and begin again with Step 1.

▶ **2.** Press the **Enter** key. The rest of the word "February" is inserted in the document.

▶ **3.** Press the **spacebar**, and then type **15, 2006**.

Trouble? If February happens to be the current month, you will see a second AutoComplete suggestion displaying the current date after you press the spacebar. To ignore that AutoComplete suggestion, continue typing the rest of the date as instructed in Step 3.

▶ **4.** Click one of the blank lines below the date. Depending on how your computer is set up, you may see a dotted underline below the date. (You will learn the meaning of this underline later in this tutorial.) You have finished entering the date. See Figure 1-23.

Date entered in the document ◀ | **Figure 1-23**

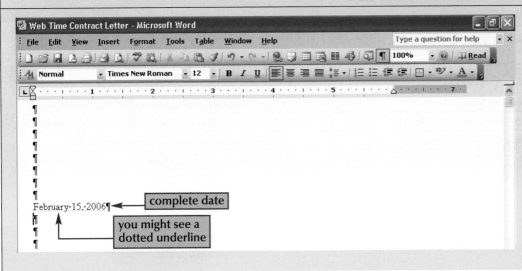

Moving the Insertion Point Around a Document

When you scroll a document, you change the part of the document that is displayed on the screen. But to change the location in the document where new text will appear when you type, you need to move the insertion point. In the last section, you moved the insertion point by scrolling up and then clicking where you wanted to insert new lines and text. You can also use the arrow keys on your keyboard, ←, →, ↑, and ↓, to move the insertion point one character at a time to the left or right, or one line at a time up or down. In addition, you can press a combination of keys to move the insertion point. As you become more experienced with Word, you'll decide which method you prefer.

Megan asks you to add her middle initial to the signature line. Before you can do that, you need to make sure you're comfortable moving the insertion point around the document. To see how quickly you can move through the document, you'll use keystrokes to move the insertion point to the beginning and end of the document.

To move the insertion point with keystrokes:

1. Press the **Ctrl** key and hold it down while you press the **Home** key. The insertion point moves to the beginning of the document.

2. Press the **Page Down** key to move the insertion point down to the top of the next screen.

3. Press the ↓ key several times to move the insertion point down one line at a time, and then press the → key several times to move the insertion point to the right one character at a time.

4. Press the **Ctrl+End** keys. The insertion point moves to the end of the document.

5. Use the arrow keys to position the insertion point to the right of the "n" in "Megan."

6. Press the **spacebar**, and then type the letter **L** followed by a period.

Figure 1-24 summarizes the keystrokes you can use to move the insertion point around the document. When you simply need to display a part of a document, you'll probably want to use the vertical scroll bar. But when you actually need to move the insertion point to a specific spot, it's helpful to use these special keystrokes.

Figure 1-24 | **Keystrokes for moving the insertion point**

Press	To move the insertion point
← or →	Left or right one character at a time
↑ or ↓	Up or down one line at a time
Ctrl+← or Ctrl+→	Left or right one word at a time
Ctrl+↑ or Ctrl+↓	Up or down one paragraph at a time
Home or End	To the beginning or to the end of the current line
Ctrl+Home or Ctrl+End	To the beginning or to the end of the document
Page Up or Page Down	To the previous screen or to the next screen
Alt+Ctrl+Page Up or Alt+Ctrl+Page Down	To the top or to the bottom of the document window

Using the Undo and Redo Commands

To undo (or reverse) the very last thing you did, click the **Undo button** on the Standard toolbar. If you want to restore your original change, the **Redo button** reverses the action of the Undo button (or redoes the undo). To undo more than your last action, you can click the Undo list arrow on the Standard toolbar. This list shows your most recent actions. Undo reverses the action only at its original location. You can't delete a word or phrase, move the surrounding text, and then undo the deletion at a different location.

Megan asks you to undo the addition of her middle initial, to see how the signature line looks without it.

To undo the addition of the letter "L":

▶ 1. Place the mouse pointer over the **Undo** button 🄐 on the Standard toolbar. The label "Undo Typing" appears in a ScreenTip, indicating that your most recent action involved typing. See Figure 1-25.

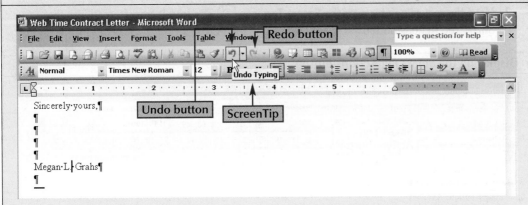

▶ 2. Click the **Undo** button 🄐. The letter "L," the period, and the space you typed earlier are deleted.

Trouble? If something else changes, you probably made another edit or change to the document between the addition of Megan's middle initial and the undo. Click the Undo button on the Standard toolbar until the letter "L," the period, and the space following it are deleted. If a list of possible changes appears under the Undo button, you clicked the list arrow next to the Undo button rather than the Undo button itself. Press the Esc key to close the list.

As she reviews the signature line, Megan decides that she does want to include her middle initial after all. Instead of retyping it, you'll redo the undo.

▶ 3. Place the mouse pointer over the **Redo** button 🄒 on the Standard toolbar and observe the "Redo Typing" ScreenTip.

▶ 4. Click the **Redo** button 🄒. Megan's middle initial (along with the period and an additional space) are reinserted into the signature line.

▶ 5. Click the **Save** button 🄓 on the Standard toolbar to save your changes to the document.

Your letter is nearly finished. All that remains is to remove the straight dotted underlines and then print the letter.

Removing Smart Tags

A straight dotted underline below a date or address indicates that Word has inserted a Smart Tag in the document. A **Smart Tag** is a feature that allows you to perform actions (such as sending e-mail or scheduling a meeting) that would normally require a completely different program. When you point to Smart Tag text, a Smart Tag Actions button appears, which you can click to open a menu with commands related to that item. (For example, you might click a Smart Tag on an address to add that address to your e-mail address book.) You don't really need Smart Tags in this document, though, so you will delete them. (Your computer may not be set up to show Smart Tags at all, or it might show them on dates but not addresses. If you do not see any Smart Tags in your document, simply read the following steps.)

To remove the Smart Tags from the document:

1. Scroll up so you can see the inside address. If you see a straight dotted underline below the street address (2015 Dubuque Avenue), position the mouse pointer over that line. A Smart Tag icon ⓘ appears over the street address.

2. Move the mouse pointer over the **Smart Tag** icon ⓘ. The icon is transformed into the Smart Tag Actions button ⓘ ▾, as shown in Figure 1-26.

Figure 1-26 ▶ Displaying the Smart Tag Actions button

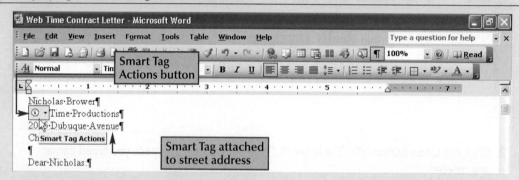

3. Click the **Smart Tag Actions** button ⓘ ▾. A menu of commands related to addresses appears.

4. Click **Remove this Smart Tag**. The Smart Tag menu closes. The address is no longer underlined, indicating that the Smart Tag has been removed. Depending on how your computer is set up, the Smart Tag on the street address may have been the only one in your document. But it's possible you see others.

5. Remove any other Smart Tags in the document, including any on the date or elsewhere in the inside address.

6. Click the **Save** button 🖫 on the Standard toolbar.

Previewing and Printing a Document

Do you think the letter is ready to print? You could find out by clicking the Print button on the Standard toolbar and then reviewing the printed page. With that approach, however, you risk wasting paper and printer time. For example, if you failed to insert enough space for the company letterhead, you would have to add more space, and then print the letter all over again. To avoid wasting paper and time, you should first display the document in the **Print Preview window**. By default, the Print Preview window shows you the full page; there's no need to scroll through the document.

To preview the document:

1. Proof the document one last time and correct any new errors. Always remember to proof your document immediately before printing it.

2. Replace "Megan L. Grahs" with your first and last name, at the end of the letter. This will ensure that you will be able to identify your copy of the letter.

3. Click the **Print Preview** button 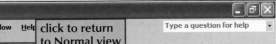 on the Standard toolbar. The Print Preview window opens and displays a full-page version of your letter, as shown in Figure 1-27. This shows how the letter will fit on the printed page. The Print Preview toolbar includes a number of buttons that are useful for making changes that affect the way the printed page will look.

Full page displayed in Print Preview window ◄ | **Figure 1-27**

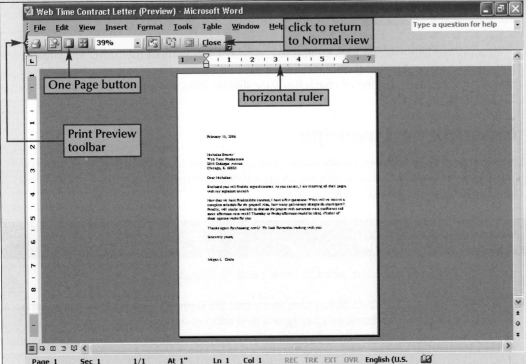

Trouble? If your letter in the Print Preview window is smaller and off to the left rather than centered in the window, click the One Page button on the Print Preview toolbar.

Trouble? If you don't see a ruler above the document, your ruler is not displayed. To show the ruler in the Print Preview window, click View on the menu bar and then click Ruler.

4. Click the **Close** button on the Print Preview toolbar to return to Normal view.

5. Click the **Save** button on the Standard toolbar.

Note that it is especially important to preview documents if your computer is connected to a network so that you don't keep a shared printer tied up with unnecessary printing. In this case, the text looks well spaced and the letterhead will fit at the top of the page. You're ready to print the letter.

When printing a document, you have two choices. You can use the Print command on the File menu, which opens the Print dialog box in which you can adjust some printer settings. Or, if you prefer, you can use the Print button on the Standard toolbar, which prints the document using default settings, without opening a dialog box. In these tutorials, the first time you print from a shared computer, you should check the settings in the Print dialog box and make sure the number of copies is set to 1. After that, you can use the Print button.

To print the letter document:

1. Make sure your printer is turned on and contains paper.

2. Click **File** on the menu bar, and then click **Print**. The Print dialog box opens.

3. Make sure the Printer section of the dialog box shows the correct printer. If you're not sure what the correct printer is, check with your instructor or technical support person. Also, make sure the number of copies is set to 1.

   Trouble? If the Print dialog box shows the wrong printer, click the Name list arrow, and then select the correct printer from the list of available printers.

4. Click the **OK** button. Assuming your computer is attached to a printer, the letter prints.

Your printed letter should look similar to Figure 1-9, but without the Art4U letterhead. The word wraps, or line breaks, might not appear in the same places on your letter because the size and spacing of characters vary slightly from one printer to the next.

Creating an Envelope

After you print the letter, Megan asks you to print an envelope in which to mail the contracts. Creating an envelope is a simple process because Word automatically uses the inside address from the letter as the address on the envelope.

Reference Window	**Printing an Envelope**

- Click Tools on the menu bar, point to Letters and Mailings, and then click Envelopes and Labels.
- In the Envelopes and Labels dialog box, verify that the Delivery address box contains the correct address. If necessary, you can type a new address or edit the existing one.
- If necessary, type a return address. If you are using preprinted stationery that already includes a return address, click the Omit check box to insert a check.
- To print the envelope immediately, insert an envelope in your printer, and then click Print.
- To store the envelope along with the rest of the document, click Add to Document.
- To print the envelope after you have added it to the document, open the Print dialog box and print the page containing the envelope.

Megan tells you that your printer is not currently stocked with envelopes. She asks you to create the envelope and add it to the document. Then she will print the envelope later, when she is ready to mail the contracts to Web Time Productions.

To create an envelope:

1. Click **Tools** on the menu bar, point to **Letters and Mailings**, and then click **Envelopes and Labels**. The Envelopes and Labels dialog box opens, as shown in Figure 1-28. By default, Word uses the inside address from the letter as the delivery address. Depending on how your computer is set up, you might see an address in the Return address box. Because Megan will be using Art4U's printed envelopes, you don't need to include a return address on this envelope.

Envelopes and Labels dialog box | **Figure 1-28**

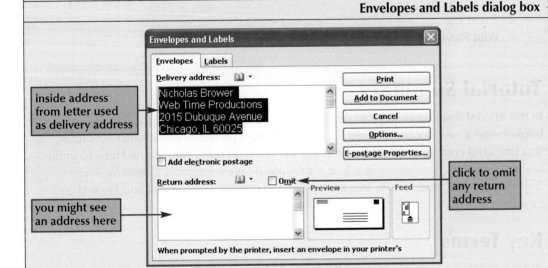

inside address from letter used as delivery address

you might see an address here

click to omit any return address

2. Click the **Omit** check box to insert a check, if necessary.

3. Click the **Add to Document** button. The dialog box closes, and you return to the Document window. The envelope is inserted at the top of the document, above a double line with the words "Section Break (Next Page)." The double line indicates that the envelope and the letter are two separate parts of the document. The envelope will print in the standard business envelope format. The letter will still print on standard 8.5 x 11-inch paper. (You'll have a chance to print an envelope in the exercises at the end of this tutorial.)

4. Click the **Save** button on the Standard toolbar.

You are finished with the letter and the envelope, so you can close the document.

To close the document:

1. Click the **Close Window** button ☒ on the menu bar. The Web Time Contract Letter document closes.

   Trouble? If you see a dialog box with the message "Do you want to save the changes to 'Web Time Contract Letter?'," click the Yes button.

2. Close any other open documents without saving them.

Congratulations on creating your first letter in Microsoft Word. You'll be able to use the skills you learned in this tutorial to create a variety of professional documents.

Review

Session 1.2 Quick Check

1. True or False: The term "word wrap" refers to automatic line breaking.
2. Explain how to enter the name of a month using AutoComplete.
3. What button can you use to reverse your most recent edit immediately?
4. List the steps required to print an envelope.
5. In your own words, define each of the following:
   a. scrolling
   b. AutoComplete
   c. Redo button
   d. Smart Tag
   e. Print Preview

Review

Tutorial Summary

In this tutorial you learned how to set up your Word window to match the figures in this book, create a new document from scratch, and type a professional-looking cover letter. You practiced correcting errors, and moving the insertion point. You learned how to undo and redo changes, how to insert a date with AutoComplete and how to remove Smart Tags from a document. Finally, you previewed and printed a document, and created an envelope.

Key Terms

AutoComplete
AutoCorrect
AutoCorrect Options button
default settings
nonprinting characters

Print Preview window
Redo button
scroll
Smart Tag

Spelling and Grammar
   checker
Undo button
word wrap

Practice

Practice the skills you learned in the tutorial using the same case scenario.

Review Assignments

There are no Data Files needed for the Review Assignments.

Megan received an e-mail from Nicholas Brower at Web Time Productions, confirming their plans for a conference call. Megan has e-mailed the graphic artists at Art4U, informing them about the call. To make sure everyone remembers, she would like you to post a memo on the bulletin board in the break room. She also asks you to create an envelope so the memo can be mailed to freelance artists who work outside the Art4U offices. Create the memo shown in Figure 1-29 by completing the following steps. The steps show quotation marks around text you type; do not include the quotation marks in your letter.

Figure 1-29

Art4U, Inc.
5725 Mesa Avenue
Tucson, AZ 85703
Art4U@Earth-World-Art.com

TO: Art4U Staff Artists

FROM: Megan L. Grahs

DATE: February 20, 2006

SUBJECT: Conference Call

Please plan to join us for a conference call at 3 p.m. on Friday, March 1. Nicholas Brower, president of Web Time Productions, will be taking part, as will five of his company's most experienced Web page designers. This will be your chance to ask the designers some important questions.

You will be able to join the call from your desk by dialing an 800 number and a special access code. You'll receive both of these numbers via e-mail the day of the call.

1. Make sure a new blank document is open.
2. Compare your screen to the checklist in Figure 1-8 and change any settings if necessary. In particular, make sure that nonprinting characters are displayed and the Getting Started task pane is open.
3. Press the Enter key eight times to insert enough space for the company letterhead.
4. Type "TO:" in capital letters, and then press the spacebar.
5. Turn off capitalization if you turned it on in Step 4, and then type "Art4U Staff Artists". Throughout the rest of this exercise, turn capitalization on and off as needed.
6. Press the Enter key twice, type "FROM:", press the spacebar, turn off capitalization, and then type your name.

7. Press the Enter key twice, type "DATE:", and then press the spacebar.
8. Enter the date February 20, 2006 using AutoComplete when possible to reduce the amount of typing required.
9. Press the Enter key twice, type "SUBJECT:", press the spacebar, type "Conference Call", and then press the Enter key three times.
10. Continue typing the rest of the memo as shown in Figure 1-29. (You will have a chance to correct any typing errors later.) Ignore any AutoCorrect suggestions that are not relevant to the text you are typing.
11. Save your work as **Call Memo** in the Tutorial.01\Review folder provided with your Data Files.
12. Practice using the keyboard to move the insertion point around the document. Use the arrow keys so the insertion point is positioned immediately to the left of the "A" in "Art4U" in the "TO" line.
13. Type "All" and a space, so the TO line reads "TO: All Art4U Staff Artists".
14. Undo the change and then redo it.
15. Scroll to the beginning of the document and proofread your work.
16. Correct any misspelled words marked by wavy red lines. If the correct spelling of a word does not appear in the shortcut menu, close the list, and then make the correction yourself. Remove any red wavy lines below words that are actually spelled correctly. Then correct any grammatical or other errors indicated by wavy green lines. Delete any extra words or spaces.
17. Remove any Smart Tags.
18. Save your most recent changes.
19. Preview and print the memo.
20. Add an envelope to the document. Use your own address as the delivery address. Do not include a return address.
21. Save your changes and close the Call Memo document. If any other documents are open, close them without saving any changes.

Apply

Apply the skills you learned to create a letter about a health care lecture.

Case Problem 1

There are no Data Files needed for this Case Problem.

Wingra Family Practice Clinic You are a nurse at Wingra Family Practice Clinic. You have organized a lunchtime lecture series for the clinic staff in which regional medical professionals will discuss topics related to pediatric healthcare. You have hired your first speaker and need to write a letter confirming your agreement and asking a few questions. Create the letter by completing the following steps. The steps show quotation marks around text you type; do not include the quotation marks.

1. Open a new blank document if one is not already open, and then check your screen to make sure your settings match those shown earlier in Figure 1-8.
2. Locate the Undo and Redo buttons on the Standard toolbar and be prepared to use them as necessary as you work on the letter.
3. Type your name, press Enter, and then type the following address:
   Wingra Family Practice Clinic
   2278 Norwood Place
   Middleton, WI 52247
4. Press the Enter key four times, and then type "May 8, 2007" as the date.

5. Press the Enter key four times, and using the proper business letter format, type this inside address:
Dr. Susanna Trevay
James Madison Medical Center
56 Ingersoll Drive
Madison, WI 53788

6. Double space after the inside address (that is, press the Enter key twice), type the salutation "Dear Dr. Trevay:", and then insert a blank line.

7. Type the paragraph as follows: "Thank you so much for agreeing to lecture about early childhood vaccinations on Friday, May 25. Before I can publicize your talk, I need some information. Please call by Tuesday with your answers to the following questions:"

8. Save your work as **Lecture Series Letter** in the Tutorial.01\Cases folder provided with your Data Files.

9. Insert one blank line, and then type these questions on separate lines with one blank line between each:
Which vaccines will you cover in detail?
Will you discuss common immune responses to vaccine antigens?
Will you provide hand-outs with suggested vaccination schedules?

10. Move the insertion point to the beginning of the third question (which begins "Will you provide..."). Insert a new line, and add the following as the new third question in the list: "Would you be willing to take questions from the audience?"

11. Correct any spelling or grammar errors indicated by red or green wavy lines. Because "Wingra" is spelled correctly, use the shortcut menu to remove the wavy red line under the word "Wingra" and prevent Word from marking the word as a misspelling. Repeat to ignore "Trevay," "Ingersoll," and any other words that are spelled correctly but that are marked as misspellings.

12. Insert a blank line after the last question, and type the complimentary closing "Sincerely," (including the comma).

13. Press the Enter key four times to leave room for the signature, and type your full name. Then press the Enter key and type "Wingra Family Practice Clinic". Notice that "Wingra" is not marked as a spelling error this time.

14. Scroll up to the beginning of the document, and then remove any Smart Tags in the letter.

15. Save your changes to the letter, and then preview it using the Print Preview button.

16. Print the letter, and then close the document.

Case Problem 2

Apply

Apply the skills you learned to create a letter informing a client about a new investment program.

There are no Data Files needed for this Case Problem.

Pear Tree Investment Services As a financial planner at Pear Tree Investment Services, you are responsible for keeping your clients informed about new investment options. You have just learned about a program called HigherEdVest, which encourages parents to save for their children's college education. Write a letter to a client introducing the program and asking him to call for more information. Create the letter by completing the following steps. The steps show quotation marks around text you type; do not include the quotation marks in your letter.

1. Open a new, blank document if one is not already open, and then check your screen to make sure your settings match those shown earlier in Figure 1-8.

2. Locate the Undo and Redo buttons on the Standard toolbar and be prepared to use them as necessary as you work on the letter.

Explore

3. Press the Enter key until the insertion point is positioned about two inches from the top of the page. (Remember that you can see the exact position of the insertion point, in inches, in the status bar.)

4. Type the name of the current month. (If an AutoComplete suggestion appears, accept it to complete the name of the month.) Press the spacebar. After you press the spacebar, an AutoComplete suggestion appears with the current date. Accept the suggestion.

5. Press the Enter key four times after the date, and, using the proper business letter format, type the inside address: "Joseph Robbins, 5788 Rugby Road, Hillsborough, CO 77332".

6. Double space after the inside address (that is, press the Enter key twice), type the salutation "Dear Joseph:", and then double space again.

7. Write one paragraph introducing the HigherEdVest program, explaining that you think the client might be interested, and asking him to call your office at 555-5555 for more details.

8. Insert a blank line and type the complimentary closing "Sincerely,".

9. Press the Enter key four times to leave room for the signature, and then type your name and title.

10. Save the letter as **HigherEdVest Letter** in the Tutorial.01\Cases folder provided with your Data Files.

11. Remove any Smart Tags. Reread your letter carefully, and correct any errors. Use the arrow keys to move the insertion point, as necessary.

12. Save any new changes, and then preview and print the letter.

Explore

13. Create an envelope for the letter. Click the Omit check box if necessary to deselect it, and then, for the return address, type your own address. Add the envelope to the document. If you are asked if you want to save the return address as the new default return address, click No. If your computer is connected to a printer that is stocked with envelopes, click File on the menu bar, click Print, click the Pages option button, type 1 in the Pages text box, and then click OK.

14. Save your work, and then close the document.

Create

Use your skills to create the congratulatory letter shown in Figure 1-30.

Case Problem 3

There are no Data Files needed for this Case Problem.

Boundary Waters Technical College Liza Morgan, professor of e-commerce at Boundary Waters Technical College in northern Minnesota, was recently honored by the Northern Business Council for her series of free public seminars on developing Web sites for nonprofit agencies. She also was recently named Teacher of the Year by a national organization called Women in Technology. As one of her former students, you decide to write a letter congratulating her on these honors. To create the letter, complete the following steps:

1. Open a new blank document if one is not already open, and then check your screen to make sure your settings match those in Figure 1-8.

2. Create the letter shown in Figure 1-30. Replace "Your Name" with your first and last name.

Figure 1-30

August 13, 2006

Professor Liza Morgan
Department of Business Administration
Boundary Waters Technical College
1010 Sturgeon Drive
Blue Pines, Minnesota 50601

Dear Professor Morgan:

I was happy to hear about your recent honors. You certainly deserve to be recognized
for your Web site development seminars. As a grateful former student, I heartily endorse
your Teacher of the Year award. Congratulations!

Sincerely,

Your Name

3. Save the document as **Congratulations Letter** in the Tutorial.01\Cases folder provided
   with your Data Files.
4. Correct any typing errors, remove any Smart Tags, and then preview and print
   the letter.
5. Create an envelope, using your address as the return address, and then add the
   envelope to the document. (*Hint*: Click the Omit check box to deselect it if it is
   selected before attempting to type the return address.) Do not save the return address
   as the default.
6. Save the document and close it.

Challenge

Go beyond what you've learned to write a memo for a small e-business company.

Case Problem 4

There are no Data Files needed for this Case Problem.

Head for the Hills You are the office manager for Head for the Hills, a small company that sells hiking equipment over the Internet. The company has just moved to a new building, which requires a special security key card after hours. Some employees have had trouble getting the key cards to work properly. You decide to hold a meeting to explain the security policies for the new building and to demonstrate the key cards. But first you need to post a memo announcing the meeting. The recently ordered letterhead (with the company's new address) has not yet arrived, so you will use a Word template to create the memo. Word provides templates—that is, models with predefined formatting—to help you create complete documents (including a professional-looking letterhead) quickly. To create the memo, do the following steps. The steps show quotation marks around text you type; do not include the quotation marks in your letter.

1. Open a new blank document if one is not already open, and then check your screen to make sure your settings match those in Figure 1-8.
2. Open the New Document task pane. You see a number of options related to creating new documents.

Explore
3. In the "Templates" section, click On my computer. The Templates dialog box opens.

Explore
4. Click the Memos tab, click Professional Memo, and then click the OK button. A memo template opens containing generic, placeholder text that you can replace with your own information.

5. Display the template in Normal view, if it is not already. Click immediately to the right of the last "e" in the text "Company Name Here" (at the top of the document), press the Backspace key repeatedly to delete the text, and type "Head for the Hills".
6. Click the text "Click here and type name" in the To: line, and type "All Employees". Click the text after "From:", and replace it with your name.
7. Click the text after "CC:", press Delete to delete the placeholder text, and then delete the entire "CC:" line. Note that Word inserts the current date automatically after the heading "Date."
8. Click the text after "Re:", and then type "Using key cards".
9. Delete the placeholder text that begins "How to Use..." but do not delete the paragraph mark (¶) at the end of the line, and then type "Meeting Tomorrow".

Explore
10. Delete the text in the body of the letter but do not delete the paragraph mark (¶) at the end of the paragraph, and then type a paragraph announcing the meeting, which is scheduled for tomorrow at 2 p.m. in the Central Conference Room.
11. Save the letter as **Key Card Meeting Memo** in the Tutorial.01\Cases folder provided with your Data Files.

Explore
12. To make it easier to review your work, you can change the Zoom setting in Normal view. Click the Zoom box in the Standard toolbar, type 110%, and then press the Enter key. Continue to type values in the Zoom text box until the document fills the window.
13. Review the memo. Correct any typos and delete any Smart Tags. Save the memo again, preview it, and then print it.
14. Close the document.

Research

Go to the Web to find information you can use to create documents.

Internet Assignments

The purpose of the Internet Assignments is to challenge you to find information on the Internet that you can use to work effectively with this software. The actual assignments are updated and maintained on the Course Technology Web site. Log on to the Internet and use your Web browser to go to the Student Online Companion for New Perspectives Office 2003 at **www.course.com/np/office2003**. Click the Internet Assignments link, and then navigate to the assignments for this tutorial.

Assess

SAM Assessment and Training

If you have a SAM user profile, you may have access to hands-on instruction, practice, and assessment of the skills covered in this tutorial. Log in to your SAM account and go to your assignments page to see what your instructor has assigned.

Reinforce

Lab Assignments

The New Perspectives Labs are designed to help you master some of the key concepts and skills presented in this text. The steps for completing this Lab are located on the Course Technology Web site. Log on to the Internet and use your Web browser to go to the Student Online Companion for New Perspectives Office 2003 at **www.course.com/np/office2003**. Click the Lab Assignments link, and then navigate to the assignments for this tutorial.

Review

Quick Check Answers

Session 1.1

1. (1) Plan the content, purpose, organization, and look of your document. (2) Create and then edit the document. (3) Format the document to make it visually appealing. (4) Preview and then print the document.
2. a. symbols you can display on-screen but that don't print
   b. controls the document's on-screen magnification
   c. settings that control the size and shape of the characters that appear when you start typing
   d. standard settings
3. Click the Normal View button.
4. Right-click a toolbar or the menu bar, and then click Standard.
5. False
6. False
7. .doc

Session 1.2

1. True
2. Type the first few characters of the month. When an AutoComplete suggestion appears, press the Enter key.
3. Undo
4. Click Tools on the menu bar, point to Letters and Mailings, and then click Envelopes and Labels. In the Envelopes and Labels dialog box, verify that the Delivery address contains the correct address. If necessary, you can type a new address or edit the existing one. If necessary, type a return address. If you are using preprinted stationery that already includes a return address, click the Omit check box to insert a check. To print the envelope immediately, insert an envelope in your printer, and then click Print. To store the envelope along with the rest of the document, click Add to Document. To print the envelope after you have added it to the document, open the Print dialog box, and then print the page containing the envelope.
5. a. the means by which text at the bottom of the document shifts out of view when you display the top of the document, and text at the top shifts out of view when you display the bottom of a document
   b. a feature that automatically enters dates and other regularly used items
   c. a button that redoes changes
   d. a window in which you can see how the document will look when printed
   e. a feature that that allows you to perform actions (such as sending e-mail or scheduling a meeting) that would normally require a completely different program.

Objectives

Session 2.1
- Check spelling and grammar
- Select and delete text
- Move text within the document
- Find and replace text

Session 2.2
- Change margins, line spacing, alignment, and paragraph indents
- Copy formatting with the Format Painter
- Change fonts and adjust font sizes
- Emphasize points with bullets, numbering, bold, underlining, and italic
- Preview formatted text
- Add a comment to a document
- Use the Research task pane

Editing and Formatting a Document

Preparing an FAQ Document

Case

Long Meadow Gardens

Marilee Brigham is the owner of Long Meadow Gardens, a landscape and gardening supply company. The firm's large nursery provides shrubs and trees to professional landscape contractors throughout the Minneapolis/St. Paul area. At the same time, Long Meadow Gardens' retail store caters to home gardeners, who often call the store with questions about planting and caring for their purchases.

Marilee has noticed that retail customers tend to ask the same set of questions. To save time, she would like to create a series of handouts designed to answer these common questions. (Such a document is sometimes known as an FAQ—which is short for "frequently asked questions.") The company's chief horticulturist, Peter Chi, has just finished creating an FAQ containing information on planting trees. Now that Marilee has commented on and corrected the draft, Peter asks you to make the necessary changes and print the document.

In this tutorial, you will edit the FAQ document according to Marilee's comments. You will open a draft of the document, resave it, and edit it. You will check the document's grammar and spelling, and then move text using two different methods. You will also find and replace one version of the company name with another.

Next, you will change the overall look of the document by changing margins and line spacing, indenting and justifying paragraphs, and copying formatting from one paragraph to another. You'll create a bulleted list to emphasize the species of water-tolerant trees and a numbered list for the steps involved in removing the burlap from around the base of a tree. Then you'll make the title more prominent by centering it, changing its font, and enlarging it. You'll add bold to the questions to set them off from the rest of the text and underline an added note about how to get further

Student Data Files

▼ **Tutorial.02**

information. Finally, before you print the FAQ document, you will add a comment, and look up information using the Research task pane.

Session 2.1

Reviewing the Document

Marilee's editing marks and notes on the first draft are shown in Figure 2-1. You'll begin by opening the first draft of the document, which has the filename FAQ.

Figure 2-1 ▷ **Draft of FAQ with Marilee's edits (page 1)**

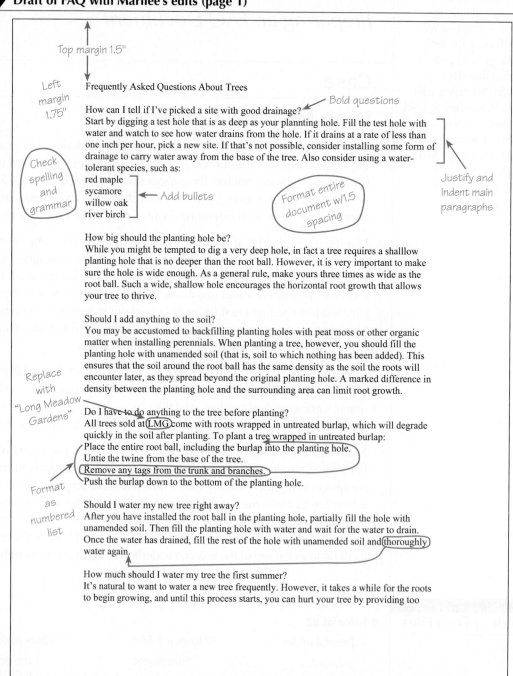

Top margin 1.5"

Left margin 1.75"

Frequently Asked Questions About Trees

Bold questions

How can I tell if I've picked a site with good drainage?
Start by digging a test hole that is as deep as your plannting hole. Fill the test hole with water and watch to see how water drains from the hole. If it drains at a rate of less than one inch per hour, pick a new site. If that's not possible, consider installing some form of drainage to carry water away from the base of the tree. Also consider using a water-tolerant species, such as:

Check spelling and grammar

red maple
sycamore
willow oak
river birch

Add bullets

Format entire document w/1.5 spacing

Justify and Indent main paragraphs

How big should the planting hole be?
While you might be tempted to dig a very deep hole, in fact a tree requires a shalllow planting hole that is no deeper than the root ball. However, it is very important to make sure the hole is wide enough. As a general rule, make yours three times as wide as the root ball. Such a wide, shallow hole encourages the horizontal root growth that allows your tree to thrive.

Should I add anything to the soil?
You may be accustomed to backfilling planting holes with peat moss or other organic matter when installing perennials. When planting a tree, however, you should fill the planting hole with unamended soil (that is, soil to which nothing has been added). This ensures that the soil around the root ball has the same density as the soil the roots will encounter later, as they spread beyond the original planting hole. A marked difference in density between the planting hole and the surrounding area can limit root growth.

Replace with "Long Meadow Gardens"

Do I have to do anything to the tree before planting?
All trees sold at LMG come with roots wrapped in untreated burlap, which will degrade quickly in the soil after planting. To plant a tree wrapped in untreated burlap:
Place the entire root ball, including the burlap into the planting hole.
Untie the twine from the base of the tree.
Remove any tags from the trunk and branches.
Push the burlap down to the bottom of the planting hole.

Format as numbered list

Should I water my new tree right away?
After you have installed the root ball in the planting hole, partially fill the hole with unamended soil. Then fill the planting hole with water and wait for the water to drain. Once the water has drained, fill the rest of the hole with unamended soil and thoroughly water again.

How much should I water my tree the first summer?
It's natural to want to water a new tree frequently. However, it takes a while for the roots to begin growing, and until this process starts, you can hurt your tree by providing too

Figure 2-1 (cont.)

Draft of FAQ with Marilee's edits (page 2)

much moisture. To avoid ~~any~~ root damage ~~or problems,~~ water once a week. In times of heavy rainfall (more than 2 inches a week) don't water your tree at all.

Is mulch necessary?
You should definitely add some mulch, which helps prevent drying and discourages weeds. But take care not to add too much mulch. Too or three inches are all you need. You can choose from organic mulches (shredded bark, cocoa shells, composts) or ornamental gravel. To prevent damage from disease and pests, push the mulch back from the tree's base, forming a circle about 2 inches out from the trunk. Never use black plastic beneath mulch because it prevents the roots from getting the air and water they need. If you want an extra barrier to prevent weeds, use porous landscape cloth.

Any of our sales associates here at LMG would be happy to answer your questions about planting and caring for your tree. Call us at (501) 555-2325, from 10 A.M. to 8 P.M., seven days a week. For details on our upcoming series of horticulture classes, call 9 A.M. to 5 P.M, Monday through Friday.

Note:

insert Marilee's name

To open the document:

1. Start Word, and then verify that the Getting Started task pane is displayed.

2. In the Open section of the Getting Started task pane, click the **Open** button 🖼. You may have to point to the down arrow at the bottom of the task pane to scroll down in order to display the Open button. (Depending on how your computer is set up, the label next to this button might read "More" or "Open.") The Open dialog box opens, as shown in Figure 2-2. (Note that you could also use the Open button on the Standard toolbar to open this dialog box.)

Figure 2-2 ▶ Open dialog box

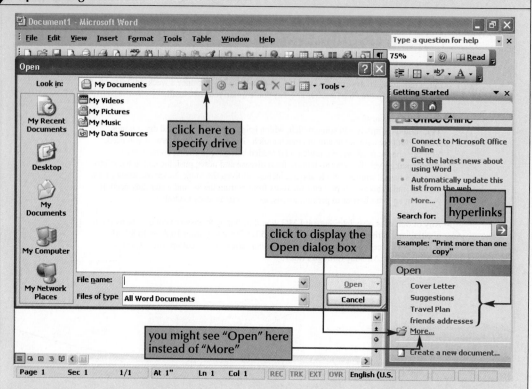

3. Click the **Look in** list arrow, and then navigate to the Tutorial.02 folder included with your Data Files.

4. Double-click the **Tutorial.02** folder, and then double-click the **Tutorial** folder.

5. Click **FAQ** to select the file, if necessary.

   Trouble? If you see "FAQ.doc" in the folder, Windows is configured to display file extensions. Click FAQ.doc and continue with Step 6. If you can't find the file with or without the file extension, make sure you're looking in the Tutorial subfolder within the Tutorial.02 folder included with your Data Files, and check to make sure the Files of type text box displays All Word Documents or All Files. If you still can't locate the file, ask your instructor or technical support person for help.

6. Click the **Open** button. The document opens with the insertion point at the beginning of the document. Notice that the document consists of a series of questions and answers.

7. Verify that the document is displayed in Normal view, and then scroll down until you can see the question "Is mulch necessary?" Notice the dotted line in the middle of the preceding paragraph. This line shows where Word has inserted a page break, dividing the document into two pages. See Figure 2-3. Word automatically inserts a page break (called an **automatic page break**) whenever your text fills up all the available lines on a page. In Normal view, a page break is represented by the dotted line shown in Figure 2-3. In some views, page breaks are not visible at all.

Document with automatic page break < **Figure 2-3**

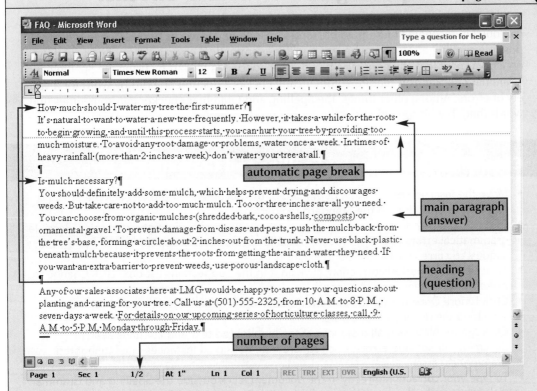

8. Check that your screen matches Figure 2-3. If necessary, click the **Show/Hide ¶** button ¶ to display nonprinting characters. This will make formatting elements (paragraph marks, spaces, and so forth) visible and easier to change.

Now that you've opened the document, you can save it with a new name. To avoid altering the original file, FAQ, you will save the document using the filename Tree FAQ. Saving the document with another filename creates a copy of the file and leaves the original file unchanged in case you want to work through the tutorial again.

To save the document with a new name:

1. Click **File** on the menu bar, and then click **Save As**. The Save As dialog box opens with the current filename highlighted in the File name text box. You could type an entirely new filename, or you could edit the current one.

2. Click to the left of "FAQ" in the File name text box, type **Tree**, and then press the **spacebar**.

3. Verify that the Tutorial.02\Tutorial folder is selected in the Save in box.

4. Click the **Save** button. The document is saved with the new filename "Tree FAQ".

Now you're ready to begin working with the document. First, you will check it for spelling and grammatical errors.

Using the Spelling and Grammar Checker

When typing a document, Word highlights possible spelling and grammatical errors. You can quickly recognize these possible errors by looking for words underlined in red (for possible spelling errors) or green (for possible grammatical errors). When you're working on a document that someone else typed, it's a good idea to start by using the Spelling and Grammar checker. This feature automatically checks a document word by word for a variety of errors. Among other things, the Spelling and Grammar checker can sometimes find words that, though spelled correctly, are not used properly.

Reference Window

Checking a Document for Spelling and Grammatical Errors

- Move the insertion point to the beginning of the document, and then click the Spelling and Grammar button on the Standard toolbar.
- In the Spelling and Grammar dialog box, review any errors highlighted in color. Possible grammatical errors appear in green; possible spelling errors appear in red. Review the suggested corrections in the Suggestions list box.
- To accept a suggested correction, click on it in the Suggestions list box, click Change to make the correction, and then continue searching the document for errors.
- Click Ignore Once to skip the current instance of the highlighted text and continue searching the document for errors.
- Click Ignore All to skip all instances of the highlighted text and continue searching the document for spelling errors. Click Ignore Rule to skip all instances of a highlighted grammatical error.
- To type your correction directly in the document, click outside the Spelling and Grammar dialog box, make the correction, and then click Resume in the Spelling and Grammar dialog box.
- To add an unrecognized word to the dictionary, click Add to dictionary.

The Spelling and Grammar Checker compares the words in your document to the default dictionary that is installed automatically with Word. If you regularly use terms that are not included in the main dictionary, you can create a custom dictionary and then select it as the new default dictionary. A custom dictionary includes all the terms in the main dictionary, plus any new terms that you add. To create a custom dictionary and select it as the new default dictionary, you would follow these steps:

1. Click **Tools** on the menu bar, click **Options**, click the **Spelling & Grammar** tab, and then click **Custom Dictionaries**. The Custom Dictionaries dialog box opens.
2. Click **New**. The Create Custom Dictionary dialog box opens.
3. Type a name for the custom dictionary in the File name text box, and click **Save**. You return to the Custom Dictionaries dialog box.
4. In the **Dictionary list** box, click the new custom dictionary to select it, click **Change Default**, and then click **OK**.

You'll see how the Spelling and Grammar checker works as you check the Tree FAQ document for mistakes.

To check the Tree FAQ document for spelling and grammatical errors:

1. Press **Ctrl+Home** to verify that the insertion point is located at the beginning of the document, to the left of the "F" in "Frequently Asked Questions."

2. Click the **Spelling and Grammar** button on the Standard toolbar. The Spelling and Grammar dialog box opens with the word "About" highlighted in green, indicating a possible grammatical error. The word "about" (with a lowercase "a") is suggested as a possible replacement. The line immediately under the dialog box title bar indicates the possible type of problem, in this case, Capitalization. See Figure 2-4. Prepositions of five or more letters are capitalized in titles so no change is required here.

   Trouble? If you see the word "plannting" selected instead of "About," your computer is not set up to check grammar. Click the Check grammar check box to insert a check, and then click Cancel to close the Spelling and Grammar dialog box. Repeat Steps 1 and 2.

Spelling and Grammar dialog box ◄ **Figure 2-4**

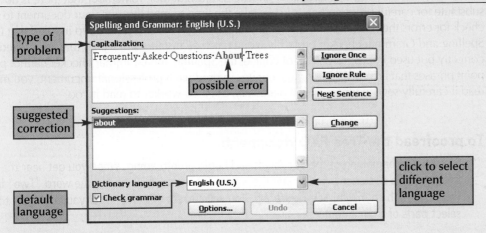

3. Click the **Ignore Rule** button. The word "plannting" is highlighted in red, with "planting," "planning," and "plantings" listed as possible corrections.

4. Verify that "planting" is highlighted in the Suggestions list box, and then click the **Change** button. "Planting" is inserted into the document, and the misspelled word "shalllow" is highlighted in the document.

5. Verify that "shallow" is selected in the Suggestions list box, and then click the **Change** button. The word "composts" is highlighted in green, with "and composts" listed as a possible correction. The type of problem "Comma Use" has to do with using a comma without "and" before the last item in a list. Marilee likes the list as it stands, so you'll ignore this suggestion.

6. Click the **Ignore Rule** button. You click Ignore Rule to ignore the rule throughout the entire document. (You can click Ignore Once to ignore a grammatical rule in the currently selected text.)

The last sentence of the document is selected. According to the type of problem listed at the top of the dialog box, the highlighted text is a sentence fragment. In this case, Word is correct. The word "call" lacks a direct object—that is, you need to indicate whom the reader should call. You can fix this problem by clicking outside the Spelling and Grammar dialog box and typing the change directly in the document.

7. Click outside the Spelling and Grammar dialog box just to the right of "call," press the **spacebar**, type **Marilee Brigham**, and then click the **Resume** button in the Spelling and Grammar dialog box. A message box opens indicating that the spelling and grammar check is complete. Notice that the last sentence is no longer a sentence fragment; that is because "Marilee Brigham" completes the sentence.

   Trouble? If you don't see the word "call," the Spelling and Grammar checker dialog box is covering it. Click the title bar of the Spelling and Grammar dialog box, and drag the dialog box out of the way.

8. Click the **OK** button. The Spelling and Grammar dialog box closes. You return to the Tree FAQ document.

Although the Spelling and Grammar checker is a useful tool, remember that there is no substitute for careful proofreading. Always take the time to read through your document to check for errors the Spelling and Grammar checker might have missed. Keep in mind that the Spelling and Grammar checker probably won't catch *all* instances of words that are spelled correctly but used improperly. And, of course, the Spelling and Grammar checker cannot pinpoint phrases that are confusing or inaccurate. To produce a professional document, you must read it carefully several times, and, if necessary, ask a co-worker to read it, too.

To proofread the Tree FAQ document:

1. Scroll to the beginning of the document and begin proofreading. When you get near the bottom of the document, notice that the word "Too" is used instead of the word "Two" in the paragraph on mulch. See Figure 2-5. You will correct this error after you learn how to select parts of a document.

Figure 2-5 ▶ **Word "Too" used incorrectly**

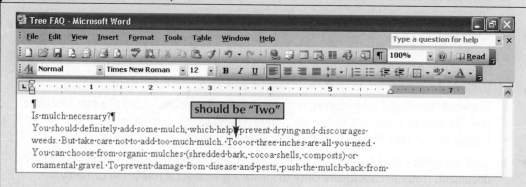

2. Finish proofreading the Tree FAQ document.

To make all of Marilee's changes, you need to learn how to select parts of a document.

Selecting Parts of a Document

Before you can do anything to text (such as deleting, moving, or formatting it), you often need to highlight, or **select** it. You can select text by using the mouse or the keyboard, although the mouse is usually easier and more efficient. With the mouse you can quickly select a line or paragraph by clicking the **selection bar** (the blank space in the left margin area of the Document window). You can also select text using various combinations of keys. Figure 2-6 summarizes methods for selecting text with the mouse and the keyboard. The notation "Ctrl+Shift" means you press and hold the two keys at the same time. Note that you will use the methods described in Figure 2-6 as you work on the Tree FAQ document.

Methods for selecting text | Figure 2-6

To Select	Mouse	Keyboard	Mouse and Keyboard
A word	Double-click the word.	Move the insertion point to the beginning of the word, hold down Ctrl+Shift, and then press →.	
A line	Click in the selection bar next to the line.	Move the insertion point to the beginning of the line, hold down Shift, and then press →.	
A sentence	Click at the beginning of the sentence, then drag the pointer until the sentence is selected.		Press and hold down the Ctrl key, and click within the sentence.
Multiple lines	Click and drag in the selection bar next to the lines.	Move the insertion point to the beginning of the first line, hold down Shift, and then press → until all the lines are selected.	
A paragraph	Double-click in the selection bar next to the paragraph, or triple-click within the paragraph.	Move the insertion point to the beginning of the paragraph, hold down Ctrl+Shift, and then press ↓.	
Multiple paragraphs	Click in the selection bar next to the first paragraph in the group, and then drag in the selection bar to select the paragraphs.	Move the insertion point to the beginning of the first paragraph, hold down Ctrl+Shift, and then press ↓ until all the paragraphs are selected.	
An entire document	Triple-click in the selection bar.	Press Ctrl+A.	Press and hold down the Ctrl key and click in the selection bar.
A block of text	Click at the beginning of the block, then drag the pointer until the entire block is selected.		Click at the beginning of the block, press and hold down the Shift key, and then click at the end of the block.
Nonadjacent blocks of text	Press and hold the Ctrl key, then drag the mouse pointer to select multiple blocks of nonadjacent text.		

Deleting Text

When editing a document, you frequently need to delete text. You already have experience using the Backspace and Delete keys to delete a few characters. To delete an entire word or multiple words, you select the text. After you select the text, you can either replace it with something else by typing over it, or delete it by pressing the Delete key. You need to delete the word "Too" and replace it with "Two," so you'll use the first method now.

To replace "Too" with "Two":

1. Press **Ctrl+End**. The insertion point moves to the end of the document.

2. Press and hold the **Ctrl** key while you press the ↑ key three times. The insertion point is now positioned at the beginning of the paragraph that begins "You should definitely add some mulch." (The status bar indicates that this is line 5 of page 2.)

3. In the second line of the paragraph, double-click the word **Too** (in the phrase "Too or three inches"). The entire word is highlighted.

4. Type **Two**. The selected word is replaced with the correction. The sentence now correctly reads: "Two or three inches are all you need."

Next, Marilee wants you to delete the phrase "or problems" and the word "any" in the paragraph before the one you've just corrected. Peter explains that you can do this quickly by selecting multiple items and then pressing Delete. As you'll see in the following steps, selecting parts of a document by clicking and dragging takes a little practice, so don't be concerned if you don't get it right the first time. You can always try again.

To select and delete multiple items:

1. Press the ↑ key five times. As shown in Figure 2-7, the insertion point is now located in the sentence that begins "To avoid any root damage or problems." The status bar indicates that this is line 1 of page 2.

Figure 2-7 **Text to be deleted**

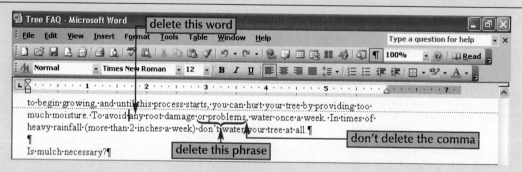

2. Double-click the word **any**. The word and the space following it are selected.

3. Press and hold the **Ctrl** key, click to the left of "or" and drag to select the phrase "or problems," and then release the **Ctrl** key. Do not select the comma after the word "problems." At this point the word "any" and the phrase "or problems" should be selected.

   Trouble? If you don't get Step 3 right the first time (for instance, if you accidentally selected the word "damage"), click anywhere in the document and then repeat Steps 2 and 3.

4. Press the **Delete** key. The selected items are deleted and the words around them move in to fill the space. As you can see in Figure 2-8, you still need to delete the extra space before the comma.

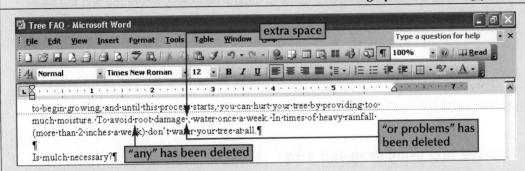

Trouble? If you deleted the wrong text, click the Undo button [↺] (not the Redo button) on the Standard toolbar to reverse your mistake, and then begin again with Step 2.

Trouble? If your screen looks slightly different from Figure 2-8, don't be concerned. The text may wrap differently on your monitor. Just make sure you deleted the correct text.

5. Click to the right of the word "damage," and then press the **Delete** key. The extra space is deleted.

6. Scroll down to display the last line of the document (if necessary), drag the mouse pointer to select "Marilee Brigham," press the **Delete** key, press the **spacebar**, and then type your first and last name. This change will make it easier for you to retrieve your document if you print it on a network printer used by other students.

You have edited the document by replacing "Too" with "Two" and by removing the text that Marilee marked for deletion. Now you are ready to make the rest of the edits she suggested.

Moving Text within a Document

One of the most useful features of a word-processing program is the ability to move text. For example, Marilee wants to reorder the four points Peter made in the section "Do I have to do anything to the tree before planting?" on page 1 of his draft. You could reorder the list by deleting an item and then retyping it at a new location, but it's easier to select and then move the text. Word provides several ways to move text: drag and drop, cut and paste, and copy and paste.

Dragging and Dropping Text

One way to move text within a document is called drag and drop. With **drag and drop**, you select the text you want to move, press and hold down the mouse button while you drag the selected text to a new location, and then release the mouse button.

Reference Window	**Dragging and Dropping Text**

- Select the text you want to move.
- Press and hold down the mouse button until the drag-and-drop pointer appears, and then drag the selected text to its new location.
- Use the dotted insertion point as a guide to determine exactly where the text will be inserted.
- Release the mouse button to drop the text at the insertion point.

Marilee wants you to change the order of the items in the list on page 1 of the document. You'll use the drag-and-drop method to reorder these items. At the same time, you'll practice using the selection bar to highlight a line of text.

To move text using drag and drop:

1. Scroll up until you see "Do I have to do anything to the tree before planting?" (line 29 of page 1). In the list of steps involved in planting a tree, Marilee wants you to move the third step ("Remove any tags from the trunk and branches.") to the top of the list.

2. Move the pointer to the selection bar to the left of the line "Remove any tags from the trunk and branches." The pointer changes from an I-beam ⌶ to a right-facing arrow ⌰.

3. Click to the left of the line "Remove any tags from the trunk and branches." The line is selected. Notice that the paragraph mark at the end of the line is also selected. See Figure 2-9.

Figure 2-9	Selected text to drag and drop

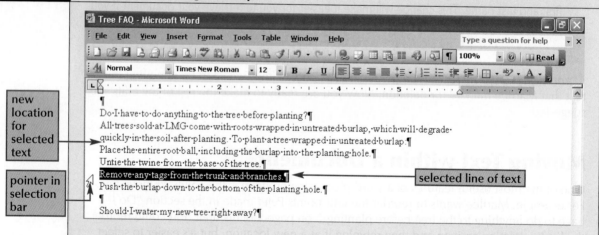

4. Position the pointer over the selected text. The pointer changes from a right-facing arrow ⌰ to a left-facing arrow ⌰.

5. Press and hold down the mouse button until the drag-and-drop pointer ⌰ appears. Note that a dotted insertion point appears within the selected text. (You may have to move the mouse pointer slightly left or right to see the drag-and-drop pointer or the dotted insertion point.)

6. Drag the selected text up until the dotted insertion point appears to the left of the word "Place." Make sure you use the dotted insertion point, rather than the mouse pointer, to guide the text to its new location. The dotted insertion point indicates exactly where the text will appear when you release the mouse button. See Figure 2-10.

Moving text with drag-and-drop pointer

Figure 2-10

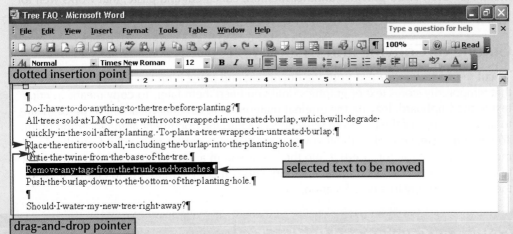

7. Release the mouse button. The selected text moves to its new location as the first step in the list. A Paste Options button appears near the newly moved text, as shown in Figure 2-11. When you move the mouse pointer over the Paste Options button, it changes to include a list arrow.

Paste Options button

Figure 2-11

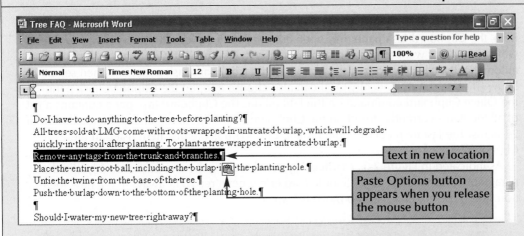

Trouble? If the selected text moves to the wrong location, click the Undo button ⟲ on the Standard toolbar, and then repeat Steps 2 through 7. Remember to hold down the mouse button until the dotted insertion point appears to the left of the word "Place."

Trouble? If you don't see the Paste Options button, your computer is not set up to display it. Read Step 8, and then continue with Step 9.

8. Click the **Paste Options** button 📋 ▾. A menu of text-moving commands appears. These commands are useful when you are inserting text that looks different from the surrounding text. For instance, suppose you selected text formatted in the Times New Roman font and then dragged it to a paragraph formatted in the Arial font. You could then use the Match Destination Formatting command to format the moved text in Arial.

9. Deselect the highlighted text by clicking anywhere in the document. The Paste Options menu closes, but the button remains visible. It will disappear as soon as you perform another task.

Dragging and dropping works well if you're moving text a short distance in a document. However, Word provides another method, called cut and paste, that works well for moving text both long and short distances.

Cutting or Copying and Pasting Text

To **cut** means to remove text from the document and place it on the **Clipboard**, a feature that temporarily stores text or graphics until you need them later. To **copy** means to copy text to the Clipboard, leaving the original material in its original location. To **paste** means to transfer a copy of the text from the Clipboard into the document at the insertion point. To **cut and paste**, you select the text you want to move, cut (or remove) it from the document, and then paste (or insert) it into the document in a new location. If you don't want to remove the text from its original location, you can copy it (rather than cutting it), and then paste the copy in a new location.

Reference Window | **Cutting or Copying and Pasting Text**

- Select the text you want to cut or copy.
- To remove the text, click the Cut button on the Standard toolbar.
- To make a copy of the text, click the Copy button on the Standard toolbar.
- Move the insertion point to the target location in the document.
- Click the Paste button on the Standard toolbar.

Depending on how your computer is set up, when you cut or copy more than one item, the **Clipboard task pane** may open automatically, making it easier for you to select which items you want to paste into the document. (To have the Clipboard task pane open automatically, click Options at the bottom of the Clipboard task pane, and then select Show Clipboard Automatically.) You can also choose to open the Clipboard task pane via the Office Clipboard command on the Edit menu. The Clipboard task pane contains a list of all the items currently stored on the Clipboard. The Clipboard can store a maximum of 24 items. The last item cut or copied to the Clipboard is the first item listed in the Clipboard task pane.

As indicated in Figure 2-1, Marilee suggested moving the word "thoroughly" (in the paragraph under the heading "Should I water my new tree right away?") to a new location. You'll use cut and paste to move this word.

To move text using cut and paste:

1. If necessary, scroll down until you can see the paragraph below the heading "Should I water my new tree right away?" near the bottom of page 1.

2. Double-click the word **thoroughly**. As you can see in Figure 2-12, you need to move this word to the end of the sentence.

Text to move using cut and paste | **Figure 2-12**

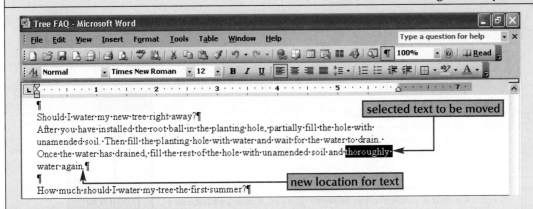

3. Click the **Cut** button on the Standard toolbar to remove the selected text from the document.

4. If the Clipboard task pane opens, click its **Close** button for now. You'll have a chance to use the Clipboard task pane shortly.

5. Click between the "n" in "again" and the period that follows it. The insertion point marks the position where you want to move the text.

6. Click the **Paste** button on the Standard toolbar. The word "thoroughly" appears in its new location, along with a Paste Options button. Note that Word also included a space before the word, so that the end of the sentence reads "and water again thoroughly." The Paste Options button that appeared in the previous set of steps (when you dragged text to a new location) disappears.

   Trouble? If the Paste Options buttons on your computer do not behave exactly as described in these steps—for instance, if they do not disappear as described—this is not a problem, just continue with the tutorial.

Peter mentions that he'll be using the paragraph on mulch and the paragraph on watering for the FAQ he plans to write on flowering shrubs. He asks you to copy that information and paste it in a new document that he can use as the basis for the new FAQ. You can do this using copy and paste. In the process you'll have a chance to use the Clipboard task pane.

To copy and paste text:

1. Click **Edit** on the menu bar, and then click **Office Clipboard**. The Clipboard task pane opens on the right side of the Document window. It contains the word "thoroughly," which you copied to the Clipboard in the last set of steps. See Figure 2-13.

Figure 2-13 ▶ **Clipboard task pane**

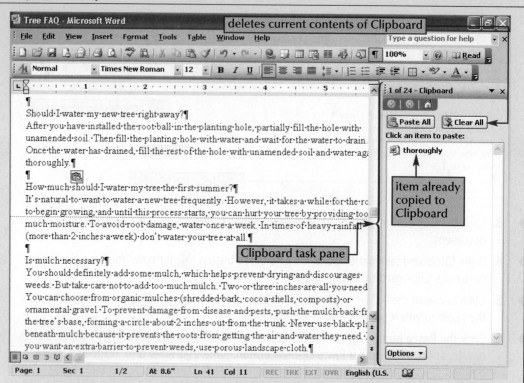

2. Click the **Clear All** button near the top of the task pane. The current contents of the Clipboard are deleted, and you see the following message on the Clipboard task pane: "Clipboard empty. Copy or cut to collect items."

3. Move the mouse pointer to the selection bar and double-click next to the paragraph that begins "After you have installed the root ball." The entire paragraph is selected.

4. Click the **Copy** button 🖺 on the Standard toolbar. The first part of the paragraph appears in the Clipboard task pane.

5. If necessary, scroll down until you can see the paragraph below the heading "Is mulch necessary?"

6. Select the paragraph below the heading (the paragraph that begins "You should definitely add . . . ").

7. Click the **Copy** button 🖺 on the Standard toolbar. The first part of the paragraph appears in the Clipboard task pane, as shown in Figure 2-14. Note the Clipboard icon 🖺 on the Windows taskbar indicating that the Clipboard task pane is currently active.

   Trouble? If you do not see the Clipboard icon in the task pane, click the Options button at the bottom of the Clipboard task pane, and then click Show Office Clipboard Icon on Taskbar. When a check mark is next to this option, the Clipboard icon appears in the far right side of the Windows taskbar to the left of the time.

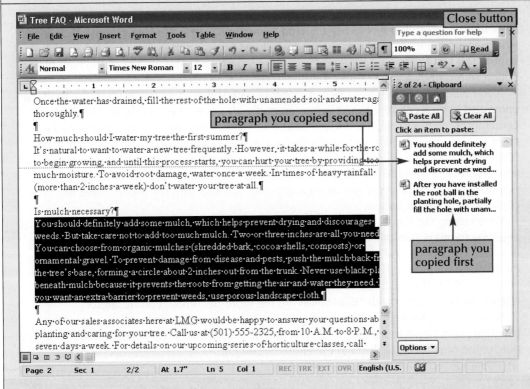

8. Click the **New Blank Document** button on the Standard toolbar. A new, blank document opens. The Clipboard icon on the Windows taskbar indicates that although the Clipboard task pane is no longer visible, it is still active.

9. Double-click the **Clipboard** icon on the right side of the Windows taskbar. The Clipboard task pane is now visible.

Now you can use the Clipboard task pane to insert the copied text into the new document.

To insert the copied text into the new document:

1. In the Clipboard task pane, click the item that begins "You should definitely add . . . " The text is inserted in the document.

2. Press the **Enter** key to insert a blank line, and then click the item that begins "After you have installed the root ball . . . " in the task pane. The text is inserted in the document.

3. Save the document as **Flowering Shrub FAQ** in the Tutorial.02\Tutorial folder, and then close the document. You return to the Tree FAQ document, where the Clipboard task pane is still open. You are finished using the Clipboard task pane, so you will delete its contents.

4. Click the **Clear All** button on the Clipboard task pane. The copied items are removed from the Clipboard task pane.

5. Click the **Close** button on the Clipboard task pane. The Clipboard task pane closes.

6. Click anywhere in the document to deselect the highlighted paragraph.

7. Save the document.

Finding and Replacing Text

When you're working with a longer document, the quickest and easiest way to locate a particular word or phrase is to use the **Find command**. To use the Find command, you type the text you want to find in the Find what text box, and then you click the Find Next button. The text in the Find what text box is the search text. After you click the Find Next button, Word finds and highlights the search text.

If you want to replace characters or a phrase with something else, you use the **Replace command**, which combines the Find command with a substitution feature. The Replace command searches through a document and substitutes the search text with the replacement text you specify. As you perform the search, Word stops and highlights each occurrence of the search text. You must determine whether or not to substitute the replacement text. If you want to substitute the highlighted occurrence, you click the Replace button. If you want to substitute every occurrence of the search text with the replacement text, you click the Replace All button.

When using the Replace All button with single words, keep in mind that the search text might be found within other words. To prevent Word from making incorrect substitutions in such cases, it's a good idea to select the Find whole words only check box along with the Replace All button. For example, suppose you want to replace the word "figure" with "illustration." Unless you select the Find whole words only check box, Word replaces "figure" in "configure" with "illustration" so the word becomes "conillustration."

As you search through a document, you can search from the current location of the insertion point down to the end of the document, from the insertion point up to the beginning of the document, or through the entire document.

Reference Window | **Finding and Replacing Text**

- Click Edit on the menu bar, and then click either Find or Replace.
- To find text, click the Find tab. To find and replace text, click the Replace tab.
- Click the More button to expand the dialog box to display additional options (including the Find whole words only option). If you see the Less button, the additional options are already displayed.
- In the Search list box, select Down if you want to search from the insertion point to the end of the document, select Up if you want to search from the insertion point to the beginning of the document, or select All to search the entire document.
- Type the characters you want to find in the Find what text box.
- If you are replacing text, type the replacement text in the Replace with text box.
- Click the Find whole words only check box to search for complete words. Click the Match case check box to insert the replacement text using the same case specified in the Replace with text box.
- Click the Find Next button.
- Click the Replace button to substitute the found text with the replacement text and find the next occurrence.
- Click the Replace All button to substitute all occurrences of the found text with the replacement text.

Marilee wants the company initials, LMG, to be spelled out as "Long Meadow Gardens" each time they appear in the text. You'll use the Replace command to make this change quickly and easily.

To replace "LMG" with "Long Meadow Gardens":

1. Press **Ctrl+Home** to move the insertion point to the beginning of the document.

2. Click **Edit** on the menu bar, and then click **Replace**. The Find and Replace dialog box opens.

3. If you see a **More** button, click it to display the additional search options. (If you see a Less button, the additional options are already displayed.) Also, click the **Search** list arrow, and then click **All** if it is not already selected in order to search the entire document.

4. Click the **Find what** text box, type **LMG**, press the **Tab** key, and then type **Long Meadow Gardens** in the Replace with text box.

   Trouble? If you already see the text "LMG" and "Long Meadow Gardens" in your Find and Replace dialog box, someone has recently performed these steps on your computer. Skip Step 4 and continue with Step 5.

5. Click the **Find whole words only** check box to insert a check.

6. Click the **Match case** check box to insert a check. This ensures that Word will insert the replacement text using initial capital letters, as you specified in the Replace with text box. Your Find and Replace dialog box should look like Figure 2-15.

Find and Replace dialog box ◀ **Figure 2-15**

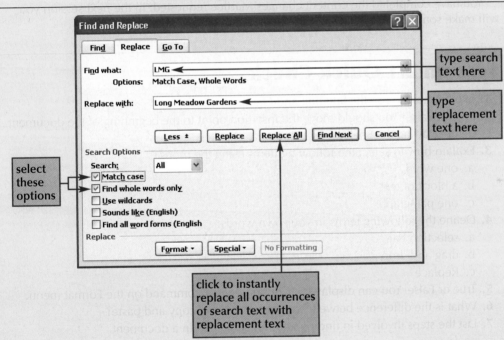

7. Click the **Replace All** button to replace all occurrences of the search text with the replacement text. When Word finishes making the replacements, you see a message box telling you that two replacements were made.

8. Click the **OK** button to close the message box, and then click the **Close** button in the Find and Replace dialog box to return to the document. The full company name has been inserted into the document, as shown in Figure 2-16. (You may have to scroll down to see this section.)

Figure 2-16 ▶ **Document with "Long Meadow Gardens" inserted**

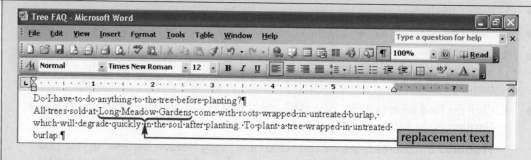

9. Save the document.

Note that you can also search for and replace formatting, such as bold and special characters, in the Find and Replace dialog box. Click in the Find what text box, enter the search text, click the Format button, click Font to open the Font dialog box, and then select the formatting for the search text. Repeat this process for the replacement text, and then complete the search or replacement operation as usual.

You have completed the content changes Marilee requested. In the next session you will make some changes that will affect the document's appearance.

Review

Session 2.1 Quick Check

1. Explain how to use the Spelling and Grammar checker.
2. True or False: You should move the insertion point to the beginning of the document before starting the Spelling and Grammar checker.
3. Explain how to select the following items using the mouse:
   a. one word
   b. a block of text
   c. one paragraph
4. Define the following terms in your own words:
   a. selection bar
   b. drag and drop
   c. Replace
5. True or False: You can display the Clipboard via a command on the Format menu.
6. What is the difference between cut and paste, and copy and paste?
7. List the steps involved in finding and replacing text in a document.

Session 2.2

Changing Margins and Page Orientation

By default, text in a Word document is formatted in **portrait orientation**, which means the page is longer than it is wide (like a typical business letter). In Portrait orientation, the default margins are 1.25 inches for the left and right margins and 1 inch for the top and bottom margins. In **landscape orientation**, the page is wider than it is long, with slightly different margins, so that text spans the widest part of the page.

When working with margins, note that the numbers on the ruler indicate the distance in inches from the left margin, not from the left edge of the paper. You can change both page margins and page orientation from within the Page Setup dialog box.

Changing Margins and Page Orientation for the Entire Document

- With the insertion point anywhere in your document and no text selected, click File on the menu bar, and then click Page Setup.
- If necessary, click the Margins tab to display the margin settings.
- Click the Landscape icon if you want to switch to Landscape orientation.
- Use the arrows to change the settings in the Top, Bottom, Left, or Right text boxes, or type a new margin value in each text box.
- Make sure the Apply to list box displays Whole document.
- Click the OK button.

You need to change the top margin to 1.5 inches and the left margin to 1.75 inches, per Marilee's request. The left margin needs to be wider than usual to allow space for making holes so that the document can be inserted in a three-ring binder. In the next set of steps, you'll change the margins using the Page Setup command. You can also change margins in Print Layout view by dragging an icon on the horizontal ruler. You'll have a chance to practice this technique in the Case Problems at the end of this tutorial.

To change the margins in the Tree FAQ document:

1. If you took a break after the previous session, make sure Word is running, the Tree FAQ document is open in Normal view, and nonprinting characters are displayed.
2. Press **Ctrl+Home** to move the insertion point to the top of the document.
3. Click **File** on the menu bar, and then click **Page Setup** to open the Page Setup dialog box.
4. Click the **Margins** tab, if it is not already selected, to display the margin settings. Portrait orientation is selected by default. The Top margin setting is selected. See Figure 2-17. As you complete the following steps, keep an eye on the document preview, which changes to reflect changes you make to the margins.

Page Setup dialog box | Figure 2-17

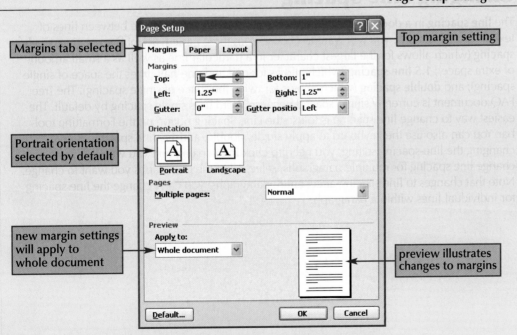

Margins tab selected

Top margin setting

Portrait orientation selected by default

new margin settings will apply to whole document

preview illustrates changes to margins

5. Type **1.5** to change the Top margin setting. (You do not have to type the inches symbol.)

6. Press the **Tab** key twice to select the Left text box and highlight the current margin setting. The text area in the Preview box moves down to reflect the larger top margin.

7. Verify that the insertion point is in the Left text box, type **1.75**, and then press the **Tab** key. The left margin in the Preview box increases.

8. Make sure the **Whole document** option is selected in the Apply to list box, and then click the **OK** button to return to your document. Notice that the right margin on the ruler has changed to reflect the larger left margin setting and the resulting reduced page area. The document text is now 5.5 inches wide. See Figure 2-18.

Figure 2-18 ▶ **Ruler after setting left margin to 1.75 inches**

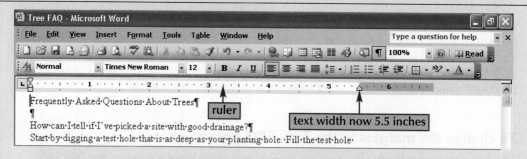

Trouble? If a double dotted line and the words "Section Break" appear in your document, Whole document wasn't specified in the Apply to list box. If this occurs, click the Undo button 🔄 on the Standard toolbar and repeat Steps 2 through 8, making sure you select the Whole document option in the Apply to list box.

Next, you will change the amount of space between lines of text.

Changing Line Spacing

The **line spacing** in a document determines the amount of vertical space between lines of text. In most situations, you will want to choose from three basic types of line spacing: **single spacing** (which allows for the largest character in a particular line as well as a small amount of extra space); **1.5 line spacing** (which allows for one and one-half times the space of single spacing); and **double spacing** (which allows for twice the space of single spacing). The Tree FAQ document is currently single-spaced because Word uses single spacing by default. The easiest way to change line spacing is to use the Line Spacing button on the Formatting toolbar. You can also use the keyboard to apply single, double, and 1.5 line spacing. Before changing the line-spacing setting, you need to click in the paragraph you want to change. To change line spacing for multiple paragraphs, select all of the paragraphs you want to change. Note that changes to line spacing affect entire paragraphs; you can't change the line spacing for individual lines within a paragraph.

Changing Line Spacing in a Document

- Click in the paragraph you want to change, or select multiple paragraphs.
- Click the list arrow next to the Line Spacing button on the Formatting toolbar, and then click the line spacing you want.

or

- Click in the paragraph you want to change, or select multiple paragraphs.
- Press Ctrl+1 for single spacing, Ctrl+5 for 1.5 line spacing, or Ctrl+2 for double spacing.

Marilee thinks the document will be easier to read with more spacing between the lines. She has asked you to change the line spacing for the entire Tree FAQ document to 1.5 line spacing. You will begin by selecting the entire document.

To change the document's line spacing:

1. Triple-click in the selection bar to select the entire document.

2. Move the mouse pointer over the **Line Spacing** button ‎ on the Formatting toolbar to display its ScreenTip. You see the text "Line Spacing (1)," indicating that single spacing is currently selected.

3. Click the **Line Spacing** list arrow ‎ on the Formatting toolbar. A list of line spacing options appears, as shown in Figure 2-19. To double space the document, you click 2.0, while to triple space it, you click 3.0. In this case, you need to apply 1.5 line spacing.

Line Spacing list box | **Figure 2-19**

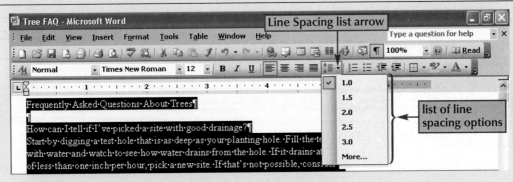

4. Click **1.5**. Notice the additional space between every line of text in the document.

5. Move the mouse pointer over the **Line Spacing** button ‎ on the Formatting toolbar to display a ScreenTip that reads "Line Spacing (1.5)." This tells you that 1.5 spacing is currently selected.

6. Click the title to deselect the text.

Now you are ready to make formatting changes that affect individual paragraphs.

Aligning Text

As you begin formatting individual paragraphs in the Tree FAQ document, keep in mind that in Word, a **paragraph** is defined as any text that ends with a paragraph mark symbol (¶). A paragraph can be a group of words that is many lines long, a single word, or even a blank line, in which case you see a paragraph mark alone on a single line. (The Tree FAQ document includes one blank paragraph before each question heading.)

The term **alignment** refers to how the text of a paragraph lines up horizontally between the margins. By default, text is aligned along the left margin but is **ragged**, or uneven, along the right margin. This is called **left alignment**. With **right alignment**, the text is aligned along the right margin and is ragged along the left margin. With **center alignment**, text is centered between the left and right margins and is ragged along both the left and right margins. With **justified alignment**, full lines of text are spaced between both the left and the right margins and the text is not ragged. Text in newspaper columns is often justified. The easiest way to apply alignment settings is by using the alignment buttons on the Formatting toolbar.

Marilee indicates that the title of the Tree FAQ should be centered and that the main paragraphs should be justified. First, you'll center the title.

To center-align the title:

▶ 1. Verify that the insertion point is located in the title "Frequently Asked Questions About Trees" at the beginning of the document.

▶ 2. Click the **Center** button ▤ on the Formatting toolbar. The text centers between the left and right margins. See Figure 2-20.

Figure 2-20 | **Centered title**

Next, you'll justify the text in the first two main paragraphs.

To justify the first two paragraphs using the Formatting toolbar:

▶ 1. Click anywhere in the paragraph that begins "Start by digging a test hole . . . "

▶ 2. Click the **Justify** button ▤ on the Formatting toolbar. The paragraph text spreads out so that it lines up evenly along the left and right margins.

▶ 3. Scroll down so you can move the insertion point to anywhere in the paragraph that begins "While you might be tempted . . . "

▶ 4. Click the **Justify** button ▤ on the Formatting toolbar again. The text is evenly spaced between the left and right margins. See Figure 2-21.

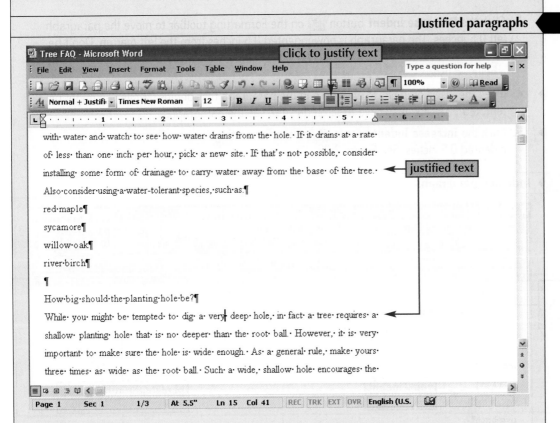

You'll justify the other paragraphs later. Now that you've learned how to change the paragraph alignment, you can turn your attention to indenting a paragraph.

Indenting a Paragraph

When you become a more experienced Word user, you might want to do some paragraph formatting, such as a **hanging indent** (where all lines except the first line of the paragraph are indented from the left margin) or a **right indent** (where all lines of the paragraph are indented from the right margin). You can select these types of indents on the Indents and Spacing tab of the Paragraph dialog box. To open this dialog box, you click Format on the menu bar and then click Paragraph.

In this document, though, you need to indent only the main paragraphs 0.5 inches from the left margin. This left indent is a simple paragraph indent. You can use the Indent buttons on the Formatting toolbar to increase or decrease paragraph indenting quickly. According to Marilee's notes, you need to indent all of the main paragraphs.

To indent a paragraph using the Increase Indent button:

1. Press **Ctrl+Home**, and then click anywhere in the paragraph that begins "Start by digging a test hole . . . "

2. Click the **Increase Indent** button 🔢 on the Formatting toolbar twice. (Don't click the Decrease Indent button by mistake.) The entire paragraph moves right 0.5 inches each time you click the Increase Indent button. The paragraph is indented 1 inch, 0.5 inches more than Marilee wants.

3. Click the **Decrease Indent** button on the Formatting toolbar to move the paragraph left 0.5 inches. The paragraph is now indented 0.5 inches from the left margin. Don't be concerned about the list of tree species. You will indent the list later, when you format it as a bulleted list.

4. Move the insertion point to anywhere in the paragraph that begins "While you might be tempted . . . " You may have to scroll down to see the paragraph.

5. Click the **Increase Indent** button on the Formatting toolbar. The paragraph is indented 0.5 inches. See Figure 2-22.

Figure 2-22 | **Indented paragraphs**

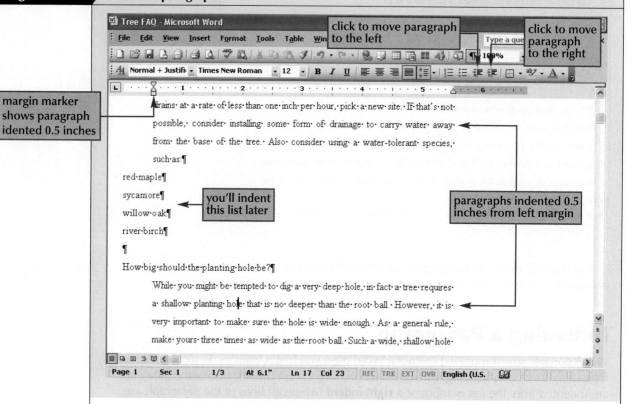

You can continue to indent and then justify each paragraph, or simply use the Format Painter command. The Format Painter allows you to copy both the indentation and alignment changes to all paragraphs in the document.

Using the Format Painter

The **Format Painter** makes it easy to copy all the formatting features of one paragraph to other paragraphs. You can use this button to copy formatting to one or multiple items.

Using the Format Painter

- Select the item whose formatting you want to copy.
- To copy formatting to one item, click the Format Painter button, and then use the mouse pointer to select the item you want to format.
- To copy formatting to multiple items, double-click the Format Painter button, and then use the mouse pointer to select each item you want to format. When you are finished, click the Format Painter button again to deselect it.

Use the Format Painter now to copy the formatting of the second paragraph to other main paragraphs. You'll begin by moving the insertion point to the paragraph whose format you want to copy.

To copy paragraph formatting with the Format Painter:

1. Verify that the insertion point is located in the paragraph that begins "While you might be tempted . . . "

2. Double-click the **Format Painter** button on the Standard toolbar. The Format Painter button will stay highlighted until you click the button again. When you move the pointer over text, the pointer changes to to indicate that the format of the selected paragraph can be painted (or copied) onto another paragraph.

3. Scroll down, and then click anywhere in the paragraph that begins "You may be accustomed . . . " The format of the third paragraph shifts to match the format of the first two main paragraphs. See Figure 2-23. All three paragraphs are now indented and justified. The Format Painter pointer is still visible.

Formats copied with Format Painter ◄ **Figure 2-23**

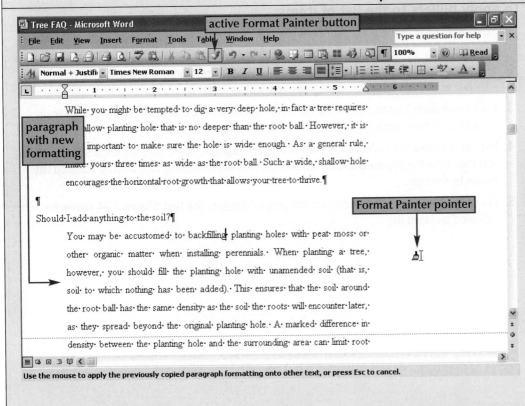

Use the mouse to apply the previously copied paragraph formatting onto other text, or press Esc to cancel.

▶ **4.** Scroll down to click the remaining paragraphs that are preceded by a question heading. Take care to click only the paragraphs below the question headings. Do not click the document title, the one-line questions, the lists, or the last paragraph in the document.

Trouble? If you click a paragraph and the formatting doesn't change to match the second paragraph, you single-clicked the Format Painter button rather than double-clicked it. Move the insertion point to a paragraph that has the desired format, double-click the Format Painter button, and then repeat Step 4.

Trouble? If you accidentally click a title or one line of a list, click the Undo button 🔄 on the Standard toolbar to return the line to its original formatting. Then select a paragraph that has the desired format, double-click the Format Painter button 🖌, and finish copying the format to the desired paragraphs.

▶ **5.** After you are finished formatting paragraphs with the Format Painter pointer, click the **Format Painter** button 🖌 on the Standard toolbar to turn off the feature.

▶ **6.** Save the document.

All the main paragraphs in the document are formatted with the correct indentation and alignment. Your next job is to make the lists easier to read by adding bullets and numbers.

Adding Bullets and Numbers

You can emphasize a list of items by adding a heavy dot, or **bullet**, before each item in the list. For consecutive items, you can use numbers instead of bullets. Marilee requests that you add bullets to the list of tree species on page 1 to make them stand out.

To apply bullets to the list of items:

▶ **1.** Scroll to the top of the document until you see the list of tree species below the text "Also consider using a water-tolerant species such as:".

▶ **2.** Select the four items in the list (from "red maple" to "river birch"). It doesn't matter whether or not you select the paragraph mark after "river birch."

▶ **3.** Click the **Bullets** button 📋 on the Formatting toolbar. A bullet, a dark circle, appears in front of each item. Each line indents to make room for the bullet.

▶ **4.** In order to make the bullets align with the first paragraph, make sure the list is still selected, and then click the **Increase Indent** button 📑 on the Formatting toolbar. The bulleted list moves to the right.

▶ **5.** Click anywhere within the document window to deselect the text. Figure 2-24 shows the indented bulleted list.

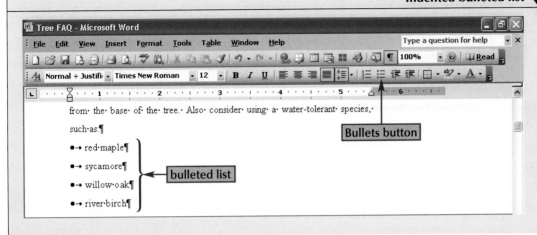

The bulleted list you just created includes the default bullet style. To select a different style of bullets (such as check marks or arrows) you can use the Bullets and Numbering command on the Format menu. You'll have a chance to try that command in the Case Problems at the end of this tutorial.

Next, you need to format the list of steps involved in planting a tree. Marilee asks you to format this information as a numbered list because this list shows sequential steps. This is an easy task thanks to the Numbering button, which automatically numbers selected paragraphs with consecutive numbers. If you insert a new paragraph, delete a paragraph, or reorder the paragraphs, Word automatically adjusts the numbers to make sure they remain consecutive.

To apply numbers to the list of steps:

1. Scroll down until you see the list that begins "Remove any tags . . . " and ends with "of the planting hole."

2. Select the entire list. It doesn't matter whether or not you select the paragraph mark at the end of the last item.

3. Click the **Numbering** button 📋 on the Formatting toolbar. Consecutive numbers appear in front of each item in the list. The list is indented, similar to the bulleted list. The list would look better if it was indented to align with the paragraph.

4. Click the **Increase Indent** button 📋 on the Formatting toolbar. The list moves to the right, so that the numbers align with the preceding paragraph.

5. Click anywhere in the document to deselect the text. Figure 2-25 shows the indented and numbered list.

Figure 2-25 ▶ **Indented numbered list**

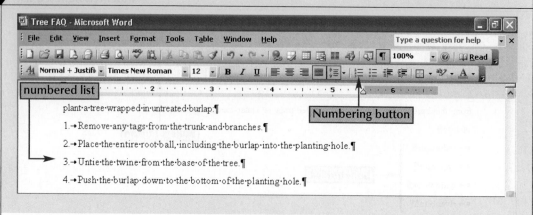

The text of the document is now properly aligned and indented. The bullets and numbers make the lists easy to read and give readers visual clues about the type of information they contain. Next, you need to adjust the formatting of individual words.

Changing the Font and Font Size

All of Marilee's remaining changes concern changing fonts, adjusting font sizes, and emphasizing text with font styles. The first step is to change the font of the title from 12-point Times New Roman to 14-point Arial. This will make the title stand out from the rest of the text.

Reference Window | **Changing the Font and Font Size**

- Select the text you want to change.
- Click the Font list arrow on the Formatting toolbar to display the list of fonts.
- Click the font you want to use.
- Click the Font Size list arrow, and then click the font size you want to use.

or

- Select the text that you want to change.
- Click Format on the menu bar, and then click Font.
- In the Font tab of the Font dialog box, select the font and font size you want to use.
- Click the OK button.

Marilee wants you to change the font of the title as well as its size and style. To do this, you'll use the Formatting toolbar. Marilee wants you to use a **sans serif font**, which is a font that does not have the small additional lines (called serifs) at the tops and bottoms of the letters. Sans serif fonts are often used in titles so they contrast with the body text. A **serif font** is a font that does include these small lines. Times New Roman is a serif font, and Arial is a sans serif font.

To change the font of the title:

1. Press **Ctrl+Home** to move the insertion point to the beginning of the document, and then click to the left of the title **Frequently Asked Questions About Trees** to select it.

2. Click the **Font** list arrow on the Formatting toolbar. A list of available fonts appears in alphabetical order, with the name of the current font in the Font text box. See Figure 2-26. Fonts that have been used recently might appear above a double line. Note that each name in the list is formatted with the relevant font. For example, "Arial" appears in the Arial font, and "Times New Roman" appears in the Times New Roman font.

Font list ◄ **Figure 2-26**

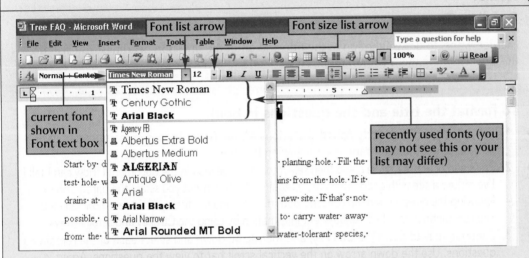

Trouble? If you don't see the fonts beginning with "A" at the top of your Font list, scroll up until you do.

3. Click **Arial** to select it as the new font. As you click, watch the font in the title change to reflect the new font.

   Trouble? If Arial doesn't appear in the font list, use another sans serif font.

4. Click the **Font Size** list arrow on the Formatting toolbar, and then click **14** in the size list. As you click, watch the title's font increase from 12 to 14 points.

5. Save your work, and then click within the title to deselect it. See Figure 2-27. Note that the font settings in the Formatting toolbar reflect the font settings of the text that is currently selected, or, if no text is selected, of the text currently containing the insertion point.

Title font and font size changed ◄ **Figure 2-27**

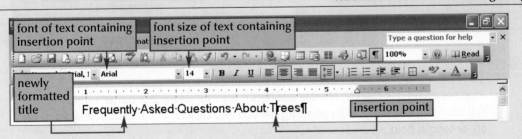

Trouble? If your font and font size settings don't match those in Figure 2-27, you might not have clicked the title. Click the title, view the font and font size settings displayed on the Formatting toolbar, and then make the necessary changes. Because of differences in fonts and monitors, the characters in your document might look different from the figure.

Emphasizing Text Using Bold, Underline, and Italic Styles

You can emphasize words in your document by formatting them with bold, underline, or italic styles. These styles help make specific thoughts, ideas, words, or phrases stand out. (You can also add special effects such as shadows to characters.) Marilee marked a few words on the document draft (shown in Figure 2-1) that need special emphasis. You add bold, underline, or italic styles by using the corresponding buttons on the Formatting toolbar. These buttons are **toggle buttons**, which means you can click them once to format the selected text, and then click again to remove the formatting from the selected text.

Bolding Text

Marilee wants to draw attention to the title and all of the question headings. You will do this by formatting them with the bold style.

To format the title and the questions in bold:

1. Select the title **Frequently Asked Questions About Trees**. It doesn't matter whether or not you select the paragraph mark following the title.

2. Press and hold the **Ctrl** key, and then select the first question in the document ("How can I tell if I've picked a site with good drainage?"). Again, whether or not you select the paragraph mark following the question is of no concern. Both the title and the first question are now selected. You can continue to select nonadjacent information by using the Ctrl key and scroll arrows.

3. Continue to hold down the **Ctrl** key, and then scroll down and select each of the remaining questions. Use the down arrow on the vertical scroll bar to view the questions. Again, whether or not you select the paragraph mark following each question is of no concern.
   Trouble? If you accidentally select something other than a question, keep the Ctrl key pressed while you click the incorrect item. This should deselect the incorrect item.

4. Release the **Ctrl** key, click the **Bold** button [B] on the Formatting toolbar, click anywhere in the document to deselect the text, and then scroll up to return to the beginning of the document. The title and the questions appear in bold, as shown in Figure 2-28.

Figure 2-28 ▶ Text in bold

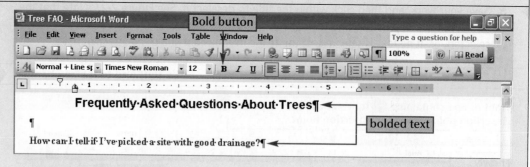

After reviewing this change, Marilee wonders if the title would look better without bold. You can easily remove bold by selecting the text and clicking the Bold button again to turn off, or toggle, bold.

5. To remove the bold, select the title, and then click the **Bold** button [B] on the Formatting toolbar. The title now appears without bold. Marilee decides she prefers to emphasize the title with bold after all.

6. Verify that the title is still selected, and then click the **Bold** button [B] on the Formatting toolbar. The title appears in bold again.

Underlining Text

The Underline button works in the same way as the Bold button. Marilee's edits indicate that the word "Note" should be inserted and underlined at the beginning of the final paragraph. Using the Underline button, you'll make both of these changes at the same time.

To underline text:

1. Press **Ctrl+End** to move the insertion point to the end of the document, then press **Ctrl+↑** to move the insertion point to the left of the word "Any" in the first line of the final paragraph.

2. Click the **Underline** button 🔘 on the Formatting toolbar to turn on underlining. The Underline button is highlighted. Whatever text you type now will be underlined on your screen and in your printed document.

3. Type **Note:** and then click the **Underline** button 🔘 on the Formatting toolbar to turn off underlining. The Underline button is no longer highlighted, and "Note:" is now underlined.

4. Press the **spacebar**. See Figure 2-29.

Word typed with underline ◀ | **Figure 2-29**

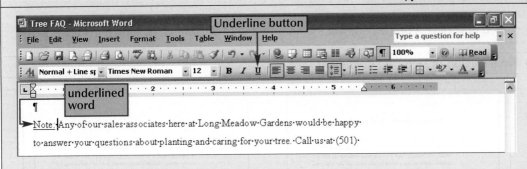

Italicizing Text

Next, you'll format each instance of "Long Meadow Gardens" in italic. This helps draw attention to the company name.

To italicize the company name:

1. Scroll up to the first question on the second page ("Do I have to do anything to the tree before planting?").

2. In the first line below the question, select **Long Meadow Gardens**.

3. Click the **Italic** button 🔘 on the Formatting toolbar. The company name changes from regular to italic text. In the next step, you'll learn a useful method for repeating the task you just performed.

4. Scroll down to the last paragraph of the document, select the company name, and then press the **F4** key. The F4 key enables you to repeat your most recent action. It is especially helpful when formatting parts of a document.

5. Save the document.

Previewing Formatted Text

You have made all the editing and formatting changes that Marilee requested for the Tree FAQ document. It's helpful to preview a document after formatting it, because the Print Preview window makes it easy to spot text that is not aligned correctly.

To preview and print the document:

1. Press **Ctrl+Home**, click the **Print Preview** button 🔍 on the Standard toolbar, click the **One Page** button 🔲 on the Print Preview toolbar if you see more than one page, and examine the first page of the document. Use the vertical scroll bar to display the second page. (If you notice any alignment or indentation errors, click the Close button on the Print Preview toolbar, correct the errors in Normal view, save your changes, and then return to the Print Preview window.)

2. Click the **Print** button 🖨 on the Print Preview toolbar. After a pause, the document prints.

3. Click the **Close** button on the Print Preview toolbar. You return to Normal view.

4. If you made any changes to the document after previewing it, save your work.

You now have a printed copy of the final Tree FAQ document, as shown in Figure 2-30.

Figure 2-30 ▶ **Final version of Tree FAQ document**

Frequently Asked Questions About Trees

How can I tell if I've picked a site with good drainage?

Start by digging a test hole that is as deep as your planting hole. Fill the test hole with water and watch to see how water drains from the hole. If it drains at a rate of less than one inch per hour, pick a new site. If that's not possible, consider installing some form of drainage to carry water away from the base of the tree. Also consider using a water-tolerant species, such as:

- red maple
- sycamore
- willow oak
- river birch

How big should the planting hole be?

While you might be tempted to dig a very deep hole, in fact a tree requires a shallow planting hole that is no deeper than the root ball. However, it is very important to make sure the hole is wide enough. As a general rule, make yours three times as wide as the root ball. Such a wide, shallow hole encourages the horizontal root growth that allows your tree to thrive.

Should I add anything to the soil?

You may be accustomed to backfilling planting holes with peat moss or other organic matter when installing perennials. When planting a tree, however, you should fill the planting hole with unamended soil (that is, soil to which nothing has been added). This ensures that the soil around the root ball has the same density as the soil the roots will encounter later, as they spread beyond the original planting hole. A marked difference in

density between the planting hole and the surrounding area can limit root growth.

Do I have to do anything to the tree before planting?

All trees sold at *Long Meadow Gardens* come with roots wrapped in untreated burlap, which will degrade quickly in the soil after planting. To plant a tree wrapped in untreated burlap:

1. Remove any tags from the trunk and branches.
2. Place the entire root ball, including the burlap into the planting hole.
3. Untie the twine from the base of the tree.
4. Push the burlap down to the bottom of the planting hole.

Should I water my new tree right away?

After you have installed the root ball in the planting hole, partially fill the hole with unamended soil. Then fill the planting hole with water and wait for the water to drain. Once the water has drained, fill the rest of the hole with unamended soil and water again thoroughly.

How much should I water my tree the first summer?

It's natural to want to water a new tree frequently. However, it takes a while for the roots to begin growing, and until this process starts, you can hurt your tree by providing too much moisture. To avoid root damage, water once a week. In times of heavy rainfall (more than 2 inches a week) don't water your tree at all.

Is mulch necessary?

You should definitely add some mulch, which helps prevent drying and discourages weeds. But take care not to add too much mulch. Two or three inches are all you need. You can choose from organic mulches (shredded

bark, cocoa shells, composts) or ornamental gravel. To prevent damage from disease and pests, push the mulch back from the tree's base, forming a circle about 2 inches out from the trunk. Never use black plastic beneath mulch because it prevents the roots from getting the air and water they need. If you want an extra barrier to prevent weeds, use porous landscape cloth.

Note: Any of our sales associates here at *Long Meadow Gardens* would be happy to answer your questions about planting and caring for your tree. Call us at (501) 555-2325, from 10 A.M. to 8 P.M., seven days a week. For details on our upcoming series of horticulture classes, call Evan Brillstein, 9 A.M. to 5 P.M., Monday through Friday.

Adding Comments

Peter reviews the Tree FAQ document and is happy with its appearance. He wonders if he should add some information about fertilizing new trees. He asks you to insert a note to Marilee about this using Word's Comment feature. A **comment** is an electronic version of a self-sticking note that you might attach to a piece of paper. To insert a comment in a Word document, select a block of text, click Comment on the Insert menu, and then type your comment in the comment box. To display a comment, place the mouse pointer over text where the comment has been inserted. Comments are very useful when you are exchanging Word documents with co-workers electronically, whether via e-mail, disks, or on CDs, because they allow you to make notes or queries without affecting the document itself.

You'll insert Peter's comment at the document title so that Marilee will be sure to see it as soon as she opens the document. It's easiest to work with comments in Print Layout view.

To add the comment to the document:

1. Click the **Print Layout View** button 📃 in the lower-left corner of the Word window, then click the **Zoom** list arrow and click **100%** in the list if it is not already selected. The document view changes, allowing you to see the document margins.

2. Scroll up and down through the document and notice that, in Print Layout view, a page break is represented by something more noticeable than a dotted line. You can actually see the end of one page and the beginning of another.

3. Scroll up to the beginning of the document, and then select the title **Frequently Asked Questions About Trees**. (Do not select the paragraph mark after the title.)

4. Click **Insert** on the menu bar, and then click **Comment**. A comment balloon appears in the right margin, with the insertion point ready for you to type your comment. The Reviewing toolbar opens, displaying buttons that are useful for working with comments. See Figure 2-31.

Inserting a comment   **Figure 2-31**

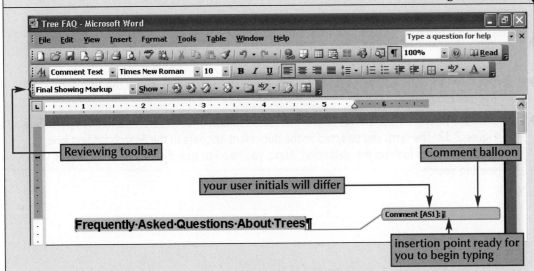

Trouble? If you can't see the entire comment balloon, scroll right to display it fully.

The comment is preceded by the user's initials and a number. Initials depend on the information entered on the Information tab in the Options dialog box. The numbers are sequential, with the first comment labeled #1, the second #2, and so on.

5. Type **Should we add a section on fertilizing new trees?** The newly typed comment is displayed in the comment balloon. Depending on the size of your monitor, you may need to scroll right to read the entire comment.

6. Click the **Normal View** button ▤ in the lower-left corner of the Word window. The title is highlighted in color with brackets around it, indicating that a comment has been inserted at this point in the document.

7. Place the mouse pointer over the title. The comment is displayed in a ScreenTip over the pointer. When you move the mouse pointer away from the title, the ScreenTip closes.

8. Save the document.

Note that to delete a comment, you can right-click the comment box in Print Layout view and click Delete Comment. To edit a comment, click in the comment box and make any deletions or additions you desire. After you insert comments in a document, you can choose to print the document with or without comments in the margin. To print the comments, select Document showing markup in the Print what list box of the Print dialog box. To print a document without comments, select Document in the Print what list box. You'll find comments useful when you need to collaborate on a document with your fellow students or co-workers.

Using the Research Task Pane

Before you finish your work for the day, Peter suggests that you use the Research task pane to look up information on plants sold at Long Meadow Gardens. The **Research task pane** provides a number of research tools, including a thesaurus, an Internet search engine, and access to the Encarta Encyclopedia and Dictionary. To take full advantage of these options, your computer must be connected to the Internet. To get started, Peter asks you to use the Research task pane to find the Latin name for "red maple."

To look up "red maple" in the Research task pane:

1. Verify that your computer is connected to the Internet. If your computer is not connected to the Internet, read, but do not attempt to perform, the following steps.

2. Use the Find command to locate and select the text "red maple". Close the Find and Replace dialog box.

3. Click the **Research** button 🔍 on the Standard toolbar. The Research task pane opens. See Figure 2-32. The term you selected in the document appears in the Search for text box, ready for you to look up the definition. Next, you need to specify the reference source you want to search.

Opening the Research task pane — **Figure 2-32**

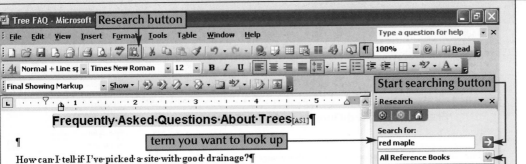

4. Verify that **All Reference Books** is selected in the list box below the Search for text box, and then click the **Start searching** button. A list of research results appears, as shown in Figure 2-33. At the top of the list is the Encarta Dictionary definition for "red maple," with the Latin name, *Acer rubrum*, at the end. If the initial search results don't provide the information you need, scroll down and click the "Can't find it?" link at the bottom of the Research task pane to display more research options. In some cases, when you click a link in the Research task pane, Internet Explorer might open a Web page with further information.

Trouble? If All Reference Books is not selected in the list box below the Search for text box, click the list arrow and select All Reference Books. At that point the search will begin; you do not have to click the Start searching button.

Figure 2-33	Research results

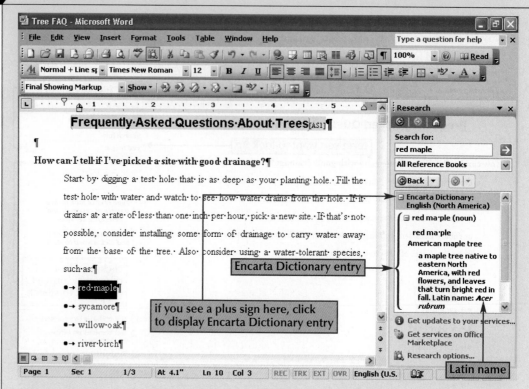

Trouble? If you see "Encarta Dictionary: English (North America)" but not the dictionary entry for "red maple," click the plus sign as indicated in Figure 2-33.

5. Click the **Close** button ☒ at the top of the Research task pane. The Research task pane closes.

6. Close the Reviewing toolbar, save, and then close the document.

In this tutorial, you have helped Peter edit and format the Tree FAQ document that will be handed out to all customers purchasing a tree at Long Meadow Gardens. Peter will e-mail the file to Marilee later so that she can review your work and read the comment you inserted.

Review

Session 2.2 Quick Check

1. What are Word's default values for the left and right margins? For the top and bottom margins?
2. Describe the steps involved in changing the line spacing in a document.
3. Describe the four types of text alignment.
4. Explain how to indent a paragraph 1 inch or more from the left margin.
5. Describe a situation in which you would use the Format Painter.
6. Explain how to transform a series of short paragraphs into a numbered list.
7. Explain how to add underlining to a word as you type it.
8. True or False: Before you can take full advantage of the Research task pane, your computer must be connected to the Internet.

Tutorial Summary

In this tutorial you learned how to use the Spelling and Grammar checker, select parts of a document, delete text, and move text within a document. You also learned how to find and replace text. Next, you focused on formatting a document, including changing margins and line spacing, aligning text, indenting paragraphs, using the Format Painter, changing the font and font size, and emphasizing text with bold, underlining, and italic styles. Finally, you learned how to add a comment to a document, preview formatted text, and look up information using the Research task pane.

Key Terms

¶	cut and paste	portrait orientation
1.5 line spacing	double spacing	ragged
alignment	drag and drop	Replace command
automatic page break	Find command	Research task pane
bullet	Format Painter	right alignment
center alignment	hanging indent	right indent
Clipboard	justified alignment	sans serif font
Clipboard task pane	landscape orientation	select
comment	left alignment	selection bar
copy	paragraph	serif font
copy and paste	paragraph symbol (¶)	single spacing
cut	paste	toggle button

Apply the skills you learned in the tutorial using the same case scenario.

Review Assignments

Data File needed for the Review Assignments: Statmnt.doc

Now that you have completed the Tree FAQ document, Marilee asks you to help her create a statement summarizing customer accounts for Long Meadow Gardens' wholesale nursery. She would also like you to create a document that contains contact information for Long Meadow Gardens. Remember to use the Undo and Redo buttons as you work to correct any errors.

1. Open the file **Statmnt** located in the Tutorial.02\Review folder included with your Data Files, and then check your screen to make sure your settings match those in the tutorial.
2. Save the document as **Monthly Statement** in the same folder.
3. Change the left and right margins to 1.5 inches using the Page Setup dialog box.
4. Make all edits and formatting changes shown in Figure 2-34, and then save your work.

Figure 2-34

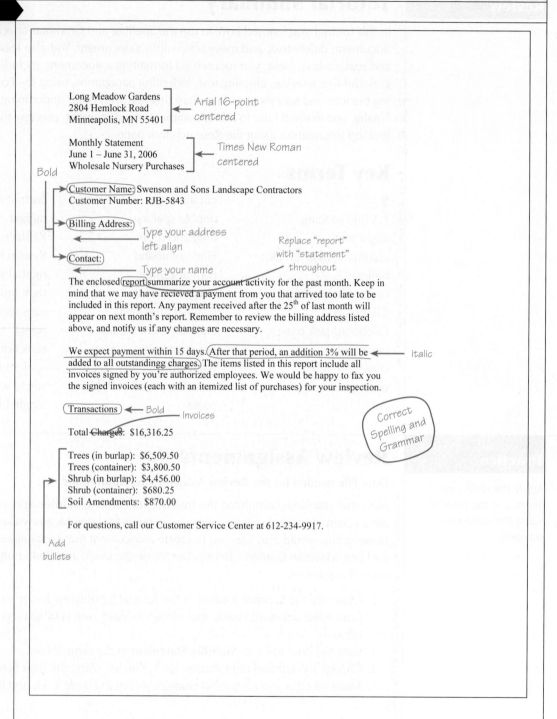

Long Meadow Gardens
2804 Hemlock Road
Minneapolis, MN 55401 ← *Arial 16-point centered*

Monthly Statement
June 1 – June 31, 2006
Wholesale Nursery Purchases ← *Times New Roman centered*

Bold

Customer Name: Swenson and Sons Landscape Contractors
Customer Number: RJB-5843

Billing Address:
Type your address left align

Contact: *Replace "report" with "statement" throughout*
Type your name

The enclosed report summarize your account activity for the past month. Keep in mind that we may have recieved a payment from you that arrived too late to be included in this report. Any payment received after the 25th of last month will appear on next month's report. Remember to review the billing address listed above, and notify us if any changes are necessary.

We expect payment within 15 days. After that period, an addition 3% will be added to all outstandingg charges. The items listed in this report include all invoices signed by you're authorized employees. We would be happy to fax you the signed invoices (each with an itemized list of purchases) for your inspection. ← *italic*

Transactions ← *Bold* *Invoices*

Total Charges: $16,316.25

Correct Spelling and Grammar

Trees (in burlap): $6,509.50
Trees (container): $3,800.50
Shrub (in burlap): $4,456.00
Shrub (container): $680.25
Soil Amendments: $870.00

For questions, call our Customer Service Center at 612-234-9917.

Add bullets

5. Proofread the document carefully to check for any additional errors. Look for and correct two errors that were not reported when you used the Spelling and Grammar checker.

6. Remove any Smart Tags in the document.

7. Move the last sentence of the document (which begins "For questions, call . . . ") to create a new paragraph, just above the heading "Transactions."

8. Select the Transactions portion of the document, from the heading "Transactions" down to the end of the document. Increase the indentation by 0.5 inch.

9. Open the Clipboard task pane. Select the company name and address at the top of the document and copy it to the Clipboard. Then copy the Customer Service Center phone number (above Transactions) to the Clipboard.

10. Open a new, blank document. Type your name on the first line, and then "Customer Service Center" on the next line. Move the insertion point to the third line. Open the Clipboard task pane, and then click the company address to insert this information at the insertion point. Be sure the insertion point is below the address, and then click the phone number to insert it in the document. Notice that text inserted from the Clipboard retains its original formatting, though the alignment may not carry over perfectly.

11. Left-align any centered text, clear the contents of the Clipboard task pane, close the task pane, and print the document.

12. Switch to Print Layout view. Then select the company name and insert the following comment: "Marilee, please let me know how you want this document formatted."

13. Save the document as **Customer Service Contact** in the Tutorial.02\Review folder. Close the document.

14. Save the Monthly Statement document, and then preview and print it.

15. Select the term "Amendments," which appears in the bulleted list at the end of the document. Open the Research task pane and look up the definition of "amendment." *Note:* you must have an active Internet connection to complete this step.

16. Type an asterisk (*) after "Amendments," and then on a blank line at the end of the document type an asterisk (*) followed by the definition of "amendment." After the definition include a sentence indicating that the definition is taken from the Encarta Dictionary.

17. Close the Research task pane and the Reviewing toolbar, save the Monthly Statement document, and then close it.

Case Problem 1

Apply

Apply the skills you learned to create a one-page advertising brochure.

Data File needed for this Case Problem: Tribune.doc

Blue Ridge Tribune The *Blue Ridge Tribune* is a student-run newspaper published through the Blue Ridge College Student Services Association. The newspaper is distributed around campus each Friday. The online version of the newspaper is posted on the Blue Ridge College Web site. Local businesses have a long-established tradition of advertising in the print version of the newspaper, and the paper's advertising manager, Noah McCormick, would like to ensure that this same tradition carries over to the online newspaper. When he sends out the monthly statements to his print advertisers, he would like to include a one-page brochure encouraging them to purchase an online ad. He typed the text about online advertising that is currently found on the Blue Ridge Tribune Web site and saved it as unformatted text in a Word document.

1. Open the file **Tribune** located in the Tutorial.02\Cases folder included with your Data Files, and save the file as **Tribune Brochure** in the same folder.

2. Correct any spelling or grammar errors. Make sure the right correction is selected in the Suggestions list box before you click Change.

3. Proofread for other errors, such as words that are spelled correctly but used incorrectly.
4. In the second to last sentence, replace "the BRT Advertising Office" with your name.
5. Change the right margin to 1.5 inches and the left margin to 2 inches.
6. Format the entire document in 12-point Times New Roman font.
7. Format the four paragraphs below "Did you know?" as a bulleted list.
8. Drag the third bullet (which begins "You can include . . . ") up to make it the first bullet in the bulleted list.
9. Format the first line of the document using a font, font size, and alignment of your choice. Use bold or italic for emphasis.
10. Format the entire document using 1.5 line spacing.
11. Save your work, preview the document, and then switch back to Normal view to make any changes you think necessary.
12. Print the document and then return to the Print Preview window. Open the Page Setup dialog box and switch to Landscape orientation. (Don't change any margin settings.) Observe the change in the Print Preview window.
13. Save the document as **Tribune Brochure Landscape** in the Tutorial.02\Cases folder and print it.
14. Switch to Print Layout view, and add a comment to the first line (*Blue Ridge Tribune*) asking Noah if he would like you to leave a printed copy of the brochure in his mailbox.
15. As Noah reviews the brochure, he wonders if the word "Web" should actually be capitalized. Use the Research task pane to look up "Web" in the Encarta Dictionary. In the first definition, you can see that "Web" is short for "World Wide Web." You will use this information to explain to Noah that indeed Web should be capitalized. Close the Research task pane.
16. Close the Reviewing toolbar, save, and then close the document.

Case Problem 2

Apply

Use your skills to format the summary document shown in Figure 2-35.

Data File needed for this Case Problem: Moths.doc

Hamilton Polytechnic Institute Finn Hansen is an associate researcher in the Department of Entomology at Hamilton Polytechnic Institute. He is working on a nationwide program that aims to slow the spread of a devastating forest pest, the gypsy moth. He has created a one-page document that will be used as part of a campaign to inform the public about current efforts to manage gypsy moths in North America. Format the document by completing the following steps.

1. Open the file **Moths** located in the Tutorial.02\Cases folder included with your Data Files, and then check your screen to make sure your settings match those in the tutorials.
2. Save the file as **Gypsy Moth Management** in the same folder.
3. Format the document as shown in Figure 2-35.

Figure 2-35

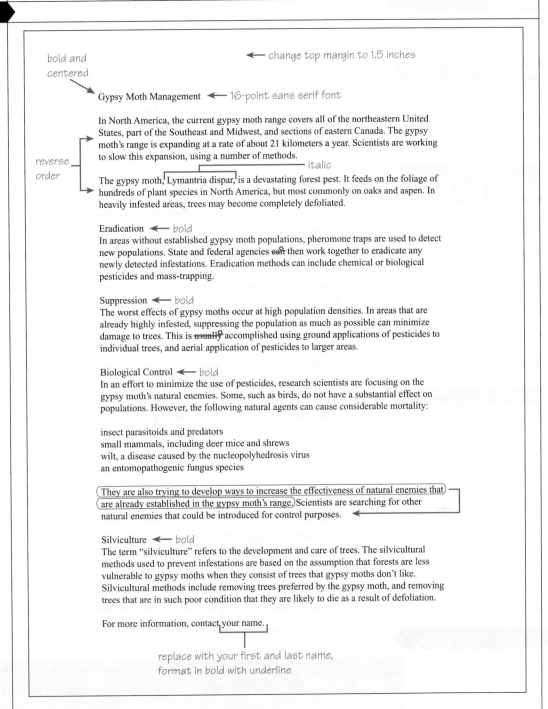

Explore

4. Change the left margin using the ruler, as follows:
   a. Make sure the horizontal ruler is displayed and the document is shown in Normal view.
   b. Select the entire document.
   c. Position the pointer on the small gray square on the ruler at the left margin. A ScreenTip with the words "Left Indent" appears.
   d. Press and hold down the mouse button. A vertical dotted line appears in the document window, indicating the current left margin. Drag the margin right to the 0.5-inch mark on the ruler, and then release the mouse button. Click anywhere to deselect the document.

Explore

5. Select the list of the four natural agents that can cause mortality in gypsy moths (in the "Biological Control" section), click Format on the menu bar, and then use the Bullets and Numbering dialog box to create a bulleted list using a square as the bullet symbol.

Explore

6. Select the headings "Eradication", "Suppression", "Biological Control", and "Silviculture". Press Ctrl+I to format the selected text in italic.
7. Use the Spelling and Grammar checker to make corrections as needed, proofread for additional errors, save, and preview the document.
8. Print the document, and then close it.

Case Problem 3

Challenge

Expand your formatting skills to create a resume for an aspiring editor.

Data File needed for this Case Problem: Resume.doc

Educational Publishing   Elena Pelliterri has over a decade of experience in education. She worked as a writing teacher, and then as a college supervisor of student teachers. Now she would like to pursue a career as sales representative for a company that publishes textbooks and other educational materials. She has asked you to edit and format her resume. Complete the resume by completing the following steps. The steps show quotation marks around text you type; do not include the quotation marks.

1. Open the file **Resume** located in the Tutorial.02\Cases folder included with your Data Files, and then check your screen to make sure your settings match those in the tutorials.
2. Save the file as **Formatted Resume** in the same folder.

Explore

3. Read the comment inserted at the first line of the document. Right-click the comment (point to the comment in the right margin and press the right mouse button), and then click Delete Comment on the shortcut menu.
4. Switch to Normal view, search for the text "your name", and replace it with your first and last name.
5. Replace all occurrences of "Aroyo" with "Arroyo".
6. Use the Spelling and Grammar checker to correct any errors in the document. Note that this document contains text that the Spelling and Grammar checker might consider sentence fragments but that are acceptable in a resume.
7. Delete the word "traveling" from the sentence below the "OBJECTIVE" heading.
8. Format the resume as described in Figure 2-36. Use one sans serif font and one serif font throughout. Be sure to pick fonts that look professional and are easy to read. Use the Format Painter to copy formatting as necessary.

Figure 2-36

Resume Element	Format
Name "Elena Pelliterri"	18-point, sans serif font, bold, with underline
Address, phone number, and e-mail address	12-point, sans serif font, bold
Uppercase headings (OBJECTIVE, EXPERIENCE, etc.)	12-point, serif font, bold, italic
Subheadings below EXPERIENCE, which begin "Rio Mesa College..." and "Middleton Public Schools..."	12-point, serif font, bold
Lists of teaching experience, educational history, and so on, below the resume headings and subheadings	12-point, serif font, bulleted list

9. Reorder the two items under the "COMPUTER SKILLS" heading so that the second item becomes the first.

Explore

10. Experiment with two special paragraph alignment options: first line and hanging. First, select the two bulleted items under the subheading "Middleton Public Schools." Click the Bullets button on the Formatting toolbar to remove the bulleted list format. Next, click Format on the menu bar, click Paragraph, and then click the Indents and Spacing tab. Click the Special list arrow in the Paragraph dialog box, and notice the special alignment options. Experiment with both the First line and the Hanging options. When you are finished, return the document to its original format by choosing the (none) option, and then reapplying the bulleted list format.

11. Save and preview the document.

12. Print the document and close it.

Explore

13. The Research task pane provides access to a variety of resources. Some (such as the Encarta Dictionary) are free, while others (such as the Encarta Encyclopedia) require you to pay a subscription fee. After you find the information you need in the Research task pane, you can copy and paste it into your document. Keep in mind that you must always cite your source when you use copyrighted material, such as the definitions from the Encarta Dictionary. To practice using the Research task pane, open a new, blank document, connect your computer to the Internet (if necessary), and open the Research task pane. Change the document's Zoom setting to 75% so you can see the entire document next to the Research task pane. Type the word "publishing" in the Search for text box, click the list arrow below the Search for text box, and select an option that interests you. Experiment by clicking topics in the Research task pane. To display a topic more fully, click the box that contains a plus sign (to the left of the topic). In some cases, when you click a topic, Internet Explorer opens (with the Research task pane on the left) to display more information.

Explore

14. When you are finished experimenting, close Internet Explorer, if necessary, and return to the Word window. Click the list arrow below the Search for text box and select Encarta Dictionary: English (North America). Scroll down and then drag the mouse pointer to select the definition that begins "the trade, profession, or activity…", press Ctrl+C to copy the information to the Clipboard, click in the document, and then use the Paste button to paste the definition into the document. Add some text explaining that you copied the definition from the Encarta Dictionary to demonstrate how to copy and paste information from the Research task pane.

15. Save the document as **Encarta Definition** in the Tutorial.02\Cases folder, print it, close the Research task pane, and close the document.

Case Problem 4

Challenge

Explore new ways to format an Invoice Authorization Form for a high-tech computer company.

Data File needed for this Case Problem: Form.doc

Gygs and Bytes Melissa Martinez is the purchasing manager for Gygs and Bytes, a wholesale distributor of computer parts based in Portland, Oregon. Most of the company's business is conducted via catalog or through the company's Web site, but local customers sometimes drop by to pick up small orders. In the past Melissa has had problems determining which of her customers' employees were authorized to sign credit invoices. To avoid confusion, she has asked all local customers to complete a form listing employees who are authorized to sign invoices. She plans to place the completed forms in a binder at the main desk, so the receptionist at Gygs and Bytes can find the information quickly.

1. Open the file **Form** located in Tutorial.02\Cases folder included with your Data Files, and save the file as **Invoice Authorization Form** in the same folder.

2. Correct any spelling or grammar errors. Ignore the name of the company "Gygs and Bytes."

Explore

3. When you type Web addresses or e-mail addresses in a document, Word automatically formats them as links. When you click a Web address formatted as a link, Windows automatically opens a Web browser (such as Microsoft Internet Explorer) and, if your computer is connected to the Internet, displays that Web page. If you click an e-mail address formatted as a link, Windows opens a program in which you can type an e-mail message. The address you clicked is automatically included as the recipient of the e-mail. You'll see how this works as you add a Web address and e-mail address to the statement. In the address at the top of the document, click at the end of the ZIP code, add a new line, and then type the address for the company's Web site: **www.G&B.com**. When you are finished, press Enter. Notice that as soon as you press Enter, Word formats the address in blue with an underline, marking it as a link. Move the mouse pointer over the link and read the ScreenTip. The company is fictitious and does not have a Web site.

Explore

4. In the line below the Web address, type G&B@worldlink.com and then press Enter. Word formats the e-mail address as a link. Press and hold the Ctrl key and then click the e-mail link. Your default e-mail program opens, displaying a window where you could type an e-mail message to Gygs and Bytes. (If your computer is not set up for e-mail, close any error messages that open.) Close the e-mail window without saving any changes. The link is now formatted in a color other than blue, indicating that the link has been clicked.

5. Change the top and left margins to 1.5 inches.

6. Center the first six lines of the document (containing the form title and the company addresses).

7. Format the first line of the document (the form title) in 16-point Arial, with italic.

8. Format lines 2 through 6 (the addresses, including the Web and e-mail addresses) in 12-point Arial.

Explore

9. Replace all instances of G&B, except the first two (in the Web and e-mail addresses), with the complete company name, Gygs and Bytes. In the Find and Replace dialog box, select the Match case check box to ensure that the replacement text is inserted exactly as you typed it in the Replace with text box. (Be sure to use the Find Next button to skip an instance of the search text.)

10. Format the blank ruled lines as a numbered list. Customers will use these blank lines to write in the names of authorized employees.

Explore

11. Format the entire document using 1.5 spacing. Then triple-space the numbered list (with the blank lines) and the Signature and Title lines as follows:
    a. Select the numbered list with the blank lines.
    b. Triple-space the selected text using the Line Spacing button on the Formatting toolbar.
    c. Select the "Signed:" and the "Title:" lines, and then press F4.

12. Save the document.

13. Drag "Customer Name:" up to position it before "Customer Number:".

Explore

14. Select "Customer Name:", "Customer Number:", and "Address:". Press Ctrl+B to format the selected text in bold. Note that it is sometimes easier to use this keyboard shortcut instead of the Bold button on the Formatting toolbar.

15. Delete the phrase "all employees" and replace it with "all authorized personnel".

Explore

16. Select the phrase "all authorized personnel will be required to show a photo I.D." Press Ctrl+I to format the selected text in italic. It is sometimes easier to use this keyboard shortcut instead of the Italic button on the Formatting toolbar.

17. Insert your name in the form to the right of "Customer Name:". Format your name without bold, if necessary.

18. Insert your address, left aligned, without bold, below the heading "Address:".

Explore

Explore

Explore

19. Click the Print Preview button on the Standard toolbar to check your work.
20. Click the Shrink to Fit button on the Print Preview toolbar to reduce the entire document to one page. Word reduces the font sizes slightly in order to fit the entire form on one page. Close the Print Preview window and save your work.
21. Use the Print command on the File menu to open the Print dialog box. Print two copies of the document by changing the Number of copies setting in the Print dialog box.
22. You can find out useful statistics about your documents by using the Word Count command on the Tools menu. Use this command to determine the number of words, characters (not including spaces), and paragraphs in the document, and then write these statistics in the upper-right corner of the printout.
23. Save and close the document.

Internet Assignments

Research

Go to the Web to find information you can use to create documents.

The purpose of the Internet Assignments is to challenge you to find information on the Internet that you can use to work effectively with this software. The actual assignments are updated and maintained on the Course Technology Web site. Log on to the Internet and use your Web browser to go to the Student Online Companion for New Perspectives Office 2003 at **www.course.com/np/office2003**. Click the Internet Assignments link, and then navigate to the assignments for this tutorial.

SAM Assessment and Training

Assess

If you have a SAM user profile, you may have access to hands-on instruction, practice, and assessment of the skills covered in this tutorial. Log in to your SAM account and go to your assignments page to see what your instructor has assigned.

Review

Quick Check Answers

Session 2.1

1. Click at the beginning of the document, and then click the Spelling and Grammar button on the Standard toolbar. In the Spelling and Grammar dialog box, review each error, which is displayed in color. Grammatical errors appear in green; spelling errors appear in red. Review the possible corrections in the Suggestions list box. To accept a suggested correction, click it in the Suggestions list box, and then click Change to make the correction and continue searching the document for errors.
2. True
3. a. double-click the word
   b. click at the beginning of the block, and then drag until the entire block is selected
   c. double-click in the selection bar next to the paragraph, or triple-click in the paragraph
4. a. the blank space in the left margin area of the Document window that allows you to select entire lines or large blocks of text easily
   b. the process of moving text by first selecting the text, then pressing and holding the mouse button while moving the text to its new location in the document, and finally releasing the mouse button
   c. a command on the Edit menu that is used to search for a set of characters and replace them with a different set of characters

5. False

6. Cut and paste removes the selected material from its original location and inserts it in a new location. Copy and paste makes a copy of the selected material and inserts the copy in a new location; the original material remains in its original location.

7. Click Edit on the menu bar, click Replace, type the search text in the Find what text box, type the replacement text in the Replace with text box, click Find Next, Replace, or click Replace all.

Session 2.2

1. The default top and bottom margins are 1 inch. The default left and right margins are 1.25 inches.

2. Select the text you want to change, click the Line Spacing list arrow on the Formatting toolbar, and then click the line spacing option you want. Or select the text, and then press Ctrl+1 for single spacing, Ctrl+5 for 1.5 line spacing, or Ctrl+2 for double spacing.

3. Left alignment: each line flush left, ragged right; Right alignment: each line flush right, ragged left; Center: each line centered, ragged right and left.; Justify: each line flush left and flush right.

4. To indent a paragraph, place the insertion point in the paragraph and then click the Increase Indent button on the Formatting toolbar. Each click indents the text .5 inches, so to indent 1 inch, click the button two times. Use the horizontal ruler to confirm that the text is indented to the correct position.

5. You might use the Format Painter to copy the formatting of a heading to the other headings in a document.

6. Select the paragraphs, and then click the Numbering button on the Formatting toolbar.

7. Click the Underline button on the Formatting toolbar, type the word, and then click the Underline button again to turn off underlining.

8. True

New Perspectives on
Microsoft® Office
Excel 2003

Read This Before You Begin: Tutorials 1–3

To the Student

Data Files

To complete Excel Tutorials 1 through 3, you need the starting student Data Files. Your instructor will either provide you with these Data Files or ask you to obtain them yourself.

Excel Tutorials 1 through 3 require the folders shown in the next column to complete the Tutorials, Review Assignments, and Case Problems. You will need to copy these folders from a file server, a standalone computer, or the Web to the drive and folder where you will be storing your Data Files. Your instructor will tell you which computer, drive letter, and folder(s) contain the files you need. You can also download the files by going to www.course.com; see the inside back or front cover for more information on downloading the files, or ask your instructor or technical support person for assistance.

If you are storing your Data Files on floppy disks, you will need **two** blank, formatted, high-density disks for these tutorials. Label your disks as shown, and place on them the folders indicated.

▼ **Excel 2003: Data Disk 1**

Tutorial.01 folder
Tutorial.02 folder

▼ **Excel 2003: Data Disk 2**

Tutorial.03 folder

When you begin a tutorial, refer to the Student Data Files section at the bottom of the tutorial opener page, which indicates which folders and files you need for the tutorial. Each end-of-tutorial exercise also indicates the files you need to complete that exercise.

Course Labs

The Excel tutorials feature an interactive Course Lab to help you understand spreadsheet concepts. There are Lab Assignments at the end of Tutorial 1 that relate to this lab. Contact your instructor or technical support person for assistance in accessing the lab.

To the Instructor

The Data Files and Course Labs are available on the Instructor Resources CD for this title. Follow the instructions in the Help file on the CD to install the programs to your network or standalone computer. See the "To the Student" section above for information on how to set up the Data Files that accompany this text.

You are granted a license to copy the Data Files and Course Labs to any computer or computer network used by students who have purchased this book.

System Requirements

If you are going to work through this book using your own computer, you need:

• **Computer System** Microsoft Windows 2000, Windows XP or higher must be installed on your computer. These tutorials assume a typical installation of Microsoft Excel 2003.

• **Data Files** You will not be able to complete the tutorials or exercises in this book using your own computer until you have the necessary starting Data Files.

• **Course Labs** See your instructor or technical support person to obtain the Course Lab software for use on your own computer.

Objectives

Session 1.1
- Learn about spreadsheets and how they work
- Identify major components of the Excel window
- Navigate within and between worksheets
- Enter text, dates, data, and formulas into a worksheet
- Change the size of a column or row

Session 1.2
- Select and move cell ranges
- Calculate totals with AutoSum
- Insert and delete a column or row
- Work in edit mode
- Undo an action
- Insert, move, and rename a worksheet
- Check the spelling in a workbook
- Preview and print a workbook
- Display the formulas within a worksheet

Lab

Spreadsheets

Using Excel to Manage Data

Creating a Sales Order Report

Case

Dalton Food Co-op

Sandra Dalton and her husband, Kevin, own a farm in northern Florida. Recently, Sandra has been selling produce to local families to earn extra income. When she started, Sandra kept a paper record of customer orders, and all of the data was entered into a paper ledger with the calculations done on a tabletop calculator. Several months ago, Sandra and Kevin purchased a computer for the co-op. Bundled with the other software installed on the computer was a copy of **Microsoft Office Excel 2003** (or simply **Excel**), a computer program used to enter, analyze, and present quantitative data.

Sandra, who handles most of the financial aspects of the business, has been using Excel for several months, but as the business continues to grow and its busy season approaches, she has asked you to help. She wants you to use an Excel workbook to keep track of orders recently made at the Dalton Food Co-op.

Student Data Files

▼**Tutorial.01**

▽ Tutorial folder

(no starting Data Files)

▽ Review folder

(no starting Data Files)

▽ Cases folder

Altac1.xls
Halley1.xls
Site1.xls

Session 1.1

Spreadsheets

Introducing Excel

Before you begin working with the recent orders at the co-op, you need to understand some of the key terms and concepts associated with a program such as Excel.

Understanding Spreadsheets

Excel is a computerized spreadsheet. A **spreadsheet** is an important tool used for analyzing and reporting information. Spreadsheets are often used in business for budgeting, inventory management, and decision making. For example, an accountant might use a paper-based spreadsheet like the one shown in Figure 1-1 to record a company's estimated and actual monthly cash flow.

Figure 1-1 ▷ A sample spreadsheet

Cash Flow Comparison
Actual versus Budget

	Jan-06	
	Estimated	Actual
Cash balance(start of month)	$ 1,500.00	$ 1,500.00
Receipts		
Cash sales	1700.00	1852.00
Cash expenditures		
Advertising	200.00	211.00
Wages	900.00	900.00
Supplies	100.00	81.00
Total cash expenditures	1200.00	1192.00
Net cash flow	500.00	660.00
Cash balance(end of month)	$ 2,000.00	$ 2,160.00

In this spreadsheet, the accountant has recorded the estimated and actual cash flow for the month of January. Each line, or row, in this spreadsheet displays a different cash flow value. Each column contains the predicted or actual values, or text that describes those values. The accountant has also entered the total cash expenditures, net cash flow, and closing cash balance for the month, perhaps having used a calculator to do the calculations.

Figure 1-2 shows the same spreadsheet in Excel. The spreadsheet is now laid out in a grid in which the rows and columns are easily apparent. As you will see later, calculations are also part of this electronic spreadsheet, so that total cash expenditures, net cash flow, and cash balances are calculated automatically rather than entered manually. When you change an entry in the electronic spreadsheet, the spreadsheet automatically updates any calculated values based on the entry. You can also use an electronic spreadsheet to perform a **what-if analysis** in which you change one or more of the values in the worksheet and then examine the recalculated values to determine the effect of the change. (You will have a chance to explore this feature at the end of the tutorial.) So, an electronic spreadsheet provides more flexibility in entering and analyzing your data than the paper version.

The same spreadsheet in Excel ◄ **Figure 1-2**

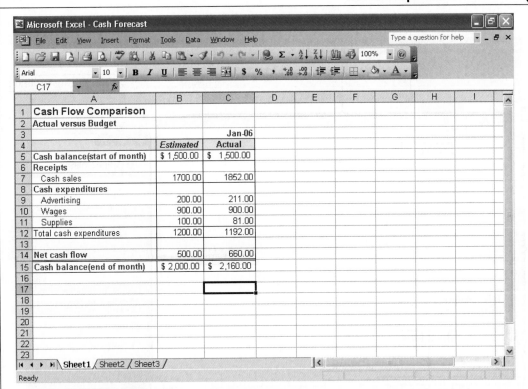

Excel stores electronic spreadsheets in files called **workbooks**. Each workbook is made up of individual **worksheets**, or **sheets**, just as a spiral-bound ledger, which an accountant would use, is made up of sheets of paper. You will learn more about multiple worksheets later in the tutorial. For now, keep in mind that the terms *worksheet* and *sheet* are often used interchangeably.

Parts of the Excel Window

Excel displays workbooks within a window that contains many tools for entering, editing, and viewing data. You will learn about some of these tools after starting Excel. By default, Excel opens with a blank workbook.

To start Excel:

1. Click the **Start** button on the taskbar, point to **All Programs**, point to **Microsoft Office**, and then click **Microsoft Office Excel 2003**. The Excel window opens. See Figure 1-3.

Figure 1-3 | **Parts of the Excel window**

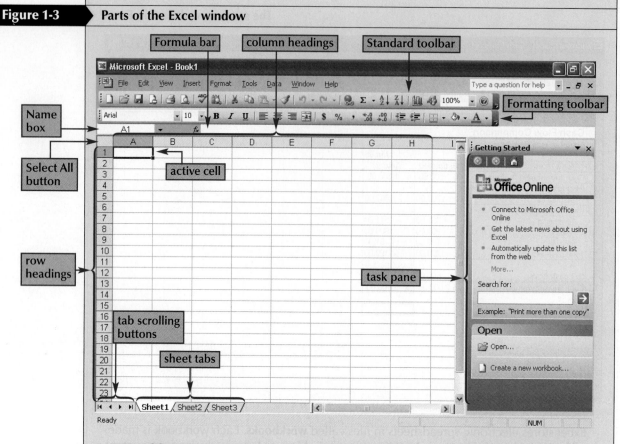

Trouble? If you don't see the Microsoft Office Excel 2003 option on the Microsoft Office submenu, look for it in a different submenu or as an option on the All Programs menu. If you still cannot find the Microsoft Office Excel 2003 option, ask your instructor or technical support person for help.

The Excel window contains many of the components that you find in other Windows programs, including a title bar, a menu bar, scroll bars, and a status bar. The Excel window also contains features that are unique to Excel. Within the Excel program window is another window, referred to as the **workbook window** or **worksheet window**. The worksheet window provides a grid of **columns** and **rows**, and the intersection of a column and row is called a **cell**. Each cell is identified by a **cell reference**, which is its column and row location. For example, the cell reference B6 indicates that the cell is located where column B and row 6 intersect. The column letter is always first in the cell reference: B6 is a correct reference; 6B is not. The cell in which you are working is called the **active cell**. Excel identifies the active cell by outlining it with a dark border. In Figure 1-3, cell A1 is the active cell. Notice that the cell reference for the active cell appears in the **Name box** next to the **Formula bar**. You can change the active cell by selecting another cell in the worksheet. As you review the layout of the Excel window shown in Figure 1-3, refer to Figure 1-4 for a description of each component.

Excel window components ◀ **Figure 1-4**

Feature	Description
Active cell	The cell in which you are currently working. A dark border outlining the cell identifies the active cell.
Column headings	The letters that appear along the top of the worksheet window. Columns are listed alphabetically from A to IV (a total of 256 possible columns).
Formula bar	The bar located immediately below the toolbars that displays the contents of the active cell. As you type or edit data, the changes appear in the Formula bar.
Name box	The box that displays the cell reference, or column and row location, of the active cell in the workbook window.
Row headings	The numbers that appear along the left side of the worksheet window. Rows are numbered consecutively from 1 to 65,536.
Select All button	Square button located at the intersection of the column and row headings that you click to select the entire contents of the worksheet.
Sheet tabs	Tabs located at the bottom of each worksheet in the workbook that display the names of the sheets. To move between worksheets, click the appropriate sheet tab.
Task pane	The pane that provides access to frequently used tasks. When you start Excel, the Getting Started task pane appears. The task pane disappears once you open a workbook. There are several task-specific panes available in Excel.
Tab scrolling buttons	Series of buttons located to the left of the sheet tabs that you can click to move between worksheets in the workbook.
Toolbars	Toolbars that provide quick access to commonly used commands. The Standard toolbar contains buttons for the most frequently used program commands, such as Save and Print. The Formatting toolbar contains buttons used to format the appearance of the workbook, such as Bold and Italics. Additional toolbars are available.

Now that you are familiar with the basic layout of an Excel window, you can try moving around within the workbook.

Navigating a Worksheet

Excel provides several ways of moving around within a worksheet. You can use your mouse to click a cell to make it the active cell, or you can use the vertical and horizontal scroll bars to display the area of the worksheet containing the cell you want to make active. You can also navigate a worksheet by using your keyboard. Figure 1-5 describes some of these keyboard shortcuts that Excel provides so you can move from cell to cell within the worksheet quickly and easily.

Shortcut keys for navigating a worksheet ◀ **Figure 1-5**

Keystroke	Action
↑, ↓, ←, →	Moves the active cell up, down, left, or right one cell
Ctrl + Home	Moves the active cell to cell A1
Ctrl + End	Moves to the last cell in the worksheet that contains data
Enter	Moves the active cell down one cell, or moves to the start of the next row in the selected range of cells
F5	Opens the Go To dialog box, in which you specify the cell you want to move to
Home	Moves the active cell to column A of the current row
Page Up, Page Down	Moves the active cell up or down one full screen
Tab, Shift + Tab	Moves the active cell to the right or left one cell

Try navigating the worksheet now.

To move around in the worksheet:

▶ 1. Click the **Close** button ☒ in the task pane to close it because you will not be using it in this session. The active cell is A1. The cell A1 is surrounded by a black border, indicating it is the active cell, and the Name box displays the cell reference A1.

▶ 2. With cell A1 the active cell, press the ↓ key on your keyboard four times to move to cell A5, and then press the → key twice to make cell C5 the active cell, as shown in Figure 1-6. Note that the column and row headings are highlighted and the cell reference appears in the Name box.

| Figure 1-6 | Making cell C5 the active cell |

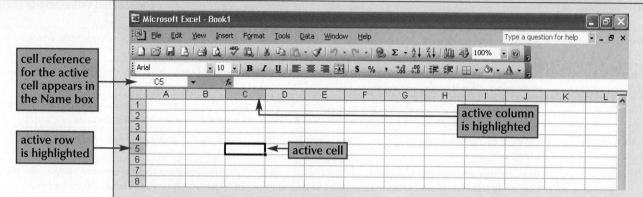

cell reference for the active cell appears in the Name box

active column is highlighted

active row is highlighted

active cell

▶ 3. Press the **Enter** key to move down one cell, and the press the **Tab** key to move to the right one cell. The active cell is now D6.

▶ 4. Press the **Page Down** key to move the display down one screen. The active cell should now be cell D29. If the actual number of columns and rows displayed on your screen differs from that shown in Figure 1-2, the active cell on your screen might not be cell D29. You will learn more about working with the number of columns and rows on your screen later in this tutorial; for now the active cell on your screen should be a screen full of rows down the worksheet.

▶ 5. Press the **Page Up** key to move the display back up one screen, making cell D6 the active cell again.

▶ 6. Press the **Home** key to move to the first cell in the current row, and then press the **Ctrl + Home** keys to make cell A1 active.

You will probably use the keyboard keys to navigate a worksheet the most frequently, but there will also be situations in which you will want to go directly to a cell on your worksheet. Although you can use the Page Up and Page Down keys or use the scroll bars, you have two other options: the Name box and the Go To dialog box. You can just click in the Name box and type the cell reference you want to go to, or you can open the Go To dialog box from any location in the worksheet by pressing the F5 function key. Try using these methods to navigate the worksheet.

To use the Go To dialog box and Name box:

▶ 1. Press the **F5** key to open the Go To dialog box, type **K55** in the Reference text box, and then click the **OK** button to make cell K55 the active cell.

▶ 2. Click in the **Name** box, type **E6**, and then press the **Enter** key to make cell E6 the active cell.

Navigating Between Worksheets

By default, a new Excel workbook contains three worksheets, labeled Sheet1, Sheet2, and Sheet3. Each sheet can be used to display different information. To move from one sheet to another, click the sheet tabs at the bottom of each sheet.

To move between worksheets:

1. Click the **Sheet2** tab. Sheet2, which is blank, appears in the workbook window. Notice that the Sheet2 tab is now white with the name "Sheet2" in a bold font. This is a visual indicator that Sheet2 is the active worksheet.

2. Click the **Sheet3** tab to move to the next worksheet in the workbook.

3. Click the **Sheet1** tab to make it the active worksheet.

Now that you have some basic skills navigating through a worksheet and a workbook, you can begin work on Sandra's worksheet.

Developing a Worksheet

Before you begin to enter data in a worksheet, you should think about the purpose of the worksheet and what will be needed to meet the challenge of that purpose. Effective worksheets are well planned and carefully designed. A well-designed worksheet should clearly identify its overall goal. It should present information in a clear, well-organized format and include all the data necessary to produce results that address the goal of the application. The process of developing a good worksheet includes the following planning and execution steps:

- Determine the worksheet's purpose, what it will include, and how it will be organized.
- Enter the data and formulas into the worksheet.
- Test the worksheet, and then edit the worksheet to correct any errors or to make modifications.
- Document the worksheet and format the worksheet's appearance.
- Save and print the complete worksheet.

To develop a worksheet that records orders made at the co-op, Sandra wants to develop a planning analysis sheet that will help her answer the following questions:

1. What is the goal of the worksheet? This helps to define its purpose or, in other words, the problem to solve.
2. What are the desired results? This information describes the output—the information required to help solve the problem.
3. What data is needed to calculate the results you want to see? This information is the input—data that must be entered.
4. What calculations are needed to produce the desired output? These calculations specify the formulas used in the worksheet.

After careful consideration of these questions, Sandra has developed the planning analysis sheet shown in Figure 1-7.

Figure 1-7   Planning analysis sheet

Planning Analysis Sheet
Author: Sandra Dalton, Dalton Food Co-op
Date: 4/26/2006

My goal
To develop a worksheet in which I can enter food co-op orders, calculating the total
quantity of the items ordered and the revenue generated.

What results do I need to see?
- A listing of each order made by customers
- The total amount of each order
- The total quantity of items ordered by all of the customers
- The total revenue generated by all of the orders

What data do I need?
- The customer's name and address
- The date of the order
- The item purchased by the customer
- The price of each item
- The quantity of items ordered by the customer

What calculations must be performed by the worksheet?
- The total amount of each order (= price of the item x the quantity ordered)
- The total quantity of items ordered (= sum of the order quantities)
- The total revenue generated by all of the orders (= sum of the total amount of each order)

Sandra also knows the information that needs to go into the worksheet, including titles, column headings, row labels, and data values. Figure 1-8 shows how Sandra wants the sales data laid out, based on a sampling of customer orders.

Figure 1-8   Sales data for co-op worksheet

Name	Address	Date	Item	Price	Qty	Total
Alison Wilkes	45 Lincoln Street Midtown, FL 80481	4/16/2006	Red Grapefruit	$14	2	
David Wu	315 Oak Lane Midtown, FL 80422	4/16/2006	Navel Oranges	$17	1	
Carl Ramirez	900 South Street Crawford, FL 81891	4/17/2006	Navel Oranges	$17	2	
Jerry Dawson	781 Tree Lane Midtown, FL 80313	4/18/2006	Deluxe Combo	$21	4	
TOTAL						

The first two columns contain the name and address of the person ordering items from the co-op. The Date and Item columns indicate the date that the order was placed and the item ordered. The Price column displays the price of the item. The Qty column indicates the quantity of each item ordered by the customer. The Total column will display the total amount of each order. The TOTAL row will display the total quantity of items ordered and the total revenue generated by all of the sales. With this information in hand, you are now ready to create Sandra's worksheet in Excel.

Entering Data into a Worksheet

A worksheet can contain the following types of data: text, numeric values, dates, and calculated values. A text entry is simply any combination of words, letters, and numbers, typically used to label key features of the worksheet. Numeric values are numbers on which calculations can be made. Numeric values do not contain alphabetic characters, but may contain characters such as commas, dollar signs, and percent signs. Dates are special numeric values recognized by Excel and can be used to determine date-related calculations. The power of Excel lies in the formulas that you can enter into the worksheet cells, whose calculated values are based on the text, dates, and numeric values entered into other cells in the workbook (or in more complicated cases, other workbooks). If those values are changed, the calculated values will also be changed.

Worksheet cells in Excel can also be formatted to improve or enhance the appearance of the cell contents or an entire worksheet. You'll learn about formatting later in Tutorial 3.

Entering Text

To insert text into a worksheet cell, you first make the cell active by using one of the navigation techniques discussed earlier, and then you type the text you want the cell to contain. Excel automatically aligns the text with the left edge of the cell.

First, you'll enter the column headings that Sandra wants across the top row of her worksheet.

To enter the column headings in row 1:

1. Press the **Ctrl + Home** keys to make cell A1 the active cell on the Sheet1 worksheet.

2. Type **Name** and then press the **Tab** key. Pressing the Tab key enters the text in the cell and moves the insertion point to the right to cell B1, making it the active cell.

3. Type **Address** in cell B1, and then press the **Tab** key again. Cell C1 becomes the active cell.

4. Enter the remaining column headings **Date**, **Item**, **Price**, **Qty**, and **Total** in cells C1 through G1. Press the **Enter** key after you type the text for cell G1. Figure 1-9 shows the column headings for the worksheet.

Entering text into the worksheet ◄ **Figure 1-9**

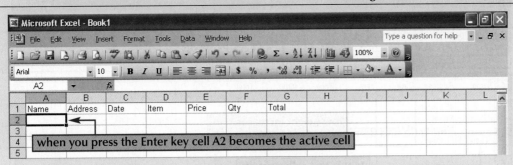

Trouble? If you make a mistake as you type, you can correct the error by clicking the cell and retyping the entry.

Note that when you press the Enter key, the active cell becomes cell A2, not cell G2. Excel recognizes that when you enter a row of data and then press the Enter key, you have completed the task of entering data in the current row, so the insertion point moves to the start of the next row. If you had started entering data in cell C1 rather than A1, pressing the Enter key would have made cell C2 the active cell.

Entering Several Lines of Text Within a Cell

In the next row, you'll enter actual sales information. One cell in this row contains the customer's address. In Sandra's records, this information is presented on two separate lines, with the street address on one line and the city, state, and ZIP code on the other. To place text on separate lines within the same cell, you press and hold the Alt key on the keyboard while pressing the Enter key.

Reference Window	**Entering Multiple Lines of Text Within a Cell**

- Click the cell in which you want to enter the text.
- Enter a line of text.
- Press and hold the Alt key, and then press the Enter key to move the insertion point to a new line within the cell.
- Enter the next line of text.
- Press the Alt + Enter keys for each new line of text you need to enter within the cell.

Try this technique now by entering the first customer's name and address.

To enter the address on two lines within a cell:

1. Verify that cell **A2** is the active cell, type **Alison Wilkes**, and then press the **Tab** key to move to column B, where you will enter the two-line address.

2. Type **45 Lincoln Street** in cell B2, but do *not* press the Tab or Enter key.

3. Press and hold the **Alt** key, and then press the **Enter** key to insert a line break, moving the insertion point to a new line within the cell.

4. Type **Midtown**, **FL 80481** on the second line of the cell, and then press the **Tab** key. Figure 1-10 shows the worksheet with the text you have entered so far.

Figure 1-10	Entering the customer name and address

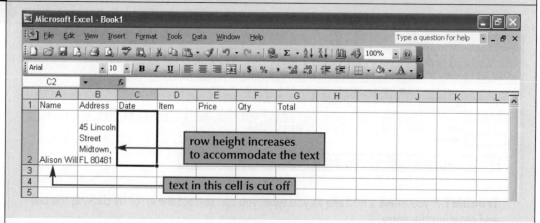

Excel has done a couple of things that you need to understand before entering more data. First, the name of the customer in cell A2 has been cut off, or truncated. When you enter more text than can be displayed within a cell, Excel will display the additional text in the cell or cells to the right as long as they are empty. If the cells to the right are not empty, Excel will truncate the display of the text when it encounters the first non-empty cell. The text itself is not affected. The complete name of the first customer is still entered in cell A2; it's just not displayed.

Second, the customer address in cell B2 does not extend into cell C2, even though that cell is empty. Instead, the height of row 2 has been increased to accommodate this text. If a cell contains multiple lines of text, Excel increases the height of the row to display all of the text entry. Note that the text in cell B2 "appears" to be on four lines, even though you entered the address on two lines. Excel wrapped the text in this way so that it would fit within the existing column width. Later in this session, you will learn how to adjust column widths and row heights to improve the worksheet's appearance.

Entering Dates

In Excel, dates are treated as numeric values, not text. This allows you to perform calculations with dates, such as determining the number of days between two dates. You'll learn how to work with date values in the next tutorial. For now, you need to know how to enter a date. You can enter a date using any of the following date formats, which are recognized by Excel:

- 4/16/2006
- 4/16/06
- 4-16-2006
- April 16, 2006
- 16-Apr-06

The appearance of a date, regardless of how you enter it in a cell, depends on the date format that has been set as the default in your version of Excel. For example, if you enter the date as the text string "April 26, 2006," Excel will automatically convert the entry to "26-Apr-2006" if the DD-MMM-YYYY format has been set as the default. You will learn about cell formats and date formats in Tutorial 3.

Sandra wants the date "4/16/2006" to appear in cell C2, so you will enter that next.

To insert the date in cell C2:

1. Verify that cell **C2** is the active cell.

2. Type **4/16/2006** and then press the **Tab** key.

   Trouble? If your computer is set up to display dates using a different date format, do not worry about their appearance at this time.

3. Type **Red Grapefruit** in cell D2, and then press the **Tab** key. Note that the text in cell D2 is completely displayed because, at this point, the cells to the right of D2 are still empty.

Entering Values

Values are numbers that represent a quantity of some type: the number of units in an inventory, stock prices, an exam score, and so on. Values can be numbers such as 378 and 25.275 or negative numbers such as –55.208. Values can also be expressed as currency such as $14.95 or as percentages such as 95%. Not all numbers are treated as values. For example, Excel treats a telephone number (1-800-555-8010) or a Social Security number (372-70-9654) as a text entry. As you type information into a cell, Excel determines whether the entry can be treated as a value, and if so, automatically right-aligns the value within the cell.

Next, you'll enter the price and quantity of the first order into cells E2 and F2.

To enter the price and quantity values:

1. Type **$14** in cell E2, and then press the **Tab** key.

2. Type **2** in cell F2, and then press the **Tab** key. Figure 1-11 shows the data for the first order. The last cell in the row is empty, but next you will enter a calculation that will give Sandra the total amount of the order.

Figure 1-11	Entering the price and quantity values

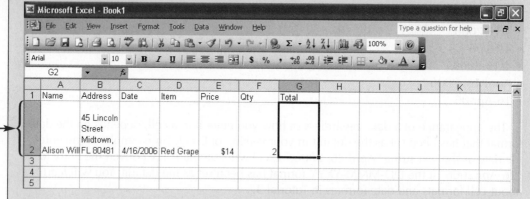

data for the first order entered

The remaining cell in this row will contain the total price of the order, which is equal to the price of the red grapefruit item multiplied by the quantity ordered. The total price of the first order is $14 multiplied by 2, or $28. Rather than entering this value into the cell, you'll let Excel calculate it for you by entering a formula.

Entering Formulas

The single most important reason for using a spreadsheet is to perform calculations on data. To accomplish that goal, you need to enter formulas. A **formula** is a mathematical expression that calculates a value. Excel formulas always begin with an equal sign (=) followed by an expression that describes the calculation to be done. A formula can contain one or more **arithmetic operators**, such as +, –, *, or /. For example, the formula =A1+A2 calculates the sum by adding the values of cells A1 and A2. Figure 1-12 gives examples of some other Excel formulas. Note that, by convention, cell references appear in uppercase letters, but this is not a requirement for Excel formulas. You can type the formula using either upper- or lowercase letters, and Excel will automatically convert the cell references to uppercase.

	Sample Excel formulas using arithmetic operators		Figure 1-12

Operation	Operator	Example	Description
Addition	+	=10+A5	Adds 10 to the value in cell A5
		=B1+B2+B3	Adds the values of cells B1, B2, and B3
Subtraction	–	=C9–B2	Subtracts the value in cell B2 from the value in cell C9
		=1–D2	Subtracts the value in cell D2 from 1
Multiplication	*	=C9*B9	Multiplies the value in cell C9 by the value in cell B9
		=E5*0.06	Multiplies the value in cell E5 by 0.06
Division	/	=C9/B9	Divides the value in cell C9 by the value in cell B9
		=D15/12	Divides the value in cell D15 by 12
Exponentiation	^	=B5^3	Raises the value in cell B5 to the third power
		=3^B5	Raises 3 to the power specified in cell B5

Entering a Formula

Reference Window

- Click the cell where you want the formula result to appear.
- Type = and then type the expression that calculates the value you want.
- For a formula that includes cell references, such as B2 or D78, type the cell reference, or use the mouse or arrow keys to select each cell.
- When the formula is complete, press the Enter key (or press the Tab key or click the Enter button on the Formula bar).

If an expression contains more than one arithmetic operator, Excel performs the calculation in the order of precedence. The **order of precedence** is a set of predefined rules that Excel follows to calculate a formula by determining which operator is applied first, which operator is applied second, and so forth. First, Excel performs exponentiation (^). Second, Excel performs multiplication (*) or division (/). Third, Excel performs addition (+) or subtraction (–).

For example, because multiplication has precedence over addition, the formula =3+4*5 results in the value *23*. If the expression contains two or more operators with the same level of precedence, Excel applies them from left to right in the expression. In the formula =4*10/8, Excel first multiplies *4* by *10* and then divides the result by *8* to produce the value *5*.

When building a formula, you must add parentheses to change the order of operations. Excel will calculate any expression contained within the parentheses before any other part of the formula. The formula =(3+4)*5 first calculates the value of *3+4* and then multiplies the total by *5*, resulting in the value *35*. (Note that without the parentheses, Excel would produce a value of *23*, as noted in the previous paragraph.) Figure 1-13 shows other examples of Excel formulas using the order of precedence rules.

Figure 1-13 ▶ **Examples illustrating order of precedence rules**

Formula (A1=50, B1=10, C1=5)	Order of precedence rule	Result
=A1+B1*C1	Multiplication before addition	100
=(A1+B1)*C1	Expression inside parentheses executed before expression outside	300
=A1/B1–C1	Division before subtraction	0
=A1/(B1–C1)	Expression inside parentheses executed before expression outside	10
=A1/B1*C1	Two operators at same precedence level, leftmost operator evaluated first	25
=A1/(B1*C1)	Expression inside parentheses executed before expression outside	1

Using what you know about formulas, you'll enter a formula in cell G2 to calculate the total amount of Alison Wilke's order.

To enter a formula to calculate the total amount of the first order:

▶ 1. Verify that cell **G2** is the active cell.

▶ 2. Type **=E2*F2** (the price of the item multiplied by the quantity ordered). Note that as you type the cell reference, Excel surrounds each cell with a different colored border that matches the color of the cell reference in the formula. As shown in Figure 1-14, Excel surrounds cell E2 with a blue border, matching the blue used for the cell reference. Green is used for the F2 cell border and cell reference.

Figure 1-14 ▶ **Typing a formula into the active cell**

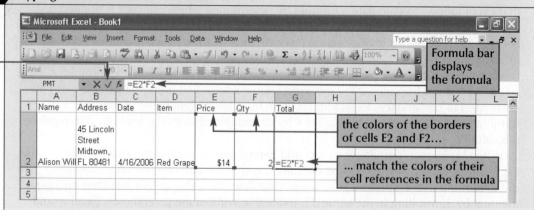

▶ 3. Press the **Enter** key. The total amount of the first order displayed in cell G2 is $28. Note that the value is displayed as currency because one of the components of the formula (cell E2) is a currency value. As you can see, the result of the formula is displayed in the worksheet. To see the formula itself, you need to select the cell and examine the formula in the Formula bar.

You can also enter formulas interactively by clicking each cell. In this technique, you type = (an equal sign) to begin the formula, and then click each cell that needs to be entered in the formula. Using this point-and-click method reduces the possibility of error caused by typing an incorrect cell reference.

Next, you'll enter the data for the second order, and then enter the formula =E3*F3 (the price of the item multiplied by the quantity ordered) using the point-and-click method.

To enter the same formula using the point-and-click method:

1. Enter **David Wu** in cell A3, **315 Oak Lane** on one line in cell B3 and **Midtown, FL 80422** on a second line in the cell, **4/16/2006** in cell C3, **Navel Oranges** in cell D3, **$17** in cell E3, and **1** in cell F3. Be sure to press the Alt + Enter keys to enter the address information on two separate lines as you did for the address in cell B2.

2. Make sure cell **G3** is the active cell, and then type **=** (but do *not* press the Enter or Tab key). When you type the equal sign, Excel knows that you are entering a formula. Any cell that you click from now on will cause Excel to insert the reference of the selected cell into the formula until you complete the formula by pressing the Enter or Tab key or by clicking the Enter button on the Formula bar (refer to Figure 1-14).

3. Click cell **E3**. Note that the cell is highlighted in the same color as the cell reference that now appears in the formula in cell G3.

4. Type ***** to enter the multiplication operator.

5. Click cell **F3** to enter this cell reference, and then press the **Enter** key. Cell G3 now contains the formula =E3*F3 and displays the value $17, which is the total amount of the second order.

Using AutoComplete

As you continue to work with Excel, you may find yourself entering the same text in different rows in the worksheet. To help make entering repetitive text easier, Excel provides the **AutoComplete** feature. Once you enter text in a worksheet, Excel tries to anticipate the text you are about to enter by displaying text that begins with the same letter as a previous entry. For example, two people—David Wu and Carl Ramirez—have ordered a box of navel oranges. You have already entered the data for David Wu's order. When you enter the data for Carl Ramirez's order, you will see how AutoComplete works.

To enter text using AutoComplete:

1. Enter **Carl Ramirez** in cell A4, **900 South Street Crawford, FL 81891** in cell B4 on two separate lines within the cell, and **4/17/2006** in cell C4. Do *not* enter the item for Carl's order yet.

2. Make sure cell **D4** is the active cell, and then type **N**. Note that Excel anticipates the entry by displaying "Navel Oranges," which is text you have already entered beginning with the letter N. See Figure 1-15. At this point, you can accept Excel's suggestion by pressing the Enter or Tab key to complete the text entry and to exit the cell. To override Excel's suggestion, you simply keep typing the text you want to enter into the cell.

Figure 1-15 | **Entering text with the AutoComplete feature**

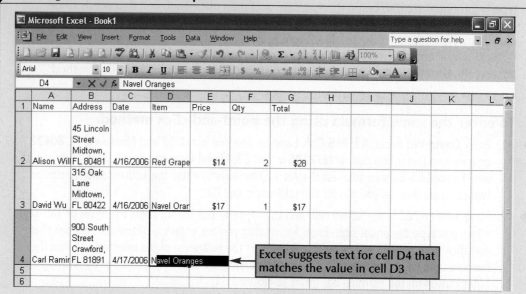

Trouble? If your version of Excel is not set up to use AutoComplete, you will not see the suggested text; therefore you must type "Navel Oranges".

3. Press the **Tab** key to accept Excel's AutoComplete suggestion and to move to cell E4.

4. Type **$17** in cell E4, press the **Tab** key, type **2** in cell F4, and then press the **Tab** key to move to cell G4.

5. Enter **=E4*F4** in cell G4 by typing the formula or by using the point-and-click method. Note that from now on in this text, when you are instructed to "enter" something versus "type" it, use the method that you most prefer; that is, press the Enter key, press the Tab key, or click the Enter button on the Formula bar. Clicking the Enter button not only enters the value in the cell, but also keeps that cell as the active cell.

Excel does not apply AutoComplete to dates or values. However, you can use another feature, AutoFill, to automatically fill in formulas. You'll learn more about AutoFill in the next tutorial.

Now you'll enter the last co-op order into the worksheet.

To enter the last order into the worksheet:

1. Enter **Jerry Dawson** in cell A5, **781 Tree Lane Midtown, FL 80313** in cell B5, **4/18/2006** in cell C5, **Deluxe Combo** in cell D5, **$21** in cell E5, and **4** in cell F5. (Remember to enter the address on two lines.)

2. In cell G5, enter the formula **=E5*F5**. Figure 1-16 shows the completed worksheet.

	A	B	C	D	E	F	G	H	I	J	K	L
1	Name	Address	Date	Item	Price	Qty	Total					
2	Alison Will	45 Lincoln Street Midtown, FL 80481	4/16/2006	Red Grape	$14	2	$28					
3	David Wu	315 Oak Lane Midtown, FL 80422	4/16/2006	Navel Orar	$17	1	$17					
4	Carl Ramir	900 South Street Crawford, FL 81891	4/17/2006	Navel Orar	$17	2	$34					
5	Jerry Daws	781 Tree Lane Midtown, FL 80313	4/18/2006	Deluxe Co	$21	4	$84					
6												
7												
8												
9												

Changing the Size of a Column or Row

The default sizes of the columns and rows in an Excel worksheet may not always accommodate the information you need to enter. You can change the width of one column or multiple columns or the height of one row or multiple rows. Excel provides several methods for changing the width of a column or the height of a row. You can click the dividing line of the column or row, or you can drag the dividing line to change the width of the column or the height of the row. Heights and widths are expressed in terms of the number of characters that can be displayed in the cell, as well as the number of screen pixels, which are small units of measurement that appear as tiny dots on the screen.

Changing the Column Width or Row Height

Reference Window

- Click the column or row heading whose width or height you want to change.
- Click Format on the menu bar, point to Column or Row, and then click Width or Height (or click AutoFit or AutoFit Selection to make the column or row as large as the longest entry of the cells).
- In the Column Width or Row Height dialog box, enter the new column width or row height, and then click the OK button.

or

- Drag the column or row heading dividing line to the right or up to increase the column width or row height, or drag the dividing line to the left or down to decrease the column width or row height.

or

- Double-click the column or row heading dividing line to make the column or row as large as the longest entry of the cells in the column or row.

You'll use the drag technique to increase the width of the columns in which the data display has been truncated. As you drag the dividing line, a ScreenTip appears and displays the column width in characters and pixels.

To change the width of columns in the worksheet:

1. Move the mouse pointer to the dividing line between the column A and column B headings until the pointer changes to ✛.

2. Click and drag the pointer to the right to a length of about **20** characters (or **145 pixels**). See Figure 1-17.

Figure 1-17	Increasing the width of column A

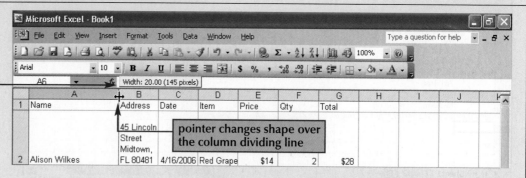

ScreenTip showing the width in characters and pixels

pointer changes shape over the column dividing line

3. Release the mouse button. All the names in column A should now be visible.

   Trouble? If the text in column A is still truncated, drag the dividing line further to the right.

4. Move the mouse pointer to the dividing line between column B and column C until the pointer changes to ✛, and then increase the width of column B to **25** characters (or **180** pixels).

5. Use your mouse to increase the width of column D to **15** characters (or **110** pixels).

Changing the width of the columns does not affect the height of the rows. However, now that column A is wider and the rows are taller, there is a great deal of empty space. To remove the empty space, you'll resize the rows. Rather than choosing a size for the rows, you'll let Excel make the adjustment automatically. If you double-click the dividing line of a column or row heading, the column width or row height adjusts to match the length of the longest entry in that column or row. You'll use this technique now to modify the height of the second row in the worksheet.

To change the height of the second row:

1. Move the mouse pointer to the dividing line between the second and third rows until the pointer changes to ✛.

2. Double-click the dividing line between the second and third rows. See Figure 1-18.

Changing the height of the second row | **Figure 1-18**

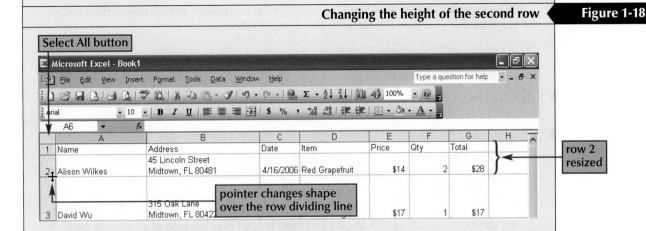

You can continue modifying the height of the remaining rows using this technique, but, for a worksheet containing a large amount of data, that would be extremely time-consuming. Another approach is to select the entire worksheet and then double-click the dividing line between any two row headings. When you do that, Excel changes the height of the rows to accommodate the data in them and reduces the amount of empty space. You can use this approach to resize columns, too.

You can select the entire worksheet by clicking the Select All button. You'll use this approach now to change the height of the remaining rows in the co-op order worksheet.

To change the height of the remaining rows:

▶ 1. Click the **Select All** button located at the junction of the row and column headings (see Figure 1-18). The row and column headings are displayed in black or dark blue, and all of the worksheet cells are displayed in light blue, indicating that the entire worksheet has been selected.

▶ 2. Move the mouse pointer to a dividing line between any two rows until the pointer changes to ✛.

▶ 3. Double-click the dividing line. Excel resizes the height of all the rows.

▶ 4. Click cell **A1** to make it the active cell and to remove the blue highlighting from the worksheet. Figure 1-19 shows the revised layout of the sheet.

Adjusting the height of the worksheet rows | **Figure 1-19**

You've entered the data that Sandra wanted in the worksheet. Before proceeding further, she suggests that you save the file with the name "Dalton".

To save the workbook:

▶ 1. Click **File** on the menu bar, and then click **Save**. The Save As dialog box opens with the current workbook name, which is "Book1," in the File name text box.

▶ 2. Navigate to the Tutorial.01\Tutorial folder included with your Data Files.

   Trouble? If you don't have the Excel 2003 Data Files, you need to get them before you can proceed. Your instructor will either give you the Data Files or ask you to obtain them from a specified location (such as a network drive). In either case, be sure that you make a backup copy of your Data Files before you start using them, so that the original files will be available on your copied disk in case you need to start over because of an error or problem. If you have any questions about the Data Files, see your instructor or technical support person for assistance.

▶ 3. Replace the default filename with **Dalton**, make sure that **Microsoft Office Excel Workbook** is displayed in the Save as type list box, and then click the **Save** button. Excel saves the workbook with the name "Dalton" and closes the Save As dialog box. The new workbook name appears in the title bar of the Excel window.

   Trouble? If your computer has been set up to display file extensions, the filename "Dalton.xls" will appear in the title bar.

By default, Excel saves the workbook in Microsoft Excel Workbook format, and for most of the work you will do in this text, you will use this file format. If you are creating a workbook that will be read by applications other than Excel (or earlier versions of Excel), you can save your workbook in a different file format by following these steps:

1. Open the Save or Save As dialog box.
2. Display the location in which you want to save the file, and enter a filename, if necessary.
3. Click the Save as type list arrow, and then select the file format you want to apply.
4. Click the Save button.

Figure 1-20 describes some of the file formats in which you can save your workbooks.

| Figure 1-20 | Some of the formats supported by Excel |

Format	Description
Microsoft Excel 4.0, 5.0, 97, 2000, 2002 Workbook	Saves the workbook in an earlier version of Excel
Single File Web Page	Saves the workbook as a single Web page file (MHTML file) that can be read by Internet Explorer 4.0 or later
Template	Saves the workbook as a template to be used for creating other Excel workbooks
Web Page	Saves the workbook in separate files that are used as the basis for a Web site, in a format that is readable by most browsers
XML Spreadsheet	Saves the workbook as an XML document

Sandra has some other changes to the workbook that she wants you to make. You'll continue working with the worksheet in the next session.

Session 1.1 Quick Check

1. A(n) _____ is the place on the worksheet where a column and row intersect.
2. Cell _____ refers to the intersection of the fourth column and second row.
3. What combination of keys can you press to make A1 the active cell in the worksheet?
4. To make Sheet2 the active worksheet, you _____.
5. Indicate whether Excel treats the following cell entries as text, a value, or a formula.
   a. 11/09/2006
   b. Net Income
   c. 321
   d. C11*225
   e. 201-19-1121
   f. =D1-D9
   g. 44 Evans Avenue
6. How do you enter multiple lines of text within a cell?
7. What formula would you enter to divide the value in cell E5 by the value in cell E6?

Session 1.2

Working with Ranges

Sandra has had a chance to study your work from the previous session. She likes the layout of her data, but she wants to have a title at the top of the worksheet that displays information about the sheet's contents. To make room for the title, you have to move the contents of the worksheet down a few rows. Before you attempt that, you have to first understand how Excel works with groups of cells.

A group of worksheet cells is called a **cell range**, or just **range**. Ranges can be either adjacent or nonadjacent. An **adjacent range** is a single rectangular block, such as all of the data entered in cells A1 through G5 of the Dalton workbook. A **nonadjacent range** consists of two or more separate adjacent ranges. For example, a nonadjacent range might be composed of the names of the customers in the cell range A1 through A5 and the total price of their orders in the cell range G1 through G5.

Just as a cell reference indicates the location of a cell on the worksheet, a **range reference** indicates the location and size of a cell range. For adjacent ranges, the range reference identifies the cells in the upper-left and lower-right corners of the rectangle, with the individual cell references separated by a colon. For example, the range reference for the order data you entered in the last session was A1:G5 because it included the range of cells from A1 through G5. If the range is nonadjacent, a semicolon separates the rectangular blocks A1:A5 and G1:G5, as in A1:A5;G1:G5. This nonadjacent range references the customer names in the range A1:A5 and the total amounts of their orders in the range G1:G5.

Selecting Ranges

Once you know how to select ranges of cells, you can move and copy the data anywhere in the worksheet or workbook.

Reference Window

Selecting Adjacent or Nonadjacent Ranges of Cells

To select an adjacent range of cells:
- Click a cell in the upper-left corner of the rectangle that comprises the adjacent range.
- Press and hold the left mouse button, and then drag the pointer through the cells you want selected.
- Release the mouse button.

To select a nonadjacent range of cells:
- Select an adjacent range of cells.
- Press and hold the Ctrl key, and then select another adjacent cell range.
- With the Ctrl key still pressed, continue to select other cell ranges until all of the ranges are selected.
- Release the mouse button and the Ctrl key.

To see how to select ranges, you'll start by selecting all of the cells containing order information.

To select the order data:

1. If you took a break at the end of the previous session, make sure that Excel is running and that the Dalton workbook is open.

2. Click cell **A1** on the Sheet1 worksheet, press and hold the left mouse button, and then drag the pointer to cell **G5**.

3. Release the mouse button. All the cells in the range A1:G5 are now highlighted, indicating that they are selected. See Figure 1-21.

Figure 1-21 ▶ Selecting the range A1:G5

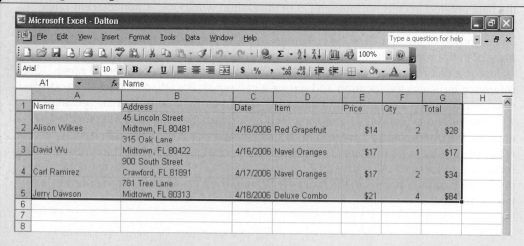

4. Click any cell in the worksheet to deselect the range.

Now try selecting the nonadjacent range A1:A5;G1:G5.

To select the nonadjacent range A1:A5;G1:G5:

▶ **1.** Select the range **A1:A5**, press and hold the **Ctrl** key, select the range **G1:G5**, and then release the mouse button and the Ctrl key. See Figure 1-22 for the selected nonadjacent range.

Selecting the nonadjacent range A1:A5;G1:G5 ◄ **Figure 1-22**

▶ **2.** Click any cell in the worksheet to deselect the range.

Other Selection Techniques

You can also select large cell ranges that extend beyond the borders of the workbook window. When this situation occurs, Excel automatically scrolls the workbook window horizontally or vertically to display additional cells in the worksheet. Selecting a large cell range using the mouse drag technique can be slow and frustrating. For this reason, Excel provides keyboard shortcuts that enable you to quickly select large blocks of data without having to drag through the worksheet to select the necessary cells. Figure 1-23 describes some of these selection techniques.

Other range selection techniques ◄ **Figure 1-23**

To Select...	Action
A large range of cells	Click the first cell in the range, press and hold down the Shift key, and then click the last cell in the range. All of the cells between the first and last cell are selected.
All cells on the worksheet	Click the Select All button, the gray rectangle in the upper-left corner of the worksheet where the row and column headings meet.
All cells in an entire row or column	Click the row or column heading.
A range of cells containing data	Click the cell where you want to begin the selection of the range, press and hold down the Shift key, and then double-click the side of the cell in the direction that you want to extend the selection. Excel selects all adjacent cells that contain data, extending the selection of the range to the first empty cell.

Try some of the techniques described to select ranges of cells in the Dalton workbook.

To select a range of cells using keyboard shortcuts:

▶ 1. Click cell **A1** to make it the active cell.

▶ 2. Press and hold the **Shift** key, click cell **A5**, and then release the Shift key. Note that all of the cells between A1 and A5 are selected.

   Trouble? If the range A1:A5 is not selected, try again, but make sure you hold the Shift key while you click cell A5.

▶ 3. Click cell **A1** to make it the active cell again. Note that you don't have to deselect one range before clicking another cell.

▶ 4. Press and hold the **Shift** key, move the pointer to the bottom edge of cell A1 until the mouse pointer changes to ⬚, and then double-click the bottom edge of cell **A1**. The selection extends to cell A5, the last cell before the empty cell A6.

▶ 5. With the Shift key still pressed, move the pointer to the right edge of the selection until, once again, the pointer changes to ⬚, double-click the right edge of the selection, and then release the Shift key. The selection extends to the last nonblank column in the worksheet, selecting the range A1:G5.

▶ 6. Click the **A** column heading. All of the cells in column A are selected. Note that you didn't have to deselect the range A1:G5.

▶ 7. Click the **1** row heading. All of the cells in the first row are selected.

Moving a Selection of Cells

Now that you know various ways to select a range of cells, you can move the co-op data down a few rows in the worksheet. To move a cell range, you first select it; then you position the pointer over the selection border, and drag the selection to a new location. Try this technique to move the order data from the cell range A1:G5 to the cell range A5:G9.

To move the order data:

▶ 1. Select the range **A1:G5**, and then move the pointer over the bottom border of the selection until the pointer changes to ⬚.

▶ 2. Press and hold the left mouse button, changing the pointer to ⬚, and then drag the selection down four rows. A ScreenTip appears indicating the new range reference of the selection. See Figure 1-24.

Moving the selection to the range A5:G9 | **Figure 1-24**

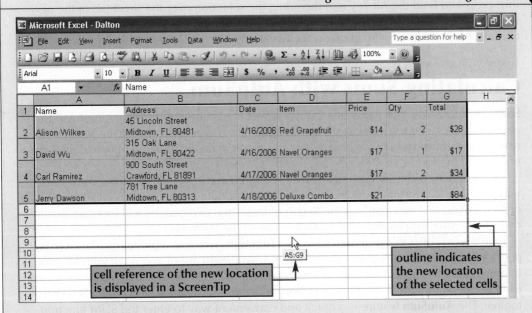

3. When the ScreenTip displays "A5:G9," release the left mouse button. The order data is now moved to range A5:G9.

   Trouble? If you selected the wrong range or moved the selection to the wrong location, click the Undo button 🔄 on the Standard toolbar, and then repeat Steps 1 through 3.

4. Click cell **A1** to remove the selection and to make cell A1 the active cell so you can enter the new titles in the worksheet.

5. Type **Dalton Food Co-op** in cell A1, **List of Orders** in cell A2, **April, 2006** in cell A3, and then press the **Enter** key. Note that moving the cell range had no impact on the values in the worksheet; the values shown by the formulas in column G are also unchanged. This is because Excel automatically updated the cell references in the formulas to reflect the new location of the data. To confirm this, you'll examine the formula in cell G6.

6. Click cell **G6** and observe what is displayed in the Formula bar. The formula in cell G6 is now =E6*F6. Recall that when you originally entered Alison Wilke's order, the formula for this cell was =E2*G2 because the order was originally placed in the second row of the worksheet. When you moved the data, Excel automatically updated the formula to reflect the new location of Alison Wilke's order.

The technique you used to move the cell range is called "drag and drop." You can also use the drag-and-drop technique to copy a cell range. Copying a range of cells is similar to moving a range, except that you must press the Ctrl key while you drag the selection to its new location. A copy of the original data will then appear at the location of the pointer when you release the mouse button. You'll learn more about copying and pasting in the next two tutorials.

A cell range can also be moved from one worksheet in the workbook to another. To do this, press and hold the Alt key and then drag the selection over the sheet tab of the new worksheet. Excel will automatically make that worksheet the active sheet, so you can drag the selection into its new location on the worksheet.

Calculating Sums with AutoSum

Sandra reminds you that she wants the worksheet to also display summary information about the co-op orders, including the total number of items ordered and the amount of revenue generated from those orders. You could calculate the total quantity and total revenue using the formulas =F6+F7+F8+F9 and =G6+G7+G8+G9.

One problem with this approach is that as Sandra adds new orders to the worksheet, you will have to constantly update these formulas, adding cell references for the new orders. As you add more orders, the length of these two expressions will increase dramatically, increasing the possibility of making errors in the formulas.

One way to solve this problem is to use a **function**, which is a predefined formula that performs calculations using specific values. You will learn about and work with functions in more detail in the next tutorial. In this case, you'll insert one of Excel's most commonly used Financial functions, the SUM function, using the AutoSum button on the Standard toolbar. The **AutoSum** feature is a quick and convenient way to enter the SUM function. You use the **SUM function** to calculate the sum of values in a cell range. In this case, you want to calculate the sum of the values in the range F6:F9 and in the range G6:G9.

Now, you'll use AutoSum to calculate the total quantity and total revenue of the ordered items, putting these values in cells F10 and G10.

To calculate the total order quantity and revenue:

1. Click cell **A10**, type **TOTAL**, and then press the **Tab** key five times to move to cell F10.

2. With cell F10 as the active cell, click the **AutoSum** button Σ on the Standard toolbar. Excel automatically inserts the SUM function in the active cell and selects a cell range that it anticipates is the range of cells to be summed. See Figure 1-25. A ScreenTip also appears, showing the form of the SUM function. The mode indicator in the status bar changes to Point, indicating that you can point to the cell references. In this case, the range that Excel has selected for you is the correct range of cells, so all you need to do is indicate that you accept the range. You can complete the function and move to the next cell by pressing the Tab key.

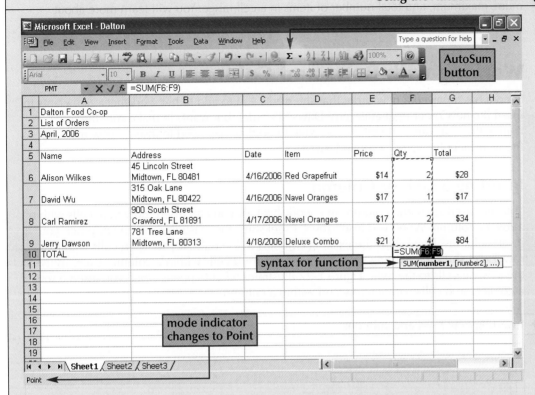

3. Press the **Tab** key to move to cell G10. The result of the formula *=SUM(F6:F9)* appears in cell F10, and you are in position to calculate the next set of values.

4. Click the **AutoSum** button [Σ] on the Standard toolbar to enter the SUM function in cell G10, and then press the **Enter** key to complete the formula *=SUM(G6:G9)*, accepting the range that Excel highlighted. See Figure 1-26. Nine items were sold, for a total of $163.

Calculating the total quantity and total income for the co-op ▶ **Figure 1-26**

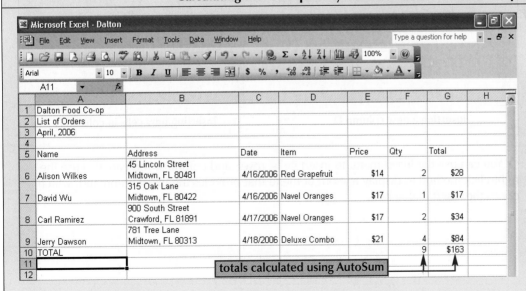

You can use AutoSum to calculate other summary values, such as the average, minimum, maximum, and total number of items in a cell range. You will learn more about using AutoSum to summarize values in Tutorial 2.

Working with Rows and Columns

Sandra has received a new order that she wants you to add to her worksheet. She wants to insert the new order right after Jerry Dawson's order, but wants to make sure the row containing the total values is still the last row. To do this, you need to insert a new row into the worksheet between row 9 and row 10.

Inserting a Row or Column

You can insert rows and columns in a worksheet, or you can insert individual cells within a row or column. When you insert rows, Excel shifts the existing rows down. When you insert columns, Excel shifts the existing columns to the right. If you insert cells within a row, Excel shifts the existing cells down; if you insert cells within a column, Excel shifts the existing cells to the right. Figure 1-27 illustrates what happens when you insert a row, a column, and cells within a row and within a column.

Figure 1-27   **Inserting new rows and columns**

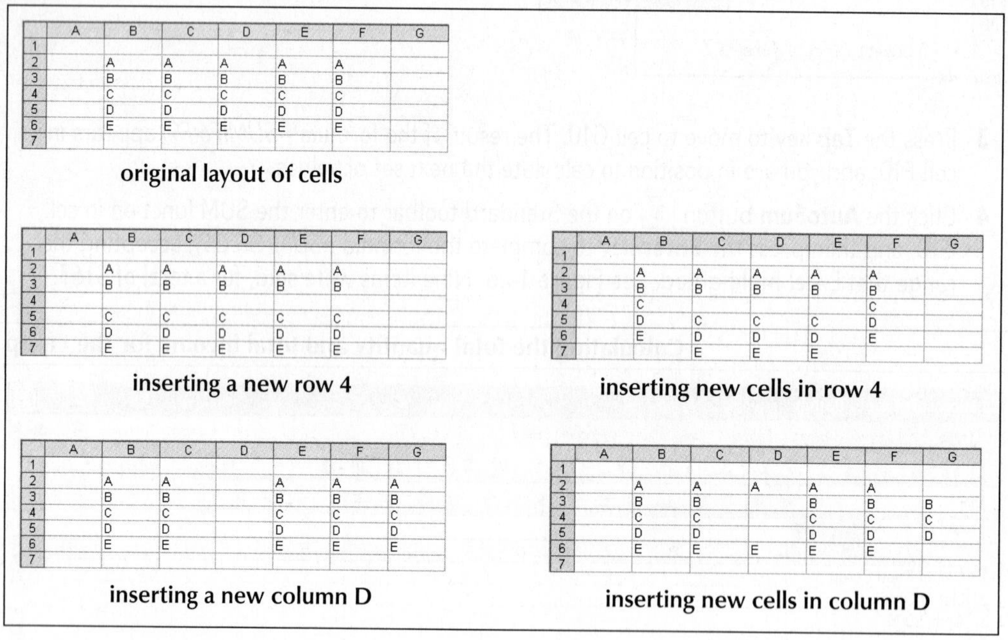

original layout of cells

inserting a new row 4

inserting new cells in row 4

inserting a new column D

inserting new cells in column D

You can use the Insert menu to insert cells, rows, and columns. You can also use the right-click method to display a shortcut menu that provides the Insert command, which opens the Insert dialog box.

Inserting a Row or Column into a Worksheet

- Select a cell where you want to insert the new row or column.
- Click Insert on the menu bar, and then click Rows or Columns.

or

- Right-click a cell where you want to insert a new row or column, and then click Insert on the shortcut menu.
- In the Insert dialog box, click the Entire row or Entire column option button, and then click the OK button.

To insert multiple rows or columns, you select a cell range that contains multiple rows or columns before applying the Insert command. For example, to insert two new blank rows, select two rows or any portion of two rows. To insert three blank columns, select three columns or any portion of three columns.

Sometimes you might need to insert individual cells, rather than an entire row or column, into a worksheet. To insert cells into a row or column, you must select the number of cells you want to insert, and then open the Insert dialog box. In this dialog box you indicate how Excel should shift the existing cells to accommodate the cells you want to insert.

Inserting Cells into a Worksheet

- Select a cell range equal to the number of cells you want to insert.
- Click Insert on the menu bar, and then click Cells; or right-click the selected range, and then click Insert on the shortcut menu.
- Click the Shift cells right option button to insert the new cells into the row, or click the Shift cells down button to insert the new cells into the column.

Sandra wants the data for the new order to be entered above the TOTAL row, row 10. You'll use the right-click method to insert a new row 10, and then you'll enter the data.

To insert a new row 10:

1. Right-click cell **A10**, which is where you want to insert the new row.

2. Click **Insert** on the shortcut menu. The Insert dialog box opens. See Figure 1-28.

Insert dialog box ◄ | **Figure 1-28**

3. Click the **Entire row** option button, and then click the **OK** button. Excel inserts a new row 10 and shifts the calculations of the total values down one row.

4. Enter the data for Karen Paulson's order into row 10, as shown in Figure 1-29. Make sure that you press the Tab key to move from cell to cell and press the Alt + Enter keys to enter the address on two lines within cell B10.

Figure 1-29 | **Data entered in the new row 10**

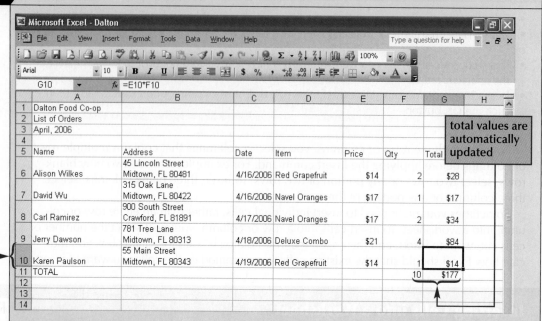

Note that Excel automatically inserts the formula *=E10*F10* into cell G10 for you. Excel recognizes that you are inserting a new set of values into a list of values and assumes that you intend to use the same formulas for the new order that you used for the previous ones. Also note that the calculations of the total quantity of items ordered and the total revenue from those orders have been updated. The functions now calculate the sums in the cell ranges F6:F10 and G6:G10. You'll learn more about how such formulas are automatically adjusted by Excel in the next tutorial.

Deleting a Row or Column

Sandra has also learned that David Wu has canceled his co-op order. You have two options for removing data from a worksheet. If you simply want to erase the contents of a cell, you can **clear** the cell, without actually removing the cell from the worksheet. If you want to remove not only the contents of the cells from the worksheet, but also the cells themselves, you can **delete** a cell range, and Excel then shifts the contents of the adjacent cells into the location of the deleted cells.

To clear the contents of a cell or range of cells, you select the range and then select the Clear command on the Edit menu or on the shortcut menu that you display by right-clicking the selection. Pressing the Delete key on the keyboard also clears the contents of the selected cells, without removing the cells themselves. To delete cells and their contents, you select the range and then choose the Delete command on the Edit menu, or right-click the selected cells, and click Delete on the shortcut menu. To adjust the adjacent cells, Excel opens the Delete Cells dialog box, which you can select to shift the remaining cells left or up, or choose to delete the entire row.

Because David Wu has canceled his order, you'll delete it from the worksheet.

To delete the row that contains David Wu's order:

1. Click the row heading for row **7**, which contains the data you want to delete.

2. Click **Edit** on the menu bar, and then click **Delete**. Excel deletes the row and shifts the next row up. See Figure 1-30. The total calculations in cells F10 and G10 are automatically updated to reflect the fact that David Wu's order has been deleted.

Deleting a row from the worksheet   **Figure 1-30**

Editing Your Worksheet

When you work in Excel, you might make mistakes that you want to correct or undo. Sandra has noticed such a mistake in the Dalton workbook. The price for the Deluxe Combo box should be $23, not $21. You could simply clear the value in cell E8 and then type the correct value. However, there may be times when you will not want to change the entire contents of a cell, but merely edit a portion of the entry, especially if the cell contains a large block of text or a complicated formula. To edit the cell contents, you need to work in **edit mode**.

When you are working in edit mode, some of the keyboard shortcuts you've been using perform differently. For example, the Home, Delete, Backspace, and End keys do not move the insertion point to different cells in the worksheet; rather they move the insertion point to different locations within the cell. The Home key, for example, moves the insertion point to the beginning of whatever content has been entered into the cell. The End key moves the insertion point to the end of the cell's content. The left and right arrow keys move the insertion point backward and forward through the cell's content. The Backspace key deletes the character immediately to the left of the insertion point, and the Delete key deletes the character to the right of the insertion point.

Editing a Cell

- Switch to edit mode by double-clicking the cell, clicking the cell and pressing the F2 key, or clicking the cell and then clicking in the Formula bar.
- Use the Home, End, ←, or → keys to move the insertion point within the cell's content, or use the Delete and Backspace keys to erase characters.
- Press the Enter key when finished, or if you are working in the Formula bar, click the Enter button.

You'll switch to edit mode and then change the value in cell E8.

To edit the value in cell E8:

1. Double-click cell **E8**. Note that the mode indicator in the status bar switches from Ready to Edit. Also note that the value 21 appears in the cell, not $21. This is because the cell contains a numeric value, not a text string. The dollar sign ($) is used to format the value. You'll learn more about formats in Tutorial 3.

2. Press the **End** key to move the blinking insertion point to the end of the cell.

3. Press the **Backspace** key once to delete the 1 character, type **3** to update the value, and then press the **Enter** key to accept the change. The value $23 appears in cell E8, and the total amount of this order in cell G8 changes to $92. Note that the mode indicator on the status bar switches back to Ready.

If you make a mistake as you type in edit mode, you can press the Esc key or click the Cancel button on the Formula bar to cancel all changes you made while in edit mode.

Undoing an Action

As you revise your worksheet, you may find that you need to undo one of your changes. To undo an action, click the Undo button on the Standard toolbar. As you work, Excel maintains a list of your actions, so you can undo most of the actions you perform in your workbook during the current session. To reverse more than one action, click the list arrow next to the Undo button and click the action you want to undo from the list. To see how this works, you'll use the Undo button to remove the edit you just made to cell E8.

To undo your last action:

1. Click the **Undo** button 🔄 on the Standard toolbar. The value $21 appears again in cell E8, indicating that your last action, editing the value in this cell, has been undone.

If you find that you have gone too far in undoing your previous actions, you can go forward in the action list and redo those actions. To redo an action, you click the Redo button on the Standard toolbar. Now you'll use the Redo button to return the value in cell E8 to $23.

To redo your last action:

1. Click the **Redo** button 🔁 on the Standard toolbar. The value in cell E8 changes back to $23.

Through the use of edit mode and the Undo and Redo buttons, you should be able to correct almost any mistake you make in your Excel workbook. The Undo and Redo commands are also available on the Edit menu or by using the shortcut keys Ctrl + Z, to undo an action, and Ctrl + Y, to redo an action.

Working with Worksheets

By default, Excel workbooks contain three worksheets, labeled Sheet1, Sheet2, and Sheet3. You can add new worksheets or remove old ones. You can also give your worksheets more descriptive names. In the Dalton workbook, there is no data entered in the Sheet2 or Sheet3 worksheets. Sandra suggests that you remove these sheets from the workbook.

Adding and Removing Worksheets

To delete a worksheet, you first select its sheet tab to make the worksheet the active sheet; then right-click the sheet tab and choose Delete from the shortcut menu. Try this now by deleting the Sheet2 and Sheet3 worksheets.

To delete the Sheet2 and Sheet3 worksheets:

1. Click the **Sheet2** tab to make Sheet2 the active sheet.

2. Right-click the sheet tab, and then click **Delete** on the shortcut menu. Sheet2 is deleted and Sheet3 becomes the active sheet.

3. Right-click the **Sheet3** tab, and then click **Delete**. There is now only one worksheet in the workbook.

After you delete the two unused sheets, Sandra informs you that she wants to include a description of the workbook's content and purpose. In other words, Sandra wants to include a **documentation sheet**, a worksheet that provides information about the content and purpose of the workbook. A documentation sheet can be any information that you feel is important, for example, the name of the person who created the workbook or instructions on how to use the workbook. A documentation sheet is a valuable element if you intend to share the workbook with others. The documentation sheet is often the first worksheet in the workbook, though in this case, Sandra wants to place it at the end of the workbook.

To insert a new worksheet, you can either use the Worksheet command on the Insert menu or the right-click method. Both methods insert a new worksheet *before* the active sheet.

To insert a new worksheet in the workbook:

1. Click **Insert** on the menu bar, and then click **Worksheet**. A new worksheet with the name "Sheet4" is placed at the beginning of your workbook. Your worksheet might be named Sheet2 or another name.

Sandra wants the documentation sheet to include the following information:

- The name of the co-op
- The date that this workbook was originally created
- The person who created the workbook
- The purpose of the workbook

You'll add this information to the new sheet in the Dalton workbook.

To insert the documentation information in the new worksheet:

▶ 1. Click cell **A1**, if necessary, type **Dalton Food Co-op**, and then press the **Enter** key twice.

▶ 2. Type **Date:** in cell A3, and then press the **Tab** key.

▶ 3. Enter the *current date* in cell B3, and then press the **Enter** key.

▶ 4. Type **Created By:** in cell A4, and then press the **Tab** key.

▶ 5. Enter *your name* in cell B4, and then press the **Enter** key.

▶ 6. Type **Purpose:** in cell A5, and then press the **Tab** key.

▶ 7. Type **To enter orders for the Dalton Food Co-op** in cell B5, and then press the **Enter** key.

▶ 8. Increase the width of column A to **15** characters (**110** pixels). Figure 1-31 shows the completed documentation sheet.

Figure 1-31 ▶ Completed documentation sheet

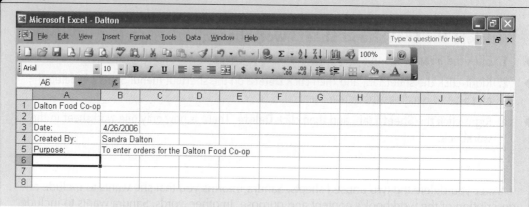

Renaming a Worksheet

The current sheet names, "Sheet4" and "Sheet1," are not very descriptive. Sandra suggests that you rename Sheet4 "Documentation" and Sheet1 "Orders." To rename a worksheet, you double-click the sheet tab to select the sheet name, and then you type a new name for the sheet. Sheet names cannot exceed 31 characters in length, including blank spaces.

To rename the worksheets:

▶ 1. Double-click the **Sheet4** tab. Note that the name of the sheet is selected.

▶ 2. Type **Documentation** and then press the **Enter** key. The width of the sheet tab adjusts to the length of the name you type.

▶ 3. Double-click the **Sheet1** tab.

▶ 4. Type **Orders** and then press the **Enter** key. Both worksheets are renamed.

Moving a Worksheet

You can change the placement of the worksheets in the workbook. To move the position of a worksheet in the workbook, click the sheet tab and then drag and drop it to a new location relative to the other worksheets. You can also make a copy of a worksheet using a similar drag-and-drop technique. To create a copy of a worksheet, press the Ctrl key as you drag and drop the sheet tab of the worksheet you want duplicated.

Reference Window

Moving or Copying a Worksheet

- Click the sheet tab of the worksheet you want to move (or copy).
- Drag the sheet tab along the row of sheet tabs until the small arrow appears in the new location. To create a copy of the worksheet, press and hold the Ctrl key as you drag the sheet tab to the new location.
- Release the mouse button. Release the Ctrl key if necessary.

Try this now by switching the location of the Documentation and Orders worksheets.

To reposition the worksheets:

1. Click the **Orders** tab, and then press and hold the left mouse button so the pointer changes to ▯ and a small arrow appears in the upper-left corner of the tab.

2. Drag the pointer to the left of the sheet tab for the Documentation sheet, and then release the mouse button. The Documentation sheet is now the second sheet in the workbook, but Sandra would prefer that the documentation sheet be the first sheet.

3. Click the **Orders** tab, and then drag the sheet tab to the right of the Documentation sheet tab to place it back in its original location.

When you create a copy of a worksheet, you move the copy of the original worksheet to a new location, while the original sheet remains at its initial position.

Using the Spell Checker

One of Excel's editing tools is the **Spell Checker**. This feature checks the words in the workbook against the program's internal dictionary. If the Spell Checker comes across a word not in its dictionary, it displays the word in a dialog box along with a list of suggested replacements. You can replace the word with one from the list, or you can choose to ignore the word and go to the next word that might be misspelled. You can also add the word to the dictionary to prevent it from being flagged in the future. There are words that are not included in the online dictionary (for example, some uncommon personal names or last names). The Spell Checker will stop at these words. You can then choose to ignore all occurrences of the word, change the word, or add the word to the dictionary. Excel checks the spelling on the current worksheet only.

To see how the Spell Checker works, you'll make an intentional spelling error in the Orders worksheet.

To check the spelling in the Orders sheet:

1. Make sure the Orders sheet is the active sheet, and then click cell **G5**. You will enter the error in this cell.

2. Type **Totale** and then click cell **A1**. The Spell Checker always starts at the active cell in the worksheet. You can start from other cells, and the Spell Checker will cycle back to the first cell in the worksheet to continue checking each cell for spelling errors. However, you will find it helpful and more efficient to begin spell checking with the first cell in the sheet, cell A1.

3. Click the **Spelling** button on the Standard toolbar. The Spelling dialog box opens, with the first word that the spell checker does not recognize, "Totale." See Figure 1-32.

Figure 1-32	Spelling dialog box

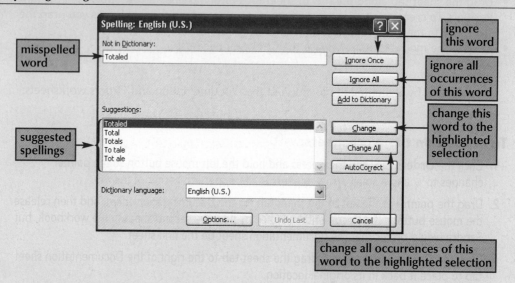

4. Click **Total** in the list of suggestions, and then click the **Change** button. The word "Totale" changes to "Total," and then Spell Checker continues to look for other potential spelling errors. There shouldn't be any other errors in this workbook.

   Trouble? If there are any other errors (you may have misspelled a name, address, or item), fix them before continuing to the next step.

5. Click the **OK** button to close the Spell Checker.

Previewing and Printing a Worksheet

Sandra would like a printed hard copy of the Dalton workbook for her records. You can print the contents of your workbook either by using the Print command on the File menu or by clicking the Print button on the Standard toolbar. If you use the Print command, Excel opens the Print dialog box in which you can specify which worksheets you want to print, the number of copies, and the print quality. If you click the Print button, your worksheet will print using the options already set in the Print dialog box. If you want to change a setting, you must open the Print dialog box using the File menu.

Before sending a worksheet to the printer, you should preview how the worksheet will appear as a printed page. You can display the worksheet in the Print Preview window either by selecting the Print Preview command on the File menu or by clicking the Print Preview button on the Standard toolbar. You can also click the Preview button in the Print dialog box. Previewing the printout is a helpful way to avoid printing errors.

If you are printing to a shared printer on a network, other people might be sending print jobs at the same time you do. To avoid confusion, you will print the contents of both the Documentation sheet and the Orders sheet. You will use the Print command on the File menu because you need to print the entire workbook and not just the active worksheet (which is the default print setting).

To open the Print dialog box:

▶ 1. Click **File** on the menu bar, and then click **Print** to open the Print dialog box.

▶ 2. Click the **Name** list box, and then select the printer to which you want to print, if it is not already selected.

Now you need to select what to print. To print the complete workbook, select the Entire workbook option button. To print the active worksheet, select the Active sheet(s) option button. To print the selected cells on the active sheet, click the Selection option button.

▶ 3. Click the **Entire workbook** option button.

▶ 4. Make sure **1** appears in the Number of copies list box, since you only need to print one copy of the workbook. Figure 1-33 shows the Print dialog box.

Print dialog box ◀ **Figure 1-33**

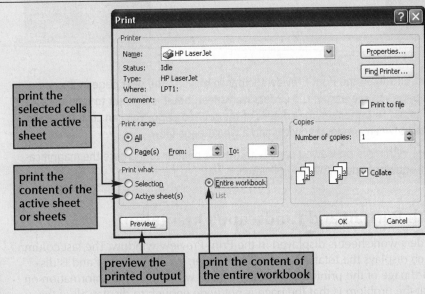

print the selected cells in the active sheet

print the content of the active sheet or sheets

preview the printed output

print the content of the entire workbook

Next you will preview the worksheet to ensure that it looks correct before printing it.

To preview the workbook before printing it:

▶ 1. Click the **Preview** button in the Print dialog box. Excel displays a preview of the first full page of the worksheet, in this case the Documentation sheet, as it will appear printed. As you can see from the status bar in Figure 1-34, this is the first of three pages.

Trouble? If the status bar on your screen indicates that there are just two pages, you can still complete the steps.

Figure 1-34 ▶ Print Preview window

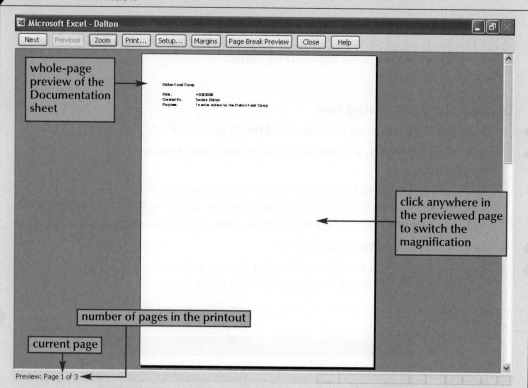

whole-page preview of the Documentation sheet

click anywhere in the previewed page to switch the magnification

number of pages in the printout

current page

2. Click the **Next** button on the Print Preview toolbar to move to the next page in the preview. On this page you see part of the Orders worksheet, but it is difficult to read because the text is so small. To better see the content of the printed page, you can click the preview page to switch between a magnified view and a whole-page view.

3. Click anywhere within the previewed page with the 🔍 pointer to increase the magnification, and click again to reduce the magnification.

Working with Portrait and Landscape Orientation

Not all of the Orders worksheet is displayed in the Print Preview window. The last column in the sheet, which displays the total amount of each order, has been cut off and is displayed on the third page of the printout. Naturally Sandra wants all of the information on a single sheet, but the problem is that the page is not wide enough to display all of this information. One way of solving this problem is to change the orientation of the page. There are two types of page orientations: portrait and landscape. In **portrait orientation** the page is taller than it is wide. In **landscape orientation** the page is wider than it is tall. In many cases, you will want to print your worksheets in landscape orientation. You'll choose this option for the Orders worksheet.

To print in landscape orientation:

1. Click the **Setup** button on the Print Preview toolbar. The Page Setup dialog box opens.

2. Verify that the Page tab is selected in the dialog box, and then click the **Landscape** option button. See Figure 1-35.

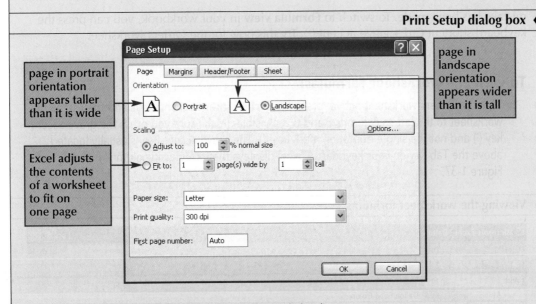

page in portrait orientation appears taller than it is wide

Excel adjusts the contents of a worksheet to fit on one page

page in landscape orientation appears wider than it is tall

▶ 3. Click the **OK** button to close the Page Setup dialog box.

▶ 4. If necessary, click anywhere within the previewed page to switch the magnification back to a whole-page view. As shown in Figure 1-36, the entire Orders worksheet is now displayed on the second (and last) page of this printout.

Orders sheet in landscape orientation ◄ **Figure 1-36**

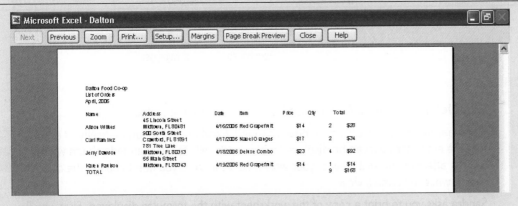

▶ 5. Click the **Print** button on the Print Preview toolbar to print the workbook and close the Print Preview window.

Note that the Documentation sheet is printed in portrait orientation, whereas the Orders worksheet is printed in landscape orientation. Changing the orientation only affects the worksheet currently displayed in the Print Preview window; it does not apply to other sheets in the workbook.

Printing the Worksheet Formulas

Sandra examines the printout and notices that none of the formulas are displayed. This is to be expected since most of the time you're only interested in the final results and not the formulas used to calculate those results. In some cases, you will want to view the formulas used in developing your workbook. This is particularly useful in situations where the results were not what you expected, and you want to examine the formulas to see if a mistake has been made. To switch to **Formula view** in your workbook, you can press the keyboard shortcut Ctrl + grave accent (`). Try this now for the Orders worksheet.

To view the worksheet formulas:

1. With the Orders worksheet active, press the **Ctrl + `** (grave accent) keys and then scroll the worksheet to the left so columns F and G are visible. (Make sure you press the grave accent key (`) and not the single quotation mark key ('). The grave accent key is usually located above the Tab key on your keyboard.) Excel displays the formulas in columns F and G. See Figure 1-37.

Figure 1-37 ▶ **Viewing the worksheet formulas**

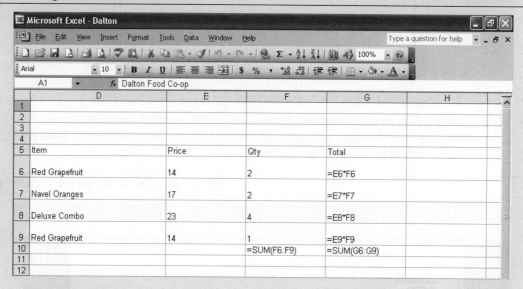

Trouble? If the Formula Auditing toolbar appears, close the toolbar.

Note that the column widths have been changed. Excel does this automatically to ensure that the entire formula can be displayed within each cell. These changed column widths will not affect the normal view of your worksheet as long as you don't change the column widths while in Formula view.

Sandra asks you to print a copy of the worksheet with the formulas displayed. First, you'll preview the worksheet.

2. Click the **Print Preview** button 🔍 on the Standard toolbar. Excel displays a preview of the Orders worksheet in Formula view. Not all of the contents of the worksheet in this view are displayed on a single page. To fit the printout to a single page, you will change the setup of the page using the Page Setup dialog box.

3. Click the **Setup** button on the Print Preview toolbar. The Page Setup dialog box opens.

4. Click the **Fit to** option button to fit the Orders worksheet on one page, and then click the **OK** button. The Formula view of the Orders worksheet should now fit on a single page.

5. Click the **Print** button on the Print Preview toolbar to print the worksheet and close the Print Preview window.

Trouble? If the Print Preview window closes and the Print dialog box opens, click the OK button to print the worksheet.

As you may have noticed while you were working in Print Preview and the Page Setup dialog box, there are a lot of options for choosing what to print and how to print. You'll examine more of these options in Tutorial 3. For now, you can switch the Orders worksheet back to Normal view and save and then close the file.

To complete your work:

▶ 1. Press the **Ctrl +** ` (grave accent) keys to switch the worksheet back to Normal view. The keyboard shortcut Ctrl + ` (grave accent) works as a toggle, so you can display or hide the formulas by pressing this combination of keys.

▶ 2. Save your changes to the Dalton workbook, and then close it.

You give Sandra the hard copy of the Dalton workbook. If she needs to add new information to the workbook or if she needs you to make further changes to the structure of the workbook, she'll contact you.

Session 1.2 Quick Check

Review

1. Describe the two types of cell ranges in Excel.
2. How do you write the cell reference for the rectangular group of cells that extends from cell A5 through cell F8?
3. The _____ button provides a quick way to enter the SUM function.
4. When you insert a new row into a worksheet, the existing rows are shifted

   _____.
5. When you insert a new column into a worksheet, the existing columns are shifted

   _____.
6. How do you change the name of a worksheet?
7. How does clearing a cell differ from deleting a cell?
8. What keyboard shortcut do you press to display the worksheet formulas?

Tutorial Summary

Review

In this tutorial, you learned the basics of spreadsheets and Excel. You learned about the major components of the Excel window. You also learned how to navigate within a worksheet and between worksheets in an Excel workbook. You learned how to enter text, dates, values, and formulas into a worksheet and were introduced to functions using the AutoSum button. Within the workbook, you practiced selecting and moving cell ranges. You saw how to insert new rows and columns into a workbook and how to modify the size of a column or row. You learned how to create new worksheets, rename them, and move them around the workbook. You learned how to check the spelling in a workbook, and finally, you learned how to print the contents of a workbook in different orientations and how to print the formulas in that workbook.

Key Terms

active cell	edit mode	sheet
adjacent range	formula	sheet tab
argument	Formula bar	Spell Checker
arithmetic operator	Formula view	spreadsheet
AutoComplete	function	SUM function
AutoSum	landscape orientation	tab scrolling buttons
cell	Name box	value
cell range	nonadjacent range	what-if analysis
cell reference	order of precedence	workbook
clear	portrait orientation	workbook window
column	range	worksheet
delete	range reference	worksheet window
documentation sheet	row	

Practice

Practice the skills you learned in the tutorial using the same case scenario.

Review Assignments

There are no Data Files needed for the Review Assignments.

Sandra has another set of orders she wants you to enter into a new Excel workbook. The data is shown in Figure 1-38.

Figure 1-38

Name	Address	Date	Item	Price	Qty
Wendy Battle	313 Oak Street Midtown, FL 80481 (833) 555-1284	5/1/2006	Deluxe Combo	$23	2
Eugene Burch	25 Fourth Street Cabot, FL 81121 (833) 555-3331	5/1/2006	Red Grapefruit	$14	4
Nicole Sweeny	312 Olive Street Midtown, FL 81241 (833) 555-9811	5/3/2006	Deluxe Combo	$23	1
Amy Yang	315 Maple Street Midtown, FL 80440 (833) 555-3881	5/4/2006	Navel Oranges	$17	3

Note that Sandra has added the phone numbers of the customers to her data. She wants the phone numbers entered into the customer address cell, but on a different line within that cell. To complete this task:

1. Start Excel and open a blank workbook. In the range A1:F5, enter the labels and data from Figure 1-38. Make sure that the address information is inserted with the street address on the first line; the city, state, and ZIP code on the second line; and the phone number on the third line.
2. In cell G1, enter the label "Total."
3. In the cells below G1, enter formulas to calculate the total amount of each order.
4. In cell A6, enter the label "TOTAL."

5. In cell F6, use the AutoSum button to calculate the total quantity of items ordered, and in cell G6, use the AutoSum button to calculate the total revenue generated by these orders.

6. Move sales data from the range A1:G6 to the range A5:G10.

7. In cell A1, enter the text "Dalton Food Co-op." In cell A2, enter the text "List of Orders." In cell A3, enter the text "May, 2006."

8. Change the width of columns A and B to 20 characters (or 145 pixels) each. Change the width of column D to 15 characters (or 110 pixels). Change the width of column G to 10 characters (or 75 pixels).

9. Select all of the cells in the worksheet, and then reduce the amount of empty space in the rows by reducing the row height to the height of the data contained in the rows.

10. Change the name of the worksheet to "Orders".

11. Create a worksheet named "Documentation" at the beginning of the workbook and, in the Documentation sheet, enter the following:
    - Cell A1: Dalton Food Co-op
    - Cell A3: Date:
    - Cell B3: *current date*
    - Cell A4: Created By:
    - Cell B4: *your name*
    - Cell A5: Purpose:
    - Cell B5: To enter May orders for the Dalton Food Co-op

12. Increase the width of column A in the Documentation worksheet to 20 characters.

13. Check the spelling on both worksheets, correcting any errors found.

14. Delete any empty worksheets from the workbook.

15. Print the contents of the workbook with the Documentation sheet in portrait orientation and the Orders worksheet in landscape orientation.

16. Display the formulas in the Orders worksheet. Preview the worksheet before printing it, and set up the worksheet to print as a single page.

17. Save the workbook as **Dalton2** in the Tutorial.01\Review folder included with your Data Files.

18. Insert the following new order in the Orders worksheet directly below Amy Yang's order:
    - Name: Chad Reynolds
    - Address: 100 School Lane
                Midtown, FL 80411
                (833) 555-4425
    - Date: 5/5/2006
    - Item: Navel Oranges
    - Price: $17
    - Qty: 2

19. Remove Amy Yang's order from the worksheet, and change the quantity ordered by Eugene Burch from 4 to 3.

20. Check the spelling in the Orders worksheet again, correcting any errors found.

21. Print the contents and formulas of the Orders worksheet again.

22. Save the workbook as **Dalton3** in the Tutorial.01\Review folder, and then close the workbook.

Case Problem 1

Data File needed for this Case Problem: Altac1.xls

Altac Bicycles Deborah York is a financial consultant for Altac Bicycles, an online seller of bicycles and bicycle equipment. She has entered some financial information in an Excel workbook, which she needs for a report she is writing. She has asked that you enter the remaining data and some formulas to complete the workbook. To complete this task:

1. Open the **Altac1** workbook located in the Tutorial.01\Cases folder included with your Data Files, and then save the workbook as **Altac2** in the same folder.
2. Insert two rows at the top of the Sheet1 worksheet, and then enter the following text on two separate lines within cell A1:
   Altac Bicycles
   Financial Data*
3. Insert five rows below the Expenses label in row 9, and then enter the following labels and data in the appropriate cells in columns B, C, D, and E, beginning on row 10:

Figure 1-39

Research	1,602	1,481	1,392
Sales and Marketing	2,631	2,012	1,840
Administrative	521	410	324
Research and Development	491	404	281
Total Operating Expenses			

4. Increase the width of column A to 18 characters and the width of column B to 25 characters. Decrease the height of row 1 to 30.
5. Rename Sheet1 "Financial Data".
6. Using the AutoSum feature, calculate the total operating expenses for each year.
7. For each year, enter formulas that calculate the following values:
   - gross margin, which is the difference between the net sales and the cost of sales
   - operating income, which is the difference between the gross margin and the total operating expenses
   - pre-tax income, which is the sum of the operating income and the other income
   - net income, which is the difference between the pre-tax income and the income taxes
8. Move the contents of range G4:K9 to range A22:E27. (*Note*: The worksheet window will automatically scroll as you move the selection down and to the left.)
9. For each year, enter a formula that calculates the net income per share, which is the net income divided by the number of shares.
10. Switch to Sheet2, and then enter the following text in the cells indicated:
    - Cell A1: Altac Bicycles
    - Cell A3: Date:
    - Cell B3: *current date*
    - Cell A4: Created By:
    - Cell B4: *your name*
    - Cell A5: Purpose:
    - Cell B5: Financial data for Altac Bicycles for 2006, 2005, and 2004
11. Increase the width of column A to 18 characters and the width of column B to 15 characters. Rename the sheet as "Documentation" and then move the sheet to the first position in the workbook.
12. Delete any empty worksheets, and then check the spelling in the workbook. Correct any errors found.
13. Save the changes you have made to the workbook, print the contents of the entire workbook in portrait orientation, and then close the workbook.

Apply

Use the skills you have learned to create a balance sheet for a food retailer.

Case Problem 2

Data File needed for this Case Problem: Halley1.xls

Halley Food Co.   Michael Li is working on the annual financial report for Halley Food Corporation, one of the biggest food retailers in the country. He has entered some financial data in an Excel workbook and would like you to complete the workbook by entering the remaining data and the formulas needed to calculate the total values.

To complete this task:

1. Open the **Halley1** workbook located in the Tutorial.01\Cases folder included with your Data Files, and then save the workbook as **Halley2** in the same folder.
2. Insert one row at the top of the worksheet, and then enter the following text on two separates lines within cell A1:
   Halley Food Co.
   Balance Sheet
3. Increase the width of column A to 30 characters, the width of column B to 20 characters, and the width of column C to 26 characters. Decrease the height of row 1 to 30.
4. Move range H3:I9 to B28:C34. (*Note:* The worksheet window will automatically scroll as you move the selection down and to the left.)
5. Enter the following data in columns D, E, and F for the shareholders' equity for each year:

Figure 1-40

Preferred and common stock	5,557	4,821	3,515
Retained earnings	5,666	4,007	3,401
Other comprehensive income	289	203	187

6. Using the AutoSum feature, calculate the totals for the current assets and the totals for the other assets for each year.
7. In row 17, enter formulas to calculate the total assets for each year, which is the sum of the total current assets and the total other assets.
8. Using the AutoSum feature, calculate the totals for the current liabilities and the totals for the shareholders' equity for each year.
9. In row 34, enter formulas to calculate the total liabilities and shareholders' equity for each year, which is the sum of the total current liabilities, the minority interest, and the total shareholders' equity for each year.
10. Rename Sheet1 as "Balance Sheet."
11. Switch to Sheet2, and then enter the following information in the cells indicated:
    - Cell A1: Halley Food Co.
    - Cell A3: Date:
    - Cell B3: *current date*
    - Cell A4: Created By:
    - Cell B4: *your name*
    - Cell A5: Purpose:
    - Cell B5: Balance sheet for Halley Food Co.
12. Resize column A to 20 characters and column B to 40 characters.
13. Rename Sheet2 as "Documentation" and move it to the beginning of the workbook. Delete the empty sheet.
14. Use the Spell Checker to correct any spelling errors in the workbook, and then print the entire workbook in landscape orientation.
15. Save your changes to the workbook, and then close it.

Challenge

Challenge yourself by going beyond what you've learned to create a worksheet that calculates the weighted scores of four possible locations for a new shoe factory.

Case Problem 3

Data File needed for this Case Problem: Site1.xls

Kips Shoes   Kips Shoes is planning to build a new factory. The company has narrowed the site down to four possible cities. Each city has been graded on a 1-to-10 scale for four categories: the size of the local market, the quality of the labor pool, the local tax base, and the local operating expenses. Each of these four factors is given a weight, with the most important factor given the highest weight. After the sites are analyzed, the scores for each factor will be multiplied by their weights, and then a total weighted score will be calculated.

Gwen Sanchez, the senior planning manager overseeing this project, has entered the weights and the scores for each city into an Excel workbook. She needs you to finish the workbook by inserting the formulas to calculate the weighted scores and the total overall score for each city. To complete this task:

1. Open the **Site1** workbook located in the Tutorial.01\Cases folder included with your Data Files, and then save the workbook as **Site2** in the same folder.
2. Switch to the Site Analysis sheet.
3. In cell B14, calculate the weighted Market Size score for Waukegan by inserting a formula that multiplies the value in cell B7 by the weight value in cell G7.
4. Insert formulas to calculate the weighted scores for the rest of the cells in the range B14:E17.

Explore

5. Select the range B18:E18, and then click the AutoSum button to calculate the sum of the weighted scores for all four of the cities. Note that you can apply the AutoSum button to more than one cell at a time. Which city has the highest weighted score?
6. Switch to the Documentation sheet, and enter your name and the date in the appropriate locations on the sheet.
7. Spell check the workbook, print the entire workbook in portrait orientation, and then save your changes to the workbook.

Explore

8. Gwen has another set of weighted scores she wants you to try. However, she doesn't want you to enter the new values in the Site Analysis worksheet, so you need to make a copy of the worksheet. To learn how to copy a worksheet, open the Excel Help task pane, and then enter "copy a worksheet" in the Search for text box. Scroll the list of topics in the Search Results task pane to locate the topic "Move or copy sheets." Open the topic, read the information about copying a sheet, and then close the Microsoft Excel Help window and the Search Results task pane.

Explore

9. Using what you learned in Step 8, create a copy of the Site Analysis worksheet, placing the new worksheet at the end of the workbook. Rename the new sheet "Site Analysis 2".
10. In the Site Analysis 2 worksheet, change the weighted scores of Market Size to 0.2 and Labor Pool to 0.4. Which city has the highest weighted score now?
11. Print the contents of the Site Analysis 2 worksheet.
12. Save the workbook as **Site3** in the Tutorial.01\Cases folder, and then close the workbook.

Create

Use Figure 1-41, which shows the "end results," to create a workbook containing monthly budget figures over a three-month period for a college student.

Case Problem 4

There are no Data Files needed for this Case Problem.

Monthly Budget   Alice Drake is a first-year student at MidWest University and has a part-time job in the admissions department. Her college-related expenses, such as tuition, books, and fees, are covered through grants and scholarships, so the money Alice makes goes towards her personal expenses. Being on her own for the first time, Alice is finding it difficult to keep within a budget. She has asked you to look at her finances and help her figure out how her money is being spent. Figure 1-41 shows the worksheet that you will create to help Alice analyze her budget.

Figure 1-41

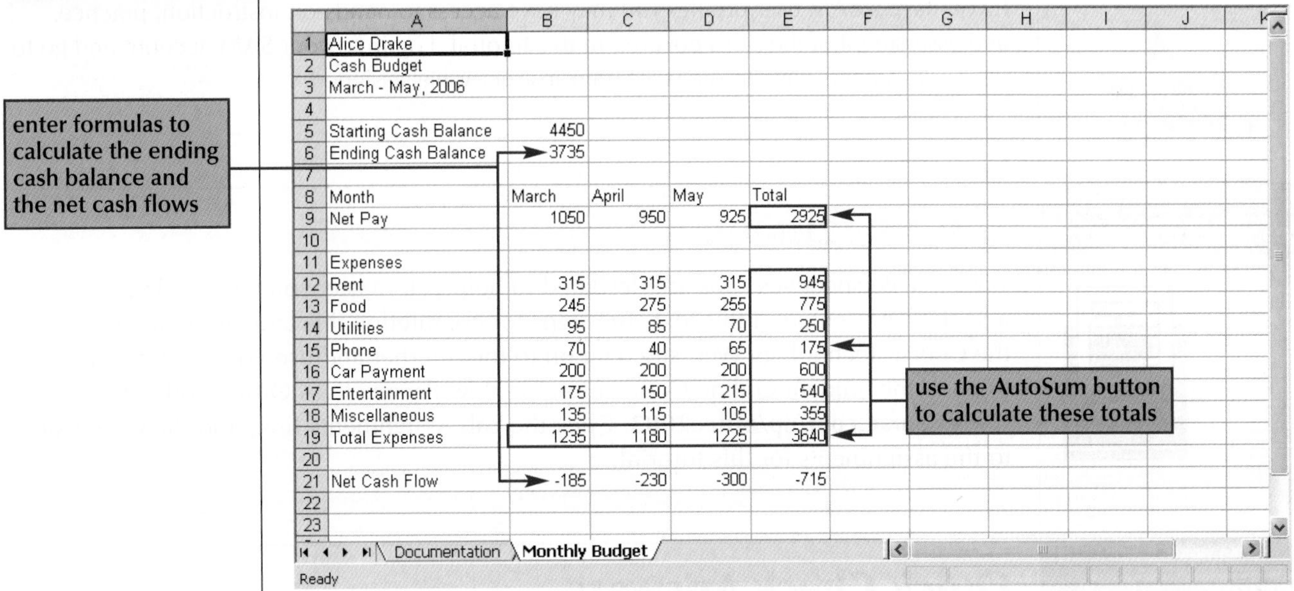

enter formulas to calculate the ending cash balance and the net cash flows

	A	B	C	D	E	F	G	H	I	J	K
1	Alice Drake										
2	Cash Budget										
3	March - May, 2006										
4											
5	Starting Cash Balance	4450									
6	Ending Cash Balance	3735									
7											
8	Month	March	April	May	Total						
9	Net Pay	1050	950	925	2925						
10											
11	Expenses										
12	Rent	315	315	315	945						
13	Food	245	275	255	775						
14	Utilities	95	85	70	250						
15	Phone	70	40	65	175						
16	Car Payment	200	200	200	600						
17	Entertainment	175	150	215	540						
18	Miscellaneous	135	115	105	355						
19	Total Expenses	1235	1180	1225	3640						
20											
21	Net Cash Flow	-185	-230	-300	-715						
22											
23											

use the AutoSum button to calculate these totals

Documentation \ **Monthly Budget** /

Ready

To complete this task:

1. Start Excel and save a new workbook with the name **Budget** in the Tutorial.01\Cases folder included with your Data Files.
2. On the Sheet1 worksheet, enter the labels and values as indicated in Figure 1-41. Note that the cells in which totals will be calculated have been marked. Do not enter the values shown; you will enter appropriate formulas next.
3. Using the AutoSum button, calculate the values for the total net pay, the total monthly expenses, and the total of each expense for the three months.
4. Enter formulas to calculate the net cash flow for each month and for all three months.
5. Enter a formula to calculate the ending cash balance, which is based on the value of the starting cash balance minus the total net cash flow over the three months. (*Hint:* Because two negatives make a positive, you need to *add* the total net cash flow to the starting cash balance.)
6. Rename Sheet1 as "Monthly Budget."
7. Create a worksheet named "Documentation" at the front of the workbook containing your name, the date, and the purpose of the workbook.
8. Delete any blank worksheets in the workbook.
9. Check the spelling on both worksheets, correcting any errors found.
10. Print the entire workbook in portrait orientation.
11. Save your changes to the workbook, and then close it.

Research

Use the Internet to find and work with data related to the topics presented in this tutorial.

Internet Assignments

The purpose of the Internet Assignments is to challenge you to find information on the Internet that you can use to work effectively with this software. The actual assignments are updated and maintained on the Course Technology Web site. Log on to the Internet and use your Web browser to go to the Student Online Companion for New Perspectives Office 2003 at **www.course.com/np/office2003**. Click the Internet Assignments link, and then navigate to the assignments for this tutorial.

Assess

SAM Assessment and Training

If you have a SAM user profile, you may have access to hands-on instruction, practice, and assessment of the skills covered in this tutorial. Log in to your SAM account and go to your assignments page to see what your instructor has assigned.

Reinforce

Lab Assignments

Spreadsheets

The New Perspectives Labs are designed to help you master some of the key concepts and skills presented in this text. The steps for completing this Lab are located on the Course Technology Web site. Log on to the Internet and use your Web browser to go to the Student Online Companion for New Perspectives Office 2003 at **www.course.com/np/office2003**. Click the Lab Assignments link, and then navigate to the assignments for this tutorial.

Review

Quick Check Answers

Session 1.1

1. cell
2. D2
3. Ctrl + Home
4. click the Sheet2 tab
5. a. value
   b. text
   c. value
   d. text (there is no equal sign indicating a formula)
   e. text
   f. formula
   g. text
6. Press the Alt + Enter keys to enter text on a new line within a cell.
7. =E5/E6

Session 1.2

1. An adjacent cell range is a rectangular block of cells. A non-adjacent cell range consists of two or more separate adjacent ranges.
2. A5:F8
3. AutoSum
4. down
5. to the right
6. Double-click the sheet tab and then type the new name to replace the highlighted sheet tab name.
7. Clearing a cell deletes the cell's contents but does not affect the position of other cells in the workbook. Deleting a cell removes the cell from the worksheet, and other cells are shifted in the direction of the deleted cell.
8. Ctrl + ` (grave accent)

Objectives

Session 2.1
- Learn about the syntax of an Excel function
- Use the SUM, AVERAGE, and MAX functions
- Copy and paste formulas
- Work with relative, absolute, and mixed references
- Change the magnification of the workbook window
- Insert a function using the Insert Function dialog box
- Use Auto Fill to insert formulas and complete a series
- Insert the current date using a Date function

Session 2.2 (Optional)
- Work with Financial functions
- Work with Logical functions

Working with Formulas and Functions

Developing a Family Budget

Case

Tyler Family Budget

As a newly married couple, Amanda and Joseph Tyler are trying to balance career, school, and family life. Amanda works full time as a legal assistant, and Joseph is in a graduate program at a nearby university. He recently was hired as a teaching assistant. In the summer, he is able to take on other jobs that bring additional income to the family. The couple also just moved into a new apartment. Although Joseph's and Amanda's salaries for the past year were greater than the years before, the couple seemed to have less cash on hand. This financial shortage has prompted them to take a closer look at their finances and figure out how to best manage them.

Because Amanda has agreed to take the lead role in the management of the family finances, she has set up an Excel workbook. Amanda has entered their salary amounts, which are their only income, and she has identified and entered several expenses that the family pays on a monthly basis, such as the rent and Joseph's tuition. She wants to calculate how much money they bring in and how much money they spend. She also wants to figure out their average monthly expenses and identify their greatest financial burden.

Amanda has asked for your help in completing the workbook. She wants you to insert formulas to perform the calculations she needs to get a better overall picture of the family's finances, which, in turn, should help the couple manage their money more effectively. Because the values entered cover a 12-month span, you will be able to copy and paste the formulas from one month to another and fill in series of data, such as the months of the year, rather than retyping formulas or entering each month individually. Finally, Amanda also wants the current date in her workbook, which you can enter using one of Excel's Date functions.

Student Data Files

▼ **Tutorial.02**

▽ **Tutorial folder**

Budget1.xls

▽ **Review folder**

Family1.xls

▽ **Cases folder**

Chem1.xls   Soup1.xls
Sales1.xls   Works1.xls
Sonic1.xls

Once she has a better handle on the family's finances, Amanda might want to evaluate whether buying a house would be possible in the near future, especially in light of the low interest rates that are available.

Session 2.1

Working with Excel Functions

In her budget worksheet, Amanda has already entered the couple's take-home salaries (that is, the amount of money in their paychecks minus taxes and other work-related deductions) and their expenses from the past year. You'll begin by opening her workbook so you can see what Amanda has done so far.

To open Amanda's workbook:

1. Start Excel and then open the **Budget1** workbook located in the Tutorial.02\Tutorial folder included with your Data Files.

2. On the Documentation sheet, enter *your name* in cell B3 and the *current date* in cell B4.

3. Save the workbook as **Budget2** in the Tutorial.02\Tutorial folder, and then click the **Budget** tab to make this sheet the active worksheet. See Figure 2-1. Amanda has recorded the couple's take-home salaries as income and has listed a variety of expenses in columns for each month. January's income and expenses are shown in column B, February's income and expenses are shown in column C, and so forth.

Figure 2-1	Budget worksheet

Microsoft Excel - Budget2

	A	B	C	D	E	F	G	H	I	J	K
1	Tyler Family Budget	1/1/2006 - 12/31/2006									
2											
3	MONTHLY TOTALS										
4		1/1/2006	2/1/2006	3/1/2006	4/1/2006	5/1/2006	6/1/2006	7/1/2006	8/1/2006	9/1/2006	10/1/2006
5	Income										
6	Amanda	2,400	2,400	2,400	2,400	2,400	2,400	2,400	2,400	2,400	2,400
7	Joseph	850	850	850	850	850	1,650	1,650	1,650	850	850
8	Total										
9											
10	Expenses										
11	Rent	850	850	850	850	850	850	850	850	850	850
12	Food	607	657	613	655	644	761	699	672	683	609
13	Utilities	225	210	200	175	150	130	145	165	175	175
14	Phone	58	63	63	63	59	59	64	63	64	58
15	Loan Payments	150	150	150	150	150	150	150	150	150	150
16	Car Payments	175	175	175	175	175	175	175	175	175	175
17	Insurance	50	50	50	50	50	50	50	50	50	50
18	Miscellaneous	140	191	171	135	171	272	146	182	144	140
19	Entertainment	192	160	172	166	185	310	155	164	132	150
20	Tuition	2,000	0	0	0	0	0	0	2,200	0	0
21	Books	520	0	0	0	0	0	0	572	0	0
22	Total										
23											

Documentation \ **Budget** /

Ready

Amanda would like the worksheet to calculate the family's total income and expenses for each month. She would also like to see a year-end summary that displays the family's total income and expenses for the entire year. This summary should also display the average income and expenses so that Amanda can get a picture of what a typical month looks like for her family. Amanda realizes that some expenses increase and decrease during certain months, so she would like to calculate the minimum and maximum values for each expense category, which will give her an idea of the range of these values throughout the year. All of this information will help Amanda and Joseph budget for the upcoming year.

To perform these calculations, you'll have to add several formulas to the workbook. As discussed in the previous tutorial, formulas are one of the most useful features in Excel because they enable you to calculate values based on data entered into the workbook. For more complex calculations, you can enter formulas that contain one or more functions. Recall that a function is a predefined formula that performs calculations using specific values. Each Excel function has a name and syntax. The **syntax** is the rule specifying how the function should be written. The general syntax of all Excel functions is

FUNCTION(argument1, argument2, ...)

where *FUNCTION* is the name of the Excel function and *argument1, argument2,* and so forth are **arguments** specifying the numbers, text, or cell references used by the function to calculate a value. An argument can also be an **optional argument** that is not necessary for the function to calculate a value. If an optional argument is not included, Excel assumes a default value for it. Each argument entered in a function is separated by a comma. The convention used in this text shows optional arguments within square brackets along with the argument's default value, as follows:

FUNCTION(argument1, [argument2=value2])

where *argument2* is an optional argument and *value2* is the default value for this argument. As you learn more about individual functions, you will also learn which arguments are required and which are optional.

Another convention followed in this text is to write function names in uppercase letters, but Excel recognizes the function names entered in either uppercase or lowercase letters, converting the lowercase letters to uppercase automatically.

There are 350 different Excel functions organized into the following 10 categories:

- Database functions
- Date and Time functions
- Engineering functions
- Financial functions
- Information functions
- Logical functions
- Lookup and Reference functions
- Math and Trigonometry functions
- Statistical functions
- Text and Data functions

You can learn about each function using Excel's online Help. Figure 2-2 describes some of the more important Math and Statistical functions that you may often use in your workbooks.

Figure 2-2 ▶ **Math and Statistical functions**

Function	Description
AVERAGE(*number1*, [*number2*, *number3*, ...])	Calculates the average of a collection of numbers, where *number1*, *number2*, and so forth are numeric values or cell references
COUNT(*value1*, [*value2*, *value3*, ...])	Calculates the total number of values, where *value1*, *value2*, and so forth are numeric values, text entries, or cell references
MAX(*number1*, [*number2*, *number3*, ...])	Calculates the maximum of a collection of numbers, where *number1*, *number2*, and so forth are either numeric values or cell references
MEDIAN(*number1*, [*number2*, *number3*, ...])	Calculates the median, or the number in the middle, of a collection of numbers, where *number1*, *number2*, and so forth are either numeric values or cell references
MIN(*number1*, [*number2*, *number3*, ...])	Calculates the minimum of a collection of numbers, where *number1*, *number2*, and so forth are either numeric values or cell references
ROUND(*number*, *num_digits*)	Rounds a number to a specified number of digits, where *number* is the number you want to round and *num_digits* specifies the number of digits to which you want to round the number
SUM(*number1*, [*number2*, *number3*, ...])	Calculates the sum of a collection of numbers, where *number1*, *number2*, and so forth are either numeric values or cell references

For example, the **AVERAGE function** calculates the average value of a collection of numbers. The syntax of this function is AVERAGE(*number1*, [*number2*, ...]). When you enter the arguments *(number1, number2)*, you can enter these numbers directly into the function, as in AVERAGE(3, 2, 5, 8), or you can enter the references to the worksheet cells that contain those numbers, as in AVERAGE(A1:A4). You can also enter a function as part of a larger formula. For example, the formula =*MAX(A1:A100)/100* calculates the maximum value in the cell range A1:A100 and then divides that number by 100. You can include, or "nest," one function within another. For example, in the formula =*ROUND(AVERAGE(A1:A100),1)*, the first argument in the ROUND function uses the value calculated by the AVERAGE function; the second argument is a constant. The result is a formula that calculates the average value of the numbers in the range A1:A100, rounding that value to the first decimal place.

In the previous tutorial, you calculated totals using the AutoSum button on the Standard toolbar. Although using the AutoSum feature is a quick and convenient way to calculate a value, it is only one way to perform this calculation in Excel. To determine the totals Amanda wants, you can also use the **SUM function**, which calculates the sum of a collection of numbers. The syntax of the SUM function is SUM(*number1*, [*number2*, ...]), which is similar to that of the AVERAGE function.

You'll use the SUM function now to begin calculating the values Amanda needs, starting with the values for the month of January.

To calculate the total income and expenses for January using the SUM function:

1. Click cell **B8** on the Budget worksheet, type **=SUM(B6:B7)** and then press the **Enter** key. Excel displays the value 3,250 in cell B8, indicating that the total income for the month of January is $3,250.

   You can also enter the cell range for a function by selecting the cell range rather than typing it. You'll use this method to determine the total expenses for January.

2. Click cell **B22** and then type **=SUM(** to begin the function.

3. Select the range **B11:B21** using your mouse. As you drag to select the range, its cell reference is automatically entered into the SUM function, as shown in Figure 2-3.

Entering the SUM function | Figure 2-3

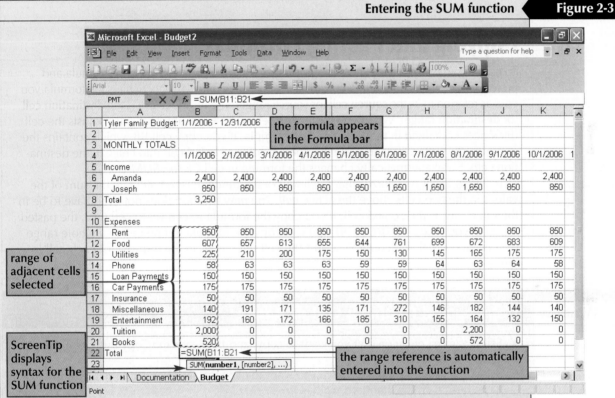

4. Press the **Enter** key to complete the formula. Note that you didn't have to type the closing parenthesis. When you press the Enter key, the closing parenthesis is inserted automatically. The value 4,967 is displayed in cell B22, indicating that the total expenses for January are $4,967.

Amanda wants to know how much money is left over at the end of each month or, in other words, the family's *net income* each month. To determine this amount, you need to enter a formula that subtracts the total monthly expenses from the total monthly income. You'll begin by calculating the net income for the month of January.

To calculate the net income for the first month:

▶ 1. Click cell **A24**, type **Net Income**, and then press the **Tab** key to move to cell B24, where you will enter the formula.

▶ 2. Type **=B8-B22** and then press the **Enter** key. Excel displays the value –1,717, which indicates that the family's net income for the month of January is a negative $1,717. Amanda and Joseph's expenses are greater than their income for that month.

Now that you've entered the formulas to calculate the total income, total expenses, and net income for January, you need to enter the same formulas for the other 11 months of the year. Entering the formulas for each of the remaining months individually would be time-consuming, but there is a quicker way.

Copying and Pasting Formulas

To use the same formula in different cells on the worksheet, you can copy the formula and paste it to a new location or locations. The cell (or range of cells) that contains the formula you copy is referred to as the **source cell** (or **source range**). The new location is the **destination cell** (or **destination range**). When you paste your selection, Excel automatically adjusts the cell references contained in the formulas. For example, if you copy cell B8, which contains the formula =SUM(B6:B7), and paste the contents of the copied cell into cell C8 (the destination cell), Excel automatically changes the formula in cell C8 to =SUM(C6:C7).

In effect, Excel recognizes that the intent of the function is to calculate the sum of the values in the two cells above the active cell. The new location does not even have to be in the same row as the copied cell. If you copy the formula in cell B8 to cell C10, the pasted formula would be =SUM(C8:C9). You can copy the formula in one cell to a whole range of cells, and Excel will correctly adjust the cell references in the formula for each cell in the range.

Reference Window	**Copying and Pasting a Cell or Range**

- Select the cell or range that you want to copy, and then click the Copy button on the Standard toolbar.
- Select the cell or range into which you want to copy the selection, and then click the Paste button on the Standard toolbar.

Next, you'll copy the formula in cell B8 to the range C8:M8 to calculate the total income for the remaining months.

To copy and paste the formula from cell B8 to the range C8:M8:

▶ 1. Click cell **B8** on the Budget worksheet, and then click the **Copy** button 🖻 on the Standard toolbar. Note that the copied cell has a moving border. This border is a visual reminder that the range has been copied and is ready to be pasted.

▶ 2. Select the range **C8:M8**, and then click the **Paste** button 🖺 on the Standard toolbar. Excel copies the formula in cell B8 into each of the cells in the range C8:M8, changing the cell references to match the location of each cell in the range. See Figure 2-4. Note that when you paste a selection, Excel automatically displays the Paste Options button. This button provides options that give you control over the paste process. You will learn more about this button in the next tutorial.

Copying the SUM function for the monthly income | **Figure 2-4**

	B	C	D	E	F	G	H	I	J	K	L	M
1	1/1/2006 - 12/31/2006											
2												
3												
4	1/1/2006	2/1/2006	3/1/2006	4/1/2006	5/1/2006	6/1/2006	7/1/2006	8/1/2006	9/1/2006	10/1/2006	11/1/2006	12/1/2006
5												
6	2,400	2,400	2,400	2,400	2,400	2,400	2,400	2,400	2,400	2,400	2,400	2,400
7	850	850	850	850	850	1,650	1,650	1,650	850	850	850	850
8	3,250	3,250	3,250	3,250	3,250	4,050	4,050	4,050	3,250	3,250	3,250	3,250
9												
10												
11	850	850	850	850	850	850	850	850	850	850	850	850
12	607	657	613	655	644	761	699	672	683	609	642	606
13	225	210	200	175	150	130	145	165	175	175	190	220
14	58	63	63	63	59	59	64	63	64	58	78	112

pasted formulas

Trouble? If your screen does not match the one shown in the figure, you may have scrolled the worksheet further to the right so column B is no longer visible. You can click the left scroll button on the horizontal scroll bar to reposition the worksheet in the workbook window to better match the one in the figure.

3. Press the **Ctrl + `** (grave accent) keys to display the formulas in the range B8:M8. Notice that the cell references in each formula refer to the income values for that particular month.

4. Press the **Ctrl + `** (grave accent) keys to return to Normal view.

You are not limited to copying a single formula from one cell. You can also copy a range of formulas. When you copy a range of cells, each of which contains a formula, and then paste the selection into a new location, Excel pastes the formulas in each cell to their corresponding locations in the new cell range. You don't have to select a range that is the same size as the range being copied. You just need to select the first, or upper leftmost, cell in the destination range, and Excel will paste the selection in a range that accommodates all the cells. Any existing text or values in the destination range will be overwritten. So, be sure you paste the selection in an area of the worksheet that can accommodate the selection without deleting existing data.

Next, you need to copy the formulas for January's total expenses and net income, which are in cells B22 and B24, to the ranges C22:M22 and C24:M24. Then Amanda will be able to see each month's total expenses and net income values. Although there is no formula in cell B23, you will select the range B22:B24 and paste the selection to range C22:M24, simplifying the process. No values will appear in row 23.

To copy and paste the formulas in the range B22:B24 to the range C22:M24:

1. Scroll the worksheet to the left, if necessary, so column B is visible, select the range **B22:B24**, and then click the **Copy** button on the Standard toolbar.

    Trouble? If the Clipboard task pane opens, close it. You will not need to use it in this tutorial.

2. Select the range **C22:M24**, and then click the **Paste** button [icon] on the Standard toolbar. Figure 2-5 shows the total expenses and net income values for each month in the Budget worksheet. Note that Excel has duplicated the two formulas from the first month in each succeeding month.

| Figure 2-5 | Copying and pasting a cell range |

total monthly expenses

17	50	50	50	50	50	50	50	50	50	50	50	50
18	140	191	171	135	171	272	146	182	144	140	147	213
19	192	160	172	166	185	310	155	164	132	150	162	200
20	2,000	0	0	0	0	0	0	2,200	0	0	0	0
21	520	0	0	0	0	0	0	572	0	0	0	0
22	4,967	2,506	2,444	2,419	2,434	2,757	2,434	5,243	2,423	2,357	2,444	2,576
23												
24	-1,717	744	806	831	816	1,293	1,616	-1,193	827	893	806	674
25												
26												

|◄ ◄ ► ►|\ Documentation \ **Budget** /

Select destination and press ENTER or choose Paste   Sum=38,150

total monthly net income values

3. Press the **Esc** key to remove the moving border from the selected range.

As you can see, Excel's ability to adjust cell references when copying and pasting formulas makes it easy to create columns or rows of formulas that share a common structure.

Using Relative and Absolute References

The type of cell reference that you just worked with is called a relative reference. A **relative reference** is a cell reference that changes when it is copied and pasted in a new location. Excel interprets the reference *relative* to the position of the active cell. For example, when you copied the formula =SUM(B6:B7) from the source cell, B8, and pasted it in the destination range, C8:M8, Excel adjusted the cell references in each pasted formula relative to the new location of the formula itself. The formula in cell C8 became =SUM(C6:C7), the formula in cell D8 became =SUM(D6:D7), and so on.

A second type of cell reference is an absolute reference. An **absolute reference** is a cell reference that doesn't change when it is copied. Excel does not adjust the cell reference because the cell reference points to a fixed, or *absolute,* location in the worksheet, and it remains fixed when the copied formula is pasted. In Excel, an absolute reference appears with a dollar sign ($) before each column and row designation. For example, $B$8 is an absolute reference, and when it is used in a formula, Excel will always point to the cell located at the intersection of column B and row 8.

Figure 2-6 provides an example in which an absolute reference is necessary to a formula. In this example, a sales worksheet records the units sold for each region as well as the overall total. If you want to calculate the percent of units sold for each region, you divide the units sold for each region by the overall total. If you use only relative references, copying the formula from the first region to the second will produce an incorrect result, because Excel shifts the location of the total sales cell down one row. To correct this problem, you use an absolute cell reference, fixing the location of the total sales cell at cell B8. In the example, this means changing the formula in cell C4 from =B4/B8 to =B4/$B$8.

Using relative and absolute references ◄ **Figure 2-6**

Formulas Using Relative References

	A	B	C	D
1	Sales			
2				
3	Regions	Units Sold	Percent	
4	Region 1	2,238	=B4/B8	
5	Region 2	1,321		
6	Region 3	3,093		
7	Region 4	1,905		
8	Total	8,557		
9				
10				

	A	B	C	D
1	Sales			
2				
3	Regions	Units Sold	Percent	
4	Region 1	2,238	0.26154026	
5	Region 2	1,321	=B5/B9	
6	Region 3	3,093		
7	Region 4	1,905		
8	Total	8,557		
9				
10				

When the formula is copied, the relative reference to the cell (B8) is shifted down and now points to an incorrect cell (B9).

Formulas Using Absolute References

	A	B	C	D
1	Sales			
2				
3	Regions	Units Sold	Percent	
4	Region 1	2,238	=B4/$B$8	
5	Region 2	1,321		
6	Region 3	3,093		
7	Region 4	1,905		
8	Total	8,557		
9				
10				

	A	B	C	D
1	Sales			
2				
3	Regions	Units Sold	Percent	
4	Region 1	2,238	0.26154026	
5	Region 2	1,321	=B5/$B$8	
6	Region 3	3,093		
7	Region 4	1,905		
8	Total	8,557		
9				
10				

When the formula is copied, the absolute reference to the cell ($B$8) continues to point to that cell.

Another type of reference supported by Excel is the mixed reference. A **mixed reference** contains both relative and absolute cell references. A mixed reference for cell B8 is either $B8 or B$8. In the case of the mixed reference $B8, the column portion of the reference remains fixed, but the row number adjusts as the formula is copied to a new location. In the B$8 reference, the row number remains fixed, whereas the column portion adjusts to each new cell location.

As you enter a formula that requires an absolute reference or a mixed reference, you can type the dollar sign for the column and row references as needed. If you have already entered a formula and need to change the type of cell reference used, you can switch to edit mode and then press the **F4** key. As you press this function key, Excel cycles through the different references for the cell in the formula at the location of the insertion point. Pressing the F4 key changes a relative reference to an absolute reference, then to a mixed reference for the row, then to a mixed reference for the column, and then back to a relative reference.

In Amanda's family budget, monthly expenses vary greatly throughout the year. For example, tuition is a major expense, and that bill must be paid once in January and once in August. Amanda knows that the family has more entertainment and miscellaneous expenses during the month of December than at other times. The family's monthly income also fluctuates as Joseph brings in more income during the summer months than at other times. Amanda would like her budget worksheet to keep a running total of the family's net income as it progresses through the year. For example, she knows that the family will start the year with less money because of the tuition bill in January. Amanda wonders how many months pass before they recover from that major expense and begin saving money again.

One way to calculate the running total is to add the net income values of consecutive months. For example, to figure out how much money the family has saved or lost after two months, you add the net income for January to the net income for February, using the formula =SUM(B24:C24). To figure out the total net income for the first three months, you use the formula =SUM(B24:D24); through the first four months the formula will be =SUM(B24:E24), and so on.

The starting point of the range in the formula needs to be fixed at the cell that contains the net income for January, cell B24. To be sure that the formula points to cell B24, you need to use the absolute reference $B$24. The ending cell of the range will shift as you copy the formula to the other months in the worksheet. You need to use a relative reference for the ending cell in the range so that Excel will adjust the reference as the formula is copied. The formula for the running total through the first two months will be =SUM($B$24:C24). When you paste this formula to the other months of the year, Excel will adjust the cell range to calculate the total for all of the months up to that point.

To calculate the running total using an absolute reference to cell B24:

1. Click cell **A25**, type **Running Total**, and then press the **Tab** key twice to move to column C.

2. Type **=SUM(B24:C24)** in cell C25, and then press the **Enter** key. Excel displays the value –973, showing that the family's expenses exceed their income by $973 through the first two months of the year.

   Now you'll change the formula to use an absolute reference for cell B24 by selecting it in the formula and pressing the F4 key.

3. Double-click cell **C25** to switch to edit mode, and then double-click **B24** within the formula to select the cell reference.

4. Press the **F4** key to change the cell reference from B24 to $B$24. See Figure 2-7.

Figure 2-7	Entering an absolute reference

17	Insurance	50	50	50	50	50	50	50	50	50	50
18	Miscellaneous	140	191	171	135	171	272	146	182	144	140
19	Entertainment	192	160	172	166	185	310	155	164	132	150
20	Tuition	2,000	0	0	0	0	0	0	2,200	0	0
21	Books	520	0	0	0	0	0	0	572	0	0
22	Total	4,967	2,506	2,444	2,419	2,434	2,757	2,434	5,243	2,423	2,357
23											
24	Net Income	-1,717	744	806	831	816	1,293	1,616	-1,193	827	893
25	Running Total		=SUM($B$24:C24)								
26			SUM(**number1**, [number2], ...)								
27											
28			absolute reference entered by pressing the F4 key								
29											

Documentation / **Budget**

Edit

Trouble? If you pressed the F4 key too many times and passed the absolute reference, continue pressing the F4 key to cycle through the options until $B$24 is displayed in the formula.

5. Press the **Enter** key when the correct reference is displayed. Excel displays the value –973.

   Now you can copy this formula to the remaining months of the year.

6. Click cell **C25**, and then click the **Copy** button on the Standard toolbar. The moving border indicates that cell C25 has been copied.

7. Select the range **D25:M25**, and then click the **Paste** button on the Standard toolbar. Excel copies the formula to the remaining cells, as shown in Figure 2-8. The amount shown for each month represents the cash on hand that the family accumulated during the year, up to and including that month. So, for example, at the end of the year, after paying all expenses, they have a total of $6,396.

Running total of the family's net income | **Figure 2-8**

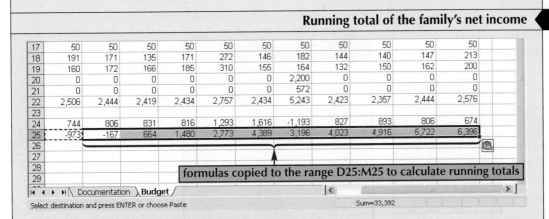

	17	50	50	50	50	50	50	50	50	50	50	50
	18	191	171	135	171	272	146	182	144	140	147	213
	19	160	172	166	185	310	155	164	132	150	162	200
	20	0	0	0	0	0	0	2,200	0	0	0	0
	21	0	0	0	0	0	0	572	0	0	0	0
	22	2,506	2,444	2,419	2,434	2,757	2,434	5,243	2,423	2,357	2,444	2,576
	23											
	24	744	806	831	816	1,293	1,616	-1,193	827	893	806	674
	25	-973	-167	664	1,480	2,773	4,389	3,196	4,023	4,916	5,722	6,396
	26											
	27											
	28											
	29											

formulas copied to the range D25:M25 to calculate running totals

Documentation / Budget

Select destination and press ENTER or choose Paste   Sum=33,392

8. Press the **Ctrl +** ` (grave accent) keys to examine the pasted formulas in the range D25:M25. The use of absolute and relative references ensures the integrity of the formula copied in each cell used to calculate the running net income total.

9. Press the **Ctrl +** ` (grave accent) keys to return to Normal view.

Working with Other Paste Options

So far you've used the Paste button to paste formulas from a source cell or range to a destination cell or range. When Excel pastes the contents of a selected cell or range, it also pastes any formatting applied to the source cell (you'll learn about formatting in the next tutorial). If you want more control over how Excel pastes the data from the source cell, you can click the list arrow next to the Paste button and choose one of the available paste options. Figure 2-9 describes each of these options.

Paste options | **Figure 2-9**

Option	Description
Formulas	Pastes the formula(s), but not the formatting, of the source cell range
Values	Pastes the value(s), but not the formula(s) or formatting, of the source cell range
No Borders	Pastes the formula(s) and formatting of the source cell range, but not the format of the cell range's borders
Transpose	Pastes the formula(s) and formatting of the source cell range, except changes the orientation so that rows in the source cell range become columns, and columns become rows
Paste Link	Pastes a link to the cell(s) in the source cell range, including the formatting used
Paste Special	Opens a dialog box displaying more paste options

For example, if you want to paste the value calculated by the formula in a cell but not the formula itself, you use the Values option. This is useful in situations in which you want to "freeze" a calculated value and remove the risk of it being changed by inadvertently changing another value in the worksheet. For even more control over the paste feature, you can select the Paste Special option. When you select this option, the Paste Special dialog box opens, as shown in Figure 2-10.

Figure 2-10 ▶ Paste Special dialog box

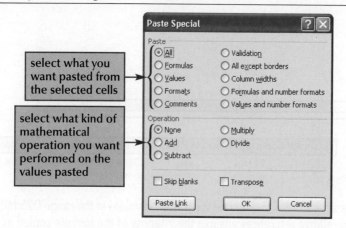

Using this dialog box, you can not only specify exactly which parts of the source cell or range—formulas, values, or formats—you want to paste, but also specify a mathematical operation you want performed as part of the paste action. For example, you can copy the value of one cell and add that value to cells in the destination range.

Another method that gives you control over the paste process is provided by the Paste Options button, which appears each time you paste a selection. By clicking this icon, you can choose from a variety of options that determine how the pasted data should be formatted. You'll explore this feature more in the next tutorial.

Changing the Magnification of a Worksheet

As you learned in Tutorial 1, an Excel worksheet can have 256 columns and more than 65,000 rows of data. You also learned that you can freeze columns and rows, so as you scroll through the data in the worksheet, the column and row headings remain visible. The number of columns and rows displayed in the workbook window depends on the zoom magnification set for the worksheet. The default zoom magnification setting is 100%. You can change this setting using the Zoom command on the View menu or the Zoom button on the Standard toolbar. Changing the zoom magnification setting allows you to see more or less of the worksheet at one time. If you decrease the magnification, you will see more of the data in the worksheet, but the data will be smaller and may be more difficult to read. If you increase the magnification, you will see less of the data in the worksheet, but the data will be larger and easier to read.

Reference Window

Changing the Zoom Magnification of the Workbook Window

- Click View on the menu bar, and then click Zoom.
- Click the option button for the percent magnification you want to apply, and then click the OK button.

or

- Click the Zoom list arrow on the Standard toolbar, and then click the percent option you want to apply.

You can change the magnification of the workbook window from 10% up to 400% or enter a percent not offered, for example, 65%, to further customize the display of your workbook window. You can also select a zoom magnification specific to the content of your worksheet. To do this, you select the worksheet's content and then choose the Selection option in the Zoom dialog box or on the Zoom list. Excel displays the content of the selection at a magnification that fills the entire workbook window.

Before continuing, Amanda wants to review the work done so far. Try changing the magnification so more of the worksheet is displayed at one time.

To change the zoom setting for the workbook window:

1. Press the **Ctrl + Home** keys to make cell A1 the active cell.

2. Click **View** on the menu bar, and then click **Zoom** to open the Zoom dialog box.

3. Click the **75%** option button in the list of options, and then click the **OK** button. At this setting, all the data in the worksheet is displayed in the workbook window, as shown in Figure 2-11.

Budget worksheet at 75 percent magnification | **Figure 2-11**

indicates the current zoom magnification setting

	A	B	C	D	E	F	G	H	I	J	K	L	
1	Tyler Family Budget: 1/1/2006 - 12/31/2006												
2													
3	MONTHLY TOTALS												
4		1/1/2006	2/1/2006	3/1/2006	4/1/2006	5/1/2006	6/1/2006	7/1/2006	8/1/2006	9/1/2006	10/1/2006	11/1/2006	12/1/2006
5	Income												
6	Amanda	2,400	2,400	2,400	2,400	2,400	2,400	2,400	2,400	2,400	2,400	2,400	2,400
7	Joseph	850	850	850	850	850	1,650	1,650	1,650	850	850	850	850
8	Total	3,250	3,250	3,250	3,250	3,250	4,050	4,050	4,050	3,250	3,250	3,250	3,250
9													
10	Expenses												
11	Rent	850	850	850	850	850	850	850	850	850	850	850	850
12	Food	607	657	613	655	644	761	699	672	683	609	642	606
13	Utilities	225	210	200	175	150	130	145	165	175	175	190	220
14	Phone	58	63	63	63	59	59	64	63	64	58	78	112
15	Loan Payments	150	150	150	150	150	150	150	150	150	150	150	150
16	Car Payments	175	175	175	175	175	175	175	175	175	175	175	175
17	Insurance	50	50	50	50	50	50	50	50	50	50	50	50
18	Miscellaneous	140	191	171	135	171	272	146	182	144	140	147	213
19	Entertainment	192	160	172	166	185	310	155	164	132	150	162	200
20	Tuition	2,000	0	0	0	0	0	0	2,200	0	0	0	0
21	Books	520	0	0	0	0	0	0	572	0	0	0	0
22	Total	4,967	2,506	2,444	2,419	2,434	2,757	2,434	5,243	2,423	2,357	2,444	2,576
23													
24	Net Income	-1,717	744	806	831	816	1,293	1,616	-1,193	827	893	806	674
25	Running Total		-973	-167	664	1,480	2,773	4,389	3,196	4,023	4,916	5,722	6,396
26													
27													

More of the worksheet is visible; however, reading the individual cell values is more difficult, so you will change the magnification back to 100%.

4. Click the **Zoom** list arrow `100%` on the Standard toolbar, and then click **100%** to return to this higher magnification. Although the overall appearance of your screen may differ from the figures in this text, the data is not affected.

From examining the running totals, Amanda has learned several important facts. One of the family's largest expenses is Joseph's tuition, which is paid in January and August. She has also learned that the family does not recover from this January expense and show a positive overall net income until the month of April, when the total savings amount for the year up to that point is $664. Therefore, with their current income and expenses, it takes four months to "catch up" with the tuition expenditure in January, which leaves the family short on cash during February and March. The good news is that the total net income at the end of 12 months is $6,396, which represents the amount of money the family is able to save for the entire year.

Amanda now wants to know the family's total income and its total yearly expenses. You'll place these calculations in a table below the monthly figures. First, you will copy the income and expense categories to a new cell range.

To copy the income and expense categories:

▶ 1. Click cell **A27**, type **YEAR-END SUMMARY**, and then press the **Enter** key.

▶ 2. Copy the range **A5:A24** and paste it into the range **A29:A48**. If you want to remove the selection border from the copied range, you can press the Esc key. The selection border will disappear as soon as you select another range.

   Now you will enter the formula to calculate the total income for the family over the entire year.

▶ 3. Click cell **B28**, type **Total**, and then press the **Enter** key twice. You will enter the formula to calculate Amanda's salary for the year.

▶ 4. Type **=SUM(B6:M6)** in cell B30, and then press the **Enter** key. The amount 28,800 appears in the cell.

   Now you will copy this formula to calculate Joseph's yearly income, the couple's combined income, and the yearly totals for the expense categories.

▶ 5. Click cell **B30** to select this cell again, and then click the **Copy** button 🖹 on the Standard toolbar.

▶ 6. Select the range **B31:B32**, press and hold the **Ctrl** key, select the range **B35:B46**, click cell **B48**, and then release the mouse button and the Ctrl key. The nonadjacent range B31:B32;B35:B46;B48 should now be selected.

▶ 7. Click the **Paste** button 🖹 on the Standard toolbar. As shown in Figure 2-12, the total values for all income and expense categories should now be pasted in the worksheet.

| Figure 2-12 | Year-end totals for income and expenses |

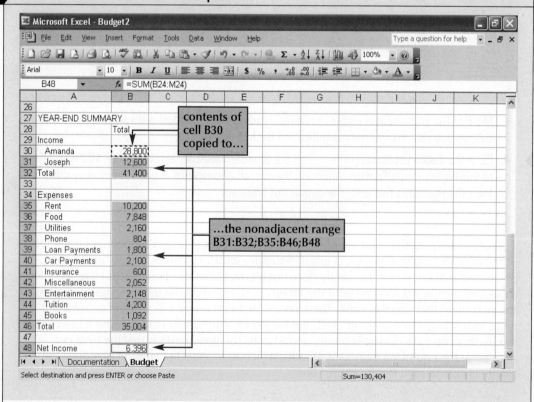

From these calculations, Amanda can quickly see that her family's yearly income is $41,400, whereas their yearly expenses total $35,004. Their largest expense is rent—a total of $10,200 per year.

Using the Insert Function Dialog Box

It's easier for Amanda to plan a budget if she knows approximately how much the family makes and spends each month. So your next task is to add a column that calculates the monthly averages for each of the income and expense categories. Rather than typing the function directly into the cell, you may find it helpful to use the Insert Function button on the Formula bar. Clicking this button displays a dialog box from which you can choose the function you want to enter. Once you choose a function, another dialog box opens, which displays the function's syntax. In this way, Excel makes it easy for you to avoid making mistakes. Try this now by entering the AVERAGE function using the Insert Function dialog box.

To insert the AVERAGE function:

▶ 1. Click cell **C28**, type **Average**, and then press the **Enter** key.

▶ 2. Click cell **C30** and then click the **Insert Function** button 𝑓𝑥 on the Formula bar. The Insert Function dialog box opens. See Figure 2-13.

Insert Function dialog box ◄ | **Figure 2-13**

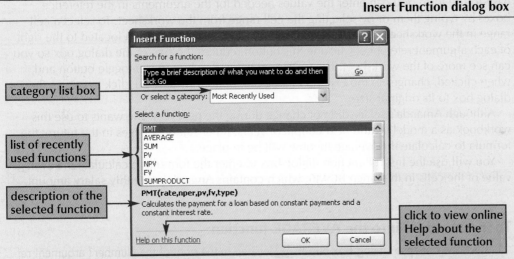

category list box

list of recently used functions

description of the selected function

click to view online Help about the selected function

The Insert Function dialog box shows a list of the most recently used functions. As you can see from Figure 2-13, one of these is the AVERAGE function. However, your list may be different and might not include the AVERAGE function. You can display a different function list using the category list box. Try this now to display a list of the Statistical functions supported by Excel.

▶ 3. Click the **Or select a category** list arrow, and then click **Statistical**. Excel displays a list of Statistical functions. See Figure 2-14.

Figure 2-14 ▶ **Excel's Statistical functions**

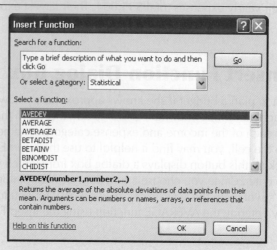

> **4.** Click **AVERAGE** in the list, and then click the **OK** button. The Function Arguments dialog box opens.

The Function Arguments dialog box provides the syntax of the selected function in an easy-to-use form. You can enter the values needed for the arguments in the reference boxes by typing them or by selecting the cell range from the worksheet. To select a cell range in the worksheet, you can click the Collapse Dialog Box button located to the right of each argument reference. Clicking this button reduces the size of the dialog box so you can see more of the worksheet. The Collapse Dialog Box button is a toggle button and, when clicked, changes to the Expand Dialog box button, which you click to restore the dialog box to its original size.

Although Amanda's salary did not change during the past year, she wants to use this workbook as a model for the next couple of years. If her salary changes in the future, the formula to calculate the average income will be in place.

You will use the Insert Function dialog box to enter the formula to calculate the average value of the cells in the range B6:M6, which contains Amanda's monthly salary amount.

To insert values into the AVERAGE function:

> **1.** Click the **Collapse Dialog Box** button 🖳 located to the right of the Number1 argument reference box. The Function Arguments dialog box reduces in size to let you see more of the worksheet, and the Collapse Dialog Box button changes to the Expand Dialog Box button.
>
> **Trouble?** If the collapsed dialog box is still in the way of the range you need to select, drag the dialog box to another location on the worksheet.
>
> **2.** Select the range **B6:M6** on the worksheet, and then click the **Expand Dialog Box** button 🔲 to restore the Function Arguments dialog box to its original size, as shown in Figure 2-15.

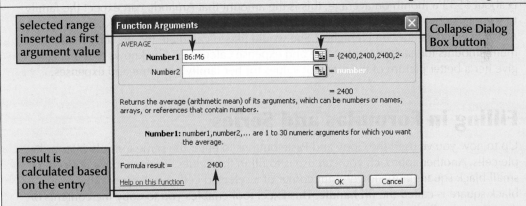

selected range inserted as first argument value

Collapse Dialog Box button

result is calculated based on the entry

3. Click the **OK** button. The value 2,400 appears in C30.

Now you will copy the formula to calculate the average of other income and expense categories.

To copy the AVERAGE function into the remaining cells:

1. Click cell **C30**, if necessary, and then click the **Copy** button 📋 on the Standard toolbar.

2. Select the nonadjacent range **C31:C32;C35:C46;C48**, and then click the **Paste** button 📋 on the Standard toolbar. Figure 2-16 shows the monthly averages in Amanda's budget.

Year-end average values ◄ **Figure 2-16**

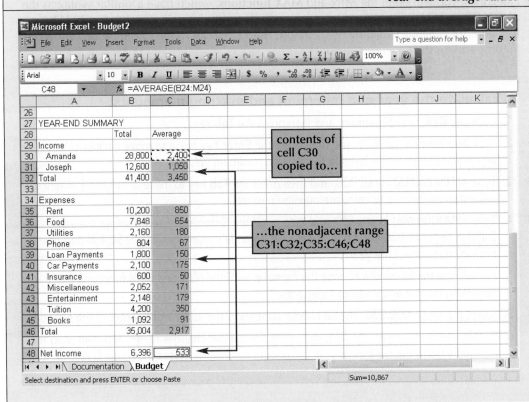

contents of cell C30 copied to...

...the nonadjacent range C31:C32;C35:C46;C48

On average, the couple makes $3,450 per month and spends $2,917. Their net income is about $533 a month on average; this is the amount that Amanda can expect the family to save. It is obvious that expenses for some months will be higher than expected. Amanda wonders how much higher? She would like to calculate the maximum and minimum amounts for each of the income and expense categories. She knows that this will give her a better picture of the range of values for her family's income and expenses.

Filling in Formulas and Series

Up to now you've used the Copy and Paste buttons to enter the same formula into multiple cells. Another approach you can use is to fill in the values. You may have noticed a small black square in the lower-right corner of a selected cell or cell range. That small black square is called the **fill handle**. This Excel tool enables you to copy the contents of the selected cells simply by dragging the fill handle over another adjacent cell or range of cells rather than going through the two-step process of clicking the Copy and Paste buttons. This technique is also referred to as **Auto Fill**.

Reference Window	**Copying Formulas Using the Fill Handle**

- Select the cell or range that contains the formula or formulas you want to copy.
- Drag the fill handle in the direction you want to copy the formula(s), and then release the mouse button.
- To select a specific fill option, click the Auto Fill Options button, and then select the option you want to apply to the selected range.

To calculate the maximum and minimum amounts for each of the income and expense categories, you will enter the **MIN** and **MAX functions**, which have a similar syntax as the AVERAGE and SUM functions. Once you enter the formulas using the MIN and MAX functions for Amanda's income, you can use Auto Fill to fill in the formulas for Joseph's income and for the expense categories.

To calculate the year-end minimum and maximum amounts:

1. Click cell **D28**, type **Minimum**, and then press the **Tab** key.

2. Type **Maximum** in cell E28, and then press the **Enter** key twice to move back to column D where you will enter the formula to calculate minimum values.

3. Type **=MIN(B6:M6)** in cell D30, and then press the **Tab** key to move to column E where you will enter the formula to calculate maximum values.

4. Type **=MAX(B6:M6)** in cell E30, and then press the **Enter** key. Excel displays the value 2,400 in both cell D30 and cell E30 because Amanda's monthly salary is $2,400 and does not vary throughout the year.

   You will use the fill handle to copy the formulas with the MIN and MAX functions into the remaining income and expense categories.

5. Select the range **D30:E30**. The fill handle appears in the lower-right corner of the selection.

6. Position the pointer over the fill handle until the pointer changes to ✛, and then drag the fill handle down the worksheet until the selection border encloses the range **D30:E48**.

7. Release the mouse button. The Auto Fill Options button appears, and by default Excel copies the formulas and formats found in the source range, D30:E30, into the destination range. Note that rows 33, 34, and 47 contain zeros. This is because those rows correspond to empty cells in the monthly table. You can delete the MIN and MAX functions in those cells.

8. Select the nonadjacent range **D33:E34;D47:E47**, and then press the **Delete** key to clear the contents of the selected cells. Figure 2-17 shows the minimum and maximum values for each income and expense category.

Year-end minimum and maximum values ◄ **Figure 2-17**

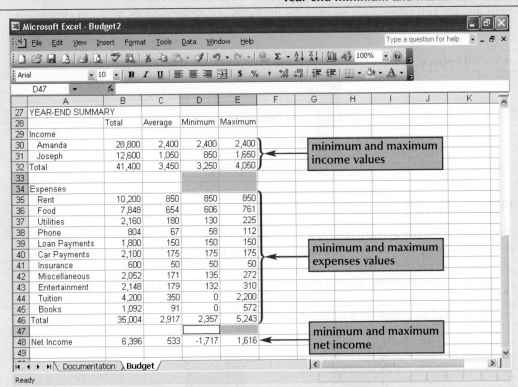

These calculations provide Amanda with an idea of the range of possible values in her budget. From these figures she can see that the maximum amount the family earned in a single month was $4,050 (cell E32), while the maximum amount the family spent in a single month was $5,243 (cell E46). How frugal can the family be? Based on her calculations, the lowest amount the family spent in a given month was $2,357 (cell D46). Amanda has also discovered that the most the family was able to save in a month was $1,616 (cell E48), while their largest deficit was $1,717—which occurred in the month of January, when a tuition payment was due. If the average values in column C give Amanda a picture of what a "typical" month looks like, the values in columns D and E give her an idea of the extremes in the family budget.

If you have a large selection to fill, you may find it difficult to use the fill handle feature of Auto Fill. If you don't want to use the fill handle, you can select the cell range that you want to fill and then use the Fill command on the Edit menu. Excel provides a list of Fill commands that you can use to fill in the selected range.

Auto Fill Options

When you use Auto Fill with formulas, Excel copies not only the formulas but also the formatting applied to the copied cell or range. However, there may be times when you only want the values in a cell copied, or maybe just the formatting. You can control what Excel does when you use the fill handle to copy formulas. When you release the mouse button, a button appears at the lower-right corner of the cell range. This is the Auto Fill Options button. Clicking this button provides a list of available options that you can choose to specify how Excel should handle the pasted selection.

The Auto Fill default option is to copy both the formulas and the formats of selected cells into the cell range. To copy only the formulas or just the formats, you can choose one of the other Auto Fill options, as shown in Figure 2-18.

| Figure 2-18 | Auto Fill options |

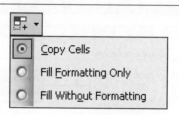

Filling a Series

The Auto Fill feature can also be used to continue a series of values, dates, or text based on an established pattern. As shown in Figure 2-19, to create a list of sequential numbers, you enter the first few numbers of the sequence and then drag the fill handle, completing the sequence. In this case, a list of numbers from 1 to 10 is quickly generated.

| Figure 2-19 | Using Auto Fill to complete a series of numbers |

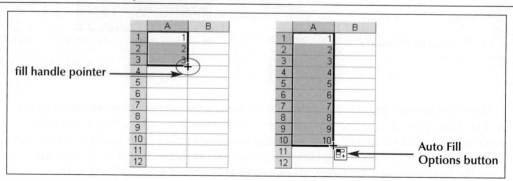

The series does not have to be numeric. It can also contain text and dates. Figure 2-20 shows a few examples of other series that can be completed using the Auto Fill feature.

Applying Auto Fill to different series | **Figure 2-20**

Type	Initial Selection	Extended Series
Values	1, 2, 3	4, 5, 6, ...
	2, 4, 6	8, 10, 12, ...
Dates and Times	Jan	Feb, Mar, Apr, ...
	January	February, March, April, ...
	Jan, Apr	Jul, Oct, Jan, ...
	15-Jan, 15-Feb	15-Mar, 15-Apr, 15-May, ...
	12/30/2005	12/31/2005, 1/1/2006, 1/2/2006, ...
	12/31/2005, 1/31/2006	2/28/2006, 3/31/2006, 4/30/2006, ...
	Mon	Tue, Wed, Thu, ...
	Monday	Tuesday, Wednesday, Thursday, ...
	11:00 AM	12:00 PM, 1:00 PM, 2:00 PM, ...
Patterned Text	1st period	2nd period, 3rd period, 4th period, ...
	Region 1	Region 2, Region 3, Region 4, ...
	Quarter 3	Quarter 4, Quarter 1, Quarter 2, ...
	Qtr3	Qtr4, Qtr1, Qtr2, ...

Amanda would like to replace dates in the Budget worksheet with the abbreviations of each month. Rather than directly typing this text, you will insert the abbreviations using the fill handle.

To fill in the abbreviations for the months of the year:

1. Press the **Ctrl + Home** keys to make the columns on the left and the top rows visible.

2. Click cell **B4**, type **Jan**, and then click the **Enter** button ✓ on the Formula bar. Because "Jan" is a commonly used abbreviation for January, Excel will recognize it as a month without your having to type in "Feb" for the next month in the series.

3. Position the pointer over the fill handle in the lower-right corner of cell B4 until the pointer changes to ✛.

4. Drag the fill handle over the range **B4:M4**, and then release the mouse button. Excel fills in the abbreviation for each month in the range of cells, as shown in Figure 2-21. As you drag the fill handle, ScreenTips for the month abbreviations appear.

Filling in the month abbreviations | **Figure 2-21**

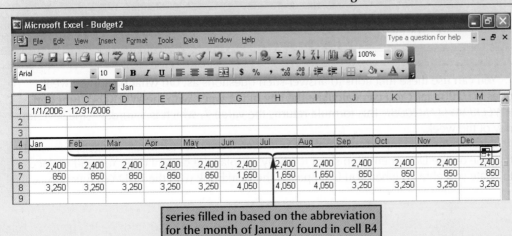

series filled in based on the abbreviation for the month of January found in cell B4

Excel provides other techniques for automatically filling in values and text. You can even create your own customized fill series. You can use Excel's online Help to explore other Auto Fill options.

Working with Date Functions

Entering the current date in a worksheet might not always address a date-related issue or need. If you want the current date to always appear in your workbook, versus the date you may have entered when you created the workbook, you can use a Date function rather than re-entering the current date each time you open the workbook. The **Date functions** provided by Excel store and calculate dates as numeric values, representing the number of days since January 1, 1900. For example, when you enter the date 1/1/2008 into a worksheet cell, you are actually entering the value 39448, because that date is 39,448 days after January 1, 1900. This method of storing dates allows you to work with dates using the same formulas you would use to work with any value. If you want to determine the number of days between two dates, you simply subtract one date from the other.

Excel automatically updates the values returned by the TODAY() and NOW() functions whenever you reopen the workbook. The **TODAY() function** displays the current date based on your computer's internal clock; the **NOW() function** displays both the date and time. If you want a permanent date (reflecting when the workbook was initially created, for example), enter the date directly into the cell without using either function.

If you have additional tasks to perform with a date or time, you can use one of the functions listed in Figure 2-22.

Figure 2-22 ▷ **Date and Time functions**

Function	Description
DATE(*year*, *month*, *day*)	Creates a date value for the date represented by the *year*, *month*, and *day* arguments
DAY(*date*)	Extracts the day of the month from the *date* value
MONTH(*date*)	Extracts the month number from the *date* value, where 1=January, 2=February, and so forth
YEAR(*date*)	Extracts the year number from the *date* value
WEEKDAY(*date*, [*return_type*])	Calculates the day of the week from the *date* value, where 1=Sunday, 2=Monday, and so forth. To choose a different numbering scheme, set the optional *return_type* value to "1" (1=Sunday, 2=Monday, ...), "2" (1=Monday, 2=Tuesday, ...), or "3" (0=Monday, 1=Tuesday, ...).
NOW()	Displays the current date and time
TODAY()	Displays the current date

You can use these functions to answer such questions as: On what day of the week does 1/1/2008 fall? You can calculate the day of the week with the **WEEKDAY function** as =*WEEKDAY(1/1/2008)*. This formula returns the value 7, which is Saturday—the seventh day of the week.

Because Amanda intends to use this worksheet as a model for future budgets, she wants the date on the Documentation sheet to always display the current date. You will replace the date you entered when you first opened the workbook with the TODAY() function.

To enter the TODAY() function on the Documentation sheet:

▶ 1. Switch to the Documentation sheet.

▶ 2. Click cell **B4**, type **=TODAY()**, and then click the **Enter** button ☑ on the Formula bar. Note that there are no arguments in the TODAY() function, but you still have to include the opening and closing parentheses, and there are no spaces between the parentheses. Excel displays the current date as shown in Figure 2-23.

Inserting the current date ◀ | **Figure 2-23**

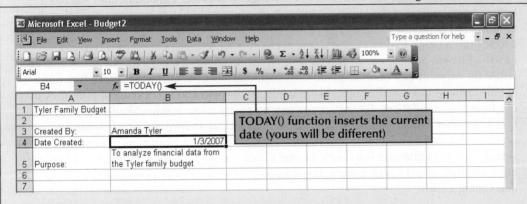

You have completed your work on the Budget2 workbook.

▶ 3. Save your changes to the workbook, and then close it.

Using Math and Statistical functions, you have been able to calculate the monthly and end-of-year values Amanda requested. With these values in place, Amanda has a better picture of the family's finances, and she is more confident about how she will manage the family budget in the year to come.

Session 2.1 Quick Check | Review

1. What is the function you enter to calculate the minimum value in the range B1:B50?
2. Cell A10 contains the formula =A1+B1. When you copy the content of cell A10 and paste it into cell B11, what formula is inserted into the destination cell?
3. Cell A10 contains the formula =$A$1+B1. When you copy the content of cell A10 and paste it into cell B11, what formula is inserted into the destination cell?
4. Express the reference to cell A1 as (a) a relative reference, (b) an absolute reference, and (c) a mixed reference (both possibilities).
5. List the steps you use in Excel to create a series of odd numbers from 1 to 99 in column A of your worksheet.
6. To display the current date in a workbook each time you reopen it, you enter the _____ function in the cell where you want the date to appear.

Session 2.2

(**Note:** This session presents topics related to Financial functions and Logical functions. This session *is optional and may be skipped* without loss of continuity of the instruction.)

Working with Financial Functions

After reviewing the figures calculated in the Budget worksheet, Amanda thinks she has a better understanding of the family finances. Now she would like to determine whether the family could afford the monthly payments required to purchase a house if they were to take a loan from a bank. To do this, she wants to create a worksheet containing a "typical" month's income and expenses, and then she wants to use an Excel Financial function to calculate the monthly payments required for a loan of $175,000. Excel's **Financial functions** are the same as those widely used in the world of business and accounting to perform various financial calculations. For instance, these functions allow you to calculate the depreciation of an asset, determine the amount of interest paid on an investment, compute the present value of an investment, and so on. Although she is not a business or financial professional, Amanda's question is a financial one: Given the family budget, how great a loan payment can they afford if they want to buy a home? There are four principal factors involved in negotiating a loan:

- The size of the loan
- The length of time in which the loan must be repaid
- The interest rate charged by the lending institution
- The amount of money to be paid to the lending institution in periodic installments, called *payment periods*. (For most home loans, payments are due monthly, so the payment period is a month.)

To be sure, this is a simplified treatment of loans. Often other issues are involved, such as whether payments are due at the beginning of the payment period or at the end. For the purposes of this exercise, the above are the major factors on which Amanda will concentrate for now. Once you know any three of these factors, you can use Excel to calculate the value of the remaining fourth. Amanda is interested in a loan with the following conditions:

- The size of the loan is equal to $175,000.
- The length of time to repay the loan is equal to 30 years.
- The annual interest rate is equal to 5.5%.

She wants to calculate the fourth value—the monthly payment required by the lending institution to pay back the loan. To answer this question, you'll add a new worksheet to her workbook in which she can analyze various loan possibilities.

To create the Loan Analysis worksheet:

1. If you took a break after the last session, make sure that Excel is running and that the Budget2 workbook is open.

2. Insert a new worksheet at the end of the workbook named **Loan Analysis**, and then save the workbook as **Budget3** in the Tutorial.02\Tutorial folder included with your Data Files.

3. Click cell **A1**, type **LOAN ANALYSIS**, and then press the **Enter** key.

   Now you need to copy the labels and the average values from the Budget worksheet, which you completed in the previous session.

4. Switch to the Budget worksheet, select the nonadjacent range **A29:A48;C29:C48**, and then click the **Copy** button 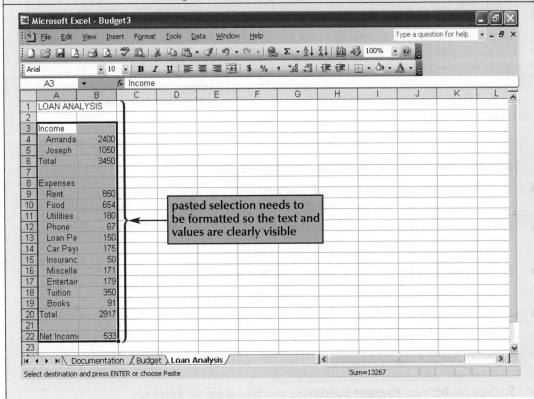 on the Standard toolbar.

5. Switch to the Loan Analysis worksheet, and then click cell **A3** to make it the active cell. Rather than pasting the formulas into this worksheet, you will simply paste the values.

6. Click the **Paste** list arrow on the Standard toolbar, and then click **Values** in the list of paste options. Excel pastes the labels from column A in the Budget worksheet into column A on the Loan Analysis worksheet and also pastes the average values from column C in the Budget worksheet into column B in the current worksheet. See Figure 2-24.

Pasting the income and expense categories and the average values | **Figure 2-24**

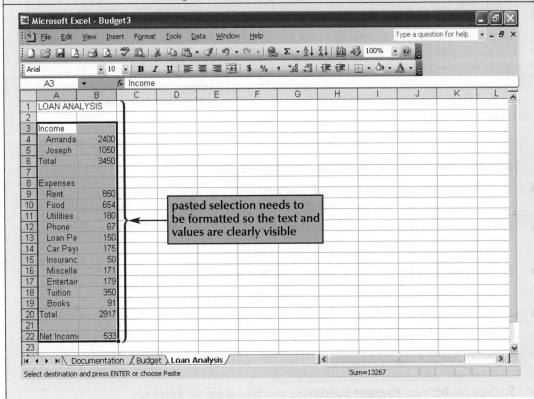

Excel pastes the cells as an adjacent range, not as a nonadjacent range. The result is that the values pasted from column C are shifted to the left into column B—right next to the labels in column A. These are the values you will need; their new location is not an issue. You will have to make some minor changes to the data, but first you need to increase the width of the columns so the values are easier to read. Then you will insert the formulas back into cells B6, B20, and B22 to calculate the total income, total expenses, and net income for a typical month.

To modify the layout of the worksheet and replace some of the values with formulas:

1. Click cell **A1** to remove the selection highlight from the pasted range.

2. Increase the width of column A to **18** characters (**131** pixels) and the width of column B to **10** characters (**75** pixels).

3. Click cell **B6**, click the **AutoSum** button Σ on the Standard toolbar, and then press the **Enter** key. Excel inserts the formula *=SUM(B4:B5)* into cell B6 to calculate the total average monthly income.

4. Click cell **B20**, click the **AutoSum** button Σ on the Standard toolbar, and then press the **Enter** key. Excel inserts the formula *=SUM(B9:B19)* into cell B20 to calculate the total average monthly expenses.

5. Click cell **B22**, type **=B6-B20** to calculate the average monthly net income, and then press the **Enter** key.

Now that you've entered the average monthly income and expense values for Amanda's budget and have widened the columns, you can enter the conditions for the loan. When you enter the amount of the loan, you will enter it as a negative value rather than as a positive value. The reason that you enter it as a negative value is because the loan is the amount owed to the lending institution; therefore, it is an expense. As you'll see later, Excel's Financial functions require loans to be entered as negative values because they represent negative cash flow. You will enter the labels and the conditions in columns D and E.

To enter the conditions of the loan in the worksheet:

1. Click cell **D3**, type **Loan Conditions**, and then press the **Enter** key to move to the next row where you will enter the Loan Amount label and the loan amount as a negative value.

2. Type **Loan Amount** in cell D4, press the **Tab** key, and then enter **-175,000** in cell E4.

   Next you will enter the length of the loan in years.

3. Type **Length of Loan** in cell D5, press the **Tab** key, and then enter **30** in cell E5.

   Now you will enter the annual interest rate, which is 5.5%.

4. Type **Annual Interest Rate** in cell D6, press the **Tab** key, and then enter **5.5%** in cell E6. Note that Excel may enter a zero, which doesn't change the value of the percentage.

   Next, you will enter the conditions under which the loan is to be repaid. In this case, you will assume that payments are due monthly.

5. Click cell **D8**, type **Payment Conditions**, and then press the **Enter** key.

   You will enter the number of payments to be made each year, which is 12.

6. Type **Payments per Year** in cell D9, press the **Tab** key, type **12** in cell E9, and then press the **Enter** key.

   Next you will enter the formula to calculate the total number of payments required to pay back the loan, which is the length of the loan (found in cell E5) multiplied by the payments per year (found in cell E9).

7. Type **Total Payments** in cell D10, press the **Tab** key, type **=E5*E9** in cell E10, and then press the **Enter** key.

8. Type **Payment Amount** in cell D11, and then press the **Tab** key.

   Before you continue, you will widen the columns so information is clearly visible.

9. Increase the width of column D to **18** characters (**131** pixels) and the width of column E to **10** characters (**75** pixels). Figure 2-25 shows the Loan Analysis worksheet with the values, loan conditions, and payment conditions entered.

Entering conditions for the loan and the monthly payments | **Figure 2-25**

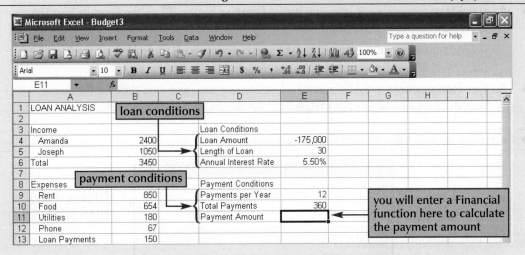

Paying off this loan will require 12 payments per year for 30 years, or 360 total payments. But how much will Amanda have to pay each month? To answer that question, you can use one of Excel's Financial functions.

Using the PMT Function

The monthly payment required to pay off a loan can be determined using the **PMT function**. The syntax of the PMT function is

=PMT(*rate*, *nper*, *pv*, [*fv*=0], [*type*=0])

where *rate* is the interest rate per payment period (determined by dividing the annual interest rate by the number of payment periods in a year), *nper* is the total number of payments, and *pv* is the present value of the future payments that will be made. In the case of a loan, the *pv* argument must be entered as a negative number. There are two optional parameters in this function: *fv* and *type*. The *fv* parameter indicates the future value of the loan and has a default value of 0. A future value of 0 means that the loan is paid off completely. The *type* parameter specifies whether payments are due at the beginning of the period (*type*=1) or at the end (*type*=0). The default value of the *type* parameter is 0.

Note that you can also use the PMT function for investments in which a specified amount of money is saved each month at a specified interest rate. In that case, the value of the *pv* argument would be positive since it represents an investment (a positive cash flow) rather than a loan (a negative cash flow).

Because the PMT function, like many Excel functions, has several required arguments, in addition to some optional arguments, you might not always remember all of the function's arguments and the order in which they should be entered. To make your task easier, you'll use the Insert Function dialog box to determine the payment amount for the loan Amanda is considering.

To select the PMT function using the Insert Function dialog box:

▶ **1.** With E11 as the active cell, click the **Insert Function** button f_x on the Formula bar. The Insert Function dialog box opens.

To locate the PMT function, you'll enter a text description of this function in the Search for a function text box.

▶ **2.** Type **loan payment** in the Search for a function text box, and then click the **Go** button. Excel displays a list of functions related to loan payments. See Figure 2-26.

Figure 2-26	Searching for functions related to loan payments

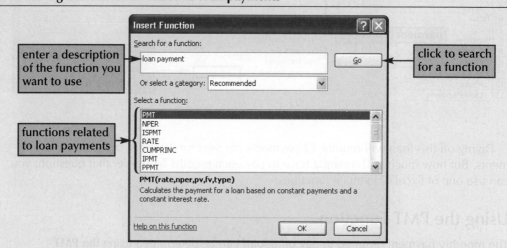

enter a description of the function you want to use

click to search for a function

functions related to loan payments

▶ **3.** Verify that **PMT** is selected in the list of functions, read the description provided in the lower portion of the dialog box, and then click the **OK** button. The Function Arguments dialog box for the PMT function opens, as shown in Figure 2-27.

Figure 2-27	Function Arguments dialog box for the PMT function

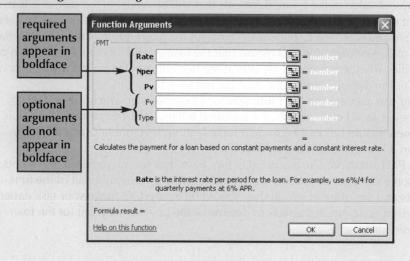

required arguments appear in boldface

optional arguments do not appear in boldface

Note that, in the Function Arguments dialog box, required arguments are displayed in a boldfaced font, whereas optional arguments are not. Neither the Fv nor Type argument is displayed in a bold font. You will use this dialog box to enter values for the PMT function's arguments. The first argument that you will enter is for the rate, which is determined by dividing the annual interest rate by the number of payment periods in a year.

To enter values for the PMT function:

▶ 1. Click the **Collapse Dialog Box** button located to the right of the Rate box.

▶ 2. Click cell **E6** to enter the cell reference for the annual interest rate.

   To determine the rate, you will divide the value in cell E6 by the number of payment periods in a year (cell E9).

▶ 3. Type **/** (the division sign), and then click cell **E9** to enter the cell reference.

▶ 4. Click the **Expand Dialog Box** button to restore the Function Arguments dialog box. The expression E6/E9 should now appear in the Rate box.

   Next you will enter the value for the second argument, the *nper* argument, which is the total number of payments that need to be made for the 30-year loan. This number is displayed in cell E10.

▶ 5. Click in the **Nper** box, and then enter **E10** either by typing it directly into the reference box or by selecting the cell from the workbook.

   Finally, you will enter the *pv* (present value) argument. In the case of a loan, the present value is the amount of the loan Amanda's family is seeking. This value is stored in cell E4.

▶ 6. Click in the **Pv** box, and then enter **E4** using the method you prefer. Figure 2-28 shows the completed Function Arguments dialog box and illustrates how this dialog box relates to the function that will be inserted into cell E11.

Entering the PMT function | **Figure 2-28**

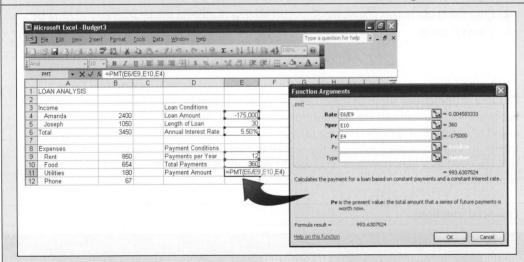

▶ 7. Click the **OK** button. Excel displays the value $993.63 in cell E11. Therefore, the required monthly payment is $993.63 for a loan of $175,000 at a 5.5% annual interest rate for 30 years.

   To see how this would affect Amanda's family budget, you will enter this information into the Expenses portion of the worksheet.

▶ 8. Click cell **A9**, type **House Payment** to replace the word "Rent," and then press the **Tab** key.

   Now you will enter a formula in cell B9 so the value House Payment is equal to the value Payment Amount.

▶ 9. Type **=E11** in cell B9, and then press the **Enter** key. The average total monthly expenses are recalculated.

If Amanda and Joseph were to buy a home with a $175,000 mortgage under the loan conditions specified in this workbook, their average monthly expenses would increase from $2,917 to $3,060.63 (cell B20), and the amount of money they could save each month would drop from $533 to about $389 (cell B22). By replacing the rent expense with the monthly home loan payment, Amanda can quickly gauge the effects of the loan on the family budget. Because the differences don't seem too unreasonable, Amanda now wants you to increase the size of the loan to $250,000, but keep all of the other factors constant.

To explore a what-if analysis for the mortgage:

▶ 1. Click cell **E4**, type **-250,000** as the new loan amount, being sure to enter this as a negative value, and then press the **Enter** key. Under this scenario, the monthly payment increases to about $1,419 and the family's monthly expenses increase to about $3,486, which is more than they make in a typical month. Obviously a loan of this size is more than they can afford.

▶ 2. Click the **Undo** button 🔄 on the Standard toolbar to restore the worksheet to its previous condition.

This time Amanda wants to know what would happen if the interest rate changed. To determine the difference between the low interest rate of 5.5% and a higher one, you will change the interest rate to 6.5%.

▶ 3. Click cell **E6**, type **6.5%**, and then press the **Enter** key. Excel calculates the monthly payment to be about $1,106. Amanda can see that if the interest rate increases by 1%, then the monthly payment increases by about $113. She wants you to change the interest rate back to 5.5%.

▶ 4. Click the **Undo** button 🔄 on the Standard toolbar to change the interest rate back to its previous value.

The PMT function is just one of the many Financial functions supported by Excel. Figure 2-29 describes some of the other functions that can be used for mortgage analysis. For example, you can use the PV function to calculate the size of the loan that Amanda could afford given a specific interest rate, monthly payment, and total number of payments. If Amanda wanted to know the size of the loan she could afford by using the $850 rent payment as a loan payment, you would enter the formula =PV(5.5%/12,360,850), which would return the value –$149,703.50, or a total loan of almost $150,000.

Figure 2-29 ▶ **Financial functions**

Function	Description
PMT(*rate*, *nper*, *pv*, [*fv*=0], [*type*=0])	Calculates the payments required each period on a loan or investment, where *rate* is the interest rate per period, *nper* is the total number of periods, *pv* is the present value or principal of the loan, *fv* is the future value of the loan, and *type* indicates whether payments should be made at the end of the period (0) or the beginning (1)
PV(*rate*, *nper*, *pmt*, [*fv*=0], [*type*=0])	Calculates the present value of a loan or investment based on periodic, constant payments
NPER(*rate*, *pmt*, *pv*, [*fv*=0], [*type*=0])	Calculates the number of periods required to pay off a loan or investment
RATE(*nper*, *pmt*, *pv*, [, *fv*=0], [*type*=0])	Calculates the interest rate of a loan or investment based on periodic, constant payments

You can use the other functions described in Figure 2-29 to calculate the interest rate and the total number of payment periods. Once again, if you know three of the conditions for the loan, there is an Excel function that you can use to calculate the value of the fourth.

From the calculations you have performed, Amanda now knows that a monthly mortgage payment of $993 is required to pay off a $175,000 loan in 30 years at 5.5% interest. This leaves the family with a net income of about $390 per month. The question remains whether Amanda feels that the mortgage is affordable. Amanda knows that she and Joseph will have to purchase a second car soon, that there are other expenses on the horizon, and that a new house will, no doubt, bring with it additional expenses that she may not have considered yet, such as property taxes. To prepare for those new future expenses, Amanda wants the family's net income to exceed their expenses by about $5,000 per year.

Does her current budget, with a home loan payment of $993 per month, meet that requirement? To find out, you will enter the amount of money Amanda feels that the family needs to save each year and a formula to calculate if they can achieve this goal.

To calculate the family's yearly net income:

▶ 1. Click cell **D13**, type **Is the loan affordable?** and then press the **Enter** key.

You will enter the amount Amanda wants the family to save each year.

▶ 2. Type **Required Savings** in cell D14, press the **Tab** key, type **5,000** in cell E14, and then press the **Enter** key.

Next, you'll enter the formula to calculate how much the family saved in one year using the average monthly net income multiplied by 12 months.

▶ 3. Type **Calculated Savings** in cell D15, press the **Tab** key, type **=B22*12** in cell E15, and then press the **Enter** key. See Figure 2-30. Note that the value in cell E15 shows five places to the right of the decimal. You'll learn how to specify the number of decimal places in Tutorial 3.

Calculating the yearly savings ◀ **Figure 2-30**

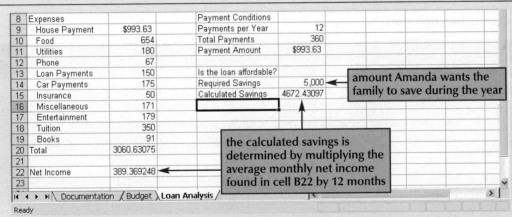

Under the proposed loan and assuming only the current expenses, the family could save about $4,672 per year, which is less than Amanda had hoped. So, Amanda would need to look at getting a smaller loan or hope that interest rates decrease in the future.

Amanda appreciates the type of information the worksheet provides, but she is concerned about getting lost in all of the numbers. She would like the worksheet to display a simple text message: "Yes" if the loan is affordable given the conditions she has set for the budget and "No" if otherwise. To add such a feature to the worksheet, you'll need to use a Logical function.

Working with Logical Functions

A **Logical function** is a function that tests, or evaluates, whether a condition in the workbook is true or false. The condition is usually entered as an expression. For example, the expression A1=10 would be true if cell A1 contains the value 10; otherwise, the expression is false.

Using the IF Function

The most commonly used Logical function is the **IF function**, which has the following syntax:

=IF(*logical_test*, *value_if_true*, [*value_if_false*])

where *logical_test* is an expression that is either true or false, *value_if_true* is the value displayed in the cell if the logical test is true, and *value_if_false* is the value displayed if the logical test is false. Note that the *value_if_false* argument is optional, though in most cases you will use it so that the function covers both possibilities.

For example, the formula =*IF(A1=10, 20, 30)* tests whether the value in cell A1 is equal to 10. If the expression A1=10 is true, the function displays the value 20 in the cell containing the function; otherwise, the cell displays the value 30. You can also construct logical tests that involve text values. The formula =*IF(A1="Retail", B1, B2)* tests whether cell A1 contains the text "Retail"; if it does, the function returns the value of cell B1; otherwise, it returns the value of cell B2.

Expressions in the logical test always include a comparison operator. A **comparison operator** indicates the relationship between two values. Figure 2-31 describes the comparison operators supported by Excel.

| Figure 2-31 | Comparison operators |

Operator	Example	Description
=	A1 = B1	Tests whether the value in cell A1 *is equal to* the value in cell B1
>	A1 > B1	Tests whether the value in cell A1 *is greater than* the value in cell B1
<	A1 < B1	Tests whether the value in cell A1 *is less than* the value in cell B1
>=	A1 >= B1	Tests whether the value in cell A1 *is greater than or equal to* the value in cell B1
<=	A1 <= B1	Tests whether the value in cell A1 *is less than or equal to* the value in cell B1
<>	A1 <> B1	Tests whether the value in cell A1 *is not equal to* the value in cell B1

You'll use the IF function to display a text message in the worksheet indicating whether a $175,000 loan is affordable. In this case, the logical expression will test whether the value in cell E14 (the required savings) is less than the value in cell E15 (the calculated savings). The expression is E14 < E15. If this expression is true, then the loan is affordable for Amanda's family; otherwise, it is not. You will now enter the formula that includes the IF function =*IF(E14 < E15, "Yes", "No")*.

To insert the IF function to evaluate whether the loan is affordable:

▶ **1.** Click cell **D16**, type **Conclusion**, and then press the **Tab** key.

▶ **2.** In cell E16, type **=IF(E14<E15,"Yes","No")** and then press the **Enter** key. The text "No" appears in cell E16, indicating that the value in cell E14 is not less than the value in cell E15, and, therefore, the conditions of the mortgage are not acceptable to Amanda.

Amanda asks you to reduce the size of the loan to $165,000 to see whether this amount changes the conclusion about the mortgage's affordability.

▶ **3.** Click cell **E4**, type **-165,000** as the new loan amount, and then press the **Enter** key. As shown in Figure 2-32, the monthly payment drops to about $936 and the net yearly savings rise to about $5,354. Cell E16 displays the text string "Yes," indicating that this loan does satisfy Amanda's conditions for affordability.

Inserting a Logical function | **Figure 2-32**

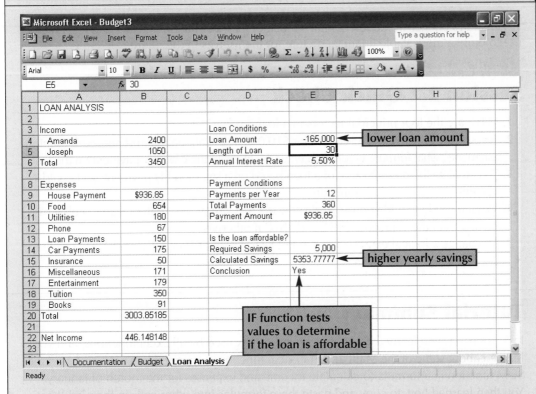

Now Amanda knows that buying a house is something that her family budget can support in the near future if she and Joseph manage their budget well. You will now save and close the Budget3 workbook.

▶ **4.** Save your changes to the workbook, and then close it.

Excel has several other Logical functions that you can use to create more complicated tests. Figure 2-33 describes the syntax of each of these functions.

Figure 2-33 ▶ **Logical functions**

Function	Description
IF(*logical_test*, *value_if_true*, [*value_if_false*])	Returns the value *value_if_true* if the *logical_test* expression is true and *value_if_false* if otherwise
AND(*logical1*, [*logical2*, *logical3*, ...])	Returns the value TRUE if all *logical* expressions in the function are true and FALSE if otherwise
OR(*logical1*, [*logical2*, *logical3*, ...])	Returns the value TRUE if any *logical* expression in the function is true and FALSE if otherwise
FALSE()	Returns the value FALSE
TRUE()	Returns the value TRUE
NOT(*logical*)	Returns the value FALSE if the *logical* expression is true and the value TRUE if the *logical* expression is false

Amanda's budget workbook contains much of the information that she and Joseph can use to build a more stable financial picture for themselves in the future.

Review

Session 2.2 Quick Check

1. What are the four principal factors in a loan?
2. If you were to take a five-year loan for $10,000 at 7% annual interest rate, with monthly payments, what formula would you enter to calculate the monthly payment on the loan?
3. To calculate the present value of a loan based on a set, monthly payment, you could use the _____ function.
4. What formula would you use to display the text string "Yes" if the value in cell A1 is greater than the value in cell B1 and "No" if otherwise?
5. To change a logical expression from FALSE to TRUE or from TRUE to FALSE, use the _____ function.

Review

Tutorial Summary

In Session 2.1, you learned about the general syntax used by all Excel functions, and you learned about some of the Math and Statistical functions supported by Excel. You used the SUM function in a formula to calculate income and expenses for the month of January. You then learned how to copy and paste these formulas into other cells in the worksheet to calculate total figures for every month of the year. You learned the difference between the three types of cell references—relative, absolute, and mixed—and then you used an absolute reference to calculate a running total of the net income. You learned about the AVERAGE, MIN, and MAX functions, and then used them to summarize the entire year's budget figures. Once you entered the formulas that used these functions, you learned how to copy and paste the formulas using the Auto Fill feature. You also learned how to change the magnification of the workbook window so you can see more or less of the data in a worksheet. Finally, you used the TODAY() function to display the current date in the Documentation sheet.

In Session 2.2, you learned about the PMT function, which is a Financial function supported by Excel. You used the PMT function to calculate the monthly payment required to pay off a specified mortgage. You also learned about one of Excel's most commonly used Logical functions, the IF function. You used the IF function to display a text string indicating whether a loan was affordable.

Key Terms

Session 2.1	MAX function	TODAY() function
absolute reference	MIN function	WEEKDAY function
argument	mixed reference	*Session 2.2*
Auto Fill	NOW() function	comparison operator
AVERAGE function	optional argument	Financial function
Date function	relative reference	IF function
destination cell	source cell	Logical function
destination range	source range	PMT function
F4 key	SUM function	
fill handle	syntax	

Practice

Practice the skills you learned in Session 2.1 using the same case scenario.

Review Assignments

Data File needed for the Review Assignments: Family1.xls

Amanda appreciates the work you did on her family budget. Her friends Ken and Ava Giles have examined the workbook you created and have asked you to create a similar workbook for their budget.

Once you have completed a budget worksheet for the Giles family, they may want you to help them determine if they can afford to purchase their dream house in the country. The mortgage would be substantially higher than the family's current mortgage, but with Ava now working full time, the couple feels that they may be able to afford the higher mortgage. They would like you to create a workbook that will help them to determine if purchasing the house is possible.

To complete this task:

1. Open the **Family1** workbook located in the Tutorial.02\Review folder included with your Data Files, and then save the workbook as **Family2** in the same folder.
2. In the Documentation sheet, enter your name in cell B3, and then enter the current date in cell B4 using the TODAY() function.
3. Switch to the Budget worksheet, and then enter the formulas in the ranges C7:N7 and C14:N14 to calculate the total income and expenses, respectively, for each month. (*Hint*: Enter the formula in cells C7 and C14 first, and then copy and paste the formulas to the other cells in the ranges.)
4. In the range C16:N16, enter a formula to calculate the family's net income. (*Hint*: Enter the formula in cell C16 first, and then copy and paste the formula to the other cells in the range.)
5. In the range D17:N17, enter a formula using the SUM function to calculate the running total for net income from February through December. (*Hint*: Use an absolute reference for the appropriate cell reference.)
6. In the range C4:N4, use Auto Fill to fill in the month names January, February, March, and so forth.

Practice the skills you learned in Session 2.2 using the same case scenario.

7. In the range C21:F23, enter a formula to calculate the total, average, minimum, and maximum values of the two incomes.

8. In the range C25:F30, enter a formula to calculate the total, average, minimum, and maximum values of each expense category.

9. In the range C32:F32, enter a formula to calculate the total, average, minimum, and maximum values for net income.

10. Print the contents of the Budget worksheet, and save the changes you have made. If you are not continuing with the remaining steps, close the workbook.

    (**Note:** The following steps are *optional*. You should attempt them only if you have completed **Session 2.2** in the tutorial.)

11. Save the workbook as **Family3** to the Tutorial.02\Review folder.

12. Add a worksheet named "Loan Analysis" to the end of the workbook, and then enter the text "Loan Analysis" in cell A1 of the worksheet.

13. Switch to the Budget worksheet, copy the nonadjacent range A21:B32;D21:D32, switch to the Loan Analysis worksheet, and then paste the values, but not the formulas, into range A3:C14, using the Paste Special option. Increase the width of columns A and C to 12 characters (89 pixels) each, and column B to 15 characters (110 pixels). Edit the entries in cells C5, C12, and C14 so they contain formulas that calculate the total income, total expense, and net income.

14. Enter the following labels in the cells as indicated:
    - Cell E3: Loan Conditions
    - Cell E4: Loan Amount
    - Cell E5: Length of Loan
    - Cell E6: Annual Interest Rate
    - Cell E8: Payment Conditions
    - Cell E9: Payments per Year
    - Cell E10: Total Payments
    - Cell E11: Payment Amount

15. Widen column E to 21 characters (152 pixels).

16. In the range F4:F9, enter values for the following loan and payment conditions:
    - Loan Amount = –300,000
    - Years = 15
    - Annual Interest Rate = 6%
    - Payments per Year = 12

17. In cell F10, enter a formula to calculate the total number of payments. In cell F11, enter a formula using the PMT function to calculate the monthly loan payment.

18. In cell C8, enter the formula to make the mortgage expense equal to the result of the calculation in cell F11.

19. Enter the following labels in the cells as indicated:
    - Cell E13: Is the loan affordable?
    - Cell E14: Minimum Loan Payment
    - Cell E15: Conclusion

20. The family does not want a monthly loan payment greater than $2,500. Enter this value into cell F14, and then in cell F15 enter a formula using the IF function to display the text string "Yes" if the monthly payment is less than or equal to the value you entered in cell F14, and "No" if otherwise. Is the loan affordable under the loan conditions you have entered?

21. Print the contents of the Loan Analysis worksheet.

22. Change the loan from a 15-year loan to a 20-year loan. What effect does this have on the monthly loan payment and the conclusion about the affordability of the loan? Print the contents of the revised Loan Analysis worksheet.
23. Save your changes to the workbook, and then close it.

Apply

Using what you have learned in Session 2.1, create a grading sheet for a chemistry class.

Case Problem 1

Data File needed for this Case Problem: Chem1.xls

Chemistry 303 Karen Raul is a professor of chemistry at MidWest University. She has started using Excel to calculate the final grades for students in her Chemistry 303 course. The final score is a weighted total of the scores given for a student's homework, lab work, exams, and final exam. Karen needs your help in creating the formulas to calculate the final score and to calculate the class averages. One way of calculating a weighted sum is to multiply each value by the corresponding weight. For example, consider the following sample exam scores:

- Exam 1 = 84
- Exam 2 = 80
- Exam 3 = 83
- Final exam = 72

If the first three exams are each given a weight of 20% and the final exam is weighted 40%, then the weighted sum is:

$84*0.2 + 80*0.2 + 83*0.2 + 72*0.4 = 78.2$

Karen has entered the weights of the exam scores for each of her students. She needs you to calculate the weighted score as well as some statistics for each exam, including the average score, the maximum and minimum score, and the range of scores.

To complete this task:

1. Open the **Chem1** workbook located in the Tutorial.02\Cases folder included with your Data Files, and then save the workbook as **Chem2** in the same folder.
2. In the Documentation sheet, enter your name in cell B3 and then enter the current date in cell B4 using the TODAY() function. Increase the width of column B to display the date, if necessary.
3. Switch to the Grades worksheet and, in cell F7, enter a formula using cell references to calculate the weighted sum of the four exam scores using the exam values in cells B7, C7, D7, and E7 and the weights in cells B4, C4, D4, and E4.
4. In the formula in cell F7, change the cell references for cells B4, C4, D4, and E4 from relative to absolute references.
5. Use Auto Fill to copy the formula in cell F7 into the range F7:F42.
6. In cell B44, enter a formula using the COUNT function to count the Exam 1 scores in range B7:B42. In cell B45, enter a formula using the AVERAGE function to calculate the average of the Exam 1 scores in range B7:B42. In cell B46, enter a formula using the MAX function to calculate the maximum Exam 1 scores in the same range. In cell B47, enter a formula using the MIN function to calculate the minimum Exam 1 score for the same. In cell B48, enter a formula to calculate the range of the Exam 1 scores (equal to the maximum score minus the minimum score).
7. Copy and paste the formulas in range B44:B48 into the range C44:F48 to calculate the same statistics for the other three exams and the weighted total of all the exams.
8. Print the contents of the Grades sheet in landscape orientation.
9. Save your changes, and then submit the completed workbook and printout to your instructor.

Apply

Using what you have learned in Session 2.1, create a workbook that summarizes regional sales information.

Case Problem 2

Data Files needed for this Case Problem: Sales1.xls, Works1.xls

Wizard Works Andrew Howe manages orders for Wizard Works, an online seller of custom fireworks. Andrew has asked you to help him use Excel to develop some reports for an upcoming meeting. Andrew's first project is to create a sales report for three different types of Wizard Works products sold in four different regions. After you enter the sales data, Andrew wants you to calculate the total, average, minimum, and maximum sales for each product and for each region, and then for all products and all regions. You will also need to calculate the percentage of sales for each product.

To complete this task:

1. Open the **Sales1** workbook located in the Tutorial.02\Cases folder included with your Data Files, and then save the workbook as **Sales2** in the same folder.
2. Enter your name and the date in the Documentation sheet.
3. Switch to the Sales Summary sheet, and enter the sales data shown in Figure 2-34.

Figure 2-34 ▶ **Units Sold**

Region	Fountains	Firecrackers	Rockets
Region 1	1503	1380	814
Region 2	1081	1873	1103
Region 3	1773	2415	644
Region 4	2289	2103	1474

4. For each product, enter formulas to calculate the total sales for all regions, the average sales per region, and the maximum and minimum sales over all the regions.
5. For each product, enter a formula that uses absolute cell references to calculate the percentage of units sold per region.
6. Summarize the sales for all three of these Wizard Works products by calculating the total, average, maximum, and minimum units sold for all products in all regions.
7. Calculate the percent of units sold for all products in each region.
8. Print the Sales Summary worksheet in landscape orientation, and then save your changes to the workbook.

   (**Note:** The following steps are *optional*. You should attempt them only if you completed **Session 2.2** in the tutorial.)

Using what you learned in Session 2.2, create a worksheet that determines shipping costs and discounts for customer orders.

Andrew also needs your help calculating the total costs of customer orders. You need to compute the total cost of each order, which includes the shipping cost and special discount offered by the store. Customers can choose one of two shipping options: Standard shipping, which costs $8.95 or Express shipping, which costs $14.95. Wizard Works also offers a 5% discount for orders that are more than $200 (not including the shipping cost). You need to enter formulas that use the IF function to determine the shipping cost and discount, if applicable, in order to calculate the total cost of each order.

9. Open the **Works1** workbook located in the Tutorial.02\Cases folder, and then save the workbook as **Works2** in the same folder.
10. Enter your name and the date in the Documentation sheet, and then switch to the Orders sheet.
11. In cell F7, calculate the cost of each product ordered, which is equal to the price of the product multiplied by the quantity.

12. Copy the formula in cell F7 into the cells F8:F9, F15:F19, and F25:F26.

13. In cell F10, calculate the sum of the values in the range F7:F9. In cell F20, calculate the sum of the values in the range F15:F19. In cell F27, calculate the sum of the values in the range F25:F26.

14. In cell F11, enter a formula that uses the IF function to calculate the shipping cost for the order. If the text in cell G11 is equal to "Standard," then the shipping cost is equal to the value in cell D2; otherwise, the shipping cost is equal to the value in cell F2. Change the cell references in the formula for cells D2 and F2 to absolute references.

15. Copy the formula in cell F11 into cells F21 and F28.

16. In cell F12, enter a formula that uses the IF function to calculate the discount. If the value in cell F10 is greater than 200, then the discount is equal to F10 multiplied by the value in cell D4; otherwise, the discount value is 0. Change the cell reference in this formula for cell D4 to an absolute reference.

17. Copy the formula in cell F12 into cells F22 and F29.

18. In cell F13, enter a formula to calculate the total cost of the order, which is equal to the cost of the products ordered plus the shipping cost minus the discount.

19. Copy the formula in cell F13 into cells F23 and F30.

20. Print the resulting Orders worksheet in landscape orientation.

21. Save your changes, and then submit the completed workbook and printout to your instructor.

Challenge

Go beyond what you learned in Session 2.2 to use the IF function as you create a payroll worksheet.

Case Problem 3

Data File needed for this Case Problem: Sonic1.xls

Sonic Sounds   Jeff Gwydion manages the payroll at Sonic Sounds. He has asked you for help in setting up an Excel worksheet to store payroll information. The payroll contains three elements: each employee's salary, 401(k) contribution, and health insurance cost. The company's 401(k) contribution is 3% of an employee's salary for those who have worked for the company at least one year; otherwise, the company's contribution is zero. Sonic Sounds also supports two health insurance plans: Premier and Standard. The cost of the Premier plan is $6,500, and the cost of the Standard plan is $5,500. The workbook has already been set up for you. Your job is to enter the formulas to calculate the 401(k) contributions and health insurance costs for each employee. Figure 2-35 shows the worksheet as it will appear at the end of this exercise.

Figure 2-35

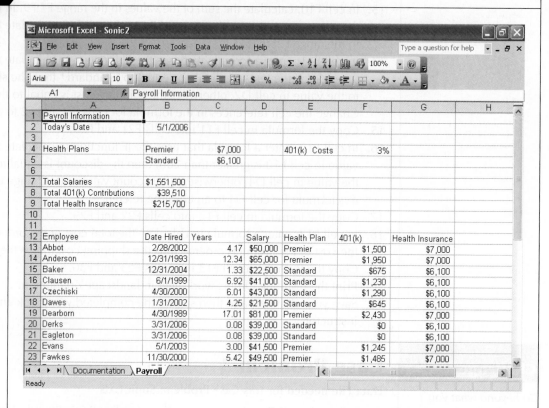

To complete this task:

1. Open the **Sonic1** workbook located in the Tutorial.02\Cases folder included with your Data Files, and then save the workbook as **Sonic2** in the same folder.

2. In the Documentation sheet, enter your name and then enter the date using the TODAY() function.

3. Switch to the Payroll worksheet. In cell C13, enter a formula to calculate the number of years the first employee has worked at Sonic Sounds. Use an absolute reference for cell B2. Divide the difference by 365. (*Hint:* You need to subtract the date the employee was hired from the current date, which is in cell B2, and then divide the difference by the number of days in a year. For the purposes of this exercise, do not try to account for leap years.)

4. Use Auto Fill to calculate the number of years the remaining employees in the table have worked for the company.

Explore

5. In the range F13:F45, insert a formula to calculate the 401(k) contributions for each employee. The formula should determine that if the number of years employed is greater than or equal to 1, then the contribution is equal to the contribution percentage in cell F4 multiplied by the employee's salary; otherwise, the contribution is zero.

Explore

6. In the range G13:G45, enter a formula to calculate the health insurance cost for each employee by testing whether the name of the employee's plan is equal to the name of the health plan in cell B4. If it is, then the cost of the health plan is equal to the value of cell C4; otherwise, the cost is equal to the value of cell C5.

7. In the range B7:B9, enter the formulas to calculate the total salaries, 401(k) contributions, and health insurance costs.

8. Print the contents of the Payroll worksheet.

9. Rework the analysis, assuming that the cost of the Premier plan has risen to $7,000 and the cost of the Standard plan has risen to $6,100.
10. Print the revised Payroll worksheet.
11. Save your changes to the workbook, and then close it.

Challenge

Go beyond what you learned in Session 2.2. Use the PMT, PPMT, and IPMT functions to create a payment schedule for a small business.

Case Problem 4

Data File needed for this Case Problem: Soup1.xls

The Soup Shop Ken Novak is the owner of a diner in Upton, Ohio, named The Soup Shop. Business has been very good lately, so Ken is considering taking out a loan to cover the cost of upgrading and expanding the diner. Ken wants your help in creating an Excel workbook that provides detailed information about the loan. He would like the workbook to calculate the monthly payment needed for a five-year, $125,000 loan at 6.5% interest. Ken believes that the expansion will increase business, so he also wants to know how much he would save on interest payments by paying off the loan after one, two, three, or four years.

To do this type of calculation, you need to know what part of each monthly payment is used to reduce the size of the loan (also referred to as payments toward the principal) and what part is used for paying interest on the loan. Excel provides two functions to calculate these values, both of which are similar to the PMT function used to calculate the total monthly payment. To calculate how much of a monthly payment is used to pay off the principal, you use the PPMT function, which has the following syntax:

=PPMT(*rate, period, nper, pv* [,*fv*=0] [,*type*=0])

where *rate* is the interest rate period, *period* is the payment period you want to examine (such as the first period, the second period, and so forth), *nper* is the total number of payment periods, *pv* is the amount of the loan, *fv* is the future value of the loan (assumed to be zero), and *type* indicates whether the payment is due at the beginning (*type*=1) or at the end (*type*=0) of the month. The function to calculate how much of the monthly payment is used for paying the interest is the IPMT function, which has a similar syntax:

=IPMT(*rate, period, nper, pv* [,*fv*=0] [,*type*=0])

As with the PMT function, the value of the *pv* argument should be negative when you are working with loans—as you are in this case.

Ken wants you to use these two functions to create a payment schedule that indicates for each of the 60 months of the loan, how much of the monthly payment is being used to pay off the loan and how much is being used to pay interest on the loan. You can then use this schedule to discover how much Ken could save in interest charges by paying off the loan early. Figure 2-36 shows the worksheet as it will appear at the end of this exercise.

Figure 2-36

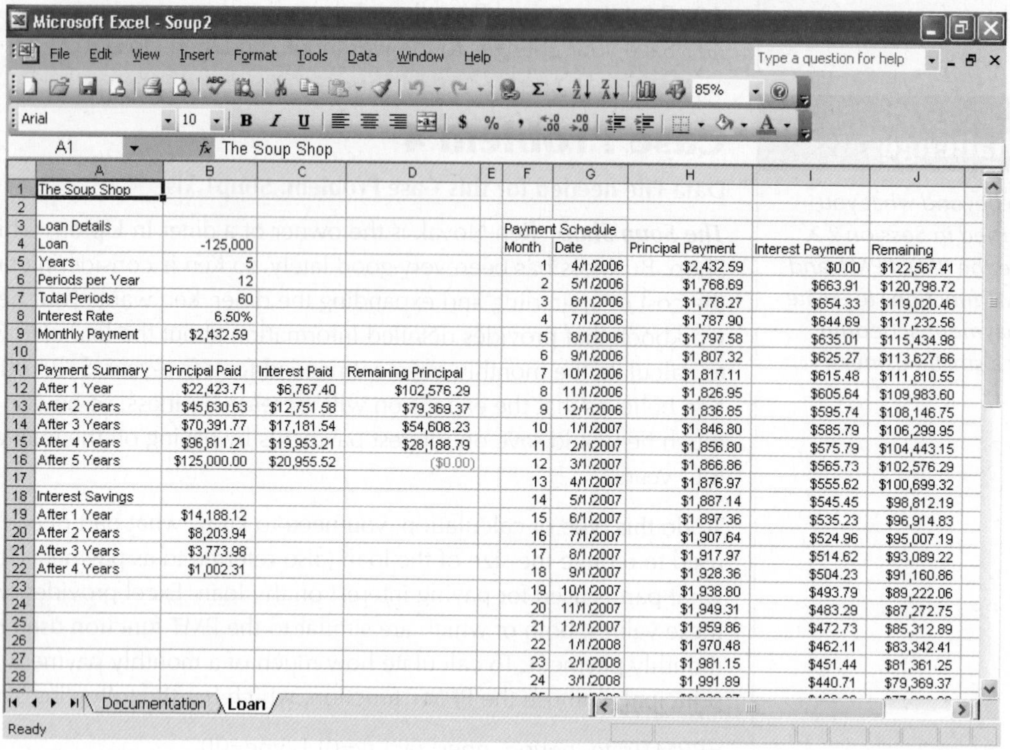

Microsoft Excel - Soup2

	A	B	C	D	E	F	G	H	I	J
1	The Soup Shop									
2										
3	Loan Details					Payment Schedule				
4	Loan	-125,000				Month	Date	Principal Payment	Interest Payment	Remaining
5	Years	5				1	4/1/2006	$2,432.59	$0.00	$122,567.41
6	Periods per Year	12				2	5/1/2006	$1,768.69	$663.91	$120,798.72
7	Total Periods	60				3	6/1/2006	$1,778.27	$654.33	$119,020.46
8	Interest Rate	6.50%				4	7/1/2006	$1,787.90	$644.69	$117,232.56
9	Monthly Payment	$2,432.59				5	8/1/2006	$1,797.58	$635.01	$115,434.98
10						6	9/1/2006	$1,807.32	$625.27	$113,627.66
11	Payment Summary	Principal Paid	Interest Paid	Remaining Principal		7	10/1/2006	$1,817.11	$615.48	$111,810.55
12	After 1 Year	$22,423.71	$6,767.40	$102,576.29		8	11/1/2006	$1,826.95	$605.64	$109,983.60
13	After 2 Years	$45,630.63	$12,751.58	$79,369.37		9	12/1/2006	$1,836.85	$595.74	$108,146.75
14	After 3 Years	$70,391.77	$17,181.54	$54,608.23		10	1/1/2007	$1,846.80	$585.79	$106,299.95
15	After 4 Years	$96,811.21	$19,953.21	$28,188.79		11	2/1/2007	$1,856.80	$575.79	$104,443.15
16	After 5 Years	$125,000.00	$20,955.52	($0.00)		12	3/1/2007	$1,866.86	$565.73	$102,576.29
17						13	4/1/2007	$1,876.97	$555.62	$100,699.32
18	Interest Savings					14	5/1/2007	$1,887.14	$545.45	$98,812.19
19	After 1 Year	$14,188.12				15	6/1/2007	$1,897.36	$535.23	$96,914.83
20	After 2 Years	$8,203.94				16	7/1/2007	$1,907.64	$524.96	$95,007.19
21	After 3 Years	$3,773.98				17	8/1/2007	$1,917.97	$514.62	$93,089.22
22	After 4 Years	$1,002.31				18	9/1/2007	$1,928.36	$504.23	$91,160.86
23						19	10/1/2007	$1,938.80	$493.79	$89,222.06
24						20	11/1/2007	$1,949.31	$483.29	$87,272.75
25						21	12/1/2007	$1,959.86	$472.73	$85,312.89
26						22	1/1/2008	$1,970.48	$462.11	$83,342.41
27						23	2/1/2008	$1,981.15	$451.44	$81,361.25
28						24	3/1/2008	$1,991.89	$440.71	$79,369.37

Documentation | Loan

Ready

To complete this task:

1. Open the **Soup1** workbook located in the Tutorial.02\Cases folder included with your Data Files, and then save the workbook as **Soup2** in the same folder.
2. Enter your name and the current date in the Documentation sheet.
3. Switch to the Loan worksheet, and then in the range B4:B8, enter the following loan details:
   - Loan Amount = –125,000
   - Years = 5
   - Periods per Year = 12
   - Interest Rate = 6.5% (annually)

   In cell B7, enter a formula to calculate the total number of payment periods.
4. In cell B9, enter a formula using the PMT function to calculate the total monthly payment required to pay off the loan. Assume that payments are made at the beginning of each period, *not* at the end, which is the default. (*Hint*: Use the *fv* and *type* arguments.)
5. In the range F5:F64, enter the numbers 1 through 60 using Auto Fill. Each number indicates the payment period in the payment schedule.
6. Ken would like his payment schedule to include the dates on which the payments are due. In cell G5, enter the date 4/1/2006. This is the due date for the first payment. In cell G6, enter the date 5/1/2006. This is the due date for the second payment. Use the Auto Fill to enter the rest of the due dates into the range G7:G64.

Explore

7. In cell H5, enter a formula using the PPMT function to calculate the amount of the first month's payment devoted to reducing the principal of the loan. The details of the loan should reference the appropriate cells in the B4:B8 range of the worksheet using absolute references. The period number should reference the value in cell F5 using a relative reference. Be sure to indicate in the function that the payments are made at the beginning, not the end, of the month.

Explore

Explore

8. In cell I5, enter a formula using the IPMT function to calculate the amount of the first month's payment that is used for paying the interest on the loan.

9. In cell J5, enter a formula that calculates the amount of the principal remaining to be paid. Ken would like this expressed as a positive value. To calculate this value, construct a formula that is equal to the *negative* of the value in cell B4 (the amount of the loan) minus the running total of the principal payments. To calculate a running total of the principal payments, use the formula =SUM($H$5:H5). Note that this formula uses both an absolute reference and a relative reference, much like the running total example in the tutorial.

10. Using Auto Fill, copy the formulas in the range H5:J5 to the range H5:J64. (*Hint:* The value displayed in cell J64 should be $0.00, indicating that the loan is completely paid off. Also, the interest payment for the last month should be $13.11.)

11. In cell B12, enter a formula to calculate the total amount of payments made to the principal in the first 12 months of the schedule. In cell C12, enter a formula to calculate the total amount of the interest payments. In cell D12, enter a formula to calculate the amount of the remaining principal. Once again, Ken wants this expressed as a positive value, so the formula must subtract the value in cell B12 from the *negative* of the value in cell B4.

12. Repeat Step 11 for the range B13:D13, calculating the totals for the first 24 months. In the range B14:D14, calculate the totals for the first 36 months. In the range B15:D15, calculate the 48-month totals. In the range B16:D16, calculate the 60-month totals.

13. In the range B19:B22, enter a formula to calculate the amount of money Ken would save in interest payments if he paid off the loan after one year, two years, three years, and four years.

Explore

14. Preview the worksheet before printing it. Open the Page Setup dialog box, change the page orientation of the worksheet to landscape orientation, and then select the option so the worksheet will print on one page. Preview the worksheet again and then print it.

15. Save your changes to the workbook and then close it.

Internet Assignments

Research

Use the Internet to find and work with data related to the topics presented in this tutorial.

The purpose of the Internet Assignments is to challenge you to find information on the Internet that you can use to work effectively with this software. The actual assignments are updated and maintained on the Course Technology Web site. Log on to the Internet and use your Web browser to go to the Student Online Companion for New Perspectives Office 2003 at **www.course.com/np/office2003**. Click the Internet Assignments link, and then navigate to the assignments for this tutorial.

SAM Assessment and Training

Assess

If you have a SAM user profile, you may have access to hands-on instruction, practice, and assessment of the skills covered in this tutorial. Log in to your SAM account and go to your assignments page to see what your instructor has assigned.

Review

Quick Check Answers

Session 2.1

1. =MIN(B1:B50)
2. =B2+C2
3. =$A$1+C2
4. (a) A1 (b) $A$1 (c) $A1 and A$1
5. Enter the values 1 and 3 in the first two rows of column A. Select the two cells and then drag the fill handle down over the range A1:A99, completing the series.
6. TODAY()

Session 2.2

1. the loan amount, the interest rate, the number of payment periods, and the payment due each period
2. =PMT(7%/12,5*12,10000)
3. PV
4. =IF(A1>B1, "Yes", "No")
5. NOT

Objectives

Session 3.1
- Format data using the Comma, Currency, and Percent styles
- Copy and paste formats using the Format Painter
- Modify and apply number formatting styles
- Change font type, style, size, and color
- Change alignment of cell contents
- Apply borders and background colors and patterns

Session 3.2
- Merge a range of cells into a single cell
- Hide rows, columns, and worksheets
- Add a background image to a worksheet
- Format worksheet tabs
- Clear and replace formats
- Create and apply styles
- Apply an AutoFormat
- Set up a worksheet for printing
- Add headers and footers to printouts

Developing a Professional-Looking Worksheet

Formatting a Sales Report

Case

NewGeneration Monitors

NewGeneration Monitors is a computer equipment company that specializes in computer monitors. Joan Sanchez, sales manager, has been entering sales data for three of the company's monitors into an Excel workbook. She plans on including the sales data in a report to be presented later in the week. Joan has made no attempt to change or enhance the presentation of this data. She has simply entered the numbers. She needs you to transform her raw figures into a presentable report.

To create a professional-looking document, you will learn how to work with Excel's formatting tools to modify the appearance of the data in each cell, the cell itself, and the entire worksheet. You will also learn how to format printouts, create headers and footers, and control which parts of the worksheet are printed on which pages.

Student Data Files

▼**Tutorial.03**

▽ **Tutorial folder**
Back.jpg
Sales1.xls

▽ **Review folder**
Region1.xls

▽ **Cases folder**
Blades1.xls
Frosti1.xls
Packing1.xls

Session 3.1

Formatting Worksheet Data

The data for Joan's sales report has already been stored in an Excel workbook. Before going further, you will open the workbook and save it with a new filename.

To open the Sales report workbook:

1. Start Excel and then open the **Sales1** workbook located in the Tutorial.03\Tutorial folder included with your Data Files.

2. On the Documentation worksheet, enter *your name* in cell B3, and enter the *current date* in cell B4.

3. Save the workbook as **Sales2** in the Tutorial.03\Tutorial folder.

4. Click the **Sales** tab to display the unformatted worksheet, shown in Figure 3-1.

| Figure 3-1 | The unformatted Sales worksheet |

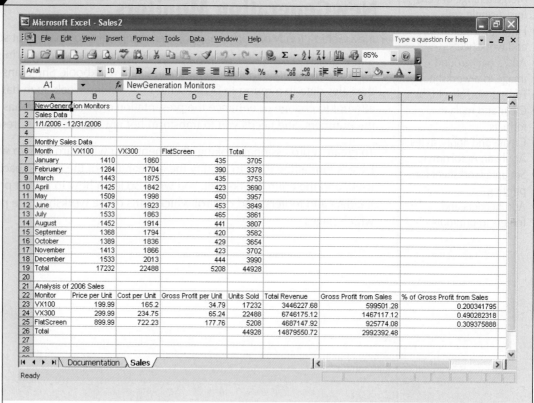

The Sales worksheet contains two tables. The table in the upper portion of the worksheet displays the monthly sales figures for three of NewGeneration's monitors: the VX100, the VX300, and the FlatScreen. The other table presents an analysis of these sales figures. Although the data in the worksheet is accurate and complete, the numbers are not as easy to read as they could be, which also makes interpreting the data more difficult. To help improve the readability of the data presented in a worksheet, you can change its appearance by formatting it.

Formatting is the process of changing the appearance of your workbook. A properly formatted workbook can be easier to read, appear more professional, and help draw attention to the important points you want to make. Formatting only changes the appearance of the data; it does not affect the data itself. For example, if a cell contains the value 0.124168, and you format the cell to display only up to the thousandths digit (so the value appears as 0.124), the cell still contains the precise value, even though you cannot see it displayed in the worksheet.

Unless you specify different formatting, Excel automatically displays numbers in the worksheet cells using the **General number format**, which, for the most part, formats numbers just the way you enter them. There are some exceptions to this approach. For example, if the cell is not wide enough to show the entire number, the General number format rounds numbers that contain decimals and uses scientific notation for large numbers.

If you don't want to use the General number format, you can choose from a wide variety of number formats. Formats can be applied using either the Formatting toolbar or the Format menu. Formats can also be copied from one cell to another, giving you the ability to apply a common format to different cells in your worksheet.

Using the Formatting Toolbar

The Formatting toolbar is one of the fastest ways to format a worksheet. By clicking a single button on the Formatting toolbar, you can increase or decrease the number of decimal places displayed in a selected range of cells, and display a value as currency with a dollar sign or a percentage with a percent sign. You also can use the Formatting toolbar to change the font type (for example, Times New Roman or Arial), style (such as bold), color, or size.

When Joan entered the monthly sales figures for the three monitors, she was concerned with entering the figures as accurately and as efficiently as possible and wasn't concerned with the appearance of the numbers in the worksheet. She entered the sales figures without including a comma to separate the thousands from the hundreds and so forth. Now, to make the numbers easier to read, Joan wants all the values to appear with commas, and for the figures that are whole numbers, she doesn't want any zeros after the decimal point (also referred to as "trailing zeros"). She believes that these changes will make the worksheet easier to read.

To insert commas in the figures in Joan's worksheet, you will apply the Comma style using its button on the Formatting toolbar. By default, Excel automatically adds two decimal places to the numbers that you have formatted with the Comma style. You will then need to use the Decrease Decimal button on the Formatting toolbar to change the number of decimal places displayed in a number.

To apply the Comma style and remove the trailing zeros:

1. Select the range **B7:E19** in the Sales worksheet.

2. Click the **Comma Style** button ⧉ on the Formatting toolbar. Excel adds the comma separator to each of the values in the table and displays the values with two digits to the right of the decimal point.

   Trouble? If you do not see the Comma Style button ⧉ on the Formatting toolbar, click the Toolbar Options button ⧉ on the Formatting toolbar, point to Add or Remove Buttons, point to Formatting, and then click ⧉ on the menu of available buttons.

   Because Joan wants whole numbers displayed without trailing zeros, you will remove any that are displayed.

3. Click the **Decrease Decimal** button ⧉ on the Formatting toolbar twice to remove the zeros. Figure 3-2 shows the worksheet with the formatting changes you have made so far.

Figure 3-2	▶	Applying the Comma style

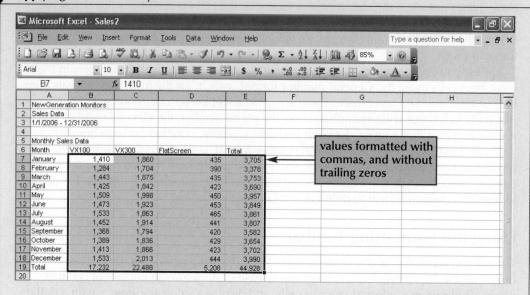

Joan wants the price and production cost of each monitor as well as last year's total sales and gross profit displayed using dollar signs, commas, and two decimal places. A quick and easy way to format the values with these attributes is to use the Currency style, which is available as a button on the Formatting toolbar. When you apply the Currency style, Excel adds a dollar sign and comma separator to the value and displays two decimal places. Try applying the Currency style to the total sales and profit values.

To apply the Currency style:

1. Select the nonadjacent range **B23:D25;F23:G26**.

   Trouble? To select a nonadjacent range, select the first range, press and hold the Ctrl key, and then select the next range.

2. Click the **Currency Style** button 〔$〕 on the Formatting toolbar. As shown in Figure 3-3, Excel adds the dollar signs and commas, and keeps two decimal places to display the values as currency. Also note that the alignment of the dollar signs is along the left edge of the cell and the decimal points are aligned vertically.

Figure 3-3	▶	Applying the Currency style

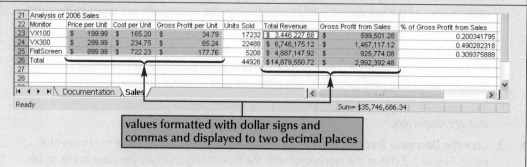

Finally, the range H23:H25 displays the percentage that each monitor contributes to the overall profit from sales. Joan wants these values displayed with a percent sign and two decimal places. To format a value as a percent, you can apply the Percent style. By default, Excel does not display any decimal places with the Percent style; therefore, you will need to increase the number of decimal places displayed.

To apply the Percent style and increase the number of decimal places:

1. Select the range **H23:H25**.

2. Click the **Percent Style** button [%] on the Formatting toolbar. The values appear with percent signs and without zeros.

3. Click the **Increase Decimal** button on the Formatting toolbar twice to display the percentages to two decimal places. Figure 3-4 shows the values in column H formatted with percent signs and to two decimal places.

Applying the Percent style ◄ | **Figure 3-4**

	Monitor	Price per Unit	Cost per Unit	Gross Profit per Unit	Units Sold	Total Revenue	Gross Profit from Sales	% of Gross Profit from Sales
21	Analysis of 2006 Sales							
22	Monitor	Price per Unit	Cost per Unit	Gross Profit per Unit	Units Sold	Total Revenue	Gross Profit from Sales	% of Gross Profit from Sales
23	VX100	$ 199.99	$ 165.20	$ 34.79	17232	$ 3,446,227.68	$ 599,501.28	20.03%
24	VX300	$ 299.99	$ 234.75	$ 65.24	22488	$ 6,746,175.12	$ 1,467,117.12	49.03%
25	FlatScreen	$ 899.99	$ 722.23	$ 177.76	5208	$ 4,687,147.92	$ 925,774.08	30.94%
26	Total				44928	$14,879,550.72	$ 2,992,392.48	
27								
28								

|◄ ◄ ► ►| \ Documentation \ Sales /

Ready   Sum=100.00%

values formatted with percent signs
and displayed to two decimal places

By displaying the percentages, you can quickly see that one monitor, the VX300, accounts for almost half of the profit from monitor sales.

Copying Formats

As you look over the sales figures, you see that one area of the worksheet still needs to be formatted. The Units Sold column in the range E23:E26 still does not display the comma separator you used with the sales figures. To fix a formatting problem like this one, you can use the Format Painter button located on the Standard toolbar. When you use the **Format Painter** option, you "paint" a format from one cell to another cell or to a range of cells. This is a fast and efficient way of copying a format from one cell to another.

Copying Formatting Using the Format Painter   Reference Window

- Select the cell or range whose formatting you want to apply to other cells.
- To apply the formatting to one cell or an adjacent range of cells, click the Format Painter button on the Standard toolbar, and then click the destination cell or drag the Format Painter pointer over the adjacent range.
- To apply the formatting to nonadjacent ranges, double-click the Format Painter button on the Standard toolbar, and then drag the Format Painter pointer over the first range and then over the other ranges you want to format.

You will use the Format Painter button to copy the format used in the sales figures and to paste that format into the range E23:E26.

To copy the formatting to the range E23:E26 using the Format Painter button:

1. Select cell **B7**, which contains the formatting that you want to copy. You do not have to copy the entire range, because the range is formatted in the same way.

2. Click the **Format Painter** button 🖋 on the Standard toolbar. As you move the pointer over the worksheet area, the pointer changes to ⊕🖌.

3. Drag the pointer over the range **E23:E26** to apply the modified Comma style format to the sales figures.

Another approach is to use the fill handle discussed in Tutorial 2 to fill in the format (not the values) from one cell to another. To use this approach, you have click the Auto Fill Options button and select the Fill Formatting option. This technique only works when the cell or cells that you want to format are adjacent to the cell containing the format you want to copy. You can also use the Paste Special command from the Copy and Paste buttons to paste only the format of a selected group of cells into a new range of cells. This technique was also discussed in Tutorial 2. One of the advantages of the Format Painter button is that it does what these two methods do, but it does so in fewer steps. However, you should use the approach with which you feel most comfortable.

The Format Painter button and the buttons on the Formatting toolbar are fast and easy ways to copy and apply cell formats, but on occasion you will need more control over your formatting choices than is provided by these toolbar buttons. In those cases, you will need to use the Format Cells dialog box.

Using the Format Cells Dialog Box

Joan agrees that formatting the values has made the worksheet easier to read, but she has a few other suggestions. She does not like the way the currency values are displayed with the dollar signs placed at the left edge of the cell, leaving a large blank space between the dollar sign and the numbers, which is characteristic of values that use an accounting format. She would rather see the dollar sign placed directly to the left of the dollar amounts, which would eliminate the blank space.

The convenience of the Formatting toolbar's one-click access to many of the formatting tasks you will want to perform does have its limits. As you can see in the worksheet, when you use the Formatting toolbar, you cannot specify how the format is applied. To make the change that Joan suggests, you will open the Format Cells dialog box, which gives you more control over the formatting by providing categories of formats from which you can choose and modify to suit your needs.

To open the Format Cells dialog box:

▶ **1.** Select the nonadjacent range **B23:D25;F23:G26**.

▶ **2.** Click **Format** on the menu bar, and then click **Cells**. The Format Cells dialog box opens, as shown in Figure 3-5. In addition to the General format category, there are 11 number format categories from which to choose.

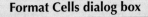

Format Cells dialog box ◄ **Figure 3-5**

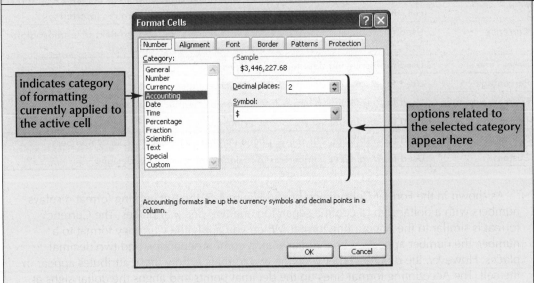

The Format Cells dialog box contains the following six tabs, each dedicated to a different set of format properties. You can apply the options available in this dialog box to any cell or range of cells that you select. The six tabs are:

- **Number:** Provides options for formatting the appearance of numbers, including dates and numbers treated as text (for example, telephone numbers)
- **Alignment:** Provides options for controlling how data is aligned within a cell
- **Font:** Provides options for selecting font types, sizes, and styles and other formatting attributes, such as underlining and colors
- **Border:** Provides options for adding borders around cells
- **Patterns:** Provides options for creating and applying background colors and patterns to cells
- **Protection:** Provides options for locking or hiding cells to prevent other users from modifying their contents

Excel supports several categories of number formats, ranging from Accounting, which you applied using the Currency Style button, to Scientific, which might be used for recording engineering data. Figure 3-6 describes the number format categories.

Figure 3-6 ▷ **Number format categories**

Category	Description
General	Default format that displays numbers as they are entered
Number	Used for a general display of numbers, with options for the formatting of negative numbers and the number of decimal places
Accounting	Used for displaying monetary values with dollar signs aligned at the left edge of the cell, the decimal points aligned vertically, and comma separators inserted
Currency	Used for displaying monetary values with dollar signs aligned next to leftmost digit and comma separators inserted (decimal points are not aligned)
Date, Time	Used for displaying date and time values
Percentage	Used for displaying decimal values as percentages
Fraction, Scientific	Used for displaying values as fractions or in scientific notation
Text	Used for displaying values as text strings
Special	Used for displaying ZIP codes, phone numbers, and social security numbers
Custom	Used for displaying numbers used in coding or specialized designs

As shown in the Format Cells dialog box in Figure 3-5, the Accounting format displays numbers with a dollar sign, a comma separator, and two decimal places. The Currency format is similar to the Accounting format. When you apply the Currency format to a number, the number appears with a dollar sign, a comma separator, and two decimal places. However, the difference between the two formats is how these attributes appear in the cell. The Accounting format lines up the decimal points and aligns the dollar signs at the left edge of the cell border (creating blank spaces between the dollar signs and the values, as you saw earlier). The Currency format aligns the dollar sign closer to the number, which removes the blank spaces. Joan prefers the Currency format, so you will apply this format to the nonadjacent range that you already selected.

To modify and apply the Currency format:

1. On the Number tab, click **Currency** in the Category list box. The Format Cells dialog box displays the options available for customizing the Currency category and provides a preview of the selected format. As shown in the Negative numbers list box, Excel displays negative currency values either with a minus sign (-) or with a combination of a red font and parentheses. Joan wants negative currency values to be displayed with a minus sign, which is one of the variations of the Currency format available to you.

2. Click the first entry in the Negative numbers list box, and then click the **OK** button. Excel changes the format of the currency values, removing the blank spaces between the dollar signs and the values and changing the alignment of the decimal points.

By using the Format Cells dialog box, you can control the formatting to ensure that text and values are displayed the way you want them to be.

Changing Font Type, Size, Style, and Color

A **font** is a set of characters that use the same typeface, style, and size. A **typeface** is the specific design of a set of printed characters, including letters, numbers, punctuation marks, and symbols. Some of the more commonly used fonts are Arial, Times Roman, and Courier. Each font can be displayed using one of the following **font styles**: regular, *italic*, **bold**, or ***bold italic***. Fonts can also be displayed with special effects, such as ~~strikeout~~, underline, and color.

Fonts can also be rendered in different sizes. **Font sizes** are measured using points. A **point** is a unit of measurement used in printing and is equal to approximately 1/72 of an inch. By default, Excel displays characters using a 10-point Arial font in a regular style. To change the font used in a selected cell, you either click the appropriate buttons on the Formatting toolbar or select options in the Format Cells dialog box.

In the logo that the company uses on all its correspondence and advertising materials, the name "NewGeneration Monitors" appears in a large Times New Roman font, which is a serif font. Characters that are designed as **serif fonts** have small lines stemming from and at an angle to the upper and lower ends of the character. **Sans serif fonts** do not include the small lines. A serif font is considered easier to read than a sans serif font. Joan wants the title in cell A1 to reflect this company-wide format, so you will format the title accordingly.

To change the font and font size of the title:

1. Click cell **A1** to make it the active cell.

2. Click the **Font** list arrow Arial on the Formatting toolbar, scroll down the list of available fonts, and then click **Times New Roman**.

   Trouble? If you do not have the Times New Roman font installed on your computer, choose a different Times Roman font or choose MS Serif or another serif font in the list.

3. Click the **Font Size** list arrow 10 on the Formatting toolbar, and then click **18**. Figure 3-7 shows the revised format for the title in cell A1.

Changing the font and font size | **Figure 3-7**

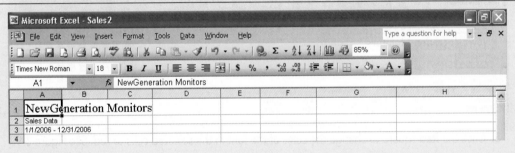

Joan wants the column titles of both tables displayed in bold font and the word "Total" in both tables displayed in italics. To make these modifications, you will again use the Formatting toolbar.

To apply the bold and italic styles:

1. Select the nonadjacent range **A6:E6;A22:H22**.

2. Click the **Bold** button ⊞ on the Formatting toolbar. The titles in the two tables now appear in a boldface font.

   Trouble? Some of the title text may appear truncated within their cells. You'll fix this problem shortly.

3. Select the nonadjacent range **A19;A26**.

4. Click the **Italic** button _I_ on the Formatting toolbar. The word "Total" in cells A19 and A26 is now italicized.

Joan points out that NewGeneration's logo usually appears in a red font. Color is another one of Excel's formatting tools and can dramatically enhance the presentation of your data if you have a color printer. Excel provides a palette of 40 different colors. If the color you want is not listed, you can modify Excel's color configuration to create a different color palette. Excel's default color settings will work for most situations, so in this case you will not modify Excel's color settings. You will apply a red color to the name of the company and the two subtitles, which describe the contents of this worksheet.

To change the font color of the title to red:

1. Select the range **A1:A3**.

2. Click the **Font Color** list arrow ▲ ▾ on the Formatting toolbar to display a color palette, and then position the pointer over the Red square (third row, first column from the left) on the palette, as shown in Figure 3-8.

Figure 3-8	Choosing a font color

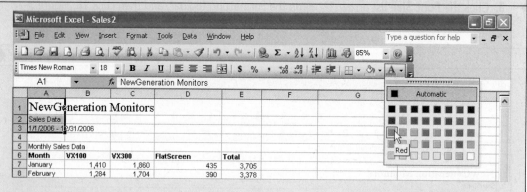

3. Click the **Red** square to change the color of the font in the selected cells to red. See Figure 3-9.

Figure 3-9	Changing the font color of a cell

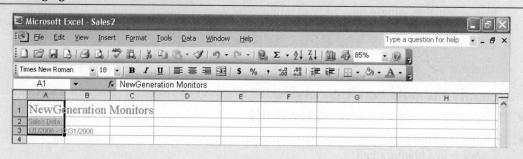

Aligning Cell Contents

When you enter numbers and formulas into a cell, Excel automatically aligns them with the cell's right edge and bottom border. Text entries are aligned with the left edge and bottom border. The default Excel alignment does not always create the most readable worksheets. As a general rule, you should center column titles, and format columns of numbers so that the decimal places are lined up within a column. You can change horizontal alignment using the alignment tools on the Formatting toolbar or the options on the Alignment tab in the Format Cells dialog box.

Next, you will center the column titles above the values in each column in the two tables.

To center the column titles:

▶ 1. Select the nonadjacent range **B6:E6;B22:H22**.

▶ 2. Click the **Center** button ☰ on the Formatting toolbar. Excel centers the text in the selected cells in each column.

The Formatting toolbar also provides the Align Left button and the Align Right button so that you can left-align and right-align cell contents. If you want to align cell contents vertically, you have to open the Format Cells dialog box and choose the vertical alignment options on the Alignment tab.

Another alignment option available in the Format Cells dialog box is to center text across a range of cells. Joan wants the text in the cell range A1:A3 to be centered at the top of the worksheet across the first eight columns of the worksheet. This time you will open the Format Cells dialog box to make this formatting change.

To center the titles and subtitles across the first eight columns of the worksheet:

▶ 1. Select the range **A1:H3**.

▶ 2. Click **Format** on the menu bar, and then click **Cells** to open the Format Cells dialog box.

▶ 3. Click the **Alignment** tab.

▶ 4. Click the **Horizontal** list arrow in the Text alignment pane, click **Center Across Selection**, and then click the **OK** button. See Figure 3-10.

Centering text within and across columns ◀ **Figure 3-10**

text is centered across the first eight columns of the worksheet

The text in these cells is centered horizontally across the selection. Note that centering the text does not affect the location. The title and subtitles are still placed in cells A1 through A3. In general, you should only use this approach for text that is in the leftmost column of the selection, and there should be no text in any other column. If you had text in column B in the previous set of steps, then that text would have been centered across columns B through H, and the text in column A would have remained where it was.

Indenting and Wrapping Text

Sometimes you will want a cell's contents offset, or indented, a few spaces from the cell's edge. This is particularly true for text entries that are aligned with the left edge of the cell. Indenting is often used for cell entries that are considered "subsections" of your worksheet. Joan wants you to indent the names of the months in the range A7:A18 and the monitor titles in the range A23:A25. You will indent the text using one of the indent buttons on the Formatting toolbar.

To indent the months and monitor titles:

1. Select the nonadjacent range **A7:A18;A23:A25**.

2. Click the **Increase Indent** button 🔳 on the Formatting toolbar. Excel shifts the contents of the selected cells to the right. See Figure 3-11.

| Figure 3-11 | Indenting text within cells |

Clicking the Increase Indent button increases the amount of indentation by roughly one character. To decrease or remove an indentation, click the Decrease Indent button or modify the Indent value using the Format Cells dialog box.

If you enter text that is too wide for a cell, Excel either extends the text into the adjoining cells (if the cells are empty) or truncates the display of the text (if the adjoining cells contain text or values). To avoid cutting off the display of text in a cell, you can widen the columns, or place the text on several lines using the method you learned in Tutorial 1 (pressing the Alt key to move to a second line with a cell). You can also have Excel wrap the text within the cell for you. To wrap text within a cell, you click the Wrap text check box on the Alignment tab of the Format Cells dialog box.

Joan notes that some of the column titles in the second table are long. For example, the "Cost per Unit" label in cell C22 is much longer than the values below it. This formatting has caused some of the columns to be wider than they need to be. Another problem is that the text for some cells has been truncated because the columns are not wide enough. Joan suggests that you wrap the text within the column titles and then change the width of the columns where necessary. To make this change, you will use the Format Cells dialog box.

To have Excel automatically wrap text within a cell:

1. Select the range **A22:H22**.

2. Click **Format** on the menu bar, and then click **Cells** to open the Format Cells dialog box.

3. Make sure that the Alignment tab is selected, select the **Wrap text** check box in the Text control pane, and then click the **OK** button. The text in many of the selected cells now appears on two rows within the cells.

4. Change the width of columns **A** and **D** to about **12** characters (**89** pixels) each, columns **B** and **C** to about **10** characters (**75** pixels) each, columns **F** and **G** to about **13** characters (**96** pixels) each, and column **H** to about **17** characters (**124** pixels) each. See Figure 3-12.

Wrapping text and resizing the worksheet columns — **Figure 3-12**

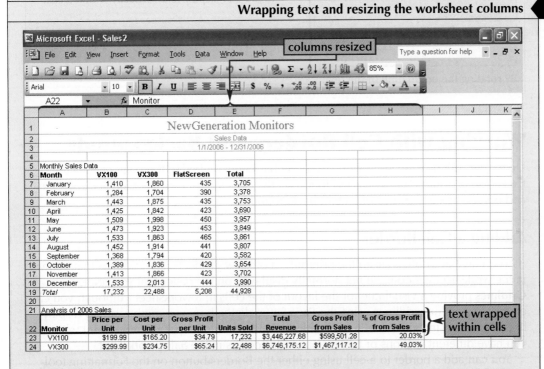

Trouble? If your screen does not match Figure 3-12, resize the columns so the values are easy to read. If some of the text is still hidden, you may need to resize the height of row 22 by dragging the bottom row border down (see Tutorial 1 for a description of resizing rows and columns).

Other Formatting Options

Excel supports even more formatting options than have been discussed so far. For example, instead of wrapping the text, you can have Excel shrink it to fit the size of the cell. If you reduce the cell later on, Excel will automatically resize the text to match. You can also rotate the contents of the cell, displaying the cell entry at almost any angle (see Figure 3-13). Joan does not need to use either of these options in her workbook, but they might be useful later for another project.

Figure 3-13 ▶ **Rotating text within a cell**

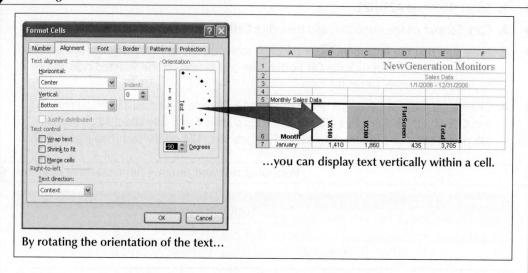

By rotating the orientation of the text…

…you can display text vertically within a cell.

Working with Cell Borders and Backgrounds

Up to now, all the formatting you have done has been applied to the contents of a cell. Excel also provides a range of tools to format the cells themselves. Specifically, you can add borders to cells and color a cell's background.

Adding a Cell Border

As you may have noticed from the printouts of other worksheets, the gridlines that appear in the worksheet window are not normally displayed on the pages that you print. **Gridlines** provide a visual cue for the layout of the cells in a worksheet. Although you can choose to print the gridlines using the Page Setup dialog box, you might want to display borders around individual cells in a worksheet. This would be particularly useful when you have different sections or tables in a worksheet, as in the Sales worksheet.

You can add a border to a cell using either the Borders button on the Formatting toolbar or the options on the Border tab in the Format Cells dialog box. The Borders button allows you to create borders quickly, whereas the Format Cells dialog box lets you further refine your choices. For example, you can specify the style, thickness, and color using the options available in the Format Cells dialog box.

Joan wants you to place a border around each cell in the two tables in the worksheet. You'll select the appropriate border style from the list of available options on the Borders palette.

To create a grid of cell borders in the two tables:

▶ **1.** Select the nonadjacent range **A6:E19;A22:H26**.

▶ **2.** Click the **Borders** list arrow 🔲 ▾ on the Formatting toolbar, then move the pointer over the gallery of borders to highlight the All Borders option as shown in Figure 3-14.

Border options ◀ **Figure 3-14**

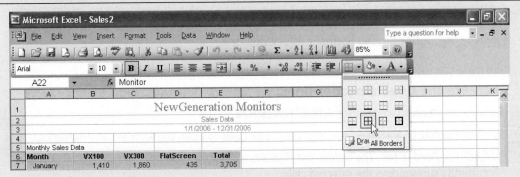

▶ **3.** Click the **All Borders** option (third row, second column from the left) in the borders gallery. A thin border appears around each cell in the selected range.

▶ **4.** Click any cell to deselect the range and to see the applied border.

You can also place a border around the entire range itself (and not the individual cells) by selecting a different border style. Try this by creating a thick border around the cell range.

To create a thick border around a selected range:

▶ **1.** Select the nonadjacent range **A6:E19;A22:H26** again.

▶ **2.** Click the **Borders** list arrow 🔲 ▾ on the Formatting toolbar, and then click the **Thick Box Border** option (third row, fourth column from the left) in the borders gallery.

▶ **3.** Click any cell to deselect the range so you can see the thick border applied to the tables. The interior borders should be unchanged.

If you want a more interactive way of drawing borders on your worksheet, you can use the Draw Borders button, which is another option on the borders gallery. To see how this option works, you will add a thick black line under the column titles in both of the tables.

To draw borders using the Draw Borders button:

▶ **1.** Click the **Borders** list arrow 🔲 ▾ on the Formatting toolbar, and then click the **Draw Borders** button 🖉 at the bottom of the borders gallery. The pointer changes to 🖉, and a floating Borders toolbar opens with four tools. The Draw Border button (currently selected) on the Borders toolbar draws a border line on the worksheet; the Erase Border button erases border lines; the Line Style button specifies the style of the border line; and the Line Color button specifies the line color.

▶ **2.** Click the **Line Style** list arrow ▭ ▾ to display a list of line style options, and then click the **thick line** option (the ninth from the top) in the list.

3. Click and drag the pointer over the lower border of the range **A6:E6**. The lower border thickens, matching the top border in thickness.

4. Click and drag the pointer over the lower border of the range **A22:H22**. The lower border thickens.

5. Click the **Close** button ☒ on the floating Borders toolbar to close it.

Finally, you will add a double line above the Total row in each table. You will add the line using the options in the Format Cells dialog box.

To create the double border lines:

1. Select the nonadjacent range **A18:E18;A25:H25**.

2. Click **Format** on the menu bar, and then click **Cells** to open the Format Cells dialog box.

3. Click the **Border** tab. The Border tab displays a diagram showing what borders, if any, are currently surrounding the selected cells.

   The bottom border is currently a single thin line. You want to change this to a double line.

4. Click the **double line** style in the Style list box located on the right side of the tab, and then click the **bottom border** in the border diagram to apply the double-line style. The bottom border changes to a double line. See Figure 3-15.

Figure 3-15	Border tab in the Format Cells dialog box

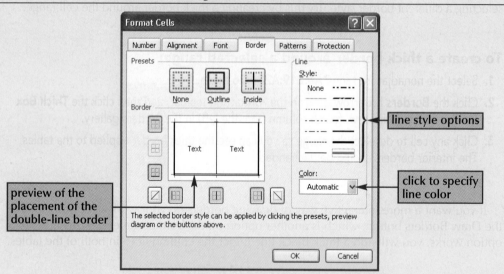

5. Click the **OK** button to close the dialog box, and then click cell **A1** to deselect the ranges. Figure 3-16 shows all of the border styles you've applied to the two tables.

Border styles applied to the worksheet | **Figure 3-16**

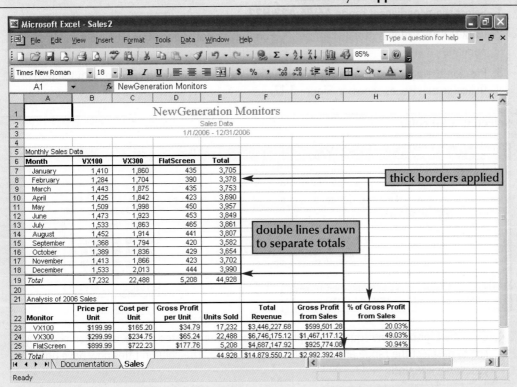

You can also specify a color for the cell borders by using the Color list box located on the Border tab (see Figure 3-15). Joan does not need to change the border colors, but she would like you to change the background color for the column title cells. When you copy the formatting of a cell, any border that you have applied is also copied.

Applying Background Colors and Patterns

Patterns and color can be used to turn a plain worksheet full of numbers and labels into a powerful presentation of information that captures your attention and adds visual emphasis to the different sections of the worksheet. If you have a color printer or a color projection device, you might want to take advantage of Excel's color tools. By default, worksheet cells are not filled with any color (the white you see in your worksheet is not a fill color for the cells). To change the background color in a worksheet, you can use the Fill Color button on the Formatting toolbar, or you can use the Format Cells dialog box, which also provides patterns that you can apply to the background. When choosing to apply color to a worksheet, you must always give consideration to the availability of a color printer. Also, if you plan to print a worksheet as an overhead, black print on a clear overhead transparency is easier to read than other colors.

Joan wants to change the background color of the worksheet. When she prints her report later in the week, she will be using the company's color laser printer. Therefore, she would like you to explore using background color in the column titles for the two sales tables. She suggests that you try formatting the column titles with a light-yellow background.

To apply a fill color to the column titles:

1. Select the nonadjacent range **A6:E6;A22:H22**.

2. Click the **Fill Color** button list arrow 🎨 ▾ on the Formatting toolbar. The color palette appears.

3. Position the pointer over the **Light Yellow** square (fifth row, third column from the left) on the color palette, as shown in Figure 3-17.

Figure 3-17 ▶ Selecting a fill color

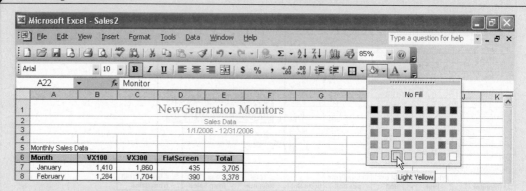

4. Click the **Light Yellow** square to apply the color to the selected range, and then click any cell to deselect the range and to see the applied color. The column titles now have light-yellow backgrounds.

Joan would also like to investigate whether you can apply a pattern to the fill background. Excel supports 18 different fill patterns. To create and apply a fill pattern, you have to open the Format Cells dialog box.

To apply a fill pattern to the column titles:

1. Select the nonadjacent range **A6:E6;A22:H22**.

2. Click **Format** on the menu bar, click **Cells** to open the Format Cells dialog box, and then click the **Patterns** tab to display the options provided.

3. Click the **Pattern** list arrow to display a gallery of patterns and a palette of colors that you can apply to the selected pattern. The default pattern color is black. First, you will choose a crosshatch pattern, which is a pattern using crossed diagonal lines.

4. Click the **50% Gray** pattern (first row, third column) in the pattern gallery, as shown in Figure 3-18.

Selecting a fill pattern | **Figure 3-18**

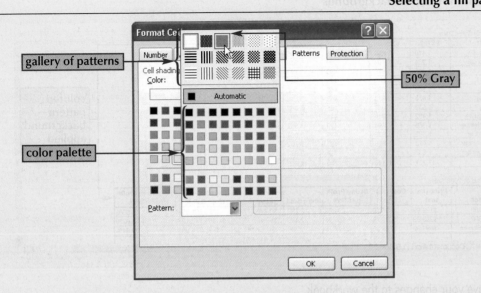

5. Click the **OK** button, and then click any cell to deselect the ranges and to see the pattern.

The background pattern you have chosen overwhelms the text in these column titles. You can improve the appearance by changing the color of the pattern itself from black to a light orange.

To change the pattern color:

1. Select the range **A6:E6;A22:H22**. The default (or automatic) color of a selected pattern is black, but you want to choose a brighter and lighter color for the pattern.

2. Click **Format** on the menu bar, and then click **Cells** to open the Format Cells dialog box again. The Patterns tab should be displayed automatically because it is the last set of options you used.

3. Click the **Pattern** list arrow to display the gallery of patterns and the color palette.

4. Click the **Light Orange** square (third row, second column) in the color palette, click the **OK** button to close the dialog box, and then click cell **A1** to deselect the range and to see the color applied to the pattern. See Figure 3-19. The column titles now appear in a light-orange patterned background. The pattern and the color do not overwhelm the column titles.

Figure 3-19 ▶ **Cells with formatted backgrounds**

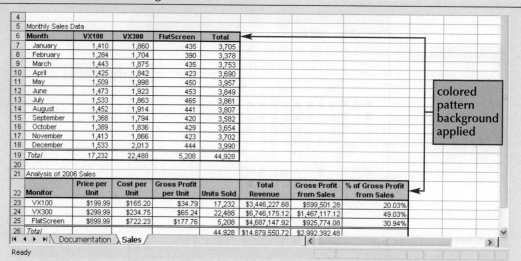

5. Save your changes to the workbook.

Joan is pleased with the progress you have made. In the next session, you will explore other formatting features.

Review

Session 3.1 Quick Check

1. Describe two ways of applying the Currency style to cells in your worksheet.
2. If the number 0.05765 has been entered into a cell, what will Excel display if you:
   a. format the number using the Percent style with one decimal place?
   b. format the number using the Currency style with two decimal places and a dollar sign?
3. Which two buttons can you use to copy a format from one cell range to another?
4. A long text string in one of your worksheet cells has been truncated. List three ways to correct this problem.
5. How do you center the contents of a single cell across a range of cells?
6. Describe three ways of creating a cell border.
7. How would you apply a colored background pattern to a selected cell range?

Session 3.2

Formatting the Worksheet

In the previous session, you formatted individual cells within the worksheet. Excel also provides tools for formatting the columns and rows in a worksheet. You will explore some of these tools as you continue to work on Joan's sales report.

Merging Cells into One Cell

Joan has several other formatting changes that she would like you to make to the Sales worksheet. She wants you to format the titles for the two tables in her report so that they are centered in a bold font above the tables. You could do this by centering the cell title across a cell range, as you did for the title in the last session. Another way is to merge several cells into one cell and then center the contents of that single cell. Merging a range of cells into a single cell removes all of the selected cells from the worksheet, except the cell in the upper-left corner of the range. Any content in the other cells of the range is deleted. To merge a range of cells into a single cell, you can use the Merge cells check box on the Alignment tab in the Format Cells dialog box or click the Merge and Center button on the Formatting toolbar.

To merge and center the cell ranges containing the table titles:

▶ 1. If you took a break after the previous session, make sure that Excel is running and that the Sales2 workbook is open.

▶ 2. In the Sales worksheet, select the range **A5:E5**.

▶ 3. Click the **Merge and Center** button ⊞ on the Formatting toolbar. The cells in the range A5:E5 are merged into a single cell whose cell reference is A5. The text in the merged cell is centered as well.

▶ 4. Click the **Bold** button **B** on the Formatting toolbar.

▶ 5. Select the range **A21:H21**, click the **Merge and Center** button ⊞ on the Formatting toolbar, and then click the **Bold** button **B** on the Formatting toolbar.

▶ 6. Click cell **A1** to deselect the range. Figure 3-20 shows the merged and centered table titles.

Merging and centering cells ◀ **Figure 3-20**

To split a merged cell back into individual cells, regardless of the method you used to merge the cells, you select the merged cell and then click the Merge and Center button again. You can also merge and unmerge cells using the Alignment tab in the Format Cells dialog box.

Hiding Rows, Columns and Worksheets

Sometimes Joan does not need to view the monthly sales for the three monitors. She does not want to remove this information from the worksheet, but she would like the option of temporarily hiding that information. Excel provides this capability. Hiding a row or column does not affect the data stored there, nor does it affect any other cell that might have a formula referencing a cell in the hidden row or column. Hiding part of your worksheet is a good way of temporarily concealing nonessential information, allowing you to concentrate on the more important data contained in your worksheet. To hide a row or column, first you must select the row(s) or column(s) you want to hide. You can then use the Row or Column option on the Format menu or right-click the selection to open its shortcut menu.

You will hide the monthly sales figures in the first table in the worksheet.

To hide the monthly sales figures:

▶ 1. Select the headings for rows **7** through **18**.

▶ 2. Right-click the selection, and then click **Hide** on the shortcut menu. Excel hides rows 7 through 18. Note that the total sales figures in the range B19:E19 are not affected by hiding the monthly sales figures. See Figure 3-21.

| Figure 3-21 | **Hiding worksheet rows** |

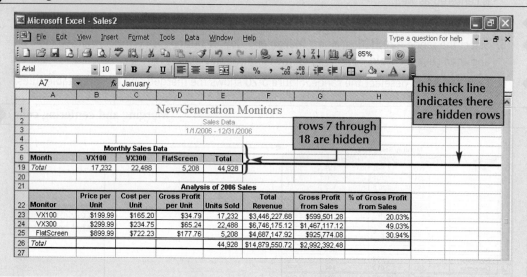

To unhide a hidden row or column, you must select the headings of the rows or columns that border the hidden area; then you can use the right-click method or the Row or Column command on the Format menu to choose the Unhide option. You will let Joan know that it is easy to hide any row or column that she does not want to view. But for now you will redisplay the hidden sales figures.

To unhide the monthly sales figures:

▶ 1. Select the row headings for rows **6** and **19**.

▶ 2. Right-click the selection, and then click **Unhide** on the shortcut menu. Excel redisplays rows 7 through 18.

▶ 3. Click cell **A1** to deselect the rows.

Hiding and unhiding a column follows the same process, except that you select the worksheet column headings rather than the row headings. For example, to hide column B, you select the column heading B. To unhide the column, you must select columns A and C.

On other occasions Joan would like to hide an entire worksheet. This could occur in situations where a worksheet contains detailed information and she only wants to display the summary figures from another sheet. To show how to hide an entire worksheet, you should suggest that she hide the documentation sheet located at the front of the workbook.

To hide the Documentation sheet:

► 1. Click the **Documentation** sheet tab to make it the active sheet.

► 2. Click **Format** on the menu bar, point to **Sheet**, and then click **Hide**.

The Documentation sheet disappears from the workbook. It is still present in the workbook, it is just hidden at this point. Excel maintains a list of the hidden worksheets in the current workbook, so you can always select one of those sheets to be redisplayed. Do this now to unhide the Documentation sheet.

To unhide the Documentation sheet:

► 1. Click **Format** on the menu bar, point to **Sheet**, and then click **Unhide**. Excel displays the Unhide dialog box, listing all hidden worksheets in the workbook.

► 2. Verify that **Documentation** is selected in the list of hidden worksheets, and click the **OK** button. The Documentation sheet should be redisplayed in the workbook and made the active sheet.

► 3. Click the **Sales** sheet tab to return to the Sales worksheet.

Adding a Background Image

In the previous session you learned how to create a background color for individual cells within the worksheet. Excel also allows you to use an image file as a background for a worksheet. The image from the file is tiled repeatedly until the images fill up the entire worksheet. Images can be used to give the background a textured appearance, like that of granite, wood, or fibered paper. The background image does not affect the format or content of any cell in the worksheet, and if you have already defined a background color for a cell, Excel displays the color on top, hiding that portion of the image.

Adding a Background Image to the Worksheet

Reference Window

- Click Format on the menu bar, point to Sheet, and then click Background.
- Locate the image file that you want tiled over the worksheet background.
- Click the Insert button.

If you add a background and then decide against it, you can remove the background image by clicking Format on the menu bar, pointing to Sheet, and then clicking Delete Background. The image will automatically be removed.

Joan wants you to experiment with using a background image for the Sales worksheet. You will add the image file that she has selected.

To add a background image to the worksheet:

1. Click **Format** on the menu bar, point to **Sheet**, and then click **Background**. The Sheet Background dialog box opens.

2. Navigate to the Tutorial.03\Tutorial folder, click the **Back** image file, and then click the **Insert** button. The Back image file is applied repeatedly to, or is "tiled over," the worksheet, creating a textured background for the Sales sheet. Notice that the tiling is hidden in the cells that already contain a background color. To make the sales figures easier to read, you'll change the background color of those cells to white.

3. Select the nonadjacent range **A7:E19;A23:H26**.

4. Click the **Fill Color** list arrow [icon] on the Formatting toolbar, click the **White** square (lower-right corner) in the color palette, and then click cell **A1** to deselect the range, making the background image easier to see. Figure 3-22 shows the Sales worksheet with the formatted background.

Figure 3-22 ▶ **Inserting a background image**

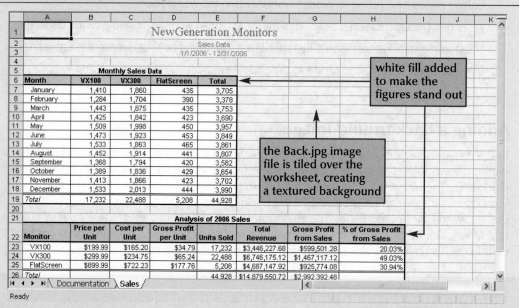

Note that you cannot apply a background image to all of the sheets in a workbook at the same time. If you want to apply the same background to several sheets, you must format each sheet separately.

Formatting Sheet Tabs

In addition to the sheet background, you can also format the background color of worksheet tabs. This color is only visible when the worksheet is not the active sheet in the workbook. By default, the tab of the active sheet in a workbook is white. If you change the color of a tab, the tab changes to white with a narrow colored stripe at the bottom of the tab when the sheet is active. You can use tab colors to better organize the various sheets in your workbook. For example, worksheets that contain sales information could be formatted with blue tabs, whereas sheets that describe the company's cash flow or budget could be formatted with green tabs. To explore how to color worksheet tabs, you will change the tab color of the Sales worksheet to light orange.

To change the tab color:

▶ 1. Right-click the **Sales** tab, and then click **Tab Color** on the shortcut menu. The Format Tab Color dialog box opens.

▶ 2. Click the **Light Orange** square (third row, second column from the left) in the color palette, and then click the **OK** button. Because the Sales sheet is the active worksheet, the tab is white with a light-orange horizontal stripe at the bottom of the tab.

▶ 3. Switch to the Documentation sheet so you can see the light-orange color of the Sales sheet tab, and then switch to the Sales sheet again.

Clearing and Replacing Formats

Sometimes you might want to change or remove some of the formatting from your workbooks. As you experiment with different formats, you can use the Undo button on the Standard toolbar to remove formatting choices that did not work out as well as you expected. Another choice is to clear the formatting from the selected cells, returning the cells to their previous format. To see how this option works, you will remove the formatting from the company name in cell A1 on the Sales worksheet.

To clear the formatting from cell A1:

▶ 1. Make sure cell **A1** is selected.

▶ 2. Click **Edit** on the menu bar, point to **Clear**, and then click **Formats**. Excel removes the formatting that was applied to the text and removes the formatting that merged the cells and then centered the text across the range.

▶ 3. Click the **Undo** button ⟲ on the Standard toolbar to undo your action, restoring the formats you cleared.

Sometimes you will want to make a formatting change that applies to several different cells. If those cells are scattered throughout the workbook, you may find it time consuming to search for and replace the formats for each individual cell. If the cells share a common format that you want to change, you can use the Find and Replace command to locate the formats and modify them.

Finding and Replacing a Format

- Click Edit on the menu bar, and then click Replace.
- Click the Options >> button, if necessary, to display the format choices.
- Click the top Format list arrow, and then click Format.
- Specify the format you want to find in the Find Format dialog box, and then click the OK button.
- Click the bottom Format list arrow, and then click Format.
- Enter the new format, which will replace the old format, and then click the OK button.
- Click the Replace All button to replace all occurrences of the old format; click the Replace button to replace the currently selected cell containing the old format; or click the Find Next button to find the next occurrence of the old format before replacing it.
- Click the Close button.

In the Sales worksheet, the table titles and column titles are displayed in a bold font. After seeing how the use of color has made the worksheet come alive, Joan wants you to change the titles to a boldface blue. Rather than selecting the cells that contain the table and column titles and formatting them, you will replace all occurrences of the boldface text with blue boldface text.

To find and replace formats:

1. Click **Edit** on the menu bar, and then click **Replace**. The Find and Replace dialog box opens. You can use this dialog box to find and replace the contents of cells. In this case, you will use it only for finding and replacing formats, leaving the contents of the cells unchanged.

2. Click the **Options >>** button to display additional find and replace options. See Figure 3-23. The dialog box expands to display options that allow you to find and replace cell formats. It also includes options to determine whether to search within the active sheet or the entire workbook. Currently no format options have been set.

| Figure 3-23 | Find and Replace dialog box |

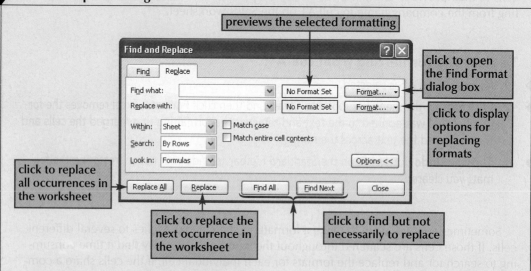

previews the selected formatting

click to open the Find Format dialog box

click to display options for replacing formats

click to replace all occurrences in the worksheet

click to replace the next occurrence in the worksheet

click to find but not necessarily to replace

Trouble? If the button on your workbook appears as Options <<, the additional options are already displayed, and you do not need to click any buttons.

3. Click the top **Format** button to open the Find Format dialog box. Here is where you specify the format you want to search for. In this case, you are searching for cells that contain boldface text.

4. Click the **Font** tab, and then click **Bold** in the Font style list box. See Figure 3-24.

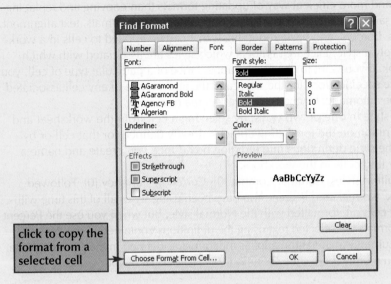

click to copy the format from a selected cell

5. Click the **OK** button.

Next, you will specify the new format that you want to use to replace the boldface text. In this case, you will specify blue boldface text.

6. Click the bottom **Format** button to open the Replace Format dialog box again, and then click **Bold** in the Font style list box.

7. Click the **Color** list box, click the **Blue** square (second row, sixth column from the left) in the color palette, and then click the **OK** button.

8. Click the **Replace All** button to replace all boldface text in the worksheet with blue bold-face text. Excel indicates that it has completed its search and made 15 replacements.

9. Click the **OK** button, and then click the **Close** button to close the Find and Replace dialog box. See Figure 3-25. The boldface text has been replaced with blue boldface text.

	Month	VX100	VX300	FlatScreen	Total				
5		Monthly Sales Data							
6	Month	VX100	VX300	FlatScreen	Total				
7	January	1,410	1,860	435	3,705				
8	February	1,284	1,704	390	3,378				
9	March	1,443	1,875	435	3,753				
10	April	1,425	1,842	423	3,690				
11	May	1,509	1,998	450	3,957				
12	June	1,473	1,923	453	3,849				
13	July	1,533	1,863	465	3,861				
14	August	1,452	1,914	441	3,807				
15	September	1,368	1,794	420	3,582				
16	October	1,389	1,836	429	3,654				
17	November	1,413	1,866	423	3,702				
18	December	1,533	2,013	444	3,990				
19	*Total*	17,232	22,488	5,208	44,928				

bold formatting found and replaced with bold blue formatting

	Monitor	Price per Unit	Cost per Unit	Gross Profit per Unit	Units Sold	Total Revenue	Gross Profit from Sales	% of Gross Profit from Sales
21				Analysis of 2006 Sales				
22	Monitor	Price per Unit	Cost per Unit	Gross Profit per Unit	Units Sold	Total Revenue	Gross Profit from Sales	% of Gross Profit from Sales
23	VX100	$199.99	$165.20	$34.79	17,232	$3,446,227.68	$599,501.28	20.03%
24	VX300	$299.99	$234.75	$65.24	22,488	$6,746,175.12	$1,467,117.12	49.03%
25	FlatScreen	$899.99	$722.23	$177.76	5,208	$4,687,147.92	$925,774.08	30.94%
26	*Total*				44,928	$14,879,550.72	$2,992,392.48	

Documentation \ Sales

Ready

Using Styles

If you have several cells that employ the same format, you can create a style for those cells. This can be a faster and more efficient way of updating formats than copying and replacing formats. A **style** is a saved collection of formatting options—number formats, text alignment, font sizes and colors, borders, and background fills—that can be applied to cells in a worksheet. When you apply a style, Excel remembers which styles are associated with which cells in the workbook. If you want to change the appearance of a particular type of cell, you need only modify the specifications for the style, and the appearance of any cell associated with that style will be automatically changed to reflect the new style.

You can create a style in one of two ways: by selecting a cell from the worksheet and basing the style definition on the formatting choices already defined for that cell or by manually entering the style definitions into a dialog box. Once you create and name a style, you can apply it to cells in the workbook.

Excel has eight built-in styles: Comma, Comma [0], Currency, Currency [0], Followed Hyperlink, Hyperlink, Normal, and Percent. You have been using styles all of this time without knowing it. Most cells are formatted with the Normal style, but when you use the Percent Style button, Excel formats the selected text using the definitions contained in the Percent style. Similarly, the Currency Style button applies the format as defined in the Currency style. As you'll see, you can modify these style definitions or create some of your own.

Creating a Style

Joan wants you to further modify the appearance of the worksheet by changing the background color of the months in the first table and the monitor names in the second table to yellow. Rather than applying new formatting to the cells, you will create a new style called "Category" and then apply the new style to the category columns of the tables in the worksheet. You will create the style using the format already applied to cell A7 as a basis.

To create a style using a formatted cell:

1. Click cell **A7** to select it. The format applied to this cell becomes the basis of the new style that you want to create.

2. Click **Format** on the menu bar, and then click **Style**. The Style dialog box opens. All of the formatting options associated with the style of the active cell are listed. For example, the font is 10-point Arial. The check boxes indicate whether these various formatting categories are part of the style definition. If you deselect one of the formatting categories, such as Border, then that category will not be part of the style definition.

   To create a new style for this cell, you simply type a different name into the list box.

3. Type **Category** in the Style name list box, as shown in Figure 3-26. At this point, cell A7 is no longer formatted using the Normal style; rather it is formatted using the Category style you just created.

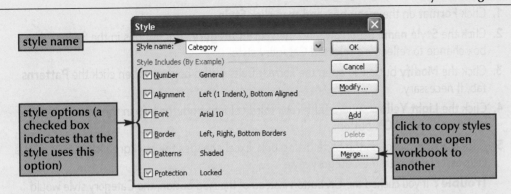

style name

style options (a checked box indicates that the style uses this option)

click to copy styles from one open workbook to another

Now you will modify the properties of this style.

4. Click the **Border** check box to deselect it. Category style will not include any border format options.

   Next, you will modify the pattern of the style.

5. Click the **Modify** button to open the Format Cells dialog box, and then click the **Patterns** tab.

6. Click the **Yellow** square (fourth row, third column from the left) in the color palette, and then click the **OK** button to close the Format Cells dialog box and redisplay the Style dialog box.

   If you click the OK button in the Style dialog box, the style definition changes and is applied to the active cell and the Style dialog box closes. If you click the Add button in the dialog box, the style change is saved and applied, but the Style dialog box remains open for further style changes.

7. Click the **OK** button to save the new style and apply it to the background color of cell A7.

Now you need to apply this style to other cells in the workbook.

Applying a Style

To apply a style to cells in a worksheet, you first select the cells you want associated with the style and then open the Style dialog box.

To apply the Category style:

1. Select the nonadjacent range **A8:A18;A23:A25**.

2. Click **Format** on the menu bar, and then click **Style**. The Style dialog box opens.

3. Click the **Style name** list arrow, and then click **Category**. The formatting options change to reflect the associated options for the selected style.

4. Click the **OK** button to close the dialog box and apply the Category style to the selected range, and then click cell **A1** to deselect the cells. A yellow background color is applied to all of the month and monitor cells in the two tables.

The yellow background appears a bit too strong. You decide to change it to a light-yellow background. Since all the month and monitor cells are now associated with the Category style, you need only modify the definition of the Category style to make this change.

To modify the Category style:

1. Click **Format** on the menu bar, and then click **Style**.
2. Click the **Style name** list arrow, and then click **Category**. The options in the Style dialog box change to reflect the selected Category style.
3. Click the **Modify** button to open the Format Cells dialog box, and then click the **Patterns** tab, if necessary.
4. Click the **Light Yellow** square (fifth row, third column from the left) in the color palette, and then click the **OK** button.
5. Click the **Add** button in the Style dialog box. Excel changes the background color of all the cells associated with the Category style.

   Trouble? If you clicked the OK button instead of the Add button, the Category style would have been applied to the active cell as well as the ranges formatted with the Category style. Click the Undo on the Standard toolbar to undo the application of the Category style to cell A2, and then skip Step 6.
6. Click the **Close** button. See Figure 3-27. The updated Category style is applied to the ranges using that format.

Figure 3-27 **Category style in the Sales worksheet**

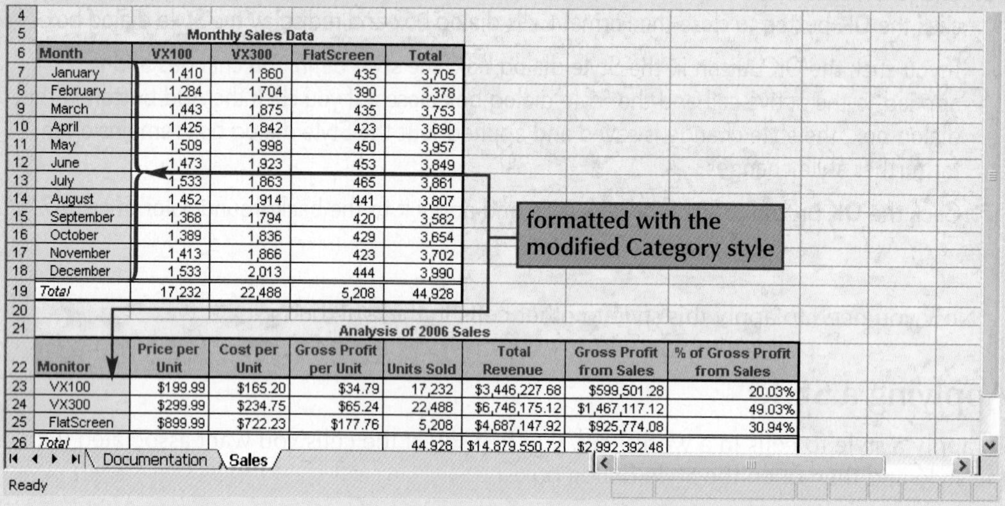

Monthly Sales Data

Month	VX100	VX300	FlatScreen	Total
January	1,410	1,860	435	3,705
February	1,284	1,704	390	3,378
March	1,443	1,875	435	3,753
April	1,425	1,842	423	3,690
May	1,509	1,998	450	3,957
June	1,473	1,923	453	3,849
July	1,533	1,863	465	3,861
August	1,452	1,914	441	3,807
September	1,368	1,794	420	3,582
October	1,389	1,836	429	3,654
November	1,413	1,866	423	3,702
December	1,533	2,013	444	3,990
Total	17,232	22,488	5,208	44,928

Analysis of 2006 Sales

Monitor	Price per Unit	Cost per Unit	Gross Profit per Unit	Units Sold	Total Revenue	Gross Profit from Sales	% of Gross Profit from Sales
VX100	$199.99	$165.20	$34.79	17,232	$3,446,227.68	$599,501.28	20.03%
VX300	$299.99	$234.75	$65.24	22,488	$6,746,175.12	$1,467,117.12	49.03%
FlatScreen	$899.99	$722.23	$177.76	5,208	$4,687,147.92	$925,774.08	30.94%
Total				44,928	$14,879,550.72	$2,992,392.48	

The Category style becomes part of the Sales2 workbook, but it is not available to other workbooks. However, you can copy styles from one workbook to another. Copying styles allows you to create a collection of workbooks that share a common look and feel.

To copy styles from one workbook to another, open the workbook containing your customized styles, and then open the workbook into which you want to copy the styles. Open the Styles dialog box, click the Merge button, and select the first workbook. All of the styles in that workbook will be copied into the second workbook for use on that workbook's contents. Note that if you make changes to the style definitions later on, you will have to copy them again. Excel will not automatically update styles across workbooks.

Using AutoFormat

Excel's **AutoFormat** feature provides a gallery of 17 predefined formats that you can select and apply to your worksheet cells. Rather than spending time testing different combinations of fonts, colors, and borders, you can apply an existing format to your worksheet.

You have done a lot of work already formatting the data in the Sales worksheet to give it a more professional and polished look, but you decide to see how the formatting you have done compares to one of Excel's AutoFormat designs.

You'll apply an AutoFormat design to the sales figures table so that you can compare a predefined format to the format you have worked on.

To apply an AutoFormat design to the table:

► 1. Select the range **A5:E19**.

► 2. Click **Format** on the menu bar, and then click **AutoFormat**. The AutoFormat dialog box opens. See Figure 3-28. The dialog box displays a preview of how each format will appear when applied to cells in a worksheet.

AutoFormat gallery ◄ **Figure 3-28**

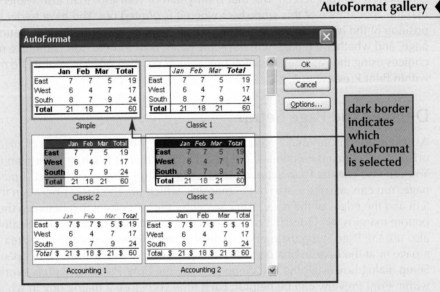

► 3. Click **Classic 3** in the list of available designs, click the **OK** button, and then click cell **A1** to remove the highlighting from the table. Figure 3-29 shows the appearance of the Classic 3 design to the cells containing the monthly sales data.

Applying an AutoFormat ◄ **Figure 3-29**

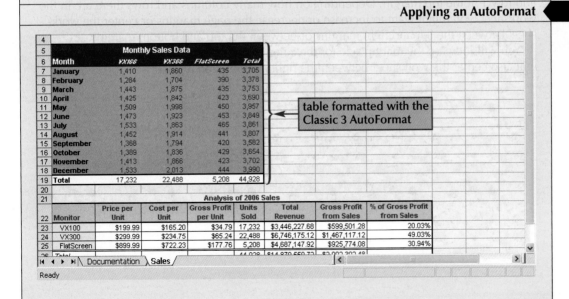

The colors and contrast of the AutoFormat design do not complement the background, so you will revert to the format you created.

▶ **4.** Click the **Undo** button 🔄 on the Standard toolbar to remove the AutoFormat design.

Although you will not use AutoFormat in this case, you can see how an AutoFormat design can be a starting point. You could start with an AutoFormat design and then make modifications to the worksheet to fit your own needs.

Formatting the Printed Worksheet

You have settled on an appearance for the Sales worksheet—at least the appearance that is displayed on your screen. But that is only half of your job. Joan also wants you to format the appearance of this worksheet when it is printed out. You have to decide on the position of the report on the page, the size of the page margins, the orientation of the page, and whether the page will have any headers or footers. You can make many of these choices using the Page Setup dialog box, which you can open from the File menu or from within Print Preview.

Defining the Page Setup

As you learned in Tutorial 1, you can use the Page Setup dialog box to change the page orientation, which determines if the page is wider than it is tall or taller than it is wide. You can also use the Page Setup dialog box to control how a worksheet is placed on a page. You can adjust the size of the **margins**, which are the spaces between the page content and the edges of the page. You can center the worksheet text between the top and bottom margins (horizontally) or between the right and left margins (vertically). You can also use the Page Setup dialog box to display text that will appear in the area at the top of a page or at the bottom of a page for each page of a worksheet. You can open the Page Setup dialog box using the File menu or using the Print Preview toolbar. Working from within Print Preview can be helpful. Each time you close a dialog box in which you have made a change or selected an option, you will see how that action impacts the worksheet before printing it.

By default, Excel places a one-inch margin above and below the report and a ¾-inch margin to the left and right. Excel also aligns column A in a worksheet at the left margin and row 1 at the top margin. Depending on how many columns and rows there are in the worksheet, you might want to increase or decrease the page margins or center the worksheet between the left and right margins or between the top and bottom margins.

You will increase the margin size for the Sales worksheet to one inch all around. You will also center the worksheet between the right and left margins.

To change the margins and positioning of the worksheet:

1. Click the **Print Preview** button ![icon] on the Standard toolbar. The Print Preview window opens, displaying the worksheet as it will appear on the printed page.

2. Click the **Setup** button on the Print Preview toolbar, and then click the **Margins** tab. The Margins tab, as shown in Figure 3-30, provides a diagram that shows you the placement of the worksheet on the page. In addition to adjusting the sizes of the margins, you can also adjust the positioning of the worksheet on the printout.

Margins tab in the Page Setup dialog box ◄ **Figure 3-30**

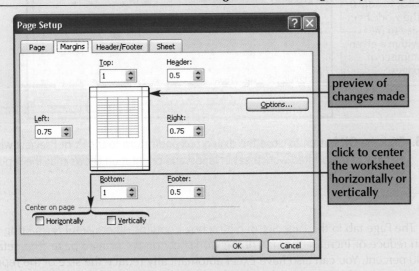

3. Click the **Left** up arrow to set the size of the left margin to **1** inch, and then click the **Right** up arrow to increase the size of the right margin to **1** inch.

4. Click the **Horizontally** check box, and then click the **OK** button to close the Page Setup dialog box and return to Print Preview.

Note that this printout does not fit on a single page. As indicated in the status line located in the lower-left corner of the Print Preview window, the worksheet covers two pages instead of one; two columns of the bottom table have been moved to the second page. You could try to reduce the left and right margins, so the worksheet fits on a single page, but as you learned in Tutorial 1, you also can change the page orientation to landscape, making the worksheet page wider than it is tall. This will accommodate all the columns of the bottom table so all the data will fit on the same page.

To change the page orientation:

1. Click the **Setup** button on the Print Preview toolbar to open the Page Setup dialog box again.

2. Click the **Page** tab and then click the **Landscape** option button, as shown in Figure 3-31.

Figure 3-31 ▶ **Changing the page orientation**

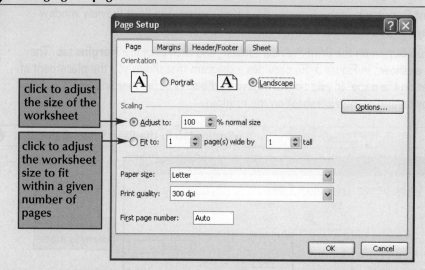

click to adjust the size of the worksheet

click to adjust the worksheet size to fit within a given number of pages

▶ **3.** Click the **OK** button to close the dialog box and return to the Print Preview window. The preview of the printed worksheet in landscape orientation shows that the report will fit on a single page.

The Page tab in the Page Setup dialog box contains other useful formatting features. You can reduce or increase the size of the worksheet on the printed page. The default size is 100 percent. You can also have Excel automatically reduce the size of the report to fit within a specified number of pages.

Working with Headers and Footers

Joan wants you to add a header and footer to the report. A **header** is text printed in the top margin of every worksheet page. A **footer** is text printed at the bottom of every page. Headers and footers can add important information to your printouts. For example, you can create a header that displays your name and the date the report was created. If the report covers multiple pages, you can use a footer to display the page number and the total number of pages. You use the Page Setup dialog box to add headers and footers to a worksheet.

Excel tries to anticipate headers and footers that you might want to include in your worksheet. Clicking the Header or Footer list arrow displays a list of possible headers or footers (the list is the same for both). For example, the "Page 1" entry inserts the page number of the worksheet prefaced by the word "Page" in the header; the "Page 1 of ?" displays the page number and the total number of pages. Other entries in the list include the name of the worksheet or workbook.

If you want to use a header or footer not available in the lists, you click the Custom Header or Custom Footer button and create your own header and footer. The Header dialog box and the Footer dialog box are similar. Each dialog box is divided into three sections: left, center, and right. If you want to enter information such as the filename or the date into the header or footer, you can either type the text or click one of the format buttons located above the three section boxes. Figure 3-32 describes the format buttons and the corresponding format codes.

Header/Footer formatting buttons | **Figure 3-32**

Button	Name	Formatting Code	Action
A	Font	None	Sets font, text style, and font size
	Page Number	&[Page]	Inserts page number
	Total Pages	&[Pages]	Inserts total number of pages
	Date	&[Date]	Inserts current date
	Time	&[Time]	Inserts current time
	File Path	&[Path]&[File]	Inserts path and filename
	Filename	&[File]	Inserts filename
	Tab Name	&[Tab]	Inserts name of active worksheet
	Insert Picture	&[Picture]	Inserts an image file
	Format Picture	None	Opens the Format Picture dialog box

Joan wants a header that displays the filename at the left margin and today's date at the right margin. She wants a footer that displays the name of the workbook author, with the text aligned at the right margin of the footer. You'll create the header and footer now.

To add a custom header and footer to the workbook:

1. Click the **Setup** button on the Print Preview toolbar, and then click the **Header/Footer** tab. The Header/Footer dialog box opens.

2. Click the **Custom Header** button. The Header dialog box opens. See Figure 3-33.

Header dialog box | **Figure 3-33**

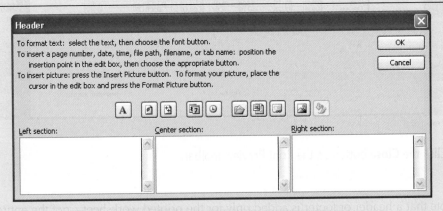

3. In the Left section box, type **Filename:** and then press the **spacebar**.

4. Click the **Filename** button to insert the format code. The formatting code for the name of the file "&[File]" appears after the text that you entered.

5. Click the **Right section** box, and then click the **Date** button. Excel inserts the &[Date] format code into the section box.

6. Click the **OK** button to close the Header dialog box, and then click the **Custom Footer** button to open the Footer dialog box, which duplicates the layout of the Header dialog box. Now you will create a footer that centers the page number and the total number of pages at the bottom of the printout.

7. Click the **Center section** box, type **Page**, press the **spacebar**, click the **Page Number** button [image], press the **spacebar**, type **of**, press the **spacebar**, and then click the **Total Pages** button [image]. The text and codes in the Center section should appear as "Page &[Page] of &[Pages]"—which, if the worksheet was divided into five pages, would appear as "Page 1 of 5."

Next, you will enter the workbook author in the right section of the footer.

8. Click the **Right section** box, type **Prepared by:**, press the **spacebar**, and then type your name.

9. Click the **OK** button to return to the Page Setup dialog box, which provides a preview of the custom header and footer that you created, and then click the **OK** button to return to Print Preview. As shown in Figure 3-34, the worksheet now is displayed with the new header and footer.

Figure 3-34	Preview of the custom header and footer

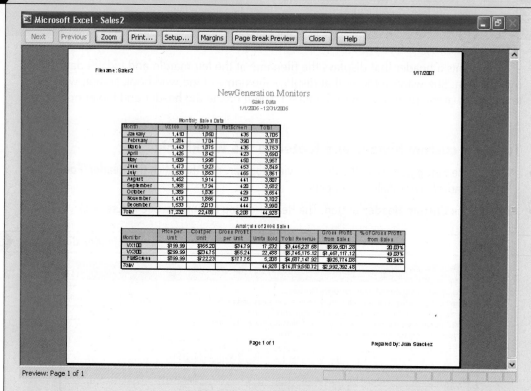

10. Click the **Close** button on the Print Preview toolbar.

Note that a header or footer is added only for the printed worksheet—not the entire workbook. You can define different headers and footers for each sheet in your workbook.

Working with the Print Area and Page Breaks

When you displayed the worksheet in the Print Preview window, how did Excel know which parts of the active worksheet you were going to print? The default action is to print all parts of the active worksheet that contain text, formulas, or values, which will not always be what you want. If you want to print only a part of the worksheet, you can define a **print area** that contains the content you want to print. To define a print area, you must first select the cells you want to print, and then select the Print Area command on the File menu.

A print area can include an adjacent range or nonadjacent ranges. You can also hide rows or columns in the worksheet in order to print nonadjacent ranges. For her report, Joan might decide against printing the sales analysis information. To remove those cells from the printout, you will define a print area that excludes the cells for the second table.

To define the print area:

1. Select the range **A1:H19**.

2. Click **File** on the menu bar, point to **Print Area**, and then click **Set Print Area**. Excel places a dotted black line around the selected cells of the print area. This is a visual indicator of what parts of the worksheet will be printed.

3. Click the **Print Preview** button 🔍 on the Standard toolbar. The Print Preview window displays only the first table. The second table has been removed from the printout because it is not in the defined print area.

4. Click the **Close** button on the Print Preview toolbar.

Another way to preview the print areas in your worksheet is through **page break preview**, which displays a view of the worksheet as it is divided up into pages. Anything outside of the print area is grayed out. Try previewing the contents of the Sales worksheet using page break preview.

To switch to page break preview:

1. Click cell **A1** to remove the selection.

2. Click **View** on the menu bar, and then click **Page Break Preview**. The workbook window adjusts to display the worksheet with any page break inserted in it and the Welcome to Page Break Preview dialog box, as shown in Figure 3-35. The dialog box serves to remind you that you can adjust the page breaks. A page number appears as a watermark on each page to be printed out. Notice that the second table is grayed out because it is not part of the printed area of the worksheet.

Figure 3-35 | **Using Page Break Preview**

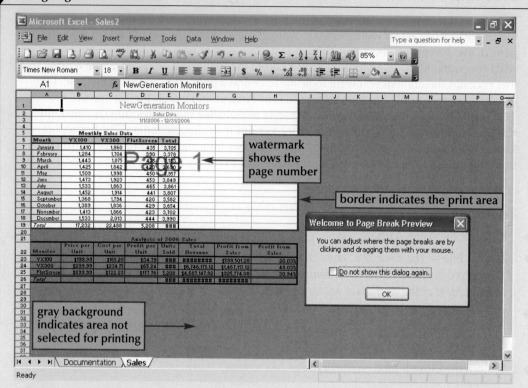

> **3.** Click the **OK** button to close the dialog box before you change the dimensions of the printed area to include the other table.

> **4.** Position the pointer at the bottom border of the print area (located at row 19) until the pointer changes to ↕, and then click the border and drag it down to row **26**. The print area has now been expanded to the cell range A1:H26.
>
>   **Trouble?** If you are unsure of the location of the bottom border, click row 19 to make the border easier to see, and then repeat Step 3.

> **5.** Click **View** on the menu bar, and then click **Normal** to switch back to Normal view.

Another approach that Joan might take is to place the two tables on separate pages. You can do this for her by inserting a **page break**, which forces Excel to place a portion of a worksheet on a new page. Before you insert a page break, you need to indicate where in the worksheet you want the break to occur. If you select a cell in the worksheet, the page break will be placed directly above and to the left of the cell. Selecting a row or a column places the page break directly above the row or directly to the left of the column. You will place a page break directly above row 20, which will separate the first sales table from the second.

To insert a page break:

> **1.** Click row **20**, click **Insert** on the menu bar, and then click **Page Break**. Another black dotted line appears—this time above row 20, indicating there is a page break at this point in the print area.

2. Click cell **A1** to remove the selection, click **View** on the menu bar, click **Page Break Preview**, and then click the **OK** button to close the Welcome to Page Break Preview dialog box. As shown in Figure 3-36, the second table will now appear on page 2 of the printout.

Inserting a page break ◄ **Figure 3-36**

3. Click **View** on the menu bar, and then click **Normal** to return to Normal view.

As Joan reviews the preview of the worksheet, she notices that the name of the company, "NewGeneration Monitors," and the two subtitles appear on the first page, but not on the second. That is not surprising because the range that includes the titles and subtitles is limited to the first page of the printout. However, Joan would like to have this information repeated on the second page.

You can repeat information, such as the company name, by specifying which cells in the print area should be repeated on each page. This is particularly useful in long tables that extend over many pages. In such cases, you can have the column titles repeated for each page of the printout.

To set rows or columns to repeat on each page, you will open the Page Setup dialog box from the worksheet window.

To repeat the first three rows on each page:

1. Click **File** on the menu bar, click **Page Setup**, and then click the **Sheet** tab. The Sheet tab displays options you can use to control how the worksheet is printed. Note that the print area you have defined is already entered into the Print area box. Because Joan wants the first three rows of the worksheet to be repeated on each printed page, you will have to select them.

2. Click the **Rows to repeat at top** box, move your pointer over to the worksheet, and then click and drag over the range **A1:A3**. A flashing border appears around the first three rows in the worksheet. This is a visual indicator that the contents of the first three rows will be repeated on all pages of the printout. In the Rows to repeat at top box, the cell reference $1:$3 appears. See Figure 3-37.

Figure 3-37 ▶ **Sheet tab of the Page Setup dialog box**

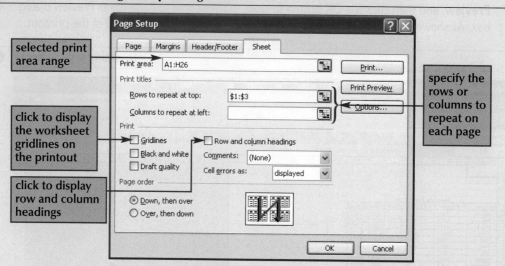

selected print area range

click to display the worksheet gridlines on the printout

click to display row and column headings

specify the rows or columns to repeat on each page

Trouble? If the Page Setup dialog box is in the way, you can move it to another location in the workbook window, or you can select the range using the Collapse Dialog Box button.

3. Click the **Print Preview** button, and then click the **Next** button on the Print Preview toolbar to display the second page of the printout. Now the title and two subtitles appear on this page as well. See Figure 3-38.

Figure 3-38 ▶ **Second page of the printout**

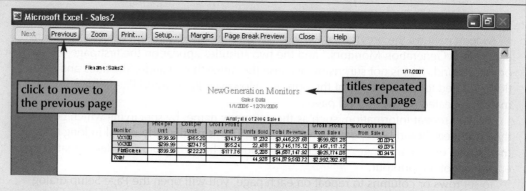

click to move to the previous page

titles repeated on each page

4. Click the **Print** button on the Print Preview toolbar, make sure the settings in the Print dialog box are correct, and then click the **OK** button.

For now, your work is done. When you save the workbook, your printing options are saved along with the file, so you will not have to re-create the print format in the future.

5. Save your changes to the workbook, and then close it.

Note that the Sheet tab also provides other options, such as the ability to print the worksheet's gridlines or row and column headings. You can also have Excel print the worksheet in black and white or draft quality. If there are multiple pages in the printout, you can indicate whether the pages should be ordered going down the worksheet first and then across, or across first and then down.

You show the final version of the workbook and the printout to Joan. She is very happy with the way in which you have formatted her report. She will spend some time going over the printout and will get back to you with any further changes she wants you to make.

Review

Session 3.2 Quick Check

1. Describe two ways of merging a range of cells into one.
2. How do you clear a format from a cell without affecting the underlying data?
3. How do you add a background image to the active worksheet?
4. To control the amount of space between the content on a page and its edges, you can adjust the page's _____.
5. By default, Excel prints what part of the active worksheet?
6. How do you define a print area? How do you remove a print area?
7. How do you insert a page break into your worksheet?

Review

Tutorial Summary

In this tutorial, you learned how to use Excel's formatting tools to design your worksheet. You saw how to quickly format cells using the buttons on the Formatting toolbar, and you learned how the Format Cells dialog box can give you even more control over the appearance of your worksheet. You saw how to create and edit cell borders using the Borders button and the Draw Borders button. You also learned how to change cell backgrounds using colors and patterns and external graphic files. The tutorial also demonstrated how to apply the formats in one cell range to another through the use of the Format and Replace dialog box and through styles. Finally, you learned how to format the appearance of your printed worksheet through the use of customized headers, footers, and print areas.

Key Terms

AutoFormat	General number format	point
font	gridline	print area
font size	header	sans serif font
font style	margin	serif font
footer	page break	style
Format Painter	page break preview	typeface
formatting		

Practice

Review Assignments

Data File needed for the Review Assignments: Region1.xls

Joan Sanchez has another report that she wants to format. The report displays regional sales for the three monitor brands you worked on earlier. As before, Joan wants to work on the overall appearance of the worksheet so the printout of the report is polished and professional looking. Figure 3-39 shows a preview of the worksheet you'll create for Joan.

Practice the skills you learned in the tutorial using the same case scenario.

Figure 3-39

	A	B	C	D	E	F	G
1			NewGeneration Monitors				
2			Regional Sales Report				
3			1/1/2006 - 12/31/2006				
4							
5	Sales by Region						
6	Region	VX100	VX300	Flatscreen	Total		
7	Northeast	1,723	2,248	520	4,491		
8	East	3,446	4,497	1,041	8,984		
9	Southeast	2,067	2,698	624	5,389		
10	Midwest	1,723	2,248	520	4,491		
11	Southwest	1,378	1,799	416	3,593		
12	West	4,308	5,622	1,302	11,232		
13	Canada	1,378	1,799	416	3,593		
14	Europe	861	1,124	260	2,245		
15	Asia	348	453	109	910		
16	Total	17,232	22,488	5,208	44,928		
17							
18	Regional Analysis						
19			Region	Units Sold	Total Sales	Profit from Sales	% of Profit
20			Domestic	14,645	$ 2,928,853	$ 509,499	17.03%
21		VX100	Foreign	2,587	$ 517,374	$ 90,001	3.01%
22			Total	17,232	$ 3,446,227	$ 599,500	20.03%
23			Domestic	19,112	$ 5,733,408	$ 1,246,866	41.67%
24		VX300	Foreign	3,376	$ 1,012,766	$ 220,250	7.36%
25			Total	22,488	$ 6,746,174	$ 1,467,116	49.03%
26			Domestic	4,423	$ 3,980,655	$ 786,232	26.27%
27		Flatscreen	Foreign	785	$ 706,492	$ 139,541	4.66%
28			Total	5,208	$ 4,687,147	$ 925,773	30.94%
29			Domestic	38,180	$12,642,918	$ 2,542,598	84.97%
30		Total	Foreign	6,748	$ 2,236,632	$ 449,793	15.03%
31			Total	44,928	$14,879,550	$ 2,992,391	100.00%
32							

To format the report:

1. Open the **Region1** workbook located in the Tutorial.03\Review folder included with your Data Files.
2. Enter your name and the current date in the Documentation sheet, and then save the workbook as **Region2** in the Tutorial.03\Review folder.
3. Switch to the Regional Sales worksheet.
4. Format the text in cell A1 with a 20-point, italicized, red, Times New Roman font. Format the text in cells A2 and A3 with a red font. Select the range A1:F3, and center the text across the selection. Do not merge the cells.
5. Select the range A5:E16, and then apply the List 2 format from the AutoFormat gallery.
6. Change the format of all values in the Sales by Region table to display a comma separator, but no decimal places. Resize column E to about 14 characters.
7. Change the format of the Units Sold values in the second table to display a comma separator, but no decimal places.
8. Indent the region names in the range A7:A15 by one character.
9. Display the text in cell A18 in bold.
10. Change the format of the values in the Total Sales and Profit from Sales columns to display a dollar sign on the left edge of the cell and no decimal places.
11. Change the format of the values in the % of Profit column to display a percent sign and two decimal places.
12. Allow the text in the range B19:F19 to wrap to a second line of text. Bold and center the text within each cell.

13. Merge and center the cells in the range A20:A22, and change the vertical text alignment to center. (*Hint*: Use the correct Text alignment option in the Format Cells dialog box to vertically align the text; see Figure 3-13.) Apply this format to the cells in the following ranges: A23:A25, A26:A28, and A29:A31.

14. Change the background color of the cells in the range A19:F19;A20:A31 to Sea Green (third row, fourth column of the color palette). Change the font color to white.

15. Change the background color of the cells in the range B20:F31 to white. Change the background color of the cells in the range B22:F22;B25:F25;B28:F28;B31:F31 to Light Green (fifth row, fourth column of the color palette).

16. Apply a thin black border to each of the cells in the range A19:F31.

17. Place a double line on the bottom border of the cells in the range B22:F22;B25:F25;B28:F28.

18. Set the print area as the range A1:F31. Insert a page break above row 18. Repeat the first three rows of the worksheet on every page of any printouts you produce from this worksheet.

19. Set up the page to print in portrait orientation with one-inch margins on all sides. Center the contents of the worksheet horizontally on the page.

20. Add a footer with the following text in the Left section box of the footer (with the date on a separate line): "Filename: *the name of the file*" and "Date: *current date*," and then the following text in the Right section box of the footer: "Prepared by: *your name*." In the Center section, place the text "Page *page_number* of *total_pages*" where *page_number* is the number of the page and *total_pages* is the total number of pages in the printout.

21. Add a header with the text "Regional Sales Report" displayed in the Center section using a 14-point Times New Roman font with a double underline. (*Hint*: Select the text in the Center section, and then click the Font button in the Footer dialog box to open the Format Cells dialog box.)

22. Preview the two-page worksheet, and then print it.

23. Save your changes to the workbook and then close it.

Apply

Use the skills you have learned to format a sales report.

Case Problem 1

Data File needed for this Case Problem: Frosti1.xls

FrostiWear Linda Young is a sales manager for FrostiWear, a new and successful online store for winter clothing. She is in charge of tracking the sales figures for FrostiWear's line of gloves. She's created a workbook containing the sales figures for three glove models organized by month and region for the past year. She would like your help in formatting the sales report and the printed output. Figure 3-40 shows a preview of the formatted worksheet you'll create for Linda.

Figure 3-40

		Region 1	Region 2	Region 3	Region 4	Region 5	Total

FrostiWear
Sales Report
Units Sold: 1/2007 - 12/2007

		Region 1	Region 2	Region 3	Region 4	Region 5	Total
PolyFleece Mitts	Jan	1,150	1,690	930	2,850	1,210	7,830
	Feb	1,100	2,200	680	2,340	1,100	7,420
	Mar	1,070	1,290	960	2,740	1,180	7,240
	Apr	780	1,520	720	2,170	1,180	6,370
	May	1,070	1,370	700	1,940	1,210	6,290
	Jun	670	1,300	780	3,430	1,170	7,350
	Jul	1,390	1,590	1,240	2,230	1,430	7,880
	Aug	1,310	1,730	610	2,560	960	7,170
	Sep	1,100	1,820	370	3,040	1,100	7,430
	Oct	1,350	2,010	750	2,430	1,230	7,770
	Nov	680	1,620	780	3,210	1,230	7,520
	Dec	1,120	1,170	670	1,920	1,310	6,190
	Total	12,790	19,310	9,190	30,860	14,310	86,460
		Region 1	Region 2	Region 3	Region 4	Region 5	Total
ArticBlast Gloves	Jan	790	1,160	620	2,590	760	5,920
	Feb	1,010	1,170	610	1,950	1,010	5,750
	Mar	710	1,270	600	2,050	930	5,560
	Apr	890	1,190	750	2,030	980	5,840
	May	990	1,340	660	2,670	1,040	6,700
	Jun	990	1,280	620	2,330	800	6,020
	Jul	780	1,180	690	2,260	920	5,830
	Aug	800	1,220	560	2,460	900	5,940
	Sep	810	1,150	670	2,500	970	6,100
	Oct	760	1,070	630	2,350	1,040	5,850
	Nov	770	1,140	630	2,540	1,080	6,160
	Dec	850	1,370	590	2,490	1,060	6,360
	Total	10,150	14,540	7,630	28,220	11,490	72,030
		Region 1	Region 2	Region 3	Region 4	Region 5	Total
Glomitts	Jan	340	780	280	1,670	600	3,670
	Feb	460	810	280	1,770	480	3,800
	Mar	410	820	310	1,490	460	3,490
	Apr	490	890	330	1,610	650	3,970
	May	470	960	290	1,580	540	3,840
	Jun	480	740	340	1,780	640	3,980
	Jul	470	760	320	1,500	640	3,690
	Aug	490	690	340	1,610	600	3,730
	Sep	420	780	340	1,660	680	3,880
	Oct	460	820	350	1,800	660	4,090
	Nov	550	830	440	1,250	590	3,660
	Dec	400	790	220	1,620	540	3,570
	Total	5,440	9,670	3,840	19,340	7,080	45,370

To complete this task:

1. Open the **Frosti1** workbook located in the Tutorial.03\Cases folder included with your Data Files, and then save the workbook as **Frosti2** in the same folder.

2. In the Documentation sheet, enter your name and the current date. Format the date so that it is displayed as *Weekday, Month Day, Year* where *Weekday* is the day of the week, *Month* is the full month name, *Day* is the day of the month, and *Year* is the four-digit year.

3. Switch to the Glove Sales worksheet. Merge the cells in the range A1:H1 into a single cell. Display the cell text in a bold white 20-point Arial font on a sky blue background. Center the text horizontally. Repeat this formatting for the cell range A2:H2 and A3:H3, except make the text size 12 points.

Explore

4. Merge range A4:A17 into a single cell. Display the text in a yellow 16-point bold Arial font on a sky blue background. Change the orientation of the text to 90 degrees, and then align the contents of the cell horizontally and vertically. (*Hint*: For more information on aligning text within a cell, read the Help topics "Indent text in a cell" and "Position data in a cell.") Apply the formatting of cell A4 to cells A18 and A32.

5. Select the noncontiguous range B4:H4;B4:B17. Display the cell text in yellow on a blue background. Right-align the contents of cells B4:B17 and indent the contents of those cells one unit. Center the contents of the cells B4:G4.

6. Select the range C5:G16. Display the contents of these cells using blue text on a light turquoise background. Apply this same formatting to cell H17.

7. Select the noncontiguous range B17:H17;H4:H17 and display the contents of those cells in bold.

8. Apply borders to the sales report as follows. First select the range C5:G16 and apply the All Borders border style to those cells. Select the range B4:G16 and apply a thick box border to the range. Also apply thick outside borders to the cell ranges B17:H17 and H4:H17 and the cell A4.

9. Copy the cell range A4:H17 and paste the format of this cell range into the range A18:H45.

10. Define the cell range A1:H45 as the print area. Repeat the first three rows on each page of the printout. Insert a page break at rows 18 and 32.

11. Create a horizontally centered header for the printout displaying the text, "FrostiWear Sales Report." Create a footer on the right corner of the page displaying your name on one line, the date on the second line, and the workbook filename on the third. Insert a centered footer displaying the text, "Page *page* of *pages*," where *page* is the page number and *pages* is the number of pages in the printout.

12. Set the orientation of the printout to landscape. Horizontally center the contents of each printed page.

13. Print the contents of the Glove Sales worksheet.

14. Save and close the workbook.

Apply

Use the skills you have learned to create a packing slip for GrillRite Grills.

Case Problem 2

Data File needed for this Case Problem: Packing1.xls

GrillRite Grills   Brian Simpko is a shipping manager at GrillRite Grills. He uses an Excel worksheet to calculate and provide shipping and order information in GrillRite's packages. He asks for your help formatting the worksheet to develop a packing slip that customers will find informative and easy to read. Figure 3-41 shows a preview of the formatted worksheet you'll create for Brian.

Figure 3-41

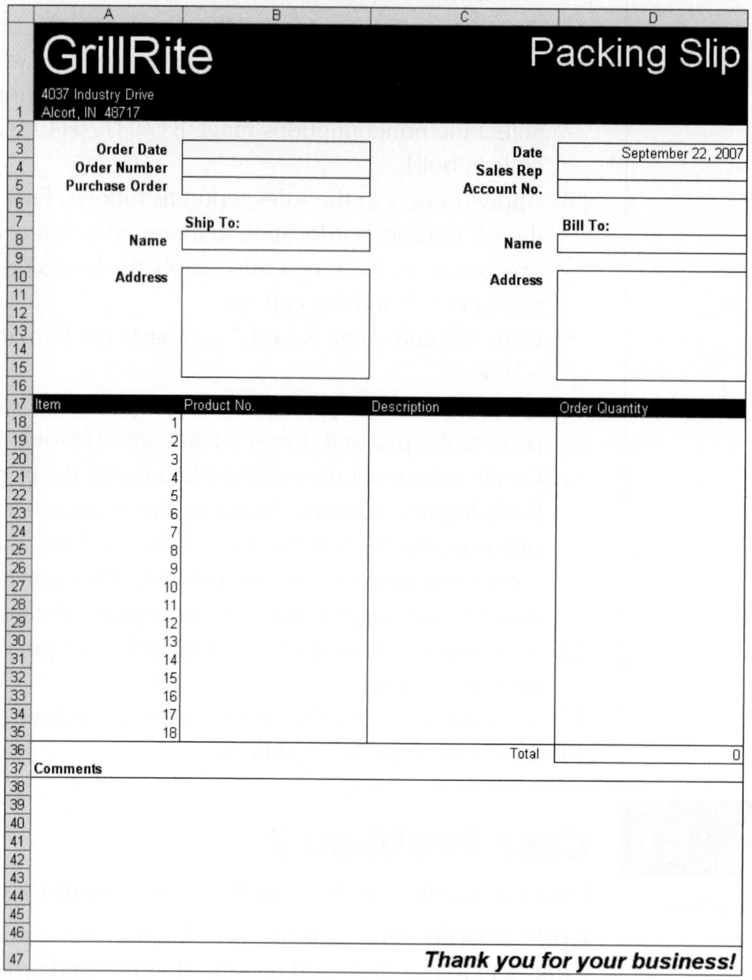

To complete this task:

1. Open the **Packing1** workbook located in the Tutorial.03\Cases folder included with your Data Files, and then save the workbook as **Packing2** in the same folder. Enter your name and the date in the Documentation sheet, and then switch to the Packing Slip sheet.
2. Select all of the cells in the worksheet and set the background color to white.
3. Select the cell range A1:D1, and change the background color to black and the font color to white. Merge cells A1 and B1. Within cell A1 select the text "GrillRite" and increase the font size to 36 points. Set the font size of the text in cell D1 to 28 points. Vertically align the contents of cells A1 and D1 with the top of the cell. Right-align the contents of cell D1.
4. Select the noncontiguous cell range A3:A5;C3:C5 and display the text in bold. Right-align the text and increase the indent by one character.

5. Change the format of the date in cell D3 to *month day, year* where *month* is the full name of the month, *day* is the day of the month, and *year* is the 4-digit year value.
6. Select the noncontiguous cell range B3:B5;D3:D5 and add borders around each cell in the range.
7. Display the text in cells B7, D7, A8, A10, C8, and C10 in bold. Right-align the text in cells A8, A10, C8, and C10 and indent one character. Add borders around cells B8 and D8.

8. Select the cell range B10:B15. Merge the cells and then place a border around the merged cell. Vertically align the contents of this cell with the top of the cell. Repeat these steps for the cell range D10:D15.

9. Select the cell range A17:D17 and change the background color to black and the font color to white. Place a border around the cell ranges A18:A35, B18:B35, C18:C35, and D18:D35. Place a border around cell D36. Right-align the contents of cell C36 and increase the indent by one character.

10. Display the text in cell A37 in bold. Select the cell range A38:D46 and merge the cells. Change the vertical alignment of the merged cells to top. Place a border around the merged cell. Display the text in cell D47 in a 16-point bold italic font. Right-align the contents of the cell.

11. Set the print area to the range A1:D47. Set the left and right margins to 0.5 inches. Display your name, the date, and the filename on separate lines in the lower-left footer.

12. Print the formatted Packing Slip worksheet in the portrait orientation.

13. Save and close the workbook.

Challenge

Using Figure 3-42 as your guide, challenge yourself by experimenting with more formatting techniques to enhance a worksheet presenting regional sales figures.

Case Problem 3

Data File needed for this Case Problem: Blades1.xls

Davis Blades Andrew Malki is a financial officer at Davis Blades, a leading manufacturer of roller blades. He has recently finished entering data for the yearly sales report. Andrew has asked you to help him with the design of the main table in the report. A preview of the format you will apply is shown in Figure 3-42.

Figure 3-42

Davis Blades

Sales Report
1/1/2006 - 12/31/2006

Units Sold		Northeast	East	Southeast	Midwest	Southwest	West	All Regions
Black Hawk	Qtr 1	641	748	733	676	691	783	4,272
	Qtr 2	708	826	811	748	763	866	4,722
	Qtr 3	681	795	780	719	734	833	4,542
	Qtr 4	668	779	764	705	720	816	4,452
	Total	2,698	3,148	3,088	2,848	2,908	3,298	17,988
Blademaster	Qtr 1	513	598	587	541	552	627	3,418
	Qtr 2	567	661	648	598	611	693	3,778
	Qtr 3	545	636	624	575	587	666	3,633
	Qtr 4	534	623	611	564	576	653	3,561
	Total	2,159	2,518	2,470	2,278	2,326	2,639	14,390
The Professional	Qtr 1	342	399	391	361	368	418	2,279
	Qtr 2	378	441	432	399	407	462	2,519
	Qtr 3	363	424	416	383	391	444	2,421
	Qtr 4	356	415	407	376	384	435	2,373
	Total	1,439	1,679	1,646	1,519	1,550	1,759	9,592
All Models	Qtr 1	1,496	1,745	1,711	1,578	1,611	1,828	9,969
	Qtr 2	1,653	1,928	1,891	1,745	1,781	2,021	11,019
	Qtr 3	1,589	1,855	1,820	1,677	1,712	1,943	10,596
	Qtr 4	1,558	1,817	1,782	1,645	1,680	1,904	10,386
	Total	6,296	7,345	7,204	6,645	6,784	7,696	41,970

To complete this task:

1. Open the **Blades1** workbook located in the Tutorial.03\Cases folder included with your Data Files, and then save the file as **Blades2** in the same folder.

2. Enter your name and the current date in the Documentation sheet, and then switch to the Sales worksheet.

3. Change the font of the title in cell A1 to a 16–point, dark blue, boldface, Times New Roman font. Change the subtitles in cells A2 and A3 to an 8-point, blue font. Reduce the height of row 2 and row 3 to 12 characters.

4. Add a solid black bottom border to the range A1:K1.

5. Format the text in cell A5 in a 12-point, blue, Arial font. Vertically align the text in this cell with the bottom of the cell.

Explore

6. Merge the cells in the range A6:A10, and align the contents of the cell vertically at the top of the cell. Repeat this for the following ranges: A11:A15, A16:A20, and A21:A25.

7. Change the background color of the cell range A6:I10 to light yellow. Change the background color of the range A11:I15 to light green. Change the background color of the range A16:I20 to light turquoise. Change the background color of the range A21:I25 to pale blue.

8. Reverse the color scheme for the subtotal values in the range B10:I10, so that instead of black on light yellow, the font color is light yellow on a black background. Reverse the subtotal values for the other products in the table.

9. Apply the borders, as shown in Figure 3-42, to the cells in the range A6:I25.

Explore

10. Rotate the column titles in the range C5:I5 by 45 degrees. Align the contents of each cell along the bottom-right corner of the cell. Change the background color of these cells to white, and then add a border to each cell.

Explore

11. Open the Options dialog box from the Tools menu. Deselect the Row & column headings and Gridlines options to remove the row and column headings and gridlines from the Sales worksheet window.

12. Set the print area as the range A1:K25.

13. Leave the page orientation as portrait, but center the worksheet horizontally on the page.

14. Create a custom footer with the text "Filename: *the name of the file*" left-aligned and with the text "Prepared by: *your name*" and "*the current date*" right-aligned, with your name and date on separate lines.

15. Preview the worksheet and then print it.

16. Save your changes to the workbook and then close it.

Case Problem 4

Create

Using Figure 3-43 as a guide, test your knowledge of formatting by creating your own design for a payroll worksheet.

There are no Data Files needed for this Case Problem.

Oritz Marine Services Vince DiOrio is an information systems major at a local college. He works three days a week at a nearby marina, Oritz Marine Services, to help pay for his tuition. Vince works in the business office, and his responsibilities range from making coffee to keeping the company's books.

Recently, Jim Oritz, the owner of the marina, asked Vince if he could help computerize the payroll for the employees. He explained that the employees work a different number of hours each week at different rates of pay. Jim now does the payroll manually, and finds it time consuming. Moreover, whenever he makes an error, he is annoyed at having to take the additional time to correct it. Jim is hoping that Vince can help him.

Vince immediately agrees to help. He tells Jim that he knows how to use Excel and that he can build a worksheet that will save him time and reduce errors. Jim and Vince meet to review the present payroll process and discuss the desired outcome of the payroll spreadsheet. Figure 3-43 displays the type of information that Jim records in the spreadsheet.

Figure 3-43

Employee	Hours	Pay Rate	Gross Pay	Federal Withholding	State Withholding	Total Deductions	Net Pay
Bramble	16	9.50					
Cortez	30	10.50					
DiOrio	25	12.50					
Fulton	20	9.50					
Juarez	25	12.00					
Smiken	10	9.00					
Smith	30	13.50					
Total							

To complete this task:

1. Create a new workbook named **Payroll1**, and save it in the Tutorial.03\Cases folder included with your Data Files.
2. Name two worksheets "Documentation" and "Payroll," and then delete the third sheet.
3. On the Documentation sheet, include the name of the company, your name as the author of the workbook, the date the workbook is being created, and a brief description of the purpose of the workbook.
4. On the Payroll worksheet, enter the payroll table shown in Figure 3-43.
5. Enter the formulas to calculate total hours, gross pay, federal withholding tax, state withholding tax, total deductions, and net pay, using the following information:
   a. Gross pay is equal to the number of hours multiplied by the pay rate.
   b. Federal withholding tax is equal to 15% of the gross pay.
   c. State withholding tax is equal to 4% of the gross pay.
   d. Total deductions are the sum of federal and state withholdings.
   e. Net pay is equal to the difference between the gross pay and the total amount of deductions.
6. Format the appearance of the payroll table using the techniques you learned in this tutorial. The appearance of the payroll table is up to you; however, do not use an AutoFormat design to format the table.
7. Format the printed page, setting the print area and inserting an appropriate header and footer. Only a few employees are entered into the table at present. However, after Jim Oritz approves your layout, many additional employees will be added, which will cause the report to cover multiple pages. Format your printout so that the worksheet title and column titles appear on every page.
8. Preview your worksheet, and then print it. Save your changes.
9. Add the following new employees to the worksheet. The employee list should be in alphabetical order, so these new employees should be inserted at the appropriate places in the sheet:

Name	Hours	Pay Rate
Carls	20	10.50
Lopez	35	11.50
Nelson	20	9.50

10. Preview the revised worksheet, and then print it.
11. Save this revised workbook as **Payroll2** in the Tutorial.03\Cases folder, and then close the workbook.

Research

Use the Internet to find and work with data related to the topics presented in this tutorial.

Internet Assignments

The purpose of the Internet Assignments is to challenge you to find information on the Internet that you can use to work effectively with this software. The actual assignments are updated and maintained on the Course Technology Web site. Log on to the Internet and use your Web browser to go to the Student Online Companion for New Perspectives Office 2003 at **www.course.com/np/office2003**. Click the Internet Assignments link, and then navigate to the assignments for this tutorial.

Assess

SAM Assessment and Training

If you have a SAM user profile, you may have access to hands-on instruction, practice, and assessment of the skills covered in this tutorial. Log in to your SAM account and go to your assignments page to see what your instructor has assigned.

Review

Quick Check Answers

Session 3.1

1. Click the Currency Style button on the Formatting toolbar; or click Format on the menu bar, click Cells, click the Number tab, and then select Currency from the Category list box.
2. a. 5.8%
   b. $0.06
3. Format Painter button and Copy button
4. Increase the width of the column; decrease the font size of the text; or select the Shrink to fit check box or the Wrap text check box on the Alignment tab in the Format Cells dialog box.
5. Select the range, click Cells on the Format menu, click the Alignment tab, and then select Center Across Selection in the Horizontal list box.
6. Use the Borders button on the Formatting toolbar; use the Draw Borders button in the Border gallery; or click Cells on the Format menu, click the Border tab, and then choose the border options in the dialog box.
7. Click Cells on the Format menu, click the Patterns tab, click the Pattern list arrow, and then select the pattern type and color.

Session 3.2

1. Select the cells and either click the Merge and Center button on the Formatting toolbar; or click Cells on the Format menu, click the Alignment tab, and then click the Merge cells check box.
2. Select the cell, click Edit on the menu bar, point to Clear, and then click Formats.
3. Click Format on the menu bar, point to Sheet, and then click Background. Locate and select an image file to use for the background, and then click the Insert button.
4. margins
5. Excel prints all parts of the active worksheet that contain text, formulas, or values.
6. To define a print area, select a range in the worksheet, click File on the menu bar, point to Print Area, and then click Set Print Area. To remove a print area, point to Print Area on the File menu, and then click Clear Print Area.
7. Select the first cell below the row at which you want to insert the page break, and then select Page Break on the Insert menu.

New Perspectives on
Microsoft® Office
Access 2003

Read This Before You Begin: Tutorials 1–3

To the Student

Data Files

To complete Access Tutorials 1 through 3, you need the starting student Data Files. Your instructor will either provide you with these Data Files or ask you to obtain them yourself.

Access Tutorials 1 through 3 require the folders shown to complete the Tutorials, Review Assignments, and Case Problems. You will need to copy these folders from a file server, a standalone computer, or the Web to the drive and folder where you will be storing your Data Files. Your instructor will tell you which computer, drive letter, and folder(s) contain the files you need. You can also download the files by going to www.course.com; see the inside back or front cover for more information on downloading the files, or ask your instructor or technical support person for assistance.

If you are storing your Data Files on floppy disks, you will need **six** blank, formatted, high-density disks for these tutorials. Label your disks as shown, and place on them the folders indicated.

> **Access 2003: Data Disk 1** - Brief\Tutorial folder
> **Access 2003: Data Disk 2** - Brief\Review folder
> **Access 2003: Data Disk 3** - Brief\Case1 folder
> **Access 2003: Data Disk 4** - Brief\Case2 folder
> **Access 2003: Data Disk 5** - Brief\Case3 folder
> **Access 2003: Data Disk 6** - Brief\Case4 folder

The Data Files you work with in each tutorial build on the work you did in the previous tutorial. For example, when you begin Tutorial 3, you will use the Data Files that resulted after you completed Tutorial 2.

Course Labs

The Access tutorials feature an interactive Course Lab to help you understand database concepts. There are Lab Assignments at the end of Tutorial 1 that relate to this lab. Contact your instructor or technical support person for assistance in accessing the lab.

To the Instructor

The Data Files and Course Labs are available on the Instructor Resources CD for this title. Follow the instructions in the Help file on the CD to install the programs to your network or standalone computer. See the "To the Student" section above for information on how to set up the Data Files that accompany this text.

You are granted a license to copy the Data Files and Course Labs to any computer or computer network used by students who have purchased this book.

System Requirements

If you are going to work through this book using your own computer, you need:

- **Computer System** Microsoft Windows 2000 operating system with Service Pack 3 or later, Windows XP recommended. These tutorials assume a typical installation of Microsoft Access 2003.

- **Data Files** You will not be able to complete the tutorials or exercises in this book using your own computer until you have the necessary starting Data Files.

- **Course Labs** See your instructor or technical support person to obtain the Course Lab software for use on your own computer.

Objectives

Session 1.1
- Define the terms field, record, table, relational database, primary key, and foreign key
- Open an existing database
- Identify the components of the Access and Database windows
- Open and navigate a table
- Learn how Access saves a database

Session 1.2
- Open an existing query, and create, sort, and navigate a new query
- Create and navigate a form
- Create, preview, and navigate a report
- Learn how to manage a database by backing up, restoring, compacting, and converting a database

Lab

Databases

Student Data Files

Introduction to Microsoft Access 2003

Viewing and Working with a Table Containing Employer Data

Case

Northeast Seasonal Jobs International (NSJI)

During her high school and college years, Elsa Jensen spent her summers working as a lifeguard for some of the most popular beaches on Cape Cod, Massachusetts. Throughout those years, Elsa met many foreign students who had come to the United States to work for the summer, both at the beaches and at other seasonal businesses, such as restaurants and hotels. Elsa formed friendships with several students and kept in contact with them beyond college. Through discussions with her friends, Elsa realized that foreign students often have a difficult time finding appropriate seasonal work, relying mainly on "word-of-mouth" references to locate jobs. Elsa became convinced that there must be an easier way.

Several years ago, Elsa founded Northeast Seasonal Jobs, a small firm located in Boston that served as a job broker between foreign students seeking part-time, seasonal work and resort businesses located in New England. Recently Elsa expanded her business to include resorts in the eastern provinces of Canada, and consequently she changed her company's name to Northeast Seasonal Jobs International (NSJI). At first the company focused mainly on summer employment, but as the business continued to grow, Elsa increased the scope of operations to include all types of seasonal opportunities, including foliage tour companies in the fall and ski resorts in the winter.

Elsa depends on computers to help her manage all areas of NSJI's operations, including financial management, sales, and information management. Several months ago the company upgraded to Microsoft Windows and **Microsoft Office Access 2003** (or simply **Access**), a computer program used to enter, maintain, and retrieve related data in a format known as a database. Elsa and her staff use Access to

▼ **Brief**

▽ Tutorial folder	▽ Review folder	▽ Case1 folder
Seasonal.mdb	Seasons.mdb	Videos.mdb

▽ Case2 folder	▽ Case3 folder	▽ Case4 folder
Fitness.mdb	Redwood.mdb	GEM.mdb

maintain data such as information about employers, positions they have available for seasonal work, and foreign students seeking employment. Elsa recently created a database named Seasonal to track the company's employer customers and data about their available positions. She asks for your help in completing and maintaining this database.

Session 1.1

Databases

Introduction to Database Concepts

Before you begin working on Elsa's database and using Access, you need to understand a few key terms and concepts associated with databases.

Organizing Data

Data is a valuable resource to any business. At NSJI, for example, important data includes employers' names and addresses, and available positions and wages. Organizing, storing, maintaining, retrieving, and sorting this type of data are critical activities that enable a business to find and use information effectively. Before storing data on a computer, however, you must organize the data.

Your first step in organizing data is to identify the individual fields. A **field** is a single characteristic or attribute of a person, place, object, event, or idea. For example, some of the many fields that NSJI tracks are employer ID, employer name, employer address, employer phone number, position, wage, and start date.

Next, you group related fields together into tables. A **table** is a collection of fields that describe a person, place, object, event, or idea. Figure 1-1 shows an example of an Employer table consisting of four fields: EmployerID, EmployerName, EmployerAddress, and PhoneNumber.

Figure 1-1	Data organization for a table of employers

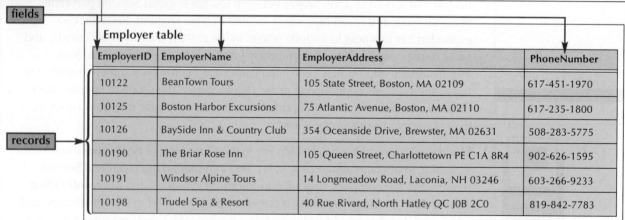

Employer table

EmployerID	EmployerName	EmployerAddress	PhoneNumber
10122	BeanTown Tours	105 State Street, Boston, MA 02109	617-451-1970
10125	Boston Harbor Excursions	75 Atlantic Avenue, Boston, MA 02110	617-235-1800
10126	BaySide Inn & Country Club	354 Oceanside Drive, Brewster, MA 02631	508-283-5775
10190	The Briar Rose Inn	105 Queen Street, Charlottetown PE C1A 8R4	902-626-1595
10191	Windsor Alpine Tours	14 Longmeadow Road, Laconia, NH 03246	603-266-9233
10198	Trudel Spa & Resort	40 Rue Rivard, North Hatley QC J0B 2C0	819-842-7783

The specific value, or content, of a field is called the **field value**. In Figure 1-1, the first set of field values for EmployerID, EmployerName, EmployerAddress, and PhoneNumber are, respectively: 10122; BeanTown Tours; 105 State Street, Boston, MA 02109; and 617-451-1970. This set of field values is called a **record**. In the Employer table, the data for each employer is stored as a separate record. Figure 1-1 shows six records; each row of field values is a record.

Databases and Relationships

A collection of related tables is called a **database**, or a **relational database**. NSJI's Seasonal database contains two related tables: the Employer and NAICS tables, which Elsa created. (The NAICS table contains North American Industry Classification System codes, which are used to classify businesses according to their activities.) In Tutorial 2, you will create a Position table to store information about the available positions at NSJI's employer clients.

Sometimes you might want information about employers and their available positions. To obtain this information, you must have a way to connect records in the Employer table to records in the Position table. You connect the records in the separate tables through a **common field** that appears in both tables.

In the sample database shown in Figure 1-2, each record in the Employer table has a field named EmployerID, which is also a field in the Position table. For example, BaySide Inn & Country Club is the third employer in the Employer table and has an EmployerID field value of 10126. This same EmployerID field value, 10126, appears in three records in the Position table. Therefore, BaySide Inn & Country Club is the employer with these three positions available.

Database relationship between tables for employers and positions **Figure 1-2**

Employer table

EmployerID	EmployerName	EmployerAddress	PhoneNumber
10122	BeanTown Tours	105 State Street, Boston, MA 02109	617-451-1970
10125	Boston Harbor Excursions	75 Atlantic Avenue, Boston, MA 02110	617-235-1800
10126	BaySide Inn & Country Club	354 Oceanside Drive, Brewster, MA 02631	508-283-5775
10190	The Briar Rose Inn	105 Queen Street, Charlottetown PE C1A 8R4	902-626-1595
10191	Windsor Alpine Tours	14 Longmeadow Road, Laconia, NH 03246	603-266-9233
10198	Trudel Spa & Resort	40 Rue Rivard, North Hatley QC J0B 2C0	819-842-7783

primary keys

common field

foreign key

three positions for BaySide Inn & Country Club

Position table

PositionID	PositionTitle	EmployerID	Hours/Week
2040	Waiter/Waitress	10126	32
2045	Tour Guide	10122	24
2053	Host/Hostess	10190	24
2066	Lifeguard	10198	32
2073	Pro Shop Clerk	10126	24
2078	Ski Patrol	10191	30
2079	Day Care	10191	35
2082	Reservationist	10125	40
2111	Kitchen Help	10126	32

Each EmployerID value in the Employer table must be unique, so that you can distinguish one employer from another and identify the employer's specific positions available in the Position table. The EmployerID field is referred to as the primary key of the Employer table. A **primary key** is a field, or a collection of fields, whose values uniquely identify each record in a table. In the Position table, PositionID is the primary key.

When you include the primary key from one table as a field in a second table to form a relationship between the two tables, it is called a **foreign key** in the second table, as shown in Figure 1-2. For example, EmployerID is the primary key in the Employer table and a foreign key in the Position table. Although the primary key EmployerID has unique values in the Employer table, the same field as a foreign key in the Position table does not necessarily have unique values. The EmployerID value 10126, for example, appears three times in the Position table because the BaySide Inn & Country Club has three available positions. Each foreign key value, however, must match one of the field values for the primary key in the other table. In the example shown in Figure 1-2, each EmployerID value in the Position table must match an EmployerID value in the Employer table. The two tables are related, enabling users to connect the facts about employers with the facts about their employment positions.

Relational Database Management Systems

To manage its databases, a company purchases a database management system. A **database management system (DBMS)** is a software program that lets you create databases and then manipulate data in them. Most of today's database management systems, including Access, are called relational database management systems. In a **relational database management system**, data is organized as a collection of tables. As stated earlier, a relationship between two tables in a relational DBMS is formed through a common field.

A relational DBMS controls the storage of databases on disk and facilitates the creation, manipulation, and reporting of data, as illustrated in Figure 1-3. Specifically, a relational DBMS provides the following functions:

- It allows you to create database structures containing fields, tables, and table relationships.
- It lets you easily add new records, change field values in existing records, and delete records.
- It contains a built-in query language, which lets you obtain immediate answers to the questions you ask about your data.
- It contains a built-in report generator, which lets you produce professional-looking, formatted reports from your data.
- It protects databases through security, control, and recovery facilities.

| Figure 1-3 | Relational database management system |

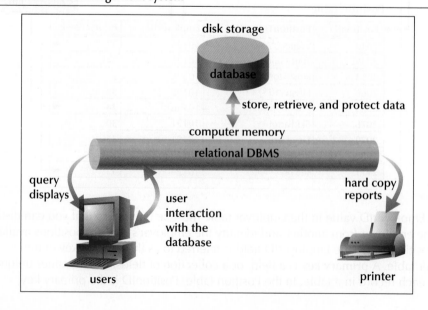

A company such as NSJI benefits from a relational DBMS because it allows users working in different departments to share the same data. More than one user can enter data into a database, and more than one user can retrieve and analyze data that was entered by others. For example, NSJI will store only one copy of the Employer table, and all employees will be able to use it to meet their specific requests for employer information.

Finally, unlike other software programs, such as spreadsheets, a DBMS can handle massive amounts of data and can easily form relationships among multiple tables. Each Access database, for example, can be up to two gigabytes in size and can contain up to 32,768 objects (tables, queries, and so on).

Opening an Existing Database

Now that you've learned some database terms and concepts, you're ready to start Access and open the Seasonal database.

To start Access:

1. Click the **Start** button on the taskbar, point to **All Programs**, point to **Microsoft Office**, and then click **Microsoft Office Access 2003**. The Access window opens. See Figure 1-4.

   Trouble? If you don't see the Microsoft Office Access 2003 option on the Microsoft Office submenu, look for it on a different submenu or as an option on the All Programs menu. If you still cannot find the Microsoft Office Access 2003 option, ask your instructor or technical support person for help.

Microsoft Access window | **Figure 1-4**

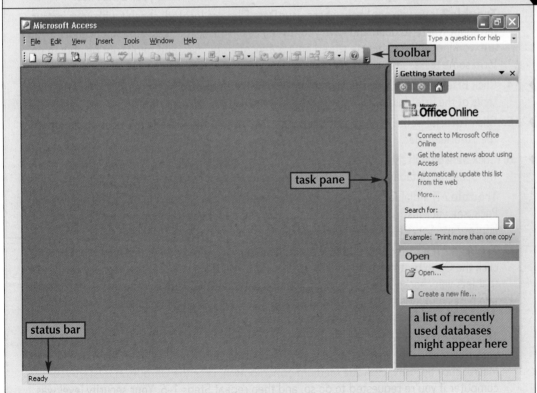

Trouble? If the Access program window on your computer is not maximized, click the Maximize button on the program window title bar.

When you start Access, the Access window contains the Getting Started task pane, which allows you to create a new database or to open an existing database. The "Create a new file" option in the task pane provides options for you to create a new database on your own, or to use one of the available online templates and let Access guide you through the steps for creating one of the standard databases provided by Microsoft.

In this case you need to open an existing database, the Seasonal database, which Elsa already created. To open an existing database, you can select the name of a database in the list of recently opened databases (if the list appears), or select a database in the Open dialog box. You need to open an existing database—the Seasonal database included with your Data Files.

To open the Seasonal database:

1. Make sure you have created your copy of the Access Data Files, and that your computer can access them. For example, if you are using a removable disk, place the disk in the appropriate disk drive.

   Trouble? If you don't have the Access Data Files, you need to get them before you can proceed. Your instructor will either give you the Data Files or ask you to obtain them from a specified location (such as a network drive). In either case, be sure that you make a backup copy of your Data Files before you start using them, so that the original files will be available on your copied disk in case you need to start over because of an error or problem. If you have any questions about the Data Files, see your instructor or technical support staff for assistance.

2. In the Open section of the task pane, click the **Open** option. The Open dialog box is displayed.

   Trouble? If your task pane doesn't provide an Open option, click the More option to display the Open dialog box.

3. Click the **Look in** list arrow, and then click the drive that contains your Data Files.

   Trouble? If you do not know where your Data Files are located, consult with your instructor about where to open and save your Data Files. Note that Access slows noticeably if you are working with a database stored on a 3 ½-inch floppy disk, and might not be able to perform some tasks, such as compacting and converting a database.

4. Click **Brief** in the list box (if necessary), and then click the **Open** button to display the contents of the Brief folder.

5. Click **Tutorial** in the list box, and then click the **Open** button to display a list of the files in the Tutorial folder.

6. Click **Seasonal** in the list box, and then click the **Open** button. The task pane closes, and the Seasonal database opens in the Access window. See Figure 1-5.

   Trouble? If a dialog box opens with a message about installing the Microsoft Jet Service Pack, see your instructor or technical support person for assistance. You must have the appropriate Service Pack installed in order to open and work with Access databases safely.

   Trouble? If a dialog box opens, warning you that the Seasonal database may not be safe, click the Open button. Your security level is set to Medium, which is the security setting that lets you choose whether or not to open a database that contains macros, VBA, or certain types of queries. The Seasonal database does not contain objects that will harm your computer, so you can safely open the database.

   Trouble? If a dialog box opens, warning you that Access can't open the Seasonal database due to security restrictions, click the OK button, click Tools on the menu bar, point to Macro, click Security, click the Medium option button, click the OK button, restart your computer if you're requested to do so, and then repeat Steps 1–6. Your security level was set to High, which is the security setting that lets you open a database that contains macros, VBA, or certain types of queries only from trusted sources. Because the Seasonal database does not contain objects that will harm your computer, you need to change the security setting to Medium and then safely open the Seasonal database.

Access and Database windows ◀ **Figure 1-5**

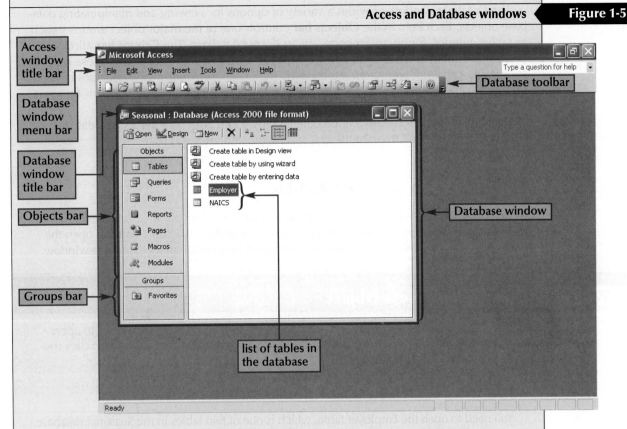

Trouble? The filename on your screen might be Seasonal.mdb instead of Seasonal, depending on your computer's default settings. The extension ".mdb" identifies the file as a Microsoft Access database.

Trouble? If Tables is not selected in the Objects bar of the Database window, click it to display the list of tables in the database.

Before you can begin working with the database, you need to become familiar with the components of the Access and Database windows.

Exploring the Access and Database Windows

The **Access window** is the program window that appears when you start the program. The **Database window** appears when you open a database; this window is the main control center for working with an open Access database. Except for the Access window title bar, all window components now on your screen are associated with the Database window (see Figure 1-5). Most of these window components—including the title bars, window sizing buttons, menu bar, toolbar, and status bar—are the same as the components in other Windows programs.

Notice that the Database window title bar includes the notation "(Access 2000 file format)." By default, databases that you create in Access 2003 use the Access 2000 database file format. This feature ensures that you can use and share databases originally created in Access 2003 without converting them to a format for an earlier version of Access, and vice versa. (You'll learn more about database file formats and converting databases later in this tutorial.)

The Database window provides a variety of options for viewing and manipulating database objects. Each item in the **Objects bar** controls one of the major object groups—such as tables, queries, forms, and reports—in an Access database. The **Groups bar** allows you to organize different types of database objects into groups, with shortcuts to those objects, so that you can work with them more easily. The Database window also provides buttons for quickly creating, opening, and managing objects, as well as shortcut options for some of these tasks.

Recall that Elsa has already created the Employer and NAICS tables in the Seasonal database. She asks you to open the Employer table and view its contents.

Opening an Access Table

As noted earlier, tables contain all the data in a database. Tables are the fundamental objects for your work in Access. To view, add, change, or delete data in a table, you first open the table. You can open any Access object by using the Open button in the Database window.

Reference Window	**Opening an Access Object**

- In the Objects bar of the Database window, click the type of object you want to open.
- If necessary, scroll the object list box until the object name appears, and then click the object name.
- Click the Open button in the Database window.

You need to open the Employer table, which is one of two tables in the Seasonal database.

To open the Employer table:

1. In the Database window, click **Employer** to select it (if necessary).
2. Click the **Open** button in the Database window. The Employer table opens in Datasheet view on top of the Database and Access windows. See Figure 1-6.

Employer table displayed in Datasheet view ◄ **Figure 1-6**

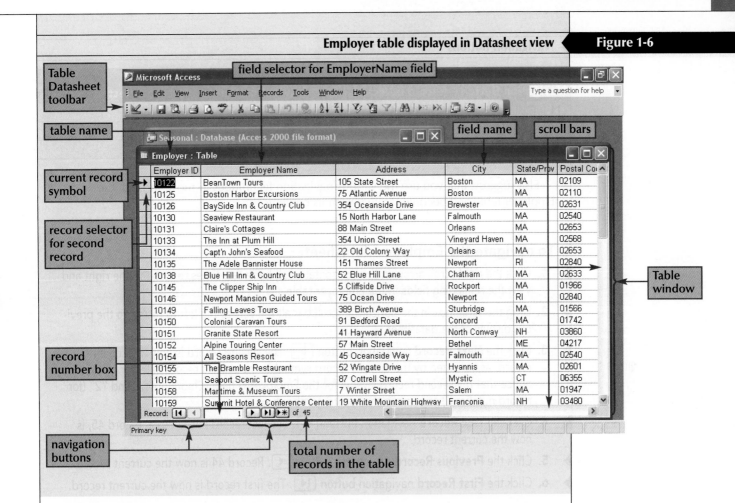

Table Datasheet toolbar

field selector for EmployerName field

table name

field name

scroll bars

current record symbol

record selector for second record

record number box

navigation buttons

Table window

total number of records in the table

Employer ID	Employer Name	Address	City	State/Prov	Postal Co
10122	BeanTown Tours	105 State Street	Boston	MA	02109
10125	Boston Harbor Excursions	75 Atlantic Avenue	Boston	MA	02110
10126	BaySide Inn & Country Club	354 Oceanside Drive	Brewster	MA	02631
10130	Seaview Restaurant	15 North Harbor Lane	Falmouth	MA	02540
10131	Claire's Cottages	88 Main Street	Orleans	MA	02653
10133	The Inn at Plum Hill	354 Union Street	Vineyard Haven	MA	02568
10134	Capt'n John's Seafood	22 Old Colony Way	Orleans	MA	02653
10135	The Adele Bannister House	151 Thames Street	Newport	RI	02840
10138	Blue Hill Inn & Country Club	52 Blue Hill Lane	Chatham	MA	02633
10145	The Clipper Ship Inn	5 Cliffside Drive	Rockport	MA	01966
10146	Newport Mansion Guided Tours	75 Ocean Drive	Newport	RI	02840
10149	Falling Leaves Tours	389 Birch Avenue	Sturbridge	MA	01566
10150	Colonial Caravan Tours	91 Bedford Road	Concord	MA	01742
10151	Granite State Resort	41 Hayward Avenue	North Conway	NH	03860
10152	Alpine Touring Center	57 Main Street	Bethel	ME	04217
10154	All Seasons Resort	45 Oceanside Way	Falmouth	MA	02540
10155	The Bramble Restaurant	52 Wingate Drive	Hyannis	MA	02601
10156	Seaport Scenic Tours	87 Cottrell Street	Mystic	CT	06355
10158	Maritime & Museum Tours	7 Winter Street	Salem	MA	01947
10159	Summit Hotel & Conference Center	19 White Mountain Highway	Franconia	NH	03480

Record: 1 of 45

Primary key

Datasheet view shows a table's contents as a **datasheet** in rows and columns, similar to a table or spreadsheet. Each row is a separate record in the table, and each column contains the field values for one field in the table. Each column is headed by a field name inside a field selector, and each row has a record selector to its left. Notice that the field names are displayed with spaces between words—such as "Employer ID" instead of "EmployerID" and "Employer Name" instead of "EmployerName." (You'll learn how to change the display of field names later in this text.) Clicking a **field selector** or a **record selector** selects that entire column or row (respectively), which you then can manipulate. A field selector is also called a **column selector**, and a record selector is also called a **row selector**.

Navigating an Access Datasheet

When you first open a datasheet, Access selects the first field value in the first record. Notice that this field value is highlighted and that a darkened triangle symbol, called the current record symbol, appears in the record selector to the left of the first record. The **current record symbol** identifies the currently selected record. Clicking a record selector or field value in another row moves the current record symbol to that row. You can also move the pointer over the data on the screen and click one of the field values to position the insertion point.

The Employer table currently has 13 fields and 45 records. To view fields or records not currently visible in the datasheet, you can use the horizontal and vertical scroll bars shown in Figure 1-6 to navigate the data. The **navigation buttons**, also shown in Figure 1-6, provide another way to move vertically through the records. Figure 1-7 shows which record becomes the current record when you click each navigation button. The **record number box**, which appears between the two sets of navigation buttons, displays the current record number. The total number of records in the table appears to the right of the navigation buttons.

Figure 1-7	Navigation buttons

Navigation Button	Record Selected	Navigation Button	Record Selected
⏮	First record	⏭	Last record
◀	Previous record	▶✱	New record
▶	Next record		

Elsa suggests that you use the various navigation techniques to move through the Employer table and become familiar with its contents.

To navigate the Employer datasheet:

1. Click the right scroll arrow in the horizontal scroll bar a few times to scroll to the right and view the remaining fields in the Employer table.

2. Drag the scroll box in the horizontal scroll bar all the way to the left to return to the previous display of the datasheet.

3. Click the **Next Record** navigation button ▶. The second record is now the current record, as indicated by the current record symbol in the second record selector. Also, notice that the second record's value for the EmployerID field is highlighted, and "2" (for record number 2) appears in the record number box.

4. Click the **Last Record** navigation button ⏭. The last record in the table, record 45, is now the current record.

5. Click the **Previous Record** navigation button ◀. Record 44 is now the current record.

6. Click the **First Record** navigation button ⏮. The first record is now the current record.

Printing a Datasheet

At times you might want a printed copy of the records in a table. You can use the Print button 🖨 on the Table Datasheet toolbar to print the contents of a table. You can also use the Print command on the File menu to display the Print dialog box and select various options for printing.

Reference Window	**Printing a Datasheet**

- Open the table datasheet you want to print.
- Click the Print button on the Table Datasheet toolbar to print the table with default settings; or click File on the menu bar, and then click Print to display the Print dialog box and select the options you want for printing the datasheet.

Elsa does not want a printed copy of the Employer table, so you do not need to print the datasheet at this time.

Saving a Database

Notice the Save button 🖫 on the Table Datasheet toolbar. Unlike the Save buttons in other Office programs, this Save button does not save the active document (database) to your disk. Instead, you use the Save button to save the design of an Access object, such as a table, or to save datasheet format changes. Access does not have a button or option you can use to save the active database. Similarly, you cannot use the Save As option on the File menu to save the active database file with a new name, as you can with other Office programs.

Access saves changes to the active database to your disk automatically, when a record is changed or added and when you close the database. If your database is stored on a removable disk, such as a floppy disk, *you should never remove the disk while the database file is open*. If you remove the disk, Access will encounter problems when it tries to save the database, which might damage the database.

You're done working with the Employer table for now, so you can close it.

To close the Employer table:

1. Click the **Close** button ☒ on the Employer Table window to close the table. You return to the Database window.

Now that you've become familiar with database concepts and Access, opened the Seasonal database that Elsa created, and navigated an Access table, Elsa wants you to work with the data stored in the Seasonal database and to create database objects including a query, form, and report. You will complete these tasks in Session 1.2.

Session 1.1 Quick Check

1. A(n) _____ is a single characteristic of a person, place, object, event, or idea.
2. You connect the records in two separate tables through a(n) _____ that appears in both tables.
3. The _____, whose values uniquely identify each record in a table, is called a(n) _____ when it is placed in a second table to form a relationship between the two tables.
4. In a table, the rows are also called _____, and the columns are also called _____.
5. The _____ identifies the selected record in an Access table.
6. Describe two methods for navigating a table.
7. Explain how the saving process in Access is different from saving in other Office programs.

Session 1.2

Working with Queries

A **query** is a question you ask about the data stored in a database. In response to a query, Access displays the specific records and fields that answer your question. When you create a query, you tell Access which fields you need and what criteria Access should use to select the records. Then Access displays only the information you want, so you don't have to navigate through the entire database for the information. In the Seasonal database, for example, Elsa might create a query to display only those records for employers located in Boston.

Before creating a new query, you will open a query that Elsa created recently so that she could view information in the Employer table in a different way.

Opening an Existing Query

Queries that you create and save appear in the Queries list of the Database window. To see the results of a query, you open, or run, the query. Elsa created and saved a query named Contacts in the Seasonal database. This query shows all the fields from the Employer table, but in a different order. Elsa suggests that you open this query to see its results.

To open the Contacts query:

1. If you took a break after the previous session, make sure that Access is running and that the Seasonal database is open.

2. Click **Queries** in the Objects bar of the Database window to display the Queries list. The Queries list box contains one object—the Contacts query. See Figure 1-8.

Figure 1-8 List of queries in the Seasonal database

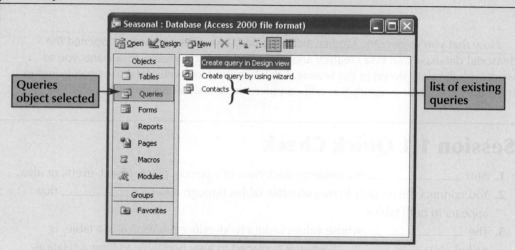

Now you will run the Contacts query by opening it.

3. Click **Contacts** to select it, and then click the **Open** button in the Database window. Access displays the results of the query in Datasheet view. See Figure 1-9.

Figure 1-9 Results of running the Contacts query

Notice that the query displays the fields from the Employer table, but in a different order. For example, the first and last names of each contact, as well as the contact's phone number, appear next to the employer name. This arrangement lets Elsa view pertinent contact information without having to scroll through the table. Rearranging the display of table data is one task you can perform with queries, so that table information appears in an order more suited to how you want to work with the information.

4. Click the **Close** button ⊠ on the Query window title bar to close the Contacts query.

Even though a query can display table information in a different way, the information still exists in the table as it was originally entered. If you opened the Employer table, it would still show the fields in their original order.

Zack Ward, the director of marketing at NSJI, wants a list of all employers so that his staff can call them to check on their satisfaction with NSJI's services and recruits. He doesn't want the list to include all the fields in the Employer table (such as PostalCode and NAICSCode)—only the employer's contact information. To produce this list for Zack, you need to create a query using the Employer table.

Creating, Sorting, and Navigating a Query

You can design your own queries or use an Access **Query Wizard**, which guides you through the steps to create a query. The Simple Query Wizard allows you to select records and fields quickly, and it is an appropriate choice for producing the employer list Zack wants. You can choose this wizard either by clicking the New button to open a dialog box listing several wizards for creating a query, or by double-clicking the "Create query by using wizard" option, which automatically starts the Simple Query Wizard.

To start the Simple Query Wizard:

1. Double-click **Create query by using wizard**. The first Simple Query Wizard dialog box opens. See Figure 1-10.

First Simple Query Wizard dialog box ◄ **Figure 1-10**

Because Contacts is the only query object in the Seasonal database, it is listed in the Tables/Queries box by default. You need to base the query you're creating on the Employer table.

> **2.** Click the **Tables/Queries** list arrow, and then click **Table: Employer** to select the Employer table as the source for the new query. The Available Fields list box now lists the fields in the Employer table.

You need to select fields from the Available Fields list box to include them in the query. To select fields one at a time, click a field and then click the [>] button. The selected field moves from the Available Fields list box on the left to the Selected Fields list box on the right. To select all the fields, click the [>>] button. If you change your mind or make a mistake, you can remove a field by clicking it in the Selected Fields list box and then clicking the [<] button. To remove all selected fields, click the [<<] button.

Each Simple Query Wizard dialog box contains buttons on the bottom that allow you to move to the previous dialog box (Back button), move to the next dialog box (Next button), or cancel the creation process (Cancel button) and return to the Database window. You can also finish creating the object (Finish button) and accept the wizard's defaults for the remaining options.

Zack wants his list to include data from only the following fields: EmployerName, City, StateProv, ContactFirstName, ContactLastName, and Phone. You need to select these fields to include them in the query.

To create the query using the Simple Query Wizard:

> **1.** Click **EmployerName** in the Available Fields list box, and then click the [>] button. The EmployerName field moves to the Selected Fields list box.

> **2.** Repeat Step 1 for the fields **City**, **StateProv**, **ContactFirstName**, **ContactLastName**, and **Phone**, and then click the **Next** button. The second, and final, Simple Query Wizard dialog box opens and asks you to choose a name for your query. This name will appear in the Queries list in the Database window. You'll change the suggested name (Employer Query) to "EmployerList."

> **3.** Click at the end of the highlighted name, use the **Backspace** key to delete the word "Query" and the space after "Employer," and then type **List**. Now you can view the query results.

> **4.** Click the **Finish** button to complete the query. Access displays the query results in Datasheet view.

> **5.** Click the **Maximize** button 🔲 on the Query window title bar to maximize the window. See Figure 1-11.

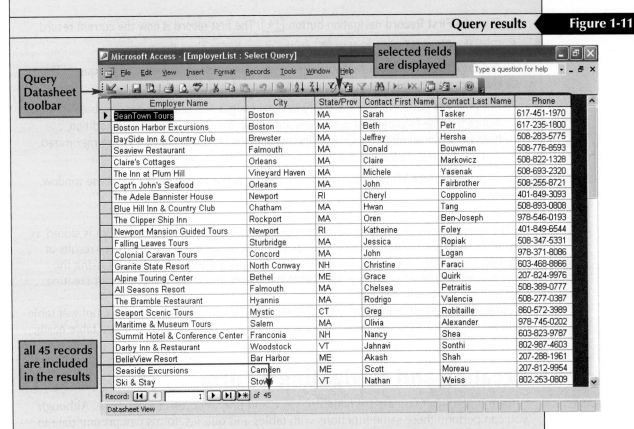

The datasheet displays the six selected fields for each record in the Employer table. The fields are shown in the order you selected them, from left to right.

The records are currently listed in order by the primary key field (EmployerID from the Employer table). This is true even though the EmployerID field is not included in the display of the query results. Zack prefers the records listed in order by state or province, so that his staff members can focus on all records for the employers in a particular state or province. To display the records in the order Zack wants, you need to sort the query results by the StateProv field.

To sort the query results:

1. Click to position the insertion point anywhere in the State/Prov column. This establishes the State/Prov column as the current field.

2. Click the **Sort Ascending** button on the Query Datasheet toolbar. Now the records are sorted in ascending alphabetical order by the values in the State/Prov column. All the records for Connecticut (CT) are listed first, followed by the records for Massachusetts (MA), Maine (ME), and so on.

   Notice that the navigation buttons are located at the bottom of the window. You navigate a query datasheet in the same way that you navigate a table datasheet.

3. Click the **Last Record** navigation button . The last record in the query datasheet, for the Darby Inn & Restaurant, is now the current record.

4. Click the **Previous Record** navigation button . Record 44 in the query datasheet is now the current record.

▶ **5.** Click the **First Record** navigation button ⏮. The first record is now the current record.

▶ **6.** Click the **Close Window** button ✕ on the menu bar to close the query.

A dialog box opens and asks if you want to save changes to the design of the query. This dialog box opens because you changed the sort order of the query results.

▶ **7.** Click the **Yes** button to save the query design changes and return to the Database window. Notice that the EmployerList query now appears in the Queries list box. In addition, because you maximized the Query window, now the Database window is also maximized. You need to restore the window.

▶ **8.** Click the **Restore Window** button 🗗 on the menu bar to restore the Database window.

The query results are not stored in the database; however, the query design is stored as part of the database with the name you specified. You can re-create the query results at any time by running the query again. You can also print the query datasheet using the Print button, just as you can to print a table datasheet. You'll learn more about creating and running queries in Tutorial 3.

After Zack views the query results, Elsa asks you to create a form for the Employer table so that her staff members can use the form to enter and work with data in the table easily.

Creating and Navigating a Form

A **form** is an object you use to maintain, view, and print records in a database. Although you can perform these same functions with tables and queries, forms can present data in many customized and useful ways.

In Access, you can design your own forms or use a Form Wizard to create your forms automatically. A **Form Wizard** is an Access tool that asks you a series of questions, and then creates a form based on your answers. However, an **AutoForm Wizard** does not ask you questions. Instead, it places all the fields from a selected table (or query) on a form automatically, and then displays the form on the screen, making it the quickest way to create a form.

Elsa wants a form for the Employer table that will show all the fields for one record at a time, with fields listed one below another in a column. This type of form will make it easier for her staff to focus on all the data for a particular employer. You'll use the AutoForm: Columnar Wizard to create the form.

To create the form using an AutoForm Wizard:

▶ **1.** Click **Forms** in the Objects bar of the Database window to display the Forms list. The Forms list box does not contain any forms yet.

▶ **2.** Click the **New** button in the Database window to open the New Form dialog box. See Figure 1-12.

New Form dialog box ◄ **Figure 1-12**

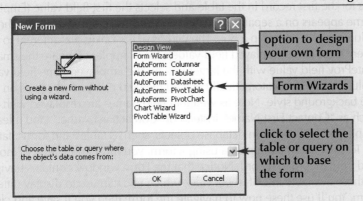

option to design your own form

Form Wizards

click to select the table or query on which to base the form

The top list box provides options for designing your own form or creating a form using one of the Form Wizards. In the bottom list box, you choose the table or query that will supply the data for the form.

► 3. Click **AutoForm: Columnar** to select this AutoForm Wizard.

► 4. Click the list arrow for choosing the table or query on which to base the form, and then click **Employer**.

► 5. Click the **OK** button. The AutoForm Wizard creates the form and displays it in Form view. See Figure 1-13.

Form created by the AutoForm: Columnar Wizard ◄ **Figure 1-13**

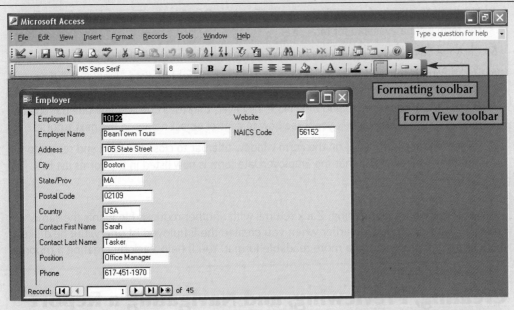

Formatting toolbar

Form View toolbar

Trouble? The placement of the Form View and Formatting toolbars might be different on your screen. If you want your screen to match the figures, you can use the mouse to drag a toolbar to a new location, using the dotted line at the left edge of a toolbar. However, the position of any toolbar does not affect your ability to complete the steps.

Trouble? The background of your form might look different from the one shown in Figure 1-13, depending on your computer's settings. If so, don't worry. You will learn how to change the form's style later in this text. For now, continue with the tutorial.

The form displays one record at a time in the Employer table. Access displays the field values for the first record in the table and selects the first field value (EmployerID). Each field name appears on a separate line (spread over two columns) and on the same line as its field value, which appears in a box. The widths of the boxes are different to accommodate the different sizes of the displayed field values; for example, compare the small box for the StateProv field value with the larger box for the EmployerName field value. The AutoForm: Columnar Wizard automatically placed the field names and values on the form and supplied the background style. Note as well that field names are displayed with spaces between them, such as "Contact First Name" instead of "ContactFirstName." (You'll learn how to control the display of field names in database objects, such as tables and forms, later in this text.)

To view and maintain data using a form, you must know how to move from field to field and from record to record. Notice that the Form window contains navigation buttons, similar to those available in Datasheet view, which you can use to display different records in the form. You'll use these now to navigate the form; then you'll save and close the form.

To navigate, save, and close the form:

1. Click the **Next Record** navigation button ▶. The form now displays the values for the second record in the Employer table.

2. Click the **Last Record** navigation button ▶| to move to the last record in the table. The form displays the information for record 45, Lighthouse Tours.

3. Click the **Previous Record** navigation button ◀ to move to record 44.

4. Click the **First Record** navigation button |◀ to return to the first record in the Employer table.

   Next, you'll save the form with the name "EmployerData" in the Seasonal database. Then the form will be available for later use.

5. Click the **Save** button 🖫 on the Form View toolbar. The Save As dialog box opens.

6. In the Form Name text box, click at the end of the highlighted word "Employer," type **Data**, and then press the **Enter** key. Access saves the form as EmployerData in the Seasonal database and closes the dialog box. Note, however, that the Form window title bar still displays the name "Employer"; you'll see how to control object names in the next tutorial.

7. Click the **Close** button ⊠ on the Form window title bar to close the form and return to the Database window. Note that the EmployerData form is now listed in the Forms list box.

After attending a staff meeting, Zack returns with another request. He wants the same employer list you produced earlier when you created the EmployerList query, but he'd like the information presented in a more readable format. You'll help Zack by creating a report.

Creating, Previewing, and Navigating a Report

A **report** is a formatted printout (or screen display) of the contents of one or more tables in a database. Although you can print data appearing in tables, queries, and forms, reports provide you with the greatest flexibility for formatting printed output. As with forms, you can design your own reports or use a Report Wizard to create reports automatically. Like other wizards, a **Report Wizard** guides you through the steps of creating a report.

Zack wants a report showing the same information contained in the EmployerList query that you created earlier. However, he wants the data for each employer to be grouped together, with one employer record below another, as shown in the report sketch in Figure 1-14.

EmployerList

Employer Name _____
City _____
State/Prov _____
Contact First Name _____
Contact Last Name _____
Phone _____

Employer Name _____
City _____
State/Prov _____
Contact First Name _____
Contact Last Name _____
Phone _____

To produce the report for Zack, you'll use the AutoReport: Columnar Wizard, which is similar to the AutoForm: Columnar Wizard you used earlier when creating the EmployerData form. An **AutoReport Wizard**, like an AutoForm Wizard, places all the fields from a selected table (or query) on a report, making it the quickest way to create a report.

To create the report using the AutoReport: Columnar Wizard:

▶ **1.** Click **Reports** in the Objects bar of the Database window, and then click the **New** button in the Database window to open the New Report dialog box, which is similar to the New Form dialog box you saw earlier.

▶ **2.** Click **AutoReport: Columnar** to select this wizard for creating the report.

Because Zack wants the same data as in the EmployerList query, you need to choose that query as the basis for the report.

▶ **3.** Click the list arrow for choosing the table or query on which to base the report, and then click **EmployerList**.

▶ **4.** Click the **OK** button. The AutoReport Wizard creates the report and displays it in Print Preview, which shows exactly how the report will look when printed.

To view the report better, you'll maximize the window and change the Zoom setting so that you can see the entire page.

▶ **5.** Click the **Maximize** button ▣ on the Report window title bar, click the **Zoom** list arrow (to the right of the value 100%) on the Print Preview toolbar, and then click **Fit**. The entire first page of the report is displayed in the window. See Figure 1-15.

Figure 1-15 First page of the report in Print Preview

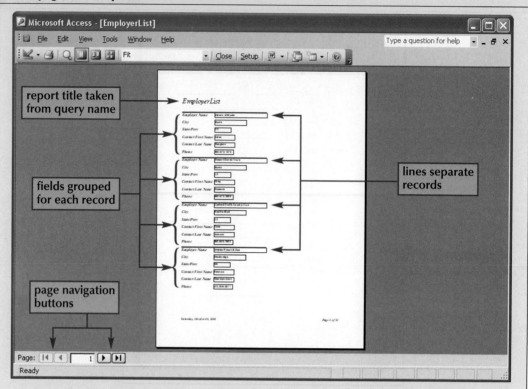

Trouble? The fonts used in your report might look different from the ones shown in Figure 1-15, depending on your computer's settings. If so, don't worry. You will learn how to change the report's style later in this text.

Each field from the EmployerList query appears on its own line, with the corresponding field value to the right and in a box. Horizontal lines separate one record from the next, visually grouping all the fields for each record. The name of the query—EmployerList—appears as the report's title.

Notice that the Print Preview window provides page navigation buttons at the bottom of the window, similar to the navigation buttons you've used to move through records in a table, query, and form. You use these buttons to move through the pages of a report.

6. Click the **Next Page** navigation button ▶. The second page of the report is displayed in Print Preview.

7. Click the **Last Page** navigation button ▶️ to move to the last page of the report. Note that this page contains the fields for only one record. Also note that the box in the middle of the navigation buttons displays the number "12"; there are 12 pages in this report.

Trouble? Depending on the printer you are using, your report might have more or fewer pages, or might have more than one record on the last page. If so, don't worry. Different printers format reports in different ways, sometimes affecting the total number of pages and the number of records per page.

8. Click the **First Page** navigation button ◀️ to return to the first page of the report.

Zack likes how the report looks, and he wants to show it to his staff members to see if they approve of the format. He would like a printout of the report, but he doesn't need the entire report printed—only the first page.

Printing Specific Pages of a Report

After creating a report, you typically print it to distribute it to others who need to view the report's contents. You can choose to print the entire report, using the Print toolbar button or the Print menu option, or you can select specific pages of a report to print. To specify certain pages to print, you must use the Print option on the File menu. In this case, you will print only the first page of the EmployerList report.

Note: To complete the following steps, your computer must be connected to a printer.

To print only the first page of the report:

▶ 1. Click **File** on the menu bar, and then click **Print**. The Print dialog box opens. See Figure 1-16.

Print dialog box ◀ **Figure 1-16**

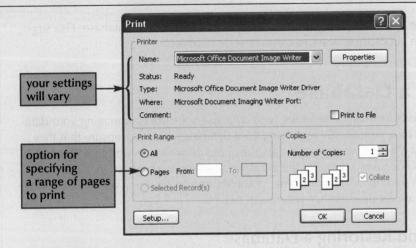

The Print dialog box provides options for printing all the pages in the report or a specified range of pages. In this case, you will print just the first page of the report, so you need to specify a range of "From" page 1 "To" page 1.

Trouble? The settings shown for the Name, Type, and Where options in your Print dialog box will vary from those shown in the figure, depending on the printer you are using.

▶ 2. In the Print Range section, click the **Pages** option button. Notice that the insertion point now appears in the From box so that you can specify the first page to be printed.

▶ 3. Type **1**, press the **Tab** key to move to the To box, and then type **1**. These settings will cause only the first page of the report to be printed.

▶ 4. Click the **OK** button. The first page of the EmployerList report prints on your selected printer.

Trouble? If your report did not print, make sure that your computer is connected to a printer, and that the printer is turned on and ready to print. Then repeat Steps 1 through 4.

At this point, you could close the report without saving it because you can easily re-create it at any time. In general, it's best to save an object—report, form, or query—only if you antic-ipate using the object frequently or if it is time-consuming to create, because these objects use considerable storage space on your disk. However, Zack wants to keep the report until he receives feedback from his staff members about its layout, so he asks you to save it.

To close and save the report:

1. Click the **Close Window** button ⊠ on the menu bar. *Do not* click the Close button on the Print Preview toolbar.

   Trouble? If you clicked the Close button on the Print Preview toolbar, you switched to Design view. Simply click the Close Window button ⊠ on the menu bar, and then continue with the steps.

   A dialog box opens and asks if you want to save the changes to the report design.

2. Click the **Yes** button. The Save As dialog box opens.

3. Click to the right of the highlighted text in the Report Name text box, type **Report**, and then click the **OK** button. Access saves the report as "EmployerListReport" and returns to the Database window.

Now that you've become familiar with the objects in the Seasonal database, Elsa suggests that you learn about some ways to manage your database.

Managing a Database

One of the main tasks involved in working with database software is managing your databases and the data they contain. By managing your databases, you can ensure that they operate in the most efficient way, that the data they contain is secure, and that you can work with the data effectively. Some of the activities involved in database management include backing up and restoring a database, compacting and repairing a database, and converting a database for use in other versions of Access.

Backing up and Restoring a Database

Backing up a database is the process of making a copy of the database file to protect your database against loss or damage. Experienced database users make it a habit to back up a database before they work with it for the first time, keeping the original data intact, and to make frequent backups while continuing to work with a database. Because a floppy disk can hold only the smallest of databases, it is not practical to store backup copies on a floppy disk. Most users back up their databases on tapes, recordable CDs, or hard disks.

With previous versions of Access, you could only make a backup copy using one of the following methods: Windows Explorer, My Computer, Microsoft Backup, or other backup software. With Access 2003, however, a new Back Up Database option enables you to back up your database file from within the Access program, while you are working on your database. Figure 1-17 shows the Save Backup As dialog box, which opens when you choose the Back Up Database option from the File menu.

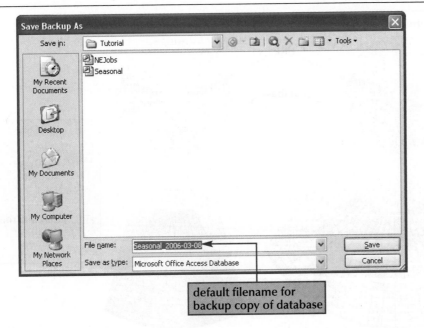

default filename for
backup copy of database

   The Save Backup As dialog box is similar to the standard Save As dialog box found in Windows programs. Notice that the default filename for the backup copy consists of the same filename as the database you are backing up (in this example, "Seasonal") plus the current date. This file naming system makes it easy for you to keep track of your database backups and when they were created. (You will not actually back up the Seasonal database here; if you are working off a floppy disk, you will not have enough room on the disk to hold both the original database and its backup copy.)

   To restore a backup database file, choose the same method you used to make the backup copy. For example, if you used the Microsoft Backup tool (which is one of the System Tools available from the All Programs menu and Accessories submenu in Windows), you must choose the Restore option for this tool to copy the database file to your database folder. If the existing database file and the backup copy have the same name, restoring the backup copy might replace the existing file. If you want to save the existing file, rename it before you restore the backup copy.

Compacting and Repairing a Database

Whenever you open an Access database and work in it, the size of the database increases. Further, when you delete records and when you delete or replace database objects—such as queries, forms, and reports—the space that had been occupied on the disk by the deleted or replaced records or objects does not automatically become available for other records or objects. To make the space available, you must compact the database. **Compacting** a database rearranges the data and objects in a database to decrease its file size. Unlike making a backup copy of a database file, which you do to protect your database against loss or damage, you compact a database to make it smaller, thereby making more space available on your disk and letting you open and close the database more quickly. Figure 1-18 illustrates the compacting process.

Figure 1-18

Compacting a database

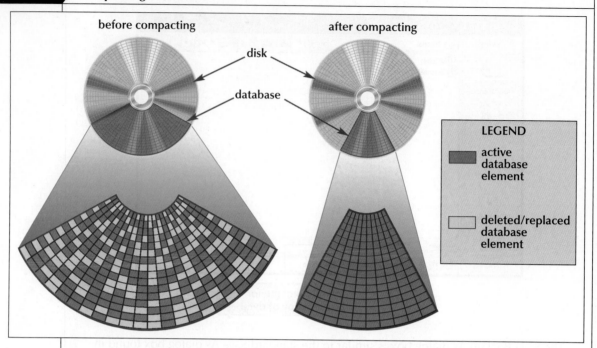

When you compact a database, Access repairs the database at the same time. In many cases, Access detects that a database is damaged when you try to open it and gives you the option to compact and repair it at that time. For example, the data in your database might become damaged, or corrupted, if you exit the Access program suddenly by turning off your computer. If you think your database might be damaged because it is behaving unpredictably, you can use the "Compact and Repair Database" option to fix it. With your database file open, point to the Database Utilities option on the Tools menu, and then choose the Compact and Repair Database option.

Compacting a Database Automatically

Access also allows you to set an option for your database file so that every time you close the database, it will be compacted automatically.

Reference Window

Compacting a Database Automatically

- Make sure the database file you want to compact automatically is open.
- Click Tools on the menu bar, and then click Options.
- Click the General tab in the Options dialog box.
- Click the Compact on Close check box to select it.
- Click the OK button.

You'll set the Compact on Close option now for the Seasonal database. Then, every time you subsequently close the Seasonal database, Access will compact the database file for you. After setting this option, you'll close the database.

Important: Because Access copies the database file and then compacts it on the same disk, you might run out of storage space if you compact a database stored on a floppy disk. Therefore, it is strongly recommended that you set the Compact on Close option *only* if your database is stored somewhere other than a floppy disk. However, if you must work with the Seasonal database on a floppy disk, per your instructor's requirements, you must also compact the database so that it will fit on the disk as you progress through the tutorials. Consult with your instructor or technical support staff to see if they recommend your using the Compact on Close option while working from a floppy disk.

To set the option for compacting the Seasonal database:

1. Make sure the Seasonal Database window is open.
2. Click **Tools** on the menu bar, and then click **Options**. The Options dialog box opens.
3. Click the **General** tab in the dialog box, and then click the **Compact on Close** check box to select it. See Figure 1-19.

General tab of the Options dialog box ◄ **Figure 1-19**

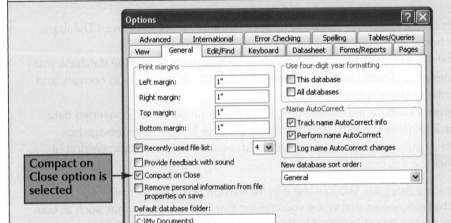

Compact on Close option is selected

4. Click the **OK** button to set the option.

   Trouble? If you are working from a floppy disk, you might receive message or warning dialog boxes when setting this option. Click OK and continue with the tutorial. See your instructor or technical support staff if you have problems with this option.

5. Click the **Close Window** button ☒ on the menu bar. Access closes the Seasonal database file and compacts it automatically.

Note: If the database you are compacting is located on a floppy disk, it is very important that you *wait until the compacting procedure is complete before removing the floppy disk.* Wait until the light on the floppy disk drive goes off and the whirring noise made by the floppy disk drive stops. If you remove the disk before compacting has finished, you could damage your database.

Converting an Access 2000 Database

Another important database management task is **converting** a database so that you can work with it in a different version of Access. As noted earlier in this tutorial, the default file format for databases you create in Access 2003 is Access 2000. This enables you to work with the database in either the Access 2000, 2002, or 2003 versions of the software without having to convert it. This compatibility makes it easy for multiple users working with different versions of the software to share the same database and work more efficiently.

Sometimes, however, you might need to convert an Access 2000 database to another version. For example, if you need to share an Access 2000 database with a colleague who works on a laptop computer with Access 97 installed on it, you could convert the Access 2000 database to the Access 97 format. Likewise, you might want to convert an Access 2000 database to the Access 2002 file format if the database becomes very large. The Access 2002 file format is enhanced so that large databases run faster than in earlier versions of Access, making it more efficient for you to work with the information contained in them.

To convert a database, you would follow these steps (note that you will not actually convert a database now):

1. Make sure that Access is running (the database you want to convert can be open or closed).
2. Click Tools on the menu bar, point to Database Utilities, point to Convert Database, and then choose the format you want to convert to.
3. In the Database to Convert From dialog box (which appears only if the database you want to convert is closed), select the name of the database you want to convert, and then click the Convert button.
4. In the Convert Database Into dialog box, enter a new name for the converted database in the File name text box, and then click the Save button. If a message box opens with a caution about not being able to share files with a specific version of Access, click the OK button.

After converting a database, you can use it in the version of Access to which you converted the file. Note, however, that when you convert to a previous file format, such as converting from the Access 2000 file format to the Access 97 file format, you might lose some of the advanced features of the newer version and you might need to make some adjustments to the converted database. Simple databases, such as the Seasonal database, generally retain their data and formatting when converted. However, you could lose data and other information from more complex databases when you convert them to an earlier file format.

With the Employer and NAICS tables in place, Elsa can continue to build the Seasonal database and use it to store, manipulate, and retrieve important data for NSJI. In the following tutorials, you'll help Elsa complete and maintain the database, and you'll use it to meet the specific information needs of other NSJI employees.

Review

Session 1.2 Quick Check

1. A(n) _____ is a question you ask about the data stored in a database.
2. Unless you specify otherwise, the records resulting from a query are listed in order by the _____.
3. The quickest way to create a form is to use a(n) _____.
4. Describe the form created by the AutoForm: Columnar Wizard.
5. After creating a report, the AutoReport Wizard displays the report in _____.
6. _____ a database rearranges the data and objects in a database to decrease its file size.

Review

Tutorial Summary

In this tutorial, you learned the basic concepts associated with databases, including how data is organized in a database and the functions of a relational database management system. You also learned how the Database window is the main control center for your work in Access, giving you options for viewing and manipulating all the objects in a database—tables, queries, forms, reports, and so on. By opening and navigating a table datasheet, you saw how the fields and records in a table are displayed and organized. Using various wizards, you also learned how to create queries, forms, and reports quickly in order to view and work with the data stored in a table in different ways. Finally, you were introduced to some of the important tasks involved in managing a database, including backing up, compacting, and converting a database.

Key Terms

Access	Database window	query
Access window	datasheet	Query Wizard
AutoForm Wizard	Datasheet view	record
AutoReport Wizard	field	record number box
backing up	field selector	record selector
column selector	field value	relational database
common field	foreign key	relational database
compacting	form	management system
converting	Form Wizard	(RDBMS)
current record symbol	Groups bar	report
database	navigation buttons	Report Wizard
database management	Objects bar	row selector
system (DBMS)	primary key	table

Practice

Take time to practice the skills you learned in the tutorial using the same case scenario.

Review Assignments

Data File needed for the Review Assignments: Seasons.mdb

In the Review Assignments, you'll work with the Seasons database, which is similar to Elsa's database that you worked with in the tutorial. Complete the following steps:

1. Open the **Seasons** database, which is located in the Brief\Review folder provided with your Data Files.
2. Open the **Employers** table.
3. Use the appropriate navigation buttons to move to the last record in the table, and then up three records from the last record. Write down the field values for all the fields in this record.
4. Move back to the first record in the table, print the table datasheet, and then close the table.
5. Use the Simple Query Wizard to create a query that includes the City, EmployerName, ContactFirstName, ContactLastName, and Phone fields (in that order) from the **Employers** table. Name the query **EmployerPhoneList**. Sort the query results in ascending order by City. Print the query results, and then close and save the query.
6. Use the AutoForm: Columnar Wizard to create a form for the **Employers** table. Save the form as **EmployerInfo**, and then close the form.
7. Use the AutoReport: Columnar Wizard to create a report based on the **Employers** table. Print the first page of the report, and then close the report and save it as **Employers**.

8. Set the option for compacting the **Seasons** database on close. (*Note*: If you are working from a floppy disk, check with your instructor or technical support staff to confirm that you should set this option.)
9. Close the Seasons database.

Apply

Use the skills you learned in the tutorial to work with the data contained in a video photography database.

Case Problem 1

Data File needed for this Case Problem: Videos.mdb

Lim's Video Photography Several years ago, Youngho Lim left his position at a commercial photographer's studio and started his own business, Lim's Video Photography, located in San Francisco, California. Youngho quickly established a reputation as one of the area's best videographers, specializing in digital video photography. Youngho offers customers the option of storing edited videos on CD or DVD. His video shoots include weddings and other special events, as well as recording personal and commercial inventories for insurance purposes.

As his business continues to grow, Youngho relies on Access to keep track of information about clients, contracts, and so on. Youngho recently created an Access database named Videos to store data about his clients. You'll help Youngho complete and maintain the Videos database. Complete the following:

1. Open the **Videos** database, which is located in the Brief\Case1 folder provided with your Data Files.
2. Open the **Client** table, print the table datasheet, and then close the table.
3. Use the Simple Query Wizard to create a query that includes the ClientName, Phone, and City fields (in that order) from the **Client** table. Name the query **ClientList**. Print the query results, and then close the query.
4. Use the AutoForm: Columnar Wizard to create a form for the **Contract** table. Save the form as **ContractInfo**, and then close it.
5. Use the AutoReport: Columnar Wizard to create a report based on the **Contract** table. Print the first page of the report, and then close the report and save it as **Contracts**.
6. Set the option for compacting the **Videos** database on close. (*Note*: If you are working from a floppy disk, check with your instructor or technical support staff to confirm that you should set this option.)
7. Close the Videos database.

Apply

Apply what you learned in the tutorial to work with the data for a new business in the health and fitness industry.

Case Problem 2

Data File needed for this Case Problem: Fitness.mdb

Parkhurst Health & Fitness Center After many years working in various corporate settings, Martha Parkhurst decided to turn her lifelong interest in health and fitness into a new business venture and opened the Parkhurst Health & Fitness Center in Richmond, Virginia. In addition to providing the usual fitness classes and weight training facilities, the center also offers specialized programs designed to meet the needs of athletes—both young and old—who participate in certain sports or physical activities. Martha's goal in establishing such programs is twofold: to help athletes gain a competitive edge through customized training, and to ensure the health and safety of all participants through proper exercises and physical preparation.

Martha created the Fitness database in Access to maintain information about the members who have joined the center and the types of programs offered. She needs your help in working with this database. Complete the following:

1. Open the **Fitness** database located in the Brief\Case2 folder provided with your Data Files.
2. Open the **Member** table, print the table datasheet, and then close the table.
3. Use the Simple Query Wizard to create a query that includes the FirstName, LastName, DateJoined, and Phone fields (in that order) from the **Member** table. Name the query **MemberList**.

> **Explore**

4. Sort the query results in descending order by the DateJoined field. (*Hint*: Use a tool-bar button.)
5. Print the query results, and then close and save the query.
6. Use the AutoForm: Columnar Wizard to create a form for the **Member** table. Save the form as **MemberInfo**, and then close it.
7. Use the AutoReport: Columnar Wizard to create a report based on the **Member** table. Maximize the Report window and change the Zoom setting to Fit.
8. Print just the first page of the report, and then close and save the report as **Members**.
9. Set the option for compacting the **Fitness** database on close. (*Note:* If you are working from a floppy disk, check with your instructor or technical support staff to confirm that you should set this option.)
10. Close the Fitness database.

Case Problem 3

> **Challenge**
>
> *Use what you've learned, and go a bit beyond, to work with a database that contains information about a zoo.*

Data File needed for this Case Problem: Redwood.mdb

Redwood Zoo   The Redwood Zoo is a small zoo located in the picturesque city of Gig Harbor, Washington, on the shores of Puget Sound. The zoo is ideally situated, with the natural beauty of the site providing the perfect backdrop for the zoo's varied exhibits. Although there are larger zoos in the greater Seattle area, the Redwood Zoo is considered to have some of the best exhibits of marine animals. The newly constructed polar bear habitat is a particular favorite among patrons.

Michael Rosenfeld is the director of fundraising activities for the Redwood Zoo. The zoo relies heavily on donations to fund both ongoing exhibits and temporary displays, especially those involving exotic animals. Michael created an Access database named Redwood to keep track of information about donors, their pledges, and the status of funds. You'll help Michael maintain the Redwood database. Complete the following:

1. Open the **Redwood** database, which is located in the Brief\Case3 folder provided with your Data Files.

> **Explore**

2. Use the "Type a question for help" box to ask the following question: "How do I rename an object?" Click the topic "Rename a database object" and read the displayed information. Close the Microsoft Office Access Help window and the task pane. Then, in the Redwood database, rename the **Table1** table as **Donor**.
3. Open the **Donor** table, print the table datasheet, and then close the table.

> **Explore**

4. Use the Simple Query Wizard to create a query that includes all the fields in the **Donor** table *except* the MI field. (*Hint:* Use the [>>] and [<] buttons to select the necessary fields.) Name the query **Donors**.

> **Explore**

5. Sort the query results in descending order by the Class field. (*Hint:* Use a toolbar button.) Print the query results, and then close and save the query.

Explore

6. Use the AutoForm: Columnar Wizard to create a form for the **Fund** table. Open the Microsoft Access Help task pane. (*Hint:* Click Help on the menu bar, and then click Microsoft Office Access Help.) Type the keywords "find a specific record in a form" in the Search for text box, and then click the Start searching button. Select the topic "Find a record in a datasheet or form," then choose the topic related to finding a record by record number. Read the displayed information. Close the Microsoft Office Access Help window and the task pane. Use the record number box to move to record 7 (Polar Bear Park), and then print the form for the current record only. (*Hint:* Use the Selected Record(s) option in the Print dialog box to print the current record.) Save the form as **FundInfo**, and then close it.

7. Use the AutoReport: Columnar Wizard to create a report based on the **Donor** table. Maximize the Report window and change the Zoom setting to Fit.

Explore

8. Use the View menu to view all seven pages of the report at the same time in Print Preview.

9. Print just the first page of the report, and then close and save it as **Donors**.

10. Set the option for compacting the **Redwood** database on close. (*Note*: If you are working from a floppy disk, check with your instructor or technical support staff to confirm that you should set this option.)

Explore

11. Convert the **Redwood** database to Access 2002–2003 file format, saving the converted file as **Redwood2002** in the Brief\Case3 folder. Then convert the **Redwood** database to Access 97 file format, saving the converted file as **Redwood97** in the Brief\Case3 folder. Using Windows Explorer or My Computer, view the contents of your Brief\Case3 folder, and note the file sizes of the three versions of the Redwood database. Describe the results.

12. Close the Redwood database.

Challenge

Work with the skills you've learned, and explore some new skills, to manage the data for a luxury rental company.

Case Problem 4

Data File needed for this Case Problem: GEM.mdb

GEM Ultimate Vacations As guests of a friend, Griffin and Emma MacElroy spent two weeks at a magnificent villa in the south of France. This unforgettable experience stayed with them upon returning to their home in a suburb of Chicago, Illinois. As a result, they decided to open their own agency, GEM Ultimate Vacations, which specializes in locating and booking luxury rental properties, primarily in Europe. Recently, Griffin and Emma expanded their business to include properties in Africa as well.

From the beginning, Griffin and Emma used computers to help them manage all aspects of their business. They recently installed Access and created a database named GEM to store information about guests, properties, and reservations. You'll work with the GEM database to manage this information. Complete the following:

1. Open the **GEM** database located in the Brief\Case4 folder provided with your Data Files.

2. Open the **Guest** table.

Explore

3. Open the Microsoft Access Help task pane. (*Hint*: Click Help on the menu bar, and then click Microsoft Office Access Help.) Type the keyword "print" in the Search for text box, and then click the Start searching button. Scroll down the list, click the topic "Set page setup options for printing," and then click "For a table, query, form, or report." Read the displayed information. Close the Microsoft Office Access Help window and the task pane. Set the option for printing in landscape orientation, and then print the **Guest** table datasheet. Close the table.

4. Use the Simple Query Wizard to create a query that includes the GuestName, City, StateProv, and Phone fields (in that order) from the **Guest** table. Name the query **GuestInfo**.

Explore

5. Sort the query results in descending order by StateProv. (*Hint*: Use a toolbar button.)

6. Print the query results, and then close and save the query.

Explore

7. Use the AutoForm: Columnar Wizard to create a form for the **Guest** table. Use the Microsoft Access Help task pane to search for information on how to find a specific record in a form. Select the topic "Find a record in a datasheet or form in Access," then choose the topic related to finding a record by record number. Read the displayed information. Close the Microsoft Office Access Help window and the task pane. Use the record number box to move to record 16, and then print the form for the current record only. (*Hint*: Use the Selected Record(s) option in the Print dialog box to print the current record.) Save the form as **GuestInfo**, and then close it.

Explore

8. Use the AutoReport: Tabular Wizard to create a report based on the **Guest** table. Maximize the Report window and change the Zoom setting to Fit. Use the Two Pages button on the Print Preview toolbar to view both pages of the report in Print Preview. Print the first page of the report in landscape orientation, and then close and save the report as **Guests**.

9. Set the option for compacting the **GEM** database on close. (*Note*: If you are working from a floppy disk, check with your instructor or technical support staff to confirm that you should set this option.)

Explore

10. Convert the **GEM** database to Access 2002–2003 file format, saving the converted file as **GEM2002** in the Brief\Case4 folder. Then convert the **GEM** database to Access 97 file format, saving the converted file as **GEM97** in the Brief\Case4 folder. Using Windows Explorer or My Computer, view the contents of your Brief\Case4 folder, and note the file sizes of the three versions of the GEM database. Describe the results.

11. Close the GEM database.

Internet Assignments

Research

Use the Internet to find and work with data related to the topics presented in this tutorial.

The purpose of the Internet Assignments is to challenge you to find information on the Internet that you can use to work effectively with this software. The actual assignments are updated and maintained on the Course Technology Web site. Log on to the Internet and use your Web browser to go to the Student Online Companion for New Perspectives Office 2003 at **www.course.com/np/office2003**. Click the Internet Assignments link, and then navigate to the assignments for this tutorial.

SAM Assessment and Training

Assess

If you have a SAM user profile, you may have access to hands-on instruction, practice, and assessment of the skills covered in this tutorial. Log in to your SAM account and go to your assignments page to see what your instructor has assigned.

Reinforce

Lab Assignments

The New Perspectives Labs are designed to help you master some of the key concepts and skills presented in this text. The steps for completing this Lab are located on the Course Technology Web site. Log on to the Internet and use your Web browser to go to the Student Online Companion for New Perspectives Office 2003 at **www.course.com/np/office2003**. Click the Lab Assignments link, and then navigate to the assignments for this tutorial.

Review

Quick Check Answers

Session 1.1

1. field
2. common field
3. primary key; foreign key
4. records; fields
5. current record symbol
6. Use the horizontal and vertical scroll bars to view fields or records not currently visible in the datasheet; use the navigation buttons to move vertically through the records.
7. Access saves changes to the active database to disk automatically, when a record is changed or added and when you close the database. You use the Save button in Access only to save changes to the design of an object, such as a table, or to the format of a datasheet—not to save the database file.

Session 1.2

1. query
2. primary key
3. AutoForm Wizard
4. The form displays each field name to the left of its field value, which appears in a box; the widths of the boxes represent the size of the fields.
5. Print Preview
6. Compacting

Objectives

Creating and Maintaining a Database

Creating the Northeast Database, and Creating, Modifying, and Updating the Position Table

Case

Northeast Seasonal Jobs International (NSJI)

The Seasonal database contains two tables—the Employer table and the NAICS table. These tables store data about NSJI's employer customers and the NAICS codes for pertinent job positions, respectively. Elsa Jensen also wants to track information about each position that is available at each employer's place of business. This information includes the position title and wage. Elsa asks you to create a third table, named Position, in which to store the position data.

Because this is your first time creating a new table, Elsa suggests that you first create a new database, named "Northeast," and then create the new Position table in this database. This will keep the Seasonal database intact. Once the Position table is completed, you then can import the Employer and NAICS tables from the Seasonal database into your new Northeast database.

Some of the position data Elsa needs is already stored in another NSJI database. After creating the Position table and adding some records to it, you'll copy the records from the other database into the Position table. Then you'll maintain the Position table by modifying it and updating it to meet Elsa's specific data requirements.

Student Data Files

▼ **Brief**

▽ **Tutorial folder**
NEJobs.mdb

▽ **Review folder**
Elsa.mdb

▽ **Case1 folder**
Events.mdb
Videos.mdb *(cont.)*

▽ **Case2 folder**
Fitness.mdb *(cont.)*
Products.mdb

▽ **Case3 folder**
Pledge.mdb
Redwood.mdb *(cont.)*

▽ **Case4 folder**
GEM.mdb *(cont.)*
Property.xls
Reserve.mdb

Guidelines for Designing Databases

A database management system can be a useful tool, but only if you first carefully design the database so that it meets the needs of its users. In database design, you determine the fields, tables, and relationships needed to satisfy the data and processing requirements. When you design a database, you should follow these guidelines:

- **Identify all the fields needed to produce the required information.** For example, Elsa needs information about employers, NAICS codes, and positions. Figure 2-1 shows the fields that satisfy these information requirements.

Figure 2-1	Elsa's data requirements

EmployerID	ContactFirstName
PositionID	ContactLastName
PositionTitle	Position
EmployerName	Wage
Address	HoursPerWeek
City	NAICSCode
StateProv	NAICSDesc
PostalCode	StartDate
Country	EndDate
Phone	ReferredBy
Openings	Website

- **Group related fields into tables.** For example, Elsa grouped the fields relating to employers into the Employer table and the fields related to NAICS codes into the NAICS table. The other fields are grouped logically into the Position table, which you will create, as shown in Figure 2-2.

Figure 2-2	Elsa's fields grouped into tables

Employer table	NAICS table	Position table
EmployerID	NAICSCode	PositionID
EmployerName	NAICSDesc	PositionTitle
Address		Wage
City		HoursPerWeek
StateProv		Openings
PostalCode		ReferredBy
Country		StartDate
ContactFirstName		EndDate
ContactLastName		
Position		
Phone		
Website		

- **Determine each table's primary key.** Recall that a primary key uniquely identifies each record in a table. Although a primary key is not mandatory in Access, it's usually a good idea to include one in each table. Without a primary key, selecting the exact record that you want can be a problem. For some tables, one of the fields, such as a Social Security or credit card number, naturally serves the function of a primary key. For other tables, two or more fields might be needed to function as the primary key. In these cases, the primary key is referred to as a **composite key.** For example, a school grade table would use a combination of student number and course code to serve as the primary key. For a third category of tables, no single field or combination of fields can uniquely identify a record in a table. In these cases, you need to add a field whose sole purpose is to serve as the table's primary key. For Elsa's tables, EmployerID is the primary key for the Employer table, NAICSCode is the primary key for the NAICS table, and PositionID will be the primary key for the Position table.

- **Include a common field in related tables.** You use the common field to connect one table logically with another table. For example, Elsa's Employer and Position tables will include the EmployerID field as a common field. Recall that when you include the primary key from one table as a field in a second table to form a relationship, the field is called a foreign key in the second table; therefore, the EmployerID field will be a foreign key in the Position table. With this common field, Elsa can find all positions available at a particular employer; she can use the EmployerID value for an employer and search the Position table for all records with that EmployerID value. Likewise, she can determine which employer has a particular position available by searching the Employer table to find the one record with the same EmployerID value as the corresponding value in the Position table.

- **Avoid data redundancy.** When you store the same data in more than one place, **data redundancy** occurs. With the exception of common fields to connect tables, you should avoid redundancy because it wastes storage space and can cause inconsistencies, if, for instance, you type a field value one way in one table and a different way in the same table or in a second table. Figure 2-3, which contains portions of potential data to be stored in the Employer and Position tables, shows an example of incorrect database design that has data redundancy in the Position table; the EmployerName field is redundant, and one value was entered incorrectly, in three different ways.

Incorrect database design with data redundancy | **Figure 2-3**

Employer table

Employer ID	Employer Name	Address	Phone
10122	BeanTown Tours	105 State Street, Boston, MA 02109	617-451-1970
10125	Boston Harbor Excursions	75 Atlantic Avenue, Boston, MA 02110	617-235-1800
10126	BaySide Inn & Country Club	354 Oceanside Drive, Brewster, MA 02631	508-283-5775
10190	The Briar Rose Inn	105 Queen Street, Charlottetown PE C1A 8R4	902-626-1595
10191	Windsor Alpine Tours	14 Longmeadow Road, Laconia, NH 03246	603-266-9233
10198	Trudel Spa & Resort	40 Rue Rivard, North Hatley QC J0B 2C0	819-842-7783

data redundancy

Position table

Position ID	Employer ID	Employer Name	Position Title	Hours/Week
2040	10126	DaySide Inn & Country Club	Waiter/Waitress	32
2045	10122	BeanTown Tours	Tour Guide	24
2053	10190	The Briar Rose Inn	Host/Hostess	24
2066	10198	Trudel Spa & Resort	Lifeguard	32
2073	10126	Baside Inn & Country Club	Pro Shop Clerk	24
2078	10191	Windsor Alpine Tours	Ski Patrol	30
2079	10191	Windsor Alpine Tours	Day Care	35
2082	10125	Boston Harbor Excursions	Reservationist	40
2111	10126	BaySide Inn Club	Kitchen Help	32

inconsistent data

- **Determine the properties of each field.** You need to identify the **properties**, or characteristics, of each field so that the DBMS knows how to store, display, and process the field values. These properties include the field's name, maximum number of characters or digits, description, valid values, and other field characteristics. You will learn more about field properties later in this tutorial.

The Position table you need to create will contain the fields shown in Figure 2-2, plus the EmployerID field as a foreign key. Before you create the new Northeast database and the Position table, you first need to learn some guidelines for setting field properties.

Guidelines for Setting Field Properties

As just noted, the last step of database design is to determine which values to assign to the properties, such as the name and data type, of each field. When you select or enter a value for a property, you **set** the property. Access has rules for naming fields, choosing data types, and setting other properties for fields.

Naming Fields and Objects

You must name each field, table, and other object in an Access database. Access then stores these items in the database, using the names you supply. It's best to choose a field or object name that describes the purpose or contents of the field or object, so that later you can easily remember what the name represents. For example, the three tables in the Northeast database will be named Employer, NAICS, and Position, because these names suggest their contents.

The following rules apply to naming fields and objects in Access:

- A name can be up to 64 characters long.
- A name can contain letters, numbers, spaces, and special characters, except for a period (.), exclamation mark (!), accent grave (`), and square brackets ([ ]).
- A name cannot start with a space.
- A table or query name must be unique within a database. A field name must be unique within a table, but it can be used again in another table.

In addition, experienced users of databases follow these conventions for naming fields and objects:

- Capitalize the first letter of each word in the name.
- Avoid extremely long names because they are difficult to remember and reference.
- Use standard abbreviations, such as Num for Number, Amt for Amount, and Qty for Quantity.
- Avoid using spaces or special characters in names. According to standard database naming conventions, spaces and special characters should not be included in names. However, you can change how a field name is displayed in database objects—tables, forms, reports, and so on—by setting the field's Caption property. (You'll learn about setting the Caption property later in this tutorial.)

Assigning Field Data Types

You must assign a data type for each field. The **data type** determines what field values you can enter for the field and what other properties the field will have. For example, the Position table will include a StartDate field, which will store date values, so you will assign the date/time data type to this field. Then Access will allow you to enter and manipulate only dates or times as values in the StartDate field.

Figure 2-4 lists the 10 data types available in Access, describes the field values allowed for each data type, explains when you should use each data type, and indicates the field size of each data type.

Data types for fields | **Figure 2-4**

Data Type	Description	Field Size
Text	Allows field values containing letters, digits, spaces, and special characters. Use for names, addresses, descriptions, and fields containing digits that are not used in calculations.	0 to 255 characters; 50 characters default
Memo	Allows field values containing letters, digits, spaces, and special characters. Use for long comments and explanations.	1 to 65,535 characters; exact size is determined by entry
Number	Allows positive and negative numbers as field values. Numbers can contain digits, a decimal point, commas, a plus sign, and a minus sign. Use for fields that you will use in calculations, except calculations involving money.	1 to 15 digits
Date/Time	Allows field values containing valid dates and times from January 1, 100 to December 31, 9999. Dates can be entered in mm/dd/yy (month, day, year) format, several other date formats, or a variety of time formats, such as 10:35 PM. You can perform calculations on dates and times, and you can sort them. For example, you can determine the number of days between two dates.	8 bytes
Currency	Allows field values similar to those for the number data type. Unlike calculations with number data type decimal values, calculations performed using the currency data type are not subject to round-off error.	Accurate to 15 digits on the left side of the decimal separator and to 4 digits on the right side
AutoNumber	Consists of integers with values controlled by Access. Access automatically inserts a value in the field as each new record is created. You can specify sequential numbering or random numbering, which guarantees a unique field value, so that such a field can serve as a table's primary key.	9 digits
Yes/No	Limits field values to yes and no, on and off, or true and false. Use for fields that indicate the presence or absence of a condition, such as whether an order has been filled or whether an employee is eligible for the company dental plan.	1 character
OLE Object	Allows field values that are created in other programs as objects, such as photographs, video images, graphics, drawings, sound recordings, voice-mail messages, spreadsheets, and word-processing documents. These objects can be linked or embedded.	1 gigabyte maximum; exact size depends on object size
Hyperlink	Consists of text used as a hyperlink address. A hyperlink address can have up to three parts: the text that appears in a field or control; the path to a file or page; and a location within the file or page. Hyperlinks help you to connect your application easily to the Internet or an intranet.	Up to 64,000 characters total for the three parts of a hyperlink data type
Lookup Wizard	Creates a field that lets you look up a value in another table or in a predefined list of values.	Same size as the primary key field used to perform the lookup

Setting Field Sizes

The **Field Size property** defines a field value's maximum storage size for text, number, and AutoNumber fields only. The other data types have no Field Size property because their storage size is either a fixed, predetermined amount or is determined automatically by the field value itself, as shown in Figure 2-4. A text field has a default field size of 50 characters; you can also set its field size by entering a number from 0 to 255. For example, the PositionTitle and ReferredBy fields in the Position table will be text fields with a size of 30 characters each. This field size will accommodate the values that will be entered in each of these fields (titles and names, respectively).

When you use the number data type to define a field, you should set the field's Field Size property based on the largest value that you expect to store in that field. Access processes smaller data sizes faster, using less memory, so you can optimize your database's performance and its storage space by selecting the correct field size for each field. For example, it would be wasteful to use the Long Integer setting when defining a field that will store only whole numbers ranging from 0 to 255, because the Long Integer setting will use four bytes of storage space. A better choice would be the Byte setting, which uses one byte of storage space to store the same values. Field Size property settings for number fields are as follows:

- **Byte:** Stores whole numbers (numbers with no fractions) from 0 to 255 in one byte
- **Integer:** Stores whole numbers from −32,768 to 32,767 in two bytes
- **Long Integer** (default): Stores whole numbers from −2,147,483,648 to 2,147,483,647 in four bytes
- **Single:** Stores positive and negative numbers to precisely seven decimal places and uses four bytes
- **Double:** Stores positive and negative numbers to precisely 15 decimal places and uses eight bytes
- **Replication ID:** Establishes a unique identifier for replication of tables, records, and other objects and uses 16 bytes
- **Decimal:** Stores positive and negative numbers to precisely 28 decimal places and uses 12 bytes

Setting Field Captions

The **Caption property** specifies how a field name will appear in datasheets and in other database objects, such as forms and reports. If you don't specify a caption, Access uses the field name as the default column heading in datasheets and as the default label in forms and reports. Because field names should not include spaces, some names might be difficult to read. For example, the Position table will include a field named "HoursPerWeek." This name looks awkward and might be confusing to users of the database. By setting the Caption property for this field to "Hours/Week," you can improve the readability of the field name displayed.

Elsa documented the design for the new Position table by listing each field's name, data type, size (if applicable), caption (if applicable), and description, as shown in Figure 2-5. Note that Elsa assigned the text data type to the PositionID, PositionTitle, EmployerID, and ReferredBy fields; the currency data type to the Wage field; the number data type to the HoursPerWeek and Openings fields; and the date/time data type to the StartDate and EndDate fields.

Figure 2-5	Design for the Position table

Field Name	Data Type	Field Size	Caption	Description
PositionID	Text	4	Position ID	Primary key
PositionTitle	Text	30	Position Title	
EmployerID	Text	5	Employer ID	Foreign key
Wage	Currency			Rate per hour
HoursPerWeek	Number	Integer	Hours/Week	Work hours per week
Openings	Number	Integer		Number of openings
ReferredBy	Text	30	Referred By	
StartDate	Date/Time		Start Date	Month/day/year
EndDate	Date/Time		End Date	Month/day/year

With Elsa's design in place, you're ready to create the new Northeast database and the Position table.

Creating a New Database

Access provides different ways for you to create a new database: you can use a Database Wizard, create a blank database, copy an existing database file, or use one of the database templates available on the Microsoft Web site. When you use a **Database Wizard**, the wizard guides you through the database creation process and provides the necessary tables, forms, and reports for the type of database you choose—all in one operation. Using a Database Wizard is an easy way to start creating a database, but only if your data requirements closely match one of the supplied templates. When you choose to create a blank database, you need to add all the tables, forms, reports, and other objects after you create the database file. Creating a blank database provides the most flexibility, allowing you to define objects in the way that you want, but it does require that you define each object separately. Whichever method you choose, you can always modify or add to your database after you create it.

The following steps outline the process for creating a new database using a Database Wizard:

1. If necessary, click the New button on the Database toolbar to display the New File task pane.
2. In the Templates section of the task pane, click the "On my computer" option. The Templates dialog box opens.
3. Click the Databases tab, and then choose the Database Wizard that most closely matches the type of database you want to create. Click the OK button.
4. In the File New Database dialog box, choose the location in which to save the new database, specify its name, and then click the Create button.
5. Complete each of the wizard dialog boxes, clicking the Next button to move through them after making your selections.
6. Click the Finish button when you have completed all the wizard dialog boxes.

None of the Database Wizards matches the requirements of the new Northeast database, so you'll use the Blank Database option to create it.

To create the Northeast database:

1. Start Access, and make sure your Data Files are in the proper location.
2. In the Open section of the Getting Started task pane, click **Create a new file**. The New File task pane is displayed.
3. Click **Blank database**. The File New Database dialog box opens. This dialog box is similar to the Open dialog box.
4. Click the **Save in** list arrow, and then click the drive that contains your Data Files.
5. Navigate to the **Brief\Tutorial** folder, and then click the **Open** button.
6. In the File name text box, double-click the text **db1** to select it, and then type **Northeast**.

   Trouble? If your File name text box contains an entry other than "db1," select whatever text is in this text box, and continue with the steps.
7. Click the **Create** button. Access creates the Northeast database in the Brief\Tutorial folder included with your Data Files, and then displays the Database window for the new database with the Tables object selected.

Now you can create the Position table in the Northeast database.

Creating a Table

Creating a table involves naming the fields and defining the properties for the fields, specifying a primary key for the table, and then saving the table structure. You will use Elsa's design (Figure 2-5) as a guide for creating the Position table in the Northeast database.

To begin creating the Position table:

► 1. Click the **New** button in the Database window. The New Table dialog box opens. See Figure 2-6.

Figure 2-6	New Table dialog box

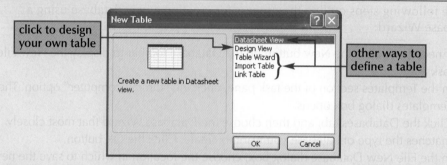

Trouble? If the New File task pane opens, you clicked the New button [ ] on the Database toolbar instead of the New button in the Database window. Click the Close button to close the task pane, and then repeat Step 1.

In Access, you can create a table from entered data (Datasheet View), define your own table (Design View), use a wizard to automate the table creation process (Table Wizard), or use a wizard to import or link data from another database or other data source (Import Table or Link Table). For the Position table, you will define your own table.

► 2. Click **Design View** in the list box, and then click the **OK** button. The Table window opens in Design view. (Note that you can also double-click the "Create table in Design view" option in the Database window to open the Table window in Design view.) See Figure 2-7.

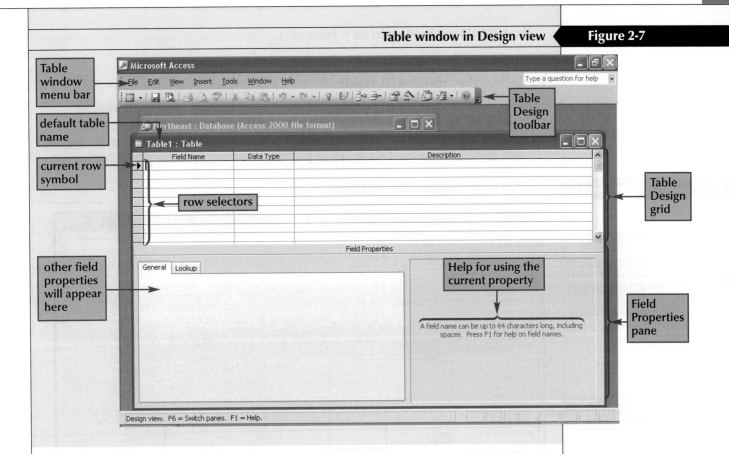

You use **Design view** to define or modify a table structure or the properties of the fields in a table. If you create a table without using a wizard, you enter the fields and their properties for your table directly in the Table window in Design view.

Defining Fields

Initially, the default table name, Table1, appears on the Table window title bar, the current row symbol is positioned in the first row selector of the Table Design grid, and the insertion point is located in the first row's Field Name text box. The purpose or characteristics of the current property (Field Name, in this case) appear in the right side of the Field Properties pane. You can display more complete Help information about the current property by pressing the **F1 key**.

You enter values for the Field Name, Data Type, and Description field properties in the Table Design grid. You select values for all other field properties, most of which are optional, in the Field Properties pane. These other properties will appear when you move to the first row's Data Type text box.

Defining a Field in a Table

Reference Window

- In the Database window, select the table, and then click the Design button to open the Table window in Design view.
- Type the field name.
- Select the data type.
- Type or select other field properties, as appropriate.

The first field you need to define is PositionID.

To define the PositionID field:

▶ 1. Type **PositionID** in the first row's Field Name text box, and then press the **Tab** key (or press the **Enter** key) to advance to the Data Type text box. The default data type, Text, appears highlighted in the Data Type text box, which now also contains a list arrow, and field properties for a text field appear in the Field Properties pane. See Figure 2-8.

| **Figure 2-8** | **Table window after entering the first field name** |

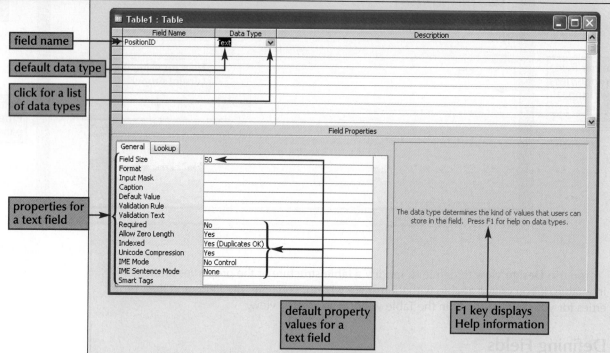

field name

default data type

click for a list of data types

properties for a text field

default property values for a text field

F1 key displays Help information

Notice that the right side of the Field Properties pane now provides an explanation for the current property, Data Type. You can display Help information about the current property by pressing the F1 key.

Trouble? If you make a typing error, you can correct it by clicking to position the insertion point, and then using either the Backspace key to delete characters to the left of the insertion point or the Delete key to delete characters to the right of the insertion point. Then type the correct text.

Because the PositionID numbers will not be used in calculations, you will assign the text data type (as opposed to the number data type) to the PositionID field.

▶ 2. Press the **Tab** key to accept Text as the data type and to advance to the Description text box.

Next you'll enter the Description property value as "Primary key." You can use the **Description property** to enter an optional description for a field to explain its purpose or usage. A field's Description property can be up to 255 characters long, and its value appears on the status bar when you view the table datasheet. Note that specifying "Primary key" for the Description property does *not* establish the current field as the primary key; you use a toolbar button to specify the primary key, which you will do later in this session.

3. Type **Primary key** in the Description text box.

Notice the Field Size property for the text field. The default setting of "50" is displayed. You need to change this number to "4" because all PositionID values at NSJI contain only 4 digits.

4. Double-click the number **50** in the Field Size property box to select it, and then type **4**.

By default, the Caption property for a field is blank. You need to set this property for the PositionID field to display "Position ID" as the column or label name in tables, forms, reports, and so on. (Refer to the Access Help system for a complete description of all the properties available for the different data types.)

5. Click to position the insertion point in the Caption property box, and then type **Position ID**. The definition of the first field is completed. See Figure 2-9.

PositionID field defined **Figure 2-9**

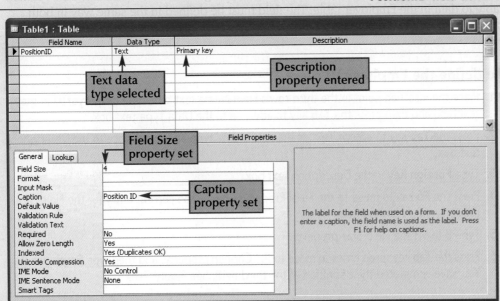

Elsa's Position table design shows PositionTitle as the second field. You will define PositionTitle as a text field with a Field Size of 30, which is a sufficient length for any title values that will be entered. You'll also set the Caption property for this field.

To define the PositionTitle field:

1. In the Table Design grid, place the insertion point in the second row's Field Name text box, type **PositionTitle** in the text box, and then press the **Tab** key to advance to the Data Type text box.

2. Press the **Tab** key to accept Text as the field's data type.

According to Elsa's design (Figure 2-5), you do not need to enter a description for this field. If you've assigned a descriptive field name and the field does not fulfill a special function (such as primary key), you usually do not enter a value for the optional Description property. PositionTitle is a field that does not require a value for its Description property.

Next, you'll change the Field Size property to 30. Note that when defining the fields in a table, you can move between the Table Design grid and the Field Properties pane of the Table window by pressing the **F6 key**.

3. Press the **F6** key to move to the Field Properties pane. The current entry for the Field Size property, 50, is highlighted.

4. Type **30** to set the Field Size property.

   Finally, you need to set the Caption property for the field. In addition to clicking to position the insertion point in a property's box, you can press the Tab key to move from one property to the next.

5. Press the **Tab** key three times to move to the Caption property, and then type **Position Title**. You have completed the definition of the second field.

The third field in the Position table is the EmployerID field. Recall that this field will serve as the foreign key in the Position table, allowing you to relate data from the Position table to data in the Employer table. The field must be defined in the same way in both tables—that is, a text field with a field size of 5.

To define the EmployerID field:

1. Place the insertion point in the third row's Field Name text box, type **EmployerID** in the text box, and then press the **Tab** key to advance to the Data Type text box.

2. Press the **Tab** key to accept Text as the field's data type and to advance to the Description text box.

3. Type **Foreign key** in the Description text box.

4. Press the **F6** key to move to the Field Properties pane. The current entry for the Field Size property, 50, is highlighted.

5. Type **5** to set the Field Size property.

6. Press the **Tab** key three times to move to the Caption property, and then type **Employer ID**. You have completed the definition of the third field. See Figure 2-10.

Figure 2-10	Table window after defining the first three fields

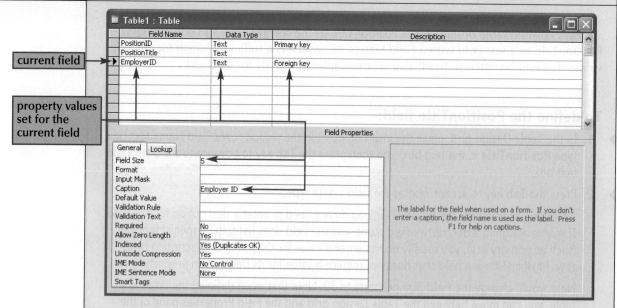

The fourth field is the Wage field, which will display values in the currency format.

To define the Wage field:

1. Place the insertion point in the fourth row's Field Name text box, type **Wage** in the text box, and then press the **Tab** key to advance to the Data Type text box.

2. Click the **Data Type** list arrow, click **Currency** in the list box, and then press the **Tab** key to advance to the Description text box.

3. Type **Rate per hour** in the Description text box.

   Elsa wants the Wage field values to be displayed with two decimal places, and she does not want any value to be displayed by default for new records. So, you need to set the Decimal Places and Default Value properties accordingly. The **Decimal Places property** specifies the number of decimal places that will be displayed to the right of the decimal point.

4. Click the **Decimal Places** text box to position the insertion point there. A list arrow appears on the right side of the Decimal Places text box.

   When you position the insertion point or select text in many Access text boxes, Access displays a list arrow, which you can click to display a list box with options. You can display the list arrow and the list box simultaneously if you click the text box near its right side.

5. Click the **Decimal Places** list arrow, and then click **2** in the list box to specify two decimal places for the Wage field values.

   Next, notice the **Default Value property**, which specifies the value that will be automatically entered into the field when you add a new record. Currently this property has a setting of 0. Elsa wants the Wage field to be empty (that is, to contain *no* default value) when a new record is added. Therefore, you need to delete the 0 so that Access, by default, will display no value in the Wage field for a new record.

6. Select **0** in the Default Value text box either by dragging the pointer or double-clicking the mouse, and then press the **Delete** key.

The next two fields in the Position table—HoursPerWeek and Openings—are number fields with a field size of Integer. Also, for each of these fields, Elsa wants the values displayed with no decimal places, and she does not want a default value displayed for the fields when new records are added. You'll define these two fields next.

To define the HoursPerWeek and Openings fields:

1. Position the insertion point in the fifth row's Field Name text box, type **HoursPerWeek** in the text box, and then press the **Tab** key to advance to the Data Type text box.

2. Click the **Data Type** list arrow, click **Number** in the list box, and then press the **Tab** key to advance to the Description text box.

3. Type **Work hours per week** in the Description text box.

4. Click the right side of the **Field Size** text box, and then click **Integer** to choose this setting. Recall that the Integer field size stores whole numbers in two bytes.

5. Click the right side of the **Decimal Places** text box, and then click **0** to specify no decimal places.

6. Move to the Caption property, and then type **Hours/Week**.

7. Select the value **0** in the Default Value text box, and then press the **Delete** key.

8. Repeat the preceding steps to define the **Openings** field as the sixth field in the Position table. For the Description, enter the text **Number of openings**. You do not have to set the Caption property for the Openings field.

According to Elsa's design (Figure 2-5), the final three fields to be defined in the Position table are ReferredBy, a text field, and StartDate and EndDate, both date/time fields. You'll define these three fields next.

To define the ReferredBy, StartDate, and EndDate fields:

▶ 1. Position the insertion point in the seventh row's Field Name text box, type **ReferredBy** in the text box, press the **Tab** key to advance to the Data Type text box, and then press the **Tab** key again to accept the default Text data type.

▶ 2. Change the default Field Size of 50 to **30** for the ReferredBy field.

▶ 3. Set the Caption property for the field to **Referred By**.

▶ 4. Position the insertion point in the eighth row's Field Name text box, type **StartDate**, and then press the **Tab** key to advance to the Data Type text box.

▶ 5. Click the **Data Type** list arrow, click **Date/Time** to select this type, press the **Tab** key, and then type **Month/day/year** in the Description text box.

Elsa wants the values in the StartDate field to be displayed in a format showing the month, the day, and a four-digit year, as in the following example: 03/11/2006. You use the Format property to control the display of a field value.

▶ 6. In the Field Properties pane, click the right side of the **Format** text box to display the list of predefined formats. As noted in the right side of the Field Properties pane, you can either choose a predefined format or enter a custom format.

Trouble? If you see a list arrow instead of a list of predefined formats, click the list arrow to display the list.

None of the predefined formats matches the exact layout Elsa wants for the StartDate values. Therefore, you need to create a custom date format. Figure 2-11 shows some of the symbols available for custom date and time formats. (A complete description of all the custom formats is available in Help.)

Figure 2-11	Symbols for some custom date formats

Symbol	Description
/	date separator
d	day of the month in one or two numeric digits, as needed (1 to 31)
dd	day of the month in two numeric digits (01 to 31)
ddd	first three letters of the weekday (Sun to Sat)
dddd	full name of the weekday (Sunday to Saturday)
w	day of the week (1 to 7)
ww	week of the year (1 to 53)
m	month of the year in one or two numeric digits, as needed (1 to 12)
mm	month of the year in two numeric digits (01 to 12)
mmm	first three letters of the month (Jan to Dec)
mmmm	full name of the month (January to December)
yy	last two digits of the year (01 to 99)
yyyy	full year (0100 to 9999)

Elsa wants the dates to be displayed with a two-digit month (mm), a two-digit day (dd), and a four-digit year (yyyy). You'll enter this custom format now.

7. Click the **Format** list arrow to close the list of predefined formats, and then type **mm/dd/yyyy**. See Figure 2-12.

Specifying the custom date format Figure 2-12

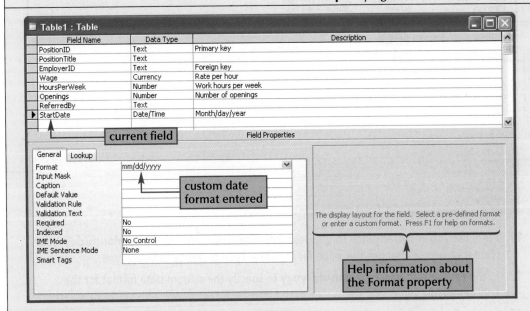

8. Set the Caption property for the field to **Start Date**.

   Next, you'll define the ninth and final field, EndDate. This field will have the same definition and properties as the StartDate field.

9. Place the insertion point in the ninth row's Field Name text box, type **EndDate**, and then press the **Tab** key to advance to the Data Type text box.

   You can select a value from the Data Type list box as you did for the StartDate field. Alternately, you can type the property value in the text box or type just the first character of the property value.

10. Type **d**. The value in the ninth row's Data Type text box changes to "date/Time," with the letters "ate/Time" highlighted. See Figure 2-13.

Figure 2-13 **Selecting a value for the Data Type property**

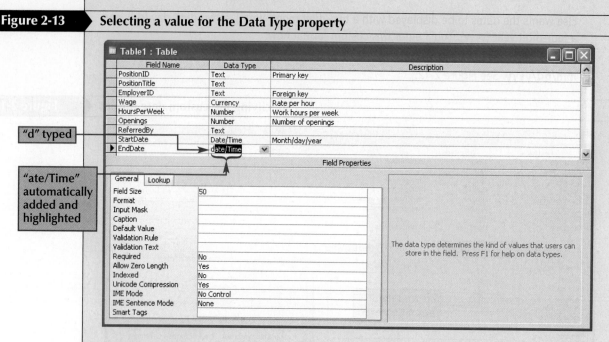

"d" typed

"ate/Time"
automatically
added and
highlighted

▶ **11.** Press the **Tab** key to advance to the Description text box, and then type **Month/day/year**.
Note that Access changes the value for the Data Type property to Date/Time.

▶ **12.** In the Format text box, type **mm/dd/yyyy** to specify the custom date format for the
EndDate field.

▶ **13.** Set the Caption property for the field to **End Date**.

You've finished defining the fields for the Position table. Next, you need to specify the
primary key for the table.

Specifying the Primary Key

Although Access does not require a table to have a primary key, including a primary key
offers several advantages:

- A primary key uniquely identifies each record in a table.
- Access does not allow duplicate values in the primary key field. If a record already
  exists with a PositionID value of 1320, for example, Access prevents you from adding
  another record with this same value in the PositionID field. Preventing duplicate values
  ensures the uniqueness of the primary key field.
- When a primary key has been specified, Access forces you to enter a value for the primary key field in every record in the table. This is known as **entity integrity**. If you do
  not enter a value for a field, you have actually given the field what is known as a **null
  value**. You cannot give a null value to the primary key field because entity integrity prevents Access from accepting and processing that record.
- Access stores records on disk in the same order as you enter them but displays them in
  order by the field values of the primary key. If you enter records in no specific order,
  you are ensured that you will later be able to work with them in a more meaningful, primary key sequence.
- Access responds faster to your requests for specific records based on the primary key.

Specifying a Primary Key for a Table

- In the Table window in Design view, click the row selector for the field you've chosen to be the primary key.
- If the primary key will consist of two or more fields, press and hold down the Ctrl key, and then click the row selector for each additional primary key field.
- Click the Primary Key button on the Table Design toolbar.

According to Elsa's design, you need to specify PositionID as the primary key for the Position table.

To specify PositionID as the primary key:

1. Position the pointer on the row selector for the PositionID field until the pointer changes to a ➡ shape. See Figure 2-14.

Specifying PositionID as the primary key ◀ **Figure 2-14**

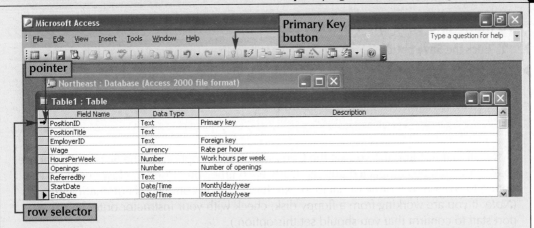

2. Click the mouse button. The entire first row of the Table Design grid is highlighted.
3. Click the **Primary Key** button 🔑 on the Table Design toolbar, and then click a row other than the first to deselect the first row. A key symbol appears in the row selector for the first row, indicating that the PositionID field is the table's primary key. See Figure 2-15.

PositionID selected as the primary key ◀ **Figure 2-15**

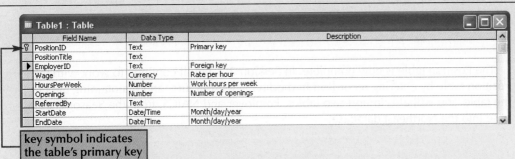

If you specify the wrong field as the primary key, or if you later change your mind and do not want the designated primary key field to be the table's primary key, you can select the field and then click the Primary Key button on the Table Design toolbar again, which will remove the key symbol and the primary key designation from the field. Then you can choose another field to be the primary key, if necessary.

You've defined the fields for the Position table and specified its primary key, so you can now save the table structure.

Saving the Table Structure

The last step in creating a table is to name the table and save the table's structure on disk. Once the table is saved, you can use it to enter data in the table.

Reference Window

Saving a Table Structure

- Click the Save button on the Table Design toolbar.
- Type the name of the table in the Table Name text box of the Save As dialog box.
- Click the OK button (or press the Enter key).

According to Elsa's plan, you need to save the table you've defined as "Position."

To name and save the Position table:

▶ 1. Click the **Save** button 🔲 on the Table Design toolbar. The Save As dialog box opens.

▶ 2. Type **Position** in the Table Name text box, and then press the **Enter** key. Access saves the table with the name Position in the Northeast database. Notice that Position now appears instead of Table1 in the Table window title bar.

Recall that in Tutorial 1 you set the Compact on Close option for the Seasonal database so that it would be compacted automatically each time you closed it. Now you'll set this option for your new Northeast database, so that it will be compacted automatically. (*Note*: If you are working from a floppy disk, check with your instructor or technical support staff to confirm that you should set this option.)

To set the option for compacting the Northeast database automatically:

▶ 1. Click **Tools** on the menu bar, and then click **Options**. The Options dialog box opens.

▶ 2. Click the **General** tab in the dialog box, and then click the **Compact on Close** check box to select it.

▶ 3. Click the **OK** button to set the option.

The Position table is now complete. In Session 2.2, you'll continue to work with the Position table by entering records in it, modifying its structure, and maintaining data in the table. You will also import two tables, Employer and NAICS, from the Seasonal database into the Northeast database.

Session 2.1 Quick Check

1. What guidelines should you follow when designing a database?
2. What is the purpose of the Data Type property for a field?
3. For which three types of fields can you assign a field size?
4. You use the _____ property to specify how a field name appears in datasheets, forms, and reports.
5. In Design view, which key do you press to move between the Table Design grid and the Field Properties pane?
6. A(n) _____ value, which results when you do not enter a value for a field, is not permitted for a primary key.

Session 2.2

Adding Records to a Table

You can add records to an Access table in several ways. A table datasheet provides a simple way for you to add records. As you learned in Tutorial 1, a datasheet shows a table's contents in rows and columns. Each row is a separate record in the table, and each column contains the field values for one field in the table. If you are currently working in Design view, you first must change from Design view to Datasheet view in order to view the table's datasheet.

Elsa asks you to add the two records shown in Figure 2-16 to the Position table. These two records contain data for positions that have recently become available at two employers.

Records to be added to the Position table ◄ **Figure 2-16**

PositionID	PositionTitle	EmployerID	Wage	HoursPerWeek	Openings	ReferredBy	StartDate	EndDate
2021	Waiter/Waitress	10155	9.50	30	1	Sue Brown	6/30/2006	9/15/2006
2017	Tour Guide	10149	15.00	20	1	Ed Curran	9/21/2006	11/1/2006

To add the records in the Position table datasheet:

1. If you took a break after the previous session, make sure that Access is running and that the Position table of the Northeast database is open in Design view. To open the table in Design view from the Database window, right-click the **Position** table, and then click **Design View** on the shortcut menu.

   Access displays the fields you defined for the Position table in Design view. Now you need to switch to Datasheet view so that you can enter the two records for Elsa.

2. Click the **View** button for Datasheet view 🔳 on the Table Design toolbar. The Table window opens in Datasheet view. See Figure 2-17.

Figure 2-17 ▶ Table window in Datasheet view

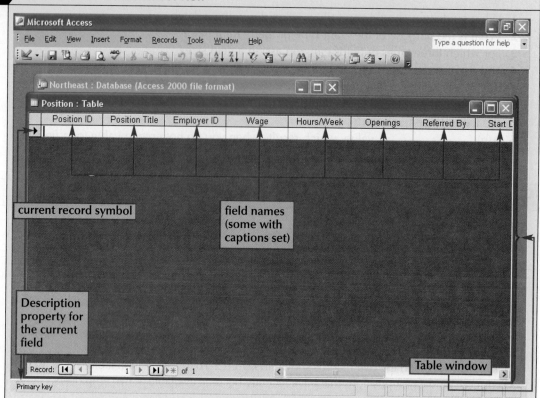

The table's nine fields appear at the top of the datasheet, with captions displayed for those fields whose Caption property you set. Some of the field names might not be visible, depending on the size of your monitor. The current record symbol in the first row's record selector identifies the currently selected record, which contains no data until you enter the first record. The insertion point is located in the first row's PositionID field, whose Description property appears on the status bar.

▶ 3. Type **2021**, which is the first record's PositionID field value, and then press the **Tab** key. Each time you press the Tab key, the insertion point moves to the right to the next field in the record. See Figure 2-18.

Datasheet for Position table after entering the first field value   Figure 2-18

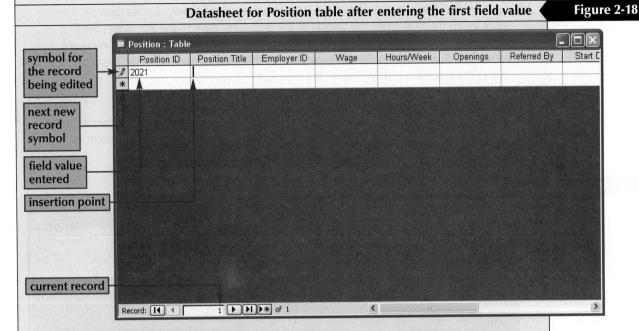

symbol for the record being edited

next new record symbol

field value entered

insertion point

current record

Trouble? If you make a mistake when typing a value, use the Backspace key to delete characters to the left of the insertion point or the Delete key to delete characters to the right of the insertion point. Then type the correct value. If you want to correct a value by replacing it entirely, drag to select the value, and then type the correct value.

The **pencil symbol** in the first row's record selector indicates that the record is being edited. The **star symbol** in the second row's record selector identifies the second row as the next one available for a new record. Notice that all the fields are initially empty; this occurs because you set the Default Value property for the fields (as appropriate) to remove any values and leave them blank.

4. Type **Waiter/Waitress** in the PositionTitle field, and then press the **Tab** key. The insertion point moves to the EmployerID field.

5. Type **10155** and then press the **Tab** key. The insertion point moves to the right side of the Wage field.

   Recall that the PositionID, PositionTitle, and EmployerID fields are all text fields and that the Wage field is a currency field. Field values for text fields are left-aligned in their boxes, and field values for number, date/time, and currency fields are right-aligned in their boxes.

6. Type **9.5** and then press the **Tab** key. Access displays the field value with a dollar sign and two decimal places ($9.50), as specified by the currency format. You do not need to type the dollar sign, commas, or decimal point (for whole dollar amounts) because Access adds these symbols automatically for you.

7. In the HoursPerWeek field, type **30**, press the **Tab** key, type **1** in the Openings field, and then press the **Tab** key.

8. Type **Sue Brown** in the ReferredBy field, and then press the **Tab** key. Depending on your monitor's resolution and size, the display of the datasheet might shift so that the next field, StartDate, is completely visible.

9. Type **6/30/2006** in the StartDate field, and then press the **Tab** key. Access displays the value as 06/30/2006, as specified by the custom date format (mm/dd/yyyy) you set for this field. The insertion point moves to the final field in the table, EndDate.

10. Type **9/15/2006** in the EndDate field, and then press the **Tab** key. Access displays the value as 09/15/2006, shifts the display of the datasheet back to the left, stores the first completed record in the Position table, removes the pencil symbol from the first row's record selector, advances the insertion point to the second row's PositionID text box, and places the current record symbol in the second row's record selector.

Now you can enter the values for the second record.

11. Refer back to Figure 2-16, and repeat Steps 3 through 10 to add the second record to the table. Access saves the record in the Position table, and moves the insertion point to the beginning of the third row. See Figure 2-19.

| Figure 2-19 | Position table datasheet after entering the second record |

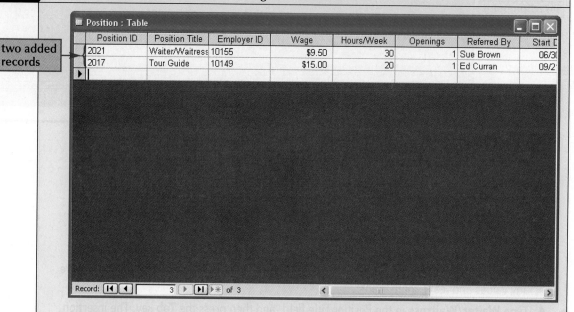

two added records

Notice that "Record 3 of 3" appears around the navigation buttons, even though the table contains only two records. Access is anticipating that you will enter a new record, which would be the third of three records in the table. If you moved the insertion point to the second record, the display would change to "Record 2 of 2."

Notice that the two records are currently listed in the order in which you entered them. However, once you close the table or change to another view, and then redisplay the table datasheet, the records will be listed in primary key order by the values in the PositionID field.

Modifying the Structure of an Access Table

Even a well-designed table might need to be modified. For example, the government at all levels and competitors place demands on a company to track more data and to modify the data it already tracks. Access allows you to modify a table's structure in Design view: you can add and delete fields, change the order of fields, and change the properties of the fields.

After holding a meeting with her staff members and reviewing the structure of the Position table and the format of the field values in the datasheet, Elsa has several changes she wants you to make to the table. First, she has decided that it's not necessary to keep track of the name of the person who originally requested a particular position, so she wants you to delete the ReferredBy field. Next, she wants the Openings field moved to the end of the table. She also wants you to add a new yes/no field, named Experience, to the table to indicate whether the available position requires that potential recruits have prior experience in that type of work. The Experience field will be inserted between the HoursPerWeek and StartDate fields. Finally, she thinks that the Wage field should remain a currency field, but she wants the dollar signs removed from the displayed field values in the datasheet so the values are easier to read. Figure 2-20 shows Elsa's modified design for the Position table.

Modified design for the Position table　　◄　**Figure 2-20**

Field Name	Data Type	Field Size	Caption	Description
PositionID	Text	4	Position ID	Primary key
PositionTitle	Text	30	Position Title	
EmployerID	Text	5	Employer ID	Foreign key
Wage	Currency			Rate per hour
HoursPerWeek	Number	Integer	Hours/Week	Work hours per week
Experience	Yes/No			Experience required
StartDate	Date/Time		Start Date	Month/day/year
EndDate	Date/Time		End Date	Month/day/year
Openings	Number	Integer		Number of openings

You'll begin modifying the table by deleting the ReferredBy field.

Deleting a Field

After you've defined a table structure and added records to the table, you can delete a field from the table structure. When you delete a field, you also delete all the values for the field from the table. Therefore, before you delete a field you should make sure that you want to do so—and that you choose the correct field to delete.

Deleting a Field from a Table Structure
Reference Window

- In the Table window in Design view, right-click the row selector for the field you want to delete, both to select the field and to display the shortcut menu.
- Click Delete Rows on the shortcut menu.

You need to delete the ReferredBy field from the Position table structure.

To delete the ReferredBy field:

1. Click the **View** button for Design view 🖊 on the Table Datasheet toolbar. The Table window for the Position table opens in Design view.

2. Position the pointer on the row selector for the ReferredBy field until the pointer changes to a ➡ shape.

3. Right-click to select the entire row for the ReferredBy field and display the shortcut menu, and then click **Delete Rows**.

   A dialog box opens asking you to confirm the deletion.

4. Click the **Yes** button to close the dialog box and to delete the field and its values from the table. See Figure 2-21.

Figure 2-21 **Table structure after deleting ReferredBy field**

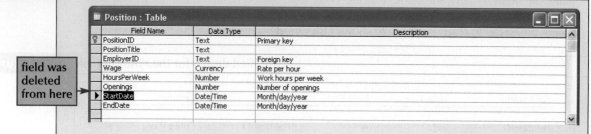

field was deleted from here

You have deleted the ReferredBy field in the Table window, but the change doesn't take place in the table on disk until you save the table structure. Because you have other modifications to make to the table, you'll wait until you finish them all before saving the modified table structure to disk.

Moving a Field

To move a field, you use the mouse to drag it to a new location in the Table window in Design view. Your next modification to the Position table structure is to move the Openings field to the end of the table, as Elsa requested.

To move the Openings field:

1. Click the **row selector** for the Openings field to select the entire row.

2. If necessary, scroll the Table Design grid so that you can see both the selected Openings field and the empty row below the EndDate field at the same time.

3. Place the pointer in the row selector for the Openings field, click the ⬚ pointer, and then drag the ⬚ pointer to the row selector below the EndDate row selector. See Figure 2-22.

Figure 2-22 **Moving a field in the table structure**

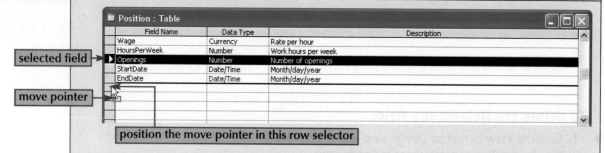

selected field

move pointer

position the move pointer in this row selector

4. Release the mouse button. Access moves the Openings field below the EndDate field in the table structure.

Trouble? If the Openings field did not move, repeat Steps 1 through 3, making sure you firmly hold down the mouse button during the drag operation.

Adding a Field

Next, you need to add the Experience field to the table structure between the HoursPerWeek and StartDate fields. To add a new field between existing fields, you must insert a row. You begin by selecting the field that will be below the new field you want to insert.

Reference Window

Adding a Field Between Two Existing Fields

- In the Table window in Design view, right-click the row selector for the row above which you want to add a new field, to select the field and display the shortcut menu.
- Click Insert Rows on the shortcut menu.
- Define the new field by entering the field name, data type, description (optional), and any property specifications.

To add the Experience field to the Position table:

1. Right-click the **row selector** for the StartDate field to select this field and display the short-cut menu, and then click **Insert Rows**. Access adds a new, blank row between the HoursPerWeek and StartDate fields. See Figure 2-23.

After inserting a row in the table structure | **Figure 2-23**

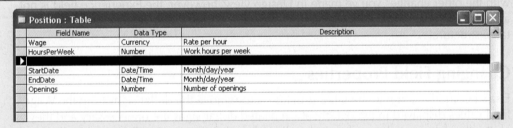

You'll define the Experience field in the new row of the Position table. Access will add this new field to the Position table structure between the HoursPerWeek and StartDate fields.

2. Click the **Field Name** text box for the new row, type **Experience**, and then press the **Tab** key.

   The Experience field will be a yes/no field that will specify whether prior work experience is required for the position.

3. Type **y**. Access completes the data type as "yes/No."

4. Press the **Tab** key to select the yes/no data type and to move to the Description text box.

   Notice that Access changes the value in the Data Type text box from "yes/No" to "Yes/No."

5. Type **Experience required** in the Description text box.

   Elsa wants the Experience field to have a Default Value property value of "No," so you need to set this property.

6. In the Field Properties pane, click the **Default Value** text box, type **no**, and then press the **Tab** key. Notice that Access changes the Default Value property value from "no" to "No." See Figure 2-24.

Figure 2-24   **Experience field added to the Position table**

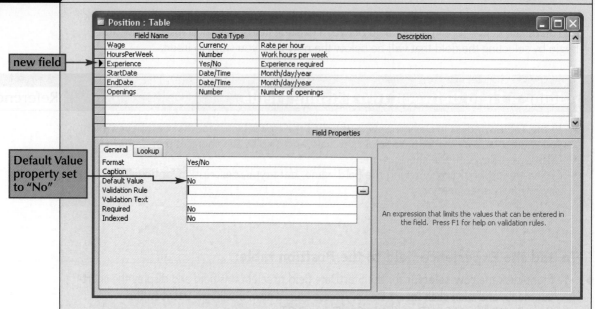

new field

Default Value
property set
to "No"

You've completed adding the Experience field to the Position table in Design view. As with the other changes you've made in Design view, however, the Experience field is not added to the Position table in the Northeast database until you save the changes to the table structure.

Changing Field Properties

Elsa's last modification to the table structure is to remove the dollar signs from the Wage field values displayed in the datasheet—repeated dollar signs are unnecessary and they clutter the datasheet. As you learned earlier when defining the StartDate and EndDate fields, you use the Format property to control the display of a field value.

To change the Format property of the Wage field:

1. Click the **Description** text box for the Wage field. The Wage field is now the current field.

2. Click the right side of the **Format** text box to display the Format list box. See Figure 2-25.

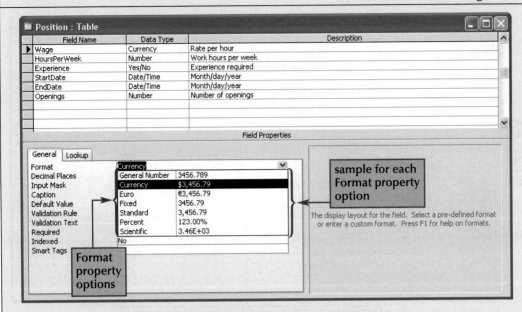

To the right of each Format property option is a field value whose appearance represents a sample of the option. The Standard option specifies the format Elsa wants for the Wage field.

3. Click **Standard** in the Format list box to accept this option for the Format property.

   Notice the Property Update Options button , which appears next to the Format property text box. This button allows you to have changes to properties take effect in other database objects.

Updating Field Property Changes

When you change a field's property in Design view, you can update the corresponding property on forms and reports that include the field you've modified. For example, in the preceding steps, you changed the Format property of the Wage field to Standard. If the Northeast database included forms or reports that contained the Wage field, you could choose to **propagate**, or update, the modified property in those forms and reports so that their Wage field values would be displayed in the Standard format.

To see the options for updating field property changes:

1. Position the pointer on the **Property Update Options** button , and then click the list arrow that appears. A menu of related options is displayed. See Figure 2-26.

| Figure 2-26 | Updating changes to field properties |

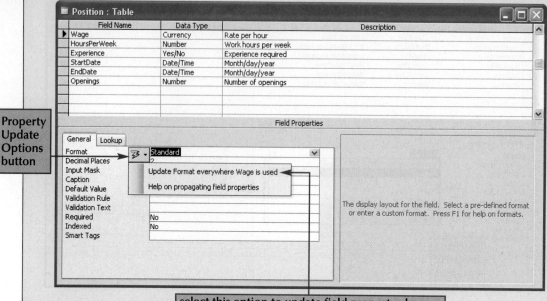

Property Update Options button

select this option to update field property changes

The "Help on propagating field properties" option takes you to a Help window for more information. The Update option allows you to select the objects you want to update with the property change.

2. Click **Update Format everywhere Wage is used**. A message box opens, indicating that no objects needed to be updated. This is because the Northeast database does not currently contain any forms or reports that might include the Wage field. If the database did contain such objects, the Update Properties dialog box would open, and you could then select the forms and reports containing the field that needs to be updated.

3. Click the **OK** button to close the message box. The Property Update Options button is no longer displayed in the Field Properties pane.

Elsa wants you to add a third record to the Position table datasheet. Before you can add the record, you must save the modified table structure, and then switch to the Position table datasheet.

To save the modified table structure, and then switch to the datasheet:

1. Click the **Save** button 🔲 on the Table Design toolbar. The modified table structure for the Position table is stored in the Northeast database. Note that if you forget to save the modified structure and try to close the table or switch to another view, Access will prompt you to save the table before you can continue.

2. Click the **View** button for Datasheet view 🔳 on the Table Design toolbar. The Position table datasheet opens. See Figure 2-27.

Datasheet for the modified Position table | **Figure 2-27**

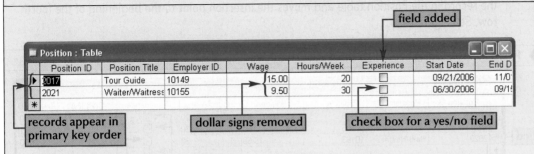

Notice that the ReferredBy field no longer appears in the datasheet, the Openings field is now the rightmost column (you might need to scroll the datasheet to see it), the Wage field values do not contain dollar signs, and the Experience field appears between the HoursPerWeek and StartDate fields. The Experience column contains check boxes to represent the yes/no field values. Empty check boxes signify "No," which is the default value you assigned to the Experience field. A check mark in the check box indicates a "Yes" value. Also notice that the records appear in ascending order based on the value in the PositionID field, the Position table's primary key, even though you did not enter the records in this order.

Elsa asks you to add a third record to the table. This record is for a position that requires prior work experience.

To add the record to the modified Position table:

▶ 1. Click the **New Record** button [▶] on the Table Datasheet toolbar. The insertion point moves to the PositionID field for the third row, which is the next row available for a new record.

▶ 2. Type **2020**. The pencil symbol appears in the row selector for the third row, and the star appears in the row selector for the fourth row. Recall that these symbols represent a record being edited and the next available record, respectively.

▶ 3. Press the **Tab** key. The insertion point moves to the PositionTitle field. Recall that "PositionTitle" is the name of the field as it is stored in the database, and "Position Title" is the value specified for this field's Caption property. (This text generally refers to fields by their field names, not by their captions.)

▶ 4. Type **Host/Hostess**, press the **Tab** key to move to the EmployerID field, type **10163**, and then press the **Tab** key again. The Wage field is now the current field.

▶ 5. Type **18.5** and then press the **Tab** key. Access displays the value as "18.50" (with no dollar sign).

▶ 6. Type **32** in the HoursPerWeek field, and then press the **Tab** key. The Experience field is now the current field.

Recall that the default value for this field is "No," which means the check box is initially empty. For yes/no fields with check boxes, you press the Tab key to leave the check box unchecked; you press the spacebar or click the check box to add or remove a check mark in the check box. Because this position requires experience, you need to insert a check mark in the check box.

▶ 7. Press the **spacebar**. A check mark appears in the check box.

▶ 8. Press the **Tab** key, type **6/15/2006** in the StartDate field, press the **Tab** key, and then type **10/1/2006** in the EndDate field.

> **9.** Press the **Tab** key, type **1** in the Openings field, and then press the **Tab** key. Access saves the record in the Position table and moves the insertion point to the beginning of the fourth row. See Figure 2-28.

Figure 2-28	Position table datasheet with third record added

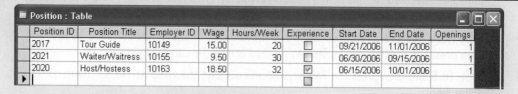

As you add records, Access places them at the end of the datasheet. If you switch to Design view and then return to the datasheet, or if you close the table and then open the datasheet, Access will display the records in primary key sequence.

For many of the fields, the columns are wider than necessary for the field values. You can resize the datasheet columns so that they are only as wide as needed to display the longest value in the column, including the field name or caption (if set). Resizing datasheet columns to their best fit improves the display of the datasheet and allows you to view more fields at the same time.

To resize the Position datasheet columns to their best fit:

> **1.** Place the pointer on the line between the PositionID and PositionTitle field names until the pointer changes to a ↔ shape.

> **2.** Double-click the pointer. The PositionID column is resized so that it is only as wide as the longest value in the column (the caption for the field name, in this case).

> **3.** Double-click the ↔ pointer on the line to the right of each remaining field name to resize all the columns in the datasheet to their best fit. See Figure 2-29.

Figure 2-29	Datasheet after resizing all columns to their best fit

Notice that all nine fields in the Position table are now visible in the datasheet if they were not visible before.

You have modified the Position table structure and added one record. Next, you need to obtain the rest of the records for this table from another database, and then import the two tables from the Seasonal database (Employer and NAICS) into your Northeast database.

Obtaining Data from Another Access Database

Sometimes the data you need for your database might already exist in another Access database. You can save time in obtaining this data by copying and pasting records from one database table into another or by importing an entire table from one database into another.

Copying Records from Another Access Database

You can copy and paste records from a table in the same database or in a different database only if the tables have the same structure—that is, the tables contain the same fields in the same order. Elsa's NEJobs database in the Brief\Tutorial folder included with your Data Files has a table named AvailablePositions that has the same table structure as the Position table. The records in the AvailablePositions table are the records Elsa wants you to copy into the Position table.

Other programs, such as Microsoft Word and Microsoft Excel, allow you to have two or more documents open at a time. However, you can have only one database open at a time for your current Access session. Therefore, you need to close the Northeast database, open the AvailablePositions table in the NEJobs database, select and copy the table records, close the NEJobs database, reopen the Position table in the Northeast database, and then paste the copied records. (*Note*: If you have a database open and then open a second database, Access will automatically close the first database for you.)

To copy the records from the AvailablePositions table:

1. Click the **Close** button ⊠ on the Table window title bar to close the Position table. A message box opens asking if you want to save the changes to the layout of the Position table. This box appears because you resized the datasheet columns to their best fit.

2. Click the **Yes** button in the message box.

3. Click the **Close** button ⊠ on the Database window title bar to close the Northeast database.

4. Click the **Open** button 🖻 on the Database toolbar to display the Open dialog box.

5. If necessary, display the list of your Data Files in the **Brief\Tutorial** folder.

6. Open the database file named **NEJobs**. The Database window opens. Notice that the NEJobs database contains only one table, the AvailablePositions table. This table contains the records you need to copy.

7. Click **AvailablePositions** in the Tables list box (if necessary), and then click the **Open** button in the Database window. The datasheet for the AvailablePositions table opens. See Figure 2-30. Note that this table contains a total of 62 records.

Figure 2-30

Datasheet for the NEJobs database's AvailablePositions table

click here to select all records

Position ID	Position Title	Employer ID	Wage	Hours/Week	Experience	Start Date	End Date	Openings
2004	Host/Hostess	10197	17.00	24	☐	07/01/2006	09/30/2006	1
2007	Tour Guide	10146	18.75	20	☑	05/15/2006	10/31/2006	2
2010	Kitchen Help	10135	13.00	40	☐	06/01/2006	10/01/2006	1
2015	Concierge	10159	22.00	40	☑	09/01/2006	03/01/2007	1
2025	Kitchen Help	10145	12.50	32	☐	07/01/2006	10/01/2006	2
2027	Waiter/Waitress	10130	10.00	32	☐	06/30/2006	10/01/2006	2
2028	Cook	10194	25.00	40	☑	08/01/2006	12/15/2006	1
2033	Lifeguard	10138	20.50	24	☑	06/15/2006	09/15/2006	1
2034	Waiter/Waitress	10162	10.25	30	☐	05/31/2006	11/01/2006	3
2036	Reservationist	10151	14.75	32	☐	10/01/2006	03/31/2007	1
2037	Gift Shop Clerk	10159	13.50	35	☐	09/01/2006	03/01/2007	1
2040	Waiter/Waitress	10126	10.50	32	☑	05/01/2006	10/01/2006	2
2041	Housekeeping	10133	12.00	40	☐	05/15/2006	10/15/2006	3
2045	Tour Guide	10122	17.00	24	☐	05/31/2006	10/01/2006	1
2048	Front Desk Clerk	10170	16.50	32	☐	07/01/2006	11/01/2006	1
2049	Pro Shop Clerk	10218	17.00	40	☑	05/01/2006	10/15/2006	1
2053	Host/Hostess	10190	15.75	24	☐	07/01/2006	09/01/2006	2
2055	Greenskeeper	10195	18.00	30	☑	06/01/2006	10/01/2006	1
2056	Reservationist	10156	15.00	24	☐	05/31/2006	10/15/2006	1
2058	Main Office Clerk	10152	14.25	32	☐	12/01/2006	04/01/2007	1

total number of records in the table

Record: |◄ ◄ 1 ► ►| ►* of 62

Elsa wants you to copy all the records in the AvailablePositions table. You can select all records by clicking the row selector for the field name row.

▶ 8. Click the **row selector** for the field name row (see Figure 2-30). All the records in the table are now highlighted, which means that Access has selected all of them.

▶ 9. Click the **Copy** button 📋 on the Table Datasheet toolbar. All the records are copied to the Clipboard.

Trouble? If a Clipboard panel opens in the task pane, click its Close button to close it, and then continue with Step 10.

▶ 10. Click the **Close** button ✕ on the Table window title bar. A message box opens asking if you want to save the data you copied to the Clipboard.

▶ 11. Click the **Yes** button in the message box. The message box closes, and then the table closes.

▶ 12. Click the **Close** button ✕ on the Database window title bar to close the NEJobs database.

To finish copying and pasting the records, you must open the Position table and paste the copied records into the table.

To paste the copied records into the Position table:

▶ 1. Click **File** on the menu bar, and then click **Northeast** in the list of recently opened databases. The Database window opens, showing the tables for the Northeast database.

▶ 2. In the Tables list box, click **Position** (if necessary), and then click the **Open** button in the Database window. The datasheet for the Position table opens.

You must paste the records at the end of the table.

▶ 3. Click the **row selector** for row four, which is the next row available for a new record. Make sure the entire row is selected (highlighted).

▶ 4. Click the **Paste** button 📋 on the Table Datasheet toolbar. A message box opens asking if you are sure you want to paste the records (62 in all).

Trouble? If the Paste button 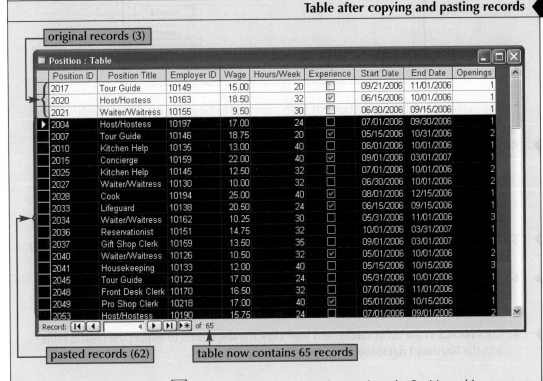 is not available, click the row selector for row four, make sure that the entire row is selected, and then repeat Step 4.

5. Click the **Yes** button. All the records are pasted from the Clipboard, and the pasted records remain highlighted. See Figure 2-31. Notice that the table now contains a total of 65 records—the three original records plus the 62 copied records.

Table after copying and pasting records ◀ **Figure 2-31**

original records (3)

Position ID	Position Title	Employer ID	Wage	Hours/Week	Experience	Start Date	End Date	Openings
2017	Tour Guide	10149	15.00	20	☐	09/21/2006	11/01/2006	1
2020	Host/Hostess	10163	18.50	32	☑	06/15/2006	10/01/2006	1
2021	Waiter/Waitress	10155	9.50	30	☐	06/30/2006	09/15/2006	1
2004	Host/Hostess	10197	17.00	24	☐	07/01/2006	09/30/2006	1
2007	Tour Guide	10146	18.75	20	☑	05/15/2006	10/31/2006	2
2010	Kitchen Help	10135	13.00	40	☐	06/01/2006	10/01/2006	1
2015	Concierge	10159	22.00	40	☑	09/01/2006	03/01/2007	1
2025	Kitchen Help	10145	12.50	32	☐	07/01/2006	10/01/2006	2
2027	Waiter/Waitress	10130	10.00	32	☐	06/30/2006	10/01/2006	2
2028	Cook	10194	25.00	40	☑	08/01/2006	12/15/2006	1
2033	Lifeguard	10138	20.50	24	☑	06/15/2006	09/15/2006	1
2034	Waiter/Waitress	10162	10.25	30	☐	05/31/2006	11/01/2006	3
2036	Reservationist	10151	14.75	32	☐	10/01/2006	03/31/2007	1
2037	Gift Shop Clerk	10159	13.50	35	☐	09/01/2006	03/01/2007	1
2040	Waiter/Waitress	10126	10.50	32	☑	05/01/2006	10/01/2006	2
2041	Housekeeping	10133	12.00	40	☐	05/15/2006	10/15/2006	3
2045	Tour Guide	10122	17.00	24	☐	05/31/2006	10/01/2006	1
2048	Front Desk Clerk	10170	16.50	32	☐	07/01/2006	11/01/2006	1
2049	Pro Shop Clerk	10218	17.00	40	☑	05/01/2006	10/15/2006	1
2053	Host/Hostess	10190	15.75	24	☐	07/01/2006	09/01/2006	2

Record: ◀◀ ◀ 4 ▶ ▶◀ ▶* of 65

pasted records (62)

table now contains 65 records

6. Click the **Close** button ☒ on the Table window title bar to close the Position table.

Importing a Table from Another Access Database

When you **import** a table from one Access database to another, you place a copy of the table—including its structure, field definitions, and field values—in the database into which you import it. There are two ways to import a table from another Access database into your current database: using the Get External Data option on the File menu, or using the Import Table Wizard, which is available in the New Table dialog box. You'll use both methods to import the two tables from the Seasonal database into your Northeast database.

To import the Employer and NAICS tables:

1. Make sure the Northeast Database window is open on your screen.

2. Click **File** on the menu bar, point to **Get External Data**, and then click **Import**. The Import dialog box opens. This dialog box is similar to the Open dialog box.

3. Display the list of files in your Brief\Tutorial folder, click **Seasonal**, and then click the **Import** button. The Import Objects dialog box opens. See Figure 2-32.

Figure 2-32 ▶ **Import Objects dialog box**

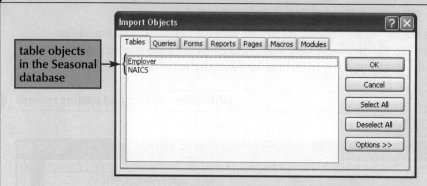

The Tables tab of the dialog box lists both tables in the Seasonal database—Employer and NAICS. Note that you can import other objects as well (queries, forms, reports, and so on).

▶ 4. Click **Employer** in the list of tables, and then click the **OK** button. The Import Objects dialog box closes, and the Employer table is now listed in the Northeast Database window.

Now you'll use the Import Table Wizard to import the NAICS table. (Note that you could also use the Select All button in the Import Objects dialog box to import all the objects listed on the current tab at the same time.)

▶ 5. Click the **New** button in the Database window, click **Import Table** in the New Table dialog box, and then click the **OK** button. The Import dialog box opens.

▶ 6. If necessary, display the list of files in your Brief\Tutorial folder, click **Seasonal**, and then click the **Import** button. The Import Objects dialog box opens, again displaying the tables in the Seasonal database.

▶ 7. Click **NAICS** in the list of tables, and then click the **OK** button to import the NAICS table into the Northeast database.

Now that you have all the records in the Position table and all three tables in the Northeast database, Elsa examines the records to make sure they are correct. She finds one record in the Position table that she wants you to delete and another record that needs changes to its field values.

Updating a Database

Updating, or **maintaining**, a database is the process of adding, changing, and deleting records in database tables to keep them current and accurate. You've already added records to the Position table. Now Elsa wants you to delete and change records.

Deleting Records

To delete a record, you need to select the record in Datasheet view, and then delete it using the Delete Record button on the Table Datasheet toolbar or the Delete Record option on the shortcut menu.

Deleting a Record

- In the Table window in Datasheet view, click the row selector for the record you want to delete, and then click the Delete Record button on the Table Datasheet toolbar (or right-click the row selector for the record, and then click Delete Record on the shortcut menu).
- In the dialog box asking you to confirm the deletion, click the Yes button.

Elsa asks you to delete the record whose PositionID value is 2015 because this record was entered in error; the position for this record does not exist. The fourth record in the table has a PositionID value of 2015. This record is the one you need to delete.

To delete the record:

1. Open the Position table in Datasheet view.

2. Right-click the **row selector** for row four. Access selects the fourth record and displays the shortcut menu. See Figure 2-33.

Deleting a record   Figure 2-33

selected record

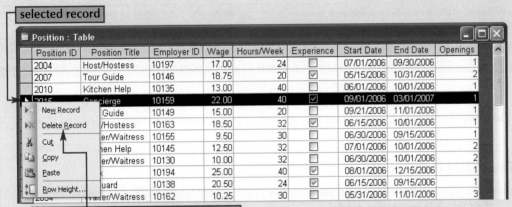

click here to delete the selected record

3. Click **Delete Record** on the shortcut menu. Access deletes the record and opens a dialog box asking you to confirm the deletion. Because the deletion of a record is permanent and cannot be undone, Access prompts you to make sure that you want to delete the record.

   Trouble? If you selected the wrong record for deletion, click the No button. Access ends the deletion process and continues to display the selected record. Repeat Steps 2 and 3 to delete the correct record.

4. Click the **Yes** button to confirm the deletion and close the dialog box.

Elsa's final update to the Position table involves changes to field values in one of the records.

Changing Records

To change the field values in a record, you must first make the record the current record. Then you position the insertion point in the field value to make minor changes or select the field value to replace it entirely. In Tutorial 1, you used the mouse with the scroll bars and the navigation buttons to navigate the records in a datasheet. You can also use keystroke combinations and the F2 key to navigate a datasheet and to select field values.

The **F2 key** is a toggle that you use to switch between navigation mode and editing mode:

- In **navigation mode**, Access selects an entire field value. If you type while you are in navigation mode, your typed entry replaces the highlighted field value.
- In **editing mode**, you can insert or delete characters in a field value based on the location of the insertion point.

Figure 2-34 shows some of the navigation mode and editing mode keystroke techniques.

Figure 2-34 ▶ **Navigation mode and editing mode keystroke techniques**

Press	To Move the Selection in Navigation Mode	To Move the Insertion Point in Editing Mode
←	Left one field value at a time	Left one character at a time
→	Right one field value at a time	Right one character at a time
Home	Left to the first field value in the record	To the left of the first character in the field value
End	Right to the last field value in the record	To the right of the last character in the field value
↑ or ↓	Up or down one record at a time	Up or down one record at a time and switch to navigation mode
Tab or Enter	Right one field value at a time	Right one field value at a time and switch to navigation mode
Ctrl+Home	To the first field value in the first record	To the left of the first character in the field value
Ctrl+End	To the last field value in the last record	To the right of the last character in the field value

The record Elsa wants you to change has a PositionID field value of 2125. Some of the values were entered incorrectly for this record, and you need to enter the correct values.

To modify the record:

▶ 1. Make sure the PositionID field value for the fourth record is still highlighted, indicating that the table is in navigation mode.

▶ 2. Press the **Ctrl+End** keys. Access displays records from the end of the table and selects the last field value in the last record. This field value is for the Openings field.

▶ 3. Press the **Home** key. The first field value in the last record is now selected. This field value is for the PositionID field.

▶ 4. Press the **↑** key. The PositionID field value for the previous record (PositionID 2125) is selected. This record is the one you need to change.

Elsa wants you to change these field values in the record: PositionID to 2124, EmployerID to 10163, Wage to 14.50, Experience to "Yes" (checked), and EndDate to 10/15/2006.

▶ 5. Type **2124**, press the **Tab** key twice, type **10163**, press the **Tab** key, type **14.5**, press the **Tab** key twice, press the **spacebar** to insert a check mark in the Experience check box, press the **Tab** key twice, and then type **10/15/2006**. The changes to the record are complete. See Figure 2-35.

Table after changing field values in a record

Figure 2-35

field values changed

	2115	Gift Shop Clerk	10154	13.00	25	☐	05/01/2006	09/30/2006	1
	2117	Housekeeping	10220	13.50	30	☐	06/30/2006	09/30/2006	3
	2118	Greenskeeper	10218	17.00	32	☐	05/01/2006	11/01/2006	1
	2120	Lifeguard	10154	19.00	32	☑	06/15/2006	09/30/2006	2
	2122	Kitchen Help	10151	13.00	35	☐	09/01/2006	03/31/2007	3
	2123	Main Office Clerk	10170	14.50	32	☐	07/01/2006	11/15/2006	1
✎	2124	Kitchen Help	10163	14.50	40	☑	06/01/2006	10/15/2006	2
	2127	Waiter/Waitress	10185	10.50	40	☐	12/01/2006	05/01/2007	1
✱						☐			

Record: ◄◄ ◄ 63 ► ►► ►✱ of 64

You've completed all of Elsa's updates to the Position table. Now you can close the Northeast database.

6. Close the Position table, and then close the Northeast database.

Elsa and her staff members approve of the revised table structure for the Position table. They are confident that the table will allow them to easily track position data for NSJI's employer customers.

Session 2.2 Quick Check

Review

1. What does a pencil symbol in a datasheet's row selector represent? A star symbol?
2. What is the effect of deleting a field from a table structure?
3. How do you insert a field between existing fields in a table structure?
4. A field with the _____ data type can appear in the table datasheet as a check box.
5. Describe the two ways in which you can display the Import dialog box, so that you can import a table from one Access database to another.
6. In Datasheet view, what is the difference between navigation mode and editing mode?

Tutorial Summary

Review

In this tutorial, you learned how to create and save a new database and how to create and save a new table in that database. With this process, you also learned some important guidelines for designing databases and tables, and for setting field properties. You worked in Design view to define fields, set properties, specify a table's primary key, and modify a table's structure. Then you worked in Datasheet view to add records to the new table, both by entering them directly in the datasheet and by copying records from another Access database. To complete the database design, you imported tables from another Access database into the new database you created. Finally, you updated the database by deleting records and changing values in records.

Key Terms

Caption property	editing mode	navigation mode
composite key	entity integrity	null value
data redundancy	F1 key	pencil symbol
data type	F2 key	propagate
Database Wizard	F6 key	properties
Decimal Places property	Field Size property	set (a property)
Default Value property	import	star symbol
Description property	maintain (a database)	update (a database)
Design view		

Practice

Take time to practice the skills you learned in the tutorial using the same case scenario.

Review Assignments

Data File needed for the Review Assignments: Elsa.mdb

Elsa needs a database to track data about the students recruited by NSJI and about the recruiters who find jobs for the students. She asks you to create the database by completing the following:

1. Start Access, and make sure your Data Files are in the proper location.
2. Create a new, blank database named **Recruits** and save it in the Brief\Review folder included with your Data Files.
3. Use Design view to create a new table using the table design shown in Figure 2-36.

Figure 2-36

Field Name	Data Type	Description	Field Size	Caption	Other Properties
SSN	Text	Primary key	30		
Salary	Currency				Format: Currency Default Value: (blank)
FirstName	Text		50	First Name	
MiddleName	Text		30	Middle Name	
LastName	Text		50	Last Name	

4. Specify SSN as the primary key field, and then save the table as **Recruiter**.
5. Add the recruiter records shown in Figure 2-37 to the **Recruiter** table.

Figure 2-37

SSN	Salary	FirstName	MiddleName	LastName
892-77-1201	40,000	Kate	Teresa	Foster
901-63-1554	38,500	Paul	Michael	Kirnicki
893-91-0178	40,000	Ryan	James	DuBrava

6. Make the following changes to the structure of the **Recruiter** table:
   a. Move the Salary field so that it appears after the LastName field.
   b. Add a new field between the LastName and Salary fields, using the following properties:

Field Name:	BonusQuota
Data Type:	Number
Description:	Number of recruited students needed to receive bonus
Field Size:	Byte
Decimal Places:	0
Caption:	Bonus Quota
Default Value:	(blank)

   c. Change the format of the Salary field so that commas are displayed, dollar signs are not displayed, and no decimal places are displayed in the field values.
   d. Save the revised table structure.
7. Use the **Recruiter** datasheet to update the database as follows:
   a. Enter these BonusQuota values for the three records: 60 for Kate Foster; 60 for Ryan DuBrava; and 50 for Paul Kirnicki.
   b. Add a record to the Recruiter datasheet with the following field values:

SSN:	899-40-2937
FirstName:	Sonia
MiddleName:	Lee
LastName:	Xu
BonusQuota:	50
Salary:	39,250

8. Close the Recruiter table, and then set the option for compacting the **Recruits** database on close. (*Note:* If you are working off a floppy disk, check with your instructor or technical support staff to confirm that you should set this option.)
9. Elsa created a database with her name as the database name. In that database, the RecruiterEmployees table has the same format as the Recruiter table you created. Copy all the records from the **RecruiterEmployees** table in the **Elsa** database (located in the Brief\Review folder provided with your Data Files) to the end of the **Recruiter** table in the **Recruits** database.
10. Delete the MiddleName field from the Recruiter table structure, and then save the table structure.
11. Resize all columns in the datasheet for the Recruiter table to their best fit.
12. Print the Recruiter table datasheet, and then save and close the table.
13. Create a table named **Student** using the Import Table Wizard. The table you need to import is named **Student**, which is one of the tables in the **Elsa** database located in the Brief\Review folder provided with your Data Files.
14. Make the following modifications to the structure of the **Student** table in the **Recruits** database:
    a. Enter the following Description property values:

StudentID:	Primary key
SSN:	Foreign key value of the recruiter for this student

    b. Change the Field Size property for both the FirstName field and the LastName field to 15.
    c. Move the BirthDate field so that it appears between the Nation and Gender fields.
    d. Change the format of the BirthDate field so that it displays only two digits for the year instead of four.
    e. Save the table structure changes. (Answer "Yes" to any warning messages about property changes and lost data.)

15. Switch to Datasheet view, and then resize all columns in the datasheet to fit the data.
16. Delete the record with the StudentID value DRI9901 from the **Student** table.
17. Save, print, and then close the Student datasheet.
18. Close the Recruits database.

Apply

Using what you learned in the tutorial, create and modify two new tables containing data about video photography events.

Case Problem 1

Data Files needed for this Case Problem: Videos.mdb (*cont. from Tutorial 1*) and Events.mdb

Lim's Video Photography Youngho Lim uses the Videos database to maintain information about the clients, contracts, and events for his video photography business. Youngho asks you to help him maintain the database by completing the following:

1. Open the **Videos** database located in the Brief\Case1 folder provided with your Data Files.
2. Use Design view to create a table using the table design shown in Figure 2-38.

Figure 2-38

Field Name	Data Type	Description	Field Size	Caption	Other Properties
ShootID	Number	Primary key	Long Integer	Shoot ID	Decimal Places: 0 Default Value: (blank)
ShootType	Text		2	Shoot Type	
ShootTime	Date/Time			Shoot Time	Format: Medium Time
Duration	Number	# of hours	Single		Default Value: (blank)
Contact	Text	person who booked shoot	30		
Location	Text		30		
ShootDate	Date/Time			Shoot Date	Format: mm/dd/yyyy
ContractID	Number	Foreign key	Integer	Contract ID	Decimal Places: 0 Default Value: (blank)

3. Specify ShootID as the primary key, and then save the table as **Shoot**.
4. Add the records shown in Figure 2-39 to the Shoot table.

Figure 2-39

ShootID	ShootType	ShootTime	Duration	Contact	Location	ShootDate	ContractID
927032	AP	4:00 PM	3.5	Ellen Quirk	Elm Lodge	9/27/2006	2412
103031	HP	9:00 AM	3.5	Tom Bradbury	Client's home	10/30/2006	2611

5. Youngho created a database named Events that contains a table with shoot data named ShootEvents. The Shoot table you created has the same format as the ShootEvents table. Copy all the records from the **ShootEvents** table in the **Events** database (located in the Brief\Case1 folder provided with your Data Files) to the end of the **Shoot** table in the **Videos** database.
6. Modify the structure of the Shoot table by completing the following:
   a. Delete the Contact field.
   b. Move the ShootDate field so that it appears between the ShootType and ShootTime fields.

7. Save the revised table structure, switch to Datasheet view, and then resize all columns in the datasheet for the Shoot table to their best fit.

8. Use the **Shoot** datasheet to update the database as follows:

   a. For ShootID 421032, change the ShootTime value to 7:00 PM, and change the Location value to Le Bistro.

   b. Add a record to the Shoot datasheet with the following field values:

ShootID:	913032
ShootType:	SE
ShootDate:	9/13/2006
ShootTime:	1:00 PM
Duration:	2.5
Location:	High School football field
ContractID:	2501

9. Switch to Design view, and then switch back to Datasheet view so that the records appear in primary key sequence by ShootID. Resize any datasheet columns to their best fit, as necessary.

10. Print the Shoot table datasheet, and then save and close the table.

11. Create a table named **ShootDesc** using the Import Table Wizard. The table you need to import is named **ShootDesc**, which is one of the tables in the **Events** database located in the Brief\Case1 folder provided with your Data Files.

12. Make the following modifications to the structure of the **ShootDesc** table in the **Videos** database:

    a. Enter the following Description property values:

ShootType:	Primary key
ShootDesc:	Description of shoot

    b. Change the Field Size property for ShootType to 2.

    c. Change the Field Size property for ShootDesc to 30.

    d. Enter the following Caption property values:

ShootType:	Shoot Type
ShootDesc:	Shoot Desc

13. Save the revised table structure (answer "Yes" to any warning messages about property changes and lost data), switch to Datasheet view, and then resize both datasheet columns to their best fit.

14. Print the ShootDesc table datasheet, and then save and close the table.

15. Close the Videos database.

Challenge

Challenge yourself by using the Table Wizard to create a new table to store data about fitness center programs.

Explore

Case Problem 2

Data Files needed for this Case Problem: Fitness.mdb (*cont. from Tutorial 1*) and Products.mdb

Parkhurst Health & Fitness Center Martha Parkhurst uses the Fitness database to track information about members who join the center and the program in which each member is enrolled. You'll help her maintain this database by completing the following:

1. Open the **Fitness** database located in the Brief\Case2 folder provided with your Data Files.

2. Use the Table Wizard to create a new table named **Program** in the **Fitness** database, as follows:

   a. Base the new table on the Products sample table, which is one of the sample tables in the Business category.

   b. Add the following fields to your table (in the order shown): ProductID, ProductDescription, and UnitPrice.

c. Click ProductID in the "Fields in my new table" list, and then use the Rename Field button to change the name of this field to ProgramID. Follow this same procedure to rename the ProductDescription field to "Description" and to rename the "UnitPrice" field to "MonthlyFee." Click the Next button.

d. Specify the name **Program** for the new table, and choose the option for setting the primary key yourself. Click the Next button.

e. Specify ProgramID as the primary key field, and select the option "Numbers and/or letters I enter when I add new records." Click the Next button.

f. In the next dialog box, click the Relationships button, select the option "The tables aren't related" (if necessary), click the OK button, and then click the Next button.

g. In the final Table Wizard dialog box, choose the option for modifying the table design. Click the Finish button.

Explore

3. Modify the structure of the Program table as follows:

a. For the ProgramID field, make the following changes:

Data Type:	Number
Description:	Primary key
Decimal Places:	0
Caption:	Program ID
Default Value:	blank (no value specified)

b. For the Description field, make the following changes:

Description:	Full programs provide access to all facilities; limited programs restrict access to certain facilities and activities
Field Size:	35

c. For the MonthlyFee field, make the following changes:

Format:	Fixed
Decimal Places:	2
Caption:	Monthly Fee

4. Add a new field as the fourth field in the table, below MonthlyFee, with the following properties:

Field Name:	PhysicalRequired
Data Type:	Yes/No
Description:	Member must have a complete physical before joining program
Caption:	Physical Required

5. Save the modified table structure.

6. Add the records shown in Figure 2-40 to the Program table.

Figure 2-40

ProgramID	Description	MonthlyFee	PhysicalRequired
201	Junior Full (ages 13–17)	$30.00	Yes
202	Junior Limited (ages 13–17)	$20.00	Yes
203	Young Adult Full (ages 18–25)	$40.00	No
204	Young Adult Limited (ages 18–25)	$25.00	No

7. Martha created a database named Products that contains a table with program data named ProgramRecords. The Program table you created has the same format as the ProgramRecords table. Copy all the records from the **ProgramRecords** table in the **Products** database (located in the Brief\Case2 folder provided with your Data Files) to the end of the **Program** table in the **Fitness** database.

8. Resize all columns in the datasheet for the Program table to their best fit.

9. For ProgramID 209, change the PhysicalRequired field value to Yes.
10. Print the Program table datasheet, and then save and close the table.
11. Close the Fitness database.

Case Problem 3

Data Files needed for this Case Problem: Redwood.mdb (*cont. from Tutorial 1*) and Pledge.mdb

Redwood Zoo   Michael Rosenfeld continues to track information about donors, their pledges, and the status of funds to benefit the Redwood Zoo. Help him maintain the Redwood database by completing the following:

1. Open the **Redwood** database located in the Brief\Case3 folder provided with your Data Files.
2. Create a table named **Pledge** using the Import Table Wizard. The table you need to import is named **PledgeRecords**, which is located in the **Pledge** database in the Brief\Case3 folder provided with your Data Files.
3. After importing the PledgeRecords table, use the shortcut menu to rename the table to **Pledge** in the Database window.
4. Modify the structure of the **Pledge** table by completing the following:
   a. Enter the following Description property values:
      PledgeID: Primary key
      DonorID: Foreign key
      FundCode: Foreign key
   b. Change the format of the PledgeDate field to mm/dd/yyyy.
   c. Change the Data Type of the TotalPledged field to Currency with the Standard format.
   d. Specify a Default Value of B for the PaymentMethod field.
   e. Specify a Default Value of F for the PaymentSchedule field.
   f. Save the modified table structure.
5. Switch to Datasheet view, and then resize all columns in the datasheet to their best fit.
6. Use the **Pledge** datasheet to update the database as follows:
   a. Add a new record to the Pledge table with the following field values:
      PledgeID: 2695
      DonorID: 59045
      FundCode: P15
      PledgeDate: 7/11/2006
      TotalPledged: 1000
      PaymentMethod: B
      PaymentSchedule: M
   b. Change the TotalPledged value for PledgeID 2499 to 150.
   c. Change the FundCode value for PledgeID 2332 to B03.
7. Print the Pledge table datasheet, and then save and close the table.
8. Close the Redwood database.

Apply

Apply the skills you learned in the tutorial to create and work with a new table containing data about donations.

Explore

Challenge

Explore two new ways to create tables containing property rental information—by importing an Excel worksheet and by entering records first in Datasheet view.

Explore

Case Problem 4

Data Files needed for this Case Problem: GEM.mdb (*cont. from Tutorial 1*), Property.xls, and Reserve.mdb

GEM Ultimate Vacations   Griffin and Emma MacElroy use the GEM database to track the data about the services they provide to the clients who book luxury vacations through their agency. You'll help them maintain this database by completing the following:

1. Open the **GEM** database located in the Brief\Case4 folder provided with your Data Files.
2. Use the Import Spreadsheet Wizard to create a new table named **Property**. The data you need to import is contained in the **Property** workbook, which is a Microsoft Excel file located in the Brief\Case4 folder provided with your Data Files.
   a. Select the Import Table option in the New Table dialog box.
   b. Change the entry in the Files of type list box to display the list of Excel workbook files in the Brief\Case4 folder.
   c. Select the **Property** file and then click the Import button.
   d. In the Import Spreadsheet Wizard dialog boxes, choose the Sheet1 worksheet; choose the option for using column headings as field names; select the option for choosing your own primary key; specify PropertyID as the primary key; and enter the table name (**Property**). Otherwise, accept the wizard's choices for all other options for the imported data.
3. Open the **Property** table and resize all datasheet columns to their best fit.
4. Modify the structure of the Property table by completing the following:
   a. For the PropertyID field, enter a Description property of "Primary key", change the Field Size property to Long Integer, set the Decimal Places property to 0, and set the Caption property to Property ID.
   b. For the PropertyName field, change the Field Size property to 45, and set the Caption property to Property Name.
   c. For the Location field, enter a Description property of "Province, city, county", and change the Field Size property to 35.
   d. For the Country field, change the Field Size property to 15.
   e. For the NightlyRate field, change the Data Type to Currency, set the Format property to Currency, set the Decimal Places property to 0, and set the Caption property to Nightly Rate.
   f. For the Bedrooms field, enter a Description property of "Number of bedrooms", change the Field Size property to Integer, and set the Decimal Places property to 0.
   g. For the Sleeps field, enter a Description property of "Number of people who can be accommodated", change the Field Size property to Integer, and set the Decimal Places property to 0.
   h. For the PropertyType field, change the Field Size property to 20, and set the Caption property to Property Type.
   i. For the Description field, change the Data Type to Memo.
   j. Save the table structure. If you receive any warning messages about lost data or integrity rules, click the Yes button.
5. Switch to Datasheet view, and then resize all datasheet columns to their best fit (if necessary).
6. Use the **Property** datasheet to update the database as follows:
   a. For PropertyID 3395, change the NightlyRate value to $750.
   b. Add a new record to the Property table with the following field values:
      PropertyID: 3675
      PropertyName: Casa de Las Palmas

Location:	Mallorca
Country:	Spain
NightlyRate:	2500
Bedrooms:	4
Sleeps:	8
PropertyType:	Villa
Description:	Private estate; multiple terraces; beautiful sea views; pool

  c. Delete the record for PropertyID 3503.

7. Print the Property table datasheet, and then save and close the table.

Explore

8. Create a new table named **Reservation**, based on the data shown in Figure 2-41 and according to the following steps:

Figure 2-41

ReservationID	GuestID	PropertyID	StartDate	EndDate	People	RentalRate
510	220	3107	5/1/07	5/15/07	6	$1000
503	209	3488	6/12/07	6/19/07	12	$2000
511	201	3142	8/20/07	8/27/07	7	$700

  a. Select the Datasheet View option in the New Table dialog box.

  b. Enter the three records shown in Figure 2-41. (Do *not* enter the field names at this point.)

  c. Switch to Design view, supply the table name, and then answer "No" if asked if you want to create a primary key.

  d. Enter the field names and properties for the seven fields, as shown in Figure 2-42.

Figure 2-42

Field Name	Data Type	Description	Field Size	Caption	Other Properties
ReservationID	Number	Primary key	Long Integer	Reservation ID	Format: (blank) Decimal Places: 0
GuestID	Number	Foreign key	Integer	Guest ID	Format: (blank) Decimal Places: 0
PropertyID	Number	Foreign key	Long Integer	Property ID	Format: (blank) Decimal Places: 0
StartDate	Date/Time			Start Date	Format: Short Date
EndDate	Date/Time			End Date	Format: Short Date
People	Number	Number of people in the party	Byte		Format: (blank) Decimal Places: 0
RentalRate	Currency	Rate per day; includes any discounts or promotions		Rental Rate	Format: Currency Decimal Places: 0

9. Specify ReservationID as the primary key, and then save the changes to the table structure.

10. Switch to Datasheet view, and then resize all datasheet columns to their best fit.

11. Emma created a database named Reserve that contains a table with reservation data named ReserveInfo. The Reservation table you created has the same format as the ReserveInfo table. Copy all the records from the **ReserveInfo** table in the **Reserve** database (located in the Brief\Case4 folder provided with your Data Files) to the end of the **Reservation** table in the **GEM** database.

12. Resize all columns in the Reservation datasheet to their best fit (if necessary).
13. Print the Reservation datasheet, and then save and close the table.
14. Close the GEM database.

Research

Use the Internet to find and work with data related to the topics presented in this tutorial.

Internet Assignments

The purpose of the Internet Assignments is to challenge you to find information on the Internet that you can use to work effectively with this software. The actual assignments are updated and maintained on the Course Technology Web site. Log on to the Internet and use your Web browser to go to the Student Online Companion for New Perspectives Office 2003 at **www.course.com/np/office2003**. Click the Internet Assignments link, and then navigate to the assignments for this tutorial.

Assess

SAM Assessment and Training

If you have a SAM user profile, you may have access to hands-on instruction, practice, and assessment of the skills covered in this tutorial. Log in to your SAM account and go to your assignments page to see what your instructor has assigned.

Review

Quick Check Answers

Session 2.1

1. Identify all the fields needed to produce the required information, group related fields into tables, determine each table's primary key, include a common field in related tables, avoid data redundancy, and determine the properties of each field.
2. The Data Type property determines what field values you can enter for the field and what other properties the field will have.
3. text, number, and AutoNumber fields
4. Caption
5. F6
6. null

Session 2.2

1. the record being edited; the next row available for a new record
2. The field and all its values are removed from the table.
3. In Design view, right-click the row selector for the row above which you want to insert the field, click Insert Rows on the shortcut menu, and then define the new field.
4. yes/no
5. Make sure the database into which you want to import a table is open, click the File menu, point to Get External Data, and then click Import; or, click the New button in the Database window, click Import Table in the New Table dialog box, and then click the OK button.
6. In navigation mode, the entire field value is selected, and anything you type replaces the field value; in editing mode, you can insert or delete characters in a field value based on the location of the insertion point.

Objectives

Session 3.1
- Learn how to use the Query window in Design view
- Create, run, and save queries
- Update data using a query
- Define a relationship between two tables
- Sort data in a query
- Filter data in a query

Session 3.2
- Specify an exact match condition in a query
- Change a datasheet's appearance
- Use a comparison operator to match a range of values
- Use the And and Or logical operators
- Use multiple undo and redo
- Perform calculations in a query using calculated fields, aggregate functions, and record group calculations

Querying a Database

Retrieving Information About Employers and Their Positions

Case

Northeast Seasonal Jobs International (NSJI)

At a recent company meeting, Elsa Jensen and other NSJI employees discussed the importance of regularly monitoring the business activity of the company's employer clients. For example, Zack Ward and his marketing staff track employer activity to develop new strategies for promoting NSJI's services. Matt Griffin, the manager of recruitment, needs to track information about available positions, so that he can find student recruits to fill those positions. In addition, Elsa is interested in analyzing other aspects of the business, such as the wage amounts paid for different positions at different employers. You can satisfy all these informational needs for NSJI by creating and using queries that retrieve information from the Northeast database.

Student Data Files

▼Brief

▽ **Tutorial folder**
  Northeast.mdb *(cont.)*

▽ **Review folder**
  Recruits.mdb *(cont.)*

▽ **Case1 folder**
  Videos.mdb *(cont.)*

▽ **Case2 folder**
  Fitness.mdb *(cont.)*

▽ **Case3 folder**
  Redwood.mdb *(cont.)*

▽ **Case4 folder**
  GEM.mdb *(cont.)*

Introduction to Queries

As you learned in Tutorial 1, a query is a question you ask about data stored in a database. For example, Zack might create a query to find records in the Employer table for only those employers located in a specific state or province. When you create a query, you tell Access which fields you need and what criteria Access should use to select the records.

Access provides powerful query capabilities that allow you to:

- display selected fields and records from a table
- sort records
- perform calculations
- generate data for forms, reports, and other queries
- update data in the tables in a database
- find and display data from two or more tables

Most questions about data are generalized queries in which you specify the fields and records you want Access to select. These common requests for information, such as "Which employers are located in Quebec?" or "How many waiter/waitress positions are available?" are called **select queries**. The answer to a select query is returned in the form of a datasheet. The result of a query is also referred to as a **recordset**, because the query produces a set of records that answers your question.

More specialized, technical queries, such as finding duplicate records in a table, are best formulated using a Query Wizard. A Query Wizard prompts you for information by asking a series of questions and then creates the appropriate query based on your answers. In Tutorial 1, you used the Simple Query Wizard to display only some of the fields in the Employer table; Access provides other Query Wizards for more complex queries. For common, informational queries, it is easier for you to design your own query than to use a Query Wizard.

Zack wants you to create a query to display the employer ID, employer name, city, contact first name, contact last name, and Web site information for each record in the Employer table. He needs this information for a market analysis his staff is completing on NSJI's employer clients. You'll open the Query window to create the query for Zack.

Query Window

You use the Query window in Design view to create a query. In Design view, you specify the data you want to view by constructing a query by example. When you use **query by example (QBE)**, you give Access an example of the information you are requesting. Access then retrieves the information that precisely matches your example.

For Zack's query, you need to display data from the Employer table. You'll begin by starting Access, opening the Northeast database (which you created in Tutorial 2), and displaying the Query window in Design view.

To start Access, open the Northeast database, and open the Query window in Design view:

▶ 1. Start Access and open the **Northeast** database which you created in Tutorial 2 and saved in the Brief\Tutorial folder provided with your Data Files.

▶ 2. Click **Queries** in the Objects bar of the Database window, and then click the **New** button. The New Query dialog box opens. See Figure 3-1.

New Query dialog box   Figure 3-1

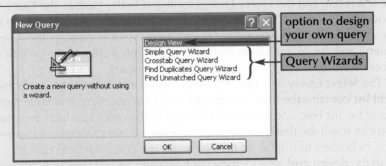

You'll design your own query instead of using a Query Wizard.

3. If necessary, click **Design View** in the list box.

4. Click the **OK** button. Access opens the Show Table dialog box on top of the Query window. (Note that you could also have double-clicked the "Create query in Design view" option in the Database window.) Notice that the title bar of the Query window shows that you are creating a select query.

   The query you are creating will retrieve data from the Employer table, so you need to add this table to the Select Query window.

5. Click **Employer** in the Tables list box (if necessary), click the **Add** button, and then click the **Close** button. Access places the Employer table's field list in the Select Query window and closes the Show Table dialog box.

   To display more of the fields you'll be using for creating queries, you'll maximize the Select Query window.

6. Click the **Maximize** button 🔲 on the Select Query window title bar. See Figure 3-2.

Select query in Design view   Figure 3-2

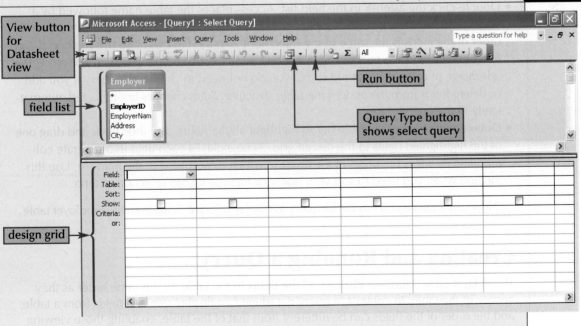

In Design view, the Select Query window contains the standard title bar, the menu bar, the status bar, and the Query Design toolbar. On the toolbar, the Query Type button shows a select query; the icon on this button changes according to the type of query you are creating. The title bar on the Select Query window displays the query type (Select Query) and the default query name (Query1). You'll change the default query name to a more meaningful one later when you save the query.

The Select Query window in Design view contains a field list and the design grid. The **field list** contains the fields for the table you are querying. The table name appears at the top of the list box, and the fields are listed in the order in which they appear in the table. You can scroll the field list to see more fields, or you can expand the field list box by dragging its borders to display all the fields and the complete field names.

In the **design grid**, you include the fields and record selection criteria for the information you want to see. Each column in the design grid contains specifications about a field you will use in the query. You can choose a single field for your query by dragging its name from the field list to the design grid. Alternatively, you can double-click a field name to place it in the next available design grid column.

When you are constructing a query, you can see the query results at any time by clicking the View button or the Run button on the Query Design toolbar. In response, Access displays the query datasheet (or recordset), which contains the set of fields and records that results from answering, or **running**, the query. The order of the fields in the query datasheet is the same as the order of the fields in the design grid. Although the query datasheet looks just like a table datasheet and appears in Datasheet view, a query datasheet is temporary, and its contents are based on the criteria you establish in the design grid. In contrast, a table datasheet shows the permanent data in a table. However, you can update data while viewing a query datasheet, just as you can when working in a table datasheet or form.

If the query you are creating includes every field from the specified table, you can use one of the following three methods to transfer all the fields from the field list to the design grid:

- Click and drag each field individually from the field list to the design grid. Use this method if you want the fields in your query to appear in an order that is different from the order in the field list.
- Double-click the asterisk in the field list. Access places the table name followed by a period and an asterisk (as in "Employer.*") in the design grid, which signifies that the order of the fields is the same in the query as it is in the field list. Use this method if you don't need to sort the query or specify conditions for the records you want to select. The advantage of using this method is that you do not need to change the query if you add or delete fields from the underlying table structure. Such changes are reflected automatically in the query.
- Double-click the field list title bar to highlight all the fields, and then click and drag one of the highlighted fields to the design grid. Access places each field in a separate column and arranges the fields in the order in which they appear in the field list. Use this method when you need to sort your query or include record selection criteria.

Now you'll create and run Zack's query to display selected fields from the Employer table.

Creating and Running a Query

The default table datasheet displays all the fields in the table, in the same order as they appear in the table. In contrast, a query datasheet can display selected fields from a table, and the order of the fields can be different from that of the table, enabling those viewing the query results to see only the information they need and in the order they want.

Zack wants the Employer table's EmployerID, EmployerName, City, ContactFirstName, ContactLastName, and Website fields to appear in the query results. You'll add each of these fields to the design grid.

To select the fields for the query, and then run the query:

▶ **1.** Drag **EmployerID** from the Employer field list to the design grid's first column Field text box, and then release the mouse button. See Figure 3-3.

Field added to the design grid ◀ **Figure 3-3**

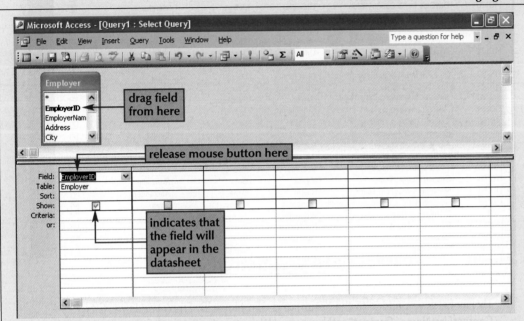

In the design grid's first column, the field name EmployerID appears in the Field text box, the table name Employer appears in the Table text box, and the check mark in the Show check box indicates that the field will be displayed in the datasheet when you run the query. Sometimes you might not want to display a field and its values in the query results. For example, if you are creating a query to show all employers located in Massachusetts, and you assign the name "EmployersInMassachusetts" to the query, you do not need to include the StateProv field value for each record in the query results—every StateProv field value would be "MA" for Massachusetts. Even if you choose not to include a field in the display of the query results, you can still use the field as part of the query to select specific records or to specify a particular sequence for the records in the datasheet.

▶ **2.** Double-click **EmployerName** in the Employer field list. Access adds this field to the second column of the design grid.

▶ **3.** Scrolling the Employer field list as necessary, repeat Step 2 for the **City**, **ContactFirstName**, **ContactLastName**, and **Website** fields to add these fields to the design grid in that order.

Trouble? If you double-click the wrong field and accidentally add it to the design grid, you can remove the field from the grid. Select the field's column by clicking the pointer ↓ on the bar above the Field text box for the field you want to delete, and then press the Delete key (or click Edit on the menu bar, and then click Delete Columns).

Having selected the fields for Zack's query, you can now run the query.

4. Click the **Run** button ⚡ on the Query Design toolbar. Access runs the query and displays the results in Datasheet view. See Figure 3-4.

Figure 3-4 ▶ **Datasheet displayed after running the query**

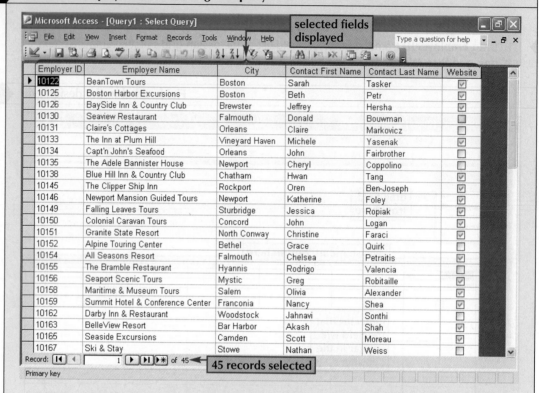

The six fields you added to the design grid—EmployerID, EmployerName, City, ContactFirstName, ContactLastName, and Website—appear in the datasheet, and the records are displayed in primary key sequence by EmployerID. Access selected a total of 45 records for display in the datasheet.

Zack asks you to save the query as "EmployerAnalysis" so that he can easily retrieve the same data again.

5. Click the **Save** button 💾 on the Query Datasheet toolbar. The Save As dialog box opens.

6. Type **EmployerAnalysis** in the Query Name text box, and then press the **Enter** key. Access saves the query with the specified name in the Northeast database and displays the name in the title bar.

When viewing the results of the query, Zack noticed a couple of changes that need to be made to the data in the Employer table. The Adele Bannister House recently developed a Web site, so the Website field for this record needs to be updated. In addition, the contact information has changed for the Alpine Touring Center.

Updating Data Using a Query

Although a query datasheet is temporary and its contents are based on the criteria in the query design grid, you can update the data in a table using a query datasheet. In this case, Zack has changes he wants you to make to records in the Employer table. Instead of making the changes in the table datasheet, you can make them in the EmployerAnalysis query datasheet. The underlying Employer table will be updated with the changes you make.

To update data using the EmployerAnalysis query datasheet:

1. For the record with EmployerID 10135 (The Adele Bannister House), click the check box in the Website field to place a check mark in it.

2. For the record with EmployerID 10152 (Alpine Touring Center), change the ContactFirstName field value to **Mary** and change the ContactLastName field value to **Grant**.

3. Click the **Close Window** button ⊠ on the menu bar to close the query. Note that the EmployerAnalysis query appears in the list of queries.

4. Click the **Restore Window** button ⊡ on the menu bar to return the Database window to its original size.

    Now you will check the Employer table to verify that the changes you made in the query datasheet were also made to the Employer table records.

5. Click **Tables** in the Objects bar of the Database window, click **Employer** in the list of tables, and then click the **Open** button. The Employer table datasheet opens.

6. For the record with EmployerID 10135, scroll the datasheet to the right to verify that the Website field contains a check mark. For the record with EmployerID 10152, scroll to the right to see the new contact information (Mary Grant).

7. Click the **Close** button ⊠ on the Employer table window to close it.

Matt also wants to view specific information in the Northeast database. However, he needs to see data from both the Employer table and the Position table at the same time. To view data from two tables at the same time, you need to define a relationship between the tables.

Defining Table Relationships

One of the most powerful features of a relational database management system is its ability to define relationships between tables. You use a common field to relate one table to another. The process of relating tables is often called performing a **join**. When you join tables that have a common field, you can extract data from them as if they were one larger table. For example, you can join the Employer and Position tables by using the EmployerID field in both tables as the common field. Then you can use a query, a form, or a report to extract selected data from each table, even though the data is contained in two separate tables, as shown in Figure 3-5. In the Positions query shown in Figure 3-5, the PositionID, PositionTitle, and Wage columns are fields from the Position table, and the EmployerName and StateProv columns are fields from the Employer table. The joining of records is based on the common field of EmployerID. The Employer and Position tables have a type of relationship called a one-to-many relationship.

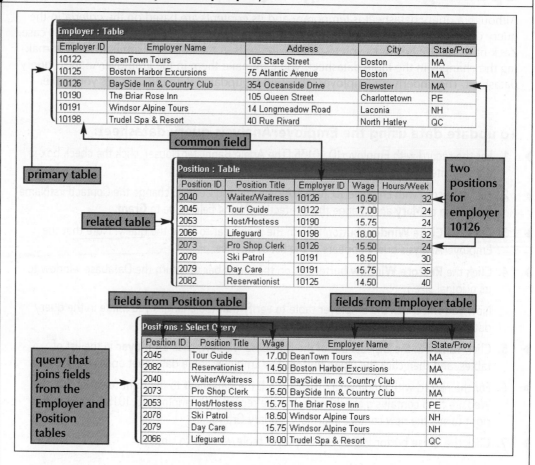

Figure 3-5 ▶ One-to-many relationship and sample query

One-to-Many Relationships

A **one-to-many relationship** exists between two tables when one record in the first table matches zero, one, or many records in the second table, and when one record in the second table matches exactly one record in the first table. For example, as shown in Figure 3-5, employers 10126 and 10191 each have two available positions, and employers 10122, 10125, 10190, and 10198 each have one available position. Every position has a single matching employer.

Access refers to the two tables that form a relationship as the primary table and the related table. The **primary table** is the "one" table in a one-to-many relationship; in Figure 3-5, the Employer table is the primary table because there is only one employer for each available position. The **related table** is the "many" table; in Figure 3-5, the Position table is the related table because there can be many positions offered by each employer.

Because related data is stored in two tables, inconsistencies between the tables can occur. Consider the following scenarios:

- Matt adds a position record to the Position table for a new employer, Glen Cove Inn, using EmployerID 10132. Matt did not first add the new employer's information to the Employer table, so this position does not have a matching record in the Employer table. The data is inconsistent, and the position record is considered to be an **orphaned record**.

- Matt changes the EmployerID in the Employer table for BaySide Inn & Country Club from 10126 to 10128. Two orphaned records for employer 10126 now exist in the Position table, and the database is inconsistent.

- Matt deletes the record for Boston Harbor Excursions, employer 10125, in the Employer table because this employer is no longer an NSJI client. The database is again inconsistent; one record for employer 10125 in the Position table has no matching record in the Employer table.

You can avoid these problems by specifying referential integrity between tables when you define their relationships.

Referential Integrity

Referential integrity is a set of rules that Access enforces to maintain consistency between related tables when you update data in a database. Specifically, the referential integrity rules are as follows:

- When you add a record to a related table, a matching record must already exist in the primary table, thereby preventing the possibility of orphaned records.
- If you attempt to change the value of the primary key in the primary table, Access prevents this change if matching records exist in a related table. However, if you choose the **cascade updates option**, Access permits the change in value to the primary key and changes the appropriate foreign key values in the related table, thereby eliminating the possibility of inconsistent data.
- When you attempt to delete a record in the primary table, Access prevents the deletion if matching records exist in a related table. However, if you choose the **cascade deletes option**, Access deletes the record in the primary table and also deletes all records in related tables that have matching foreign key values. Note, however, that you should *rarely* select the cascade deletes option, because setting this option might cause you to inadvertently delete records you did not intend to delete.

Now you'll define a one-to-many relationship between the Employer and Position tables so that you can use fields from both tables to create a query that will retrieve the information Matt needs. You will also define a one-to-many relationship between the NAICS (primary) table and the Employer (related) table.

Defining a Relationship Between Two Tables

When two tables have a common field, you can define a relationship between them in the Relationships window. The **Relationships window** illustrates the relationships among a database's tables. In this window, you can view or change existing relationships, define new relationships between tables, and rearrange the layout of the tables in the window.

You need to open the Relationships window and define the relationship between the Employer and Position tables. You'll define a one-to-many relationship between the two tables, with Employer as the primary table and Position as the related table, and with EmployerID as the common field (the primary key in the Employer table and a foreign key in the Position table). You'll also define a one-to-many relationship between the NAICS and Employer tables, with NAICS as the primary table and Employer as the related table, and with NAICSCode as the common field (the primary key in the NAICS table and a foreign key in the Employer table).

To define the one-to-many relationship between the Employer and Position tables:

▶ 1. Click the **Relationships** button [icon] on the Database toolbar. The Show Table dialog box opens on top of the Relationships window. See Figure 3-6.

Figure 3-6 | **Show Table dialog box**

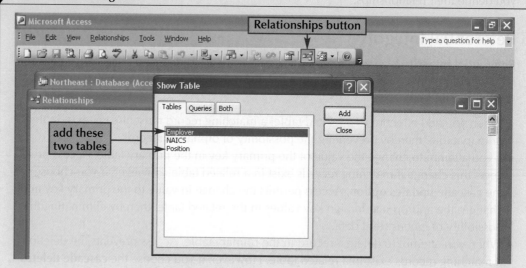

You must add each table participating in a relationship to the Relationships window.

▶ 2. Click **Employer** (if necessary), and then click the **Add** button. The Employer field list is added to the Relationships window.

▶ 3. Click **Position**, and then click the **Add** button. The Position field list is added to the Relationships window.

▶ 4. Click the **Close** button in the Show Table dialog box to close it and reveal the entire Relationships window.

So that you can view all the fields and complete field names, you'll first move the Position field list box further to the right, and then resize both field list boxes.

▶ 5. Click the Position field list title bar and drag the list to the right (see Figure 3-7), and then release the mouse button.

▶ 6. Use the ↔ pointer to drag the right side of each list box to widen it until the complete field names are displayed, and then use the ↕ pointer to drag the bottom of each list box to lengthen it until all the fields are visible. Make sure that both field list boxes no longer contain scroll bars, and that they are sized and positioned similar to those shown in Figure 3-7.

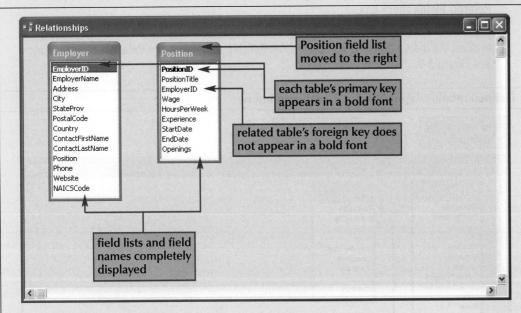

Notice that EmployerID in the Employer table appears in a bold font; this indicates that the field is the table's primary key (the same is true of PositionID in the Position table). On the other hand, the EmployerID field in the Position table is not bold, which is a reminder that this field is the foreign key in this table.

To form the relationship between the two tables, you drag the common field of EmployerID from the primary table to the related table. Then Access opens the Edit Relationships dialog box, in which you select the relationship options for the two tables.

▶ 7. Click **EmployerID** in the Employer field list, and then drag it to **EmployerID** in the Position field list. When you release the mouse button, the Edit Relationships dialog box opens. See Figure 3-8.

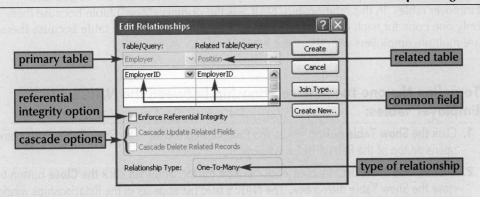

The primary table, related table, and common field appear at the top of the dialog box. The type of relationship, One-To-Many, appears at the bottom of the dialog box. When you click the Enforce Referential Integrity check box, the two cascade options become available. If you select the Cascade Update Related Fields option, Access changes the appropriate foreign key values in the related table when you change a primary key value in the primary table. You will not select the Cascade Delete Related Records option, because doing so could cause you to delete records that you did not want to delete; this option is rarely selected.

8. Click the **Enforce Referential Integrity** check box, and then click the **Cascade Update Related Fields** check box.

9. Click the **Create** button to define the one-to-many relationship between the two tables and to close the dialog box. The completed relationship appears in the Relationships window. See Figure 3-9.

| Figure 3-9 | Defined relationship in the Relationships window |

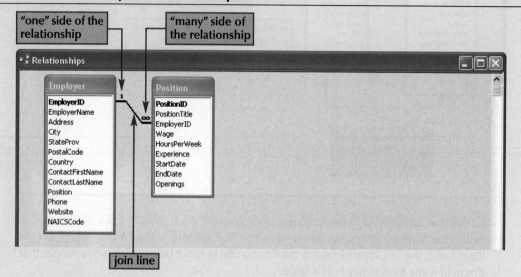

The **join line** connects the EmployerID fields, which are common to the two tables. The common field joins the two tables, which have a one-to-many relationship. The "one" side of the relationship has the digit 1 at its end, and the "many" side of the relationship has the infinity symbol ∞ at its end. The two tables are still separate tables, but you can use the data in them as if they were one table.

Now you need to define the one-to-many relationship between the NAICS and Employer tables. In this relationship, NAICS is the primary ("one") table because there is only one code for each employer. Employer is the related ("many") table because there are multiple employers with the same NAICS code.

To define the one-to-many relationship between the NAICS and Employer tables:

1. Click the **Show Table** button on the Relationship toolbar. The Show Table dialog box opens on top of the Relationships window.

2. Click **NAICS** in the list of tables, click the **Add** button, and then click the **Close** button to close the Show Table dialog box. The NAICS field list appears in the Relationships window to the right of the Position field list. To make it easier to define the relationship, you'll move the NAICS field list below the Employer and Position field lists.

3. Click the NAICS field list title bar and drag the list until it is below the Position table (see Figure 3-10), and then release the mouse button.

   Because the NAICS table is the primary table in this relationship, you need to drag the NAICSCode field from the NAICS field list to the Employer field list.

4. Click and drag the **NAICSCode** field in the NAICS field list to the **NAICSCode** field in the Employer field list. When you release the mouse button, the Edit Relationships dialog box opens.

5. Click the **Enforce Referential Integrity** check box, and then click the **Cascade Update Related Fields** check box.

6. Click the **Create** button to define the one-to-many relationship between the two tables and close the dialog box. The completed relationship appears in the Relationships window. See Figure 3-10.

Both relationships defined ◄ | **Figure 3-10**

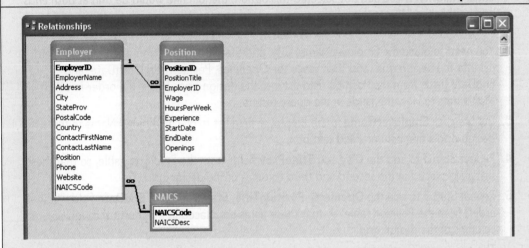

With both relationships defined, you have connected the data among the three tables in the Northeast database.

7. Click the **Save** button 🔲 on the Relationship toolbar to save the layout in the Relationships window.

8. Click the **Close** button ☒ on the Relationships window title bar. The Relationships window closes, and you return to the Database window.

You've established relationships among the three tables in the Northeast database, so you can now create queries that let Matt view data from the Employer table and the Position table at the same time.

Creating a Multi-table Query

Now that you have joined the Employer and Position tables, you can create a query to produce the information Matt wants. To help him determine his recruiting needs, Matt wants a query that displays the EmployerName, City, and StateProv fields from the Employer table and the Openings, PositionTitle, StartDate, and EndDate fields from the Position table.

To create, run, and save the query using the Employer and Position tables:

▶ 1. Click **Queries** in the Objects bar of the Database window, and then double-click **Create query in Design view**. The Show Table dialog box opens on top of the Query window in Design view.

You need to add the Employer and Position tables to the Query window.

▶ 2. Click **Employer** in the Tables list box (if necessary), click the **Add** button, click **Position**, click the **Add** button, and then click the **Close** button. The Employer and Position field lists appear in the Query window, and the Show Table dialog box closes. Note that the one-to-many relationship between the two tables is shown in the Query window. Also, notice that the join line is thick at both ends; this signifies that you selected the option to enforce referential integrity. If you had not selected this option, the join line would be thin at both ends and neither the "1" nor the infinity symbol would appear, even though there is a one-to-many relationship between the two tables.

You need to place the EmployerName, City, and StateProv fields from the Employer field list into the design grid, and then place the Openings, PositionTitle, StartDate, and EndDate fields from the Position field list into the design grid. This is the order in which Matt wants to view the fields in the query results.

▶ 3. Double-click **EmployerName** in the Employer field list to place EmployerName in the design grid's first column Field text box.

▶ 4. Repeat Step 3 to add the **City** and **StateProv** fields from the Employer table, so that these fields are placed in the second and third columns of the design grid.

▶ 5. Repeat Step 3 to add the **Openings**, **PositionTitle**, **StartDate**, and **EndDate** fields (in that order) from the Position table, so that these fields are placed in the fourth through seventh columns of the design grid.

The query specifications are completed, so you can now run the query.

▶ 6. Click the **Run** button on the Query Design toolbar. Access runs the query and displays the results in the datasheet.

▶ 7. Click the **Maximize** button on the Query window title bar. See Figure 3-11.

Figure 3-11	Datasheet for the query based on the Employer and Position tables

Only the seven selected fields from the Employer and Position tables appear in the datasheet. The records are displayed in order according to the values in the primary key field, EmployerID, even though this field is not included in the query datasheet.

Matt plans on frequently tracking the data retrieved by the query, so he asks you to save the query as "EmployerPositions."

8. Click the **Save** button 🖫 on the Query Datasheet toolbar. The Save As dialog box opens.

9. Type **EmployerPositions** in the Query Name text box, and then press the **Enter** key. Access saves the query with the specified name and displays the name in the title bar.

Matt decides he wants the records displayed in alphabetical order by employer name. Because the query displays data in order by the field value of EmployerID, which is the primary key for the Employer table, you need to sort the records by EmployerName to display the data in the order Matt wants.

Sorting Data in a Query

Sorting is the process of rearranging records in a specified order or sequence. Sometimes you might need to sort data before displaying or printing it to meet a specific request. For example, Matt might want to review position information arranged by the StartDate field because he needs to know which positions are available earliest in the year. On the other hand, Elsa might want to view position information arranged by the Openings field for each employer, because she monitors employer activity for NSJI.

When you sort data in a query, you do not change the sequence of the records in the underlying tables. Only the records in the query datasheet are rearranged according to your specifications.

To sort records, you must select the **sort field**, which is the field used to determine the order of records in the datasheet. In this case, Matt wants the data sorted by the employer name, so you need to specify EmployerName as the sort field. Sort fields can be text, number, date/time, currency, AutoNumber, yes/no, or Lookup Wizard fields, but not memo, OLE object, or hyperlink fields. You sort records in either ascending (increasing) or descending (decreasing) order. Figure 3-12 shows the results of each type of sort for different data types.

Sorting results for different data types ◀ **Figure 3-12**

Data Type	Ascending Sort Results	Descending Sort Results
Text	A to Z	Z to A
Number	lowest to highest numeric value	highest to lowest numeric value
Date/Time	oldest to most recent date	most recent to oldest date
Currency	lowest to highest numeric value	highest to lowest numeric value
AutoNumber	lowest to highest numeric value	highest to lowest numeric value
Yes/No	yes (check mark in check box) then no values	no then yes values

Access provides several methods for sorting data in a table or query datasheet and in a form. One method, clicking a toolbar sort button, lets you sort the displayed records quickly.

Using a Toolbar Button to Sort Data

The **Sort Ascending** and **Sort Descending buttons** on the toolbar allow you to sort records immediately, based on the values in the selected field. First you select the column on which you want to base the sort, and then you click the appropriate sort button on the toolbar to rearrange the records in either ascending or descending order. Unless you save the datasheet or form after you've sorted the records, the rearrangement of records is temporary.

Recall that in Tutorial 1 you used the Sort Ascending button to sort query results by the StateProv field. You'll use this same button to sort the EmployerPositions query results by the EmployerName field.

To sort the records using a toolbar sort button:

▶ 1. Click any visible EmployerName field value to establish the field as the current field (if necessary).

▶ 2. Click the **Sort Ascending** button ![Sort Ascending icon] on the Query Datasheet toolbar. The records are rearranged in ascending order by employer name. See Figure 3-13.

| Figure 3-13 | Sorting records on a single field in a datasheet |

After viewing the query results, Matt decides that he'd prefer to see the records arranged by the value in the PositionTitle field, so that he can identify the types of positions he needs to fill. He also wants to display the records in descending order according to the value of the Openings field, so that he can easily see how many openings there are for each position. In addition, he wants the Openings field values to be displayed in the rightmost column of the query results so that they stand out in the query datasheet. To produce the results Matt wants, you need to sort using two fields.

Sorting Multiple Fields in Design View

Sort fields can be unique or nonunique. A sort field is **unique** if the value of the sort field for each record is different. The EmployerID field in the Employer table is an example of a unique sort field because each employer record has a different value in this field. A sort field is **nonunique** if more than one record can have the same value for the sort field. For example, the PositionTitle field in the Position table is a nonunique sort field because more than one record can have the same PositionTitle value.

When the sort field is nonunique, records with the same sort field value are grouped together, but they are not in a specific order within the group. To arrange these grouped records in a specific order, you can specify a **secondary sort field**, which is a second field that determines the order of records that are already sorted by the **primary sort field** (the first sort field specified). Note that the primary sort field is *not* the same as a table's primary key field. A table has at most one primary key, which must be unique, whereas any field in a table can serve as a primary sort field.

Access lets you select up to 10 different sort fields. When you use the toolbar sort buttons, the sort fields must be in adjacent columns in the datasheet. You highlight the adjacent columns, and Access sorts first by the first column and then by each remaining highlighted column in order from left to right.

Matt wants the records sorted first by the PositionTitle field and then by the Openings field. The two fields are adjacent, but not in the correct left-to-right order, so you cannot use the toolbar buttons to sort them. You could move the Openings field to the right of the PositionTitle field in the query datasheet. However, you can specify only one type of sort—either ascending or descending—for selected columns in the query datasheet. This is not what Matt wants; he wants the PositionTitle field values to be sorted in ascending alphabetical order and the Openings field values to be sorted in descending order. To accomplish the differing sort orders for the PositionTitle and Openings fields, you must specify the sort fields in Design view.

In the Query window in Design view, Access first uses the sort field that is leftmost in the design grid. Therefore, you must arrange the fields you want to sort from left to right in the design grid, with the primary sort field being the leftmost. In Design view, multiple sort fields do not have to be adjacent to each other, as they do in Datasheet view; however, they must be in the correct left-to-right order.

Sorting a Query Datasheet

Reference Window

- In the query datasheet, select the column or adjacent columns on which you want to sort.
- Click the Sort Ascending button or the Sort Descending button on the Query Datasheet toolbar.

or

- In Design view, position the fields serving as sort fields from left (primary sort field) to right, and then select the sort order for each sort field.

To achieve the results Matt wants, you need to switch to Design view, move the Openings field to the right of the EndDate field, and then specify the sort order for the two fields.

To select the two sort fields in Design view:

1. Click the **View** button for Design view ◪ on the Query Datasheet toolbar to open the query in Design view.

   First, you'll move the Openings field to the right of the EndDate field, because Matt wants the Openings field to be the rightmost column in the query results. Remember, in Design view, the sort fields do not have to be adjacent, and non-sort fields can appear between sort fields. So, you will move the Openings field to the end of the query design, following the EndDate field.

2. If necessary, click the right arrow in the design grid's horizontal scroll bar a few times to scroll to the right so that both the Openings and EndDate fields are completely visible.

3. Position the pointer in the Openings field selector until the pointer changes to a ↓ shape, and then click to select the field. See Figure 3-14.

Figure 3-14 ▶ Selected Openings field

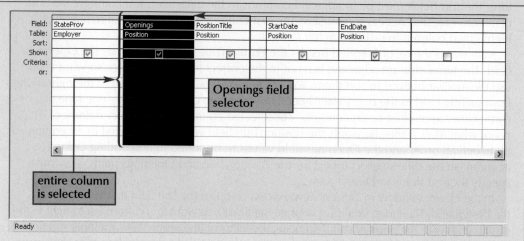

Openings field selector

entire column is selected

Ready

▶ **4.** Position the pointer in the Openings field selector, and then click and drag the pointer ☒ to the right until the vertical line on the right of the EndDate field is highlighted. See Figure 3-15.

Figure 3-15 ▶ Dragging the field in the design grid

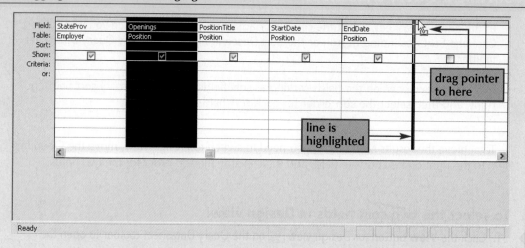

drag pointer to here

line is highlighted

Ready

▶ **5.** Release the mouse button. The Openings field moves to the right of the EndDate field.

The fields are now in the correct order for the sort. Next, you need to specify an ascending sort order for the PositionTitle field and a descending sort order for the Openings field.

▶ **6.** Click the right side of the **PositionTitle Sort** text box to display the list arrow and the sort options, and then click **Ascending**. You've selected an ascending sort order for the PositionTitle field, which will be the primary sort field. The PositionTitle field is a text field, and an ascending sort order will display the field values in alphabetical order.

▶ **7.** Click the right side of the **Openings Sort** text box, click **Descending**, and then click in one of the empty text boxes to the right of the Openings field to deselect the setting. You've selected a descending sort order for the Openings field, which will be the secondary sort field, because it appears to the right of the primary sort field (PositionTitle) in the design grid. See Figure 3-16.

Selecting two sort fields in Design view | **Figure 3-16**

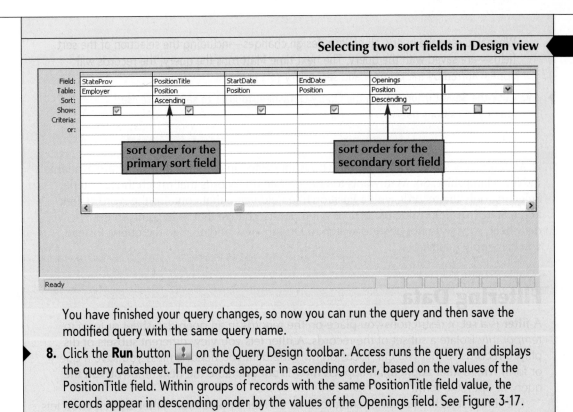

You have finished your query changes, so now you can run the query and then save the modified query with the same query name.

8. Click the **Run** button on the Query Design toolbar. Access runs the query and displays the query datasheet. The records appear in ascending order, based on the values of the PositionTitle field. Within groups of records with the same PositionTitle field value, the records appear in descending order by the values of the Openings field. See Figure 3-17.

Datasheet sorted on two fields | **Figure 3-17**

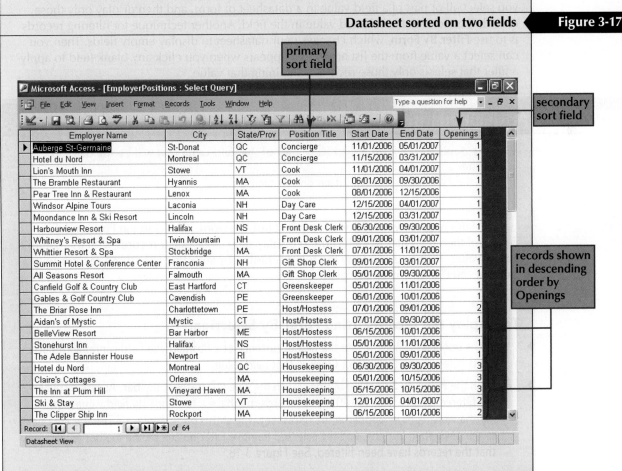

When you save the query, all of your design changes—including the selection of the sort fields—are saved with the query. The next time Matt runs the query, the records will appear sorted by the primary and secondary sort fields.

▶ 9. Click the **Save** button 🔲 on the Query Datasheet toolbar to save the revised EmployerPositions query.

Matt recently spoke with a recruit who is interested in clerk positions that are available in New Hampshire. So, Matt wants to concentrate on records that match those criteria. Selecting only the records with a PositionTitle field value that contains the word "Clerk" and a StateProv field value of "NH" is a temporary change that Matt wants in the datasheet, so you do not need to switch to Design view and change the query. Instead, you can apply a filter.

Filtering Data

A **filter** is a set of restrictions you place on the records in an open datasheet or form to *temporarily* isolate a subset of the records. A filter lets you view different subsets of displayed records so that you can focus on only the data you need. Unless you save a query or form with a filter applied, an applied filter is not available the next time you run the query or open the form.

The simplest technique for filtering records is Filter By Selection. **Filter By Selection** lets you select all or part of a field value in a datasheet or form, and then display only those records that contain the selected value in the field. Another technique for filtering records is to use **Filter By Form**, which changes your datasheet to display empty fields. Then you can select a value from the list arrow that appears when you click any blank field to apply a filter that selects only those records containing that value.

Reference Window	**Using Filter By Selection**

- In the datasheet or form, select all or part of the field value that will be the basis for the filter.
- Click the Filter By Selection button on the toolbar.

For Matt's request, you first need to select just the word "Clerk" in the PositionTitle field, and then use Filter By Selection to display only those query records with this same partial value. Then you will filter the records further by selecting only those records with a value of "NH" in the StateProv field.

To display the records using Filter By Selection:

▶ 1. In the query datasheet, locate the first occurrence of a PositionTitle field containing the word "Clerk," and then select **Clerk** in that field value.

▶ 2. Click the **Filter By Selection** button 🔽 on the Query Datasheet toolbar. Access displays the filtered results. Only the 10 query records that have a PositionTitle field value containing the word "Clerk" appear in the datasheet. The status bar's display (FLTR), the area next to the navigation buttons, and the selected Remove Filter button on the toolbar all indicate that the records have been filtered. See Figure 3-18.

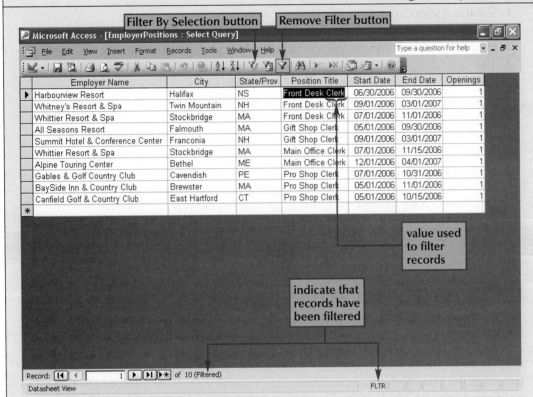

Next, Matt wants to view only those records with a StateProv value of NH, because the recruit is interested in positions in NH only.

3. Click in any StateProv field value of **NH**, and then click the **Filter By Selection** button 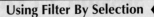 on the Query Datasheet toolbar. The filtered display now shows only the 2 records for clerk positions available in New Hampshire.

Now you can redisplay all the query records by clicking the Remove Filter button; this button works as a toggle to switch between the filtered and nonfiltered displays.

4. Click the **Remove Filter** button ⛛ on the Query Datasheet toolbar. Access redisplays all the records in the query datasheet.

5. Click the **Save** button 🖫 on the Query Datasheet toolbar, and then click the **Close Window** button ✕ on the menu bar to save and close the query and return to the Database window.

6. Click the **Restore Window** button 🗗 on the menu bar to return the Database window to its original size.

The queries you've created will help NSJI employees retrieve just the information they want to view. In the next session, you'll continue to create queries to meet their information needs.

Session 3.1 Quick Check

1. What is a select query?
2. Describe the field list and the design grid in the Query window in Design view.
3. How are a table datasheet and a query datasheet similar? How are they different?
4. The _____ is the "one" table in a one-to-many relationship, and the _____ is the "many" table in the relationship.
5. _____ is a set of rules that Access enforces to maintain consistency between related tables when you update data in a database.
6. For a date/time field, how do the records appear when sorted in ascending order?
7. True or False: When you define multiple sort fields in Design view, the sort fields must be adjacent to each other.
8. A(n) _____ is a set of restrictions you place on the records in an open datasheet or form to isolate a subset of records temporarily.

Session 3.2

Defining Record Selection Criteria for Queries

Matt wants to display employer and position information for all positions with a start date of 07/01/2006, so that he can plan his recruitment efforts accordingly. For this request, you could create a query to select the correct fields and all records in the Employer and Position tables, select a StartDate field value of 07/01/2006 in the query datasheet, and then click the Filter By Selection button to filter the query results to display only those positions starting on July 1, 2006. However, a faster way of displaying the data Matt needs is to create a query that displays the selected fields and only those records in the Employer and Position tables that satisfy a condition.

Just as you can display selected fields from a database in a query datasheet, you can display selected records. To tell Access which records you want to select, you must specify a condition as part of the query. A **condition** is a criterion, or rule, that determines which records are selected. To define a condition for a field, you place the condition in the field's Criteria text box in the design grid.

A condition usually consists of an operator, often a comparison operator, and a value. A **comparison operator** asks Access to compare the value in a database field to the condition value and to select all the records for which the relationship is true. For example, the condition >15.00 for the Wage field selects all records in the Position table having Wage field values greater than 15.00. Figure 3-19 shows the Access comparison operators.

Figure 3-19 | **Access comparison operators**

Operator	Meaning	Example
=	equal to (optional; default operator)	="Hall"
<	less than	<#1/1/99#
<=	less than or equal to	<=100
>	greater than	>"C400"
>=	greater than or equal to	>=18.75
<>	not equal to	<>"Hall"
Between ... And...	between two values (inclusive)	Between 50 And 325
In ()	in a list of values	In ("Hall", "Seeger")
Like	matches a pattern that includes wildcards	Like "706*"

Specifying an Exact Match

For Matt's request, you need to create a query that will display only those records in the Position table with the value 07/01/2006 in the StartDate field. This type of condition is called an **exact match** because the value in the specified field must match the condition exactly in order for the record to be included in the query results. You'll use the Simple Query Wizard to create the query, and then you'll specify the exact match condition.

To create the query using the Simple Query Wizard:

1. If you took a break after the previous session, make sure that Access is running, the Northeast database is open, and the Queries object is selected in the Database window.

2. Double-click **Create query by using wizard**. Access opens the first Simple Query Wizard dialog box, in which you select the tables (or queries) and fields for the query.

3. Click the **Tables/Queries** list arrow, and then click **Table: Position**. The fields in the Position table appear in the Available Fields list box. Except for the PositionID and EmployerID fields, you will include all fields from the Position table in the query.

4. Click the >> button. All the fields from the Available Fields list box move to the Selected Fields list box.

5. Scroll up and click **PositionID** in the Selected Fields list box, click the < button to move the PositionID field back to the Available Fields list box, click **EmployerID** in the Selected Fields list box, and then click the < button to move the EmployerID field back to the Available Fields list box.

   Matt also wants certain information from the Employer table included in the query results. Because he wants the fields from the Employer table to appear in the query datasheet to the right of the fields from the Position table fields, you need to click the last field in the Selected Fields list box so that the new Employer fields will be inserted below it in the list.

6. Click **Openings** in the Selected Fields list box.

7. Click the **Tables/Queries** list arrow, and then click **Table: Employer**. The fields in the Employer table now appear in the Available Fields list box. Notice that the fields you selected from the Position table remain in the Selected Fields list box.

8. Click **EmployerName** in the Available Fields list box, and then click the > button to move EmployerName to the Selected Fields list box, below the Openings field.

9. Repeat Step 8 to move the **StateProv**, **ContactFirstName**, **ContactLastName**, and **Phone** fields into the Selected Fields list box. (Note that you can also double-click a field to move it from the Available Fields list box to the Selected Fields list box.)

10. Click the **Next** button to open the second Simple Query Wizard dialog box, in which you choose whether the query will display records from the selected tables or a summary of those records. Summary options show calculations such as average, minimum, maximum, and so on. Matt wants to view the details for the records, not a summary.

11. Make sure the **Detail (shows every field of every record)** option button is selected, and then click the **Next** button to open the last Simple Query Wizard dialog box, in which you choose a name for the query and complete the wizard. You need to enter a condition for the query, so you'll want to modify the query's design.

12. Type **July1Positions**, click the **Modify the query design** option button, and then click the **Finish** button. Access saves the query as July1Positions and opens the query in Design view. See Figure 3-20.

Figure 3-20

Query in Design view

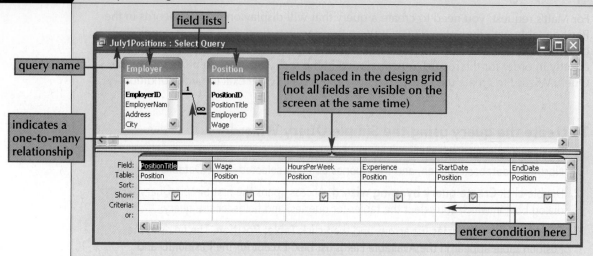

The field lists for the Employer and Position tables appear in the top portion of the window, and the join line indicating a one-to-many relationship connects the two tables. The selected fields appear in the design grid. Not all of the fields are visible in the grid; to see the other selected fields, you need to scroll to the right using the horizontal scroll bar.

To display the information Matt wants, you need to enter the condition for the StartDate field in its Criteria text box. Matt wants to display only those records with a start date of 07/01/2006.

To enter the exact match condition, and then run the query:

1. Click the **StartDate Criteria** text box, type **07/01/2006**, and then press the **Enter** key. The condition changes to #7/1/2006#.

   Access automatically placed number signs (#) before and after the condition. You must place date and time values inside number signs when using these values as selection criteria. If you omit the number signs, however, Access will include them automatically.

2. Click the **Run** button on the Query Design toolbar. Access runs the query and displays the selected field values for only those records with a StartDate field value of 07/01/2006. A total of 9 records are selected and displayed in the datasheet. See Figure 3-21.

Figure 3-21

Datasheet displaying selected fields and records

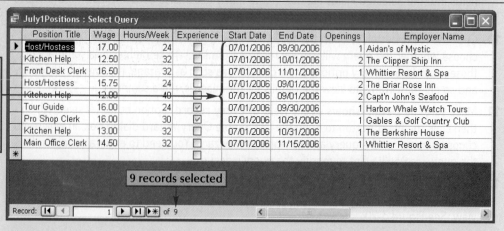

3. Click the **Save** button on the Query Datasheet toolbar to save the query.

Matt would like to see more fields and records on the screen at one time. He asks you to maximize the datasheet, change the datasheet's font size, and resize all the columns to their best fit.

Changing a Datasheet's Appearance

You can change the characteristics of a datasheet, including the font type and size of text in the datasheet, to improve its appearance or readability. As you learned in Tutorial 2, you can also resize the datasheet columns to view more columns on the screen at the same time.

You'll maximize the datasheet, change the font size from the default 10 points to 8, and then resize the datasheet columns.

To change the font size and resize columns in the datasheet:

1. Click the **Maximize** button 🔲 on the Query window title bar.

2. Click **Format** on the menu bar, and then click **Font** to open the Font dialog box.

3. Scroll the Size list box, click **8**, and then click the **OK** button. The font size for the entire datasheet changes to 8.

   Next, you need to resize the columns to their best fit, so that each column is just wide enough to fit the longest value in the column. Instead of resizing each column individually, as you did in Tutorial 2, you'll select all the columns and resize them at the same time.

4. Position the pointer in the PositionTitle field selector. When the pointer changes to a ⬇ shape, click to select the entire column.

5. Click the right arrow on the horizontal scroll bar until the Phone field is fully visible, and then position the pointer in the Phone field selector until the pointer changes to a ⬇ shape.

6. Press and hold the **Shift** key, and then click the mouse button. All the columns are selected. Now you can resize all of them at once.

7. Position the pointer at the right edge of the Phone field selector until the pointer changes to a ➕ shape. See Figure 3-22.

Preparing to resize all columns to their best fit ◄ **Figure 3-22**

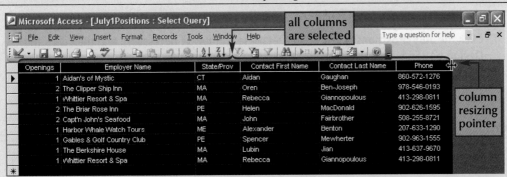

8. Double-click the mouse button. All columns are resized to their best fit, which makes each column just large enough to fit the longest *visible* value in the column, including the field name at the top of the column.

9. Scroll to the left, if necessary, so that the PositionTitle field is visible, and then click any field value box (except an Experience field value) to deselect all columns. See Figure 3-23.

| Figure 3-23 | Datasheet after changing font size and column widths |

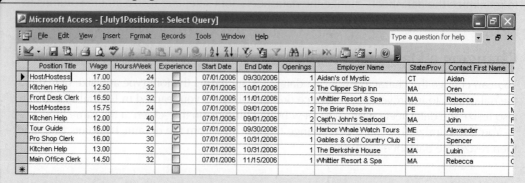

Trouble? Your screen might show more or fewer columns, depending on the monitor you are using.

10. Save and close the query. You return to the Database window.

After viewing the query results, Matt decides that he would like to see the same fields, but only for those records whose Wage field value is equal to or greater than 17.00. He needs this information when he recruits students who require a higher wage per hour for the available positions. To create the query needed to produce these results, you need to use a comparison operator to match a range of values—in this case, any Wage value greater than or equal to 17.00.

Using a Comparison Operator to Match a Range of Values

Once you create and save a query, you can click the Open button to run it again, or you can click the Design button to change its design. Because the design of the query you need to create next is similar to the July1Positions query, you will change its design, run the query to test it, and then save the query with a new name, which keeps the July1Positions query intact.

To change the July1Positions query design to create a new query:

1. Click the **July1Positions** query in the Database window (if necessary), and then click the **Design** button to open the July1Positions query in Design view.

2. Click the **Wage Criteria** text box, type **>=17**, and then press the **Tab** key three times. See Figure 3-24.

| Figure 3-24 | Changing a query's design to create a new query |

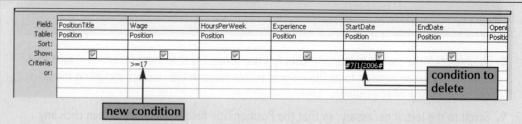

Matt's new condition specifies that a record will be selected only if its Wage field value is 17.00 or higher. Before you run the query, you need to delete the condition for the StartDate field.

3. With the StartDate field condition highlighted, press the **Delete** key. Now there is no condition for the StartDate field.

4. Click the **Run** button 🔔 on the Query Design toolbar. Access runs the query and displays the selected fields for only those records with a Wage field value greater than or equal to 17.00. A total of 19 records are selected. See Figure 3-25.

Running the modified query ◀ **Figure 3-25**

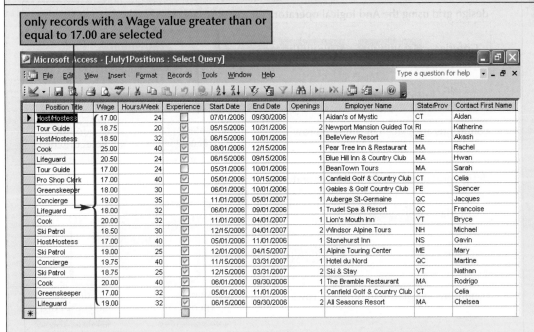

only records with a Wage value greater than or equal to 17.00 are selected

So that Matt can display this information again, as necessary, you'll save the query as HighWageAmounts.

5. Click **File** on the menu bar, and then click **Save As** to open the Save As dialog box.

6. In the text box for the new query name, type **HighWageAmounts**. Notice that the As text box specifies that you are saving the data as a query.

7. Click the **OK** button to save the query using the new name. The new query name appears in the title bar.

8. Close the Query window and return to the Database window.

Elsa asks Matt for a list of the positions with a start date of 07/01/2006 for only the employers in Prince Edward Island. She wants to increase NSJI's business activity throughout eastern Canada (Prince Edward Island in particular), especially in the latter half of the year. To produce this data, you need to create a query containing two conditions—one for the position's start date and another to specify only the employers in Prince Edward Island (PE).

Defining Multiple Selection Criteria for Queries

Multiple conditions require you to use **logical operators** to combine two or more conditions. When you want a record selected only if two or more conditions are met, you need to use the **And logical operator**. In this case, Elsa wants to see only those records with a StartDate field value of 07/01/2006 *and* a StateProv field value of PE. If you place conditions in separate fields in the *same* Criteria row of the design grid, all conditions in that row must be met in order for a record to be included in the query results. However, if you place conditions in *different* Criteria rows, a record will be selected if at least one of the conditions is met. If none of the conditions is met, Access does not select the record. When you place conditions in different Criteria rows, you are using the **Or logical operator**. Figure 3-26 illustrates the difference between the And and Or logical operators.

Figure 3-26 | Logical operators And and Or for multiple selection criteria

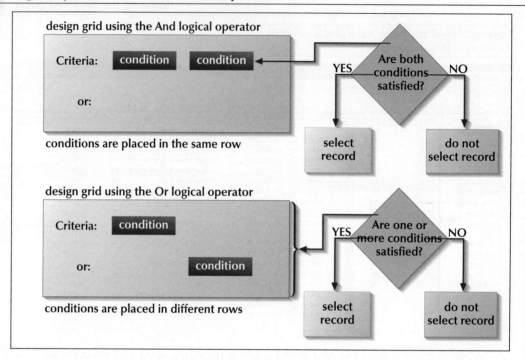

The And Logical Operator

To create Elsa's query, you need to modify the existing July1Positions query to show only the records for employers located in Prince Edward Island and offering positions starting on 07/01/2006. For the modified query, you must add a second condition in the same Criteria row. The existing condition for the StartDate field finds records for positions that start on July 1, 2006; the new condition "PE" in the StateProv field will find records for employers in Prince Edward Island. Because the conditions appear in the same Criteria row, the query will select records only if both conditions are met.

After modifying the query, you'll save it and then rename it as "PEJuly1Positions," overwriting the July1Positions query, which Matt no longer needs.

To modify the July1Positions query and use the And logical operator:

▶ 1. With the Queries object selected in the Database window, click **July1Positions** (if necessary), and then click the **Design** button to open the query in Design view.

▶ 2. Scroll the design grid to the right, click the **StateProv Criteria** text box, type **PE**, and then press the ↓ key. See Figure 3-27.

Query to find positions in PE that start on 07/01/2006 ◄ **Figure 3-27**

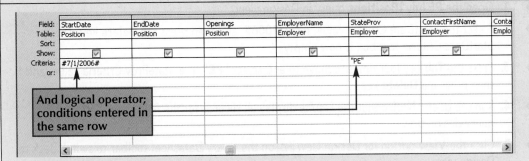

And logical operator; conditions entered in the same row

Notice that Access added quotation marks around the entry "PE"; you can type the quotation marks when you enter the condition, but if you forget to do so, Access will add them for you automatically.

The condition for the StartDate field is already entered, so you can run the query.

3. Run the query. Access displays in the datasheet only those records that meet both conditions: a StartDate field value of 07/01/2006 and a StateProv field value of PE. Two records are selected. See Figure 3-28.

Results of query using the And logical operator ◄ **Figure 3-28**

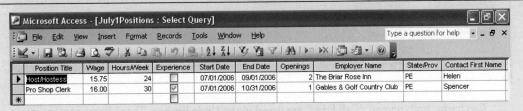

Now you can save the changes to the query and rename it.

4. Save and close the query. You return to the Database window.

5. Right-click **July1Positions** in the Queries list box, and then click **Rename** on the shortcut menu.

6. Press the **Home** key to position the insertion point to the left of the text "July," type **PE**, and then press the **Enter** key. The query name is now PEJuly1Positions.

Now Elsa can run the PEJuly1Positions query whenever she needs to know which employers in Prince Edward Island are offering positions starting on 07/01/2006.

Using Multiple Undo and Redo

Access allows you to undo and redo multiple actions when you are working in Design view for tables, queries, forms, reports, and so on. For example, when working in the Query window in Design view, if you specify multiple selection criteria for a query, you can use the multiple undo feature to remove the criteria—even after you run and save the query.

To see how this feature works, you will reopen the PEJuly1Positions query in Design view, delete the two criteria, and then reinsert them using multiple undo.

To modify the PEJuly1Positions query and use the multiple undo feature:

1. Open the **PEJuly1Positions** query in Design view.

2. Select the StartDate Criteria value, **#7/1/2006#**, and then press the **Delete** key. The StartDate Criteria text box is now empty.

3. Press the **Tab** key four times to move to and select **"PE"**, the StateProv Criteria value, and then press the **Delete** key.

4. Run the query. Notice that the results display all records for the fields specified in the query design grid.

5. Click the **View** button for Design view ▨ on the Query Datasheet toolbar to switch back to Design view.

   Now you will use multiple undo to reverse the edits you made and reinsert the two conditions.

6. Click the **list arrow** for the Undo button ↻ ▾ on the Query Design toolbar. A menu appears listing the actions you can undo. See Figure 3-29.

Figure 3-29 | **Using multiple undo**

Undo list arrow

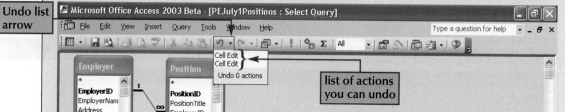

Two items, both named "Cell Edit," are listed in the Undo list box. These items represent the two changes you made to the query design—first deleting the StartDate condition and then deleting the StateProv condition. If you select an action that is below other items in the list, you will undo all the actions above the one you select, in addition to the one you select. Currently no actions are selected, so the list box indicates "Undo 0 actions."

7. Position the pointer over the second occurrence of **Cell Edit** in the list. Notice that both undo actions are highlighted, and the list box indicates that you can undo two actions.

8. Click the second occurrence of **Cell Edit**. Both actions are "undone," and the two conditions are redisplayed in the query design grid. The multiple undo feature makes it easy for you to test different criteria for a query and, when necessary, to undo your actions based on the query results.

   Notice that the Redo button and list arrow are now available. You can redo the actions you've just undone.

9. Click the **list arrow** for the Redo button ↺ ▾ on the Query Design toolbar. The Redo list box indicates that you can redo the two cell edits.

10. Click the **list arrow** for the Redo button ↺ ▾ again to close the Redo list box without selecting any option.

11. Close the query. Click the **No** button in the message box that opens, asking if you want to save your changes. You return to the Database window.

Matt has another request for information. He knows that it can be difficult to find student recruits for positions that offer fewer than 30 hours of work per week or that require prior work experience. So that his staff can focus on such positions, Matt wants to see a list of those positions that provide less than 30 hours of work or that require experience. To create this query, you need to use the Or logical operator.

The Or Logical Operator

For Matt's request, you need a query that selects a record when either one of two conditions is satisfied or when both conditions are satisfied. That is, a record is selected if the HoursPerWeek field value is less than 30 *or* if the Experience field value is "Yes" (checked). You will enter the condition for the HoursPerWeek field in the Criteria row and the condition for the Experience field in the "or" criteria row, thereby using the Or logical operator.

To display the information Matt wants to view, you'll create a new query containing the EmployerName and City fields from the Employer table and the PositionTitle, HoursPerWeek, and Experience fields from the Position table. Then you'll specify the conditions using the Or logical operator.

To create the query and use the Or logical operator:

▶ 1. In the Database window, double-click **Create query in Design view**. The Show Table dialog box opens on top of the Query window in Design view.

▶ 2. Click **Employer** in the Tables list box (if necessary), click the **Add** button, click **Position**, click the **Add** button, and then click the **Close** button. The Employer and Position field lists appear in the Query window, and the Show Table dialog box closes.

▶ 3. Double-click **EmployerName** in the Employer field list to add the EmployerName field to the design grid's first column Field text box.

▶ 4. Repeat Step 3 to add the **City** field from the Employer table, and then add the **PositionTitle**, **HoursPerWeek**, and **Experience** fields from the Position table.

   Now you need to specify the first condition, <30, in the HoursPerWeek field.

▶ 5. Click the **HoursPerWeek Criteria** text box, type **<30** and then press the **Tab** key.

   Because you want records selected if either of the conditions for the HoursPerWeek or Experience fields is satisfied, you must enter the condition for the Experience field in the "or" row of the design grid.

▶ 6. Press the ↓ key, and then type **Yes** in the "or" text box for Experience. See Figure 3-30.

| Query window with the Or logical operator | Figure 3-30 |

Or logical operator; conditions entered in different rows

▶ 7. Run the query. Access displays only those records that meet either condition: an HoursPerWeek field value less than 30 or an Experience field value of "Yes" (checked). A total of 35 records are selected.

   Matt wants the list displayed in alphabetical order by EmployerName. The first record's EmployerName field is highlighted, indicating the current field.

▶ 8. Click the **Sort Ascending** button ↓ on the Query Datasheet toolbar.

9. Resize all datasheet columns to their best fit. Scroll through the entire datasheet to make sure that all values are completely displayed. Deselect all columns when you are finished resizing them, and then return to the top of the datasheet. See Figure 3-31.

Figure 3-31 ▶ **Results of query using the Or logical operator**

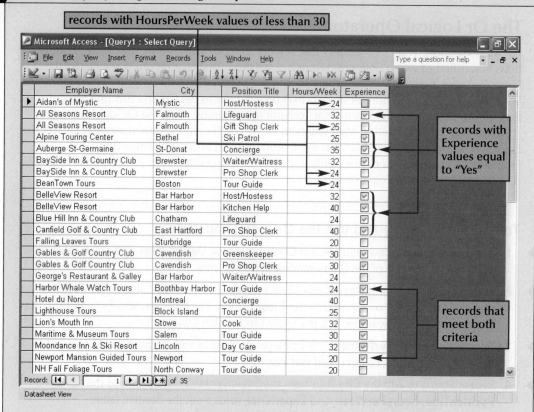

records with HoursPerWeek values of less than 30

records with Experience values equal to "Yes"

records that meet both criteria

10. Save the query with the name **HoursOrExperience**, and then close the query.

Next, Elsa wants to use the Northeast database to perform calculations. She is considering offering a 2% bonus per week to the student recruits in higher paid positions, based on employer recommendation, and she wants to know exactly what these bonuses would be.

Performing Calculations

In addition to using queries to retrieve, sort, and filter data in a database, you can use a query to perform calculations. To perform a calculation, you define an **expression** containing a combination of database fields, constants, and operators. For numeric expressions, the data types of the database fields must be number, currency, or date/time; the constants are numbers such as .02 (for the 2% bonus); and the operators can be arithmetic operators (+ – * /) or other specialized operators. In complex expressions, you can enclose calculations in parentheses to indicate which one should be performed first. In expressions without parentheses, Access calculates in the following order of precedence: multiplication and division before addition and subtraction. When operators have equal precedence, Access calculates them in order from left to right.

To perform a calculation in a query, you add a calculated field to the query. A **calculated field** is a field that displays the results of an expression. A calculated field appears in a query datasheet or in a form or report; however, it does not exist in a database. When you run a query that contains a calculated field, Access evaluates the expression defined by the calculated field and displays the resulting value in the query datasheet, form, or report.

Creating a Calculated Field

To produce the information Elsa wants, you need to open the HighWageAmounts query and create a calculated field that will multiply each Wage field value by each HoursPerWeek value, and then multiply that amount by .02 to determine the 2% weekly bonus Elsa is considering.

To enter an expression for a calculated field, you can type it directly in a Field text box in the design grid. Alternately, you can open the Zoom box or Expression Builder and use either one to enter the expression. The **Zoom box** is a large text box for entering text, expressions, or other values. To use the Zoom box, however, you must know all the parts of the expression you want to create. **Expression Builder** is an Access tool that makes it easy for you to create an expression; it contains a box for entering the expression, buttons for common operators, and one or more lists of expression elements, such as table and field names. Unlike a Field text box, which is too small to show an entire expression at one time, the Zoom box and Expression Builder are large enough to display lengthy expressions. In most cases, Expression Builder provides the easiest way to enter expressions, because you don't have to know all the parts of the expression; you can choose the necessary elements from the Expression Builder dialog box.

Reference Window

Using Expression Builder

- Open the query in Design view.
- In the design grid, position the insertion point in the Field text box of the field for which you want to create an expression.
- Click the Build button on the Query Design toolbar.
- Use the expression elements and common operators to build the expression, or type the expression directly.
- Click the OK button.

You'll begin by copying, pasting, and renaming the HighWageAmounts query, keeping the original query intact. You'll name the new query "HighWagesWithBonus." Then you'll modify this query in Design view to show only the information Elsa wants to view.

To copy the HighWageAmounts query and paste the copy with a new name:

1. Right-click the **HighWageAmounts** query in the list of queries, and then click **Copy** on the shortcut menu.

2. Right-click an empty area of the Database window, and then click **Paste** on the shortcut menu. The Paste As dialog box opens.

3. Type **HighWagesWithBonus** in the Query Name text box, and then press the **Enter** key. The new query appears in the query list, along with the original HighWageAmounts query.

Now you're ready to modify the HighWagesWithBonus query to create the calculated field for Elsa.

To modify the HighWagesWithBonus query:

1. Open the **HighWagesWithBonus** query in Design view.

   Elsa wants to see only the EmployerName, PositionTitle, and Wage fields in the query results. First, you'll delete the unnecessary fields, and then you'll move the EmployerName field so that it appears first in the query results.

2. Scroll the design grid to the right until the HoursPerWeek and EmployerName fields are visible at the same time.

3. Position the pointer on the HoursPerWeek field selector until the pointer changes to a ↓ shape, click and hold down the mouse button, drag the mouse to the right to highlight the HoursPerWeek, Experience, StartDate, EndDate, and Openings fields, and then release the mouse button.

4. Press the **Delete** key to delete the five selected fields.

5. Use this same method to delete the StateProv, ContactFirstName, ContactLastName, and Phone fields from the query design grid.

   Next, you'll move the EmployerName field to the left of the PositionTitle field so that the Wage values will appear next to the calculated field values in the query results.

6. Scroll the design grid back to the left (if necessary), select the **EmployerName** field, and then use the pointer ☒ to drag the field to the left of the PositionTitle field. See Figure 3-32.

Figure 3-32	Modified query before adding the calculated field

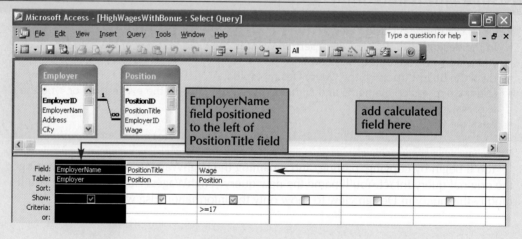

Now you're ready to use Expression Builder to enter the calculated field in the HighWagesWithBonus query.

To add the calculated field to the HighWagesWithBonus query:

1. Position the insertion point in the blank Field text box to the right of the Wage field, and then click the **Build** button ☒ on the Query Design toolbar. The Expression Builder dialog box opens. See Figure 3-33.

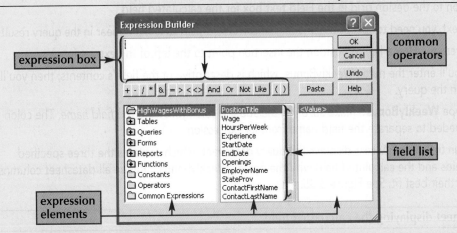

You use the common operators and expression elements to help you build an expression. Note that the HighWagesWithBonus query is already selected in the list box on the lower left; the fields included in the original version of the query are listed in the center box.

The expression for the calculated field will multiply the Wage field values by the HoursPerWeek field values, and then multiply that amount by the numeric constant .02 (which represents a 2% bonus). To include a field in the expression, you select the field and then click the Paste button. To include a numeric constant, you simply type the constant in the expression.

► 2. Click **Wage** in the field list, and then click the **Paste** button. [Wage] appears in the expression box.

To include the multiplication operator in the expression, you click the asterisk (*) button. Note that you do not include spaces between the elements in an expression.

► 3. Click the * button in the row of common operators, click **HoursPerWeek** in the field list, and then click the **Paste** button. The expression multiplies the Wage values by the HoursPerWeek values.

► 4. Click the * button in the row of common operators, and then type **.02**. You have finished entering the expression. See Figure 3-34.

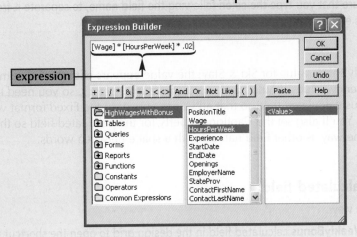

Note that you also could have typed the expression directly into the expression box, instead of clicking the field names and the operator.

5. Click the **OK** button. Access closes the Expression Builder dialog box and adds the expression to the design grid in the Field text box for the calculated field.

Next, you need to specify a name for the calculated field as it will appear in the query results.

6. Press the **Home** key to position the insertion point to the left of the expression.

You'll enter the name WeeklyBonus, which is descriptive of the field's contents; then you'll run the query.

7. Type **WeeklyBonus:**. *Make sure you include the colon following the field name.* The colon is needed to separate the field name from its expression.

8. Run the query. Access displays the query datasheet, which contains the three specified fields and the calculated field with the name "WeeklyBonus." Resize all datasheet columns to their best fit. See Figure 3-35.

Figure 3-35	Datasheet displaying the calculated field

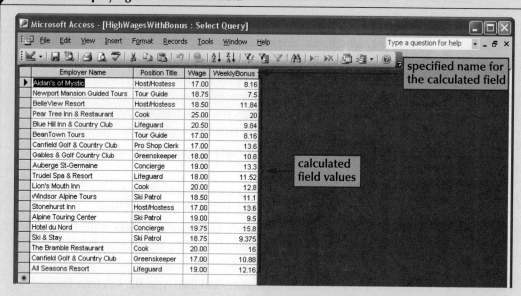

Trouble? If the calculated field name does not appear correctly, as shown in Figure 3-35, you might not have included the required colon. Switch to Design view, then repeat Steps 7 and 8, making sure that you type the colon following the field name, to separate it from the calculated field's expression.

Notice the WeeklyBonus value for Ski & Stay; the value appears with three decimal places (9.375). Currency values should have only two decimal places, so you need to format the WeeklyBonus calculated field so that all values appear in the Fixed format with two decimal places. You'll also set the Caption property for the calculated field so that it is displayed in the same way as other field names, with a space between words.

To format the calculated field:

1. Switch to Design view.

2. Right-click the **WeeklyBonus** calculated field in the design grid to open the shortcut menu, and then click **Properties**. The property sheet for the selected field opens. The property sheet for a field provides options for changing the display of field values in the datasheet.

3. Click the right side of the **Format** text box to display the list of formats, and then click **Fixed**. This format specifies no commas or dollar signs, which are unnecessary for the calculated field and would only clutter the worksheet.

4. Click the right side of the **Decimal Places** text box, and then click **2**.

5. Press the **Tab** key twice to move to the Caption property, and then type **Weekly Bonus**. See Figure 3-36.

Property sheet settings to format the calculated field ◄ **Figure 3-36**

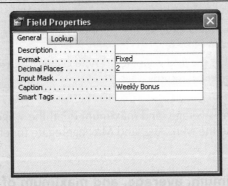

Now that you have formatted the calculated field, you can run the query.

6. Close the Field Properties window, and then save and run the query. The calculated field now displays the name "Weekly Bonus," and the value for Ski & Stay now correctly appears as 9.38.

7. Close the query.

Elsa prepares a report on a regular basis that includes a summary of information about the wages paid to student recruits. She lists the minimum hourly wage paid, the average wage amount, and the maximum hourly wage paid. She asks you to create a query to determine these statistics from data in the Position table.

Using Aggregate Functions

You can calculate statistical information, such as totals and averages, on the records selected by a query. To do this, you use the Access aggregate functions. **Aggregate functions** perform arithmetic operations on selected records in a database. Figure 3-37 lists the most frequently used aggregate functions. Aggregate functions operate on the records that meet a query's selection criteria. You specify an aggregate function for a specific field, and the appropriate operation applies to that field's values for the selected records.

Figure 3-37 ▶ **Frequently used aggregate functions**

Aggregate Function	Determines	Data Types Supported
Avg	Average of the field values for the selected records	AutoNumber, Currency, Date/Time, Number
Count	Number of records selected	AutoNumber, Currency, Date/Time, Memo, Number, OLE Object, Text, Yes/No
Max	Highest field value for the selected records	AutoNumber, Currency, Date/Time, Number, Text
Min	Lowest field value for the selected records	AutoNumber, Currency, Date/Time, Number, Text
Sum	Total of the field values for the selected records	AutoNumber, Currency, Date/TIme, Number

To display the minimum, average, and maximum of all the wage amounts in the Position table, you will use the Min, Avg, and Max aggregate functions for the Wage field.

To calculate the minimum, average, and maximum of all wage amounts:

▶ 1. Double-click **Create query in Design view**, click **Position**, click the **Add** button, and then click the **Close** button. The Position field list is added to the Query window, and the Show Table dialog box closes.

To perform the three calculations on the Wage field, you need to add the field to the design grid three times.

▶ 2. Double-click **Wage** in the Position field list three times to add three copies of the field to the design grid.

You need to select an aggregate function for each Wage field. When you click the Totals button on the Query Design toolbar, a row labeled "Total" is added to the design grid. The Total row provides a list of the aggregate functions that you can select.

▶ 3. Click the **Totals** button Σ on the Query Design toolbar. A new row labeled "Total" appears between the Table and Sort rows in the design grid. See Figure 3-38.

Figure 3-38 ▶ **Total row inserted in the design grid**

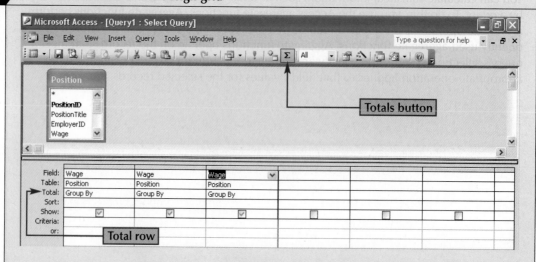

In the Total row, you specify the aggregate function you want to use for a field.

▶ **4.** Click the right side of the first column's **Total** text box, and then click **Min**. This field will calculate the minimum amount of all the Wage field values.

When you run the query, Access automatically will assign a datasheet column name of "MinOfWage" for this field. You can change the datasheet column name to a more descriptive or readable name by entering the name you want in the Field text box. However, you must also keep the field name Wage in the Field text box, because it identifies the field whose values will be calculated. The Field text box will contain the datasheet column name you specify followed by the field name (Wage) with a colon separating the two names.

▶ **5.** Position the insertion point to the left of Wage in the first column's Field text box, and then type **Minimum Wage:**. *Be sure that you type the colon following the name.*

▶ **6.** Click the right side of the second column's **Total** text box, and then click **Avg**. This field will calculate the average of all the Wage field values.

▶ **7.** Position the insertion point to the left of Wage in the second column's Field text box, and then type **Average Wage:**.

▶ **8.** Click the right side of the third column's **Total** text box, and then click **Max**. This field will calculate the maximum amount of all the Wage field values.

▶ **9.** Position the insertion point to the left of Wage in the third column's Field text box, and then type **Maximum Wage:**.

The query design is completed, so you can run the query.

▶ **10.** Run the query. Access displays one record containing the three aggregate function values. The single row of summary statistics represents calculations based on the 64 records selected by the query.

You need to resize the three columns to their best fit to see the column names.

▶ **11.** Resize all columns to their best fit, and then position the insertion point in the field value in the first column. See Figure 3-39.

Results of the query using aggregate functions ◀ **Figure 3-39**

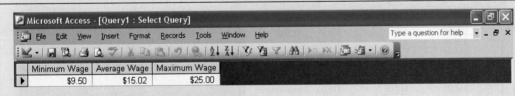

▶ **12.** Save the query as **WageStatistics**, and then close the query.

Elsa also wants her report to include the same wage statistics (minimum, average, and maximum) for each type of position. She asks you to display the wage statistics for each different PositionTitle value in the Position table.

Using Record Group Calculations

In addition to calculating statistical information on all or selected records in selected tables, you can calculate statistics for groups of records. For example, you can determine the number of employers in each state or province, or the average wage amount by position.

To create a query for Elsa's latest request, you can modify the current query by adding the PositionTitle field and assigning the Group By operator to it. The **Group By operator** divides the selected records into groups based on the values in the specified field. Those records with the same value for the field are grouped together, and the datasheet displays one record for each group. Aggregate functions, which appear in the other columns of the design grid, provide statistical information for each group.

You need to modify the current query to add the Group By operator for the PositionTitle field. This will display the statistical information grouped by position for the 64 selected records in the query. As you did earlier, you will copy the WageStatistics query and paste it with a new name, keeping the original query intact, to create the new query.

To copy and paste the query, and then add the PositionTitle field with the Group By operator:

1. Right-click the **WageStatistics** query in the list of queries, and then click **Copy** on the shortcut menu.

2. Right-click an empty area of the Database window, and then click **Paste** on the shortcut menu.

3. Type **WageStatisticsByPosition** in the Query Name text box, and then press the **Enter** key.

   Now you're ready to modify the query design.

4. Open the **WageStatisticsByPosition** query in Design view.

5. Double-click **PositionTitle** in the Position field list to add the field to the design grid. Group By, which is the default option in the Total row, appears for the PositionTitle field.

   You've completed the query changes, so you can run the query.

6. Run the query. Access displays 16 records—one for each PositionTitle group. Each record contains the three aggregate function values and the PositionTitle field value for the group. Again, the summary statistics represent calculations based on the 64 records selected by the query. See Figure 3-40.

| Figure 3-40 | Aggregate functions grouped by PositionTitle |

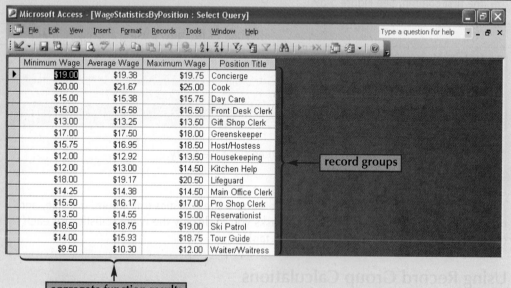

record groups

aggregate function results

7. Save and close the query, and then close the Northeast database.

   Trouble? If a dialog box opens and asks if you want to empty the Clipboard, click the Yes button.

The queries you've created and saved will help Elsa, Zack, Matt, and other employees to monitor and analyze the business activity of NSJI's employer customers. Now any NSJI staff member can run the queries at any time, modify them as needed, or use them as the basis for designing new queries to meet additional information requirements.

Session 3.2 Quick Check

Review

1. A(n) _____ is a criterion, or rule, that determines which records are selected for a query datasheet.
2. In the design grid, where do you place the conditions for two different fields when you use the And logical operator? The Or logical operator?
3. To perform a calculation in a query, you define a(n) _____ containing a combination of database fields, constants, and operators.
4. How does a calculated field differ from a table field?
5. What is an aggregate function?
6. The _____ operator divides selected records into groups based on the values in a field.

Tutorial Summary

Review

In this tutorial, you learned how to create queries in Design view, and how to run and save queries. You also learned how you can use the query datasheet to update the data contained in the underlying database table. This tutorial presented one of the most important database concepts—defining table relationships. You learned how to define a one-to-many relationship between two tables in a database, and how to enforce referential integrity as part of the relationship. After defining this relationship, you created a query based on data in the two tables. You learned how to sort and filter query results to view records in a particular order and to view different subsets of the displayed records. Using record selection criteria, you specified an exact match in a query, used a comparison operator to match a range of values, and used the And and Or logical operators to meet various requests for data retrieval. Finally, you created a calculated field in the Expression Builder dialog box to display the results of an expression in a query, and you used aggregate functions and the Group By operator to calculate and display statistical information in a query.

Key Terms

aggregate function	Filter By Form	recordset
And logical operator	Filter By Selection	referential integrity
calculated field	Group By operator	related table
cascade deletes option	join	Relationships window
cascade updates option	join line	run (query)
comparison operator	logical operator	secondary sort field
condition	nonunique sort field	select query
design grid	one-to-many relationship	sort
exact match	Or logical operator	Sort Ascending button
expression	orphaned record	Sort Descending button
Expression Builder	primary sort field	sort field
field list	primary table	unique sort field
filter	query by example (QBE)	Zoom box

Practice

Build on what you learned in the tutorial by practicing those skills using the same case scenario.

Review Assignments

Data File needed for the Review Assignments: Recruits.mdb (*cont. from Tutorial 2*)

Elsa needs information from the Recruits database, and she asks you to query the database by completing the following:

1. Open the **Recruits** database located in the Brief\Review folder provided with your Data Files.

2. Create a select query based on the **Student** table. Display the StudentID, FirstName, and LastName fields in the query results; sort in ascending order based on the LastName field values; and select only those records whose Nation value equals Ireland. (*Hint*: Do not display the Nation field values in the query results.) Save the query as **StudentsFromIreland**, run the query, and then print the query datasheet.

3. Use the **StudentsFromIreland** datasheet to update the **Student** table by changing the FirstName field value for StudentID OMA9956 to Richard. Print the query datasheet, and then close the query.

4. Define a one-to-many relationship between the primary **Recruiter** table and the related **Student** table. Resize the field lists, as necessary, to display all the field names. Select the referential integrity option and the cascade updates option for the relationship.

5. Use Design view to create a select query based on the **Recruiter** and **Student** tables. Select the fields FirstName, LastName, City, and Nation from the **Student** table, and the fields BonusQuota, Salary, and SSN from the **Recruiter** table, in that order. Sort in ascending order based on the Nation field values. Select only those records whose SSN equals "977-07-1798." (*Hint*: Do not display the SSN field values in the query results.) Save the query as **WolfeRecruits**, and then run the query. Resize all columns in the datasheet to fit the data. Print the datasheet, and then save and close the query.

6. Use Design view to create a query based on the **Recruiter** table that shows all recruiters with a BonusQuota field value between 40 and 50, and whose Salary field value is greater than 35000. (*Hint*: Refer to Figure 3-19 to determine the correct comparison operator to use.) Display all fields except SSN from the **Recruiter** table. Save the query as **BonusInfo**, and then run the query.

7. Switch to Design view for the **BonusInfo** query. Create a calculated field named RaiseAmt that displays the net amount of a 3% raise to the Salary values. The expression for the calculated field will begin with the Salary field, and add to it the result of multiplying the Salary field by .03. Display the results in descending order by RaiseAmt. Save the query as a new query named **SalariesWithRaises**, and then run the query.

8. Switch to Design view for the **SalariesWithRaises** query, and then change the format of the calculated field to the Standard format, with no decimal places. Also change the caption property of the calculated field to "Raise Amt." Run the query. Resize all columns in the datasheet to fit the data, print the query datasheet, and then save and close the query.

9. In the Database window, copy the **StudentsFromIreland** query, and then paste it with the new name **StudentsFromHollandPlusYoungerStudents**. Open the new query in Design view. Modify the query to display only those records with a Nation field value of Holland or with a BirthDate field value greater than 1/1/85. Also, modify the query to include the Nation field values in the query results. Save and run the query. Resize all columns in the datasheet to fit the data, print the query datasheet, and then save and close the query.

10. Create a new query based on the **Recruiter** table. Use the Min, Max, and Avg aggregate functions to find the lowest, highest, and average values in the Salary field. Name the three aggregate fields Lowest Salary, Highest Salary, and Average Salary, respectively. Save the query as **SalaryStatistics**, and then run the query. Resize all columns in the datasheet to fit the data, print the query datasheet, and then save and close the query.

11. Open the **SalaryStatistics** query in Design view. Modify the query so that the records are grouped by the BonusQuota field. Save the query as **SalaryStatisticsByBonusQuota**, run the query, print the query datasheet, and then close the query.

12. Close the Recruits database.

Apply

Using what you learned in the tutorial, create queries to retrieve data about video photography events.

Explore

Case Problem 1

Data File needed for this Case Problem: Videos.mdb (*cont. from Tutorial 2*)

Lim's Video Photography   Youngho Lim wants to view specific information about his clients and video shoot events. He asks you to query the Videos database by completing the following:

1. Open the **Videos** database located in the Brief\Case1 folder provided with your Data Files.

2. Define the necessary one-to-many relationships between the database tables, as follows: between the primary **Client** table and the related **Contract** table, between the primary **Contract** table and the related **Shoot** table, and between the primary **ShootDesc** table and the related **Shoot** table. (*Hint*: Add all four tables to the Relationships window, and then define the three relationships.) Resize the field lists, as necessary, to display all the field names. Select the referential integrity option and the cascade updates option for each relationship.

3. Create a select query based on the **Client** and **Contract** tables. Display the ClientName, City, ContractDate, and ContractAmt fields, in that order. Sort in ascending order based on the ClientName field values. Run the query, save the query as **ClientContracts**, and then print the datasheet.

4. Use Filter By Selection to display only those records with a City field value of Oakland in the **ClientContracts** datasheet. Print the datasheet and then remove the filter. Save and close the query.

5. Open the **ClientContracts** query in Design view. Modify the query to display only those records with a ContractAmt value greater than or equal to 600. Run the query, save the query as **ContractAmounts**, and then print the datasheet.

6. Switch to Design view for the **ContractAmounts** query. Modify the query to display only those records with a ContractAmt value greater than or equal to 600 and with a City value of San Francisco. Also modify the query so that the City field values are not displayed in the query results. Run the query, save it as **SFContractAmounts**, print the datasheet, and then close the query.

7. Close the Videos database.

Create

Follow the steps provided and use the figures as guides to create queries for a health and fitness center.

Case Problem 2

Data File needed for this Case Problem: Fitness.mdb (*cont. from Tutorial 2*)

Parkhurst Health & Fitness Center Martha Parkhurst is completing an analysis of the members enrolled in different programs in the fitness center. To help her find the information she needs, you'll query the Fitness database by completing the following:

1. Open the **Fitness** database located in the Brief\Case2 folder provided with your Data Files.
2. Define a one-to-many relationship between the primary **Program** table and the related **Member** table. Resize the field lists, as necessary, to display all the field names. Select the referential integrity option and the cascade updates option for the relationship.
3. Use Design view to create a select query based on the **Member** and **Program** tables. Display the fields FirstName, LastName, DateJoined, MonthlyFee, and PhysicalRequired, in that order. Sort in descending order based on the DateJoined field values. Select only those records with a PhysicalRequired field value of Yes. Save the query as **PhysicalsNeeded**, and then run the query. Switch to Design view and modify the query so that the PhysicalRequired values do not appear in the query results. Save the modified query, and then run the query.
4. Use the **PhysicalsNeeded** datasheet to update the **Member** table by changing the DateJoined value for the first record in the datasheet to 10/18/2007. Print the datasheet, and then close the query.

Explore

5. Use Design view to create a select query based on the **Member** and **Program** tables. For all members who joined the center between 06/01/2007 and 06/30/2007, display the MemberID, FirstName, LastName, DateJoined, Description, and MonthlyFee fields. Save the query as **JuneMembers**, run the query, print the query results, and then close the query.
6. Create and save the query whose results are shown in Figure 3-41. Print the query datasheet, and then close the query.

Figure 3-41

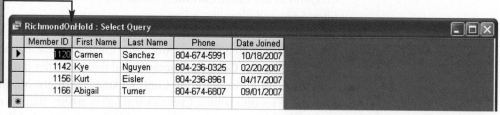

show only records for customers from Richmond whose memberships are on hold

Member ID	First Name	Last Name	Phone	Date Joined
1120	Carmen	Sanchez	804-674-5991	10/18/2007
1142	Kye	Nguyen	804-236-0325	02/20/2007
1156	Kurt	Eisler	804-236-8961	04/17/2007
1166	Abigail	Turner	804-674-6807	09/01/2007

7. Create and save the query whose results are shown in Figure 3-42. Print the query datasheet, and then close the query.

Figure 3-42

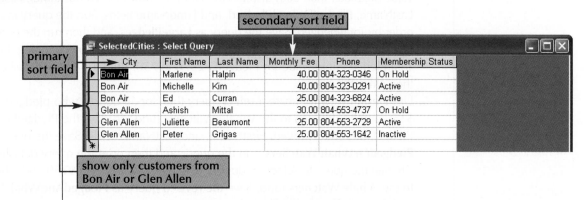

secondary sort field

primary sort field

show only customers from Bon Air or Glen Allen

8. Create and save the query whose results are shown in Figure 3-43 to display statistics for the MonthlyFee field. Print the query datasheet.

Figure 3-43

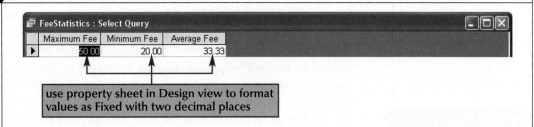

use property sheet in Design view to format values as Fixed with two decimal places

9. Change the query to display the same statistics grouped by City. (*Hint*: Use the Show Table button on the Query Design toolbar to add the **Member** table to the query.) Save the query as **FeeStatisticsByCity**. Run the query, print the query results, and then close the query.
10. Close the Fitness database.

Challenge

Use the skills you learned in the tutorial, plus some new ones, to create queries that display information about a zoo and its patrons.

Explore

Case Problem 3

Data File needed for this Case Problem: Redwood.mdb (*cont. from Tutorial 2*)

Redwood Zoo Michael Rosenfeld wants to find specific information about the donors and their pledge amounts for the Redwood Zoo. You'll help him find the information in the Redwood database by completing the following:

1. Open the **Redwood** database located in the Brief\Case3 folder provided with your Data Files.
2. Define the necessary one-to-many relationships between the database tables, as follows: between the primary **Donor** table and the related **Pledge** table, and between the primary **Fund** table and the related **Pledge** table. (*Hint*: Add all three tables to the Relationships window, and then define the two relationships.) Resize the field lists, as necessary, to display all the field names. Select the referential integrity option and the cascade updates option for each relationship.

3. Use Design view to create a select query that, for all pledges with a TotalPledged field value of greater than 200, displays the DonorID (from the **Donor** table), FirstName, LastName, PledgeID, TotalPledged, and FundName fields. Sort the query in ascending order by TotalPledged. Save the query as **LargePledges**, and then run the query.

4. Use the **LargePledges** datasheet to update the **Pledge** table by changing the TotalPledged field value for PledgeID 2976 to 750. Print the query datasheet, and then close the query.

5. Use Design view to create a select query that, for all donors who pledged less than $150 or who donated to the Whale Watchers fund, displays the PledgeID, PledgeDate, TotalPledged, FirstName, and LastName fields. Save the query as **PledgedOrWhaleWatchers**, run the query, and then print the query datasheet. Change the query to select all donors who pledged less than $150 and who donated to the Whale Watchers fund. Save the revised query as **PledgedAndWhaleWatchers**, and then run the query. Close the query.

Explore

6. Use Design view to create a select query that displays the DonorID (from the **Donor** table), TotalPledged, PaymentMethod, PledgeDate, and FundName fields. Save the query as **PledgesAfterCosts**. Create a calculated field named Overhead that displays the results of multiplying the TotalPledged field values by 15% (to account for overhead costs). Save the query, and then create a second calculated field named NetPledge that displays the results of subtracting the Overhead field values from the TotalPledged field values. Format the calculated fields as Fixed and set an appropriate caption for the NetPledge field. Display the results in ascending order by TotalPledged. Save the modified query, and then run the query. Resize all datasheet columns to their best fit, print the query results, and then save and close the query.

Explore

7. Use the **Pledge** table to display the sum, average, and count of the TotalPledged field for all pledges. Then do the following:
   a. Specify column names of Total Pledge, Average Pledge, and Number of Pledges.
   b. Change properties so that the values in the Total Pledge and Average Pledge columns display two decimal places and the Fixed format.
   c. Save the query as **PledgeStatistics**, run the query, resize all datasheet columns to their best fit, and then print the query datasheet. Save the query.
   d. Change the query to display the sum, average, and count of the TotalPledged field for all pledges by FundName. (*Hint:* Use the Show Table button on the Query Design toolbar to add the **Fund** table to the query.) Save the query as **PledgeStatisticsByFund**, run the query, print the query datasheet, and then close the query.

8. Close the Redwood database.

Challenge

Challenge yourself by creating queries, including a new type of query, for a luxury property rental agency.

Explore

Case Problem 4

Data File needed for this Case Problem: GEM.mdb (*cont. from Tutorial 2*)

GEM Ultimate Vacations Griffin and Emma MacElroy want to analyze data about their clients and the luxury properties they rent. Help them query the GEM database by completing the following:

1. Open the **GEM** database located in the Brief\Case4 folder provided with your Data Files.

2. Define the necessary one-to-many relationships between the database tables, as follows: between the primary **Guest** table and the related **Reservation** table, and between the primary **Property** table and the related **Reservation** table. (*Hint:* Add all three tables to the Relationships window, and then define the two relationships.) Select the referential integrity option and the cascade updates option for each relationship.

3. For all guests, display the GuestName, City, StateProv, ReservationID, StartDate, and EndDate fields. Save the query as **GuestTripDates**, and then run the query. Resize all datasheet columns to their best fit. In Datasheet view, sort the query results in ascending order by the StartDate field. Print the query datasheet, and then save and close the query.

4. For all guests from Illinois (IL), display the GuestName, City, StateProv, ReservationID, People, StartDate, and EndDate fields. Sort the query in ascending order by City. Save the query as **IllinoisGuests**, and then run the query. Modify the query to remove the display of the StateProv field values from the query results. Save the modified query, run the query, print the query datasheet, and then close the query.

Explore ▶

5. For all guests who are not from Illinois or who are renting a property beginning in the month of June 2007, display the GuestName, City, StateProv, ReservationID, StartDate, and PropertyID fields. (*Hint:* Refer to Figure 3-19 to determine the correct comparison operators to use.) Sort the query in descending order by StartDate. Save the query as **OutOfStateOrJune**, run the query, and then print the query datasheet. Change the query to select all clients who are not from Illinois and who are renting a property beginning in the month of June 2007. Sort the query in ascending order by StartDate. Save the query as **OutOfStateAndJune**, run the query, print the query datasheet, and then close the query.

6. For all reservations, display the ReservationID, StartDate, EndDate, PropertyID, PropertyName, People, and RentalRate fields. Save the query as **RentalCost**. Then create a calculated field named CostPerPerson that displays the results of dividing the RentalRate field values by the People field values. Display the results in descending order by CostPerPerson. Run the query. Modify the query design to set the following properties for the CostPerPerson field: Format set to Standard; Decimal Places set to 2; and Caption set to "Cost Per Person". Run the modified query, resize all datasheet columns to their best fit, print the query datasheet, and then save and close the query.

7. Use the **Reservation** table to determine the minimum, average, and maximum RentalRate values for all reservations. Then do the following:
   a. Specify column names of Lowest Rate, Average Rate, and Highest Rate.
   b. Use the property sheet for each column to format the results as Fixed with two decimal places.
   c. Save the query as **RateStatistics**, run the query, resize all datasheet columns to their best fit, print the query datasheet, and then save the query again.

Explore ▶

   d. Revise the query to show the rate statistics grouped by Country. (*Hint:* Use the Show Table button on the Query Design toolbar to add the **Property** table to the query.) Save the revised query as **RateStatisticsByCountry**, run the query, print the query datasheet, and then close the query.

Explore ▶

8. Use the "Type a question for help" box to ask the following question: "How do I create a Top Values query?" Click the topic "Show only the high or low values in a query (MDB)." Read the displayed information, and then close the Microsoft Office Access Help window and the task pane. Open the **RentalCost** query in Design view, and then modify the query to display only the top five values for the CostPerPerson field. Save the query as **TopRentalCost**, run the query, print the query datasheet, and then close the query.

9. Close the GEM database.

Research

Use the Internet to find and work with data related to the topics presented in this tutorial.

Internet Assignments

The purpose of the Internet Assignments is to challenge you to find information on the Internet that you can use to work effectively with this software. The actual assignments are updated and maintained on the Course Technology Web site. Log on to the Internet and use your Web browser to go to the Student Online Companion for New Perspectives Office 2003 at **www.course.com/np/office2003**. Click the Internet Assignments link, and then navigate to the assignments for this tutorial.

Assess

SAM Assessment and Training

If you have a SAM user profile, you may have access to hands-on instruction, practice, and assessment of the skills covered in this tutorial. Log in to your SAM account and go to your assignments page to see what your instructor has assigned.

Review

Quick Check Answers

Session 3.1

1. a general query in which you specify the fields and records you want Access to select
2. The field list contains the table name at the top of the list box and the table's fields listed in the order in which they appear in the table; the design grid displays columns that contain specifications about a field you will use in the query.
3. A table datasheet and a query datasheet look the same, appearing in Datasheet view, and can be used to update data in a database. A table datasheet shows the permanent data in a table, whereas a query datasheet is temporary and its contents are based on the criteria you establish in the design grid.
4. primary table; related table
5. Referential integrity
6. oldest to most recent date
7. False
8. filter

Session 3.2

1. condition
2. in the same Criteria row; in different Criteria rows
3. expression
4. A calculated field appears in a query datasheet, form, or report but does not exist in a database, as does a table field.
5. a function that performs an arithmetic operation on selected records in a database
6. Group By

New Perspectives on
Microsoft® Office PowerPoint® 2003

Tutorial 1   PPT 3
Creating a Presentation
Presenting Information About Humanitarian Projects

Read This Before You Begin: Tutorial 1

To the Student

Data Files

To complete PowerPoint Tutorial 1, you need the starting student Data Files. Your instructor will either provide you with these Data Files or ask you to obtain them yourself.

PowerPoint Tutorial 1 requires the folder shown in the next column to complete the Tutorial, Review Assignments, and Case Problems. You will need to copy this folder from a file server, a standalone computer, or the Web to the drive and folder where you will be storing your Data Files. Your instructor will tell you which computer, drive letter, and folder(s) contain the files you need. You can also download the files by going to www.course.com; see the inside back or front cover for more information on downloading the files, or ask your instructor or technical support person for assistance.

If you are storing your Data Files on floppy disk, you will need **one** blank, formatted, high-density disk for this tutorial. Label your disk as shown, and place on it the folder indicated.

▼**PowerPoint 2003: Data Disk**

  Tutorial.01 folder

When you begin a tutorial, refer to the Student Data Files section at the bottom of the tutorial opener page, which indicates which folders and files you need for the tutorial. Each end-of-tutorial exercise also indicates the files you need to complete that exercise.

To the Instructor

The Data Files are available on the Instructor Resources CD for this title. Follow the instructions in the Help file on the CD to install the programs to your network or standalone computer. See the "To the Student" section above for information on how to set up the Data Files that accompany this text.

You are granted a license to copy the Data Files to any computer or computer network used by students who have purchased this book.

System Requirements

If you are going to work through this book using your own computer, you need:

- **Computer System** Microsoft Windows 2000, Windows XP, or higher must be installed on your computer. These tutorials assume a complete installation of Microsoft Office PowerPoint 2003.

- **Data Files** You will not be able to complete the tutorials or exercises in this book using your own computer until you have the necessary starting Data Files.

Objectives

Creating a Presentation

Presenting Information About Humanitarian Projects

Case

Global Humanitarian, Austin Office

In 1985, a group of Austin, Texas business leaders established a nonprofit organization called Global Humanitarian. Its goal was to alleviate abject poverty in the third world through public awareness and personal involvement in sustainable self-help initiatives in third-world villages. Today, Global Humanitarian is a large umbrella organization and clearinghouse for national and international humanitarian organizations. Its five major functions are to help provide the following: entrepreneurial support, service expeditions, inventory surplus exchange, funding and grant proposals, and student internships.

The president of Global Humanitarian is Norma Flores, who sits on the board of directors and carries out its policies and procedures. The managing director of the Austin office is Miriam Schwartz, and the managing director in Latin America is Pablo Fuentes, who lives and works in Lima, Peru. Miriam wants you to use PowerPoint to develop a presentation to provide information about Global Humanitarian's current projects to potential donors, expedition participants, and student interns.

In this tutorial, you'll examine a presentation that Miriam created to become familiar with **Microsoft Office PowerPoint 2003** (or simply **PowerPoint**). You'll then create a presentation based on content that PowerPoint suggests by using the AutoContent Wizard. You'll modify the text in the presentation, and you'll add and delete slides. You'll check the spelling and style of the presentation, and then you'll view the completed slide show. Finally, you'll save the slide show and print handouts.

Student Data Files

▼**Tutorial.01**

▽ **Tutorial folder**

Lorena.ppt

▽ **Review folder**

VillageOP.ppt

▽ **Cases folder**

LASIK.ppt
Library.ppt

What Is PowerPoint?

PowerPoint is a powerful presentation graphics program that provides everything you need to produce an effective presentation in the form of on-screen slides, a slide presentation on a Web site, black-and-white or color overheads, or 35-mm photographic slides. You may have already seen your instructors use PowerPoint presentations to enhance their classroom lectures.

Using PowerPoint, you can prepare each component of a presentation: individual slides, speaker notes, an outline, and audience handouts. The presentation you'll create for Miriam will include slides, notes, and handouts.

To start PowerPoint:

▶ 1. Click the **Start** button on the taskbar, point to **All Programs**, point to **Microsoft Office**, and then click **Microsoft Office PowerPoint 2003**. PowerPoint starts and the PowerPoint window opens. See Figure 1-1.

Trouble? If you don't see the Microsoft Office PowerPoint 2003 option on the Microsoft Office submenu, look for it on a different submenu or as an option on the All Programs menu. If you still cannot find the Microsoft Office PowerPoint 2003 option, ask your instructor or technical support person for help.

Figure 1-1	Blank PowerPoint window

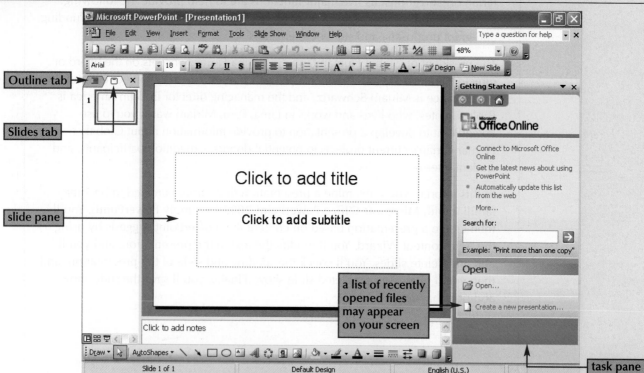

Trouble? If the PowerPoint program window is not maximized, click the Maximize ▢ button on the program window title bar.

Trouble? If the Office Assistant (an animated icon, usually a paper clip with eyes) opens when you start PowerPoint, right-click the Office Assistant, and then click Hide to close it.

Opening an Existing PowerPoint Presentation

Before you prepare the presentation on Global Humanitarian, Miriam suggests that you view an existing presentation recently prepared under Norma's and Miriam's direction as an example of PowerPoint features. When you examine the presentation, you'll learn about some PowerPoint capabilities that can help make your presentations more interesting and effective. You'll open the presentation now.

To open the existing presentation:

1. Make sure you have access to the Data Files in the Tutorial.01 folder.

    Trouble? If you don't have the PowerPoint Data Files, you need to get them before you can proceed. Your instructor will either give you the Data Files or ask you to obtain them from a specified location (such as a network drive). In either case, be sure that you make a backup copy of your Data Files before you start using them, so that the original files will be available on your copied disk in case you need to start over because of an error or problem. If you have any questions about the Data Files, see your instructor or technical support person for assistance.

2. Click the **Open** link under Open in the Getting Started task pane. The Open dialog box appears on the screen.

    Trouble? If you don't see the Open link, either click More or point to the small triangle at the bottom of the task pane to view additional links.

3. Click the **Look in** list arrow to display the list of disk drives on your computer, and then navigate to the **Tutorial.01\Tutorial** folder included with your Data Files.

4. Click **Lorena** (if necessary), and then click the **Open** button to display Miriam's presentation. The presentation opens in Normal view. See Figure 1-2.

PowerPoint window with presentation open | Figure 1-2

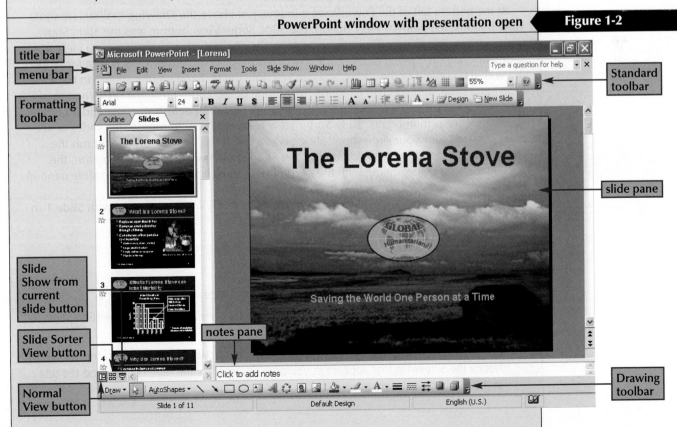

Trouble? If you see filename extensions on your screen (such as ".ppt" appended to "Lorena" in the filename), don't be concerned; they won't affect your work.

Trouble? If your screen doesn't show the Drawing toolbar, click View on the menu bar, point to Toolbars, and then click Drawing.

Trouble? If your screen shows the Standard toolbar and the Formatting toolbar on the same line, click Tools on the menu bar, click Customize, click the Options tab, click the Show Standard and Formatting toolbars on two rows check box to select it, and then click the Close button.

Switching Views and Navigating a Presentation

The PowerPoint window contains features common to all Windows programs, as well as features specific to PowerPoint. One obvious difference between the PowerPoint window and other Office programs is that the PowerPoint window is divided into sections. The section in the center of the screen, to the left of the task pane, is the slide pane. The **slide pane** shows the current slide as it will look during your slide show. Just below the slide pane is the notes pane. The **notes pane** contains notes (also called speaker notes) for the presenter; for example, the notes pane might contain specific points to cover or phrases to say during the presentation. During a slide show, the audience does not see the contents of the notes pane.

Along the left edge of the PowerPoint window, you can see two tabs, the Outline tab and the Slides tab. The **Slides tab** is on top when you first start PowerPoint. It shows a column of numbered slide **thumbnails** (miniature images) so you can see a visual representation of several slides at once. You can use the Slides tab to jump quickly to another slide in the slide pane by clicking the desired slide. The **Outline tab** shows an outline of the titles and text of each slide of your presentation.

At the bottom left of the PowerPoint window, just above the Drawing toolbar, are three view buttons: the Normal View button, the Slide Sorter View button, and the Slide Show from current slide button. These three buttons allow you to change the way you view a slide presentation. PowerPoint is currently in Normal view. Normal view is best for working with the content of the slides. You can see how the text and graphics look on each individual slide, and you can examine the outline of the entire presentation. When you switch to Slide Sorter view, the Slides and Outline tabs disappear from view and all of the slides appears as thumbnails. Slide Sorter view is an easy way to reorder the slides or set special features for your slide show. Slide Show view is the view in which you run the slide show presentation. When you click the Slide Show from current slide button, the presentation starts, beginning with the current slide (the slide currently in the slide pane in Normal view or the selected slide in Slide Sorter view).

Next you'll try switching views. PowerPoint is currently in Normal view with Slide 1 in the slide pane.

To switch views in PowerPoint:

▶ **1.** Click the **Slide 2** thumbnail in the Slides tab. Slide 2 appears in the slide pane.

▶ **2.** Click the **Next Slide** button ⬇ at the bottom of the vertical scroll bar in the slide pane. Slide 3 appears in the slide pane.

▶ **3.** Drag the scroll box in the slide pane vertical scroll bar down to the bottom of the scroll bar. Notice the ScreenTip that appears as you drag. It identifies the slide number and the title of the slide at the current position.

4. Click the **Outline** tab. The text outline of the current slide appears in the Outline tab.

5. Drag the scroll box in the vertical scroll bar of the Outline tab up to the top of the scroll bar, and then click the **slide icon** ⬜ next to Slide 3. Slide 3 again appears in the slide pane.

6. Click the **Slides** tab. The Outline tab disappears behind the Slides tab.

7. Click the **Slide Sorter View** button ⊞. Slide Sorter view appears, and Slide 3 has a colored frame around it to indicate that it is the current slide.

8. Position the pointer over the **Slide 2** thumbnail. A thin, colored frame appears around Slide 2.

9. Click the **Slide 2** thumbnail to make it the current slide.

10. Double-click the **Slide 1** thumbnail. The window switches back to Normal view and Slide 1 appears in the slide pane. You could also have clicked the Normal View button to switch back to Normal view.

Now that you're familiar with the PowerPoint window, you're ready to view Miriam's presentation.

Viewing a Presentation in Slide Show View

Slide Show view is the view you use when you present an on-screen presentation to an audience. When you click the Slide Show from current slide button or click the Slide Show command on the View menu, the slide show starts. If you click the Slide Show from current slide button, the current slide fills the screen, and if you click the Slide Show command on the View menu, the first slide fills the screen. No toolbars or other Windows elements are visible on the screen.

In Slide Show view, you move from one slide to the next by pressing the spacebar, clicking the left mouse button, or pressing the → key. Additionally, PowerPoint provides a method for jumping from one slide to any other slide in the presentation during the slide show: you can right-click anywhere on the screen, point to Go to Slide on the shortcut menu, and then click one of the slide titles in the list that appears to jump to that slide.

When you prepare a slide show, you can add special effects to the show. For example, you can add **slide transitions**, the manner in which a new slide appears on the screen during a slide show. You can also add **animations** to the elements on the slide; that is, each text or graphic object on the slide can appear on the slide in a special way or have a sound effect associated with it. A special type of animation is **progressive disclosure**, a technique in which each element on a slide appears one at a time after the slide background appears. Animations draw the audience's attention to the particular item on the screen.

You can also add a footer on the slides. A **footer** is a word or phrase that appears at the bottom of each slide in the presentation.

You want to see how Miriam's presentation will appear when she shows it in Slide Show view at Global Humanitarian's executive meeting. You'll then have a better understanding of how Miriam used PowerPoint features to make her presentation informative and interesting.

To view the presentation in Slide Show view:

1. With Slide 1 in the slide pane, click the **Slide Show from current slide** button ⬚. The slide show begins by filling the entire viewing area of the screen with Slide 1 of Miriam's presentation. Watch as the slide title moves down the slide from the top and the Global Humanitarian logo and motto gradually appear on the screen.

   As you view this first slide, you can already see some of the types of elements that PowerPoint allows you to place on a slide: text in different styles, sizes, and colors; graphics; and a background picture. You also saw an example of an animation when you watched the slide title slide down the screen and the logo and motto gradually appear.

2. Press the **spacebar**. The slide show goes from Slide 1 to Slide 2. See Figure 1-3. Notice that during the transition from Slide 1 to Slide 2, the presentation displayed Slide 2 by scrolling down from the top of the screen and covering up Slide 1.

Figure 1-3 ▶ Slide 2 in Slide Show view

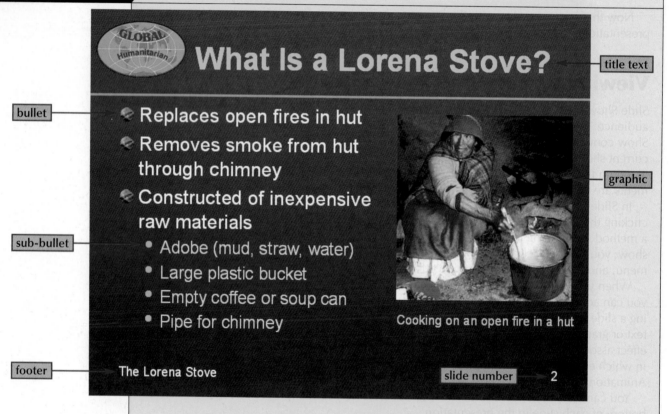

Trouble? If you missed the transition from Slide 1 to Slide 2, or if you want to see it again, press the ← key to redisplay Slide 1, and then press the spacebar to go to Slide 2 again.

Notice in Figure 1-3 that Slide 2 displays: (1) a colored background that varies in color across the slide, (2) Global Humanitarian's logo, (3) a title in large yellow text, (4) a bulleted list (with green textured bullets and white text, or solid cyan bullets with light yellow text), (5) a footer, (6) the slide number (in the lower-right corner of the slide), and (7) a photograph of a villager using an open fire.

3. Click the left mouse button to proceed to Slide 3. During the transition from Slide 2 to Slide 3, you again see the slide scroll down onto the screen from the top. Once the slide appears on the screen, you see a chart slowly appear. PowerPoint supports features for creating and customizing this type of chart, as well as graphs, diagrams, tables, and organization charts.

4. Press the **spacebar**. The title of Slide 4 appears on screen. What you don't see on the screen is a bulleted list. That's because this slide is designed for progressive disclosure. Additional slide elements will appear on screen after you press the spacebar or click on the screen.

5. Press the **spacebar** to reveal the first bulleted item on Slide 4. The item is animated to fly onto the screen from the bottom.

6. Press the **spacebar** again to reveal the next bulleted item. As this item appears, the previous item dims. Dimming the previous bulleted items helps focus the audience's attention on the current bulleted item.

7. Press the **spacebar** again to cause the last bulleted item to dim.

So far, you've seen important PowerPoint features: slide transitions, progressive disclosure, animations, and graphics (photos and drawings). Now you'll finish the presentation and see custom animations and simple drawings.

To continue viewing the slide show:

1. Press the **spacebar** to go to Slide 5, and then press the **spacebar** again. The label "Fuel chamber" and its accompanying arrow appear gradually on the screen. This is another example of an animation.

2. Press the **spacebar** three more times, pausing between each to allow the label and arrow to appear gradually on the screen.

3. Press the **spacebar** once more. A graphic labeled "smoke" comes into view, and you hear the sound of wind (or a breeze). The smoke object is an example of a user-drawn graphic.

4. Press the **spacebar** again to animate the smoke graphic and repeat the sound effect. The smoke graphic travels from the fuel chamber up the stovepipe.

5. Go to **Slide 6**. The graphic on this slide is a simple diagram drawn using drawing tools on the Drawing toolbar, which include not only shapes like circles, ovals, squares, and rectangles, but also arrows, boxes, stars, and banners.

6. Continue moving through the slide show, looking at all the slides and pausing at each one to read the bulleted items and view the graphics, until you reach Slide 11, the last slide in the slide show.

7. Press the **spacebar** to move from Slide 11. A black, nearly blank, screen appears. This signals that the slide show is over, as indicated by the line of text on the screen.

8. Press the **spacebar** one more time to return to the view from which you started the slide show, in this case, Normal view.

9. Close the current presentation by clicking the **Close Window** button ☒ on the menu bar, and then click the **No** button when asked if you want to save changes.

As you can see from this slide show, PowerPoint has many powerful features. You'll learn how to use many of these features in your own presentations as you work through these tutorials.

You're now ready to create Miriam's presentation on general information about Global Humanitarian's current projects. Before you begin, however, you need to plan the presentation.

Planning a Presentation

Planning a presentation before you create it improves the quality of your presentation, makes your presentation more effective and enjoyable, and, in the long run, saves you time and effort. As you plan your presentation, you should answer several questions: What is my purpose or objective for this presentation? What type of presentation is needed? Who is the audience? What information does that audience need? What is the physical location of my presentation? What is the best format for presenting the information contained in this presentation, given its location?

In planning your presentation, you should determine the following aspects:

- **Purpose of the presentation**: to provide general information about Global Humanitarian
- **Type of presentation**: training (how to become involved with Global Humanitarian)
- **Audience for the presentation**: potential donors, potential participants in humanitarian expeditions, and potential student interns
- **Audience needs**: to understand Global Humanitarian's mission and how to join the effort
- **Location of the presentation**: small conference rooms to large classrooms
- **Format**: oral presentation accompanied by an electronic slide show of 10 to 12 slides

You have carefully planned your presentation. Now you'll use the PowerPoint AutoContent Wizard to create it.

Using the AutoContent Wizard

PowerPoint helps you quickly create effective presentations by using a wizard, a special window that asks you a series of questions about your tasks, and then helps you perform them. The AutoContent Wizard lets you choose a presentation category, such as "Training," "Recommending a Strategy," "Brainstorming Session," or "Selling a Product or Service." After you select the type of presentation you want, the AutoContent Wizard creates a general outline for you to follow and formats the slides using a built-in design template and predesigned layouts. A **design template** is a file that contains the colors and format of the background and the font style of the titles, accents, and other text. Once you start creating a presentation with a given design template, you can change to any other PowerPoint design template or create a custom design template. A **layout** is a predetermined way of organizing the objects on a slide. You can change the layout applied to a slide or you can customize the layout of objects on a screen by moving the objects.

In this tutorial, you'll use the AutoContent Wizard to create a presentation with the goal of training employees, volunteers, and prospective donors on Global Humanitarian's mission. Because "Training" is predefined, you'll use the AutoContent Wizard, which will automatically create a title slide and standard outline that you can then edit to fit Miriam's needs.

To create the presentation with the AutoContent Wizard:

▶ 1. Click **File** on the menu bar, and then click **New**. The New Presentation task pane opens on the right side of the PowerPoint window.

▶ 2. Click the **From AutoContent wizard** link in the New Presentation task pane. The first dialog box of the AutoContent Wizard opens on top of the PowerPoint program window. The green square on the left side of the window indicates where you are in the wizard.

▶ 3. Read the information in the Start dialog box of the AutoContent Wizard, and then click the **Next** button. The next dialog box in the AutoContent Wizard appears. Note that the green square on the left side of the dialog box moved from Start to Presentation type. The Presentation type dialog box allows you to select the type of presentation you want.

4. Click the **General** button, if necessary, and then click **Training**. See Figure 1-4.

Figure 1-4

Selecting the type of presentation in the AutoContent Wizard

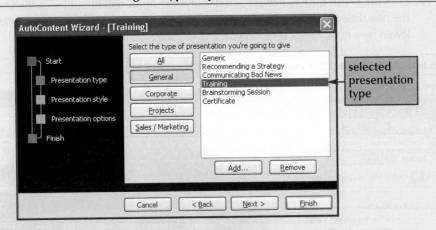

selected presentation type

5. Click the **Next** button. The Presentation style dialog box opens with the question, "What type of output will you use?" You could also change this option after you create the presentation. As noted in your plan, you want to create an on-screen presentation.

Trouble? If a dialog box opens telling you that PowerPoint can't display the template used in this document because the feature is not currently installed, you must install the Training template before continuing. If you are working on your own computer, click the Yes button. If you are working in a lab, ask your instructor or technical support person for help.

6. Click the **On-screen presentation** option button to select it, if necessary, and then click the **Next** button. The Presentation options dialog box opens. In this dialog box, you specify the title and footer (if any) of the presentation.

7. Click in the **Presentation title** text box, type **Global Humanitarian**, press the **Tab** key to move the insertion point to the **Footer** text box, and then type **Overview of Global Humanitarian**.

The title will appear on the title slide (the first slide) of the presentation. The footer will appear on every slide (except the title slide) in the presentation. If the other two options are checked, they will appear on either side of the footer on the presentation slides.

8. Click the **Date last updated** check box to clear it, and leave the **Slide number** check box checked. You don't want to clutter the screen with information that is not pertinent for the audience. See Figure 1-5.

Figure 1-5

Selecting information in the AutoContent Wizard

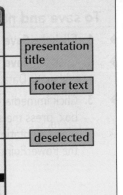

presentation title

footer text

deselected

9. Click the **Next** button. The Finish dialog box opens, letting you know that you completed the questions for the AutoContent Wizard.

10. Click the **Finish** button. PowerPoint displays the AutoContent outline in the Outline tab and the title slide (Slide 1) in the slide pane. The filename in the title bar "Presentation" followed by a number is a temporary filename. See Figure 1-6.

| Figure 1-6 | Outline and slide after completing the AutoContent Wizard |

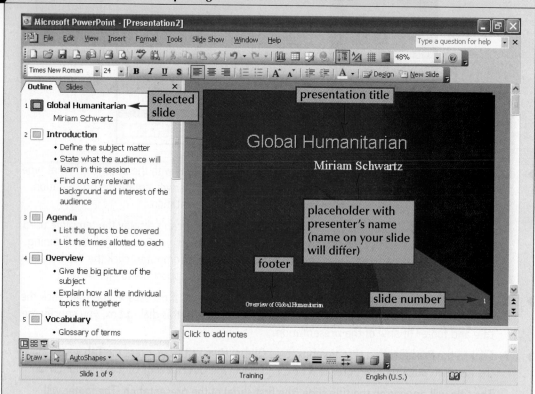

The AutoContent Wizard automatically displays the presenter's name (actually the name of the registered PowerPoint user) below the title in Slide 1. The name that appears on your screen will be different from the one shown in Figure 1-6.

Next, you'll save and name the presentation you created.

To save and name the presentation:

1. Click the **Save** button [icon] on the Standard toolbar. The Save As dialog box opens.

2. Click the **Save in** list arrow, and then navigate to the **Tutorial.01\Tutorial** folder included with your Data Files, if necessary.

3. Click immediately after Global Humanitarian, the default filename, in the **File name** text box, press the **spacebar**, type **Overview**, and then click the **Save** button. PowerPoint saves the presentation as Global Humanitarian Overview and displays that name in the title bar of the PowerPoint window.

In the next session, you'll edit the text of Miriam's presentation, as well as create notes.

Session 1.1 Quick Check

1. Describe the components of a PowerPoint presentation.
2. Name and describe the two panes and two tabs in the PowerPoint window in Normal view.
3. Define or describe the following:
   a. progressive disclosure
   b. slide transition
   c. design template
   d. layout
4. What are some of the questions that you should answer when planning a presentation?
5. Describe the purpose of the AutoContent Wizard.
6. Describe Slide Show view.

Session 1.2

Modifying a Presentation

Now that you've used the AutoContent Wizard, you're ready to edit some of the words in the presentation to fit Miriam's specific needs. You'll keep the design template, which includes the blue background and the size and color of the text, used by the AutoContent Wizard.

The AutoContent Wizard automatically creates the title slide, as well as other slides, with suggested text located in placeholders. A **placeholder** is a region of a slide, or a location in an outline, reserved for inserting text or graphics. To edit the AutoContent outline to fit Miriam's needs, you must select the placeholders one at a time, and then replace them with other text. Text placeholders are a special kind of **text box**, which is a container for text. You can edit and format text in a text box, or you can manipulate the text box as a whole. When you manipulate the text box as a whole, the text box is treated as an **object**, something that can be manipulated or resized as a unit.

When text is selected, the text box is active and appears as hatched lines around the selected text with sizing handles (small circles) at each corner and on each side of the box. You drag **sizing handles** to make a text box or other object larger or smaller on the slide. When the entire text box is selected as a single object, the text box appears as a dotted outline with sizing handles.

Many of the slides that the AutoContent Wizard created in your presentation for Global Humanitarian contain bulleted lists. A **bulleted list** is a list of paragraphs with a special character (dot, circle, box, star, or other character) to the left of each paragraph. A **bulleted item** is one paragraph in a bulleted list. Bullets can appear at different outline levels. A **first-level bullet** is a main paragraph in a bulleted list; a **second-level bullet**—sometimes called a **sub-bullet**—is a bullet beneath (and indented from) a first-level bullet. Using bulleted lists reminds both the speaker and the audience of the main points of the presentation. In addition to bulleted lists, PowerPoint also supports numbered lists. A **numbered list** is a list of paragraphs that are numbered consecutively within the body text.

When you edit the text on the slides, keep in mind that the bulleted lists aren't meant to be the complete presentation; instead, they should emphasize the key points to the audience and remind the speaker of the points to emphasize. In all your presentations, you should follow the 6 × 6 rule as much as possible: Keep each bulleted item to no more than six words, and don't include more than six bulleted items on a slide.

Creating Effective Text Presentations

- Think of your text presentation as a visual map of your oral presentation. Show your organization by using overviews, making headings larger than subheadings, including bulleted lists to highlight key points, and numbering steps to show sequences.
- Follow the 6 × 6 rule: Use six or fewer items per screen, and use phrases of six or fewer words. Omit unnecessary articles, pronouns, and adjectives.
- Keep phrases parallel.
- Make sure your text is appropriate for your purpose and audience.

Miriam reviewed your plans for your presentation and she has several suggestions for improvement. First, she wants you to replace the text that the AutoContent Wizard inserted with information about Global Humanitarian. She also wants you to delete unnecessary slides, and change the order of the slides in the presentation. You'll start by editing the text on the slides.

Editing Slides

Most of the slides in the presentation contain two placeholder text boxes. The slide **title text** is a text box at the top of the slide that gives the title of the information on that slide; the slide **body text** (also called the **main text**) is a large text box in which you type a bulleted or numbered list. In this presentation, you'll modify or create title text and body text in all but the title slide (Slide 1).

To edit the AutoContent outline to fit Miriam's needs, you must select text in each of the placeholders, and then replace that text with other text. You'll now begin to edit and replace the text to fit Miriam's presentation. The first text you'll change is the presenter's name placeholder.

To edit and replace text in the first slide:

1. If you took a break after the previous session, make sure PowerPoint is running, and then open the presentation **Global Humanitarian Overview** located in the Tutorial.01\Tutorial folder included with your Data Files. Slide 1 appears in the slide pane and the Outline tab is on top.

2. Position the pointer over the presenter's name (currently the registered PowerPoint user's name) in the slide pane so that the pointer changes to I, and then drag it across the text of the presenter's name to select the text. The text box becomes active, as indicated by the hatched lines around the box and the sizing handles at each corner and on each side of the text box, and the text becomes highlighted.

3. Type your first and last name (so your instructor can identify you as the author of this presentation), and then click anywhere else on the slide. As soon as you start to type, the selected text disappears, and the typed text appears in its place. (The figures in this book will show the name Miriam Schwartz.)

   Trouble? If PowerPoint marks your name with a red wavy underline, this indicates that the word is not found in the PowerPoint dictionary. Ignore the wavy line for now, because spelling will be covered later.

You'll now edit Slides 2 through 9 by replacing the placeholder text and adding new text, and by deleting slides that don't apply to your presentation.

To edit the text in the slides:

1. Click the **Next Slide** button ⬇ at the bottom of the vertical scroll bar in the slide pane. Slide 2 appears in the slide pane.

2. Drag across the word **Introduction** (the title text) to select it. See Figure 1-7.

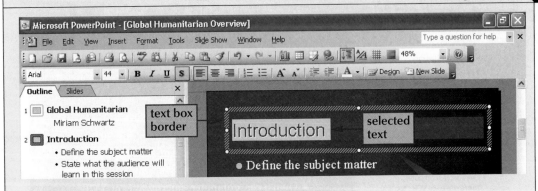

Now you're ready to type the desired title. As you perform the next step, notice not only that the words you type replace the selected text in the slide pane, but also that the slide title on the Outline tab changes.

3. Type **Are You Rich?** and then click in a blank space in the slide pane, just outside the edge of the slide, to deselect the text box. The hatched lines and sizing handles disappear. Notice that the slide title changed on the Outline tab as well.

   Trouble? If you clicked somewhere on the slide and selected another item, such as the bulleted list, click another place, preferably just outside the edge of the text box, to deselect all items.

   Now you're going to edit the text from the Outline tab.

4. In the Outline tab, select the text **Define the subject matter**. The text is highlighted by changing to white on black.

5. Type **Home has non-dirt floor: top 50%**. Don't include a period at the end of the phrase. This bulleted item is an incomplete sentence, short for "If you live in a home with a non-dirt floor, you're in the top 50% of the wealthiest people on earth."

6. Select the text of the second bulleted item in either the Outline tab or the slide pane, and then type **Home has more than one room: top 20%**. Again, don't include a period.

7. Select the text of the third bulleted item in the slide pane, and then type **Own more than one pair of shoes: top 5%**.

With the insertion point at the end of the third bulleted item, you're ready to create additional bulleted items.

To create additional bulleted items:

1. With the insertion point blinking at the end of the last bulleted item, press the **Enter** key. PowerPoint creates a new bullet and leaves the insertion point to the right of the indent after the bullet, waiting for you to type the text.

2. Type **Own a refrigerator: top 3%** and then press the **Enter** key.

3. Type **Own a car, computer, microwave, or VCR: top 1%**.

4. Click in a blank area of the slide pane to deselect the bulleted list text box. The completed Slide 2 should look like Figure 1-8.

| **Figure 1-8** | Slide 2 after adding text |

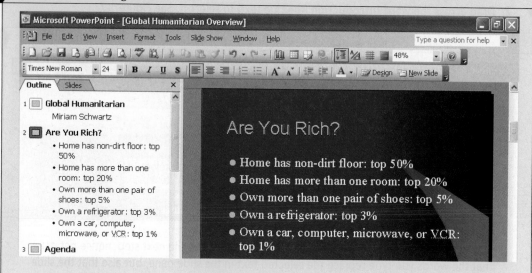

You're now ready to edit the text on another slide and create sub-bullets.

To create sub-bullets:

1. Click the **Next Slide** button at the bottom of the vertical scroll bar four times to move to Slide 6. Slide 6 appears in the slide pane and on the Outline tab.

2. Select the title text **Topic One**, and then type **How You Can Help**.

3. Select all the text in the body text placeholder, not just the text of the first bulleted item.

4. Type **Become a member of Global Humanitarian**, press the **Enter** key, and then type **Contribute to humanitarian projects**. You've added two bulleted items to the body text.

Now you'll add some sub-bullets beneath the first-level bulleted item.

5. Press the **Enter** key to insert a new bullet, and then press the **Tab** key. The new bullet changes to a sub-bullet. In this design template, sub-bullets have a dash in front of them, which you won't be able to see until you start typing the text.

6. Type **Health and Education**, and then press the **Enter** key. The new bullet is a second-level bullet, the same level as the previous bullet.

7. Type **Water and Environment**, press the **Enter** key, type **Income Generation and Agriculture**, press the **Enter** key, and then type **Leadership and Cultural Enhancement**.

Now you want the next bullet to return to the first level.

8. Press the **Enter** key to create a new, second-level bullet, and then click the **Decrease Indent** button on the Formatting toolbar. The bullet is converted to a first-level bullet. You can also press the Shift+Tab key combination to move a bullet up a level.

9. Type the remaining two first-level bulleted items: **Join a humanitarian expedition** and **Become a student intern**, and then click in a blank area of the slide to deselect the text box. See Figure 1-9.

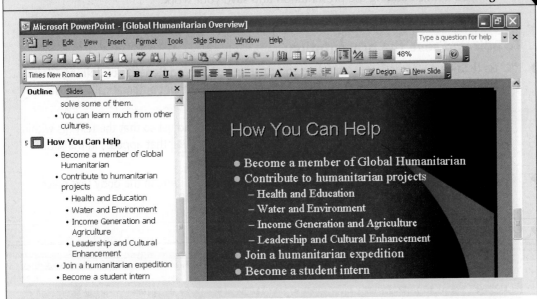

You have completed editing Slide 6. Miriam suggests that you delete the previous three slides, which are unnecessary for your presentation, before you edit the other slides.

Deleting Slides

When creating a presentation, you'll often delete slides. The AutoContent Wizard may create slides that you don't think are necessary, or you may create slides that you no longer want. You can delete slides in several ways: in Normal view, by clicking the slide thumbnail in the Slides tab or by clicking the slide icon in the Outline tab to select the slide, and then pressing the Delete key or using the Delete command on the shortcut or Edit menu; or in Slide Sorter view, by selecting the slide and then pressing the Delete key. Keep in mind that once you delete a slide, you can recover it by immediately clicking the Undo button on the Standard toolbar.

You need to delete Slide 3 ("Agenda"), Slide 4 ("Overview"), and Slide 5 ("Vocabulary").

To delete Slides 3 through 5:

1. With Slide 6 in the slide pane, click the **slide icon** [icon] next to Slide 3 ("Agenda") on the Outline tab. You might need to drag the Outline pane scroll box up to view Slide 3. This causes Slide 3 to appear in the slide pane. Now you're ready to delete the slide.

2. Right-click the Slide 3 ("Agenda") **slide icon** [icon] on the Outline tab, and then click **Delete Slide** on the shortcut menu. The entire slide is deleted from the presentation, and the rest of the slides are renumbered so that the slide that was Slide 4 becomes Slide 3, and so on. The renumbered Slide 3 ("Overview") appears in the slide pane.

3. Click the **Slides** tab. The Outline tab disappears and the Slides tab appears with thumbnails of all of the slides. With the Slides tab on top, notice that the labels identifying the Slides and Outline tabs change to icons.

4. With **Slide 3** ("Overview") selected in the Slides tab, press and hold the **Shift** key, and then click **Slide 4** on the Slides tab. Slides 3 and 4 are both selected on the Slides tab.

5. Click **Edit** on the menu bar, and then click **Delete Slide**. Both slides are deleted from the presentation. The new Slide 3, entitled "How You Can Help," now appears in the slide pane.

   Trouble? If the Delete Slide command is not on the Edit menu, click the double arrow at the bottom of the menu to display all of the commands on the menu.

Now you'll finish editing the presentation and save your work.

To edit and save the presentation:

▶ 1. Go to **Slide 4** ("Topic Two"), and then edit the title text to read **Benefits of Joining Global Humanitarian**. Notice that as you type the last word, PowerPoint automatically adjusts the size of the text to fit in the title text box.

Trouble? If the font size of the text doesn't automatically adjust so that the text fits within the body text placeholder, click the AutoFit Options button ⊞ that appears in the slide pane, and then click the AutoFit Text to Placeholder option.

▶ 2. Select all the body text, not just the text of the first bulleted item, in the body text placeholder, and then type the bulleted items shown in Figure 1-10.

Figure 1-10 | **Completed Slide 4**

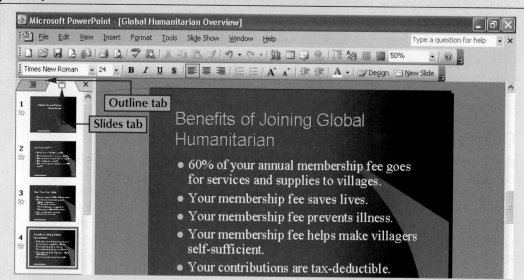

▶ 3. Go to **Slide 5**, and then modify the title and body text so that the slide looks like Figure 1-11.

Figure 1-11 | **Completed Slide 5**

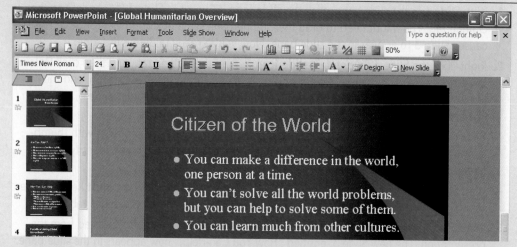

4. Delete **Slide 6** ("Where to Get More Information").

5. Click the **Save** button 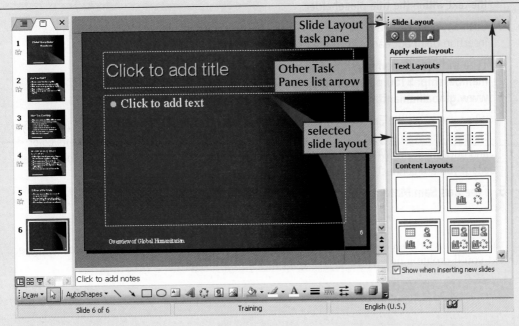 on the Standard toolbar to save the presentation.

Miriam reviews your presentation and wants you to add a slide at the end of the presentation stating what action you want your readers to take as a result of your presentation.

Adding a New Slide and Choosing a Layout

Miriam suggests that you add a new slide at the end of the presentation explaining how individuals and families can join Global Humanitarian. When you add a new slide, PowerPoint formats the slide using a slide layout. PowerPoint supports four **text layouts**: Title Slide (placeholders for a title and a subtitle, usually used as the first slide in a presentation); Title Only (a title placeholder but not a body text placeholder); Title and Text (the default slide layout, with a title and a body text placeholder); and Title and 2-Column Text (same as Title and Text, but with two columns for text). PowerPoint also supports several **content layouts**—slide layouts that contain from zero to four charts, diagrams, images, tables, or movie clips. In addition, PowerPoint supports combination layouts, called **text and content layouts**, and several other types of layouts.

When you insert a new slide, it appears after the current one, and the Slide Layout task pane appears with a default layout already selected. This default layout is applied to the new slide. To use a different layout, you click it in the Slide Layout task pane.

To insert the new slide at the end of the presentation:

1. Because you want to add a slide after Slide 5, make sure Slide 5 is still in the slide pane.

2. Click the **New Slide** button on the Formatting toolbar. The Slide Layout task pane opens with the first layout in the second row under Text Layouts selected as the default, and a new Slide 6 appears in the slide pane with the default layout applied. See Figure 1-12.

New slide added ◄ **Figure 1-12**

You'll accept the default layout for this slide. If you wanted a different layout, you would click the desired layout in the Slide Layout task pane.

Trouble? If the Slide Layout task pane does not appear, click View on the menu bar, click Task Pane, click the Other Task Panes list arrow at the top of the task pane, and then click Slide Layout. To make the Slide Layout task pane open automatically when you insert a new slide, click the Show when inserting new slides check box at the bottom of the task pane.

3. Position the pointer over the selected layout in the task pane. A ScreenTip appears, identifying this layout as the Title and Text layout.

Next you'll close the Slide Layout task pane to provide a larger view of the slide pane.

4. Click the **Close** button ☒ in the Slide Layout task pane title bar to close the task pane.

Trouble? If you accidentally click the Close button of the PowerPoint window or Presentation window, PowerPoint will ask you if you want to save the changes to your presentation. Click the Cancel button so that the presentation doesn't close, and then click the correct Close button on the task pane title bar.

The new slide contains text placeholders. On a new slide, you don't need to select the text on the slide to replace it with your text. You only need to click in the placeholder text box; the placeholder text will disappear and the insertion point will be placed in the text box, ready for you to type your text. Once you type your text, the dotted line outlining the edge of the text box will disappear. You'll add text to the new slide.

To add text to the new slide:

1. Click anywhere in the title text placeholder in the slide pane, where it says "Click to add title." The title placeholder text disappears and the insertion point blinks at the left of the title text box.

2. Type **Global Humanitarian Memmbership**. Make sure you type "Memmbership" with two *m*s in the middle. You'll correct this misspelling later. Again, the font size decreases to fit the text within the title placeholder.

3. Click anywhere in the body text placeholder. The placeholder text disappears and the insertion point appears just to the right of the first bullet.

4. Type **Individual membership: $75 per year**, press the **Enter** key, type **Family membership: $150 per year**, press the **Enter** key, type **Visit our Web site at www.globalhumanitarian.org**, and then press the **Enter** key.

When you press the Enter key after typing the Web site address, PowerPoint automatically changes the Web site address (the URL) to a link. It formats the link by changing its color and underlining it. When you run the slide show, you can click this link to jump to that Web site if you are connected to the Internet.

5. Type **Call Sam Matagi, Volunteer Coordinator, at 523–555–SERV**.

You have inserted a new slide at the end of the presentation and added text to the slide. Next you'll create a new slide by promoting text in the Outline tab.

Promoting, Demoting, and Moving Outline Text

You can modify the text of a slide in the Outline tab as well as in the slide pane. Working in the Outline tab gives you more flexibility because you can see the outline of the entire presentation, not only the single slide currently in the slide pane. Working in the Outline tab allows you to easily move text from one slide to another or to create a new slide by promoting bulleted items from a slide so that they become the title and body text on a new slide.

To **promote** an item means to increase the outline level of that item—for example, to change a bulleted item into a slide title or to change a second-level bullet into a first-level bullet. To **demote** an item means to decrease the outline level—for example, to change a slide title into a bulleted item on the previous slide or to change a first-level bullet into a second-level bullet. You'll begin by promoting a bulleted item to a slide title, thus creating a new slide.

To create a new slide by promoting outline text:

1. Click the **Outline** tab. The outline of the presentation appears.

2. Drag the scroll box in the slide pane up until the ScreenTip displays "Slide: 3 of 6" and the title "How You Can Help." Slide 3 appears in the slide pane and the text of that slide appears at the top of the Outline tab.

3. In the Outline tab, move the pointer over the bullet to the left of "Contribute to humanitarian projects" so that the pointer becomes ✛, and then click the bullet. The text for that bullet and all its sub-bullets are selected.

   Now you'll promote the selected text so that it becomes the title text and first-level bullets on a new slide.

4. Click the **Decrease Indent** button on the Formatting toolbar. PowerPoint promotes the selected text one level. Because the bullet you selected was a first-level bullet, the first-level bullet is promoted to a slide title on a new Slide 4, and the second-level bullets become first-level bullets on the new slide. See Figure 1-13.

Promoting a bulleted item to become a new slide ◄ **Figure 1-13**

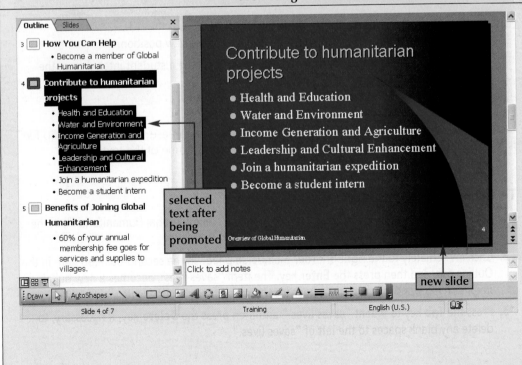

Now you'll edit this text, and then move some of the bulleted items to another slide.

5. Click anywhere to deselect the text, select the Slide 4 title text in the Outline tab, and then type **Types of Humanitarian Projects in Third-World Villages**. Notice that the title changes in the slide pane as well.

   Trouble? If all of the text on the slide becomes selected when you try to select the title text, make sure you position the pointer just to the left of the title text, and not over the slide icon, before you drag to select the text.

6. Click the bullet to the left of "Join a humanitarian expedition" (the fifth bullet in Slide 4) in the Outline tab, and then, while holding down the left mouse button, drag the bullet and its text up until the horizontal line position marker is just under the bulleted item "Become a member of Global Humanitarian" in Slide 3, as shown in Figure 1-14.

Figure 1-14	**Moving text in the Outline tab**

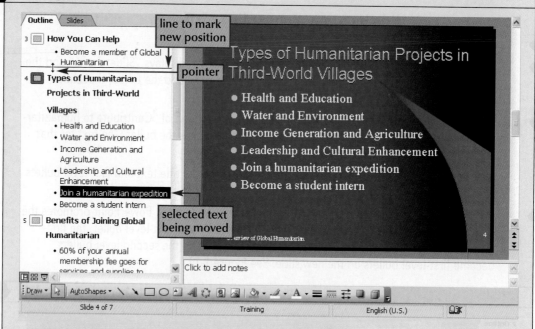

7. Release the mouse button. The bulleted item moves to the new position.

8. Using the same procedure, move the bulleted item "Become a student intern" from the end of Slide 4 to the end of Slide 3 in the Outline tab.

As you review your slides, you notice that in Slide 5, the phrase "Your membership fee" is repeated three times. You'll fix the problem by demoting some of the text.

To demote text on Slide 5:

1. Click the **slide icon** 🔲 next to Slide 5 ("Benefits of Joining Global Humanitarian") in the Outline tab.

2. Click immediately to the right of "Your membership fee" in the second bulleted item in the Outline tab, and then press the **Enter** key. The item "saves lives" becomes a new bulleted item, but you want that item to appear indented at a lower outline level.

3. Press the **Tab** key to indent "saves lives," and then press the **Delete** key, if necessary, to delete any blank spaces to the left of "saves lives."

4. Click the bullet to the left of "Your membership fee prevents illness" in the Outline tab, press and hold down the **Shift** key, and then click the bullet to the left of "Your membership fee helps make villagers self-sufficient." This selects both bulleted items at the same time.

5. Click the **Increase Indent** button on the Formatting toolbar to demote the two bulleted items. Note this has the same effect as pressing the Tab key.

6. Delete the phrase "Your membership fee" and the space after it from the two items that you just demoted. Your slide should now look like Figure 1-15.

Slide 5 after demoting text to sub-bullets | **Figure 1-15**

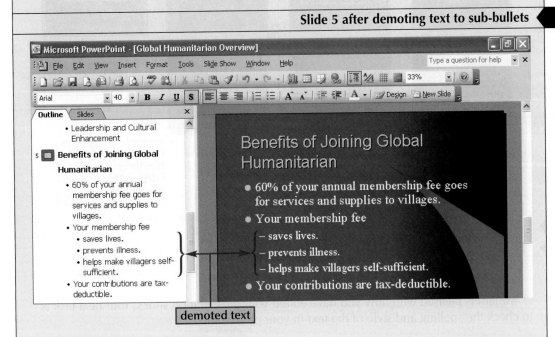

demoted text

Miriam looks at your presentation and suggests that you move the current Slide 4 ahead of Slide 3. You could make this change by clicking the slide icon and dragging it above the slide icon for Slide 3 in the Outline tab. Instead, you'll move the slide in Slide Sorter view.

Moving Slides in Slide Sorter View

In Slide Sorter view, PowerPoint displays all the slides as thumbnails, so that several slides can appear on the screen at once. This view not only provides you with a good overview of your presentation, but also allows you to easily change the order of the slides and modify the slides in other ways.

To move Slide 4:

1. Click the **Slide Sorter View** button at the bottom of the Outline tab. You now see your presentation in Slide Sorter view.

2. Click **Slide 4**. A thick colored frame appears around the slide, indicating that the slide is selected.

3. Press and hold down the left mouse button, drag the slide to the left so that the vertical line position marker appears on the left side of Slide 3, as shown in Figure 1-16.

Figure 1-16 ▶ Moving a slide in Slide Sorter view

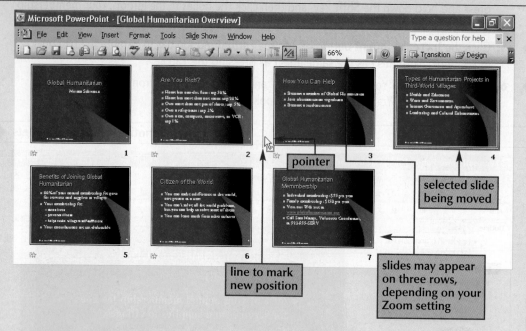

4. Release the mouse button. Slides 3 and 4 have switched places.

5. Click the **Normal View** button ▣ to return to Normal view.

Miriam is pleased with how you have edited your presentation slides. Your next task is to check the spelling and style of the text in your presentation.

Checking the Spelling and Style in a Presentation

Before you print or present a slide show, you should always perform a final check of the spelling and style of all the slides in your presentation. This will help to ensure that your presentation is accurate and professional looking.

Checking the Spelling

If PowerPoint finds a word that's not in its dictionary, the word is underlined with a red wavy line in the slide pane. When you right-click the word, suggestions for alternate spellings appear on the shortcut menu, as well as commands for ignoring the misspelled word or opening the Spelling dialog box. You can also click the Spelling button on the Standard toolbar to check the spelling in the entire presentation.

You need to check the spelling in the Global Humanitarian presentation.

To check the spelling in the presentation:

1. Go to **Slide 7**. The spelling check always starts from the current slide.

2. Click the **Spelling** button 🕮 on the Standard toolbar. The Spelling dialog box opens. The word you purposely mistyped earlier, "Memmbership," is highlighted in the Outline tab and listed in the Not in Dictionary text box in the Spelling dialog box. Two suggested spellings appear in the Suggestions list box, and the selected word in the Suggestions list box appears in the Change to text box.

▶ **3.** With "Membership" selected in the Suggestions list box and in the Change to text box, click the **Change** button. If you knew that you misspelled that word throughout your presentation, you could click the Change All button to change all of the instances of the misspelling in the presentation to the corrected spelling.

The word is corrected, and the next word in the presentation that is not in the PowerPoint dictionary, Matagi, is flagged. This word is not misspelled; it is a surname.

▶ **4.** Click the **Ignore** button. The word is not changed on the slide. If you wanted to ignore all the instances of that word in the presentation, you could click the Ignore All button. A dialog box opens telling you that the spelling check is complete.

Trouble? If another word in the presentation is flagged as misspelled, select the correct spelling in the Suggestions list, and then click the Change button. If your name on Slide 1 is flagged, click the Ignore button.

▶ **5.** Click the **OK** button. The dialog box closes.

Next, you need to check the style in the presentation.

Using the Style Checker

The **Style Checker** checks your presentation for consistency in punctuation, capitalization, and visual elements and marks problems on a slide with a light bulb. For this feature to be active, you need to turn on the Style Checker.

To turn on the Style Checker:

▶ **1.** Click **Tools** on the menu bar, click **Options** to open the Options dialog box, and then click the **Spelling and Style** tab.

▶ **2.** Click the **Check style** check box to select it, if necessary. Now you'll check to make sure the necessary Style Checker options are selected.

Trouble? If a message appears telling you that the Style Checker needs to use the Office Assistant, click the Enable Assistant button. If another message appears telling you that PowerPoint can't display the Office Assistant because the feature is not installed, click the Yes button only if you are working on your own computer. If you are in a lab, ask your instructor or technical support person for assistance.

▶ **3.** Click the **Style Options** button in the Options dialog box, click the **Slide title style** check box to select it, if necessary, click the list arrow to the right of this option, and then click **UPPERCASE**. When you run the Style Checker, it will suggest changing all of the titles to all uppercase.

▶ **4.** Click the **Body text style** check box to select it, if necessary, click the list arrow to the right of this option, and then click **Sentence case**, if necessary. When you run the Style Checker, it will check to make sure that the text in each bullet in the body text has an uppercase letter as the first letter, and that the rest of the words in the body text start with a lowercase letter.

▶ **5.** Click the bottom two check boxes under End punctuation to clear them, if necessary. Some of the bulleted lists in this presentation are complete sentences and some are not, so you want PowerPoint to allow variation in the end punctuation. See Figure 1-17.

Figure 1-17 ▶ **Style Options dialog box**

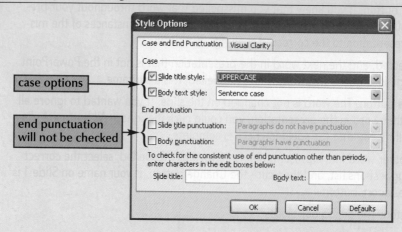

case options ▶

end punctuation
will not be checked ▶

▶ **6.** Click the **OK** button to close the Style Options dialog box, and then click the **OK** button to close the Options dialog box.

From now on, PowerPoint will check the style in your presentation as you display each slide in the slide pane. Now you'll go through your presentation and check for style problems.

To fix problems marked by the Style Checker:

▶ **1.** Go to **Slide 1**. A light bulb appears next to the title. This indicates that the Style Checker found a problem with the slide title. Since you did not type any of the titles in all uppercase letters, a light bulb will appear on every slide marking the titles as not matching the style.

▶ **2.** Click the **light bulb**. The Office Assistant appears and displays a dialog box with a description of the problem and three options from which you can choose. See Figure 1-18.

Figure 1-18 ▶ **Using the Style Checker**

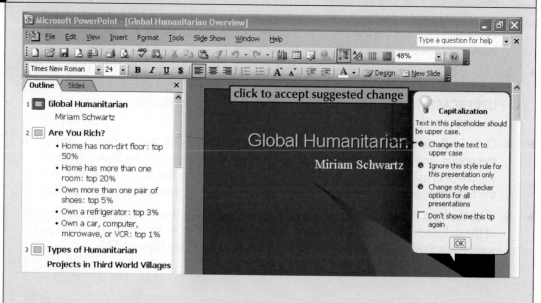

Trouble? If a message appears telling you that PowerPoint can't display the Office Assistant because the feature is not installed, click the Yes button only if you are working on your own computer. If you are in a lab, ask your instructor or technical support person for assistance.

3. Click the **Change the text to upper case** option button in the Office Assistant dialog box. All of the title text is now changed to uppercase.

4. Go to **Slide 2**.

5. Use the Style Checker to change the title text to uppercase.

6. Go to **Slide 3**, and then change the title text to uppercase. Another light bulb appears on Slide 3 next to the body text.

   Trouble? If, in this or subsequent steps, the light bulb doesn't appear by the body text, go to the next or the previous slide, and then return to the current slide as a way of telling the Style Checker to recheck the slide.

7. Click the **light bulb** to see that the error in the body text is another capitalization error, and then click the **Change the text to sentence case** option button in the Office Assistant dialog box. All the words in the bulleted items are converted to lowercase (except the first word in each bulleted item); that is, all the bulleted items are converted to sentence case.

8. Go to **Slide 4**, change the title text to uppercase, and then click the **light bulb** next to the body text. The Style Checker detects that the first bulleted item is in mixed case (the words "Global Humanitarian" are capitalized), but the organization's name should remain capitalized, so you don't need to make any changes here.

9. Click the **OK** button in the Office Assistant dialog box. PowerPoint ignores the style for that slide, and the light bulb no longer appears.

10. Correct the title and body text on Slide 5, and the title text on Slide 6, and then go to Slide 7.

11. Correct the title text on Slide 7, but do not correct the capitalization in the body text on Slide 7. The words that start with an uppercase letter in the body text on this slide are proper nouns or are part of the phone number. Now you need to turn off the Style Checker.

12. Click **Tools** on the menu bar, click **Options**, click the **Check style** check box on the Spelling and Style tab to clear it, and then click the **OK** button. The Style Checker is turned off.

As you create your own presentations, watch for the problems marked by the Style Checker. Of course, in some cases, you might want a certain capitalization that the Style Checker detects as an error. In these cases, just ignore the light bulb, or click it, and then click the OK button. The light bulb never appears on the screen during a slide show or when you print a presentation.

Using the Research Task Pane

PowerPoint enables you to use the Research task pane to search online services or Internet sites for additional help in creating a presentation. Using these resources helps you make your presentations more professional. For example, you could look up specific words in a thesaurus. A **thesaurus** contains a list of words and their synonyms, antonyms, and other related words. Using a thesaurus is a good way to add variety to the words you use or to choose more precise words. You could also look up information in online encyclopedias, news services, libraries, and business sites.

Miriam thinks the word "rich" in Slide 2 may be too informal. She asks you to find an appropriate replacement word. You'll now look for synonyms in the Office thesaurus.

To do research using the thesaurus:

1. Go to **Slide 2**, and then highlight the word **RICH** in either the Outline tab or the slide pane. Be careful not to highlight the question mark at the end of the phrase.

2. Click the **Research** button on the Standard toolbar. The Research task pane opens with the word "RICH" in the Search for text box.

3. Click the list arrow next to All Reference Books in the task pane, and then click **Thesaurus: English (U.S.)**.

4. Click the **green arrow** button next to the Search for text box to begin a search for synonyms for the word "rich," if necessary. The thesaurus provides several suggestions in a list organized so that the most relevant words are in bold, and additional synonyms are indented under the bold terms.

5. Scroll down, if necessary, to see the word "full" in boldface, and then click the **minus sign** button next to "full (adj.)." The minus sign changes to a plus sign, and the list of words under "full" collapses.

   After looking over the list, Miriam decides that "full" and "opulent" do not convey the correct meaning. She decides that "wealthy" is the most appropriate synonym.

6. Position the pointer over the word **wealthy**, indented under the bold term **wealthy (adj.)**. A box appears around the term and a list arrow appears at the right side of the box.

7. Click the list arrow on the side of the box, as shown in Figure 1-19.

Figure 1-19	Using the Thesaurus in the Research task pane

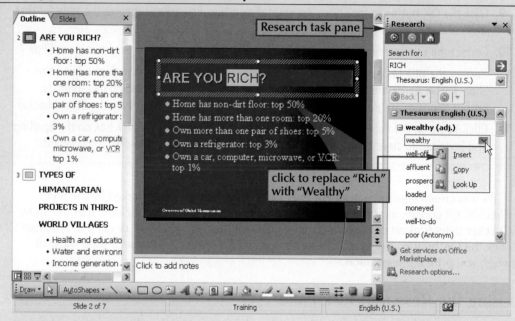

8. Click **Insert**. "WEALTHY" replaces "RICH" in the slide.

9. Close the task pane.

Creating Speaker Notes

When you show the presentation to Miriam, she is satisfied. Now you're ready to prepare the other parts of Miriam's presentation: the notes (also called speaker notes) and audience handouts (a printout of the slides). **Notes** are printed pages that contain a picture of and notes about each slide. They help the speaker remember what to say when a particular slide appears during the presentation. **Handouts** are printouts of the slides; these can be arranged with several slides printed on a page.

You'll create notes for only a few of the slides in the presentation. For example, Miriam wants to remember to acknowledge special guests or Global Humanitarian executives at any meeting where she might use this presentation. You'll create a note reminding her to do that.

To create notes:

1. Click the **Slides** tab, and then click **Slide 1** in the Slides tab. Slide 1 appears in the slide pane. The notes pane currently contains placeholder text.

2. Click in the notes pane, and then type **Acknowledge special guests and Global Humanitarian executives.** See Figure 1-20.

Notes on Slide 1 ◀ | **Figure 1-20**

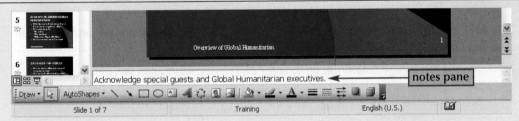

3. Click **Slide 2** in the Slides tab, click in the notes pane, and then type **Everyone in this room is in the top one percent of wealthy people who have ever lived on earth.**

4. Go to **Slide 3**, click in the notes pane, and then type **Give an example of each of these project types.** These are all the notes that Miriam wants.

5. Click the **Save** button 🖫 on the Standard toolbar to save the changes to the presentation.

Before Miriam gives her presentation, she'll print the notes of the presentation so she'll have them available during her presentations. You can now view the completed presentation to make sure that it is accurate, informative, and visually pleasing.

To view the slide show:

1. Go to **Slide 1**, and then click the **Slide Show from current slide** button 🖵 at the bottom of the Slides tab.

2. Proceed through the slide show as you did earlier, clicking the left mouse button or pressing the spacebar to advance from one slide to the next.

3. If you see a problem on one of your slides, press the **Esc** key to leave the slide show and display the current slide on the screen in Normal view, fix the problem on the slide, save your changes, and then click the **Slide Show from current slide** button 🖵 to resume the slide show from the current slide.

4. When you reach the end of your slide show, press the **spacebar** to move to the blank screen, and then press the **spacebar** again to return to Normal view.

Now you're ready to preview and print your presentation.

Previewing and Printing a Presentation

Before you give your presentation, you may want to print it. PowerPoint provides several printing options. For example, you can print the slides in color using a color printer; print in grayscale or pure black and white using a black-and-white printer; print handouts with 2, 3, 4, 6, or 9 slides per page; or print the notes pages (the speaker notes printed below a picture of the corresponding slide). You can also format and then print the presentation onto overhead transparency film (available in most office supply stores).

Usually you'll want to open the Print dialog box by clicking File on the menu bar, and then clicking Print, rather than clicking the Print button on the Standard toolbar. If you click the Print button, the presentation prints with the options chosen last in the Print dialog box. If you're going to print your presentation on a black-and-white printer, you should first preview the presentation to make sure the text will be legible. You'll use Print Preview to see the slides as they will appear when they are printed.

To preview the presentation:

▶ **1.** Go to **Slide 1**, if necessary, and then click the **Print Preview** button 🔍 on the Standard toolbar. The Preview window appears, displaying Slide 1.

▶ **2.** Click the **Options** button on the Preview toolbar, point to **Color/Grayscale**, and then click **Grayscale**. The slide is displayed in grayscale.

▶ **3.** Click the **Next Page** button 🔲 on the Preview toolbar. As you can see, part of the background graphic covers the text on Slide 2. See Figure 1-21. You'll need to remove the background from the slides so you can read them after you have printed them.

| Figure 1-21 | Slide 2 in Preview window |

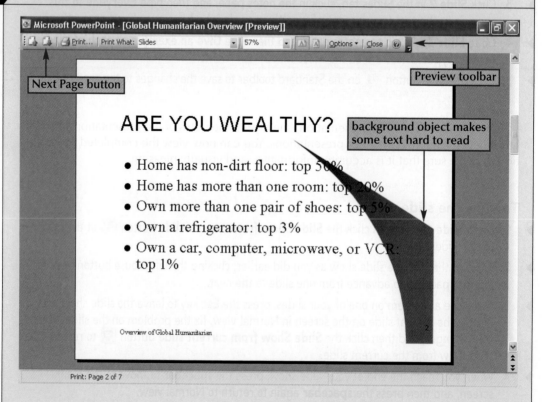

4. Click the **Close** button on the Preview toolbar to return to Normal view.

5. Click **Format** on the menu bar, click **Background** to display the Background dialog box, click the **Omit background graphics from master** check box, and then click the **Apply to All** button. The slide appears as before, but without the background graphic.

6. Click the **Print Preview** button 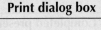 on the Standard toolbar, and then click the **Next Page** button on the Preview toolbar. You can now easily read the text on Slide 2.

7. Click the **Print What** list arrow on the Preview toolbar, and then click **Handouts (4 slides per page)**. The preview changes to display four slides on a page.

8. Click the **Print** button on the Preview toolbar. The Print dialog box opens. See Figure 1-22.

Print dialog box ◄ **Figure 1-22**

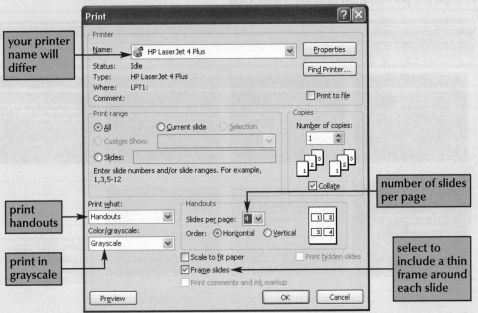

9. Compare your dialog box to the one shown in Figure 1-22, make any necessary changes, and then click the **OK** button to print the handouts on two pages. Now you're ready to print the notes.

10. Click the **Print What** list arrow on the Preview toolbar, and then click **Notes Pages**. The current slide is displayed as a notes page, with the slide on the top and the notes on the bottom.

11. Click the **Print** button on the Print Preview toolbar, click the **Slides** option button in the Print range section of the Print dialog box, and then type **1-3**. These are the only slides with notes on them, so you do not need to print all seven slides as notes pages.

12. Click the **OK** button to print the notes. Slides 1-3 print on three pieces of paper as notes pages.

13. Click the **Close** button on the Preview toolbar. The view returns to Normal view.

Your last task is to view the completed presentation in Slide Sorter view to see how all the slides look together. First, however, you'll restore the background graphics.

To restore the background graphics and view the completed presentation in Slide Sorter view:

▶ **1.** Click **Format** on the menu bar, click **Background**, click the **Omit background graphics from master** check box to clear it, and then click the **Apply to All** button. The background graphics are restored to the slides.

▶ **2.** Click the **Slide Sorter View** button ▣ at the bottom of the Slides tab. The slides appear on the screen in several rows, depending on the current zoom percentage shown in the Zoom box on the Standard toolbar and on the size of your monitor. You need to see the content on the slides better.

▶ **3.** Click the **Zoom** list arrow on the Standard toolbar, and then click **75%**. See Figure 1-23.

Figure 1-23 ▷ **Completed presentation in Slide Sorter view**

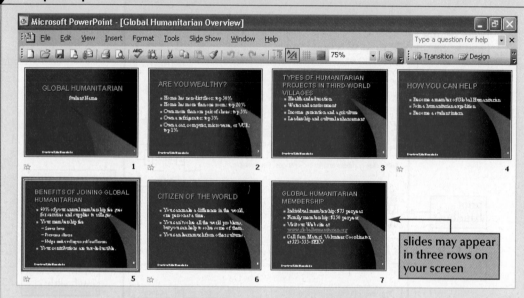

slides may appear in three rows on your screen

▶ **4.** Compare your handouts with the slides shown in Slide Sorter view.

▶ **5.** Click the **Close window** button ✕. A dialog box appears asking if you want to save your changes.

▶ **6.** Click the **Yes** button to save the changes and close the presentation.

Review

Session 1.2 Quick Check

1. Explain how to do the following in the Outline tab:
   a. move text up
   b. delete a slide
   c. change a first-level bullet to a second-level bullet

2. What does it mean to promote a bulleted item in the Outline tab? To demote a bulleted item?

3. Explain a benefit of using the Outline tab rather than the slide pane.

4. What is the Style Checker? What is an example of a consistency or style problem that it might mark?
5. What are notes? How do you create them?
6. Why is it beneficial to preview a presentation before printing it?

Review

Tutorial Summary

In this tutorial, you learned how to plan and create a PowerPoint presentation by modifying AutoContent slides. You learned how to edit the text in both the Outline tab and the slide pane; add a new slide and choose a slide layout; delete slides; and promote, demote and move text in your outline. You also learned how to check your presentation for consistency, create speaker notes, and preview and print your presentation.

Key Terms

animation	note	slide pane
body text	notes pane	slide transitions
bulleted item	numbered list	Slides tab
bulleted list	object	Style Checker
content layout	Outline tab	sub-bullet
demote	placeholder	text and content layout
design template	PowerPoint	text box
first-level bullet	progressive disclosure	text layout
footer	promote	thesaurus
handout	second-level bullet	thumbnail
layout	sizing handle	title text
main text		

Practice

Practice the skills you learned in the tutorial using the same case scenario.

Review Assignments

Data File needed for the Review Assignments: VillageOP.ppt

Miriam Schwartz, the managing director of the Austin, Texas headquarters of Global Humanitarian, asks you to prepare a PowerPoint presentation explaining the Village Outreach Program to potential donors and volunteers. She gives you a rough draft of a PowerPoint presentation. Your job is to edit the presentation. Complete the following:

1. Open the presentation **VillageOP** in the Tutorial.01\Review folder included with your Data Files.
2. Save the file as **Village Outreach Program** in the same folder.
3. In Slide 1, change the subtitle placeholder ("Global Humanitarian") to your name.
4. In Slide 2, use the Outline tab to demote the bulleted items "Health," "Education," "Clean water," and "Environment," so that they become second-level bulleted items.
5. Below the sub-bulleted item "Clean water," insert another second-level bulleted item: "Agriculture and Income-producing Projects."
6. In Slide 3, delete all occurrences of the word "the" to reduce the number of words in each bulleted item and thus approach the 6 × 6 rule.
7. Move the last bulleted item in Slide 3 ("Assist villagers in organizing health committees") in the Outline tab so it becomes the second bulleted item in the body text of Slide 3.

8. Go to Slide 5, and then promote the bulleted item "Agriculture and Income-producing Opportunities" in the Outline tab so it becomes the title of a new slide (Slide 6).
9. Return to Slide 5 and promote the last three second-level bulleted items so they become bullets on the same level as "Help villagers build."
10. In Slide 7, move the second bulleted item ("Mobilize resources") so it becomes the fourth bulleted item.
11. Add a new Slide 8 with the default Title and Text layout.
12. In Slide 8, type the slide title "Village Projects."
13. Type the following as first-level bulleted items in Slide 8: "Wells," "Water Pumps," "Greenhouses," "Lorena Stoves," "First aid supplies," and "School supplies."
14. In Slide 2, add the following speaker note: "Relate personal experiences for each topic."
15. In Slide 3, add the following speaker note: "Explain that we need volunteers, especially physicians, dentists, optometrists, and nurses."
16. Switch to Slide Sorter view, and then drag Slide 5 to the left of Slide 4.
17. Use the Research task pane to replace "Agriculture" on Slide 6 with another word, and then make this same change on Slide 2.
18. Check the spelling in the presentation and change or ignore each flagged word.
19. Turn on the Style Checker, set the Case options so that the slide title style is uppercase and the body text style is sentence case, and then examine the slides for elements that the Style Checker flags, correcting slides as appropriate. Turn off the Style Checker when you are finished.
20. View the presentation in Slide Show view. Look carefully at each slide and check the content. If you see any errors, press the Esc key to end the slide show, fix the error, and then start the slide show again.
21. Go to Slide 6. When you viewed the presentation, did you notice the typographical error "load" in the final bulleted item? (It should be "loan.") If you did not fix this error already, fix it now.
22. Save the changes to the presentation, preview the presentation in grayscale, and then print the presentation in grayscale as handouts, four slides per page.
23. Print Slides 2 and 3 as notes pages in grayscale, and then close the file.

Apply

Apply the skills you learned to create a new presentation for an e-commerce company using the AutoContent Wizard, and then modify the content.

Case Problem 1

There are no Data Files needed for this Case Problem.

e-Commerce Consultants Kendall Koester founded e-Commerce Consultants, a consulting company that helps local businesses with their e-commerce needs, including Web page design, order fulfillment, and security. Kendall hired you to prepare a presentation to businesses to sell the services of e-Commerce Consultants. Complete the following:

1. Start PowerPoint, and then start the AutoContent Wizard.
2. In the Presentation type window, select the Sales/Marketing category, and then select Selling a Product or Service.
3. In the Presentation style window, select On-screen presentation.
4. In the Presentation options window, type "Developing Strategies for Your Future" as the presentation title, and type "e-Commerce Consultants" as the footer.
5. Omit the date last updated from the presentation, but include the slide number.
6. In Slide 1, change the subtitle placeholder to your name, if necessary.
7. In Slide 2 ("Objective"), replace the slide title with "What We Offer," and replace the body text with the following first-level bulleted items: "Overcoming barriers to e-commerce," "Surviving today's shaky market," "Setting up your Web site," and "Managing your orders."

8. In Slide 3 ("Customer Requirements"), leave the title text as is, and then replace the body text with the following bulleted items: "Web site design and development," "Order taking and fulfillment," "Security," and "Other." Don't modify or delete the radial diagram on the slide.

9. In Slide 4, change the slide title to "Meeting Your Needs," and then replace the body text with the following first-level bulleted items: "Promoting your product," "Securing startup funds," "Arranging for credit card accounts," and "Answering all your questions." Don't modify or delete the three pyramid diagrams.

10. Delete Slides 5 ("Cost Analysis") and 6 ("Our Strengths").

11. In the new Slide 5 ("Key Benefits"), leave the title text as is, and then replace the body text with the following first-level bulleted items: "You can focus on your products, your services, and your bottom line."; and "We'll help you sell your product on the Internet."

12. In Slide 6 ("Next Steps"), leave the title text as is, and then replace the body text with the following first-level bulleted items: "List what you want us to do," "Draw up an agreement," "Determine a timeline," "Establish the order-fulfillment process," and "Launch the Web-based e-commerce system."

13. Save the presentation as **e-Commerce Consultants** in the Tutorial.01\Cases folder included with your Data Files.

14. In Slide 2, indent (demote) "Managing your orders" so it is a sub-bullet under "Setting up your Web site," and then add another sub-bullet, "Handling online credit."

15. In Slide 3, add the following sub-bulleted items under "Web site design and development": "know-how," "graphic design," "software," and "programming."

16. In Slide 4, insert a new first bullet "We can help by," and then make all the other phrases the sub-bullets.

17. Move the last bulleted item "Answering all your questions" up to become the first sub-bullet.

18. In Slide 6 ("Next Steps"), delete excess words like "a," "an," and "the" to achieve the 6 × 6 rule as closely as possible.

19. Add a new slide after Slide 6 with the Title and Text layout, type "Your Account Representative" as the title text, and then type the following information in five bullets: Kendall Koester, e-Commerce Consultants, 1666 Winnebago St., Pecatonica, IL 61063, 555-WEB-PAGE. The city, state, and Zip code should all be part of the same bulleted item. (Note that the first letter of "e-Commerce" changes to an uppercase letter as soon as you press the spacebar. This is PowerPoint's AutoFormat.)

20. Replace the "E" in "E-Commerce" with "e."

21. Turn on the Style Checker, set the Case options so that the slide title style is title case and the body text style is sentence case, and then go through each slide of the presentation to see if the Style Checker marks any potential problems. (Don't forget to double-check each slide by moving to the next or previous slide and then back to the current slide to recheck it.) When you see the light bulb, click it, and then assess whether you want to accept or reject the suggested change. You'll want to accept most of the suggested changes, but make sure you leave words like "Web" and "Internet" capitalized, and don't change the capitalization of the address and phone number you typed on Slide 7. Turn off the Style Checker when you are finished.

22. Check the spelling in the presentation. Correct any misspellings, and ignore any words that are spelled correctly.

23. View the presentation in Slide Show view.

24. Save the presentation, preview it in grayscale, print the presentation in grayscale as handouts with four slides per page, and then close the file.

Apply

Apply the skills you learned to modify an existing presentation for a public library outreach program.

Case Problem 2

Data File needed for this Case Problem: Library.ppt

Carriage Path Public Library   Davion McGechie is head of the Office of Community Outreach Services for the Carriage Path Public Library in Milford, Connecticut. Davion and his staff coordinate outreach services and develop programs in communities throughout the Long Island Sound. These services and programs depend on a large volunteer staff. Davion wants you to help him create a PowerPoint presentation to train his staff. Complete the following:

1. Open the file **Library** located in the Tutorial.01\Cases folder included with your Data Files, and save it as **Public Library Outreach** in the same folder.
2. In Slide 1, replace the subtitle placeholder ("Davion McGechie, Director") with your name.
3. In Slide 2, add the speaker's note "Mention that community groups include ethnic neighborhood councils, religious organizations, and civic groups."
4. Add a fourth bulleted item to Slide 2: "To implement outreach programs in the surrounding communities."
5. Move the second bulleted item ("To provide staff training") so that it becomes the last bulleted item.
6. In Slide 3, edit the second and third bulleted items so that "Four central libraries with in-depth collections" and "Six neighborhood Branch libraries" are second-level bulleted items below the main bullet.
7. Promote the bulleted item "Special Events & Programs" and its sub-bullets so that they become a new separate slide.
8. Use the Slides tab to move Slide 6 ("Branch Libraries") to become Slide 5.
9. Add a new slide after Slide 7 with the title "Volunteer Opportunities."
10. On Slide 8 (the new slide), create three bulleted items with the first line ("Literacy Tutors"), the second line ("Computer Instructors"), and the third line ("Children's Hour Story Tellers").
11. Under the third bullet, add the sub-bullets ("After-school story hour") and ("Bookmobile story hour").
12. Turn on the Style Checker, if necessary, and then go through all the slides, accepting all the suggested corrections of case (capitalization), except the following: "Deaf History Month: May," "National Literacy Month: September," "English as a Second Language (ESL)," and the names of the libraries.
13. Check the spelling in the presentation. Correct any spelling errors and ignore any words that are spelled correctly.
14. View the presentation in Slide Show view.
15. Go to Slide 2. When you viewed the presentation, did you notice the two typographical errors on this page? If you did not fix these errors, fix them now.
16. Save the presentation, preview it in grayscale, print the presentation in grayscale as handouts with four slides per page, and then close the file.

Challenge

Explore more advanced features of PowerPoint by formatting text, paragraphs, and lists, and by changing slide layouts and adding a design template.

Case Problem 3

Data File needed for this Case Problem: LASIK.ppt

Camellia Gardens Eye Center   Dr. Carol Wang, head ophthalmologist at the Camellia Gardens Eye Center in Charleston, South Carolina, performs over 20 surgeries per week using laser-assisted in situ keratomileusis (LASIK) to correct vision problems of myopia (nearsightedness), hyperopia (farsightedness), and astigmatism. She asks you to help prepare a PowerPoint presentation to those interested in learning more about LASIK. Complete the following:

1. Open the file **LASIK** located in the Tutorial.01\Cases folder included with your Data Files, and then save it as **Camellia LASIK** in the same folder.

2. In Slide 1, replace the subtitle placeholder ("Camellia Gardens Eye Center") with your name.

3. In Slide 2, move the first bulleted item down to become the third bulleted item.

4. Edit the sub-bullets "Myopia," "Hyperopia," and "Astigmatism" in the first item so they're part of the first-level bullet and there are no sub-bullets. Be sure to add commas after the first two words, and add the word "and" before the last word.

5. Add a fourth bulleted item with the text "Patients no longer need corrective lenses."

Explore ▶ 6. Still in Slide 2, center the text in the title text box. (*Hint*: Click anywhere in the title text, and then position the pointer over the buttons on the Formatting toolbar to see the ScreenTips to find a button that will center the text.)

Explore ▶ 7. In Slide 3, change the bulleted list to a numbered list. (*Hint*: Select all of the body text, and then look for a button on the Formatting toolbar that will number the list.)

Explore ▶ 8. Have PowerPoint automatically split Slide 3 into two slides. (*Hint*: First, click the AutoFit Options button in the slide pane and click the Stop Fitting Text to This Placeholder option button. Then, with the insertion point in the body text box, click the AutoFit Options button again, and then click the appropriate option.)

Explore ▶ 9. On the new Slide 4, change the numbering so it continues the numbering from Slide 3 rather than starting over at number 1. (*Hint*: Right-click anywhere in the first item in the numbered list, click Bullets and Numbering on the shortcut menu, click the Numbered tab, and then change the Start at value.)

10. At the end of the title in Slide 4, add a space and "(cont.)," the abbreviation for continued.

11. In Slide 5, demote the two bullets under "With low to moderate myopia," so they become sub-bullets.

Explore ▶ 12. Still in Slide 5, tell the PowerPoint Spell Checker to ignore all occurrences of the word "hyperopia," which is not found in PowerPoint's dictionary. (*Hint*: Right-click the word to see a shortcut menu with spelling commands.)

Explore ▶ 13. If any of the bulleted text doesn't fit on the slide, but drops below the body text box, set the text box to AutoFit. (*Hint*: Click anywhere in the text box, click the AutoFit Options button that appears, and then click the desired option.)

14. In Slide 6, join the final two bullets to become one bullet. Be sure to add a semicolon between the two bullets and change the word "Other" to lowercase.

15. In Slide 8, move the second bullet "Schedule eye exam to determine" (along with its sub-bullets) up to become the first bullet.

16. In Slide 8, edit the bulleted item ("Analysis of . . .") so that "eye pressure," "shape of cornea," and "thickness of cornea" are sub-bullets below "Analysis of."

Explore ▶ 17. Change the layout of Slide 8 so that the body text appears in two columns. (*Hint*: Click the AutoFit Options button in the slide pane, and then click Change to Two-Column Layout.) Drag the last two bullets over to the second column in the body text. (*Hint*: After you select the bulleted item, position the pointer over the selected text instead of over the bullet, and then drag the pointer to immediately after the new bullet in the second column, using the vertical line indicator that appears to help guide you.)

18. Add a new Slide 9, and then apply the Title Only layout in the Text Layout section of the Slide Layout task pane.

Explore

19. In Slide 9, add the title "Camellia Gardens Eye Center," create a new text box near the center of the slide, and then add the address "8184 Camellia Drive" on the first line, "Charleston, SC 29406" on the second line, and the phone number "(843) 555-EYES" on the third line. (*Hint*: Click the Text Box button on the Drawing toolbar, and then click on the slide at the desired location.)

Explore

20. Change the size of the text in the new text box on Slide 9 so that it's 32 points. (*Hint*: Click the edge of the text box to select the entire text box and all of its contents, and then click the Font Size list arrow on the Formatting toolbar.)

Explore

21. Turn on the Style Checker, and then set the style options for end punctuation so that the Style Checker checks to make sure that slide titles do not have end punctuation, and that paragraphs in the body text have punctuation. Set the slide title style to title case and the body text style to sentence case. Also, set the Visual Clarity options so that the maximum number of bullets should not exceed six, the number of lines per title should not exceed two, and the number of lines per bulleted item should not exceed two. (*Hint*: Use the End punctuation section of the Case and End Punctuation tab and the Legibility section of the Visual Clarity tab in the Style Options dialog box.)

Explore

22. Go through all the slides, correcting problems of case (capitalization) and punctuation. Be sure not to let the Style Checker change the case for proper nouns. Let the Style Checker correct end punctuation for complete sentences, but you shouldn't allow (or you should remove) punctuation for words or phrases that don't form complete sentences. Do not accept the Style Checker's suggestions to remove question marks in the slide titles.

Explore

23. Change the Style Options back so that the next time the Style Checker is run, only the Slide title style and Body text style options on the Case and End Punctuation tab and the Fonts options on the Visual Clarity tab are selected, and then turn off the Style Checker.

24. Check the spelling in the presentation.

Explore

25. Apply the design template called "Watermark," which has a white background with violet circles. (*Hint*: Click the Design button on the Formatting toolbar, and then use the ScreenTips in the Slide Design task pane to find the Watermark design template.) If you can't find the Watermark design template, choose a different design template.

26. View the presentation in Slide Show view.

27. Save the presentation, preview it in grayscale, print the presentation in grayscale as handouts with four slides per page, and then close the file.

Research

Use the Internet to research MP3 players and prepare a review.

Case Problem 4

There are no Data Files needed for this Case Problem.

Portable Digital Audio Players Your public speaking teacher instructs you to prepare a review of a portable digital audio player (for example, an MP3 player) for presentation to the class. If you are not familiar with portable digital audio players, your teacher suggests that you search the Internet or talk to other students for an explanation of what they are, how they work, and why so many people like them. You should then search the Internet for information or reviews about various brands and models of digital audio players. Alternatively, if you own a portable digital audio player, your instructor suggests you search the Internet for information about your player. You should organize your information into a PowerPoint presentation, with at least six slides. Complete the following:

1. Go to **www.google.com**, **yahoo.com**, or any other Web site that allows you to search the Web, and search using such terms as "digital audio player review" or "MP3 player review." You should read about various brands of players to get an idea of the most popular sellers.

2. Select one brand and model of digital audio player; search the Internet for more information and reviews about that player.

3. Use the AutoContent Wizard to begin developing slides for a presentation based on "Generic" in the General category of presentation types.

    a. Title the presentation "Review of" followed by the brand and model of your selected digital audio player. For example, the title might be "Review of Apple iPod," "Review of Rio Cali Sport MP3 Player," or "Review of Samsung Yepp YP-60V 256 MB MP3 Player."

    b. Include a footer with the text "Review of a digital audio player."

    c. Include both the date and the slide number in the footer.

4. In Slide 1, change the subtitle to your name, if necessary.

5. In Slide 2 ("Introduction"), include basic information about the digital audio player in the bulleted list. The information might include brand name, model name or number, capacity (for example, 128 MB or 256 MB), retail price, and street price.

6. In Slide 3 ("Topics of Discussion"), include categories of information used in reviewing the player, such as "General Description," "Features," "Audio File Formats," "Desktop Computer Software," "Ease of Use," "Technical Specifications," and "Reviewers' Comments."

7. Delete Slides 4 through 9. (*Hint*: Use Slide Sorter view.)

8. Create at least one slide for each topic you listed on Slide 3, and then include bulleted lists explaining that topic.

Explore ▶ 9. Use the Research Pane (by clicking the Research button on the Standard toolbar) to find additional information about the digital audio player you've chosen. (*Hint*: In the Research Pane, type the phrase "digital audio player" into the Search for text box, make sure your computer is connected to the Internet, select a research site such as eLibrary, if necessary, and click the green Start searching button.) You might want to create one or more new slides, cut and paste information into the new slides, and then edit the information into one or more appropriate bulleted lists.

10. Create a slide titled "Summary and Recommendation" as the last slide in your presentation, giving your overall impression of the player and your recommendation for whether the player is worth buying.

11. View the presentation on the Outline tab. If necessary, change the order of the bulleted items on slides, or change the order of slides.

Explore ▶ 12. If you see any slides with more than six or seven bulleted items, split the slide in two. (*Hint*: With the insertion point in the body text box, click the AutoFit Options button that appears near the lower-left corner of the text box, and click the appropriate command.)

13. Go through all the slides, correcting problems of case (capitalization), punctuation, number of bulleted items per slide, and number of lines per bulleted item. Be sure not to let the Style Checker change the case for proper nouns. Let the Style Checker correct end punctuation for complete sentences, but do not allow (or remove) punctuation for words or phrases that don't form complete sentences.

14. Check the spelling of your presentation.

15. View the presentation in Slide Show view. If you see any typographical errors or other problems, stop the slide show, correct the problems, and then continue the slide show. If you find slides that aren't necessary, delete them.

16. Save the presentation as **Digital Audio Player Review** in the Tutorial.01\Cases folder included with your Data Files.

17. Preview the presentation in grayscale, and print the presentation in grayscale as handouts with four slides per page. Print speaker notes if you created any, and then close the file.

Research

Go to the Web to find information you can use to create presentations.

Internet Assignments

The purpose of the Internet Assignments is to challenge you to find information on the Internet that you can use to work effectively with this software. The actual assignments are updated and maintained on the Course Technology Web site. Log on to the Internet and use your Web browser to go to the Student Online Companion for New Perspectives Office 2003 at **www.course.com/np/office2003**. Click the Internet Assignments link, and then navigate to the assignments for this tutorial.

Assess

SAM Assessment and Training

If you have a SAM user profile, you may have access to hands-on instruction, practice, and assessment of the skills covered in this tutorial. Log in to your SAM account and go to your assignments page to see what your instructor has assigned.

Review

Quick Check Answers

Session 1.1

1. Individual slides, speaker notes, an outline, and audience handouts.
2. The slide pane shows the slide as it will look during your slide show. The notes pane contains speaker notes. The Outline tab shows an outline of your presentation. The Slides tab displays thumbnails of each slide.
3. a. a feature that causes each element on a slide to appear one at a time
   b. the manner in which a new slide appears on the screen during a slide show
   c. a file that contains the colors and format of the background and the font style of the titles, accents, and other text
   d. a predetermined way of organizing the objects on a slide
4. What is my purpose or objective? What type of presentation is needed? What is the physical location of my presentation? What is the best format my presentation?
5. The AutoContent Wizard lets you choose a presentation category and then creates a general outline of the presentation.
6. The view you use to present an on-screen presentation to an audience.

Session 1.2

1. a. Click a slide or bullet icon, and then drag the selected item up.
   b. Right-click the slide icon of the slide to be deleted in the Outline tab, and then click Delete Slide on the shortcut menu; or, move to the slide you want to delete in the slide pane, click Edit on the menu bar, and then click Delete Slide.
   c. Click the slide or bullet icon in the Outline tab, and then click the Decrease Indent button on the Formatting toolbar.
2. Promote means to decrease the level (for example, from level two to level one) of an outline item; demote means to increase the level of an outline item.
3. In the Outline tab, you can see the text of several slides at once, which makes it easier to work with text. In the slide pane, you can see the design and layout of the slide.
4. The Style Checker automatically checks your presentation for consistency and style. For example, it will check for consistency in punctuation.
5. Notes are notes for the presenter. They appear in the notes pane in Normal view or you can print notes pages, which contain a picture of and notes about each slide.
6. By previewing your presentation, you make sure that the slides are satisfactory, and that the presentation is legible in grayscale if you use a monochrome printer.

New Perspectives on

Microsoft® Office Outlook 2003

Read This Before You Begin: Tutorial 1

To the Student

Data Files

To complete Outlook Tutorial 1, you need the starting student Data Files. Your instructor will either provide you with these Data Files or ask you to obtain them yourself.

Outlook Tutorial 1 requires the folder named "Tutorial.01" to complete the Tutorial, Review Assignments, and Case Problems. You will need to copy this folder from a file server, a standalone computer, or the Web to the drive and folder where you will be storing your Data Files. Your instructor will tell you which computer, drive letter, and folder(s) contain the files you need. You can also download the files by going to www.course.com; see the inside back or front cover for more information on downloading the files, or ask your instructor or technical support person for assistance.

If you are storing your Data Files on floppy disks, you will need **two** blank, formatted, high-density disks for this tutorial. Label your disks as shown, and place on them the folder(s) indicated.

▼ **Outlook 2003: Tutorial**
　　Tutorial.01\Tutorial folder
▼ **Outlook 2003: Exercises**
　　Tutorial.01\Review folder
　　Tutorial.01\Cases folder

When you begin this tutorial, refer to the Student Data Files section at the bottom of the tutorial opener page, which indicates which folders and files you need for the tutorial. Each end-of-tutorial exercise also indicates the files you need to complete that exercise.

To the Instructor

The Data Files are available on the Instructor Resources CD for this title. Follow the instructions in the Help file on the CD to install the programs to your network or standalone computer. See the "To the Student" section above for information on how to set up the Data Files that accompany this text.

You are granted a license to copy the Data Files to any computer or computer network used by students who have purchased this book.

System Requirements

If you are going to work through this book using your own computer, you need:

• **Computer System** Microsoft Windows 2000, Windows XP or higher must be installed on your computer. This tutorial assumes a typical installation of Microsoft Office 2003 (including Outlook and Word).

• **Data Disk** You will not be able to complete the tutorials or exercises in this book using your own computer until you have the necessary starting Data Files.

Objectives

Session 1.1
- Start and exit Outlook
- Explore the Outlook window
- Navigate between Outlook components
- Create and edit contact information
- Create and send e-mail messages

Session 1.2
- Read and respond to e-mail messages
- Attach files to e-mail messages
- File, sort, save, and archive messages

Communicating with Outlook 2003

Sending and Receiving E-mail Messages

Case

The Express Lane

The Express Lane is a complete and affordable online grocery store in the San Francisco Bay Area, specializing in natural and organic foods. Alan Gregory and Lora Shaw began The Express Lane in 1998 in response to what they saw as a growing need for more online grocery shopping services. Customers span all income and educational levels, ages, and locations.

Unlike traditional groceries, The Express Lane does not have a storefront where customers come to shop. Instead it stores both packaged goods and fresh produce in its warehouse. Customers place orders using e-mail or the company's Web site, or fax. The Express Lane staff then selects and packs the requested items, bills the customer's credit card for the cost of the groceries plus a $5 service fee, and delivers the groceries to the customer's front door within 12 to 24 hours. To coordinate these activities, The Express Lane relies on **Microsoft Outlook**, an information management and communication program.

To help manage their company's growth, Alan and Lora hire you to assist them with the variety of tasks they perform using Outlook. In this tutorial, you'll explore the Outlook window and its components. You'll use e-mail to send information about increasing an order to a supplier. You'll also set up contact information for suppliers and The Express Lane staff. Then you'll receive, read, and respond to e-mail messages. Finally you'll organize messages by filing, filtering, sorting, and archiving them.

Student Data Files

▼**Tutorial.01**

▽ Tutorial folder	▽ Review folder	▽ Cases folder
Sales.xls	Tea.doc	Amendments.doc

Exploring Outlook

Microsoft Outlook is a powerful information manager. You can use Outlook to perform a wide range of communication and organizational tasks, such as sending, receiving, and filing e-mail; organizing contact information; scheduling appointments, events, and meetings; creating a to-do list and delegating tasks; and writing notes.

There are six main components in Outlook. The **Mail** component is a message/communication tool for receiving, sending, storing, and managing e-mail. The three mail folders you will use the most often are the Inbox folder, which stores messages you have received; the Outbox folder, which stores messages you have written but not sent; and the Sent Items folder, which stores copies of messages you have sent. You also can create other folders to save and organize e-mail you've received and written. The **Calendar** component is a scheduling tool for planning appointments, events, and meetings. The **Contacts** component is an address book for compiling postal addresses, phone numbers, e-mail and Web addresses, and other personal and business information about people and businesses with whom you communicate. The **Notes** component is a notepad for jotting down ideas and thoughts that you can group, sort, and categorize. The **Tasks** component is a to-do list for organizing and tracking items you need to complete or delegate. The **Journal** component is a diary for recording your activities, such as time spent talking on the phone, sending an e-mail message, or working on a document. As you work with these components, you create items such as e-mail messages, appointments, contacts, tasks, journal entries, and notes. An **item** is the basic element that holds information in Outlook, similar to a file in other programs. Items are organized into **folders**. Unlike folders in Windows Explorer, Outlook folders are available only from within Outlook.

Starting Outlook

You start Outlook the same way as any other program—using the Start menu. If Outlook is the default e-mail program on your computer, you can also click the E-mail link in the pinned items list at the top of the Start menu to start the program.

To start Outlook:

1. Click the **Start** button on the taskbar, point to **All Programs**, point to **Microsoft Office**, and then click **Microsoft Office Outlook 2003**. After a short pause, the Outlook program window appears. The pane on the right displays **Outlook Today**, a view of Outlook that shows your appointments, tasks, and number of e-mail messages you have.

   Trouble? If you don't see the Microsoft Office Outlook 2003 option on the Microsoft Office submenu, look for it on a different submenu or as an option on the All Programs menu, or click the E-mail Microsoft Office Outlook option at the top of the Start menu. If you still can't find the Microsoft Office Outlook 2003 option, ask your instructor or technical support person for help.

   Trouble? If a dialog box opens, indicating that you need to set up an e-mail account, click the Cancel button and continue with Step 2.

   Trouble? If a dialog box opens, asking whether you want to import e-mail messages and addresses from Outlook Express or another e-mail program, click the No button.

   Trouble? If a dialog box opens, asking whether you want to make Outlook the default manager for Mail, News, and Contacts, click the No button.

   Trouble? If a dialog box opens, asking whether you want to AutoArchive your old items now, click the No button.

2. If necessary, click the **Maximize** button ▣. Figure 1-1 shows the maximized Outlook window.

Outlook Today ◀ **Figure 1-1**

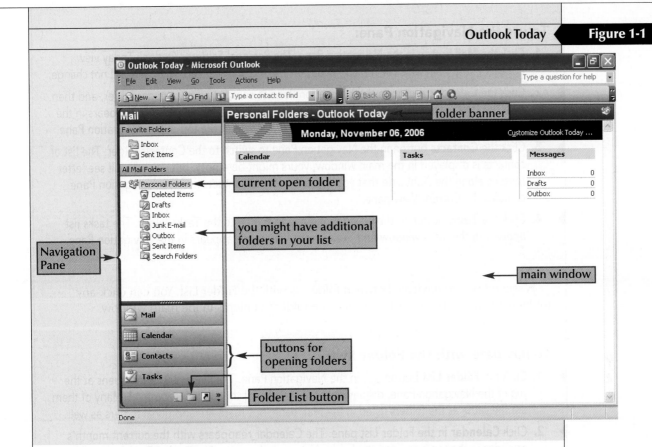

The Outlook window contains some elements that might be familiar to you from other programs, such as Word or Excel. Other elements are specific to Outlook, including:

- **Navigation Pane.** A central tool for accessing Outlook folders or files and folders on your computer or network that contains buttons to access additional panes within the Navigation Pane.
- **Folder List.** A hierarchy of the Outlook folders that you use to store and organize items; also provides a way to navigate among the Outlook folders. The Folder List is not shown in Figure 1-1; you'll work with it later in this tutorial.
- **Folder banner.** A bar at the top of the main window that displays the name of the open folder.
- **Main window.** The display of items stored in the selected folder; may be divided into panes. For example, the center pane of the Inbox main window displays a list of e-mail messages in the Inbox, and the right pane displays the contents of the selected e-mail message.

No matter which component you use, these elements of the Outlook window work in the same way. You can use the View menu to display or hide any of these elements, depending on your needs and preferences.

Navigating Between Outlook Components

You can click any button in the Navigation Pane to display that folder's contents in the main window. The Navigation Pane contains buttons for the most commonly used Outlook folders—Mail, Calendar, Contacts, Tasks, Notes, Folder List, and Shortcuts. Depending on the size of your monitor, the Notes, Folder List, and Shortcuts buttons may appear as icons at the bottom of the Navigation Pane rather than as bars with the name of the pane displayed. You click a button to display its contents in the Navigation Pane.

To use the Navigation Pane:

1. Click the **Mail** button in the Navigation Pane. The Personal Folders - Outlook Today view appears in the main window. If the Mail button was already selected, your view will not change.

2. Click the **Calendar** button in the Navigation Pane to switch to the Calendar folder, and then click the **Day** button on the Standard toolbar, if necessary. The daily planner appears in the main window, and the current month's calendar appears at the top of the Navigation Pane.

3. Click the **Contacts** button in the Navigation Pane to switch to the Contacts folder. The list of contacts is displayed in the main window; yours might be empty, but you will still see letter buttons along the right side that you use to scroll the contacts list. The Navigation Pane contains the Current View pane.

4. Click the **Tasks** button in the Navigation Pane to switch to the Tasks folder. The tasks list appears in the main window and the Current View pane appears in the Navigation Pane.

A second way to navigate between folders is with the Folder List. You can click any folder name in the Folder List to display the folder's contents in the main window.

To navigate with the Folder List:

1. Click the **Folder List** button in the Navigation Pane. The Folder List pane opens at the top of the Navigation Pane, displaying icons for each of the folders in Outlook. Many of them are the same as the folders listed in the Mail pane, but there are additional folders as well.

2. Click **Calendar** in the Folder List pane. The Calendar reappears with the current month's calendar in the top pane and the Folder List pane above the Navigation Pane buttons.

3. Click **Inbox** in the Folder List pane. The Inbox folder opens in the main window. If there are any messages in your Inbox, the contents of the selected message might appear in the Reading pane to the right of or below the main window. See Figure 1-2.

Figure 1-2	Inbox folder

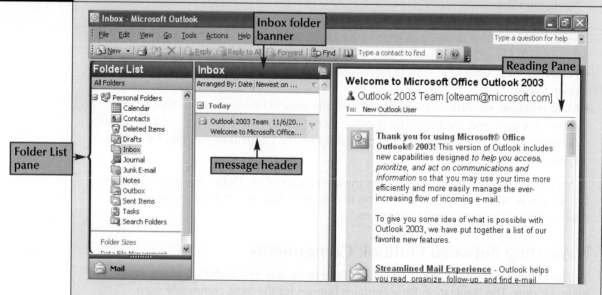

The main window currently displays the contents of the Inbox folder, where you receive, create, and send e-mail messages.

Creating and Sending E-mail Messages

E-mail, the electronic transfer of messages between computers, is a simple and inexpensive way to communicate with friends around the corner, family across the country, and colleagues in the same building or around the world. The messages you send are delivered immediately and stored until recipients can read those messages at their convenience. The Express Lane staff uses e-mail to correspond with its customers, suppliers, and each other because it is fast, convenient, and inexpensive. In addition, it saves the company the cost of paper, ink or toner, and other supplies.

Before you can send and receive e-mail messages with Outlook, you must have access to an e-mail server or Internet service provider (ISP), an e-mail address, and a password. An **e-mail address** is a user ID and a host name separated by the @ symbol. A **user ID** (or user name or account name) is a unique name that identifies you to your mail server. The **host name** consists of the name of your ISP's computer on the Internet plus its domain or level. For example, in the e-mail address "alan@theexpresslane.com," "alan" is the user ID and "theexpresslane.com" is the host name. Although many people might use the same host, each user ID is unique, enabling the host to distinguish one user from another. A **password** is a private code that you enter to access your account. (In this tutorial, you'll use your own e-mail address to send all messages.)

If you haven't already set up an Outlook mail account, you'll need to do so now by using the E-mail Accounts Wizard and completing the following steps.

To set up an Outlook mail account:

1. Click **Tools** on the menu bar, and then click **E-mail Accounts**. The first dialog box of the E-mail Accounts Wizard opens. Here, you choose whether you want to create a new account or modify an existing one.

2. Click the **Add a new e-mail account** option button, and then click the **Next** button. The Server Type dialog box of the E-mail Accounts Wizard opens and lists various server types.

3. Select the type of server you will use to access your e-mail, and then click the **Next** button. The Internet E-mail Settings dialog box varies, depending on the type of server you selected. Figure 1-3 shows the options when the POP3 server type is selected in the Server Type dialog box.

Internet E-mail Settings dialog box for POP3 server type account   ◄   **Figure 1-3**

options vary depending on the server type you selected in the previous dialog box

4. Enter the requested information in the Internet E-mail Settings dialog box, and then click the **More Settings** button. The Internet E-mail Settings dialog box opens with the General tab on top.

5. Type your name in the Mail Account text box, press the **spacebar**, and then type **E-mail Account**. This is the name by which you will refer to this e-mail account in Outlook.

6. Click the **OK** button, and then click the **Test Account Settings** button. Outlook opens the Test Account Settings dialog box and verifies that your e-mail account works.

Trouble? If you are unsure of what information to enter in the Internet E-mail Settings dialog box or if the test fails, ask your instructor or technical support person for help.

8. Click the **Close** button in the Test Account Settings dialog box, click the **Next** button in the Internet E-mail Settings dialog box, and then click the **Finish** button to set up your account based on the information you entered.

Choosing a Message Format

Outlook can send and receive messages in three formats: HTML, Rich Text, and Plain Text. Although you specify one of these formats as the default for your messages, you can always switch formats for an individual message. HTML provides the most formatting features and options (text formatting, numbering, bullets, alignment, horizontal lines, backgrounds, HTML styles, and Web pages). Rich Text provides some formatting options (text formatting, bullets, and alignment). With both HTML and Rich Text, some recipients will not be able to see the formatting if their e-mail software is not set up to handle formatted messages. Plain Text messages include no formatting, and the recipient specifies which font is used for the message. When you reply to a message, Outlook uses the same format in which the message was created, unless you specify otherwise. For example, if you reply to a message sent to you in Plain Text, Outlook sends the response in Plain Text.

You'll set the message format to HTML so you can customize your messages.

To choose a default message format:

1. Click **Tools** on the menu bar, and then click **Options**. The Options dialog box opens.

2. Click the **Mail Format** tab.

3. If necessary, click the **Compose in this message format** list arrow, and then click **HTML**.

4. If necessary, click the **Use Microsoft Office Word 2003 to edit e-mail messages** check box to insert a check mark. See Figure 1-4.

| Figure 1-4 | Mail Format tab in the Options dialog box |

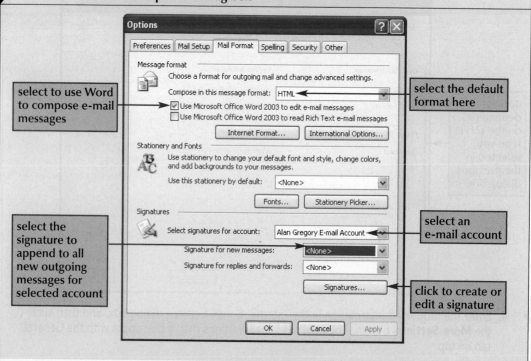

Now each time you create a message, Outlook will use the HTML format, unless you select a different format for that message. Because you selected HTML as your message format, you can customize your messages with a formatted signature. You'll do that before closing the Options dialog box.

Adding a Signature

A **signature** is text that is automatically added to every e-mail message you send. A signature can contain any text you want. For example, you might create a signature with your name, job title, company name, and phone number. The Express Lane might create a signature containing a paragraph that describes how to order groceries. You can also create more than one signature and then use the Signature button on the Standard toolbar to select which one you want to include in a particular message. If you have more than one e-mail account, you can create different signatures for each e-mail account you have set up. Although you can attach a signature to a message in any format, the HTML and Rich Text formats enable you to apply font and paragraph formatting. For now, you'll create a simple signature with your name and the company name. Note that the figures in this book will show the name Alan Gregory, whose e-mail address is alan@theexpresslane.com.

To create a signature:

1. Click the **Signatures** button on the Mail Format tab in the Options dialog box, and then click the **New** button in the Create Signature dialog box. The Create New Signature dialog box opens.

2. Type your name in the Enter a name for your new signature text box, click the **Start with a blank signature** option button if necessary, and then click the **Next** button. The Edit Signature dialog box opens with the insertion point blinking in the large text box.

3. Type your name, press the **Enter** key, and then type **The Express Lane**. See Figure 1-5.

Edit Signature dialog box | **Figure 1-5**

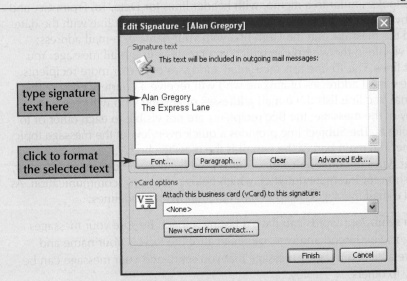

type signature text here

click to format the selected text

Next, you'll change the format of part of the signature.

4. Select **The Express Lane**, click the **Font** button, change the font to **10-point, Bold Italic, Arial**, and then click the **OK** button in the Font dialog box. The selected text is reformatted.

5. Click the **Finish** button. The Create Signature dialog box appears again, with your new signature listed and selected in the Signature box, and a preview of the selected signature.

6. Click the **OK** button to return to the Options dialog box.

   You'll add your signature to new messages you create, but not to messages you respond to.

7. Click the **Select signatures for account** list arrow, and then click your e-mail account name (your name, followed by "E-mail Account" if you set up your account in this tutorial).

8. If necessary, click the **Signature for new messages** list arrow, and then click your name.

9. If necessary, click the **Signature for replies and forwards** list arrow, and then click **<None>**.

10. Click the **Apply** button. If you had more than one e-mail account, you could click the Select signatures for account list arrow again, click the name of another e-mail account, and then repeat Steps 7 and 8 to create a signature for that account.

11. Click the **OK** button.

Using Stationery

Stationery templates are HTML files that include complementary fonts, background colors, and images for your outgoing e-mail messages. They also increase the size of your message. To use one of the stationery templates that comes with Outlook, including announcements, invitations, greetings, and other designs, you click Actions on the menu bar, point to New Mail Message Using, and then click the More Stationery command to open a dialog box with stationery options. Previously selected stationeries will appear below the More Stationery command. You also can create your own stationery. Stationery uses HTML message format, so recipients whose e-mail programs don't read HTML e-mail won't see the stationery, but they will still be able to read the text.

Creating an E-mail Message

An e-mail message looks similar to a memo, with header lines for Date, To, From, Cc, and Subject, followed by the body of the message. Outlook fills in the Date line with the date on which you send the message and the From line with your name or e-mail address; these lines are not visible in the window in which you create your e-mail message. You complete the other lines. The To line lists the e-mail addresses of one or more recipients. The Cc line lists the e-mail addresses of anyone who will receive a courtesy copy of the message. An optional Bcc line lists the e-mail addresses of anyone who will receive a blind courtesy copy of the message; the Bcc recipients are not visible to each other or to the To and Cc recipients. The Subject line provides a quick overview of the message topic, similar to a headline. The main part of the e-mail is the message body.

E-mail, like other types of communication, is governed by its own customs of behavior, called **netiquette** (short for Internet etiquette), which helps prevent miscommunication. As you write and send e-mail messages, keep in mind the following guidelines:

- **Think before you send.** Your words can have a lasting impact. Be sure your messages convey the thoughts you intend and want others to attribute to you. Your name and e-mail address are attached to every message that you send, and your message can be forwarded swiftly to others.
- **Be concise.** The recipient should be able to read and understand your message quickly.
- **Use standard capitalization.** Excessive use of uppercase is considered shouting, and exclusive use of lowercase is incorrect; both are difficult to read.
- **Check spelling and grammar.** Create and maintain a professional image by using standard spelling and grammar. What you say is just as important as how you say it.

- **Avoid sarcasm.** Without your vocal intonations and body language, a recipient may read your words with emotions or feelings you didn't intend. You can use punctuation marks and other characters to create **emoticons**—also called **smileys**—such as :-), to convey the intent of your words. (Tilt your head to the left to look at the emoticon sideways to see the "face"—in this case, a smile.) To learn additional emoticons, search the Web for emoticon or smiley dictionaries.
- **Don't send confidential information.** E-mail is not private; once you send a message, you lose control over where it may go and who might read it. Also, employers and schools usually can legally access their employees' and students' e-mail messages, even after a message is deleted from an Inbox.

Creating an E-mail Message

Reference Window

- Click the New Mail Message button on the Standard toolbar.
- Type recipient e-mail address(es) in the To text box (separate by semicolons).
- Type recipient e-mail address(es) in the Cc text box and the Bcc text box, as needed.
- Type a topic in the Subject text box, and then type the message body.
- Format the message as needed.
- Click the Send button.

You'll create an e-mail message. Although you would usually send messages to other people, you will send messages to yourself in this tutorial so you can practice sending and receiving messages.

To create an e-mail message:

1. Click the **New** button list arrow on the Standard toolbar. A list of new items you can create in Outlook appears. Because a Mail folder is the current folder, Mail Message appears at the top of the list, and is the default if you simply click the New button.

2. Click a blank area of the window to close the New button list, and then position the mouse pointer over the **New** button on the Standard toolbar. A ScreenTip appears identifying this button as the New Mail Message button. Notice that the icon next to the word New on the button is an open envelope and a piece of paper.

3. Click the **New** button on the Standard toolbar. A new Message window opens in Word with the blinking insertion point in the To text box. Your signature appears in the **message body**, where the content of your message appears; you'll type your message above the signature. Notice that the title bar indicates that this is an Untitled Message.

4. Type your e-mail address in the To text box. You could send the e-mail to multiple recipients by typing a semicolon between each address.

5. Press the **Tab** key twice to move to the Subject text box. You skipped the Cc text box because you aren't sending a courtesy copy of this e-mail to anyone.

   Trouble? If the insertion point is not in the Subject text box, then the Bcc text box is displayed. Press the Tab key again to move to the Subject text box, and then continue with Step 6.

6. Type **Peach Order** in the Subject text box, and then press the **Tab** key to move to the message body, just above the signature. As soon as you move the insertion point out of the Subject text box, the name in the title bar changes to match the contents of the Subject text box.

7. Type **Your peaches are a big hit with The Express Lane customers. Please double our order for the next three weeks.**, press the **Enter** key twice, and then type **Thank you.** (including the period).

You don't need to type your name because you included it as part of the signature. Before sending your message, however, you want to add some text formatting. You set up Outlook to use Word as your e-mail editor, which means that you have access to all the formatting features available in Word. For example, you can set bold, underline, and italics; change the font, font size, and font color; align and indent text; create a bulleted or numbered list; and even apply paragraph styles. People whose e-mail programs can't read formatted e-mail will still be able to read your messages in plain text.

To format text in an e-mail message:

1. Select the text **a big hit** in the message body. You'll make this text bold and orange.
2. Click the **Bold** button B on the Formatting toolbar.
3. Click the **Font Color** button list arrow A ⋅ on the Formatting toolbar, and then click the **Orange** tile in the second column, second row of the palette that opens.
4. Press the **Down Arrow** key to deselect the text and move the insertion point to the next line. The text is reformatted.

You could add more formatting, but a little goes a long way. Try to be judicious in your use of text formatting. Use it to enhance your message rather than overwhelm it.

Setting the Importance and Sensitivity Levels

You can add icons that appear in the message pane of the Inbox to provide clues to the recipient about the importance and sensitivity of the message. You can specify an importance level of High or Low or leave the message set at the default Normal importance level. High importance tells the recipient that the message needs prompt attention, whereas a Low importance tells the recipient that the message can wait for a response. Use the importance level appropriately. If you send all messages with a High importance, recipients will learn to disregard the status.

You'll change the message importance level to high.

To change a message importance level:

1. Click the **Importance: High** button on the Standard toolbar. The button remains selected as an indicator of the message's importance level. See Figure 1-6.

Figure 1-6	Completed e-mail message

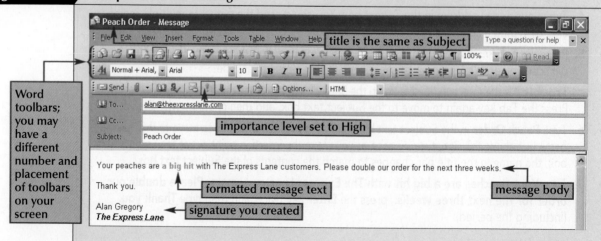

Word toolbars; you may have a different number and placement of toolbars on your screen

title is the same as Subject

importance level set to High

formatted message text

message body

signature you created

You can also change the normal sensitivity level for the message to Personal, Private, or Confidential. This is another way to help recipients determine the content of a message before reading it. To set the sensitivity level, click the Options button on the Standard toolbar in the Message window, click the Sensitivity list arrow in the Options dialog box, and then select the sensitivity level you want for the message. You'll leave the sensitivity set to Normal for this message.

Sending E-mail

There are a variety of ways you can set up Outlook for sending messages. Your messages can be sent immediately (assuming your computer is connected to your e-mail server), or you can set it up so messages remain in the Outbox until you click the Send/Receive button. You also can set up a schedule, where Outlook automatically sends and receives messages at regular intervals that you specify (such as every five minutes or every few hours).

If you are working **offline** (not connected to your e-mail server) or if you have a dial-up connection, any messages you write remain in the Outbox until you choose to send them. You select how messages are sent in the Options dialog box. You'll set these options now.

To change your message delivery options:

1. Click the **Inbox - Microsoft Outlook** button on the taskbar to return to the Inbox.

2. Click **Tools** on the menu bar, click **Options** to open the Options dialog box, and then click the **Mail Setup** tab.

3. In the Send/Receive section, click the **Send immediately when connected** check box to remove the check mark, if necessary. Now Outlook will move your completed messages into the Outbox until you choose to send them rather than immediately sending them to your e-mail server.

4. Click the **OK** button.

When you click the Send button in the Message window, the message will move to the Outbox. You must then click the Send/Receive button on the Standard toolbar to check for and deliver new messages.

To send a message to the Outbox:

1. Click the **Peach Order - Message** button on the taskbar to return to your message.

2. Click the **Send** button on the message toolbar. The Message window closes and the message moves to the Outbox. You are returned to the Outlook window.

The Outbox folder name in the Mail pane changes to boldface and is followed by [1], which indicates that there is one outgoing message. You can send and receive e-mail from any folder in the Mail pane; you'll switch to the Outbox to deliver this message.

To switch to the Outbox and send the message:

1. Click **Outbox** in the Folder List pane. The message in the Outbox folder appears in the Outbox main window. See Figure 1-7.

Figure 1-7 ▶ **Message in Outbox**

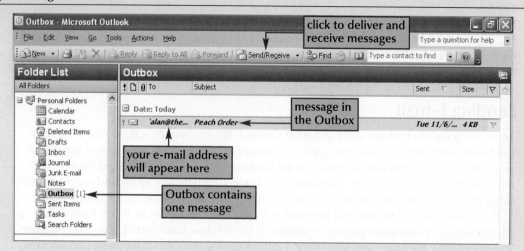

2. Click the **Send/Receive** button on the Standard toolbar to send the message. The Outlook Send/Receive Progress dialog box remains open until the message is sent. After the message is sent, the Outbox is empty and the boldface and [1] have disappeared.

   Trouble? If you are not already connected to the Internet, connect now.

   Trouble? If Outlook requests a password, you need to enter your password before you can send and receive your messages. Type your password, and then click the OK button.

A copy of the message is stored in the Sent Items folder, which provides a record of all the messages you sent. The time your e-mail takes to arrive at its destination will vary, depending on the size of the message, the speed of your Internet connection, and the number of other users on the Internet.

While sending your outgoing messages, Outlook may check your mail server for messages you have received since you last checked. If you have messages, they will be delivered to your Inbox. The message you just sent to yourself might appear in your Inbox instantly, and you might receive other messages to you that are unrelated to this tutorial.

Organizing Contact Information

The Contacts folder is an address book where you store information about the people and businesses with whom you communicate. Each person or organization is called a **contact**. You can store business-related information about each contact, including job title, phone and fax numbers, postal and Web addresses, and e-mail addresses, as well as more personal information, such as birthdays, anniversaries, and spouse and children's names.

Each piece of information you enter about a contact is called a **field**. For example, a complete contact name, such as Mr. Salvador F. Aiello, Jr., is comprised of a Title field, First field, Middle field, Last field, and Suffix field. The field's name or label identifies what information is stored in that field. You can use fields to sort, group, or look up contacts by any part of the name.

Creating Contacts

The Express Lane stores information about its suppliers and customers in the **Contacts** folder. Alan has asked you to create new contacts for several suppliers. You can start a new contact from any folder by clicking the New button list arrow on the Standard toolbar and then clicking New Contact. Instead, you'll switch to the Contacts folder.

To create a contact:

▶ 1. Click **Contacts** in the Folders List pane to display the Contacts folder. The icon on the New button changes to reflect the most likely item you'll want to create from this folder—in this case, a new contact.

▶ 2. Click the **New** button on the Standard toolbar. A new Contact window opens, displaying text boxes in which to enter the contact information.

▶ 3. Maximize the Contact window, if necessary.

Contact information is entered on two tabs. The General tab stores the most pertinent information about a contact, including the contact's name, job title and company, phone numbers, and addresses. The Details tab contains less frequently needed information, such as the names of the contact's manager, assistant, and spouse, as well as the contact's birthday, anniversary, and nickname.

Creating a Contact

Reference Window

- Click the New Contact button on the Standard toolbar to open a blank Contact window.
- Enter the contact's name, job title, company, mailing address, phone numbers, e-mail addresses, and Web site (click the down arrow to select other address, number, or e-mail options).
- Click the Details tab and enter other business or personal data as needed.
- Click the Save and New button on the Standard toolbar to create another contact (or click the Save and Close button if this is the last contact).
- If the Duplicate Contact Detected dialog box opens, select whether to add contact anyway or merge with existing contact, and then click the OK button.

You'll enter the first contact's name and company.

To enter a contact's name and company:

▶ 1. Type **Mr. Salvador F. Aiello, Jr.** in the Full Name text box, and then press the **Enter** key. The insertion point moves to the next text box (the Job title text box), and the contact name appears, last name first, in the File as text box. By default, Outlook organizes your contacts by their last names. The contact's name also appears in the title bar of the Contact window.

▶ 2. Click the **Full Name** button. The Check Full Name dialog box opens. Although you entered the contact name in one text box, Outlook stores each part of the name as a separate field. See Figure 1-8.

Figure 1-8   **Check Full Name dialog box**

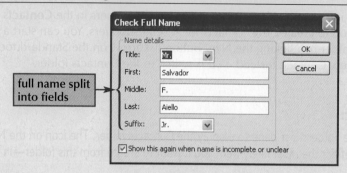

full name split into fields

3. Click the **Cancel** button to close the dialog box without making any changes. If Outlook cannot tell how to distinguish part of a name, the Check Full Name dialog box will open so that you can correct the fields.

4. Click in the **Job title** text box, and then type **President**.

5. Press the **Tab** key to move to the Company text box, and then type **Green Grocer Produce**.

Next you'll enter the contact's phone numbers. You can enter as many as 19 numbers per contact. No matter how you enter the numbers—with or without spaces, hyphens, or parentheses—Outlook formats them consistently, such as (415) 555-3928.

To enter a contact's phone numbers, mailing address, and e-mail address:

1. Click in the **Business** text box in the Phone numbers section. Clicking the Business button opens the Check Phone Number dialog box, which is similar in function and appearance to the Check Full Name dialog box.

   Trouble? If the Location Information dialog box opens, enter the appropriate information about your location, and then click the OK button. If the Phone and Modem Options dialog box opens, click the Cancel button.

2. Type **415 555 9753**, and then press the **Tab** key. Outlook formats the phone number with parentheses around the area code and a hyphen after the prefix, even though you didn't type them.

   Next to each phone number text box is a down arrow button that you can click to change the name of the phone field. Although you can display only four phone fields at a time, you can enter information in all the fields, using one text box or all four text boxes.

3. Click the **down arrow** button ⊡ next to Home, click **Assistant** to change the field label, and then enter **415-555-9752** for the phone number of Salvador's assistant.

   You'll switch to the Details tab to enter the name of Salvador's assistant, and then return to the General tab to enter his fax number, postal address, and e-mail address.

4. Click the **Details** tab, click in the Assistant's name text box, and then type **Cynthia Lopez**.

5. Click the **General** tab, and then enter **415-555-6441** as the Business Fax number.

6. Click in the **Business** text box in the Addresses section, type **12 Haymarket Blvd.**, press the **Enter** key, and then type **San Francisco, CA 94102**. You could verify that Outlook recorded the address in the correct fields by clicking the Business button, but you don't need to do so for a simple address.

As soon as you started typing the address, the This is the mailing address check box becomes checked. Outlook assumes that the first address you enter for a contact is the mailing address. You could enter additional addresses and specify any one of them as the mailing address.

7. Click in the **E-mail** text box, type your own e-mail address, and then click in the Display as text box. The e-mail address you typed becomes underlined, and the contact's name appears in the Display as text box with your e-mail in parentheses after the name. The Display as text box shows how the e-mail address will appear in the To text box of e-mail messages. You'll change the Display as text to the contact's name.

8. Select all the text in the Display as text box (including your e-mail address), and then type **Sal Aiello**. See Figure 1-9.

| Completed Contact window for Salvador F. Aiello Jr. | Figure 1-9 |

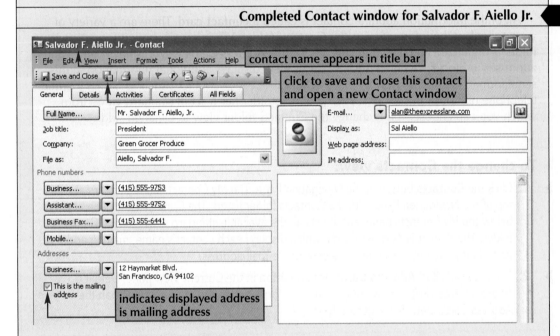

In most cases, each contact would have a unique e-mail address to which you would send e-mail messages. You have completed the contact information for Salvador. You can close his Contact window and open a new Contact window in the same step.

To create additional contacts:

1. Click the **Save and New** button on the Standard toolbar to save Salvador's contact information and open a new Contact window.

2. Enter the following information: full name **Julia Shang**, job title **Manager**, company **Foods Naturally**, business phone **415-555-1224**, business fax **415-555-4331**, and business address **19 Hillcrest Way, Novato, CA 94132**. Use your own e-mail address, but display as **Julia Shang**.

3. Click the **Save and New** button on the Standard toolbar. Outlook detects that another contact already has the same e-mail address as Julia Shang and opens the Duplicate Contact Detected dialog box. Click the **Add this as a new contact anyway** option button, and then click the **OK** button.

▶ **4.** Enter the following contact information: full name **Kelley Ming**, company **Ming Nuts Company**, business phone **415-555-9797**, and business address **2932 Post Street, San Francisco, CA 94110**. Use your own e-mail address, but display as **Kelley Ming**.

▶ **5.** Click the **Save and New** button 🖫 on the Standard toolbar, add Kelley Ming as a new contact anyway, and then enter the following contact information: full name **Alan Gregory** and company **The Express Lane**; use your e-mail address, but display as **Alan Gregory**.

▶ **6.** Click the **Save and Close** button on the Standard toolbar and add Alan Gregory as a new contact anyway to save his contact information and return to the Contacts folder. The four contacts you added appear in the Contacts main window, sorted alphabetically by last name.

All of the information about a contact is called a **contact card**. There are a variety of ways to look at the information in the Contacts folder. **Views** specify how information in a folder is organized and which details are visible. Address Cards view displays names and addresses in blocks. Detailed Address Cards view displays additional information in this same format. Phone List view displays details about your contacts, such as name, job title, telephone numbers, in columns. Each Outlook folder has a set of standard views from which you can choose. You'll change the Contacts folder view to Detailed Address Cards.

To change the Contacts view:

▶ **1.** Click the **Contacts** button in the Navigation Pane. The My Contacts pane appears at the top of the Navigation Pane with the Contacts folder listed. The Current View pane appears below the My Contacts pane, and it lists all the available standard views for the Contacts folder. The default is Address Cards, which displays each contact's name, mailing address, up to four phone numbers, and the contact's e-mail address.

▶ **2.** Click the **Detailed Address Cards** option button in the Current View pane. Detailed Address Cards view displays more contact information in the main window than the Address Cards view. See Figure 1-10.

Contacts in Detailed Address Cards view | Figure 1-10

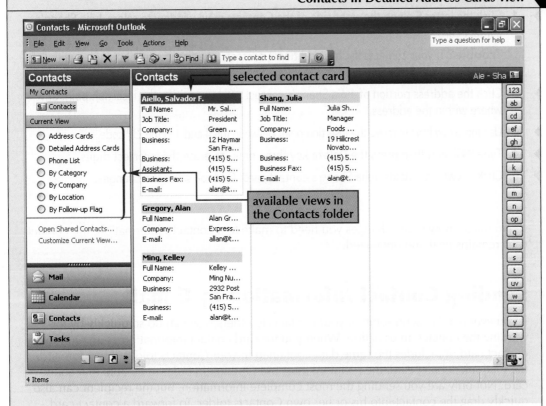

In the Address Cards and Detailed Address Cards views, Outlook organizes your contacts in the main window in alphabetical order by last name, as specified in the File as text box. When you have many contacts, you find a certain contact quickly by clicking the letter button along the right side of the main window that corresponds to the first letter of a contact's last name. Then use the scroll bar at the bottom of the window to display that contact.

Editing Contacts

Many aspects of a contact's information may change over time. A person or company may move to a new street address or be assigned a new area code. A person may change jobs periodically. You may discover that you entered information incorrectly. Rather than deleting the card and starting over, you can update the existing contact card as needed. Simply double-click the contact to open its Contact window, and edit the information as needed. You can also make the change directly in the Contacts folder from the Address Cards or Detailed Address Cards view.

Alan tells you that the ZIP code for Foods Naturally is actually 94947. You'll make this correction directly in the Detailed Address Cards view.

To edit a contact:

▶ 1. Click the letter **S** along the right side of the Contacts main window to select Julia Shang's contact card.

   Trouble? If your contacts list has additional contacts, the first contact beginning with "s" will be selected. Scroll until you can see Julia Shang's contact card.

▶ 2. Click the address portion of Julia Shang's contact card to position the insertion point anywhere within the address.

▶ 3. Use the arrow keys to move the insertion point between the 4 and 1 in the ZIP code.

▶ 4. Type **947**, and then press the **Delete** key three times to erase the incorrect digits.

▶ 5. Click anywhere outside Julia Shang's contact card. Outlook saves the changes.

No matter how many changes you need to make to a contact's information, the contact card remains neat and organized.

Sending Contact Information by E-mail

If you ever need to send some of your contacts to others, you can do so quickly by forwarding the contact information. When you forward contact information as an Outlook contact card, it includes the same data contained in your Contacts folder. If you forward the Outlook contact card, the recipient must use Outlook in order to be able to read the card. Not only are you sending the most complete information, but the recipient can also quickly drag the contact into his or her own Contacts folder. To forward a contact card, right-click the contact card in the Contacts folder, and then click Forward Items on the shortcut menu. A new Message window opens with the contact card as an attachment to the message.

If you are not sure if the recipient uses Outlook, you can send contact information as a vCard. A **vCard** is a file that contains a contact's personal information, such as the contacts name, mailing address, phone numbers, and e-mail address. The vCard files are compatible with other popular communication and information management programs. You can also use vCards to exchange contact information with handheld personal digital assistants (PDAs). To send a contact card as a vCard, click the contact card in the Contacts folder to select it, click Actions on the menu bar, and then click Forward as vCard. A new Message window opens with the vCard included as an attachment.

When you receive a forwarded contact card, you can add the contact information directly to your Contacts folder without retyping the information. Just drag the contact card from the message to the Contacts folder, and the new contact card is created.

Creating and Modifying Distribution Lists

Sometimes you'll find that you repeatedly send on e-mail message—such as a weekly progress report or company updates—to the same group of people. Rather than selecting the names one by one from the Contacts list, you can create a distribution list. A **distribution list** is a group of people to whom you frequently send the same messages, such as all suppliers. A distribution list saves time and insures that you don't inadvertently leave out someone. You can create multiple distribution lists to meet you needs, and individuals can be included in more than one distribution list.

Creating a Distribution List

- Click the New button list arrow on the Standard toolbar, and then click Distribution List.
- Click the Select Members button near the top of the Distribution List window.
- Click the Show names from the list arrow, and then click Contacts.
- Double-click the names you want to add to the distribution list, and then click the OK button.
- Click in the Name text box, and then type a contact name for the distribution list.
- Click the Save and Close button on the Standard toolbar.

Alan asks you to create a distribution list to all The Express Lane suppliers as he frequently needs to send the same information to all of them.

To create a distribution list:

1. Click the **New** button list arrow on the Standard toolbar, and then click **Distribution List**. A new Distribution List window opens.

2. Type **Suppliers** in the Name text box. This is the contact name for the distribution list.

3. Click the **Select Members** button below the Name text box. The Select Members dialog box opens.

4. If necessary, click the **Show Names from the** list arrow, and then click **Contacts**. A contact appears in the list box once for each e-mail address and fax number.

   You'll move the three suppliers into the distribution list.

5. Double-click the top **Julia Shang** entry to move the contact to the Add to distribution list box. Double-clicking the name is the same as clicking the name and then clicking the Members button.

6. Double-click the **Kelley Ming** entry and the top **Salvador F. Aiello Jr.** entry to select them as members of distribution list. See Figure 1-11.

Figure 1-11	Select Members dialog box

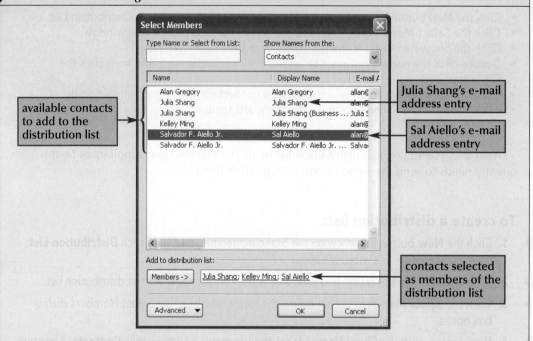

available contacts to add to the distribution list

Julia Shang's e-mail address entry

Sal Aiello's e-mail address entry

contacts selected as members of the distribution list

7. Click the **OK** button. The three suppliers appear as members of the Suppliers distribution list. See Figure 1-12.

Figure 1-12	Distribution List window for the Suppliers distribution list

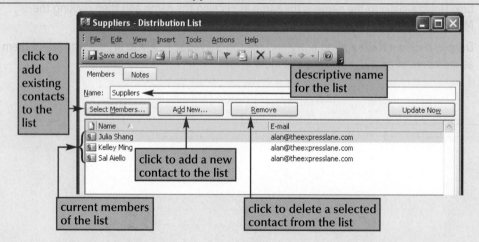

click to add existing contacts to the list

descriptive name for the list

click to add a new contact to the list

current members of the list

click to delete a selected contact from the list

8. Click the **Save and Close** button on the Standard toolbar in the Distribution List window. The list appears in the Contacts folder filed under the name of the distribution list, Suppliers. A group icon in the upper-right corner of the contact card indicates that this is a distribution list rather than a one-person contact.

You can use the Suppliers distribution list contact just as you would any one-person contact.

Modifying a Distribution List

At times, you'll need to update a distribution list. You may need to delete a contact from the distribution list or add a new contact to the distribution list. You do this by double-clicking the distribution list contact in the Contacts folder to open its Distribution List window, and then click the Select Members button to add other contacts to the list or click the Remove button to delete a selected contact from the list. Removing a contact from a distribution list only deletes the contact from the distribution list; the individual's contact card remains intact in the Contacts folder. If you need to update the information for an existing contact, you would do so in the individual's contact card. If you find that you no longer need a distribution list, you delete it just like an individual contact.

Session 1.1 Quick Check

Review

1. Describe the purposes of the Inbox and the Outbox.
2. Define e-mail and list two benefits of using it.
3. What is a signature?
4. List five types of contact information that you can store in Outlook.
5. Explain the purpose of a distribution list.

Session 1.2

Receiving E-mail

You check for new e-mail messages by clicking the Send/Receive button on the Standard toolbar. Outlook connects to your e-mail server, if necessary, sends any messages in the Outbox, and receives any incoming messages that have arrived since you last checked. New messages are delivered into the Inbox.

You'll switch to the Inbox and download the message you sent yourself earlier.

To receive e-mail:

1. If you took a break after the previous session, make sure Outlook is running.

2. Click the **Mail** button in the Navigation Pane, and then click **Inbox** in the Favorite Folders pane.

3. Click the **Send/Receive** button on the Standard toolbar.

   Trouble? If you are not already connected to the Internet, connect now.

4. Watch for the new message to appear in the Inbox. The number of new messages you receive appears within parentheses next to the Inbox folder name in the Navigation Pane. See Figure 1-13. Your Inbox might contain additional e-mail messages.

Figure 1-13   Received message in Inbox

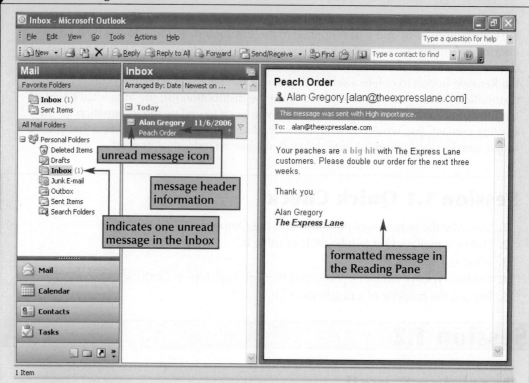

Trouble? If no messages appear, your e-mail server might not have received the message yet. Wait a few minutes, and then repeat Steps 3 and 4.

Once a message arrives, you can read it. The Inbox folder is divided into two panes. The Inbox main window displays a list of all e-mail messages that you have received, along with information about the message. The **message header** includes the sender's name, the message subject, and the date the message was received, as well as icons that indicate the message's status (such as the message's importance level and whether the message has been read). The **Reading Pane** displays the content of the selected message in a memo format. The subject, the sender, importance level, and all the recipients (except Bcc recipients) appear at the top of the memo. You can resize the panes by dragging the border between the Inbox main window and the Reading Pane left or right.

To read a message:

1. Click the **Peach Order** message in the Inbox main window to display its contents in the Reading Pane. In a moment, the mail icon changes from unread ✉ to read ✉, and the message no longer appears in boldface.

   Trouble? If the Reading Pane does not appear on your screen or if it appears on the bottom of the screen, click View on the menu bar, point to Reading Pane, and then click Right.

   Trouble? If the mail icon in the Inbox main window does not change to indicate that the message has been read, click Tools on the menu bar, click Options, click the Other tab, click the Reading Pane button, click the Mark items as read when viewed in the Reading Pane check box to select it, and then click the OK button twice.

2. Read the message in the Reading Pane. Because Outlook can view HTML messages, the formatting added to the message is visible.

   Trouble? If you don't see the HTML formatting, your mail server may not display the HTML formatting in e-mail messages. Continue with the tutorial.

You can also open a message in its own window by double-clicking the message header in the Inbox pane. After you read a message, you have several options—you can leave the message in the Inbox and deal with it later, reply to the message, forward the message to others, print it, file it, or delete it.

Replying to and Forwarding Messages

Many messages you receive require some sort of response—for example, confirmation you received the information, the answer to a question, or sending the message to another person. The quickest way to respond to messages is to use the Reply, Reply to All, and Forward features. The **Reply** feature responds to the sender, and the **Reply to All** feature responds to the sender and all recipients (including any Bcc recipients); Outlook inserts the e-mail addresses into the appropriate text boxes. The **Forward** feature sends a copy of the message to one or more recipients you specify; you enter the e-mail addresses in the To or Cc text box. With both the Reply and Forward features, the original message is included for reference, separated from your new message by a line and the original message header information. By default, any new text you type is added at the top of the message body, above the original message. This makes it simpler for recipients to read your message because they don't have to scroll through the original message text to find the new text.

You'll reply to the Peach Order message. In reality, you would respond to someone other than yourself.

To reply to a message:

1. Make sure that the **Peach Order** message is selected in the Inbox main window, and then click the **Reply** button on the Standard toolbar. A Message window opens with the receiver's name and e-mail address in the To text box (in this case, your name and address) and RE: (short for Regarding) inserted at the beginning of the Subject line. The body of the original message appears in the message body pane below a divider line, and the insertion point is blinking above the message, ready for you to type your reply.

2. If necessary, click in the message area, and then type **You will receive double shipments of peaches for the next three weeks. Thank you for your order.**, press the **Enter** key twice, and then type your name (remember that your signature is not added for replies). Your reply message appears in blue because you selected HTML format.

   Trouble? Depending on how your computer is configured, you might not see the HTML formatting.

3. Click the **Send** button on the message toolbar to move the message to the Outbox. The icon next to the message header in the Inbox main window changes to ⬛ to indicate that this message has been replied to.

Next you'll forward the message to Julia Shang, the manager at Foods Naturally. Because Julia's contact information is in the Contacts folder, you can address the message to her quickly.

To forward a message:

1. Make sure that the **Peach Order** message is selected in the Inbox main window, and then click the **Forward** button on the Standard toolbar. This time, the insertion point is in the empty To text box and FW: (for Forward) precedes the Subject line.

2. Type **Julia Shang** in the To text box, and then press the **Tab** key. A wavy red line appears below the name, indicating that multiple contact information is available for that contact.

3. Right-click **Julia Shang**, and then click **Julia Shang**, the entry with her e-mail address (do not click the Julia Shang (Business Fax) entry). When Outlook recognizes the contact name as an item in the Contacts folder with a valid e-mail address, it underlines it.

4. Click at the top of the message body, above the forwarded message, and then type **Please update The Express Lane account.**

5. Click the **Send** button on the message toolbar to move the message to the Outbox. The icon next to the message header in the Inbox main window changes to 🖳 to indicate that this message has been forwarded.

6. Click the **Send/Receive** button on the Standard toolbar, if necessary, to send the messages to your mail server.

Alan asks you to print the message for future reference.

Printing Messages

Although e-mail eliminates the need for paper messages, sometimes you'll want a printed copy of a message to file or distribute, or to read when you're not at your computer. You can use the Print button on the Standard toolbar to print a selected message with the default settings, or you can use the Print command on the File menu to open the Print dialog box, where you can verify and change settings before you print. All default print styles include the print date, user name, and page number in the footer. You'll use the Print dialog box to verify the settings and then print the Peach Order message.

To verify settings and print a message:

1. If necessary, select the **Peach Order** message in the Inbox main window.

2. Click **File** on the menu bar, and then click **Print**. The Print dialog box opens.

3. Make sure that the correct printer appears in the Name list box.

   Trouble? If you're not sure which printer to use, ask your instructor or technical support person for assistance.

4. If necessary, click **Memo Style** in the Print style section to select it.

   Memo style prints the contents of the selected item—in this case, the e-mail message. Table Style prints the view of the selected folder—in this case, the Inbox folder. Other Outlook folders display different print style options.

5. Click the **OK** button. The message prints.

In your work at The Express Lane, you'll often want to send information that is stored in a variety of files on your computer. Some of this information could be typed into an e-mail message, but many kinds of files (such as photos and spreadsheets) can't be inserted into e-mail messages. Instead, you can send files as attachments.

Working with Attachments

An **attachment** is a file that you send with an e-mail message. Attachments can be any type of file, including documents (such as a Word document, Excel workbook, or PowerPoint slide presentation), images, sounds, and programs. For example, you might send an attachment containing The Express Lane's latest sales figures to Alan for his review. Recipients can then save and open the file; the recipient must have the original program or a program that can read that file type. For example, if Alan receives a Lotus 1-2-3 spreadsheet, he can open and save it with Excel.

To attach a file to an e-mail:

1. With the Inbox folder selected, click the **New** button on the Standard toolbar to open a new Message window.

2. Click the **To** button. The Select Names dialog box opens.

3. Click **Alan Gregory** in the list of contacts, and then click the **To** button at the bottom of the dialog box. Alan's name is added to the To list..

4. Click the **OK** button.

5. Type **Latest Sales** in the Subject text box.

6. In the message body area, type **The attached Excel workbook contains the latest sales figures. It looks like we're on track. Let me know if you have any comments.**

7. Click the **Insert File** button on the Standard toolbar. The Insert File dialog box opens; it functions like the Open dialog box.

8. Change the Look in list box to the **Tutorial.01\Tutorial** folder included with your Data Files.

   Trouble? If you don't have the Outlook Data Files, you need to get them before you can proceed. Your instructor will either give you the Data Files or ask you to obtain them from a specified location (such as a network drive). In either case, be sure that you make a backup copy of your Data Files before you start using them, so that the original files will be available on your copied disk in case you need to start over because of an error or problem. If you have any questions about the Data Files, see your instructor or technical support person for assistance.

9. Double-click **Sales** in the file list. The file is attached to your e-mail message, and the Insert File dialog box closes. See Figure 1-14. The message is ready to send.

Message with attached file | **Figure 1-14**

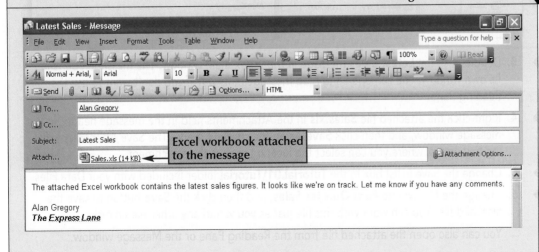

Excel workbook attached to the message

10. Click the **Send** button on the message toolbar, and then click the **Send/Receive** button on the Inbox Standard toolbar to send the message to your mail server and receive the two messages you sent earlier.

A message with an attachment may take a bit longer to send because it's larger than an e-mail message without an attachment. Messages with attached files display a paper clip icon in the message header. If the appropriate program is installed on your computer, you can open the attached file from the message itself. You can also save the attachment to your computer and then open, edit, and move it like any other file on your computer.

You can reply to or forward any message with an attachment, but the attachment is included only in the forwarded message because you will rarely, if ever, want to return the same file to the sender.

After you receive the message with the attachment, you'll save the attachment and then view it from within the message.

To save and view the message attachment:

1. If the Latest Sales message (with the attachment) is not already in your Inbox, click the **Send/Receive** button on the Standard toolbar. It might take a bit longer than usual to download the message with the attachment.

2. Click the **Latest Sales** message in the Inbox pane to view the message in the Reading Pane. The attachment icon appears below the date in the message header in the Inbox pane and the file icon and name appear in the Reading Pane. See Figure 1-15.

Figure 1-15   Message with attached file

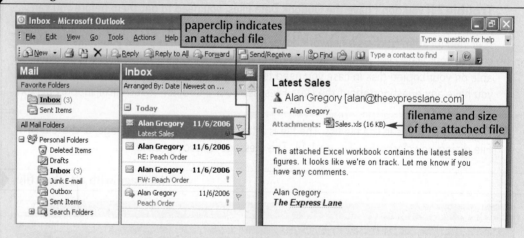

3. Double-click the **Latest Sales** message in the Inbox main window. The message opens in its own window. You can open and read messages this way if you don't want to use the Reading Pane.

4. Right-click the attached file **Sales.xls** in the Attachments field in the message header in the Message window, and then click **Save As** on the shortcut menu. The Save Attachment dialog box opens, where you can select the location to save the attachment.

5. Change the Save in list box to the **Tutorial.01\Tutorial** folder included with your Data Files.

6. Change the filename to **First Quarter Sales**, and then click the **Save** button to save the attached file. You can work with this file just as you would any other file on disk.

You can also open the attached file from the Reading Pane or the Message window.

7. Click the **Close** button ⊠ on the message window title bar, and then double-click **Sales.xls** in the Reading Pane. The Opening Mail Attachment dialog box opens, warning you that you should only open attachments from a trusted source.

Trouble? If the Opening Mail Attachment dialog box doesn't open, skip the action in Step 8, but read the step anyway.

8. Click the **Open** button. The attached file opens in its associated program—in this case, Excel. You can read, edit, format, and save the file just as you would any other Excel workbook.

Trouble? If the file opens in a spreadsheet program other than Excel, your computer might be configured to associate the file extension .xls with spreadsheet programs other than Excel. Continue with Step 9.

9. Review the sales figures, and then click the **Close** button ⊠ on the Excel window title bar to close the workbook and exit Excel.

Trouble? If a dialog box opens asking whether you want to save changes, click the No button.

So far, all the messages you received are stored in the Inbox folder.

Flagging Messages

Some messages you receive require a specific response or action. Although the subject should be informative and the message can provide explicit instructions, often a more obvious reminder would better draw attention messages that require action. A **message flag** is an icon that appears in the message header. To better organize or prioritize your messages, you can choose from six flag colors. If you add a reminder, the message flag also includes text that appears in the Reading Pane or Message window and even a deadline. In the Flag for Follow Up dialog box, you can choose from preset flag text or enter your own text, and you can select a specific due date or enter descriptive words such as "tomorrow" that Outlook converts to the correct date. Outlook will then display a reminder about the flag at the appropriate time.

You can also add a flag with preset or custom text and a deadline to messages you send to others. You would click the Message Flag button on the Standard toolbar in the Message window to open the Flag for Follow Up dialog box, and select or enter the flag text and due date.

You'll add preset flag text with a deadline of tomorrow to the message to Julia Shang.

To flag a message:

1. Right-click the **flag** icon in the Latest Sales message header in the Inbox main window. The list of available flag colors appears on the shortcut menu.

2. Click **Green Flag** on the shortcut menu. The flag color changes to green in the Inbox pane and the Follow up banner appears above the message header in the Reading Pane.

3. Right-click the **flag** icon in the message header in the Inbox main window, and then click **Add Reminder**. The Flag for Follow Up dialog box opens. See Figure 1-16.

| **Figure 1-16** | Flag for Follow Up dialog box

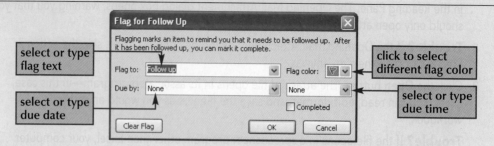

You want to set the flag message to Review and add a due date for tomorrow by 5 p.m.

4. Click the **Flag to** list arrow to display the preset flag options, and then click **Review**.

5. Click the left **Due by** list arrow to open a calendar showing this month with today's date highlighted, click the date three working days from now, click the right **Due by** list arrow, and then click **5:00 PM**.

6. Click the **OK** button. The Flag for Follow Up dialog box closes. The Follow up banner in the Reading Pane changes to reflect the selections you made in the Flag for Follow Up dialog box. See Figure 1-17.

| **Figure 1-17** | Message with flag

Once you have performed the requested action, you can mark the flag completed by clicking the flag icon in the message header until a check mark replaces the flag.

Organizing/Managing Messages

As you can readily see, messages can collect quickly in your Inbox. Even if you respond to each message as it arrives, all the original messages still remain in your Inbox. Some messages you'll want to file and store, just as you would file and store paper memos in a file cabinet. Other messages you'll want to delete.

Creating a Folder

The Folder List acts like an electronic file cabinet. You should create a logical folder structure in which to store your messages. For example, an employee of The Express Lane might create subfolders named "Customers" and "Suppliers" within the Inbox folder. You can create folders at the same level as the default folders, such as Inbox, Outbox, and Sent Messages, or you can create subfolders within these main folders. For now, you'll create one subfolder in the Inbox folder, named "Suppliers."

To create a folder in the Inbox folder:

▶ 1. Right-click the **Inbox** folder in the All Mail Folders pane, and then click **New Folder** on the shortcut menu. The Create New Folder dialog box opens.

▶ 2. Type **Suppliers** in the Name text box.

▶ 3. If necessary, click the **Folder contains** list arrow, and then click **Mail and Post Items**. You can also create subfolders to store contacts, notes, tasks, and so on.

▶ 4. Click **Inbox** in the Select where to place the folder list box if it's not already selected. See Figure 1-18.

Create New Folder dialog box ◀ **Figure 1-18**

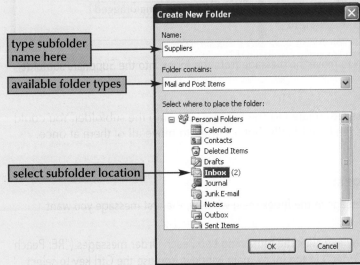

type subfolder name here

available folder types

select subfolder location

▶ 5. Click the **OK** button. The new folder appears indented under the Inbox folder in the All Mail Folders pane in the Navigation Pane.

Now you can file any messages related to The Express Lane in the new subfolder.

Filing Messages

As soon as you've dealt with a message in the Inbox, you should move it out of the Inbox; otherwise it will become cluttered, and you won't know which messages you've dealt with and which you haven't. To file a message, you can drag selected messages from one folder to another or use the Move to Folder button on the Standard toolbar.

To file messages:

▶ 1. Select the **Peach Order** message in the Inbox main window. It is the first message that you will move.

▶ 2. Drag the Peach Order message to the **Suppliers** subfolder in the All Mail Folders pane in the Navigation Pane, but do not release the mouse button. See Figure 1-19.

Figure 1-19   **Filing a message**

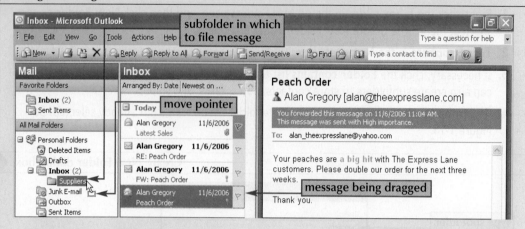

3. Release the mouse button to move the message from the Inbox into the Suppliers subfolder.

You want to move all messages related to The Express Lane into the subfolder. You could continue to move each message individually, but it's faster to move all of them at once.

To file multiple messages:

1. Click the **Latest Sales** message in the Inbox main window, the first message you want to file.

2. Press and hold the **Ctrl** key and click the remaining two Peach Order messages ("RE: Peach Order" and "FW: Peach Order") in the Inbox main window. You use the Ctrl key to select nonadjacent messages. You use the Shift key to select a range of adjacent messages.

3. Release the **Ctrl** key. The three messages are selected.

4. Drag the three selected messages from the Inbox main window into the **Suppliers** subfolder.

The Inbox is now empty of messages related to The Express Lane. However, the sales figures e-mail does not belong in the Suppliers folder. You'll create a new folder named "Sales" to file that e-mail.

To create another folder:

1. Right-click the **Inbox** main window title bar, and then click **New Folder**. The Create New Folder dialog box opens.

2. Type **Sales** in the Name text box, and then select **Mail and Post Items** in the Folder contains list box, if necessary.

3. Click **Inbox** in the Select where to place the folder list box if it's not already selected, and then click the **OK** button. The new folder appears indented under the Inbox folder in the All Mail Folders pane in the Navigation Pane.

You'll use a rule to move the sales figures message to the Sales folder.

Creating Rules

Rather than manually filing all your messages, you can create rules that specify how Outlook should process and organize them. For example, you can use rules to move messages to a folder based on their subjects, flag messages about a particular topic, or forward messages to a person or a distribution list.

Each **rule** includes three parts: the *conditions* that determine if a message is to be acted on, the *actions* that should be applied to qualifying messages, and any *exceptions* that remove a message from the qualifying group. For example, a rule might state that all messages you receive from Julia Shang (condition) are moved to the Suppliers folder (action) except for ones marked as High importance (exception). Outlook can apply rules to incoming, outgoing, or stored messages.

You can create a simple rule from common conditions and actions in the Create Rule dialog box, or use the Rules Wizard, a feature that steps you through the rule-writing process, to write more complex rules that also include exceptions. As you build a rule, you continue to refine the sentence that describes the conditions, actions, and exceptions.

If you are using Outlook with Exchange Server, you must be online to create rules.

Reference Window

Creating a Simple Rule

- Click the Create Rule button on the Standard toolbar.
- Select conditions and set their values as needed.
- Select actions and set their values as needed.
- Click the OK button.

You want to create a rule to move all sales messages related to the Sales folder. A message must be selected in order for the Create Rule button to be available. You can select any message to create a rule. Note that the information from the selected message automatically appears as conditions in the create Rule dialog box.

To create a rule:

1. Click the **Suppliers** folder in the Navigation Pane, and then click the **Latest Sales** message.
2. Click the **Create Rule** button 📩 on the Standard toolbar. The Create Rule dialog box opens.
3. Click the **Subject contains** check box to insert a check mark. The Subject text box already contains the subject from the selected message, so you do not need to replace this text.
4. Click the **Move e-mail to folder** check box. The Rules and Alerts dialog box opens.
5. Click the **plus sign** button ⊞ next to Inbox in the Choose a folder list, click **Sales**, and then click the **OK** button. The conditions and actions for this rule are set. See Figure 1-20.

Figure 1-20

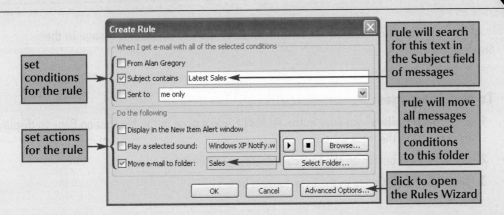

set conditions for the rule

set actions for the rule

rule will search for this text in the Subject field of messages

rule will move all messages that meet conditions to this folder

click to open the Rules Wizard

> **6.** Click the **OK** button. The Success dialog box opens, indicating that the rule "Latest Sales" has been created. You want to run the rule on the message in the Inbox folder.
>
> **Trouble?** If a dialog box opens and displays the message, "This rule is a client-only rule, and will process only if Outlook is running," then you are set up to run Outlook with Exchange. This message appears because Outlook has determined that the rule requires access to your computer to run. Click the OK button. Outlook saves the rule and adds "(client only)" after the name of the rule in the Rules and Alerts dialog box to remind you that your computer must be logged onto Exchange for the rule to be run.
>
> **7.** Click the **Run this rule now on messages already in the current folder** check box to select it, and then click the **OK** button.
>
> The rule runs on the messages in the Inbox folder and the Latest Sales message is moved to the Sales folder.
>
> **8.** Click the **Sales** folder in the All Mail Folders in the Navigation Pane to confirm that the message was moved into this folder.

After you place messages in a variety of folders, you can further arrange them.

Rearranging Messages

As your folder structure becomes more complex and you have more stored messages, it might become difficult to locate a specific message you filed. Finding, using Search Folders, sorting, and changing views provide different ways to organize your messages.

Finding Messages

Rather than searching through multiple folders, you can have Outlook find the desired message. The Find command searches the From or Subject text boxes in a single folder for text that you specify. For searches of more than one criterion or multiple folders and sub-folders, you must use the Advanced Find feature.

Reference Window | **Finding Messages**

- Open the folder you want to search.
- Click the Find button on the Standard toolbar (*or* click Tools on the menu bar, and then click Find).
- Type the search text in the Look for text box.
- Select the folder to search in the Search In list box.
- Click the Find Now button.

You'll use the Find feature to look for replies to the peach order message in the Suppliers folder.

To find messages:

> **1.** Click the **Suppliers** subfolder in the All Mail Folders pane in the Navigation Pane to display its contents in the main window.
>
> **2.** Click the **Find** button on the Standard toolbar. The Find Bar opens.
>
> **3.** Type **RE: Peach Order** in the Look for text box.

4. Make sure **Suppliers** appears in the Search In list box.

5. Click the **Find Now** button. After a moment, the one message that contains "RE: Peach Order" appears in the main window. See Figure 1-21.

Find results ◄   **Figure 1-21**

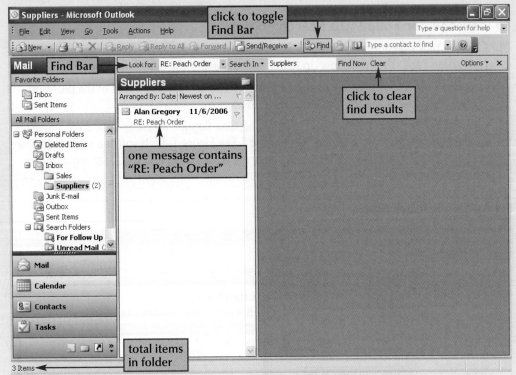

You could perform additional simple searches, but for now you're done.

6. Click the **Find** button on the Standard toolbar to close the Find Bar.

Once you close the Find Bar, all messages in that folder reappear. Another way to find specific messages is with Search Folders.

Using Search Folders

Search Folders are folders that display any e-mail messages that match specific search criteria. Any messages that meet the Search Folder's criteria are displayed in that Search Folder but remain stored in their current Outlook folders. This enables you to open one folder to view similar messages, but store them in other folders with a logical filing system. Outlook has several preset Search Folders. For example, the For Follow Up Search Folder displays any flagged messages you have stored, the Large Mail Search Folder displays any messages larger than 100 KB, and the Unread Mail Search Folder displays all messages that have an unread icon. A message can appear in more than one Search Folder. For example, a flagged message that is 200 KB and still marked as unread, will be displayed in at least three Search Folders: For Follow Up, Large Mail, and Unread Mail. You can use the existing Search Folders, customize them to better fit your needs, or create your own Search Folders.

If you delete a Search Folder, the messages that were displayed in that folder are not deleted because they are actually stored in other Outlook folders. However, if you delete an individual message from within a Search Folder, the message is also deleted from its storage folder.

You'll use Search folders to look for flagged messages and unread messages.

To view the For Follow Up Search Folder:

1. Click the **plus sign** button ⊞ next to Search Folders in the All Mail Folders pane in the Navigation Pane. The For Follow Up folder appears under the Search Folders folder.

   Trouble? If a minus sign button appears next to Search Folders instead of the plus sign button, the folder is already expanded. Skip to Step 2.

2. Click **For Follow Up** in the All Mail Folders pane. One flagged message appears in the main window under the group heading "Green Flag." See Figure 1-22. If you had more than one message flagged and used different flag colors, the messages would appear organized as different groups.

Figure 1-22	For Follow Up Search Folder

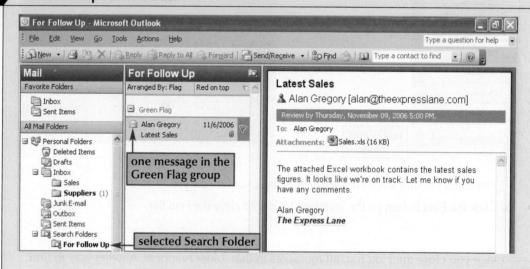

You'll use the New Search Folder dialog box to open the Unread Mail Search Folder. If you already have an Unread Mail folder in your Folder List, read, but do not complete the following set of steps.

To view the Unread Mail Search Folder:

1. Right-click **Search Folders** in the All Mail Folders pane in the Navigation pane, and then click **New Search Folder**. The New Search Folder dialog box opens. See Figure 1-23.

New Search Folder dialog box Figure 1-23

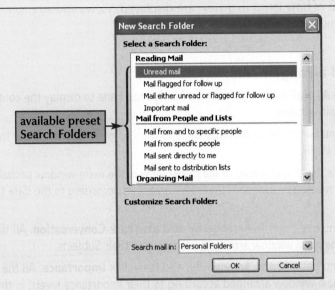

available preset
Search Folders

2. Click **Unread mail** in the Select a Search Folder list box, and then click the **OK** button. The contents of the Unread Mail Search Folder appears in the main window. The two messages you haven't yet read are listed. See Figure 1-24.

Unread Mail Search Folder Figure 1-24

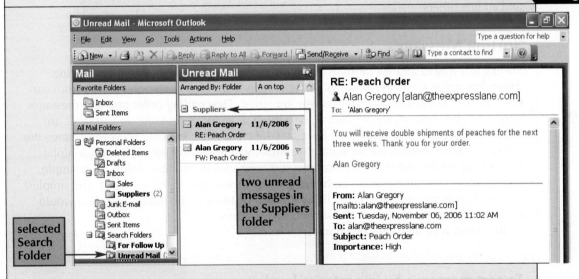

two unread
messages in
the Suppliers
folder

selected
Search
Folder

Trouble? If you see fewer or more messages, you may have inadvertently changed a message icon from unread to read when moving it to the Suppliers folder or you may have received messages unrelated to this tutorial. Continue with the tutorial.

Another way to manage files is to change the view or arrangement.

Switching Views and Arrangements

There are a variety of ways to look at items in a folder. You are already familiar with views, which specify how items in a folder are organized and which details are visible. Each

Outlook folder has a set of standard views from which you can choose. **Arrangements** are a predefined arrangement of how items in a view are displayed. Views and arrangements enable you to see the same items in a folder in different ways.

To switch views and arrangements:

▶ 1. Click **Suppliers** in the All Mail Folders pane in the Navigation Pane to display the contents of this folder in the main window.

▶ 2. Click **View** on the menu bar, point to **Arrange By**, and then point to **Current View** to display the list of default views.

▶ 3. Click **Messages**. This is the default view, so the folder view in the main window probably didn't change. All the messages appear in the folder arranged according to the date they were received.

▶ 4. Click **View** on the menu bar, point to **Arrange By**, and then click **Conversation**. All the messages appear in the main window arranged according to their Subjects.

▶ 5. Click **View** on the menu bar, point to **Arrange By**, and then click **Importance**. All the messages appear in the main window arranged according to their importance levels, in this case High or none. Each level (High, Low, or none) becomes a heading for a different group. The other arrangements display the e-mail messages in different ways.

You could further customize a view by removing some of the existing column headings and adding others.

Sorting Messages

Sorting is a way to arrange items in a specific order—either ascending or descending. **Ascending order** arranges messages alphabetically from A to Z, chronologically from earliest to latest, or numerically from lowest to highest. **Descending order** arranges messages in reverse alphabetical, chronological, or numerical order. By default, all messages are sorted in descending order by their Received date and time. You can, however, change the field by which messages are sorted; for example, you might sort e-mail messages alphabetically by sender. Alternatively, you can sort messages by multiple fields; for example, you might sort e-mail messages alphabetically by sender and then by subject. The simplest way to change the sort order is to click a column heading in the folder pane. You would press the Shift key as you click the second sort column.

You'll sort your messages by importance level.

To sort messages by importance level:

▶ 1. Click the **High on top** column heading in the main window. The sort order changes to ascending by importance, as indicated by the up arrow icon in the column heading. See Figure 1-25.

Sorted messages | **Figure 1-25**

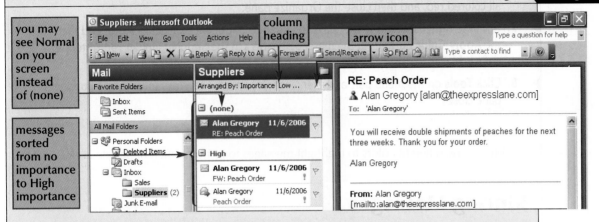

Trouble? If you don't see "on top" as part of the column heading, your main window is too narrow to display the entire column label. Click High to change the sort order to ascending by importance.

Trouble? If there is no High on top column heading, only one labeled Low on top, and the arrow icon points up, then the sort order is already ascending. Skip to Step 2.

2. Click the **Low on top** column heading in the main window. The sort order returns to descending by importance, as indicated by the down arrow icon in the column heading.

3. Click **View** on the menu bar, point to **Arrange By**, and then click **Date**.

You can sort messages in any view except Message Timeline view. Another way to make certain messages stand out is to color them.

Coloring Messages

Sometimes you'll want messages that you send to a certain person or that you receive from a certain person to stand out from all the other messages. A simple way to do this is to create a rule to change the color of the message headers in the Inbox for those messages. You choose to change all messages to or from a particular person to a color you select. You can also select a color for any messages that are sent only to you. You can set up both these rules in the Organize pane, which also provides another way to move items from one Outlook folder to another and to switch views.

You'll use the Organize pane to set up the rule to change the color of messages from yourself to Red.

To change the color of messages:

1. Click **Tools** on the menu bar, and then click **Organize**. The Ways to Organize Suppliers pane opens.

2. Click the **Using Colors** link. The options for setting colors for specific messages appear in the pane. You'll use the first sentence.

3. If necessary, click the left list arrow, and then click **from**.

4. If necessary, select the text in the text box, and then type your name.

5. If necessary, click the right list arrow, and then click **Red**. The rule is complete.

6. Click the **Apply Color** button. The rule is applied to the messages in the current folder, and all the message headers in the Suppliers folder change to red.

You'll change the message headers back to black, so that your outgoing messages are not all colored red, and then close the Organize pane.

   ▶ **7.** Click the right list arrow in the Ways to Organize Suppliers pane, click **Auto**, and then click the **Apply Color** button. All the message headers in the Suppliers folder return to the default black.

   ▶ **8.** Click **Tools** on the menu bar, and then click **Organize**. The Ways to Organize Suppliers pane closes.

You can use different colors to highlight messages to or from different people at one time.

Storing Messages

After a time, you may not need immediate access to the messages you have compiled in the Outlook folders. You can store messages in other file formats or by archiving them.

Saving Messages

You can use the Save As command to save messages and other Outlook items in other file formats so that you can save them on your hard drive or floppy disks, as you save your other files, and then delete them from Outlook. You can open such messages with other programs. For example, you can save an e-mail message as a Text Only (.txt) file that most word processing programs can read. You can also save HTML messages as HTML (.htm) files to preserve their original formatting.

Reference Window	**Saving Messages in Another File Format**

- Select the message or messages you want to save in another format.
- Click File on the menu bar, and then click Save As.
- Change the Save in location.
- Enter a new filename as needed.
- Click the Save as type list arrow, and then select the file format you want.
- Click the Save button.

You'll save the original Peach Order message as a Text Only file.

To save a message in another format:

   ▶ **1.** Click the **Peach Order** message in the main window to select it.

   ▶ **2.** Click **File** on the menu bar, and then click **Save As**. The Save As dialog box opens, with the subject listed in the File name text box.

   ▶ **3.** Change the Save in location to the **Tutorial.01\Tutorial** folder included with your Data Files.

   ▶ **4.** Click the **Save as type** list arrow to display the file formats from which you can select.

       Trouble? If your message did not retain the HTML formatting, then the format options available are Text Only, Outlook Template, Outlook Message Format, and Outlook Message Format - Unicode. Continue with Step 5.

   ▶ **5.** Click **Text Only** to select that file format.

   ▶ **6.** Click the **Save** button. The message is saved as a text file.

You or others can now open the file in Word or any other program that can read text files. The process is the same for saving and viewing files in HTML.

Archiving Mail Messages

Eventually, even the messages in your subfolders can become too numerous to manage easily. More often than not, you don't need immediate access to the older messages. Rather than reviewing your filed messages and moving older ones to a storage file, you can archive them. When you **archive** a folder, you transfer messages or other items stored in a folder (such as an attachment in the e-mail folder) to a personal folder file when the items have reached the age you specify. A **personal folders file** is a special storage file with a .pst extension that contains folders, messages, forms, and files; it can be viewed only in Outlook. Outlook calculates the age of an e-mail message from the date the message was sent or received, whichever is later. The personal folders file format for Outlook 2003 has greater storage capacity than and is incompatible with earlier versions of Outlook. However, Outlook 2003 can create and view personal folders files in both formats.

When you create an archive, your existing folder structure from Outlook is recreated in the archive file and all the messages are moved from Outlook into the archive file. If you want to archive only a subfolder, the entire folder structure is still recreated in the archive file; however, only the messages from the selected subfolder are moved into the archive file. For example, if you archive the Suppliers folder, the archive file will include both the Inbox and the Suppliers subfolder, but only the messages in the Suppliers subfolder will be moved. Any messages in the Inbox remain in the Outlook Inbox. All folders remain in place within Outlook after archiving—even empty ones.

You can manually archive a folder at any time, such as when you finish a project or event. You specify which folders to archive, the age of items to archive, and the name and location of the archive file.

To manually archive a folder:

▶ **1.** Click **File** on the menu bar, and then click **Archive**. The Archive dialog box opens. See Figure 1-26.

Archive dialog box ◀ **Figure 1-26**

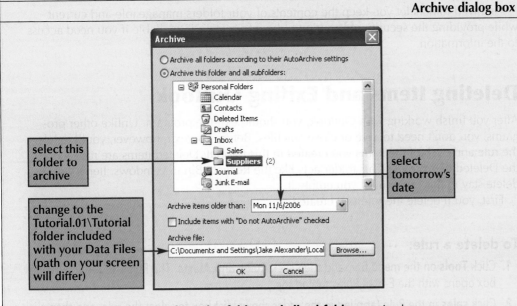

▶ **2.** If necessary, click the **Archive this folder and all subfolders** option button.

▶ **3.** If necessary, click the **plus sign** button ➕ next to Inbox to display the subfolders, and then click the **Suppliers** folder.

4. Type **tomorrow** in the Archive items older than text box, and then press the **Tab** key. Outlook will move any files dated with today's date or earlier to the archive file.

5. Click the **Browse** button. The Open Personal Folders dialog box opens.

6. Change the Save in location to the **Tutorial.01\Tutorial** folder included with your Data Files, type **Suppliers Archive** as the filename, and then click the **OK** button.

7. Click the **OK** button in the Archive dialog box.

8. Click the **Yes** button to confirm that you want to archive all the items in the folder. All the messages in the Suppliers folder are moved into the archive file you specified. The empty Suppliers folder remains in the folder structure.

9. Repeat Steps 1 through 8 to create an archive for the **Sales** folder named **Sales Archive**.

The archived folders are open and displayed in the Folders List. You can access items in your archive files several ways: you can open the file using the Open command on the File menu and then drag the items you need to a current folder; you can add the archive file to your profile; or you can restore all the items in the archive file by using the Import and Export command on the File menu. If you don't need access to the archive folders, then you can close them.

To close archive folders:

1. Click the **Folder List** button 🗀 on the Navigation Pane, and then scroll down to see the two archive folders at the end of the list.

2. Right-click the top **Archive Folders** in the Folder List, and then click **Close "Archive Folders."** The folder closes.

3. Right-click the remaining **Archive Folders** in the Folder List, and then click **Close "Archive Folders."** The folder closes.

Archived folders let you keep the contents of your folders manageable and current while providing the security of knowing older information is available if you need access to the information.

Deleting Items and Exiting Outlook

After you finish working with Outlook, you should exit the program. Unlike other programs, you don't need to save or close any files. Before you exit, however, you'll delete the rule and each of the items you created in this tutorial. Deleted items are moved into the Deleted Items folder. This folder acts like the Recycle Bin in Windows. Items you delete stay in this folder until you empty it.

First, you'll delete the rule you created.

To delete a rule:

1. Click **Tools** on the menu bar, and then click **Rules and Alerts**. The Rules and Alerts dialog box opens with the E-mail Rules tab on top.

2. Click **sales** in the Rule (applied in the order shown) list box to select the rule, and then click the **Delete** button on the toolbar at the top of the tab.

3. Click the **Yes** button to confirm the deletion, and then click the **OK** button to close the Rules and Alerts dialog box. The rule is deleted.

Next, you'll delete the folders and e-mails you created.

To delete items:

1. Click the **Suppliers** folder in the All Folders pane in the Navigation Pane.
2. Click the **Delete** button ☒ on the Standard toolbar, and then click the **Yes** button to confirm that the folder and all of its messages should be moved to the Deleted Items folder.
3. Click the **Sales** folder in the Folder List, click the **Delete** button ☒ on the Standard toolbar, and then click the **Yes** button to confirm that the folder and all of its messages should be moved to the Deleted Items folder.
4. Switch to the **Sent Items** folder, click the first message you sent in this tutorial, press and hold the **Ctrl** key as you click each additional message you sent in this tutorial, release the **Ctrl** key, and then click the **Delete** button ☒ on the Standard toolbar. The messages move to the Deleted Items folder.
5. Click the **Contacts** button in the Navigation Pane, press and hold the **Ctrl** key as you click each of the five contacts you created in this tutorial, release the **Ctrl** key, and then press the **Delete** key. The contacts you created for this tutorial are deleted.
6. Click the **plus sign** button ⊞ next to Search Folders in the Navigation pane, if necessary, click the **Unread Mail** folder, and then click the **Delete** button ☒ on the Standard toolbar.
7. Right-click the **Deleted Items** folder in the All Folders pane, click **Empty "Deleted Items" Folder** on the shortcut menu, and then click the **Yes** button to confirm the deletion. The folder empties and the items are permanently deleted.

Finally you'll remove the signature you created and exit Outlook.

To delete a signature and exit Outlook:

1. Click **Tools** on the menu bar, click **Options**, and then click the **Mail Format** tab in the Options dialog box.
2. Click the **Signatures** button, click the name of your signature in the Signature list box, and then click the **Remove** button.
3. Click the **Yes** button to confirm that you want to delete this signature.
4. Click the **OK** button in the Create Signature dialog box, and then click the **OK** button in the Options dialog box. You're ready to exit Outlook.
5. Click the **Close** button ☒ on the title bar to exit Outlook.

Alan thanks you for your help. The Express Lane can now fill all of its customers' orders for peaches until the end of the season. A happy customer means a profitable business.

Session 1.2 Quick Check

Review

1. Explain the difference between the Reply button and the Reply to All button.
2. True or False: You can save a file attached to a message, but you cannot open the attachment from within Outlook.
3. How do you move an e-mail message from the Inbox to a subfolder?
4. What is a Search Folder?
5. What is the purpose of a rule?
6. What does it mean to archive a folder?

Review

Tutorial Summary

In this tutorial, you learned about the Outlook components, started Outlook, viewed its window elements, and navigated between components. You created and sent e-mail messages. You created and organized a contact list and created a distribution group. You received, read, replied to, forwarded, and printed e-mail messages. Then you added and read attachments to e-mail messages. You organized messages in subfolders by filing them manually and using a rule to move them. You rearranged messages by changing a folders view and arrangement, and sorting them. Finally, you saved messages in other formats, archived messages within a folder, and then deleted items you created.

Key Terms

archive	Folder Banner	Outlook Today
arrangement	Folder List	password
ascending order	Forward	personal folders file
attachment	host name	Reading Pane
Calendar	item	Reply
contact	Journal	Reply to All
contact card	Mail	Search Folder
Contacts	main window	rule
descending order	message flag	signature
distribution list	message header	smiley
e-mail	Microsoft Outlook	sorting
e-mail address	Navigation Pane	stationery template
emoticon	netiquette	Tasks
field	Notes	user ID
folder	offline	vCard
		view

Practice

Practice the skills you learned in the tutorial.

Review Assignments

Data File needed for the Review Assignments: Tea.doc

Lora Shaw asks you to help her with customer communication for The Express Lane. Complete the following:

1. Create a signature that uses your name and "Customer Service Representative" as your title. Apply the signature to new messages and replies and forwards.
2. Create a new e-mail message addressed to your e-mail address with the subject "Welcome New Customer" and the message "Welcome to The Express Lane. We're sure you'll find our grocery delivery service more convenient and cheaper than your local grocery store—not to mention more healthful, because all our foods are certified organic. If you have any questions or comments, feel free to e-mail us."
3. Format the text of your e-mail in 12-point Times New Roman.
4. Send the e-mail to the Outbox and then to your mail server.
5. Create a contact card for Alan Gregory at The Express Lane with a fictional business mailing address and business phone number; use your own e-mail address.
6. Create a contact card for Lora based on Alan's contact card. Enter the same company information as on Alan Gregory's contact card. (*Hint*: To create a card with the business information entered automatically, select the contact card that contains the

business information you want to duplicate in the Contacts folder, click Actions on the menu bar, and then click New Contact from Same Company.) Type "Lora Shaw" in the Full Name text box. Type your e-mail address in the E-mail text box.

7. Create contact cards for the following three customers at their home addresses, using your e-mail address: (*Hint:* Click the down arrow button in the address section, and then click Home.)
   - Elliot Zander, 384 Leavenworth Street, San Francisco, CA 94103, 415-555-1232
   - Mai Ching, 1938 Grant Avenue, San Francisco, CA 94110, 415-555-0907
   - Lester Newhoun, 2938 Golden Gate Avenue, San Francisco, CA 94124, 415-555-6497

8. Create a distribution list named "Customers" that includes Mai Ching, Lester Newhoun, and Elliot Zander.

9. Edit Mai Ching's contact card to change the address to "1938 Presidio Street."

10. Create an e-mail message addressed to Lora Shaw. Type "Tea health benefits?" as the subject. Type "I've heard that drinking tea has health benefits. Do you have any information about this?" as the message body. Send the e-mail to the Outbox and then to your mail server.

11. Download your new messages. If the Tea health benefits? message hasn't arrived, wait a few minutes and try again.

12. Reply to the Tea health benefits? message with the text "In addition to being the world's second favorite drink to water, there is growing evidence of a link between tea and disease prevention, particularly cancer and heart disease. Check out our large selection of black, oolong, and green teas. The attached file has some information about teas. I hope this information is helpful."

13. Attach the **Tea** document located in the **Tutorial.01/Review** folder included with your Data Files to the file, and then send the message to your Outbox.

15. Forward the Tea health benefits? message to Alan Gregory with the message "Let's meet next week to talk about adding this information to our Web site." Mark it as high importance. Send the message to the Outbox.

16. Send all messages in your Outbox to your mail server.

17. Create a Mail and Post Items subfolder named "Customers" located within the Inbox.

18. Create a rule to move messages you receive from yourself to the Customers folder. Run the rule now.

19. Download your messages, and verify that the Welcome New Customer message and the three Tea health benefits? messages were filed in the Customers subfolder.

20. Add a blue flag to the Tea health benefits? message.

21. Find the messages in the Customers folder that contain the word "customer."

22. Save each of the messages that were found in HTML format to the **Tutorial.01\Review** folder included with your Data Files (if your server does not support HTML, then save the messages in Text Only format). Close the Find bar.

23. Create a new Mail flagged for follow up Search Folder, and then open the new folder.

24. Save the attachment in the RE: Tea health benefits? message as **Tea Health Benefits** in the **Tutorial.01\Review** folder included with your Data Files.

25. Print the RE: Tea health benefits? message and its attachment. (*Hint:* In the Print dialog box, select the Print attached files check box.)

26. Archive all the messages in the Customers folder to the **Tutorial.01\Review** folder included with your Data Files, using the filename **Customers Archive**. Close the archive folder.

27. Delete each Outlook item you created, including the Search Folder you created named for Follow Up1, the signature, the rule, the subfolder, the messages in the Sent Items folder, and the contacts, and then empty the Deleted Items folder.

Apply

Apply what you learned in the tutorial to send and respond to e-mail messages for a tutoring service.

Case Problem 1

Answers Anytime Answers Anytime is a unique tutoring service where students can e-mail specific questions and problem areas to subject experts and receive quick answers. The subject experts reply to students within two hours, either by e-mail message or e-mail message with an attachment. Complete the following:

1. Create a new e-mail message to your e-mail address with the subject "History questions" and the message "Please send information about the following: What is the Bill of Rights? When did women receive the right to vote? How does Rachel Carson fit into the environmental movement?" Press the Enter key after each question to place it on its own line, and then format the questions as a numbered list. Type your name at the end of the message. Send the message.

2. Create a contact card for Benji Tanago, Environmental History Expert, Answers Anytime, Pallas Road, Cincinnati, OH 45230, 513-555-6582, and your e-mail address.

3. Download your message, and then reply to the message using the following text formatted as a numbered list:

   1. See the attached document for information about the Bill of Rights.
   2. On August 26, 1920, Tennessee delivered the last needed vote and the Nineteenth Amendment was added to the Constitution. It states that "the right of citizens of the United States to vote shall not be denied by the United States or by any State on account of sex."
   3. I've forwarded this question to Benji Tanago, our resident expert on the environmental movement.

4. Attach the **Amendments** document located in the **Tutorial.01\Cases** folder included with your Data Files to the e-mail. Send the message to the Outbox.

Explore

5. Rather than retype Benji's information, you can send the contact card you just created. Switch to the Contacts folder, click Benji's contact card to select it, click Actions on the menu bar, and then click Forward as vCard. A Message window opens with the contact card included as an attachment. Enter your e-mail address in the To text box, and then send the message to the Outbox.

6. Forward the student's original message to Benji with a High importance level. Add the text "Hi, Benji. Question 3 is yours. Thanks."

Explore

7. Because you want to make sure that Benji responds in a timely manner, you want to recall the message if Benji hasn't read it within one week. Click the Options button on the toolbar in the message window, click the Expires after check box to insert a check mark, enter the date of one week from today, and then click the Close button. This option makes the message unavailable after the date you specified.

8. Send the message to the Outbox, and then send all the messages to your mail server.

9. Create a Mail and Post Items subfolder named "Answers" located in the Inbox.

10. Download your messages, and then find all messages in the Inbox related to the subject "History questions."

11. Save the messages you found as HTML files in the **Tutorial.01\Cases** folder included with your Data Files.

12. File the found messages in the Answers folder, and then close the Find bar.

13. File the message with the vCard in the Answers folder.

14. Use the Organize pane to display all the messages in the Answers folder from yourself in green.

15. Archive the Answers subfolder as **Answers Archive** in the **Tutorial.01\Cases** folder included with your Data Files. Close the archive.

16. Delete the Answers folder, the messages in the Sent Items folder, and the contact, and then empty the Deleted Items folder.

Challenge

Extend what you've learned to create e-mail invitations for a graduation party.

Explore ▶

Explore ▶

Explore ▶

Explore ▶

Explore ▶

Explore ▶

Case Problem 2

Party Planners Jace Moran, owner of Party Planners, plans events ranging from company picnics to children's birthday parties to weddings. Right now, she is working on a graduation party. The graduate hosting the party has given Jace the e-mail addresses for the entire guest list so that Jace can send the invitations using Outlook. Complete the following:

1. Create a new e-mail message to your e-mail address with an appropriate subject using an Excel worksheet as the message body. With the Inbox selected, click Actions on the menu bar, point to New Mail Message Using, point to Microsoft Office, and then click Microsoft Excel Worksheet. In column A, enter a list of foods for the party. In column B, enter the probable cost for the food. Total the cost column. Send the e-mail to the Outbox and then to your mail server. Close Excel without saving the worksheet.

2. Create contact cards for five guests. Include their names, addresses, phone numbers, and e-mail addresses. Enter your own e-mail address for each contact. Create a contact card for Jace Moran that includes her name, company name, and your e-mail address.

3. Create a distribution list named "Guests" that includes the contact cards of all the guests.

4. Edit three contacts to include one item of personal information, such as a birthday or spouse's name.

5. Use stationery to create the party invitation. From the Inbox, click Actions on the menu bar, point to New Mail Message Using, and then click More Stationery. Click an appropriate stationery in the Stationery list box, and then click the OK button.

6. Address the invitation to the Guests distribution list and to Jace. Type an appropriate subject.

7. Enter the Day, Time, and Place of the party. Format the stationery using Word's formatting features; try changing the font and color of existing text. Send the message to the Outbox and then to your mail server.

8. Create a Mail and Post Items subfolder named "Party" in the Inbox, and then move the food cost e-mail into the Party subfolder.

9. Read and print the food cost e-mail, and then add a purple flag to the message.

10. Create a rule that moves any messages with the subject you used for the invitation into the Party subfolder.

11. Switch to the Contacts folder, and then change the view to Detailed Address Cards.

12. Print the contact cards you created. If other contact cards exist in addition to the ones you created, press and hold the Ctrl key as you click the contact name for each card you created. Open the Print dialog box. Use Card Style as the Print style and, if you selected contact cards, click the Only selected items option button in the Print range. Click the OK button.

13. Create a Contacts subfolder named "Guests" located in the Contacts folder and move the contact cards you created into it. (*Hint*: Make sure you change the Folder contains list box to "Contact Items" in the Create New Folder dialog box.)

14. Export your contact list. Click File on the menu bar, and then click Import and Export. Click Export to a file, and then click the Next button. Click Microsoft Access, and then click the Next button. If necessary, click the plus button next to Contacts to display the Guests subfolder, select the subfolder, and then click the Next button. Use the Browse button to save the file as **Guest List** to the **Tutorial.01\Cases** folder included with your Data Files. Click the Next button, and then click the Finish button. The contact list is exported as an Access database.

15. Download your messages. (Note that you will only receive one message because all of the e-mail addresses for your contacts are the same.) Print the message, and then save it as an HTML file to the **Tutorial.01\Cases** folder included with your Data Files.

16. Archive the messages in the Party subfolder as **Party Archive** in the **Tutorial.01\Cases** folder included with your Data Files.

Explore

17. Expand the Archive folder files, and then copy the Guests subfolder to the archive. Click the Guests subfolder, press and hold the Ctrl key as you drag the folder to the archive file, and then release the Ctrl key. Close the archive file.

18. Delete the rule you created, the Guests subfolder, the Party subfolder, the messages in the Sent Items folder, and the contacts you created, and then empty the Deleted Items folder.

Review

Quick Check Answers

Session 1.1

1. The Inbox stores e-mail messages you have received; the Outbox stores e-mail messages you have written but not yet sent.

2. The electronic transfer of messages between computers on the Internet. It's an inexpensive way to communicate with others who are nearby or far away. You can send and read messages at your convenience.

3. Text that is automatically added to every e-mail message you send, such as your name, job title, and company name.

4. a contact's name, job title, company name and address, phone and fax numbers, as well as personal information such as birthdays, anniversaries, and children's names

5. Creates a contact card for a group of people to whom you frequently send the same messages; a distribution list saves time and insures that you don't inadvertently leave out someone.

Session 1.2

1. Reply responds to only the sender of the e-mail message; Reply to All responds to the sender and any other recipients of the e-mail message.

2. False

3. Drag the message from the Inbox pane to the subfolder in the Folder List.

4. folders that display any e-mail messages that match specific search criteria; messages are stored in their current Outlook folder.

5. specifies how Outlook should process and organize your e-mail messages.

6. moves items you selected from Outlook into a personal folder file

Glossary/Index

Note: Boldface entries include definitions.

SPECIAL CHARACTERS

> (greater than operator), EX 82
> (greater than symbol), AC 102
< (less than operator), EX 82
< (less than symbol), AC 102
() (parentheses), EX 15–16
<> (not equal to operator), EX 82
<> (not equal to symbol), AC 102
_ (space marker), WD 9
¶ (paragraph mark), WD 9
* (asterisk), EX 15
+ (plus sign), EX 15
- (minus sign), EX 15
/ (slash), EX 15
= (equal sign), AC 102, EX 82
>= (greater than or equal to operator), EX 82
>= (greater than or equal to symbol), AC 102
<= (less than or equal to operator), EX 82
<= (less than or equal to symbol), AC 102
^ (caret), EX 15

A

absolute reference(s) Cell reference that points to a specific cell and does not change when copied; appears with a dollar sign ($) before each column and row designation. EX 58, EX 59, EX 60–61

Access. *See* Microsoft Access 2003

Access window The program window that appears when you start the Access program. AC 7, AC 9

account name. *See* user ID(s)

Accounting format, EX 102

active cell The selected cell in the worksheet; indicated with a dark border. EX 6, EX 7, EX 8

active program The program you are currently using. WIN 13

address(es), e-mail, OUT 7

Address bar, FM 8

adjacent range(s) A single rectangular block that include a group of contiguous cells. EX 15, EX 23

aggregate function(s) A function that performs an arithmetic operation on selected records in a database. AC 117–119

alignment in a document The way the text of a paragraph lines up horizontally between the margins. WD 64–65

alignment of cell contents, EX 105–108

Alignment tab, Format Cells dialog box, EX 101

AND function, EX 84

And logical operator The logical operator you use in a query when you want a record selected only if two or more conditions are met. AC 107–109

animation The association of the elements on the slide with a special look or sound effect. PPT 7

application(s) Software that a computer uses to complete tasks; also called program. WIN 4

archive(ing) A feature that lets you manually transfer messages or other items stored in a folder (such as an attachment in the e-mail folder) to a personal folder file when the items have reached the age you specify. OUT 41–42

Archive dialog box, OUT 41–42

argument(s) Specifies the numbers, text, or cell references used by the function to calculate a value. EX 53

arithmetic operator(s) Symbols, such as +, -, *, or /, used in a formula to perform a arithmetic calculations. EX 14, EX 15

arrangement(s) A predefined arrangement of how items in a view are displayed. OUT 38

ascending order Arranges messages alphabetically from A to Z, chronologically from earliest to latest or numerically from lowest to highest. OUT 38

asterisk (*) multiplication operator, EX 15

attachment(s) A file that you send with an e-mail message. OUT 27–28

Auto Fill An Excel tool that enables you to copy the contents of the selected cells by dragging the fill handle over another adjacent cell or range of cells rather than using the Copy and Paste commands. EX 70

AutoComplete (Excel) A feature that anticipates the text you are about to enter by displaying text that begins with the same letter as a previous entry displays text. EX 17

AutoComplete (Word) A feature that automatically inserts dates and other regularly used items for you. WD 24–25

AutoContent Wizard, PPT 10–12

AutoCorrect A feature that automatically corrects common typing errors. WD 20–22

AutoCorrect Options button A button that is inserted into a document wherever AutoCorrect makes a change and that can be used to undo a change, or to prevent AutoCorrect from making the same change in the future. WD 21–22

AutoForm Wizard A Form Wizard that places all the fields from a selected table (or query) on a form automatically, and then displays the form on the screen, making it the quickest way to create a form. AC 18–19

AutoFormat(s) (Excel) A gallery of 17 predefined formats that you can select and apply to your worksheet cells. EX 124–126

automatic page break(s) A page break inserted automatically by Word whenever all the available lines on a page are filled with text. WD 44–45

AutoNumber data type, AC 39

AutoReport Wizard(s) A Report Wizard that places all the fields from a selected table (or query) on a report automatically, and then displays the report on the screen, making it the quickest way to create a report. AC 21–22

AutoSum Toolbar button that automatically inserts the SUM function to calculate the sum of values in a range. EX 28–30

AVERAGE function Excel function that calculates the average value of a collection of numbers. EX 54
    copying into remaining cells, EX 67
    inserting, EX 65–66
    inserting values, EX 66–67

Avg function, AC 118

B

background colors in worksheets, EX 111–112, EX 113–114

background graphics, EX 117–118

background patterns, EX 111, EX 112–113

backing up The process of making a copy of a database file to protect your database against loss or damage. AC 24–25

backup(s) A duplicate copy of important files that you need. FM 7

blank lines, inserting in documents, WD 12–13, WD 24

body text A large text box on a slide in which you type a bulleted or numbered list; also called main text. PPT 14

bolding text, WD 71

border(s) of cells, EX 108–111

Border tab, Format Cells dialog box, EX 101, EX 110

bullet(s) A heavy dot (or other graphic) before each item in a list. WD 68–69

bulleted item(s) One paragraph in a bulleted list. PPT 13
    adding, PPT 15–16

bulleted list(s) A list of paragraphs with a special character, such as a dot, to the left of each paragraph. PPT 13

buttons. *See also specific buttons*
    toggle, WD 71

C

calculated field(s) A field that displays the results of an expression in a query datasheet or a form or report, but does not exist as a field in the database. AC 112–117
    creating, AC 113–117

calculations, AC 112–120
    aggregate functions, AC 117–119
    calculated fields, AC 112–117
    group, AC 119–120
    sums, EX 28–30, EX 54–55

Calendar An Outlook folder in which you use a calendar to schedule appointments, events, and meetings. OUT 4

Caption property The property that specifies how a field name will appear in datasheets and in other database objects, such as forms and reports. AC 40

caret (^), exponentiation operator, EX 15

Task Reference

TASK	PAGE #	RECOMMENDED METHOD
Absolute reference, change press to relative	EX 58	Edit the formula, deleting the $ before the column and row references; or F4 to switch between absolute, relative, and mixed references
Access, start	AC 7	Click Start, point to All Programs, point to Microsoft Office, click Microsoft Office Access 2003
Action, redo	EX 34, WD 27	Click [icon]
Action, undo	EX 34, WD 27	Click [icon]
Actions, redo several	EX 34	Click [icon], select the action(s) to redo
Actions, undo several	EX 34	Click [icon], select the action(s) to undo
Address bar, display in My Computer window	WIN 27	Click View, point to Toolbars, click Address Bar to insert a check mark
Aggregate functions, use in a query	AC 118	Display the query in Design view, click [Σ]
Archive folder, close	OUT 41	Right-click Archive Folder in Folder List, click Close "Archive Folder"
Arrangement, switch	OUT 38	Click View, point to Arrange By, click desired arrangement
Attachment, add to e-mail	OUT 27	From Message window, click [icon], select file location, double-click file to insert
Attachment, save	OUT 28	Right-click attachment icon in Reading Pane or Message window, click Save As, select save location, enter filename, click Save
Attachment, view	OUT 28	Double-click attachment icon in Reading Pane or Message window, click Open, click OK
Auto Fill, copy formulas	EX 68	See Reference Window: Copying Formulas Using the Fill Handle
Auto Fill, create series	EX 71	Select the range, drag the fill handle down, release mouse button, click [icon], click the option button to complete series
AutoContent Wizard, run	PPT 10	Click File, click New, click From AutoContent Wizard on New Presentation task pane, follow instructions
AutoCorrect, use	WD 20	Click [icon], click correct spelling
AutoFormat, apply	EX 125	Select the range, click Format, click AutoFormat, select an AutoFormat design, click OK
AutoSum, apply	EX 28	Click the cell in which you want the final value to appear, click [Σ], select the AutoSum function to apply
Background color, apply	EX 112	Select the range, click the list arrow for [icon], select a color square in the color palette
Background pattern, apply	EX 112	Open the Format Cells dialog box, click the Patterns tab, click the Pattern list arrow, click a pattern in the pattern gallery, click OK
Boldface, add to text	WD 72	Select text, click [B]
Border, create	EX 109	Click [icon], select a border in the border gallery
Border, draw	EX 109	Click [icon], click [icon], draw the border using the Pencil tool
Bullets, add to paragraphs	WD 68	Select paragraphs, click [icon]
Calculated field, add to a query	AC 113	See Reference Window: Using Expression Builder
Cell, clear contents of	EX 32	Click Edit, point to Clear, click Contents; or press Delete
Cell, edit	EX 34	See Reference Window: Editing a Cell

TASK	PAGE #	RECOMMENDED METHOD
Cell reference, change	EX 59	Press the F4 key to cycle through the difference cell reference modes
Cells, delete	EX 32	Select the cell or range, click Edit, click Delete, select a delete option, click OK; or select the cell or range, click-right the selection, click Delete, select a delete option, click OK
Cells, insert	EX 31	See Reference Window: Inserting Cells into a Worksheet
Cells, merge	EX 115	Select the adjacent cells, open the Format Cells dialog box, click the Alignment tab, select the Merge cells check box, click OK
Cells, merge and center	EX 115	Select the adjacent cells, click 🖅
Clip art, insert	PPT 16	Change slide layout to a Content layout, click 🖼 in content placeholder, click clipart image, click OK
Clipboard task pane, open	WD 54	Click Edit, click Office Clipboard
Clipboard task pane, use to cut, copy, and paste	WD 54	See Reference Window: Cutting or Copying and Pasting Text
Column, change width	EX 19	See Reference Window: Changing the Column Width or Row Height
Column, delete	EX 32	Select the column, click Edit, click Delete; or select the column, click-right the selection, click Delete
Column, hide	EX 116	Select the headings for the columns you want to hide, right-click the selection, click Hide
Column, insert	EX 31	See Reference Window: Inserting a Row and Column into a Worksheet
Column, resize width in a datasheet	AC 64	Double-click ↔ on the right border of the column heading
Column, select	EX 25	Click the column heading of the column you want to select. To select a range of columns, click the first column heading in the range, hold down the Shift key and click the last column in the range.
Column, unhide	EX 116	Select the column headings left and right of the hidden columns, right-click the selection, click Unhide
Columns, repeat in printout	EX 133	Open the Page Setup dialog box, click the Sheet tab, click the Column to repeat at left box, click the column that contains the information you want repeated, click OK
Comment, display in Normal view	WD 76	Point to comment
Comment, insert	WD 75	Click insert, click Comment
Compressed files, extract	FM 19	Right-click compressed folder, click Extract All, click Next, select location, click Next, click Finish
Compressed folder, create	FM 19	Right-click a blank area of a folder window, point to New, click Compressed (zipped) Folder
Contact, create	OUT 15	See Reference Window: Creating a Contact
Contact, edit	OUT 20	Switch to Address Cards or Detailed Address Cards view, click in contact card, edit text as usual, click outside contact card
Contact, forward as vCard	OUT 20	Click contact card in Contacts folder, click Actions, click Forward as vCard
Contact, forward by e-mail	OUT 20	Right-click contact card in Contacts folder, click Forward
Contacts view, change	OUT 18	Click Contacts button in Navigation Pane, click option button in Current View pane
Database, compact and repair	AC 26	Click Tools, point to Database Utilities, click Compact and Repair Database

TASK	PAGE #	RECOMMENDED METHOD
Database, compact on close	AC 26	*See* Reference Window: Compacting a Database Automatically
Database, convert to another Access version	AC 28	Click Tools, point to Database Utilities, point to Convert Database, click the format to convert to
Database, create a blank	AC 41	Click Create a new file in the task pane, click Blank database, type the database name, select the drive and folder, click Create
Database, create using a wizard	AC 41	Click 🗋 on the Database toolbar, click On my computer in the task pane, click the Databases tab, select a template, click OK, type the database name, select the drive and folder, click Create, follow the instructions in the wizard
Database, open	AC 8	Click Open (or More) in the task pane, select the database to open
Datasheet, print	AC 12	Click 🖨
Datasheet view, switch to	AC 53	Click 🔳
Date, insert current	EX 72	Insert the TODAY() or NOW() function
Date, insert with AutoComplete	WD 24	Start typing date, press Enter
Dates, fill in using Auto Fill	EX 71	Select the cell containing the initial date, drag and drop the fill handle to fill in the rest of the dates. Click 📑, select option to fill in days, week-days, months, or years
Deleted Items folder, empty	OUT 43	Right-click Deleted Items folder in All Folders pane in Navigation Pane, click Empty "Deleted Items" Folder, click Yes
Design view, switch to	AC 57	Click 📐
Dictionary, create and select as default	WD 46	Click Tools, click Options, click Spelling & Grammar tab, click Custom Dictionaries, click New, type a name in the File name text box, click Save, click the name of the new dictionary, click Change Default, click OK.
Distribution list, create	OUT 21	See Reference Window: Creating a Distribution List
Distribution list, modify	OUT 23	Double-click distribution list contact in Contacts folder, click Select Members to add more contacts, click Remove to delete selected contact
Document, open	WD 43	Click 📂, select drive and folder, click filename, click open
Document, open new	WD 11	Click 🗋
Document, preview	WD 29	Click 🔍
Document, save with same name	WD 19	Click 💾
E-mail, receive	OUT 23	Switch to Mail folder, click Send/Receive button on Standard toolbar
E-mail account, set up new account	OUT 7	Click Tools, click E-mail Accounts, follow wizard to Add a new e-mail account
E-mail message, create	OUT 11	See Reference Window: Creating an E-mail Message
E-mail message, format	OUT 12	Select text, click appropriate buttons on Formatting toolbar in Message window
E-mail message, forward	OUT 26	Select message, click Forward button on Standard toolbar in Inbox, enter recipient e-mail address(es), type message, click Send button on toolbar in Message window
E-mail message, open	OUT 28	Double-click message in Inbox main window
E-mail message, print	OUT 26	Select message in Inbox main window, click File, click Print, verify printer, select print style, click OK

TASK	PAGE #	RECOMMENDED METHOD
E-mail message, read	OUT 24	Click message in Inbox main window, read message in Reading Pane
E-mail message, reply	OUT 25	Select message, click Reply button on Standard toolbar in Inbox, type reply message, click Send button on toolbar in Message window
E-mail message, send to Outbox	OUT 13	Click Send button on toolbar in Message window
E-mail message, set importance	OUT 12	Click ❗ or ⬇ on Standard toolbar in Message window
E-mail message, set sensitivity	OUT 13	Click Options button on toolbar in Message window, select sensitivity level in Sensitivity list in Options dialog box, click OK
E-mail messages, send from Outbox	OUT 13	Switch to Mail folder, click Send/Receive button on Standard toolbar
Envelope, create	WD 30	Click Tools, point to Letters and Mailings, click Envelopes and Labels, click Envelopes tab, type delivery and return addresses, click Print
Excel, start	EX 5	Click Start, point to All Programs, point to Microsoft Office, click Microsoft Office Excel 2003
Field, add to a table	AC 59	*See* Reference Window: Adding a Field Between Two Existing Fields
Field, define in a table	AC 43	*See* Reference Window: Defining a Field in a Table
Field, delete from a table	AC 57	*See* Reference Window: Deleting a Field from a Table Structure
Field, move to a new location in a table	AC 58	Display the table in Design view, click the field's row selector, drag the field with the pointer
Field property change, update	AC 61	Click the list arrow for ⿻, select option for updating field property
File, close	OFF 21	Click the Close Window button ✕ on the menu bar
File, copy	FM 16	*See* Reference Window: Copying a File or Folder in Windows Explorer or My Computer
File, delete	FM 18	Right-click the file, click Delete
File, move	FM 14	*See* Reference Window: Moving a File or Folder in Windows Explorer or My Computer
File, open	OFF 22	See Reference Window: Opening an Existing or a New File
File, print	OFF 29	See Reference Window: Printing a File
File, rename	FM 17	Right-click the file, click Rename, type the new name, press Enter
File, save	OFF 20	See Reference Window: Saving a File
File, switch between open	OFF 8	Click the taskbar button for the file you want to make active
Files, compress	FM 19	Drag files into a compressed folder
Files, sort by date	WIN 28	In Details view, click Date Modified button
Files, view details	WIN 28	Click Views button, click Details
Files, view tiles	WIN 29	Click Views button, click Tiles
Filter By Selection, activate	AC 100	*See* Reference Window: Using Filter By Selection
Find and replace text	WD 58	See Reference Window: Finding and Replacing Text
Flag, add reminder to message in Inbox	OUT 29	Right-click flag icon in message header in Inbox main window, click Add Reminder, select or type a message in Flag to list, select due date in left Due by list, select due time in right Due by list, click OK
Flag, add to message in Inbox	OUT 29	Right-click flag icon in message header in Inbox main window, click desired flag color
Flag, mark complete	OUT 30	Click flag icon in message header in Inbox until check mark appears

TASK	PAGE #	RECOMMENDED METHOD
Folder or drive contents, view in Windows Explorer	FM 10	Click ⊞
Folder, copy	FM 16	*See* Reference Window: Copying a File or Folder in Windows Explorer or My Computer
Folder, create	FM 13	*See* Reference Window: Creating a Folder Using Windows Explorer
Folder, create	OUT 31	Right-click folder in Navigation Pane, click New Folder, type folder name, select items you want to store in Folder contains list, select folder location, click OK
Folder, move	FM 14	*See* Reference Window: Moving a File or Folder in Windows Explorer or My Computer
Folder, open	WIN 31	Double-click the folder
Folder, rename	FM 17	Right-click the folder, click Rename, type the new name, press Enter
Folder List, display	OUT 6	Click 📁 in Navigation Pane
Folder List, use	OUT 6	Click folder in Folder List pane; click ⊞ to see nested folders
Folders pane, open	WIN 30	Click View, point to Explorer Bar, click Folders
Font, change color	EX 104	Select the text, click A ▾, select a color from the color palette
Font, change size	EX 103	Click 10 ▾, click a size
Font, change style	EX 103	Click **B**, click *I*, or click U
Font, change typeface	EX 103	Click Arial ▾, click a font
Font, select default	WD 8	Click Format, click Font, click Font tab, click font name
Font and font size, change	WD 70	See Reference Window: Changing the Font and Font Size
Font size, select default	WD 8	Click Format, click Font, click Font tab, click font size
Format, apply Currency Style, Percent Style, or Comma Style	EX 97	Click $, click % or click ⦁, or open the Format Cells dialog box, click the Number tab, select a style, specify style-related options, click OK
Format, clear	EX 119	Click Edit, point to Clear, click Formats
Format, copy	WD 66	Select text with desired format, double-click ✓, select paragraphs to format, click ✓
Format, copy using Format Painter	EX 99	See Reference Window: Copying Formatting Using the Format Painter
Format, decrease decimal places	EX 97	Click ⮐.00
Format, find and replace	EX 120	See Reference Window: Finding and Replacing a Format
Format, increase decimal places	EX 99	Click ⮐.00
Format Cells dialog box, open	EX 101	Click Format, click Cells
Formula, copy	EX 56	See Reference Window: Copying and Pasting a Cell or Range
Formula, copy using the fill handle	EX 68	See Reference Window: Copying Formulas Using the Fill Handle
Formula, enter using keyboard	EX 15	See Reference Window: Entering a Formula
Formula, enter using mouse	EX 15	See Reference Window: Entering a Formula
Formula, insert	EX 15	See Reference Window: Entering a Formula
Formulas, show/hide	EX 42	Press the Ctrl + ` (grave accent) keys to display or hide the formulas in the worksheet cells
Forwarded contact card, add to Contacts folder	OUT 20	Drag contact card attachment from Message window to Contacts folder

TASK	PAGE #	RECOMMENDED METHOD
Function, insert using Insert Function dialog box	EX 65	Click f_x on the Formula bar, select the function from the Insert Function dialog box, complete the Function Arguments dialog box
Getting Started task pane, open	OFF 16	Click the Home button 🏠 in the task pane
Grayscale, preview presentation in	PPT 30	Click ▣, click Grayscale
Handouts, print	PPT 31	Click File, click Print, click Print what list arrow, click Handouts, click Slides per page list arrow, click number, click OK
Header/footer, create	EX 128	Open the Page Setup dialog box, click the Header/Footer tab, click the Header list arrow or the Footer list arrow, select an available header or footer, click OK
Header/footer, create custom	EX 129	Open Page Setup dialog box, click the Header/Footer tab, click the Custom Header or Customer Footer button, complete the header/footer related boxes, click OK
Help, display topic from the Home page	WIN 32	In Help and Support, click Home in the navigation bar
Help, display topic from the Index page	WIN 33	In Help and Support, click Index in the navigation bar, scroll to locate a topic or type a keyword, double-click the topic
Help, find topic	WIN 34	In Help and Support, click in the Search box, type word or phrase, click ➡
Help, start	WIN 31	Click Start, click Help and Support
Help task pane, use	OFF 26	See Reference Window: Getting Help from the Help Task Pane
Italics, add to text	WD 73	Select text, click I
Items, delete	OUT 43	Click item, click ✕ , click Yes if necessary
Items, select multiple	OUT 43	Click first item, press and hold Ctrl key, click additional items, release Ctrl key
Line spacing, change	WD 63	Select text to change, press Ctrl+1 for single spacing, Ctrl+5 for 1.5 line spacing, or Ctrl+2 for double spacing
List box, scroll	WIN 21	Click the list arrow for the list box to display the list of options; click the scroll down or up arrow; or drag the scroll box
Logical function, insert	EX 83	Use the IF function
Magnification, changing	EX 62	See Reference Window: Changing the Zoom Magnification of the Workbook Window
Margins, change	WD 61	Click File, click Page Setup, click Margins tab, enter margin values, click OK
Menu command, select	WIN 8	Click the command on the menu; for submenus, point to a command on the menu
Message format, choose	OUT 8	Click Tools, click Options, click Mail Format tab, select HTML in the Compose in this message format list, click OK
Messages, archive manually	OUT 41	Click File, click Archive, click Archive this folder and all subfolders option button, click folder to archive, type date in Archive items older than text box, click Browse, select save in location, click OK, click OK, click Yes
Messages, color	OUT 39	Click Tools, click Organize, click Using Colors link, set options, click Apply Color
Messages, file	OUT 31	Select message or messages in main window, drag to appropriate folder or subfolder
Messages, find	OUT 34	See Reference Window: Finding Messages

TASK	PAGE #	RECOMMENDED METHOD
Messages, save	OUT 40	See Reference Window: Saving Messages in Another File Format
Messages, sort	OUT 38	Click column heading
Messages, sort by two or more columns	OUT 38	Click column heading, hold down Shift, click additional column headings, release Shift
Microsoft Office Online, use	OFF 28	Click the Connect to Microsoft Office Online link in the Help task pane
Mortgage, calculate monthly payment	EX 78	Use the PMT function
Mortgage, calculate the interest rate of	EX 80	Use the RATE function
Mortgage, calculate the number of payments	EX 80	Use the NPER function
Mortgage, calculate total value of	EX 80	Use the PV function
My Computer, open	WIN 25	Click Start, click My Computer
Navigation Pane, use	OUT 6	Click button in Navigation Pane, click folder if necessary
Nonprinting characters, show	WD 10	Click Show/ Hide ¶
Normal view, change to	WD 7	Click ≡
Notes, create	PPT 29	Click I in Notes pane, type text
Notes, print	PPT 31	Click File, click Print, click Print what list arrow, click Notes Pages, click OK
Numbering, add to paragraphs	WD 69	Select paragraphs, click ⊟
Object, open	AC 10	Click the object's type in the Objects bar, click the object's name, click Open
Object, save	AC 12	Click 🖫, type the object name, click OK
Outline text, demote	PPT 23	Click Outline tab (if necessary), click paragraph, click 🔁
Outline text, promote	PPT 21	Click Outline tab (if necessary), click paragraph, click 🔁
Page, change orientation	EX 40	Open the Page Setup dialog box, click the Page tab, click the Landscape or Portrait option button
Page, set margins	EX 127	Open the Page Setup dialog box, click the Margins tab, specify the width of the margins, click OK
Page break preview, switch to	EX 131	Click View on the menu bar, click Page Break Preview
Page orientation, change	WD 60	Click File, click Page Setup, click Margins tab, click Landscape or Portrait icon, click OK.
Page Setup dialog box, open	EX 40	Click File, click Page Setup; or click the Setup button on the Print Preview toolbar
Paragraph, decrease indent	WD 65	Click 🔁
Paragraph, indent	WD 65	Click 🔁
Paste options, select	WD 53	Click 🔁
PowerPoint, exit	PPT 12	Click ✕ on PowerPoint window
PowerPoint, start	PPT 4	Click Start button, point to All Programs, point to Microsoft Office, click Microsoft Office PowerPoint 2003
Presentation, close	PPT 9	Click ✕ on presentation window
Presentation, open	PPT 5	Click 📂, select disk and folder, click filename, click Open
Presentation, print	PPT 30	Click File, click Print, select options, click OK
Primary key, specify	AC 51	See Reference Window: Specifying a Primary Key for a Table

TASK	PAGE #	RECOMMENDED METHOD
Print area, define	EX 131	Select the range, click File, point to Print Area, click Set Print Area
Program, close	WIN 12	Click ⊠
Program, close inactive	WIN 14	Right-click the program button on the taskbar, click Close
Program, exit	OFF 30	Click the Close button ⊠ on the title bar
Program, start	WIN 11	See Reference Window: Starting a Program
Program, switch to another	WIN 14	Click the program button on the taskbar
Programs, open	OFF 5	See Reference Window: Starting Office Programs
Programs, switch between open	OFF 8	Click the taskbar button for the program you want to make active
Property sheet, open	AC 116	Right-click the object or control, click Properties
Query, define	AC 82	Click Queries in the Objects bar, click New, click Design View, click OK
Query, run	AC 86	Click ❗
Query results, sort	AC 97	See Reference Window: Sorting a Query Datasheet
Range, copy	EX 27	Select the cell or range, hold down the Ctrl key and drag the selection to the new location, release the Ctrl key and mouse button
Range, move	EX 26	Select the cell or range, drag the selection to the new location, release the mouse button
Range, select adjacent	EX 24	See Reference Window: Selecting Adjacent or Nonadjacent Ranges of Cells
Range, select nonadjacent	EX 24	See Reference Window: Selecting Adjacent or Nonadjacent Ranges of Cells
Record, add a new one	AC 63	Click ▶
Record, delete	AC 69	See Reference Window: Deleting a Record
Record, move to a specific one	AC 11	Type the record number in the record number box, press Enter
Record, move to first	AC 12	Click ◀◀
Record, move to last	AC 12	Click ▶▶
Record, move to next	AC 12	Click ▶
Record, move to previous	AC 12	Click ◀
Records, redisplay all after filter	AC 101	Click ▽
Recycle Bin, view contents of	WIN 8	Double-click the Recycle Bin icon
Redo command, use to redo multiple operations in a database object	AC 110	Click the list arrow for ↻, click the action(s) to redo
Relationship, define between database tables	AC 90	Click ◳
Relative reference, change to absolute	EX 58	Type $ before the column and row references; or press the F4 key
Report, print specific pages of	AC 23	Click File, click Print, click Pages, enter number of pages to print in the From and To boxes, click OK
Research task pane, open	WD 76	Click 📖.
Research task pane, use	OFF 17	See Reference Window: Using the Research Task Pane
Research task pane, use	WD 77	Connect to Internet, click 📖, enter text in Search for text box, verify All Reference Books is selected in box below Search for text box, click ➡.
Row, change height	EX 19	See Reference Window: Changing the Column Width or Row Height
Row, delete	EX 33	Select the row, click Edit, click Delete; or select the row, right-click the selection, click Delete

TASK	PAGE #	RECOMMENDED METHOD
Row, hide	EX 116	Select the headings for the rows you want to hide, right-click the selection, click Hide
Row, insert	EX 31	See Reference Window: Inserting a Row or Column into a Worksheet
Row, select	EX 25	Click the heading of the row you want to select. To select a range of rows, click the first row heading in the range, hold down the Shift key and click the last row in the range
Row, unhide	EX 116	Select the rows headings above and below the hidden rows, right-click the selection, click Unhide
Rows, repeat in printout	EX 133	Open the Page Setup dialog box, click the Sheet tab, click the Row to repeat at top box, click the row that contains the information
Rule, create simple	OUT 33	See Reference Window: Creating a Simple Rule
Rule, delete	OUT 42	Click Tools, click Rules and Alerts, click rule in Rule list box, click Delete, click Yes, click OK
Ruler, display	WD 8	Click View, click Ruler
ScreenTip, view	WIN 6	Position pointer over an object
Search Folder, display new	OUT 36	Right-click Search Folders in All Mail Folders pane in Navigation Pane, click New Search Folder, click desired Search Folder, click OK
Search Folder, use preset	OUT 36	Click ⊞ next to Search Folders in All Mail Folders pane in Navigation Pane, click Search Folder
Sheet tabs, format	EX 119	Right-click the sheet tab, click Tab Color, select a color from the color palette
Shortcut menu, open	WIN 9	Right-click an object
Signature, create new	OUT 9	Click Tools, click Options, click Mail Format tab, click Signatures, click New, enter a name for signature, click desired starting point option, click Next, type signature text, add font and paragraph formatting as needed, click Finish, click OK, click OK
Signature, delete	OUT 43	Click Tools, click Options, click Mail Format tab, click Signatures, click signature in Signature list box, click Remove, click Yes, click OK, click OK
Signature, select for e-mail account	OUT 10	Click Tools, click Options, click Mail Format tab, select e-mail account name in Select signatures for account list, select signature in Signature for new messages list, select signature in Signature for replies and forwards list, click Apply, repeat for other accounts, click OK
Slide, add new	PPT 19	Click the New Slide button
Slide, delete	PPT 17	In Slide Pane, click Edit, click Delete Slide. In Outline tab, click ▣, press Delete. In Slide tab, click slide, press Delete
Slide, go to next	PPT 6	Click ▼
Slide, go to previous	PPT 6	Click ▲
Slide Show, view	PPT 8	Click �☐
Slide Sorter View, switch to	PPT 7	Click ▦
Smart Tag, remove	WD 28	Click ⓘ ▾, click Remove this Smart Tag
Sort, specify ascending in datasheet	AC 96	Click ↓
Sort, specify descending in datasheet	AC 96	Click ↓

TASK	PAGE #	RECOMMENDED METHOD
Speaker Notes, create	PPT 29	Click I in Notes Pane, type text
Spelling, check	EX 38	Click ABC
Spelling, correct individual word	WD 22	Right-click misspelled word (as indicated by a wavy red line), click correctly spelled word
Spelling and grammar, check	WD 46	See Reference Window: Checking a Document for Spelling and Grammatical Errors
Standard Buttons toolbar, display in My Computer window	WIN 27	Click View, point to Toolbars, click Standard Buttons to insert a check mark
Start menu, open	WIN 7	Click Start
Stationery, create an e-mail message with	OUT 10	In Inbox, click Actions, point to New Mail Message Using, click More Stationery, select desired stationery, click OK
Style, apply	EX 123	Select the range, click Format, click Style, select a style, click OK
Style, create	EX 122	Select the cell that contains the formatting you want to use as the basis of the new style, click Format, click Style, type a name for the style, click Modify, specify format options using the Format Cells dialog box, click OK, click OK
Style, modify	EX 124	Select the range, click Format, click Style, click Modify, change style attributes, click OK
Style Checker, fix style problem	PPT 26	Click light bulb, click option to fix style problem
Style Checker, set options	PPT 25	Click Tools, click Options, click Spelling and Style tab, click Style Options, set options, click OK, click OK
Style Checker, turn on	PPT 25	Click Tools, click Options, click Spelling and Style tab, select Check style check box, click OK
Table, create in a database	AC 42	Click Tables in the Objects bar, click New, click Design View, click OK
Table, import from another Access database	AC 67	Click File, point to Get External Data, click Import, select the folder, click Import, select the table, click OK
Table, open in a database	AC 10	Click Tables in the Objects bar, click the table name, click Open
Table structure, save in a database	AC 52	See Reference Window: Saving a Table Structure
Task pane, close	OFF 15	Click the Close button ✕ on the task pane title bar
Task pane, display	OFF 15	Click View on the menu bar, click Task Pane
Task pane, navigate between	OFF 16	Click the Back button ⊕ or the Forward button ⊕ in the task pane previously opened
Task pane, open	OFF 16	Click the Other Task Panes button on the task pane title bar, click name of task pane you want to open
Task pane, open	WD 7	Click View, click Task Pane
Text, align	WD 64	Select text, click, ▤, ▤, ▤, or ▤
Text, align within a cell	EX 105	Click ▤, click ▤, or click ▤; or open Format Cells dialog box, click the Alignment tab, select a text alignment, click OK
Text, copy and paste	WD 54	Select text, click 📄 click at target location, click 📋
Text, delete	WD 50	Press Backspace to delete character to left of Insertion point; press Delete to delete character to the right, press Ctrl+Backspace to delete to beginning of word; press Ctrl+Delete to delete to end of word
Text, enter into cell	EX 11	Click the cell, type text entry, press Enter

TASK	PAGE #	RECOMMENDED METHOD
Text, enter multiple lines in a cell	EX 12	See Reference Window: Entering Multiple Lines of Text Within a Cell
Text, enter using AutoComplete	EX 17	Type the first letter of text entry you've entered in the worksheet, press Enter or Tab to complete the text entry displayed by AutoComplete
Text, increase or decrease indent of	EX 106	Click 🔳 or 🔳
Text, move by cut and paste	WD 54	Select text, click ✂ click at target location, click 📋
Text, move by drag and drop	WD 52	Select text, drag selected text to target location, release mouse button
Text, select a block of	WD 49	Click at beginning of block, press and hold Shift and click at end of block
Text, select entire document	WD 49	Press Ctrl and click in selection bar
Text, select multiple adjacent lines	WD 49	Click and drag in selection bar
Text, select multiple nonadjacent lines	WD 49	Select text, press and hold Ctrl, and select next text
Text, select multiple paragraphs	WD 49	Click and drag in selection bar
Text, select paragraph	WD 49	Double-click in selection bar next to paragraph
Text, select sentence	WD 49	Press Ctrl and click in sentence
Text, wrap in cell	EX 107	Open the Format Cells dialog box, click the Alignment tab, select the Wrap text check box, click OK
Toolbar, display	WD 7	Right-click any visible toolbar, click toolbar name
Toolbar, turn off personalized	OFF 14	Click the Toolbar Options button ⬛ on the right side of the toolbar, click the Show Buttons on Two Rows command
Type a question for help box, use	OFF 24	See Reference Window: Getting Help from the Type a Question for Help Box
Underline, add to text	WD 73	Select text, click 🔲U
Undo command, use to undo multiple operations in a database object	AC 110	Click the list arrow for ↩ , click the action(s) to undo
vCard, forward by e-mail	OUT 20	Click contact card in Contacts folder, click Actions, click Forward as vCard
View, switch	OUT 38	Click View, point to Arrange By, point to Current View, click desired view
Window, close	OFF 9	Click the Close button ❎
Window, maximize	OFF 10, WIN 17	Click 🔲
Window, minimize	OFF 10, WIN 17	Click 🔳
Window, move	WIN 18	Drag the title bar
Window, resize	WIN 18	Drag 🔳
Window, restore	OFF 10, WIN 17	Click 🔲
Windows Explorer, start	FM 9, WIN 29	Click Start, point to All Programs, point to Accessories, click Windows Explorer
Windows XP, shut down	WIN 34	Click Start, click Turn Off Computer, click Turn Off
Windows XP, start	WIN 4	Turn on the computer
Word, choose as e-mail editor	OUT 8	Click Tools, click Options, click Mail Format tab, check the Use Microsoft Office Word 2003 to edit e-mail messages check box, click OK

TASK	PAGE #	RECOMMENDED METHOD
Word, start	WD 5	Click ⟪ start ⟫, point to All Programs, point to Microsoft Office, click Microsoft Office Word 2003
Workbook, preview	EX 39	Click ⟨🔍⟩; or click the Preview button in the Print dialog box
Workbook, print	EX 39	Click ⟨🖨⟩; or click File, click Print, select printer and print-related options, click OK
Workbook, save	EX 22	Click File, click Save, locate the folder and drive where you want to save the file, type a filename, click Save
Workbook, save in a different format	EX 22	Open the Save or Save As dialog box, display the location where you want to save the file, enter a filename, click the Save as type list arrow, select the file format you want to apply, click Save
Worksheet, add background image	EX 117	See Reference Window: Adding a Background Image to the Worksheet
Worksheet, copy	EX 37	See Reference Window: Moving or Copying a Worksheet
Worksheet, delete	EX 35	Click the sheet tab, click Edit, click Delete Sheet; or right-click the sheet tab, click Delete
Worksheet, insert	EX 35	Click Insert, click Worksheet; or right-click a sheet tab, click Insert, click Worksheet icon, click OK
Worksheet, rename	EX 36	Double-click the sheet tab that you want to rename, type a new name, press Enter
Worksheets, move	EX 37	See Reference Window: Moving or Copying a Worksheet
Worksheets, move between	EX 9	Click the sheet tab for the worksheet you want to view; or click one of the tab scrolling buttons and then click the sheet tab
Zoom setting, change	WD 8	Click Zoom list arrow, click zoom selection